Beginning ASP.NET 3.5

Beginning
ASP.NET 3.5
In C# and VB

Imar Spaanjaars

Wiley Publishing, Inc.

Beginning ASP.NET 3.5: In C# and VB

Published by
Wiley Publishing, Inc.
10475 Crosspoint Boulevard
Indianapolis, IN 46256
www.wiley.com

Published simultaneously in Canada

ISBN: 978-0-470-18759-3

Manufactured in the United States of America

10 9 8 7 6 5 4 3 2

Library of Congress Cataloging-in-Publication Data

Spaanjaars, Imar.
Beginning ASP.NET 3.5 / Imar Spaanjaars.
p. cm.
Includes index.
ISBN 978-0-470-18759-3 (pbk. : web)
1. Active server pages. 2. Web sites—Design. 3. Microsoft .NET. I. Title.
TK5105.8885.A26S6815 2006
005.2'76—dc22
2007052406

To my dad — I know you'd be proud

About the Author

Imar Spaanjaars graduated in Leisure Management at the Leisure Management School in the Netherlands, but he quickly changed his career path into the Internet world.

After working for a large corporation and doing some freelance work, he now works for Design IT (`www.designit.nl`), an IT company in the Netherlands specializing in Internet and intranet applications built with Microsoft technologies like ASP.NET 3.5. As a technical director and software designer, he's responsible for designing and building medium- to large-scaled e-commerce web sites and portals.

He's also the tech lead for Dynamicweb Nederland, the Dutch branch of the popular Danish Content Management System Dynamicweb (`www.dynamicweb.nl`).

Imar has written books on ASP.NET 2.0 and Macromedia Dreamweaver, all published under the Wrox brand. He is also one of the top contributors to the Wrox Community Forum at `p2p.wrox.com`, where he shares his knowledge with fellow programmers.

Imar lives in Utrecht, the Netherlands, with his girlfriend, Fleur. You can contact him through his personal web site at `http://imar.spaanjaars.com`.

Credits

Acquisitions Director
Jim Minatel

Development Editor
Brian Herrmann

Lead Technical Editor
Peter Lanoie

Technical Editors
Alexei Gorkov
John Dunagan
Robert Searing

Editorial Manager
Mary Beth Wakefield

Production Manager
Tim Tate

Vice President and Executive Group Publisher
Richard Swadley

Vice President and Executive Publisher
Joseph B. Wikert

Project Coordinator, Cover
Lynsey Stanford

Compositor
Laurie Stewart, Happenstance Type-O-Rama

Proofreaders
Kathryn Duggan
David Parise
Rachel Gunn

Indexer
Melanie Belkin

Acknowledgments

Writing a book is probably one of the most exhausting but fun and rewarding things I have ever done. During writing you have to invest a lot of time and effort to put your ideas down into something that is worth reading by others. After the hard work is done and the book is written, the reward comes from readers like you who send me e-mails, contact me through my web site, or participate in the online discussion forums at `p2p.wrox.com` to discuss the book.

As Norman Mailer put it, writing a book is the closest that men ever get to childbearing. Although I think there is probably some truth in that statement, I also realize there is one big difference: writing a book is not something you have to do on your own. Although only my name is on the cover, I owe a lot to many people who helped me write this book.

First of all I'd like to thank Jim Minatel from Wiley for asking me to pick up this project and having faith in my ability to bring it to a good end. I would also like to thank Brian Herrmann for his editorial work. I know it wasn't always easy with the number of reviewers we had, but I think it turned out pretty well.

I am very thankful for the work done by the technical editors on this book: Alexei, John, and Rob — thanks, guys, for all your hard work! I particularly want to thank the lead technical editor, Peter Lanoie, who has made a major contribution, both in shaping the direction of the book and in assuring its technical accuracy. Thank you, Peter!

I am also very glad for the support I got from the people at Design IT. Thanks to all who have reviewed my work and participated in my discussions on the book's direction.

Another person I owe a lot to is Anne Ward from Blue Violet, a UK-based web and graphic design company. Anne has done most of the designs used in this book, which I highly appreciate. Thanks, Anne! The concert pictures you see in this book come from her good friend Nigel D. Nudds, who kindly let me use pictures from his collection.

Finally, I would like to thank my lovely girlfriend, Fleur. You may get tired of hearing it, but I really appreciate the support you have given me throughout this project. I couldn't — and wouldn't — have done it without you!

Contents

Introduction

To build effective and attractive database-driven web sites, you need two things: a solid and fast framework to run your web pages on and a rich and extensive environment to create and program these web pages. With ASP.NET 3.5 and Visual Web Developer 2008 you get both. Together they form *the* platform to create dynamic and interactive web applications.

ASP.NET 3.5 builds on top of its popular predecessor ASP.NET 2.0. While maintaining backward compatibility with sites built using this older version, the Microsoft .NET Framework 3.5 in general and ASP.NET 3.5 in particular add a lot of new, compelling features to the mix.

Continuing the path of "less code" that was entered with the 2.0 version of the .NET Framework, ASP.NET 3.5 lets you accomplish more with even less code. New features like LINQ that are added to the .NET Framework allow you to access a database with little to no handwritten code. The integration of Microsoft ASP.NET Ajax into the ASP.NET Framework and Visual Web Developer means you can now create fast-responding and spiffy web interfaces simply by dragging a few controls onto your page and setting a few properties. This book gives you an in-depth look at both of these technologies.

The support for Cascading Style Sheets (CSS), the language to lay out and format web pages, has undergone a major overhaul in Visual Web Developer. The design-time support, that shows you how a page will eventually look in the browser, has been vastly improved. Additionally, Visual Web Developer now ships with a lot of tools that make writing CSS a breeze.

However, drag-and-drop support and visual tools are not the only things you'll learn from this book. ASP.NET 3.5 and Visual Web Developer 2008 come with a great and extensive set of tools to help you program your web applications. These tools range from the new LINQ syntax that allows you to query data and databases in your web applications, to the vastly improved debugging capabilities that allow you to debug your application from client-side JavaScript all the way up into your server-side code, all with the same familiar user interface, commands, and actions.

Under the hood, ASP.NET 3.5 makes use of the same run time as version 2.0. This ensures a great backward compatibility with that version, which means that ASP.NET 2.0 applications continue to run under the new framework. But don't be fooled by the fact that the run time hasn't changed. Although the technical underpinnings needed to execute your web application haven't changed, the .NET 3.5 Framework and ASP.NET add *a lot* of new features, as you'll discover in this book.

Probably the best thing about Visual Web Developer 2008 is its price: it's available for free. Although the commercial versions of Visual Studio 2008 ship with Visual Web Developer, you can also download and install the free Express Edition. This makes Visual Web Developer 2008 and ASP.NET 3.5 probably the most attractive and compelling web development technologies available today.

Whom This Book Is For

This book is for anyone who wants to learn how to build rich and interactive web sites that run on the Microsoft platform. With the knowledge you gain from this book, you create a great foundation to build any type of web site, ranging from simple hobby-related web sites to sites you may be creating for commercial purposes.

Anyone new to web programming should be able to follow along because no prior background in web development is assumed. The book starts at the very beginning of web development by showing you how to obtain and install Visual Web Developer. The chapters that follow gradually introduce you to new technologies, building on top of the knowledge gained in the previous chapters.

Do you have a strong preference for Visual Basic over C# or the other way around? Or do you think both languages are equally cool? Or maybe you haven't made up your mind yet and want to learn both languages? Either way, you'll like this book because *all* code examples are presented in both languages!

Even if you're already familiar with previous versions of ASP.NET, with the 1.*x* versions in particular, you may gain a lot from this book. Although many concepts from ASP.NET 2.0 are brought forward into ASP.NET 3.5, you'll discover there's a host of new stuff to be found in this book, including an introduction to LINQ, the new CSS and JavaScript debugging tools, new ASP.NET controls, and integrated support for ASP.NET Ajax.

What This Book Covers

This book teaches you how to create a feature-rich, data-driven, and interactive web site. Although this is quite a mouthful, you'll find that with Visual Web Developer 2008 this isn't as hard as it seems. You'll see the entire process of building a web site, from installing Visual Web Developer 2008 in Chapter 1 all the way up to putting your web application on a live server in Chapter 18. The book is divided into 18 chapters, each dealing with a specific subject.

- **Chapter 1, "Getting Started with ASP.NET 3.5."** In this chapter you'll see how to obtain and install Visual Web Developer 2008. You'll get instructions for downloading and installing the free edition of Visual Web Developer 2008, called the Express Edition. You are also introduced to HTML, the language behind every web page. The chapter closes with an overview of the customization options that Visual Web Developer gives you.
- **Chapter 2, "Building an ASP.NET Web Site."** This chapter shows you how to create a new web site and how to add new elements like pages to it. Besides learning how to create a well-structured site, you also see how to use the numerous tools in Visual Web Developer to create HTML and ASP.NET pages.
- **Chapter 3, "Designing Your Web Pages."** Visual Web Developer comes with a host of tools that allow you to create well-designed and attractive web pages. In this chapter, you see how to make good use of these tools. Additionally, you learn about CSS, the language that is used to format web pages.
- **Chapter 4, "Working with ASP.NET Controls."** ASP.NET Server Controls are one of the most important concepts in ASP.NET. They allow you to create complex and feature-rich web sites with very little code. This chapter introduces you to the large number of server controls that are available, explains what they are used for, and shows you how to use them.

- **Chapter 5, "Programming Your ASP.NET Web Pages."** Although the built-in CSS tools and the ASP.NET Server Controls can get you a long way in creating web pages, you are likely to use a programming language to enhance your pages. This chapter serves as an introduction to programming with a strong focus on programming web pages. Best of all: all the examples you see in this chapter (and the rest of the book) are in both Visual Basic and C#, so you can choose the language you like best.
- **Chapter 6, "Creating Consistent Looking Web Sites."** Consistency is important to give your web site an attractive and professional appeal. ASP.NET helps you create consistent-looking pages through the use of master pages, which allow you to define the global look and feel of a page. Skins and themes help you to centralize the looks of controls and other visual elements in your site. You also see how to create a base page that helps to centralize programming code that you need on all pages in your site.
- **Chapter 7, "Navigation."** To help your visitors find their way around your site, ASP.NET comes with a number of navigation controls. These controls are used to build the navigation structure of your site. They can be connected to your site's central site map that defines the pages in your web site. You also learn how to programmatically send users from one page to another.
- **Chapter 8, "User Controls."** User controls are reusable page fragments that can be used in multiple web pages. As such, they are great for repeating content like menus, banners, and so on. In this chapter, you learn how to create and use user controls and enhance them with some programmatic intelligence.
- **Chapter 9, "Validating User Input."** A large part of interactivity in your site is defined by the input of your users. This chapter shows you how to accept, validate, and process user input using ASP.NET Server Controls. Additionally, you see how to send e-mail from your ASP.NET web application and how to read from text files.
- **Chapter 10, "ASP.NET Ajax."** Microsoft ASP.NET Ajax allows you to create good-looking, flicker-free web pages that close the gap between traditional desktop applications and web applications. In this chapter you learn how to use the built-in Ajax features to enhance the presence of your web pages, resulting in a smoother interaction with the web site.
- **Chapter 11, "Introduction to Databases."** Understanding how to use databases is critical to building modern web sites, as most modern web sites require the use of a database. You'll learn the basics of SQL, the query language that allows you to access and alter data in a database. In addition, you are introduced to the database tools found in Visual Web Developer that help you create and manage your SQL Server databases.
- **Chapter 12, "Displaying and Updating Data."** Building on the knowledge you gained in the previous chapter, this chapter shows you how to use the ASP.NET data-bound and data source controls to create a rich interface that enables your users to interact with the data in the database that these controls target.
- **Chapter 13, "LINQ."** LINQ is Microsoft's new solution for accessing objects, databases, XML, and more. In this chapter you'll see how to use LINQ to SQL to access SQL Server databases. Instead of writing a lot of manual code, you create a bunch of LINQ objects that do the heavy work for you. This chapter shows you what LINQ is all about, how to use the visual LINQ designer built into Visual Web Developer, and how to write LINQ queries to get data in and out of your SQL Server database.
- **Chapter 14, "Presenting Data: Advanced Topics."** While earlier chapters focused mostly on the technical foundations of working with data, this chapter looks at the same topic from a front-end perspective. You see how to change the visual appearance of your data through the use of

control styles. You also see how to interact with the data-bound controls and how to speed up your application by keeping a local copy of frequently accessed data.

- **Chapter 15, "Security in Your ASP.NET 3.5 Web Site."** Although presented quite late in the book, security is a first-class, important topic. This chapter shows you how to make use of the built-in ASP.NET features related to security. You learn about a number of application services that facilitate security. You also learn about how to let users sign up for an account on your web site, how to distinguish between anonymous and logged-on users, and how to manage the users in your system.
- **Chapter 16, "Personalizing Web Sites."** Building on the security features introduced in Chapter 15, this chapter shows you how to create personalized web pages with content targeted at individual users. You see how to configure and use the ASP.NET Profile that enables you to store personalized data for known and anonymous visitors.
- **Chapter 17, "Exception Handling, Debugging, and Tracing."** In order to understand, improve, and fix the code you write for your ASP.NET web pages you need good debugging tools. Visual Web Developer ships with great debugging support that enables you to diagnose the state of your application at run time, helping you to find and fix problems before your users do.
- **Chapter 18, "Deploying Your Web Site."** By the end of the book, you should have a web site that is ready to be shown to the world. But how exactly do you do that? What are the things you need to know and understand to put your web site out in the wild? This chapter gives the answers and provides you with a good look at configuring different production systems in order to run your final web site.

How This Book Is Structured

This book takes the time to explain concepts step-by-step using working examples and detailed explanations. Using the famous Wrox Try It Out and How It Works sections, you are guided through a task step by step, detailing important things as you progress through the task. Each Try It Out task is followed by a detailed How It Works section that explains the steps you performed in the exercise.

At the end of each chapter, you find exercises that help you test the knowledge you gained in this chapter. You'll find the answers to each question in Appendix A at the end of this book. Don't worry if you don't know all the answers to the questions. Later chapters do not assume you followed and carried out the tasks from the exercise sections of previous chapters.

What You Need to Use This Book

This book assumes you have a system that meets the following requirements:

- Capable of running Visual Web Developer. For the exact system requirements, consult the readme file that comes with the software.
- Running Windows XP Professional Edition, Windows Vista (at least the Home Premium edition), or one of the server editions of Windows.

Although you should be able to follow along with most exercises using Windows XP Home or Windows Vista Basic, some of the chapters in this book require the use of IIS, Microsoft's web server, which only ships with the Windows versions in the requirements list.

The first chapter shows you how to obtain and install Visual Web Developer 2008, which in turn installs the Microsoft .NET Framework version 3.5 and SQL Server 2005 Express Edition; all you need is a good operating system and the drive to read this book!

Conventions

To help you get the most from the text and keep track of what's happening, a number of conventions are used throughout the book.

Try It Out Conventions

The Try It Out is an exercise you should work through, following the text in the book.

1. They usually consist of a set of steps.
2. Each step has a number.
3. Follow the steps through with your copy of the code.
4. Then read the How It Works section to find out what's going on.

How It Works

After each Try It Out, the actions you carried out and the code you've typed in will be explained in detail.

> **Boxes like this one hold important, not-to-be forgotten information that is directly relevant to the surrounding text.**

Tips, hints, tricks, and asides to the current discussion are offset and placed in italics like this.

As for styles in the text:

- New terms and important words are *italicized* when they are introduced.
- URLs and code within the text are presented like this: `Request.QueryString.Get("Id")`
- Menu items that require you to click multiple submenus have a special symbol that looks like this: ➪. For example: File ➪ New ➪ Folder.
- Code or content irrelevant to the discussion is either left out completely or replaced with three subsequent dots, like this:

```
<tr>
  <td style="white-space: nowrap;">
```

```
    ... Menu items go here; not shown
  </td>
</tr>
```

The three dots are used regardless of the programming language used in the example, so you'll see it for C#, Visual Basic, HTML, CSS, and JavaScript. When you see it in code you're instructed to type into the code editor, you can simply skip the three dots and anything that follows them on the same line.

- Code shown for the first time, or other relevant code, is in the following format:

```
Dim albumOwner As String
albumOwner = "Imar"
lblOwner.Text = albumOwner
```

By contrast, less important code, or code that you have seen before, looks like this:

```
albumOwner = "Imar"
```

- Text that appears on screen often has Each Word Start With A Capital Letter, even though the original screen text uses a different capitalization. This is done to make the screen text stand out from the rest of the text.

Source Code

As you work through the examples in this book, you may choose either to type in all the code manually or to use the source code files that accompany the book. All of the source code used in this book is available for download at `www.wrox.com`. Once at the site, locate the book's title (either by using the Search box or by using one of the title lists) and click the Download Code link on the book's detail page to obtain all the source code for the book.

Because many books have similar titles, you may find it easiest to search by ISBN; for this book the ISBN is 978-0-470-18759-3.

You can download the full source for this book as a single file that you can decompress with your favorite decompression tool. If you extract the source, make sure you maintain the original folder structure that is part of the code download. The different decompression tools use different names for this feature, but look for a feature like Use Folder Names or Maintain Directory Structure. Once you have extracted the files from the code download, you should end up with a folder called Source and a folder called Resources. Then create a new folder in the root of your C drive, call it BegASPNET, and move the Source and Resources folders into this new folder so you end up with folders like C:\BegASPNET\Source and C:\BegASPNET\Resources. The source folder contains the source for each of the 18 chapters of this book and the final version of the PlanetWrox application that you'll work on throughout this book. The Resources folder contains files you need during some of the exercises in this book. If everything turned out correctly, you should end up with the structure shown in Figure I-1.

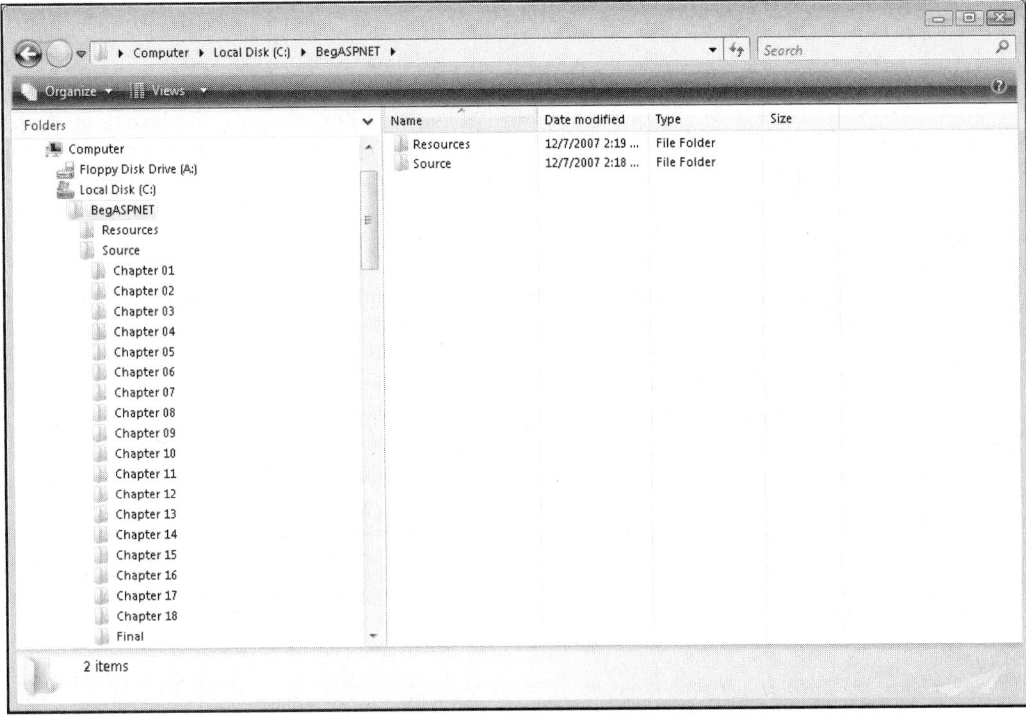

Figure I-1

Later chapters have you create folders called Site and Release inside the same C:\BegASPNET folder giving you a folder structure similar to that in Figure I-2.

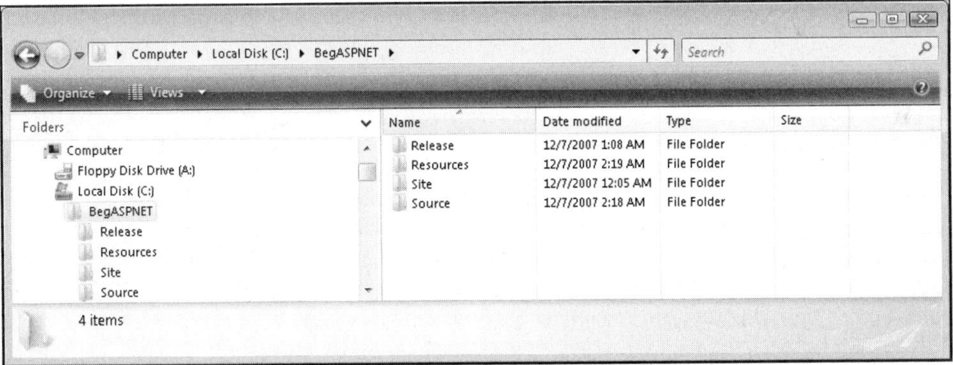

Figure I-2

The Site folder contains the site as you'll build it throughout this book, while the Release folder will contain your final version at the end of this book. Whenever you're stuck with some examples in this book, you can take a peek in the Source folder to see how things should have ended up.

If you want to run the site for a specific chapter to see how it works, be sure to open the chapter's folder in Visual Web Developer as a web site. So you should open C:\BegASPNET\Source\Chapter 13 rather than opening its parent folder C:\BegASPNET\Source.

Sticking to this structure ensures a smooth execution of the Try It Out exercises in this book. Incorrectly mixing or nesting these folders make it harder to carry out the exercises and may even lead to unexpected situations and errors. Whenever you run into an issue or error that is not explained in this book, ensure that your site structure is still closely related to the one presented here.

Errata

I have made every effort to ensure that there are no errors in the text or in the code. However, no one is perfect, and mistakes do occur. If you find an error in this book, like a spelling mistake or a faulty piece of code, I'd be very grateful for your feedback. By sending in errata you may save another reader hours of frustration and at the same time you will be helping me provide even higher quality information.

To find the errata page for this book, go to `www.wrox.com` and locate the title using the Search box or one of the title lists. Then, on the book details page, click the Book Errata link. On this page you can view all errata that has been submitted for this book and posted by Wrox editors. A complete book list including links to each book's errata is also available at `www.wrox.com/misc-pages/booklist.shtml`.

If you don't spot "your" error on the Book Errata page, go to `www.wrox.com/contact/techsupport.shtml` and complete the form there to send us the error you have found. I'll check the information and, if appropriate, post a message to the book's errata page and fix the problem in subsequent editions of the book.

p2p.wrox.com

For author and peer discussion, join the P2P forums at `p2p.wrox.com`. The forums are a web-based system for you to post messages relating to Wrox books and related technologies and interact with other readers and technology users. The forums offer a subscription feature to e-mail you topics of interest of your choosing when new posts are made to the forums. I am a frequent visitor of the Wrox forums, and I'll do my best to help you with any questions you may have about this book.

At `p2p.wrox.com` you will find a number of different forums that will help you not only as you read this book, but also as you develop your own applications. To join the forums, just follow these steps:

1. Go to `p2p.wrox.com` and click the Register Now link.
2. Read the terms of use and click Agree.

3. Complete the required information to join as well as any optional information you wish to provide and click Submit.
4. You will receive an e-mail with information describing how to verify your account and complete the joining process.

You can read messages in the forums without joining P2P but in order to post your own messages, you must join.

After you join, you can post new messages and respond to messages other users post. You'll find this book's own forum under the Books category that is available from the homepage or by clicking View All Forums on the menu on the left. You can read messages at any time on the Web. If you would like to have new messages from a particular forum e-mailed to you, click the Subscribe to this Forum icon by the forum name in the forum listing.

For more information about how to use the Wrox P2P, be sure to read the P2P FAQs for answers to questions about how the forum software works as well as many common questions specific to P2P and Wrox books. To read the FAQs, click the FAQ link on any P2P page.

Getting Started with ASP.NET 3.5

Ever since the first release of the .NET Framework 1.0 in early 2002, Microsoft has put a lot of effort and development time into ASP.NET, the part of the .NET Framework that enables you to build rich web applications. This first release meant a radical change from the older Microsoft technology to build web sites called *Active Server Pages* (ASP), now often referred to as *classic* ASP. The introduction of ASP.NET 1.0 and the associated Visual Studio .NET 2002 gave developers the following benefits over classic ASP:

- A clean separation between presentation and code. With classic ASP, your coding logic was often scattered throughout the HTML of the page, making it hard to make changes to the page later.
- A development model that was much closer to the way desktop applications are programmed. This made it easier for the many Visual Basic desktop programmers to make the switch to web applications.
- A feature-rich development tool (called Visual Studio .NET) that allowed developers to create and code their web applications visually.
- A choice between a number of *object-oriented programming* languages, of which Visual Basic .NET and C# (pronounced as C-Sharp) are now the most popular.
- Access to the entire .NET Framework, which for the first time meant that web developers had a unified and easy way to access many advanced features to work with databases, files, e-mail, networking tools, and much more.

Despite the many advantages of ASP.NET over the older model, using ASP.NET also meant an increase of complexity and the knowledge you needed to build applications with it, making it harder for many new programmers to get started with ASP.NET.

After the initial release in 2002, Microsoft released another version of the .NET Framework (called .NET 1.1) and the development IDE Visual Studio .NET in 2003. Many people saw this as a service pack for the initial release, although it also brought a lot of new enhancements in both the framework and the development tools.

In November 2005, Visual Studio 2005 and ASP.NET 2.0 were released. To the pleasant surprise of many developers around the world, Microsoft had again been able to drastically improve and expand the product, adding many features and tools that helped reduce the complexity that was introduced with ASP.NET 1.0. New wizards and smart controls made it possible to reduce the code required to build an application, decreasing the learning curve for new developers and increasing the productivity.

The current version, ASP.NET 3.5, builds on top of the successful ASP.NET 2.0 release, leaving many of the beloved features in place, while adding new features and tools in other areas.

Over the next 18 chapters, you learn how to build full-featured ASP.NET web sites using Visual Web Developer, Microsoft's development tool for ASP.NET web applications. This book guides you through the process of creating a fully functional, database-driven web, starting with a bare bones web site in this chapter, all the way down to the deployment of it to a production environment in Chapter 18.

To start off, this chapter gives you a good look at:

- Visual Web Developer 2008 Express Edition and Visual Studio 2008 and how to acquire and install them.
- Creating your first web site with Visual Web Developer.
- The way an ASP.NET page is processed and sent to the browser.
- How you can use and customize the development environment.

The chapter closes with an overview of the sample web site that comes with this book, the Planet Wrox web site. In this chapter, you'll see what the site has to offer and how to use it; the remainder of this book then shows you the inner workings of the site and how it's built.

The sample site and all the examples in this book are built with Visual Web Developer (VWD), so it's important that you have it installed on your development machine, and know how to access its most basic features. The next section shows you how to acquire and install VWD. Once you have it up and running, you'll see how to create your first web site, followed by an extensive tour through the many features of VWD.

Microsoft Visual Web Developer

Although you could theoretically write ASP.NET web applications with Notepad or another text editor alone, you really want to install a copy of Microsoft Visual Web Developer. VWD is developed specifically for building ASP.NET web sites, and as such, hosts an enormous amount of tools that will help you in rapidly creating complex ASP.NET web applications.

Visual Web Developer comes in two flavors: as a standalone and free version called Microsoft Visual Web Developer 2008 Express Edition, and as part of the larger development suite called Visual Studio 2008, which is also available in different editions, each with its own price tag. Although the Express Edition of VWD is free, it contains all the features and tools you need to create complex and feature-rich web applications. All the examples you find in the book can be built with the free Express Edition so there's no need to shell out big bucks for the commercial versions of Visual Studio 2008 to follow along with this book.

Getting VWD is easy. You can download it from the Microsoft site as discussed next.

Getting Visual Web Developer

You can get the free version of VWD from the Microsoft site at `www.microsoft.com/express/`. On the Express home page, follow the Download Now link until you reach the page that offers the downloads for the Express products, including Visual Web Developer 2008 Express Edition. From this page, you can download Visual Web Developer 2008 Express Edition as a Web Install, where you download only the installer, while the remaining files are downloaded during the installation process. Make sure you choose Visual Web Developer from the page, and not one of the other free Express products. The page also allows you to download all Express products conveniently as an ISO image that you can burn onto a DVD.

Don't be fooled by the file size of the Web Install download, which is little under 3MB. The file you downloaded is just the installer that downloads the required files over the Internet. The total download is around 1.3GB.

If you want to try out the full version of Visual Studio 2008, which also contains VWD, you can sign up for a free 90-day trial that you can get from the Microsoft site at `http://msdn2.microsoft.com/vstudio`. You can choose to download an ISO image that you'll need to burn on a DVD.

Installing Visual Web Developer Express Edition

Installing Visual Web Developer is a straightforward, although somewhat lengthy, process. Depending on your installation method, your computer and your Internet connection speed, installing VWD may take up to several hours.

Try It Out Installing Visual Web Developer 2008 Express Edition

This Try it Out exercise guides you through installing VWD Express Edition on your computer. It assumes you're using the web download option, although the process for installing the Express edition from a DVD is almost identical. The steps you need to perform to install the full versions of Visual Studio 2008 are similar as well, although the screens you'll see will be somewhat different.

No matter which version of VWD you install, it's important that you also install SQL Server 2005 Express Edition — a required component if you want to follow along with many of this book's examples. When you install the full version of Visual Studio 2008, the option to install SQL Server is included on the list with features to install that you see during setup. If you install VWD Express Edition, you get the option to choose SQL Server on the Installer Options dialog box. If you don't see SQL Server listed on these dialog boxes, you probably already have SQL Server 2005 Express Edition installed.

1. When you're installing the web version, run the file you downloaded from the Microsoft web site. Otherwise, start the setup process from the Visual Studio or Visual Web Developer DVD.
2. Once the installer has started, click Next, read and accept the license terms, and click Next once more.
3. On the Installer Options page, make sure you select both the MSDN Express Library for Visual Studio 2008 and Microsoft SQL Server 2005 Express Edition. Although these two options add

considerably to the size of the download, both of them are invaluable for building ASP.NET web applications. If you don't see the SQL Server option, you already have it installed. The Microsoft Silverlight Runtime component is optional, although it's probably a good idea to download it now because you'll see more and more web sites using Silverlight in the near future. Click Next again.

4. On the Destination Folder page, you can leave the Install in folder field set to its default if you have enough space on your primary disk. Otherwise, click the Browse button and select a different location.

5. Click the Install button. If you're using the web-based installer, the setup application will first download the files over the Internet to your computer. During the installation process, you'll see a screen (similar to Figure 1-1) that shows you the progress of the download and installation of VWD.

6. Once the application is finished installing, you may get a dialog box asking to reboot your machine. Click Restart now. Once your machine has started again, VWD is ready for use.

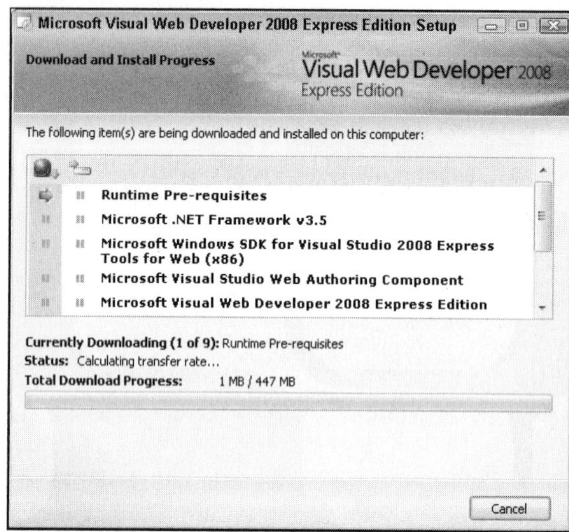

Figure 1-1

How It Works

The straightforward installation process guided you through the setup of VWD Express Edition. In the Installer Options dialog box, you selected the MSDN Library — which contains the help files for VWD — and Microsoft SQL Server 2005 Express Edition, Microsoft's free version of its database engine. SQL Server 2005 is discussed and used a lot in this book, starting with Chapter 11. Appendix B shows you how to configure security settings for the various versions of SQL Server 2005 using the free SQL Server Management Studio Express Edition.

Now that VWD is installed, it's time to fire it up and start working with it. The next section shows you how to create your very first site in VWD. You see how to create a site, add content to a web page, and view that page in your browser.

Creating Your First ASP.NET 3.5 Web Site

You probably can't wait to get started with your first ASP.NET web site, so instead of giving you a theoretical overview of web sites in VWD, the next Try It Out exercise dives right into the action and shows you how to build your first web project. Then, in the How It Works explanation and the section that follows, you get a good look of what goes on behind the scenes when you view an ASP.NET page in your browser.

Try It Out — Creating Your First ASP.NET Web Page

1. Start VWD from the Windows Start menu if you haven't done so already. The first time you start VWD, there is a long delay before you can use VWD because it's busy configuring itself. Subsequent starts of the application will go much faster.

2. If you're using a commercial version of Visual Studio, you also get a dialog box that lets you choose between different collections of settings the first time you start Visual Studio. The choice you make on that dialog box influences the layout of windows, toolboxes, menus, and shortcuts. Choose Web Development Settings because those settings are designed specifically for ASP.NET developers. You can always choose a different profile later by resetting your settings, as explained later in this chapter.

3. Once VWD is fully configured, you see the main screen appear, as shown in Figure 1-2.

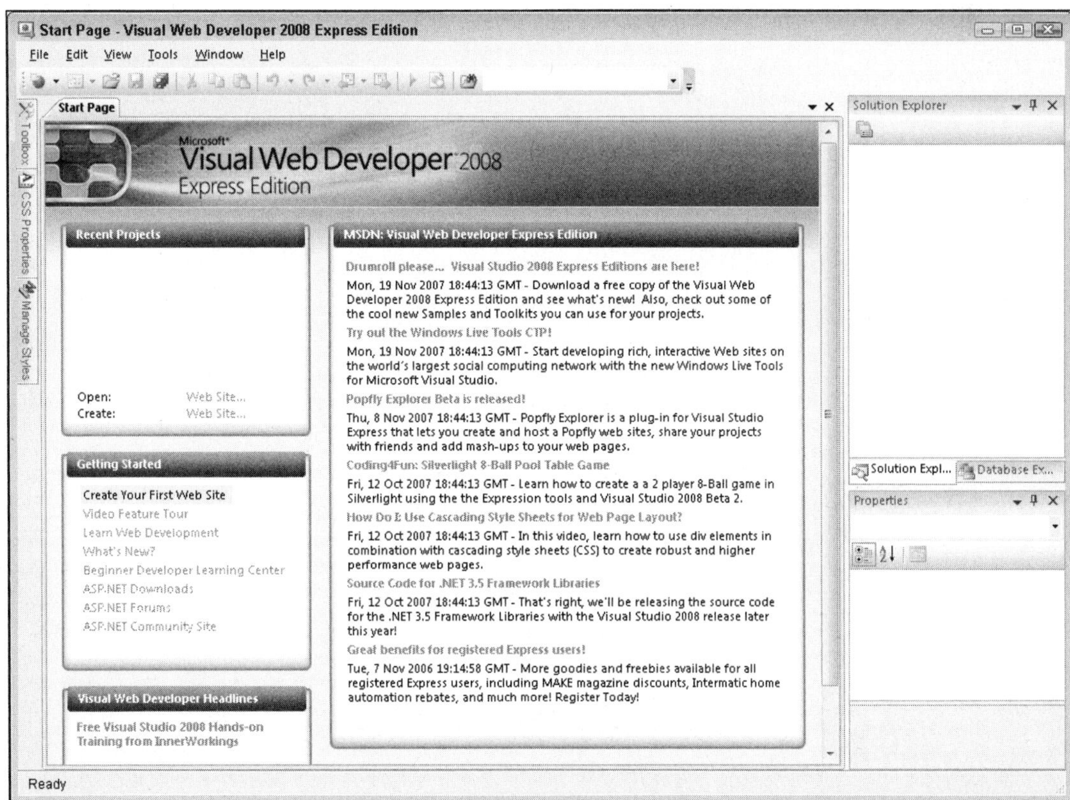

Figure 1-2

You get a full description of all the windows, toolbars, panels, and menus in the next section, so for now, just focus on creating a new web site. Click the File menu in the upper-left corner and choose New Web Site. If you're using a commercial version of Visual Studio, you may have to open the submenu New first. (Make sure you don't accidentally use the New Project menu, as that is used to create different types of .NET applications.) The New Web Site dialog box appears as shown in Figure 1-3.

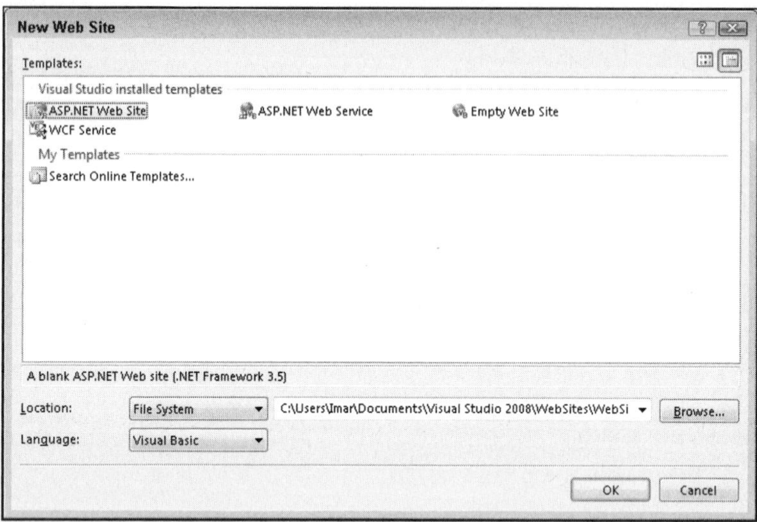

Figure 1-3

4. In the Templates section of the dialog box, verify that ASP.NET Web Site is selected. Also verify that File System is the selected option in the Location drop-down list. If you want, you could change the location on disk where the web site is stored by clicking the Browse button and choosing a new location on your computer's hard drive. For now, the default location — a folder under your Documents folder — is fine, so you can leave the location as is.

5. In the Language drop-down list, you can choose a programming language you will use mainly in your site. This book shows all examples in both Visual Basic and C# so you can choose a language to your liking.

6. Click OK. VWD creates a new web site for you that includes one standard ASP.NET page called Default.aspx, a web.config file, and an empty App_Data folder, as shown in Figure 1-4. It also opens the file Default.aspx so you can see the code for the page.

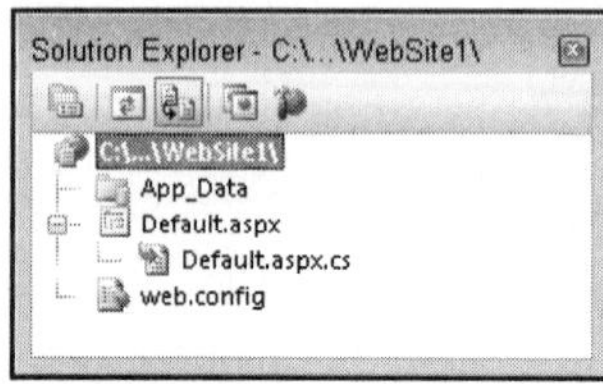

Figure 1-4

7. Between the opening and closing <div> tags in the page, type the highlighted text and code:

```
<div>
  <h1>Hello World</h1>
  <p>Welcome to Beginning ASP.NET 3.5 on <%= DateTime.Now.ToString() %></p>
</div>
```

- You'll see code formatted like this a lot more in this book. When you are instructed to type in code formatted like this with mixed background colors, you only need to type in the highlighted code. The other code should already be present in the file.
- When you see code like this in a discussion — for example, in a How it Works section — the highlighted code is the part you need to focus on, while the code with no background is less important.
- Don't worry about the code with the angle brackets (<>) in the welcome message; you'll see how it works later in this book. Although this code may not look familiar to you now, you can probably guess what it does: it writes out today's date and time.

8. From the Debug menu in VWD, choose Start Without Debugging (or press Ctrl+F5) to open the page in your default browser, as shown in Figure 1-5.

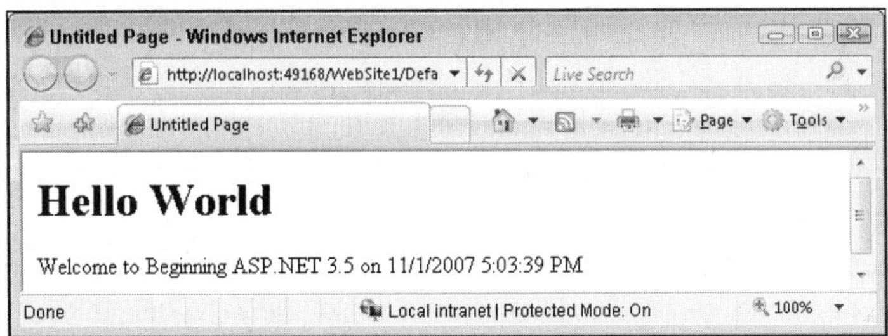

Figure 1-5

If you don't see the date and time in the page, or if you get an error, look again at the code in the welcome message. It starts with an angle bracket (<) followed by a percentage symbol and an equals sign. It closes with a single percentage sign and another angle bracket (>). Also, make sure you typed in the code exactly as shown here, including capitalization. This is especially true when you are using C#, as that language is case sensitive.

If you get an Information bar warning about Intranet settings in Internet Explorer, click the bar and choose Enable Intranet Settings. If you want to learn more about the implications of these settings first, choose What are Intranet Settings from the popup menu.

9. Notice how a little icon with a screen tip appeared in the tray bar of Windows, visible in Figure 1-6. This icon belongs to the ASP.NET Development Server. This web server has been started by VWD automatically to serve the request for your page. You'll learn more about how the web server is able to process your page later in this book.

Figure 1-6

That's it. You just created your very first ASP.NET 3.5 web site with VWD.

How It Works

Although the web page you created in the previous Try It Out is quite simple, the process that eventually results in the page being displayed in your browser isn't so simple. All by itself, the ASP.NET page (also referred to as an ASPX page because of its extension) you created in the previous Try It Out can't do much. It needs to be processed and served by a *web server* before your browser can display it. That's why VWD automatically started up the built-in ASP.NET Development Server to handle the request for the page. Next, it started up your default web browser and directed it to the address of the web server, `http://localhost:49168/WebSite1` in the Try It Out example, although the actual number in the address may change every time you start the web server as the number is randomly chosen by VWD.

It's important to realize that the ASPX file you created in VWD is not the same as the one that eventually gets displayed by the browser.

When you create a page in VWD, you add *markup* to it. The markup in an ASPX page is a combination of plain text, HTML, code for ASP.NET server controls (which you'll learn more about in this chapter and in Chapter 4), code written in Visual Basic.NET or C#, and more.

When you request an ASPX page in your browser, the web server processes the page, executes any code it finds in the file, and effectively transforms the ASP.NET markup into plain HTML that it then sends to the browser, where it is displayed. In the previous Try It Out, the resulting HTML causes the browser to display the current date and time. HTML, or HyperText Markup Language, is the language that browsers use to display a web page. You learn how HTML looks and how to use it later in this chapter.

To see how the final HTML differs from the original ASPX page, open the source for the page in your browser. In most browsers, you can bring up the source window by right-clicking the page and choosing View Source. This brings up your default text editor, showing the HTML for the page.

If you already closed your browser after the previous Try It Out, press Ctrl+F5 in VWD to open the page again.

Most of the HTML you see in the text editor is similar to the original ASPX page. However, if you look at the line that displays the welcome message and the current date and time, you'll notice a big difference. Instead of the code between the angle brackets and percentage signs, you now see the actual date and time:

```
      <h1>Hello World</h1>
      <p>Welcome to Beginning ASP.NET 3.5 on 11/1/2007 5:03:39 PM</p>
    </div>
```

When the web server processed the page, it looked up the current date and time from the local computer, and inserted it in the HTML that got sent to the browser.

In the following section, you'll see how this works in much more detail.

An Introduction to ASP.NET 3.5

When you type a web address like `www.wrox.com` in your web browser and press Enter, the browser sends a request to the web server at that address. This is done through HTTP, the *HyperText Transfer Protocol*. HTTP is the protocol by which web browsers and web servers communicate. When you send the address, you send a *request* to the server. When the server is active and the request is valid, the server accepts the request, processes it, and then sends the *response* back to the client browser. The relationship between the request and response is shown in Figure 1-7.

For simple, static files, like HTML files or images, the web server simply reads in the file from its local hard drive and sends it to the browser. However, for dynamic files, such as ASPX pages, this is obviously not good enough. If the web server were to send the ASPX file directly to the browser as a text file, you wouldn't have seen the current date and time in the browser, but instead you would have seen the actual code (`<%= DateTime.Now.ToString() %>`). So, instead of sending the file directly, the web server hands over the request to another piece of software that is able to process the page. This is done with a concept called Application Mapping or Handler Mapping, where an extension of a file (.aspx in this example) is mapped to an application that is capable of handling it. In the case of an .aspx page, the request is eventually handled and processed by the *ASP.NET runtime*, part of the Microsoft .NET Framework designed specifically to handle web requests.

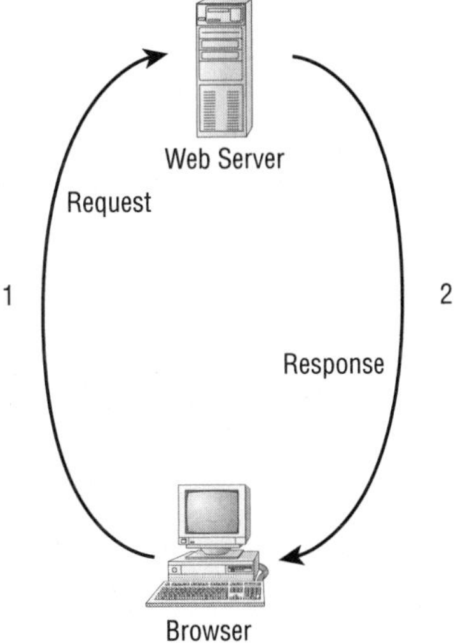

Figure 1-7

During the processing of the page, three important areas can influence the way the page eventually ends up in the browser:

- **Static text.** Any static text, like HTML, CSS, or JavaScript code you place in a page, is sent to the browser directly. You learn more about HTML, CSS, and JavaScript in this and subsequent chapters, including Chapter 3, which gives you a detailed look at CSS.
- **ASP.NET server controls.** These controls are placed in your ASPX page and when they are processed, they emit HTML that is inserted in the page. You'll learn more about server controls after the discussion of HTML in this chapter, and Chapter 4 is devoted entirely to ASP.NET server controls.
- **Programming code.** You can embed code, like Visual Basic .NET or C#, directly in a page, as you saw in the previous Try It Out. In addition, you can place code in a separate code file, called a Code Behind file. This code can be executed by the runtime automatically, or based on a user's action. Either way, execution of the code can greatly influence the way the page is displayed, by accessing databases, performing calculations, hiding or showing specific controls, and much more. Programming your ASP.NET web pages is discussed in great detail in Chapter 5.

Once the page is done processing, and all the HTML for the page has been collected, it is sent back to the browser. The browser then reads this HTML, parses it and, finally, displays the page for you to look at.

Since HTML is so critical for displaying web pages, the next section gives you an overview of HTML.

Understanding HTML

HTML is the de facto language for creating web pages and is understood by every web browser that exists today. Since the beginning of the '90s it has been the driving force of the World Wide Web, the part of the Internet that deals with web pages. HTML documents are simple text files that contain markup, a combination of text, and additional data that influences that text.

HTML Elements

HTML uses angle brackets to indicate how your content should be *rendered* (or displayed) in the browser. The angle brackets are referred to as *tags;* a pair of tags holding some text is referred to as an *element*. Take another look at the HTML you saw in the previous Try It Out where you opened the source window for the page in the browser:

```
<h1>Hello World</h1>
<p>Welcome to Beginning ASP.NET 3.5 on 11/1/2007 5:03:39 PM</p>
```

The first line of this example contains an `<h1>` element with an opening tag (`<h1>`) and a closing tag (`</h1>`). This element is used to signify a heading at level one. Notice how the element is closed with a similar tag, but with an additional forward slash (/) in it: `</h1>`. Any text between these opening and closing tags is considered part of the element, and is thus rendered as a heading. In most browsers, this means the text is rendered in a larger font. Similar to the `<h1>` tag, there are tags for creating headings up to level six, such as `<h2>`, `<h3>`, and so on.

Below the heading element, you see a <p> element, which is used to denote a paragraph. All text within the pair of <p> tags is considered part of the paragraph. By default, a browser renders a paragraph with some additional margin spacing at the bottom, although you can override that behavior.

Many tags are available in HTML; too many to cover them all here. The following table lists some of the most important tags and describes how they can be used. For a complete list of all HTML elements, take a look at the web site of the organization that maintains HTML: www.w3.org/TR/html401/index/elements.html.

Tag	Description	Example
<html>	Used to denote the start and end of the entire page.	<html> ...All other content goes here </html>
<head> <title>	Used to denote a special section of the page that contains data about the page, including its title.	<head> <title>Welcome to my site</title> </head>
<body>	Used to denote the start and end of the body of the page.	<body> Page body goes here </body>
<a>	Used to link one web page to another.	<a href="http://www.wrox.com">Visit the Wrox site</a>
<img>	Used to embed images in a page.	<img src="Logo.gif" />
<b> <i> <u>	Used to format text in a bold, italic, or underline font.	This is <b>bold text</b> while <i>this text is in italic</i>
<form> <textarea> <select> <input>	Used for input forms that allow users of a web site to submit information to the server.	<input type="text" value="Some Text" />
<table> <tr> <td>	These tags are used to create a layout with a table. The <table> tag defines the entire table, while the <tr> and <td> are used to define rows and cells, respectively.	<table> <tr> <td>This is a Cell in Column 1</td> <td>This is a Cell in Column 2</td> </tr> </table>

Continued

Continued

Tag	Description	Example
<ul> <ol> <li>	These three tags are used to create numbered or bulleted lists. The <ul> and the <ol> define the looks of the list (either unordered, with a simple bullet, or ordered, with a number), while the <li> is used to represent items in the list.	<ul> <li>First item with a bullet</li> <li>Second item with a bullet</li> </ul> <ol> <li>First item with a number</li> <li>Second item with a number</li> </ol>
<span>	This tag is used to wrap and influence other parts of the document. It appears as *inline*, so it adds no additional line break to the page.	<p>This is some normal text while <span style="color: red;">this text appears in red</span></p>
<div>	Just like the <span> tag, the <div> is used as a container for other elements. However, the <div> acts as a *block element*, which causes an explicit line break after the <div> tag by default.	<div>This is some text on 1 line</div> <div>This text is put directly under the previous text on a new line. </div>

HTML Attributes

In addition to the HTML elements, the previous table also shows you *HTML attributes*. Attributes contain additional information that changes the way a specific element behaves. For example, with the `<img>` tag that is used to display an image, the `src` attribute defines the source of that image. Similarly, the `<span>` tag contains a `style` attribute that changes the color of the text to red. The value of the `style` attribute (`color: red;`) is part of a *Cascading Style Sheet* (CSS), which is discussed in much more detail in Chapter 3. Just as with the HTML elements, there is a long list of available attributes on the W3C web site: `www.w3.org/TR/html401/index/attributes.html`.

You don't need to memorize all these elements and attributes. Most of the time, they are generated for you automatically by VWD. In other cases, where you need to enter them by hand, VWD has some great tools to help you find the right tag or attribute. This tool, called IntelliSense, is discussed later in the book.

The Difference Between HTML and XHTML

In addition to HTML, you may also run into the term XHTML. Although the two have very similar names, there are some interesting differences that you need to be aware of. XHTML is a reformulation of HTML in

XML — eXtensible Markup Language. This is a generic, text- and tag-based language used to describe data and is used as the base language for many other languages, including XHTML.

So, XHTML is in fact largely just HTML rewritten with XML rules. These rules are pretty simple, and most of the time VWD will help you get it right or show you a list of errors and suggestions on how to fix them.

Always Close Your Elements

In XHTML, all elements must be closed. So when you start a paragraph with `<p>`, you must use `</p>` somewhere later in your page to close the paragraph. This is also the case for tags that don't have their own closing tags, like `<img>` or `<br>` (to enter a line break). In XHTML, these tags are written as *self-closing tags,* where the closing slash is embedded directly in the tag itself as in `<img src="Logo.gif" />` or `<br />`.

Always Use Lower Case for Your Tag and Attribute Names

XML is case sensitive, and XHTML applies that rule by forcing you to write all your tags in lowercase. Although the tags and attributes must be in all lowercase, the actual value doesn't have to be. So, the previous example that displays the logo image is perfectly valid XHTML, despite the uppercase L in the image name.

Always Enclose Attribute Values in Quotes

Whenever you write an attribute in a tag, make sure you wrap its value in quotes. For example, when writing out the `<img>` tag and the `src` attribute, write it like this:

```
<img src="Logo.gif" />
```

and not like this:

```
<img src=Logo.gif />
```

Note that you could also use single quotes to enclose the attribute value, as in this example:

```
<img src='Logo.gif' />
```

It's also sometimes necessary to nest single and double quotes. When some special ASP.NET syntax requires the use of double quotes, you should use single quotes to wrap the attribute's value:

```
<asp:Label ID="DescriptionLabel" runat="server" Text='<%# Eval("Description") %>' />
```

You'll see this syntax used a lot more in other chapters in this book.

For consistency, this book uses double quotes where possible in all HTML that ends up in the client.

Nest Your Tags Correctly

When you write nested tags, make sure that you first close the inner tag you opened last, and then close the outer tag. Consider this correct example that formats a piece of text with both bold and italic fonts:

```
<b><i>This is some formatted text</i></b>
```

Notice how the <i> is closed before the <b> tag. Swapping the order of the closing tags leads to invalid XHTML:

```
<b><i>This is some formatted text</b></i>
```

Always Add a DOCTYPE Declaration to Your Page

A DOCTYPE gives the browser information about the kind of HTML it can expect. By default, VWD adds a DOCTYPE for XHTML 1.0 Transitional to your page:

```
<!DOCTYPE html PUBLIC "-//W3C//DTD XHTML 1.0 Transitional//EN"
       "http://www.w3.org/TR/xhtml1/DTD/xhtml1-transitional.dtd">
```

The DOCTYPE greatly influences the way browsers like Internet Explorer render the page. VWD's default DOCTYPE of XHTML 1.0 Transitional gives you a good mix between valid markup and pages that render the same in all major browsers.

> *If you want to learn more about XHTML, get a copy of* Beginning Web Programming with HTML, XHTML, and CSS, *ISBN: 978-0-7645-7078-0.*

Besides HTML, an ASP.NET web page can contain other markup as well. Most pages will have one or more ASP.NET Server Controls on the page to give it some added functionality. The next section briefly looks at these ASP.NET Server Controls, and you get an in-depth look at them in Chapter 4.

A First Look at ASP.NET Markup

To some extent, the markup for ASP.NET Server Controls is similar to that of HTML. It also has the notion of tags and attributes, using the same angle brackets and closing tags as HTML does. However, there are also some differences.

For starters, most of the ASP.NET tags start with an `asp:` prefix. For example, a button in ASP.NET looks like this:

```
<asp:Button ID="Button1" runat="server" Text="Button" />
```

Note how the tag is self-closed with the trailing slash (/) character, eliminating the need to type a separate closing tag.

Another thing you may have noticed is that the tag and attribute names are not necessarily in all lowercase. Because an ASP.NET Server Control lives on the server, it doesn't have to adhere to the XHTML rules used in the browser at the client. However, when a server control is asked to emit its HTML to a page that is configured to output XHTML, it will do so in XHTML. So, the code for the same button looks like this when rendered in the browser as XHTML:

```
<input type="submit" name="Button1" value="Button" id="Button1" />
```

Notice how the entire tag and its attributes conform to the XHTML standard.

Now that you understand the basics of an ASP.NET page and the HTML that it generates, it's time to look at VWD again. Knowing how to use the application and its many tools and windows is an important step in building fun, good-looking, and functional web sites.

A Tour of the IDE

VWD is by far the most extensive and feature-rich *integrated development environment* (IDE) for building ASP.NET web pages. The abbreviation IDE refers to the way all the separate tools you need to build complex web applications are integrated in a single environment. Instead of writing code in a text editor, compiling code at the command line, writing HTML and CSS in a separate application, and managing your database in yet another, VWD allows you to perform all of these tasks, and more, from the same environment. Besides the efficiency this brings because you don't have to constantly switch tools, this also makes it much easier to learn new areas of VWD, as many of the built-in tools work in the same way.

The Main Development Area

To get familiar with the many tools that are packed in VWD's interface, take a look at Figure 1-8. It shows the same screen you got after you created your first web site in VWD, but now it highlights some of the most important screen elements. If you had a previous version of Visual Studio installed, your screen may look different, as Visual Studio 2008 is able to import settings from older versions.

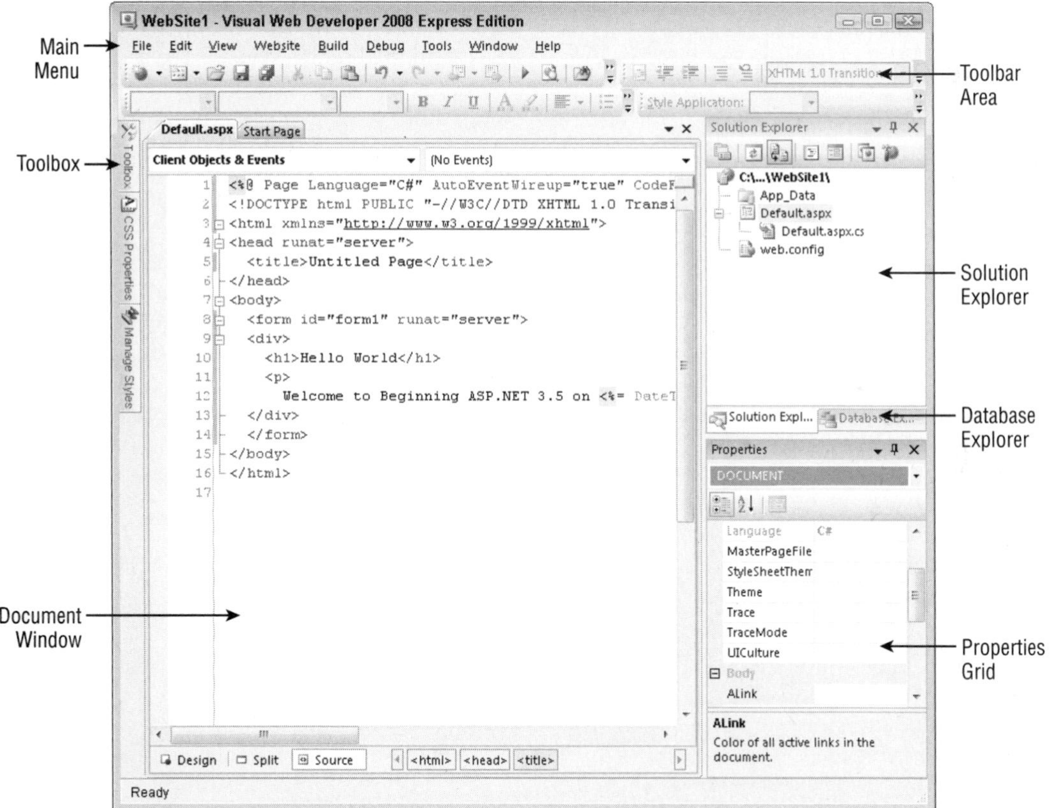

Figure 1-8

The Main Menu

At the top of the application, right below the Windows title bar, you see the main menu. This menu bar contains familiar items you find in many other Windows applications, like the File, Edit, and Help menus as well as menus that are specific to VWD, such as the Website and Debug menus. The menu changes dynamically depending on the task you're working on, so you'll see menu items appear and disappear as you work your way through the application.

The Toolbar Area

Right below the menu, you see the toolbar area that is capable of showing different toolbars that give you quick access to the most common functions in VWD. In Figure 1-8, only four of the toolbars are enabled, but VWD comes with many other toolbars that you can use in specific task-oriented scenarios. Some toolbars appear automatically when you're working on a task that requires a particular toolbar's presence, but you can also enable and disable toolbars to your liking. To enable or disable a toolbar, right-click an existing toolbar or the menu bar and choose the toolbar from the menu that appears.

The Toolbox

On the left of the main screen, tucked away at the border of VWD, you see the tab for the Toolbox. If you hover your mouse over the tab, the Toolbox folds out, giving you a chance to see what it contains. If you click the little pin icon in the upper-right corner of the Toolbox (or any of the other panels that have this pin icon), it gets pinned to the IDE so it remains open.

Just as with the menu bar and the toolbars, the Toolbox automatically updates itself to show content that is relevant to the task you're working on. When you're editing a standard ASPX page, the Toolbox shows the many controls you have available for your page. You can simply drag an item from the Toolbox and drop it on a location of your page where you want it to appear. These controls are discussed in great detail in Chapter 4.

The Toolbox contains multiple categories with tools that can be expanded and collapsed as you see fit to make it easier to find the right tool. You can also reorder the items in the list, add and remove items from the Toolbox, and even add your own tools to it. Customizing the IDE is discussed later in this chapter.

If the Toolbox is not visible on-screen, press Ctrl+Alt+X to open it or choose Toolbox from the View menu.

There are two additional tabs below the Toolbox tab: CSS Properties and Manage Styles. Both are discussed extensively in Chapter 3.

The Solution Explorer

At the right of the screen, you see the Solution Explorer. The Solution Explorer is an important window because it gives you an overview of the files that comprise your web site. Instead of placing all your files in one big folder, the Solution Explorer enables you to store files in separate folders, creating a logical and organized site structure. You can use the Solution Explorer to add new files to your site, move existing files around using drag and drop, delete files from the project, and more. Most of the functionality of the Solution Explorer is hidden behind its right-click menu, which changes depending on the item you right-clicked in the explorer window.

At the top of the Solution Explorer, you see a little toolbar that gives you quick access to some functionality related to your web site, including opening the Properties window for the selected item, refreshing the Solution Explorer window, an option to nest related files, and two buttons that allow you to copy and configure your web site. All of this functionality is discussed later in the book.

You can access the Solution Explorer by choosing View ➪ Solution Explorer from the main menu or by pressing Ctrl+Alt+L.

The Database Explorer

This window, hidden behind the Solution Explorer in Figure 1-8, enables you to work with your databases. It gives you the tools to create new databases and open existing ones, add new tables and queries to your database, and access other tools that enable you to work with the data in your database. If you have a commercial version of Visual Studio, such as Visual Studio 2008 Professional, this window is called the Server Explorer and may be located at the left of your screen.

The Database Explorer is discussed in more detail in the chapters about databases, starting with Chapter 11.

The Properties Grid

With the Properties Grid, you can view and edit the properties of many items in Visual Studio, including files in the Solution Explorer, controls on a web page, properties of the page itself, and much more. The window constantly updates itself to reflect the selected item. You can quickly open the Properties Grid by pressing F4. This same shortcut can be used to force the Properties Grid to show the details of a selected item.

The Document Window

The Document Window is the main area in the middle of the application. This is where most of the action takes place. You can use the Document Window to work with many different document formats, including ASPX and HTML files, CSS and JavaScript files, code files for VB and C#, XML and text files, and even images. In addition, you can use the same window to manage databases, create copies of your site, and view the pages in your site in the built-in mini-browser, and much more.

At the bottom of the Document Window in Figure 1-9, you see three buttons called Design, Split, and Source. These buttons appear automatically when you're working with a file that contains markup, such as ASPX and HTML pages. They allow you to open the Design View of a page (giving you an idea of how the page will look in the browser), its Markup View (the HTML and other markup), or both at the same time. How this works is explained in more detail in Chapter 2 but for now, it's important to realize you can switch between Markup View and Design View by clicking the appropriate buttons. The Markup View is also often called the Source View or Code View window. However, in order to avoid confusion, this book uses the term Markup View exclusively.

The Document Window is a tabbed window by default, which means it can host multiple documents, each one distinguished by a tab with the file name at the top of the window. The right-click menu of each tab contains some useful shortcuts for working with the file, including saving and closing it and opening the file's parent folder in Windows Explorer.

To switch between documents, you can press Ctrl+Tab or you can click the down arrow in the upper-right corner of the Document Window, as shown in Figure 1-9. Clicking the down arrow reveals a list of open documents so you can easily select one.

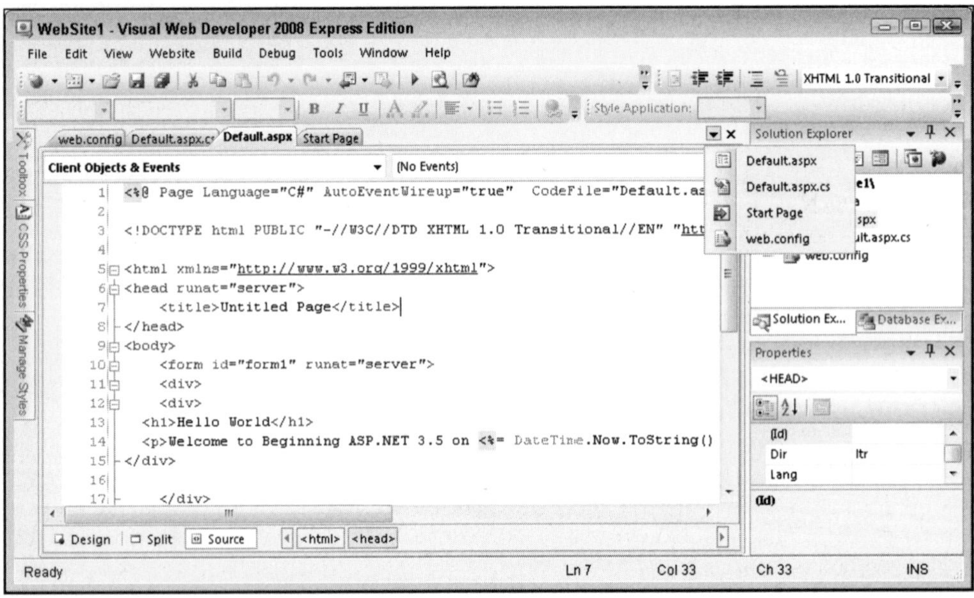

Figure 1-9

Another way to switch documents is to press Ctrl+Tab and then hold the Ctrl key down. On the window that pops ups, you can select a document you want to work with in the right hand column. You can then use the cursor keys to move up and down in the list with open documents and get a live preview of each document. This makes it super easy to select the correct file.

On the same dialog box, you see a list with all active tool windows. Clicking one of the windows in the list will show it on-screen, moving in front of other windows if necessary.

The Start Page

Whenever you start up VWD, the Start Page is loaded in the Document Window. With the Start Page, you can quickly create new web sites or open existing ones. The Start Page is also used to give you access to some common help topics and shows headlines from the Microsoft web site. The main part of the Start Page is used to display an RSS feed with information from the MSDN Visual Web Developer team.

To get a feel of how you can use all these windows, the following Try It Out shows you how to build a simple web page that contains a few ASP.NET Server Controls.

Try It Out Designing Your First ASP.NET Web Page

This Try It Out exercise guides you through creating a new web site with a single page that contains a number of ASP.NET Server Controls. You'll see how to use windows like the Start Page and the Solution Explorer, and how to use the Toolbox and the Properties Grid to add ASP.NET Server Controls to the page and change their looks.

1. Start VWD. If you don't see the Start Page, choose View ➪ Other Windows ➪ Start Page from the main menu.
2. On the Start Page, click Web Site next to the Create label in the Recent Projects area. This triggers the New Web Site dialog box. If you don't see the link to create a new web on the Start Page, choose File ➪ New Web Site or File ➪ New ➪ Web Site from VWD's main menu instead.

   Make sure that ASP.NET Web Site is selected and that File System is chosen in the Location drop-down list. Click OK to create the new site.
3. Next, right-click the new web site in the Solution Explorer. Make sure you click the uppermost element that says something like `C:\..\WebSite2\`. It's the highlighted element in Figure 1-4. From the context menu that appears, choose Add New Item.
4. In the new window that appears, click Web Form and type **ControlsDemo** as the name. The ASPX extension is added for you automatically when you click the OK button. You can leave the other settings in the dialog box at their default settings. The page should open in Markup View, showing you the default HTML, like the `<html>`, `<head>`, `<title>`, and `<body>` elements that Visual Web Developer adds there for you automatically when you create a new page.
5. Switch the page to Design View by clicking the Design button at the bottom of the Document Window.
6. If the Toolbox isn't open yet, press Ctrl+Alt+X to open it or hover your mouse over the Toolbox tab to show it and then click the pin icon to make the Toolbox visible at all times. Drag a `TextBox` and a `Button` from the Toolbox into the dashed area in the Design View of the page. You should end up with a page that looks similar to Figure 1-10.

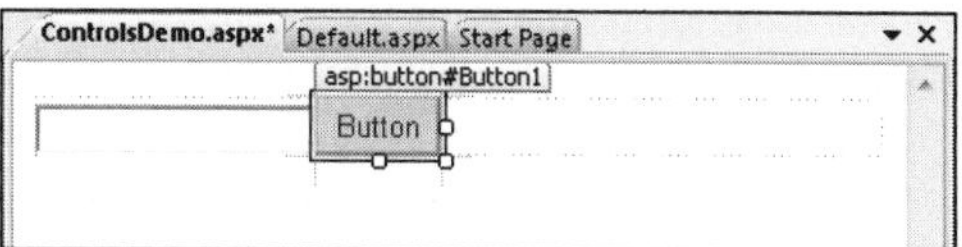

Figure 1-10

7. Right-click the button in Design View and choose Properties. In the Properties Grid, locate the Text property under the Appearance category (shown in Figure 1-11) and change it from Button to Submit Information. As soon as you press Tab or click somewhere outside the Properties Grid, the Design View of the page is updated and shows the new text on the button.

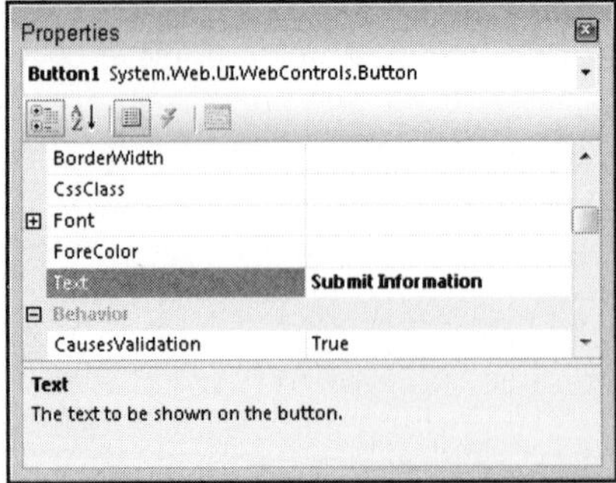

Figure 1-11

8. Press Ctrl+F5 to open the page in your default browser. Note that it's not necessary to explicitly save the changes to your page (although it's a good idea to do this often anyway using the shortcut Ctrl+S). As soon as you press Ctrl+F5 to run the page, VWD saves all changes to open documents automatically.

If you don't like this behavior, you can change it in Visual Web Developer's Options dialog box, accessible from the Tools menu. Make sure that Show All Settings is checked, and then open the Projects and Solutions node and choose Build and Run. In the Before Building list, you can change the way VWD behaves when you open a page in your browser.

9. Type some text in the text box and then click the button. Note that after the page has reloaded, the text is still displayed in the text box. Other than that, not much has happened because you didn't write any code for the button yet.

How It Works

When you dragged the `Button` and the `TextBox` from the Toolbox on the page in Design View, VWD added the corresponding code for you in Markup View automatically. Similarly, when you changed the Text property of the button in the Properties Grid, VWD automatically updated the markup for the control in Markup View. Instead of using the Properties Grid, you could also have typed the text directly between the quotation marks of the `Text` property in the code window.

After changing the `Text` property, your page should now look like this in Markup View:

```
<asp:TextBox ID="TextBox1" runat="server"></asp:TextBox>
<asp:Button ID="Button1" runat="server" Text="Submit Information" />
```

When you press Ctrl+F5 to view the page in the browser, the web server receives the request, the page is processed by the ASP.NET runtime, and the resulting HTML for the page is sent to the browser.

Take a look at the resulting HTML for the page using the browser's View Source command (rerun the page from VWD by pressing Ctrl+F5 if you already closed it). You should see code similar to this:

```
<input name="TextBox1" type="text" value="Hello World" id="TextBox1" />
<input type="submit" name="Button1" value="Submit Information" id="Button1" />
```

Just as with the earlier example, you can see that the resulting HTML is substantially different from the original ASPX markup.

After you type in some text and click the button, the same process is more or less repeated: the web server receives the request, the page is parsed, and the result gets sent back to the browser. When you click the button, you cause a *postback* to occur, where any information contained in the page — such as the text you typed in the text box — is sent back to the server. ASP.NET reacts to the postback by rendering the page again. However, this time it prepopulates controls, like the `TextBox`, with the values that were sent to the page. Postbacks are an important concept in ASP.NET, and you'll see more about them in other chapters, including Chapters 4 and 9.

VWD hosts a lot more windows and tool panels than those you have seen so far. The next section briefly touches upon some of the windows you'll most frequently use when building ASP.NET web pages. All of the windows mentioned are accessible from the main View menu in VWD.

Informational Windows

Besides the windows that are visible by default when you start VWD, there are many more windows available in VWD. You'll see most of them in action in the remainder of this book, but some are worth highlighting now.

The Error List

The Error List, which is accessible from the View menu, gives you a list of the things that are currently somehow broken in your site, including incorrect markup in your ASPX or HTML files and programming errors in VB or C# files. This window can even show you errors in XML and CSS files. The error list shows its messages in three categories — Errors, Warnings, and Messages — that signify the severity of the problem. Figure 1-12 shows the error list for a page that has some problems with its CSS and XHTML.

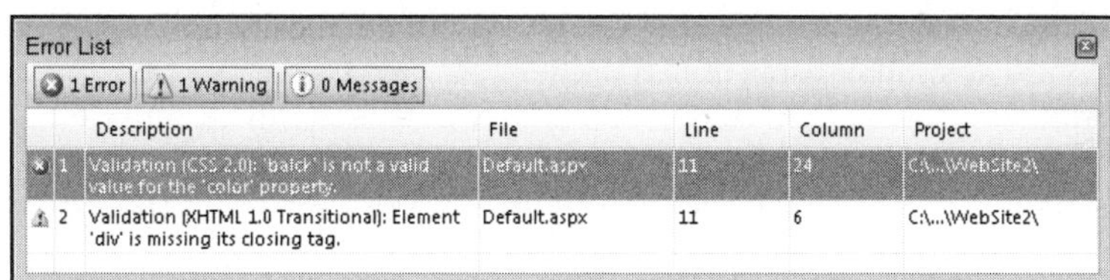

Figure 1-12

The Output Window

When you try to build your site using the Build menu, the Output window tells you whether the build succeeded or not. If the build failed, the Output window will tell you why the build failed. In the commercial versions of Visual Studio, the Output window is used for other information as well, including the status of external plug-in programs. Building web sites is discussed later in this book, including Chapter 18, which deals with deployment of your web site.

The Bookmark Window

You can add a bookmark to many code files in the Document Window by pressing Ctrl+K twice. With this shortcut key you can drop a little *breadcrumb* in the margin of a code line that you can later pick up using the Bookmark window. This allows you to quickly move around your code, which is especially useful when your site begins to grow.

The Find Results Window

The Find and Replace features of VWD are invaluable tools when it comes to managing the content of your site. You will often need to replace some text in the current document or even in the entire site. Find in Files (Ctrl+Shift+F) and Replace in Files (Ctrl+Shift+H) both output their results in the Find Results window, as shown in Figure 1-13.

Find Results 1
Replace all "SomethingOld", "SomethingNew", Subfolders, Find Results 1, "Entire Solution"
C:\Users\Imar\Documents\Visual Studio 2008\WebSites\WebSite2\Default.aspx.cs(17,9): SomethingNew
C:\Users\Imar\Documents\Visual Studio 2008\WebSites\WebSite2\StyleSheet.css(3,1):SomethingNew
C:\Users\Imar\Documents\Visual Studio 2008\WebSites\WebSite2\web.config(11,3): SomethingNew
Total replaced: 3 Matching files: 3 Total files searched: 6

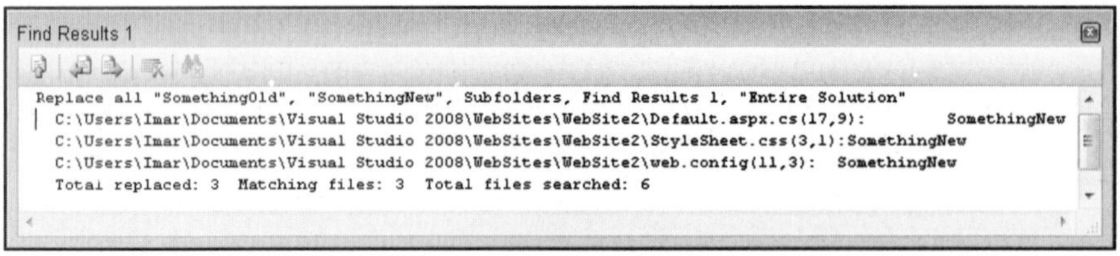

Figure 1-13

Because having several informational windows open at the same time may take up precious screen space, it's often a good idea to dock them. This way, only one of them is visible at a time, while you still have quick access to the others. You learn how to customize the IDE, including the docking of windows, next.

Customizing the IDE

Although the standard setup of VWD and its tool windows is pretty useful, there's a fair chance you want to customize the IDE to your likings. You may want to rearrange some of the windows to a location where they are easier to reach, or you may want to open additional windows you frequently use. VWD is fully customizable and allows you to tweak every little detail of the IDE. In the next section, you learn how to perform the most common customization tasks.

Rearranging Windows

To give each window the location it deserves, you can drag and drop them in the main IDE. Simply grab a window's title bar or its bottom tab and drag it in the direction of the new location. Once you start dragging, you'll see that VWD gives you visual cues as to where the window will end up (see Figure 1-14).

If you drag the window over one of the four square indicators at the sides of the indicator, VWD shows a preview of how the window will be docked *next to* an existing window. Once you drop it, the window will pop to its new location. If you drop the window on the square in the middle of the large indicator, the window will dock *with* that window, sharing the same screen space. Each window has its own tab, as can be seen with the windows at the bottom of Figure 1-14.

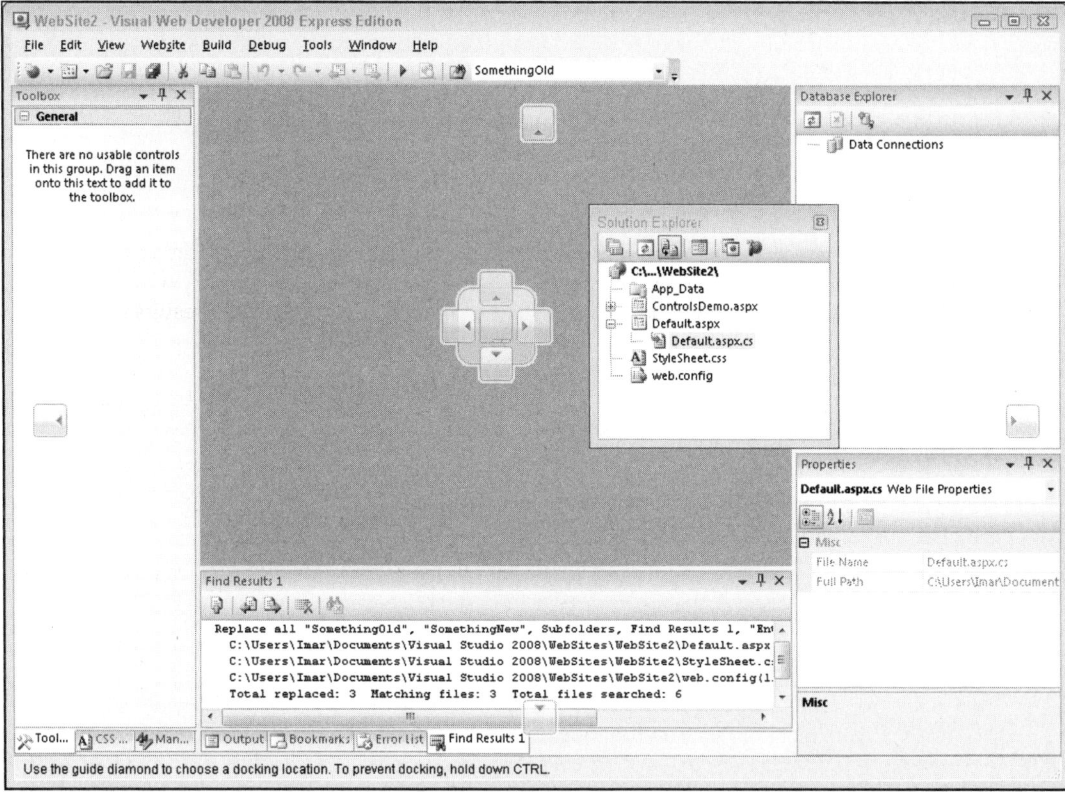

Figure 1-14

In addition to docking windows with others in the IDE, you can also have floating windows. To change a docked window into a floating one, either drag it away from its current location and drop it somewhere in the IDE without hitting one of the visual cues on the screen or choose Window ➪ Floating from the main menu.

To restore a floating panel to its previous docked location, choose Window ➪ Dockable from the main menu and then double-click its title bar.

Modifying the Toolbox

The Toolbox can be modified as well. You can reorder the items alphabetically, making them easier to find in the list. To do this, open the Toolbox (press Ctrl+Alt+X), right-click one of the items in a category (such as the TextBox under the Standard category), and choose Sort Items Alphabetically. You can also delete items from the Toolbox by right-clicking them and then choosing Delete from the context menu. Don't worry about items getting lost forever; you can reset the Toolbox again by choosing Reset Toolbox from the same menu.

You can also add your own items to the Toolbox. The most common use for this is code snippets. Simply highlight some text or code in the Document Window and drag it to the Toolbox. You can then right-click the item and choose Rename Item to give it a more meaningful name that you can easily recognize.

To avoid cluttering up the Toolbox with your own code snippets, consider creating a separate category for them. You can do this by choosing Add Tab from the Toolbox's right-click menu. Enter a name and then press Enter, and your Toolbox tab is ready for use.

In the next Try It Out exercise, you get the chance to play around with the VWD IDE so you can customize it to your liking.

Try It Out Customizing the IDE

In this exercise you'll practice with opening and rearranging the windows in the Visual Web Developer IDE. You'll also order the items in the Standard category of the Toolbox alphabetically so the controls are easier to find. Don't be afraid to mess up the IDE. A little later in this chapter, there are instructions on how to reset the IDE to the way it was when you opened it the first time.

1. If you closed your web site since the previous Try It Out, open it again, or create a new one using the Start Page or the File menu.
2. From the View menu, choose Error List to open the Error List window. Notice how it gets docked below the Document Window by default.
3. From the same View menu, choose Task List. By default, it will be docked in the same space as the Error List, with the tabs for both windows next to each other.
4. Click the tab of the Task List and while holding down your mouse button, drag the Task List away from its location in the direction of the Document Window. Once you release the window, it will appear as a floating window in the IDE. To restore the window, double-click its title bar. Notice how the tab returns to the same tab group, but possibly at a different position. To change the order in which tabs appear in a tab group, drag a tab over the other tabs and release it at the desired location.
5. If you want, you can repeat the previous steps for other windows that are visible in the IDE by default or for the ones you find under the View menu. Spend some time familiarizing yourself with all the different windows and how you can arrange them on-screen. Since you'll be working a lot with these windows in the remainder of this book, it's good to be familiar with their locations.
6. Next, open the Default.aspx page from the Solution Explorer by double-clicking it. When the page opens, the Toolbox should become visible automatically. If it doesn't, press Ctrl+Alt+X to open it.
7. The Standard category should be expanded by default, but if it isn't, click the plus symbol in the left margin of the Toolbox. Next, right-click somewhere on a control in the Standard category and choose Sort Items Alphabetically. This puts the controls in alphabetical order in the Standard category only. If you want, you can repeat this step for other categories of the Toolbox.
8. Right-click the Toolbox again and choose Add Tab. Type **HTML Fragments** as its new name and press Enter. This adds a new category to the Toolbox that behaves just like all the others.
9. With the Document Window showing the page Default.aspx in Markup View, type **<h1>** between the opening and closing `<div>` tag. Note that VWD automatically inserts the closing `<h1>` for you. You should end up with the code window looking like this:

```
<div>
<h1></h1>
</div>
```

10. Highlight the opening and closing `<h1>` tags, and then drag the selection from the Markup View window onto the new Toolbox tab you created in step 8. The selection shows up as Text: `<h1></h1>`.

11. Right-click the Toolbox item you just created, choose Rename Item, and type **Heading 1** as the name.

12. Repeat steps 9 through 11, creating headings from h2 through h6.

    From now on, whenever you need a heading in your document in Markup View, simply place the cursor in the Document Window where you want the heading to appear and then double-click the appropriate heading in the Toolbox.

How It Works

Most of the steps in this Try It Out are self-explanatory. You started off by opening a few windows that you frequently need when building web applications. You then used the drag-and-drop features of the IDE to rearrange the window layout to your personal preferences. You also rearranged the items in the Toolbox so they are easier to find.

You closed the exercise by adding a few HTML fragments to a custom tab in the Toolbox. When you drag any markup to the Toolbox, VWD creates a Toolbox item for it that contains the selected markup. Whenever you need a copy of that markup in your page, simply double-click the item or drag it from the Toolbox into the Markup View window. This is a great time saver for HTML fragments that you frequently use.

Besides the Window layout and the Toolbox, VWD allows you to customize a lot more in the IDE. The following section explains how to customize three other important IDE features: the Document Window, toolbars, and keyboard shortcuts.

Customizing the Document Window

Visual Web Developer gives you great flexibility with regard to how text is displayed in the Document Window. You can change things like font size, font color, and even the background color of the text. You can access the Font and Colors settings by choosing Tools ➪ Options, making sure that Show All Settings at the bottom of the dialog box is selected, and then choosing Environment ➪ Fonts and Colors.

One thing I like to customize in the Document Window is the tab size, which controls the number of spaces that are inserted when indenting code. To change the tab size, choose Tools ➪ Options, and then under Text Editor choose All Languages ➪ Tabs. If you don't see this option, choose Show All Settings at the bottom first. I usually set both the Tab Size and the Indent Size to 2, leaving the other settings in the Tab panel untouched.

With the exception of the Tab Size being set to 2, all screen shots in this book show the default setup of Visual Web Developer.

Customizing Toolbars

Toolbars can be customized in three ways: you can show or hide the built-in toolbars, you can add and remove buttons on existing toolbars, and you can create your own toolbars with buttons you often use.

Enabling and Disabling Toolbars

You disable and enable existing toolbars by right-clicking any existing toolbar or the menu bar and then selecting the appropriate item from the list. Once the toolbar is displayed, you can use its drag grip at the left of the toolbar to drag it to a new location. You can drag the toolbars to any location in the IDE, including to the left and right sides of the screen where they'll dock as vertical bars. You can also create them as floating toolbars and place them anywhere on the screen.

Editing Existing Toolbars

If you feel that an existing toolbar is missing an important button or that it contains buttons you rarely use, you can customize the buttons on the toolbar. To do this, right-click any toolbar or the menu bar and choose Customize. Next, make sure the toolbar you want to tweak is enabled by placing a check mark in front of it. Then switch to the Commands tab, choose a category from the list on the left, and then locate the command in the Command list at the right. You can now drag the command from the Customize window onto the toolbar.

Removing a button from a toolbar is even easier. With the Customize window still open, right-click the button and choose Delete.

While you're in the Customize dialog box, you may want to enable the Show Shortcut Keys in ScreenTips setting on the Toolbars tab. This way, the toolbars for the button show the associated keyboard shortcut so it's more likely you'll memorize and use them. Shortcut keys are often easier to use than their toolbar button or menu counterparts.

Creating Your Own Toolbars

Creating your own toolbar is useful if you want to group some functions that you frequently use. To create a new toolbar, open the customize window as explained in the previous section. Click the New button and type a name for the toolbar. When you click OK, the new toolbar is displayed on the screen. You can now start dragging commands to it the same way as when you're modifying the existing toolbars.

Customizing Keyboard Shortcuts

Another setting many developers like to change is keyboard shortcuts. Keyboard shortcuts are a good way to save time because they allow you to perform a task with a simple keyboard command instead of reaching for the mouse and selecting the appropriate item from the menu. To change the keyboard shortcuts, open the Customize dialog box again by right-clicking a toolbar or choosing it from the Tools menu. Next, click the Keyboard button. Locate the command for which you want to change the shortcut in the list with commands. Since this list contains many items, you can filter the list by typing a few letters from the command. For example, typing **print** in the Show commands containing field gives you a list of all print-related commands.

Next, in the Press shortcut keys field, type a new shortcut. VWD allows you to enter a double shortcut key for a single command. For example, you can bind the command Close All Documents to the command Ctrl+K, Ctrl+O. To perform this command, you need to press both key combinations in rapid succession. Although a double shortcut key may seem like overkill, it greatly increases the number of available shortcut keys.

Resetting Your Changes

Don't worry if you feel that you have messed up VWD by trying out the numerous customization options. There are many ways to restore VWD to its previous state.

Resetting the Window Layout

This setting, accessible from the Window menu, resets all windows to the position they were in when you first started VWD. This command is useful if you misplaced too many windows and ended up with a cluttered IDE.

Resetting the Tool Box

If you removed a button from the Toolbox by mistake or even deleted an entire tab, you can reset the Toolbox to its original state by right-clicking the Toolbox and choosing Reset Toolbox. You need to think twice before you use this command because it will also delete all your custom code snippets.

Resetting All Settings

To completely revert all VWD settings to the way they were right after installation, choose Import and Export Settings from the Tools menu. Next, choose the Reset All Settings option and click Next. If you want, you can create a backup of the existing settings; otherwise, choose No, Just Reset Settings. Finally, click Finish. This action will cause all settings to be reset to their defaults, including the Windows layout, toolbox and Toolbox customizations, shortcut keys, and everything you may have changed in the VWD Options dialog box. So, use this command only when you're really sure you want a fresh, new setup of VWD.

If you followed along with the previous Try It Out exercises, and then started experimenting with the customization possibilities, your IDE is now probably in one of two states: it either looks exactly the way you want it, or it looks like a complete mess. In the former case, you can skip the next exercise; in the latter case, stay tuned to see how easy it is to clean up the chaos.

Try It Out Resetting All Settings

The following Try It Out shows you how to reset the IDE to the state it was in when you started VWD for the first time. Make sure you really want to do this before you follow the exercise, as the next exercise will reset all important settings, including Window and Toolbox customizations and all the options you set in the Options dialog box.

1. Start the Import and Export Settings Wizard by choosing Tools ⇨ Import and Export Settings.
2. Choose the Reset All Settings option at the bottom of the screen and click Next.
3. Let VWD create a backup of your current settings by selecting the first item in the dialog box. With this backup, you can always revert to the current setup by running the Import and Export Settings Wizard again.
4. Click Finish. The wizard resets all your settings and then displays a message reporting that the settings were successfully reset.
5. Click Close to exit the wizard. You'll find that your IDE is now the same as it was the first time you started it.

How It Works

All the changes you make to the IDE are stored in an XML configuration file in your Visual Studio Settings folder, which by default is located in a folder called `Visual Studio 2008\Settings` under your main `Documents` folder in Windows.

When you choose to reset your settings, VWD overwrites your settings file with a factory default. If you chose to create a backup, an additional backup file with today's date in it is saved in the same folder. With that backup file, you can restore the settings at a later time.

With some basic knowledge about ASP.NET pages and VWD, it's time for some real action. In the next chapter, you see how to create ASP.NET web sites and web pages in much more detail. You'll learn how to organize your site in a logical and structured way, how to add the many different types of files to your site and how to use them, and how to connect the pages in your site.

However, before you can proceed to the next chapter, there is one more important topic you need to look at: the sample application that comes with this book.

The Sample Application

Building web sites is what this book is all about, so it makes a whole lot of sense that this book comes with a complete and functional sample site that is used to showcase many of the capabilities of ASP.NET.

The sample site you'll build in this book is called Planet Wrox, a site that serves as an online community for people interested in music. The site offers the following features to its visitors:

- Reviews about CDs and concerts that have been posted on the site by the administrator.
- The Gig Pics section, an online photo album where users can share pictures taken at concerts.
- The ability to switch between the different graphical themes that the site offers, giving you a chance to change the look and feel of the site without altering the content.
- Musical preferences that influence the information you see on the site.
- Access to bonus content for users who register for an account.

From an administrative perspective (that is you, as the owner of the site) the site allows you to do the following:

- Add and maintain the reviews.
- Manage the different musical genres in the system.
- Decide which users you allow to access protected content such as special photo albums.

Figure 1-15 shows the Planet Wrox home page.

Figure 1-16 shows another page from Planet Wrox, but with a different theme applied. This page allows users to enter their personal information and specify preferences with regard to their favorite musical genres.

Figure 1-15

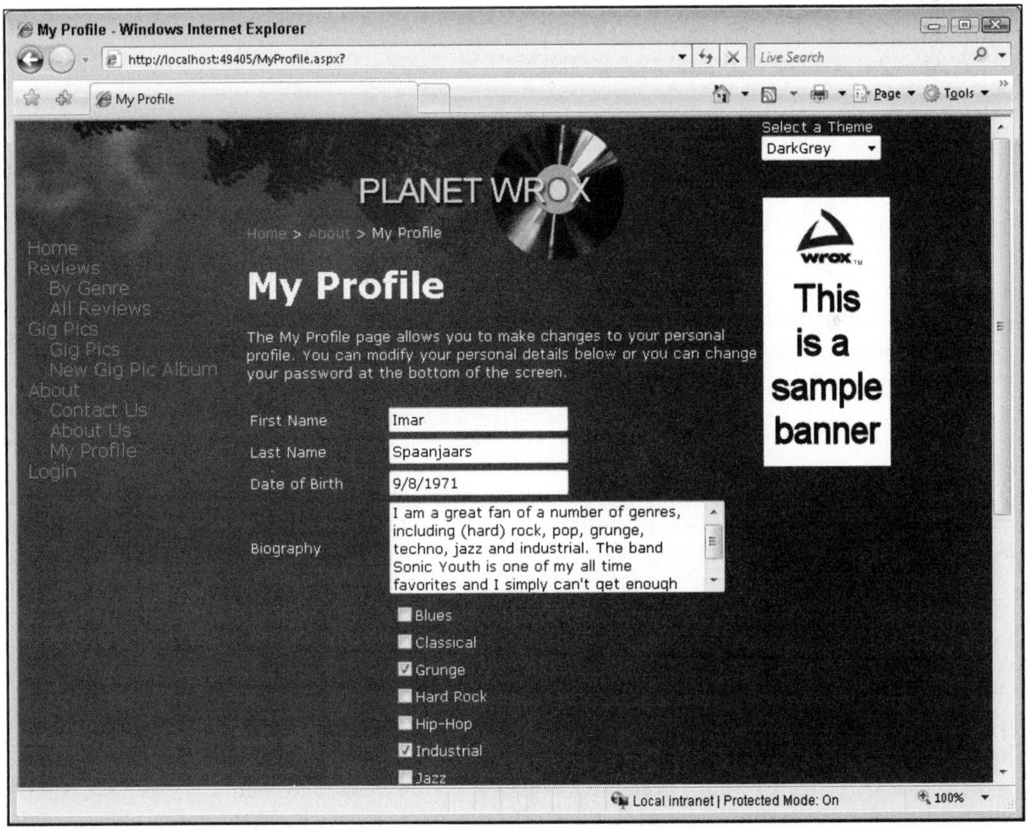

Figure 1-16

You can find an online running example of the site at `www.PlanetWrox.com`. There you can play around with the site from an end user's perspective.

You can also download the source for the sample application and all other examples from this book from the Wrox web site at `http://p2p.wrox.com/`.

By the end of this book, you'll be able to build all of the functionality from the sample site (and hopefully even more) in other web sites. Don't worry if it sounds like an awful lot of complex things. I'll guide you, step by step, from the beginning of the application all the way to the last feature. As long as you keep having fun doing this, I'm sure you'll make it all the way.

Practical Tips on Visual Web Developer

Most of the chapters in this book end with a short section with useful tips. These are tips that either didn't fit in anywhere in the text or that encourage you to further explore or test out things. Sometimes they may seem irrelevant or hard to understand at first, but you'll find that as you make your way through this book and look back at tips from previous chapters, things start to make sense. Don't worry if you don't understand certain things completely the first time you see them. Give the idea some thought and revisit the topic a few days later. Hopefully, by letting the ideas sink in a little, things start to make more sense automatically. This applies not only to the Practical Tips section, but to the entire book.

- Before you move on to the next chapter, play around with VWD some more. Add a couple of pages to your site, drag and drop some controls from the Toolbox onto your pages, and view them in your browser. That way, you'll have a better understanding of the tools and the many controls available when you start the next chapter.
- Familiarize yourself with the many options to tweak the Visual Web Developer IDE. When building web sites, you spend most of your time in this IDE, so it makes sense to tweak it as much as possible to your liking. Don't be afraid to mess it up; you can always revert to previous settings.
- Take some time to browse through the settings you find in the Options dialog box of VWD (accessible through the Tools ➪ Options menu). Many of the settings are self-explanatory and can really help further tweaking the IDE to your liking.

Summary

This chapter covered a lot of important ground to get you started with ASP.NET 3.5 and VWD. It started off with a brief history of the Microsoft .NET Framework in general and ASP.NET in particular.

You then learned how to acquire and install Visual Web Developer 2008 Express Edition. VWD is the most extensive and versatile tool available for creating ASP.NET 3.5 web pages. To enable you to work with it effectively, this chapter showed you how to use and customize the main features of the IDE. In subsequent chapters, you will use and extend this knowledge to work with the many tools found in VWD.

It's important to understand how a page in VWD makes it to your web browser. Some knowledge of the web server that serves the request and how the page is processed to deliver the final HTML in the browser is critical in understanding ASP.NET. This chapter gave you a short introduction in the way a web page is requested and served to the browser.

In the next chapter, you get a much more detailed explanation of creating web sites.

Exercises

1. Explain the differences between the markup of a page in VWD and the final HTML page in the browser.
2. Explain the difference between HTML and XHTML. How are the two related?
3. Imagine you have a number of HTML fragments that you expect to use a lot throughout the site. What's the best way to make these fragments available in VWD?
4. What are three of the ways you can reset part or all of the IDE customization settings?
5. If you want to change the property of a control on your page, for example the text of a button, which two options do you have available to make the change?

2

Building an ASP.NET Web Site

To create good-looking, functional, and successful web sites, you have to understand a number of important technologies and languages, including HTML, ASP.NET, CSS (Cascading Style Sheets), and JavaScript. This and upcoming chapters provide a solid foundation in these technologies, so you should be comfortable with the most important concepts once you've finished this book.

Besides these technologies, you also have to understand the Visual Web Developer IDE that was introduced in the previous chapter. You need to know how to create sites, add pages, and manage all the toolbars and windows that Visual Web Developer (VWD) offers you. In addition, you need to know how to build and design web pages in VWD with HTML and server controls.

This chapter shows you, in detail, how to create and manage your web sites. It also shows you how to create your ASP.NET web pages and add markup to them, allowing you to create useful web pages that can present information to the user and react to their response.

In particular, this chapter examines:

- ❑ Two different project types for building ASP.NET web sites
- ❑ The different project templates that are available to jumpstart your site development and how to use them
- ❑ The numerous different file types available in ASP.NET and what they are used for
- ❑ Ways to create structured web sites that are easy to manage, now and in the future
- ❑ How to use the designer tools to created formatted web pages

Although you already created your first ASP.NET web site in the previous chapter, this chapter starts off with another in-depth look at creating a new web site. As there are many choices to make when you start a new site, it's important to understand all the different options and pick the right one for your scenario.

Creating Web Sites with VWD 2008

The previous chapter gave you a quick overview of creating a web site in VWD. You simply chose New Web Site from the File menu, selected the standard ASP.NET Web Site template, selected a language, and clicked OK. However, there's more to the New Web Site dialog box than you saw in the previous chapter. You may have noticed that you can choose from a number of different templates that allow you to create different kind of sites. But before you look at the different templates on which you can base your new web site, you need to know a little more about the different project types that are available in VWD.

Different Project Types

Depending on the version of VWD you're using, you may have the choice between two different project types. If you're using Visual Web Developer Express Edition you only have one option: *Web Site Projects*. If you're using one of the commercial versions of Visual Studio 2008, you also have the option to create a new *Web Application Project*. Both project types are discussed next.

Web Site Projects

Web Site Projects represent a project in VWD for a web site. You create a new Web Site Project by choosing File ➪ New Web Site or File ➪ New ➪ Web Site from Visual Web Developer's main menu.

Web Site Projects were introduced in Visual Studio 2005 and provide some new flexibility in creating and working with web sites. In contrast to web sites built with earlier versions of Visual Studio .NET, a Web Site Project site is simply a Windows folder with a bunch of files and subfolders in it. There is no collective file (known as the *project file* with a `.vbproj` or `.csproj` extension) that keeps track of all the individual files in the web site. You just point VWD to a folder, and it instantly opens it as a web site. This makes it very easy to create copies of the site, move them, or even share them with others, as there are no dependencies with files on your local system. Because of the lack of a central project file, Web Site Projects are usually simply referred to as Web Sites, which is the term I use in the remainder of this book.

Besides a lot of positive feedback on this move, Microsoft also received a lot of negative response from developers who complained that Web Site Projects were too limiting for their development environment. Since there is no container file that keeps track of everything in the site, it became much harder to exclude files or folders from the site and work with source control systems — a centralized system that allows developers to work on a project collaboratively and that keeps track of changes in the project automatically. Also, Web Site Projects influenced the way web sites are compiled and deployed, making it harder for developers accustomed to the previous model to apply their knowledge and skills to the new project type.

In response to the criticism, Microsoft released the Web Application Projects in May 2006 as an add-on for Visual Studio 2005 standard edition and up. Unfortunately, Web Application Projects are not available for the Visual Web Developer Express Editions, including the new Visual Web Developer 2008. So, if you are working with the free version, you don't have much to choose: you can only use Web Site Projects.

Web Application Projects

With the new Visual Studio 2008 release, Web Application Projects are now fully integrated in the IDE. This makes it easier for developers who work in teams or who need more control over the contents of the site and their compilation and deployment processes to build web sites with Visual Studio.

In Visual Studio 2008, you create a new Web Application Project through the File ➪ New Project dialog box. In that dialog box, expand your preferred programming language (either Visual Basic or Visual C#) and then click the Web category, where you'll find a number of ASP.NET web application templates.

This book uses the Web Site Projects model exclusively, so you can follow along with all the examples, even if you're using the free Express Edition.

Now that you know about the different project types, the next thing to consider is the different *web site templates* and their options.

Choosing the Right Web Site Template

The New Web Site dialog box in VWD contains different web site templates, each one serving a distinct purpose.

Figure 2-1 shows the New Web Site dialog box in VWD. You can open this dialog box by choosing File ➪ New Web Site, or File ➪ New ➪ Web Site depending on your version of VWD.

The top section of the Templates area shows the ASP.NET web site templates that are installed by default. Each of them is discussed in the next section. The second part, labeled My Templates, contains a link to search for templates online. In addition, when you have created your own templates (which you learn how to do in Chapter 6), or have templates installed from other parties, they show up in this area as well.

From the list of available built-in templates, only the ASP.NET Web Site template is used throughout this book. The others are described briefly in the following sections so you know how they can be used.

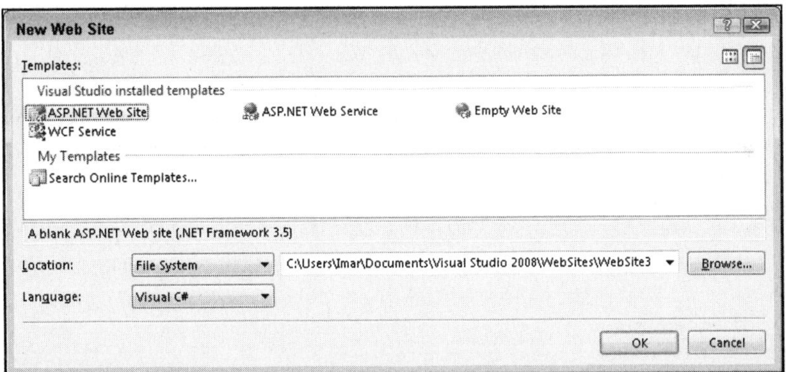

Figure 2-1

ASP.NET Web Site

This template allows you to set up a basic ASP.NET web site. It contains a simple web.config file (an ASP.NET configuration file), one Web Form (called Default.aspx), its Code Behind file, and an empty App_Data folder. The different file types are all discussed later in this chapter, and the App_Data folder is discussed in Chapter 11.

This template is a good starting point for all your ASP.NET web sites.

ASP.NET Web Service

The ASP.NET Web Service template is the starting point for new sites that contain *web services*. A web service allows you to create software on the web server that can be called by other applications located on the same machine, or on computers somewhere in the network or on the Internet. When you create a site based on this template, you get a web service file, an additional code file named after the service, and a web.config file that contains configuration information accessible to the web services.

You'll see how to create and consume a web service from a browser in Chapter 10.

WCF Service

The WCF Service template is somewhat similar to the Web Service template in that it allows you to create a web site that contains services that are callable over a network. However, *Windows Communication Foundation Services* go much further than simple web services and offer you a lot more flexibility. WCF Services are outside the scope of this book, but if you want to learn more about them, pick up the book *Professional WCF Programming: .NET Development with the Windows Communication Foundation* by Scott Klein (ISBN: 978-0-470-08984-2).

Empty Web Site

The empty web site template gives you exactly what its name implies: nothing. All you get is an empty web site as a starting point. The empty web site template is useful if you have a bunch of existing files you want to use to create a new web site.

Although it seems you have to make a clear choice up front for the right web site template, this isn't really the case. Since an ASP.NET web site in VWD is essentially just a reference to a folder, it's easy to add types from one template to another. For example, it's perfectly acceptable (and very common) to add a web service file to a standard ASP.NET web site, as you will see in Chapter 10.

Creating and Opening a New Web Site

There are a number of different ways to create new and open existing web sites. The choices you have here are largely influenced by the way you access the web site (either from the local or a remote machine), and whether you want to use the built-in web server that ships with VWD or use the web server that comes with Windows.

All the examples in this book assume that you open sites from your local hard drive and that you use the built-in web server, as it's very convenient to develop sites with it. However, Chapter 18 shows you how to use and configure *Internet Information Services*, or *IIS* for short, the advanced web server that comes with almost all editions of Windows. IIS is mostly used for production hosting of your web sites, as it's capable of serving web pages in high-traffic scenarios.

Creating New Web Sites

The next Try It Out section guides you through creating the Planet Wrox web site that will be the project you're working on in this book. All exercises in the remainder of the book assume you have this web site open in VWD, except where stated otherwise. The exercise instructs you to store your web site in a folder called `C:\BegASPNET\Site`. Take note of this folder name, because it's used throughout this book. If you decide to use a different folder, be sure to use your own location whenever you see this folder name in the book.

Try It Out — Creating a New ASP.NET 3.5 Web Site

1. Start by creating a folder called **BegASPNET** in the root of your C drive using Windows Explorer or My Computer. Inside the folder, create another folder called **Site**. You should end up with a folder called `C:\BegASPNET\Site`. If you followed the instructions from the "Introduction" of this book and unpacked the source for this book, you already have the BegASPNET folder, which in turn contains the Source and Resources folders.
2. Start Visual Web Developer 2008 and choose File ➪ New Web Site or File ➪ New ➪ Web Site, depending on your version of VWD.
3. Make sure that ASP.NET Web Site is selected under the Templates section.
4. Under Location, make sure that File System is selected. The other two options (HTTP and FTP) allow you to open a remote site running IIS with the so-called Front Page Extensions and open a site from an FTP server respectively.
5. Click the Browse button next to the Location drop-down list, browse to the folder you created in the first step of this exercise, and click Open.
6. In the Language drop-down list, choose between Visual Basic and Visual C#. All the examples in this book are shown in both programming languages, so you can choose the one you like best. Your final screen should look like the one in Figure 2-2, except for the Language drop-down list, which you may have set to Visual C# instead.
7. Click OK and VWD creates the new site for you.

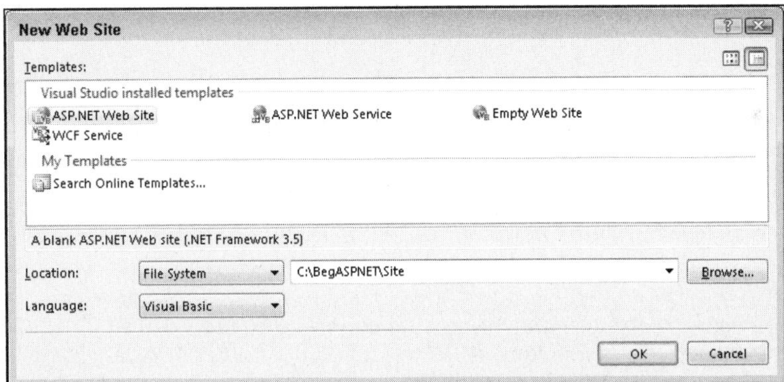

Figure 2-2

How It Works

As soon as you click OK, VWD creates a new web site for you. This new web site contains a Web Form, a Code Behind file (Default.aspx and Default.aspx.vb or Default.aspx.cs, depending on the language you chose), a configuration file (called web.config), and an empty App_Data folder. In the Solution Explorer, your web site now looks like Figure 2-3 (which has Default.aspx expanded so you can see the additional .vb file).

Since a web site based on the Web Site Project template is just a simple Windows folder that VWD looks at, the actual folder on disk contains the exact same files. No additional files are used to create the site, as shown in Figure 2-4, which shows a Windows Explorer displaying the files in the folder `C:\BegASPNET\Site`.

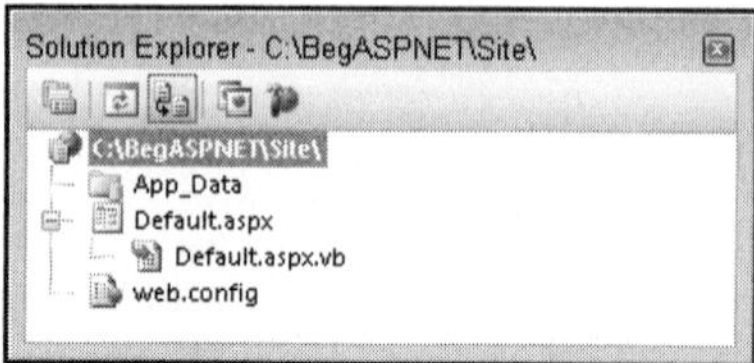

Figure 2-3

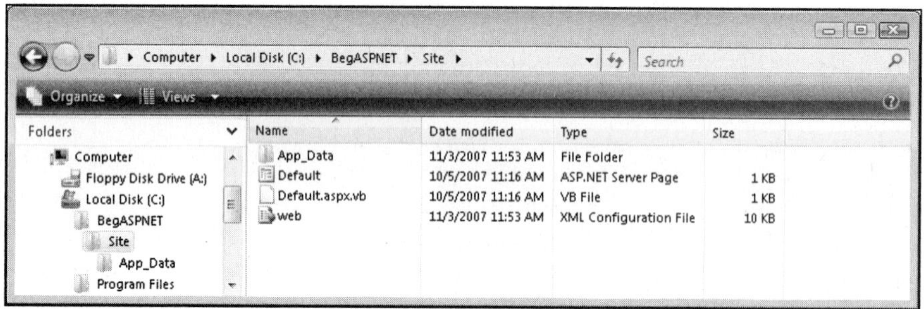

Figure 2-4

As you progress through this book, you'll add new files and folders to the site. Just as with the initial site, these additional files and folders show up in the Solution Explorer and will appear in the Windows folder at `C:\BegASPNET\Site` as well.

Opening web sites based on the Web Site Project template is very similar to creating new ones. In the next section, you get a quick overview of opening existing sites in VWD.

Opening Existing Web Sites

Just as with creating new sites, opening an existing site in VWD gives you a few options with regard to the source location of the web site. You can choose to open a site from the local file system, from a local IIS web server, from a remote server using FTP, or from a remote site using the Microsoft FrontPage Server Extensions. Figure 2-5 shows the Open Web Site dialog box in VWD.

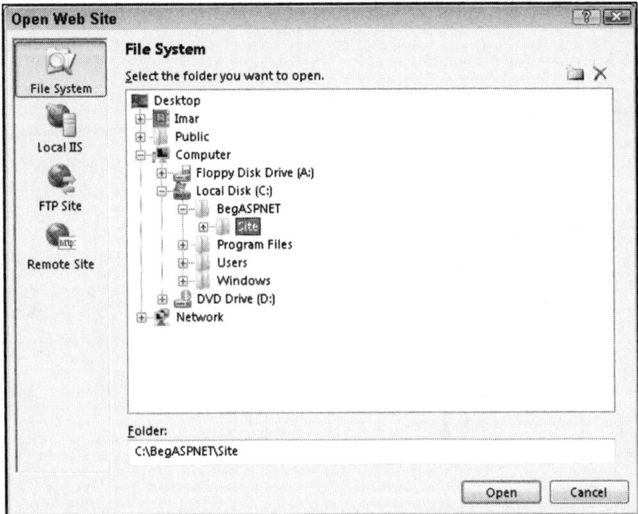

Figure 2-5

All the examples in the book assume that you always open the Planet Wrox web site from the local file system, using the File System button, which is the first button in the left column of the window. Then in the right pane, locate your web site (`C:\BegASPNET\Site` in this example) and click the Open button. The other three options are relatively straightforward.

The site you created in the previous Try It Out is a very bare-bones site since it only contains a single Web Form. To make the site more useful, you'll need to add files to it. The many file types you have at your disposal and the way they are added to the site are the next topics of discussion.

Working with Files in Your Web Site

An ASP.NET 3.5 web site consists of at least a single Web Form (a file with an `.aspx` extension), but usually it consists of a larger number of files. Many different file types are available in VWD, each offering a distinct functionality. In the next section, you'll see the most important file types that are used in VWD. In addition, you'll learn a few different ways to add these files to your site.

The Many File Types of an ASP.NET 3.5 Web Site

To give you an idea of how many different files you can use in ASP.NET, Figure 2-6 shows the dialog box that allows you to add new files to the site (accessible by right-clicking your web site in the Solution Explorer and choosing Add New Item or by choosing Website ➪ Add New Item from the main menu).

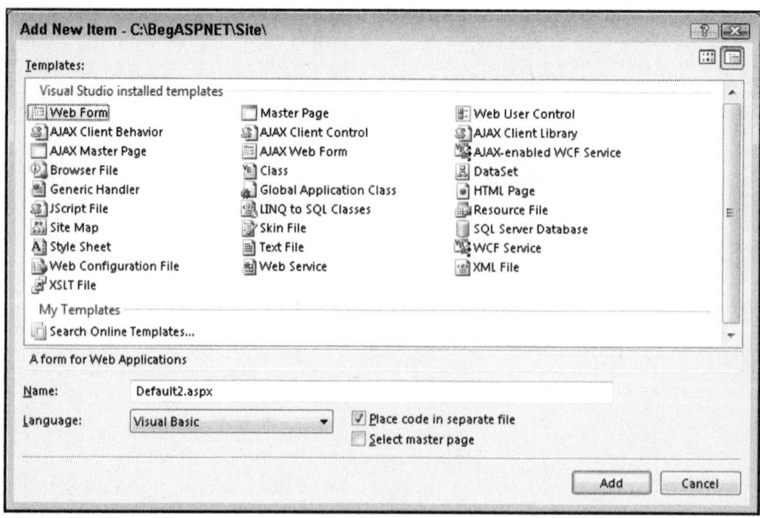

Figure 2-6

These files can be grouped in a few different categories. The most important files — the ones you'll use throughout the examples in this book — are discussed next.

Web Files

Web files are specific to web applications and can either be requested by a browser directly, or are used to build up part of the web page that is requested in the browser. The following table lists the various web files and their extensions, and describes how each file is used.

File Type	Extension	Description
Web Form and AJAX Web Form	`.aspx`	These files are the workhorses of any ASP.NET web site. Web Forms represent the pages that your users view in their browser. An AJAX Web Form is similar to a normal Web Form, but it's been prepared to work with the Ajax controls you'll learn about in Chapter 10. Web Forms are discussed in full detail later in this chapter.
Master Page and AJAX Master Page	`.master`	These files allow you to define the global structure and the look and feel of a web site. You'll see how they can be used in Chapter 6. Just as with AJAX Web Forms, the AJAX Master Page contains some code that is necessary to work with AJAX.
Web User Control	`.ascx`	Contains page fragments that can be reused in multiple pages in your site. Chapter 8 is entirely devoted to user controls.

File Type	Extension	Description
HTML Page	`.htm` / `.html`	Can be used to display static HTML in your web site.
Style Sheet	`.css`	Contains CSS code that allows you to style and format your web site. You'll learn more about CSS in the next chapter.
Web Configuration File	`.config`	Contains global configuration information that is used throughout the site. You'll see how to use the web.config later in this book.
Site Map	`.sitemap`	Contains a hierarchical representation of files in your site in an XML format. The Site Map is used for navigation and is discussed in Chapter 7.
JScript File	`.js`	Contains JavaScript (which Microsoft calls JScript) that can be executed in the client's browser.
Skin File	`.skin`	Contains design information for controls in your web site. Skins are discussed in the next chapter.

The next Try It Out shows you how to add a new master page to the site, which is used throughout the book.

Try It Out Adding Files to Your Site

1. If it is not still open, open the Planet Wrox web site you created earlier by choosing File ➪ Open Web Site. Make sure that you open the site from the File System, locate the folder that contains your site (`C:\BegASPNET\Site`), and click the Open button.
2. In the Solution Explorer, right-click your site and choose Add New Item. Make sure you click the actual site and not one of the existing files, or you won't get the correct menu item. Alternatively, you can choose File ➪ New File from Visual Web Developer's main menu.
3. In the dialog box that appears, choose Master Page. You can leave the Name set to MasterPage.master. Verify that the Language drop-down list is set to the language you want to use for this site and that Place Code in Separate File is checked. Finally, click the Add button. The master page is added to the site, and is opened automatically for you in the Document Window.

How It Works

This simple exercise showed you how to add a new item to your web site in two ways. Although at this stage the site isn't very exiting yet, the file you added forms the basis for the rest of the book.

The next sections briefly look at the remainder of the file types. Adding them to the site is identical to how you add web files. The following table describes the various types of code files.

File Type	Extension	Description
Web Service	`.asmx`	Can be called by other systems, including browsers, and can contain code that can be executed on your server. Web Services are covered in Chapter 10.
Class	`.cs / .vb`	Can contain code to program your web site. Note that Code Behind files (discussed later) also have this extension because they are essentially class files.
Global Application Class	`.asax`	Can contain code that is fired in response to interesting things that happen in your site, such as the start of the application or when an error occurs somewhere in the site. You'll see how to use this class later.

Besides the Code Files category, there is one more group of files worth looking into: Data Files.

Data Files

Data Files are used to store data that can be used in your site and in other applications. The group consists of the XML files and database files.

File Type	Extension	Description
XML File	`.xml`	Used to store data in XML format. In addition to plain XML files, ASP.NET supports a few more XML-based files, two of which you saw before: web.config and the Site Map.
SQL Server Database	`.mdf`	Files with an .mdf extension are databases that are used by Microsoft SQL Server.
LINQ to SQL Classes	`.dbml`	Used to access databases declaratively, without the need to write code. Technically, this is not a data file, as it does not contain the actual data. However, since they are tied to the database so closely, it makes sense to group them under this header. You learn more about LINQ to SQL in Chapter 13.

As you saw in the previous Try It Out, adding a new file of any of these types is really easy. It's just as easy to add existing files to the site.

Adding Existing Files

Not every file you create in your web site has to be brand new. There are cases where it makes sense to reuse files from other projects. For example, you may want to reuse a logo or a CSS file across multiple sites. You can easily add existing files by right-clicking the web site in the Solution Explorer and choosing Add Existing Item. In the dialog box that appears, you can browse for the files, and optionally select multiple files by holding down the Ctrl key. Finally, when you click Add, the files are added to the web site.

However, there is an even easier way to add files to the site, which can be a great time saver when you need to add multiple existing files and folders to your site: drag and drop. The following Try It Out shows you how this works.

Try It Out — Adding Existing Files to Your Site

1. Right-click your Windows desktop and choose New ➪ Text Document. If you don't see this option, simply create a new text document using Notepad.

2. Rename the text file as **Styles.css**. Make sure the **.txt** extension is replaced by **.css**. If you don't see the initial `.txt` extension and the icon of the file doesn't change from a text file to a CSS file (by default this is the same icon as a text file but with a gear symbol on top of it, but you may have software installed that changed the icon for CSS files), Windows is configured to hide extensions for known file types. If that's the case, open up Windows Explorer and choose Tools ➪ Folder Options in Windows XP or click the Organize button in Windows Vista and then choose Folder and Search Options. In both cases, switch to the View tab and deselect the option labeled Hide Extensions for Known File Types. You now may need to rename the file from `Styles.css.txt` to **Styles.css**.

   When you rename the file from `.txt` to `.css`, Windows may give you a warning that the file becomes unusable if you proceed. You can safely answer Yes to this question to continue.

3. Rearrange VWD so you can see part of the desktop with the CSS file as well. You can use the Restore Down button next to the big red closing X at the top of the window, to get VWD out of full screen mode.

4. Click the CSS file on the desktop and while holding down the mouse button, drag the file into the Solution Explorer. Make sure you drag the file into the Solution Explorer and not in other parts of VWD, or the file won't be added. For example, when you drag it into the Document Window, VWD will simply open the file for you, but not add it to the site.

5. When you release the mouse while over the web site node or an existing file in the Solution Explorer (shown in Figure 2-7), the CSS file will be added to you site.

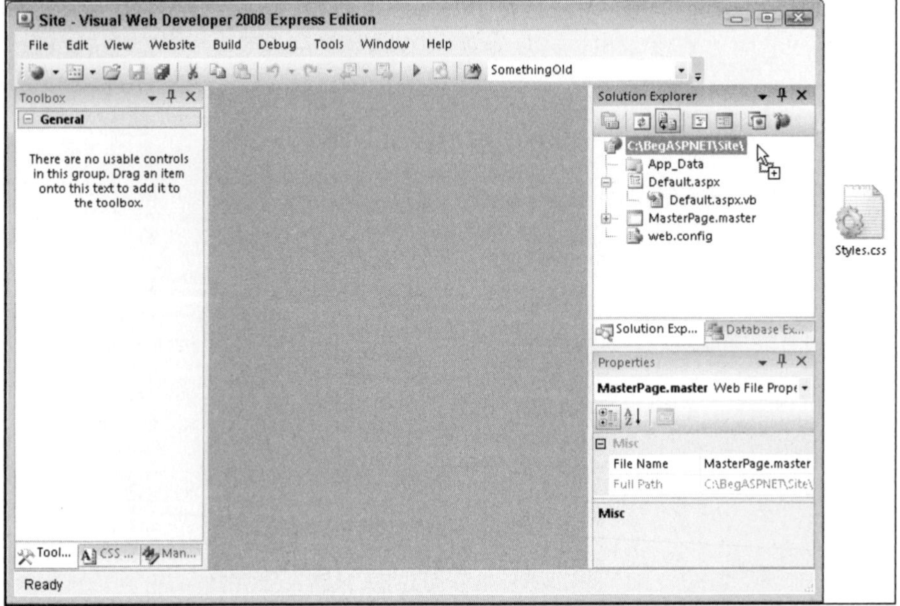

Figure 2-7

How It Works

What's important to take away from this Try It Out is that VWD creates *a copy* of the file when it adds it to the site. So, the original Styles.css file on the desktop is not affected when you make changes to the copy in VWD. This way, it's easy to drag and drop files out of existing web sites into your new one, without affecting the originals. The same applies to files you add using the Add Existing Item dialog box in VWD.

If you have added files to your web site's folder outside of VWD, they may not show up right away. You can get a fresh copy of the file list by clicking the Refresh button on the Solution Explorer's toolbar.

Organizing Your Site

Because of the many files that make up your site, it's often a good idea to group them by function in separate folders. For example, all Style Sheet files could go in a folder called Styles, `.js` files could go in Scripts, User Controls could go in a Controls folder, and master pages could be stored in a folder called MasterPages. This is a matter of personal preference, but structured and well-organized sites are easier to manage and understand. The next Try It Out explains how you can add new folders to the site and how you move files from one location to another.

Try It Out Organizing Your Web Site

1. Right-click the Planet Wrox site in the Solution Explorer and choose New Folder, as shown in Figure 2-8.

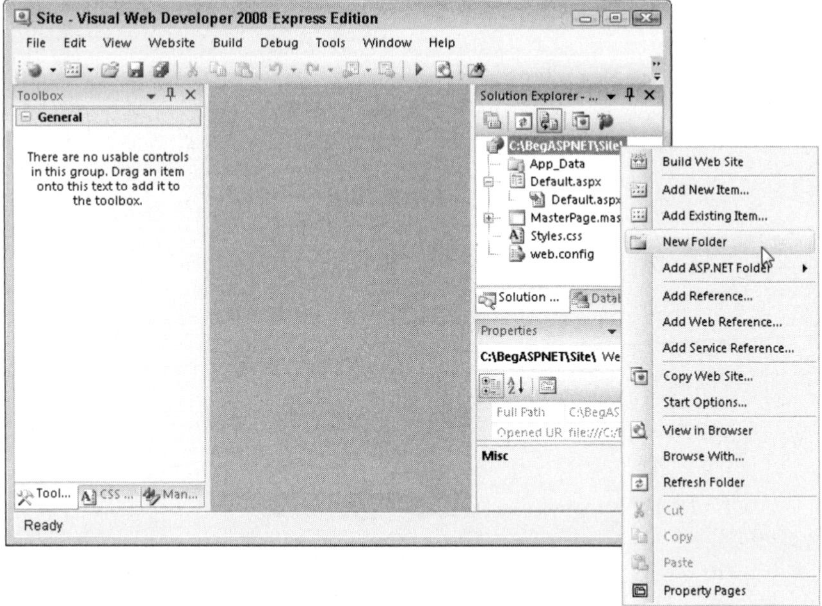

Figure 2-8

2. Type **MasterPages** as the new folder name and press Enter.
3. Create two more folders, called **Styles** and **Controls**, respectively. These folders will be used in the remainder of this book.
4. Drag the file MasterPage.master and drop it into the MasterPages folder you just created. This moves the file from the root of the site into the designated folder.
5. Drag the file Styles.css from the root of the site and drop it into the Styles folder.
6. If everything went well, your Solution Explorer should look like Figure 2-9.

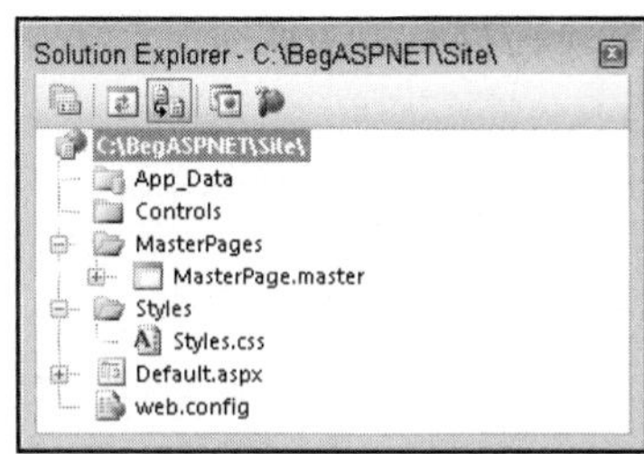

Figure 2-9

If your Solution Explorer looks different from the one shown in Figure 2-9, follow this Try It Out again until your site looks exactly the same, with the same folder structure and files in it. Future Try It Out exercises in this book assume you have the correct folders and files in your web site.

How It Works

Structure and organization are important to keep your sites manageable. Although you may be tempted to add all of your files to the root of your project, it's better not to do this. With a very small site, you may not notice any difference, but as soon as your site begins to grow, you'll find it becomes a lot harder to manage when it lacks structure. Placing related files in separate folders is the first step to an organized site. Storing files of the same type in a single folder is only one way to optimize your site. In later chapters, you'll see that separate folders are used to group files with similar functionality as well. For example, all files that are accessible only by an administrator of the site are grouped in a folder called Management.

The drag-and-drop features of VWD make it easy to reorganize your site. Simply pick up one file or multiple files and drop them in their new location. If you continue to apply these kinds of organization practices while expanding your site, you'll find that tomorrow or six months from now, you won't have any problems locating the right file when you need it.

Special File Types

Some of the files listed in the previous section require that you put them in a special folder as opposed to the optional organizational folder structure proposed in the previous section. The IDE will warn you when you try to add a file outside of its special folder, and will offer to create the folder and put the file there. For example, when you try to add a class file (with a `.vb` or `.cs` extension), you get the warning shown in Figure 2-10.

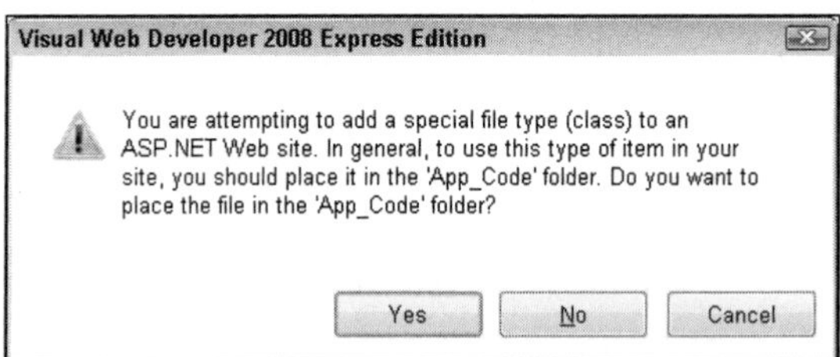

Figure 2-10

When you get this dialog box, always click Yes. Otherwise your file won't function correctly. You get similar dialog boxes for other file types, including skin and database files.

Now that you have a good understanding of the different types of files that make up your web site, it's time to look at one of them in much more detail: `.aspx` files, also known as Web Forms.

Working with Web Forms

Web Forms, represented by `.aspx` files are the core of any ASP.NET 3.5 web application. They are the actual pages that users see in their browser when they visit your site.

As you saw in the previous chapter, Web Forms can contain a mix of HTML, ASP.NET server controls, client-side JavaScript, CSS, and programming code. To make it easier to see how all this code ends up in the browser, VWD offers a number of different views on your pages.

The Different Views on Web Forms

VWD allows you to look at your Web Form from a few different angles. When you have an ASPX or HTML file open in the Document Window, you see three view buttons at the bottom of the window. With these buttons, visible in Figure 2-11, you can switch between the different views.

Source View is the default view when you open a page. Source View shows you the raw HTML and other markup for the page, and is very useful if you want to tweak the contents of a page and you have a good idea of what you want to change where. As I explained in the previous chapter, I use the term Markup View rather than Source View to refer to the markup of ASPX and HTML pages.

The Design button allows you to switch the Document Window into Design View, which gives you an idea of how the page will end up. When in Design View, you can use the Visual Aids and Formatting Marks submenus from the main View menu to control visual markers like line breaks, borders, and spaces. Both submenus offer a menu item called Show that allows you to turn all the visual aids on or off at once. Turning both off is useful if you want to have an idea of how the page ends up in the browser. You should, however, use Design View only to get *an idea* of how the page will end up. Although VWD has a great rendering engine that renders the page in Design View pretty well, you should always check your pages in different browsers as well because what you see in VWD is the markup for the page before it gets processed. Server controls on the page may emit HTML that changes the looks of the page in the browser. Therefore, it's recommended to view the page in the browser as often as possible so you can check if it's going to look the way you want it.

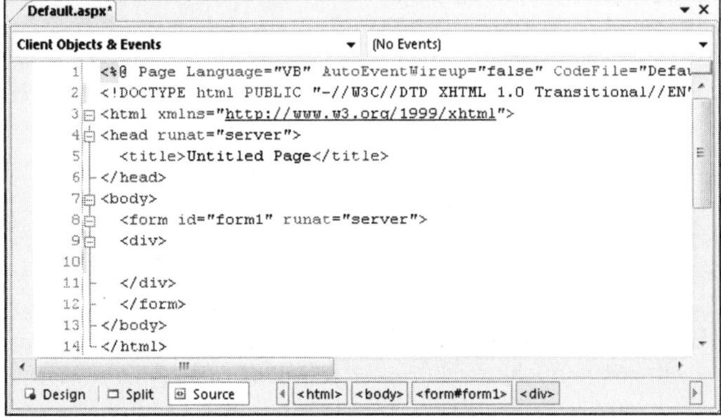

Figure 2-11

The Split button allows you to look at Design View and Markup View at the same time, as you can see in Figure 2-12.

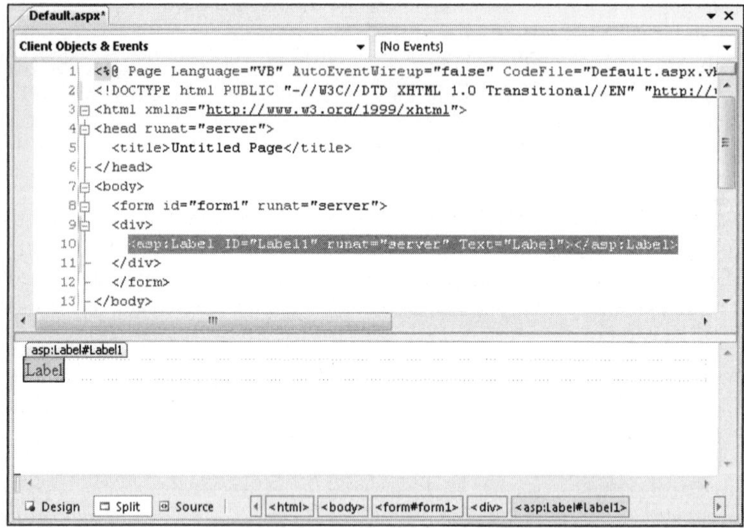

Figure 2-12

Split View is great if you want to see the code that VWD generates when you add controls to the Design View of your page. The other way around is very useful too: when you make changes to the markup of the page in Markup View, you can see how it ends up in Design View. There are times where Design View becomes out-of-sync with Markup View. If that's the case, a message appears at the top of Design View. Simply clicking the message or saving the entire page is enough to update the Design window.

If you want your pages to open in a different view than Markup View, choose Tools ➪ Options. Then choose the HTML Designer category, and on the General tab, set your preferred view.

In addition to the HTML and other markup you see in the Markup View window, a Web Form can also contain code in either C# or Visual Basic .NET. Where this code is placed depends on the type of Web Form you create. The next section explains the two options you have in more detail.

Choosing between Code Behind and Pages with Inline Code

Web Forms come in two flavors: either as an `.aspx` file with a *Code Behind* file (a file named after the Web Form with an additional `.vb` or `.cs` extension) or as `.aspx` files that have their code embedded, often referred to as Web Forms with *inline code*. Although you won't see much code until Chapter 5, it's important to understand the difference between these type of Web Forms. At first, Web Forms with inline code seem a little easier to understand. Since the code needed to program your web site is part of the very same Web Form, you can clearly see how the code relates to the file. However, as your page gets bigger and you add more functionality to it, it's often easier if you have the code in a separate file. That way, it's completely separate from the markup, allowing you to focus on the task at hand.

In the next exercise, you'll add two files that demonstrate the difference between Code Behind and inline code.

Try It Out Adding Web Forms with Code to Your Site

The files you're going to add in this exercise aren't needed for the final application. To avoid cluttering up the project, you should put them in a separate Demos folder.

1. In the Solution Explorer, right-click your web site and choose New Folder. Name the folder **Demos** and press Enter.
2. Right-click the Demos folder and choose Add New Item. In the dialog box that appears, click the Web Form template and name the file **CodeBehind.aspx**. Make sure that the check box for Place Code in Separate File is selected, and choose your programming language from the drop-down list. Finally, click the Add button. The page should open in Markup View so you can see the HTML for the page.
3. At the bottom of the Document Window, click the Design button to switch the page from Markup View into Design View. The page you see has a white background with a small, dashed rectangle at the top of it. The dashed rectangle is the `<div>` tag you saw in Markup View.
4. From the Toolbox, drag a `Label` control from the Standard category and drop it in the dashed area of the page. Remember, you can open the Toolbox with the shortcut Ctrl+Alt+X if it isn't open yet. In Design View, your screen should now look like Figure 2-13.

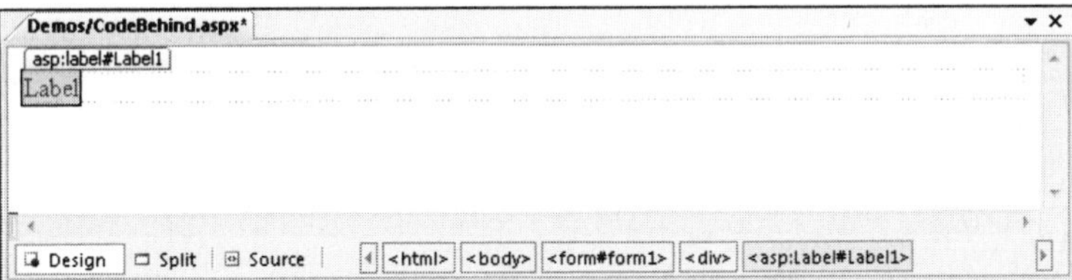

Figure 2-13

5. Double-click somewhere in the white area below the dashed line of the `<div>` tag. VWD switches from Design View into the Code Behind of the file and adds code that fires when the page loads in the browser:

VB.NET

```
Protected Sub Page_Load(ByVal sender As Object, ByVal e As System.EventArgs) _
       Handles Me.Load

End Sub
```

C#

```
protected void Page_Load(object sender, EventArgs e)
{

}
```

Although this odd syntax may look a little scary at this point, don't worry about it too much. In most cases, VWD adds it for you automatically, as you just saw. In later chapters, you'll see exactly how this code works, but for now it's important to realize that the code you're going to place between the lines that start with `Protected Sub` and `End Sub` in Visual Basic and between the curly braces in C# will be run when the page is requested in the browser. If you are using Visual Basic, you won't have the underscore that is visible in this code snippet. I added that here to split the code over two lines. You'll see why in the How It Works section after this exercise.

All code examples you'll see from now on include a Visual Basic (VB.NET) and a C# version so always pick the one that matches your programming language.

6. Place your cursor in the open line in the code that VWD created and add the highlighted line of code that assigns today's date and time to the label, which will eventually show up in the browser:

VB.NET

```
Protected Sub Page_Load(ByVal sender As Object, ByVal e As System.EventArgs) _
       Handles Me.Load
  Label1.Text = "Hello World; the time is now " & DateTime.Now.ToString()
End Sub
```

C#

```
protected void Page_Load(object sender, EventArgs e)
{
  Label1.Text = "Hello World; the time is now " + DateTime.Now.ToString();
}
```

Note that as soon as you type the **L** for `Label1`, you get a list with options to choose from. This is part of VWD's IntelliSense, a great tool that helps you rapidly write code. Instead of typing the whole word **Label1**, you simply type the letter **L** or the letters **La** and then you pick the appropriate item from the list, visible in Figure 2-14.

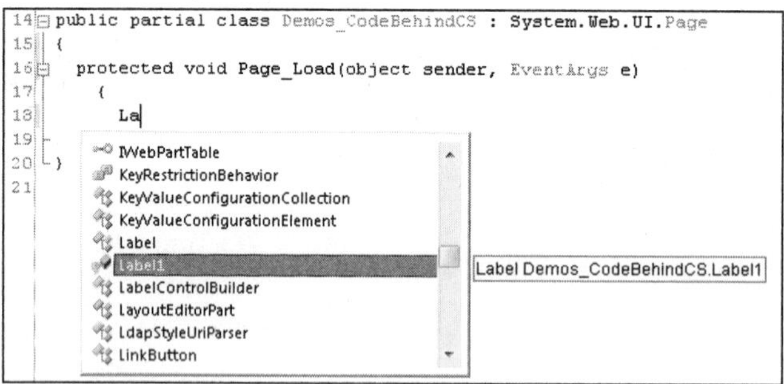

Figure 2-14

To complete the selected word, you can press Enter or Tab or even the period. In the latter case, you immediately get another list that allows you to pick the word `Text` simply by typing the first few letters, completing the word by pressing the Tab or Enter key. This feature is a real productivity tool because you can write code with a minimum of keystrokes. IntelliSense is available in many other file types as well, including ASPX, HTML, CSS, JavaScript, and XML. In many cases, the list with options pops up automatically if you begin typing. If it doesn't, press Ctrl+Spacebar to invoke it. If the list covers some of your code in the code window, press and hold the Ctrl key to make the window transparent.

7. Right-click the page in the Solution Explorer and choose View in browser. Click Yes if you get a dialog box that asks if you want to save the changes, and then the page will appear in the browser, similar to the browser window you see in Figure 2-15.

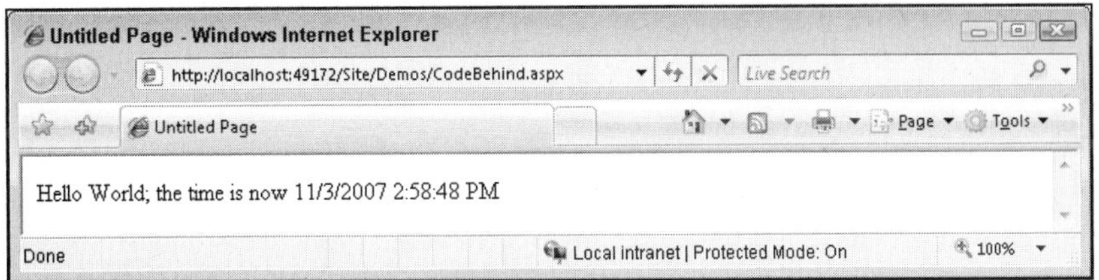

Figure 2-15

If you don't see the message with the date and time appear or you get an error on the page in the browser, make sure you saved the changes to all open pages. To save all pages at once, press Ctrl+Shift+S or click the Save All button on the toolbar (the one with the multiple purple floppy disk symbols). Additionally, make sure you typed the code for the right language. When you created this new page, you chose a programming language that applies to the entire page. You can't mix languages on a single page, so if you started with a Visual C# page, make sure you entered the C# code snippet from the Try It Out.

8. Setting up a page with inline code is very similar. Start by adding a new file to the Demos folder. Call it **InLine.aspx** and make sure you uncheck the Place Code in Separate File option.

9. Just as you did in steps 3, 4, and 5, switch the page into Design View, drag a label inside the `<div>` tag, and then double-click the page somewhere outside the `<div>` that now contains the label. Instead of opening a Code Behind file, VWD now switches your page into Markup View, and adds the `Page_Load` code directly in the page.

10. On the empty line in the code block that VWD inserted, type the highlighted line you see in step 6 of this exercise. Make sure you use the correct programming language. You should end up with the following code at the top of your `.aspx` file:

VB.NET

```
<script runat="server">
  Protected Sub Page_Load(ByVal sender As Object, ByVal e As System.EventArgs)
    Label1.Text = "Hello World; the time is now " & DateTime.Now.ToString()
  End Sub
</script>
```

C#

```
<script runat="server">
  protected void Page_Load(object sender, EventArgs e)
  {
    Label1.Text = "Hello World; the time is now " + DateTime.Now.ToString();
  }
</script>
```

11. Right-click the page in the Solution Explorer and choose View in browser. Alternatively, press Ctrl+F5 to open the page in your browser. You should see the same screen you got in step 7.

How It Works

At runtime, pages with inline code behave the same as pages that use Code Behind. In both cases, the ASP.NET runtime sees the `Page_Load` code and executes any code it finds in it. In the Try It Out, this meant setting the `Text` of `Label1` to today's date and time.

Note that in this example, the C# code looks very similar to the VB.NET code. The code that sets the `Label`'s text is almost identical in the two languages. One difference is that VB.NET uses an ampersand (&) to glue two pieces of text together, but C# uses the plus (+) character. The other difference is that in C# all code lines must be terminated with a semicolon (;) to indicate the end of a unit of code, but Visual Basic uses the line break.

That's also the reason for the additional underscore you saw in this code snippet from step 6 of the exercise:

```
Protected Sub Page_Load(ByVal sender As Object, ByVal e As System.EventArgs) _
       Handles Me.Load
  Label1.Text = "Hello World; the time is now " & DateTime.Now.ToString()
End Sub
```

Note that in your page, you won't see the underscore (_) at the end of the first line of the Visual Basic example. In Visual Basic, you can add this *line continuation character* to break up long lines over multiple lines without breaking the original meaning of this code. It was added here because the book's pages are not wide enough to show the entire code statement on a single line. You'll see more of these underscores in other Visual Basic examples in the remainder of this book. If you decide to manually type the underscore to make your own code more readable, don't forget to type an additional space before the actual underscore or your code won't work.

In C#, you don't need this character because the language itself allows you to break long lines simply by pressing Enter. This is because C# uses a semicolon to denote the end of a line instead of a line break in the source.

You opened the page in your browser using the right-click View in browser option or by pressing Ctrl+F5. With the View in browser option, you always open the page you right-click. With the Ctrl+F5 shortcut, you open the page that is currently the active document in the Document Window, the page that is currently selected in the Solution Explorer, or the file that has been set as the *start page* for the web site. Additionally, all open files are saved automatically, and the site is checked for errors before the requested page is opened in the browser.

You can assign a page as the start page by right-clicking it in the Solution Explorer and choosing Set As Start Page. If you want to control this behavior at a later stage, right-click the web site in the Solution

Explorer and choose Property Pages. In the Start Options category, you can indicate that you want the currently active page to open, or you can assign a specific page, as show in Figure 2-16.

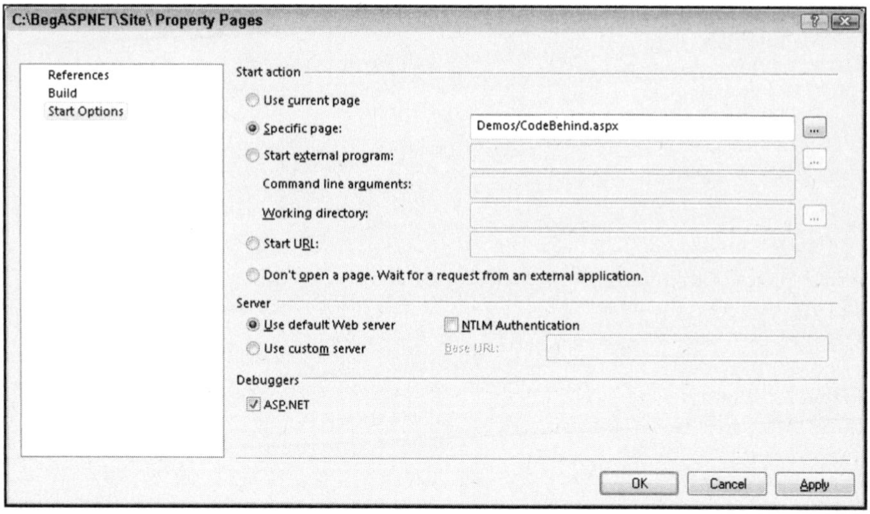

Figure 2-16

In the previous exercise, you learned how to add a page that contains a simple `Label` control. Additionally, you saw how to write some code that updates the label with today's date and time. You can ignore this code for now; it only served to demonstrate the differences between Code Behind and inline code. In Chapter 5, you'll learn more about programming in Visual Basic and C#.

To make compelling pages, you obviously need a lot more content than just a simple `Label` control that shows today's date and time. The next section shows you how to add content and HTML to your pages and how to style and format it.

Adding Markup to Your Page

There are a number of ways to add HTML and other markup to your pages. First of all, you can simply type it in the Markup View window. However, this isn't always the best option, because it forces you to type a lot of code by hand. To make it easier to insert new HTML in the page and to apply formatting to it, the Design View window offers a number of helpful tools. These tools include the Formatting toolbar and the menu items Format and Table. For these tools to be active, you need to have the document in Design View. If you're working in Split View mode, you have to make sure that the Design View part has the focus, or you'll find that most of the tools are not available.

Inserting and Formatting Text

You can type text in both Design View and in Markup View. Simply place the cursor at the desired location and start typing. When you switch to Design View, the Formatting toolbar becomes available, with the options shown in Figure 2-17.

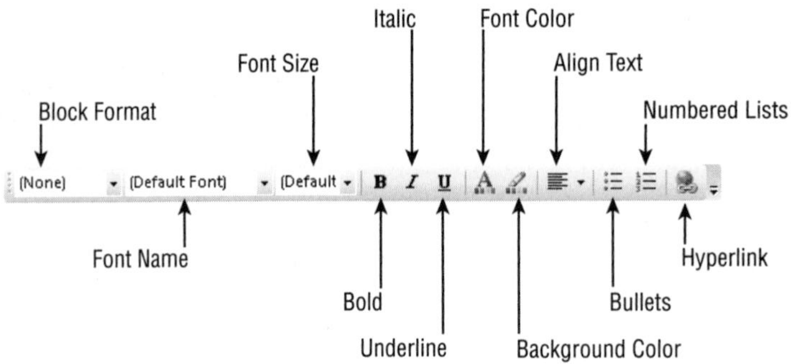

Figure 2-17

The drop-down list labeled Block Format enables you to insert HTML tags like <p> for paragraphs, <h1> through <h6> for headings, and <ul>, <ol>, and <li> tags for lists. You can choose an item from the drop-down list directly to have it inserted in your page, or you can select some text first and choose the appropriate block element from the list to wrap the selected text inside the tags.

The drop-down list labeled Font Name allows you to change the *font family*, and the Font Size drop-down list enables you to change the *font size*.

The remainder of the buttons on the toolbar function exactly the same as in other editing environments. For example, the B button formats your text with a bold font. Similarly, the I and the U buttons italicize and underline your font, respectively.

In the next Try It Out, you see how to work with these tools to create the home page of the Planet Wrox web site.

Try It Out Adding Formatted Text

In this Try It Out, you modify the page Default.aspx that was added automatically to the site when you created it. In Chapter 6, you'll modify this page once more when you start using master pages.

1. Open the page Default.aspx from the root of the site and switch to Design View using the Design button at the bottom of the Document Window.

2. Make sure the Style Application toolbar is visible. If it isn't, right-click an existing toolbar, and then select Style Application from the list. When the toolbar is visible, make sure that the Style Application drop-down list on the toolbar is set to Manual, and not to Auto.

3. Click inside the dashed rectangle until you see the glyph showing that the <div> element is currently active. At the same time, the tag navigator at the bottom of the code window should highlight the last block with the text <div> on it, as shown in Figure 2-18.

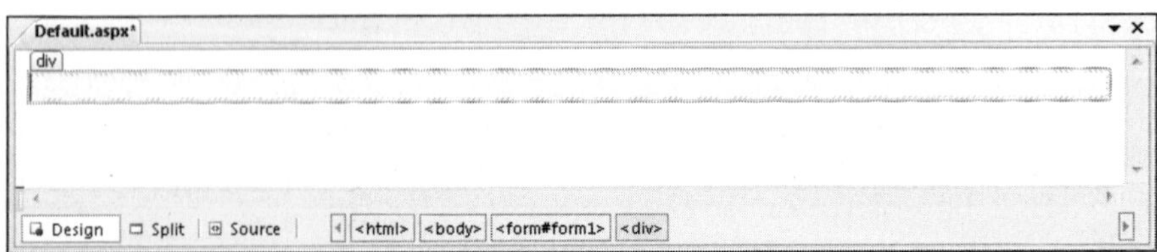

Figure 2-18

4. Type "Hi there visitor and welcome to Planet Wrox" and highlight the text using the mouse. From the Block Format drop-down list (visible in Figure 2-17) choose Heading 1 <h1>. Note that a little glyph with the text h1 appears right above the text, to indicate that VWD created a heading for you automatically. Figure 2-19 shows the Design View with the `<h1>` element.

Figure 2-19

5. Position your cursor at the end of the heading after the word `Wrox` and press Enter. A new paragraph (indicated by a little glyph with the letter `p` on it) is inserted for you so you can directly start typing.

6. Type the text shown in Figure 2-20 (or make up your own) to welcome the visitor to Planet Wrox. Select the text "paying a visit", click the Foreground Color button on the Formatting toolbar and select a different color in the dialog box that appears. Then select some other text, such as "reviews and concert pictures", and click the Bold button. When you're done, your Design View should show something similar to Figure 2-20.

Figure 2-20

The code for the home page should now look more or less similar to the following (the code has been reformatted a bit to fit the space in the book):

```
<div>
  <h1>Hi there visitor and welcome to Planet Wrox</h1>
  <p>
    We&#39;re glad you&#39;re <span class="style1">paying a visit</span> to
          <a href="http://www.PlanetWrox.com">www.PlanetWrox.com</a>,
          the coolest music community site on the Internet.
  </p>
  <p>
    Feel free to have a look around; as there are lots of interesting <b>reviews
         and concert pictures</b> to be found here.
  </p>
</div>
```

7. Open the page in your browser by pressing Ctrl+F5, or by right-clicking the page in the Solution Explorer and then choosing View in browser.

How It Works

When you use the various Formatting toolbar buttons, like Foreground Color, VWD inserts the appropriate HTML and CSS code for you. For example, when you click the B button, VWD inserts a pair of `<b>` tags around the selected text. When you click the I button, it adds a pair of `<i>` tags to italicize the text. It also inserts a `class` attribute (shown in the previous code example) that points to a class called `style1`. The code for this style has been added to the top of your file and looks similar to this:

```
<style type="text/css">
  .style1
  {
    color: #FF0000;
  }
</style>
```

Your code may look slightly different if you chose a different color. The code you see here is explained in the next chapter. For now, just remember that this code sets color of the text it is applied to as red.

The Style Application that you set at the beginning of this exercise determines where VWD adds your code. In Manual mode, you control the place where the code is added by making a choice in the Target Rule drop-down list, whereas in Auto mode, VWD makes that choice for you. Most of the examples in this book assume you set the mode to Manual.

Note that VWD replaced the apostrophe character (') in "we're" in the welcome message with its HTML-compliant variant: `'`. Using this kind of code allows you to insert characters in your page that a browser may have trouble displaying, or that have special meaning within HTML itself, like the ampersand character (&), which is written as `&`. When you type text in Design View, VWD automatically inserts the coded equivalents of relevant characters for you; however, if you type in Markup View directly, you'll have to do this yourself.

Don't worry if your code looks different from what is shown here. Many settings in VWD influence the code that is generated for you.

So far, the exercises have been concerned with adding and styling text in your page. However, VWD allows you to insert other HTML tags as well, like tables and bullets. The next section shows you how this works.

Adding Tables and Other Markup

HTML tables are great if you need to present structured or repeating data, like a list of products in a shopping cart, photos in a photo album, or input controls in a form. There is a lot of debate on the Internet about whether you should use tables to lay out your page as well. For example, if your page contains a header with a logo, a main content area, and a footer at the bottom, you could use a table with three rows to accomplish this. In general, it's considered bad practice to use tables for this purpose because they add a lot of extraneous markup to the page and are often difficult to maintain. Besides, quite often the same result can be accomplished using CSS, which you'll learn about in the next chapter. Despite the disadvantages that tables may bring, they are still an invaluable asset in your HTML toolbox when it comes to displaying tabular or otherwise structured information.

Try It Out Using the Format and Table Menus

In this exercise, you will learn how to add tables to your page using the Table menu and how to add rows and columns. Additionally, you'll learn how to add other structured elements such as bulleted lists.

1. Under the Demos folder, create a new Web Form called **TableDemo.aspx**. Make sure it uses Code Behind by checking the Place code in separate file option.
2. Switch the page to Design View, click inside the dashed rectangle that represents the standard `<div>` tag in the page, and choose Table ➪ Insert Table. The Insert Table dialog box appears, as shown in Figure 2-21.

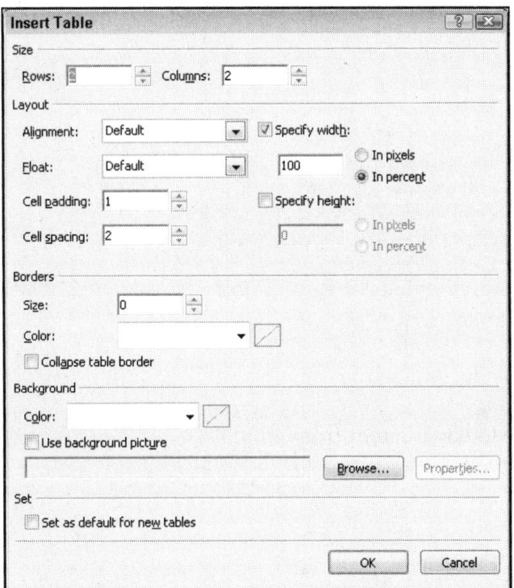

Figure 2-21

3. Set Rows to 3 and leave Columns set to 2. Leave all other settings set to their defaults and click OK. The table gets inserted in the page.
4. If you see only a single table cell, and not the entire table with three rows and two columns, you need to enable Visual Aid for tables. To do this, choose View ➪ Visual Aids ➪ Visible Borders from the main menu to turn the borders on. Your Design View should now look like Figure 2-22.

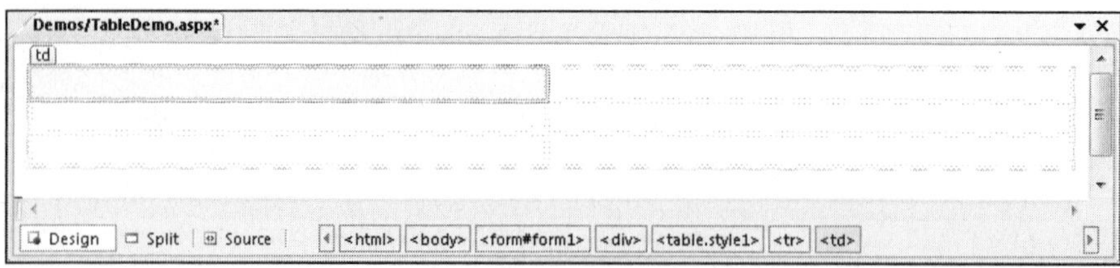

Figure 2-22

5. Drag the right border of the very first cell in the table to the left. You'll see a visual indicator showing the width of the cell. Keep dragging it to the left until it has a width of 200 pixels, as in Figure 2-23.

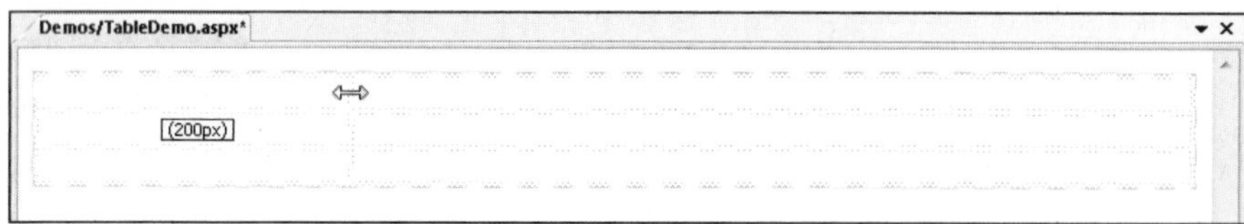

Figure 2-23

6. To add more rows or columns to the table, you can right-click an existing cell. From the pop-up menu that appears, choose Insert to add additional rows or columns at different locations. Similarly, you can use the Delete, Select, and Modify options to delete rows or columns, merge cells, and make selections. For this exercise, you don't need to add additional rows or columns, although it's okay if you had already done so.
7. Place your cursor in the first cell of the first row and type the words **Bulleted List**.
8. Place your cursor in the second cell of the first row and choose Bullets and Numbering from the Format menu.
9. Switch to the Plain Bullets tab, click the picture with the round, solid bullets (see Figure 2-24), and click OK.

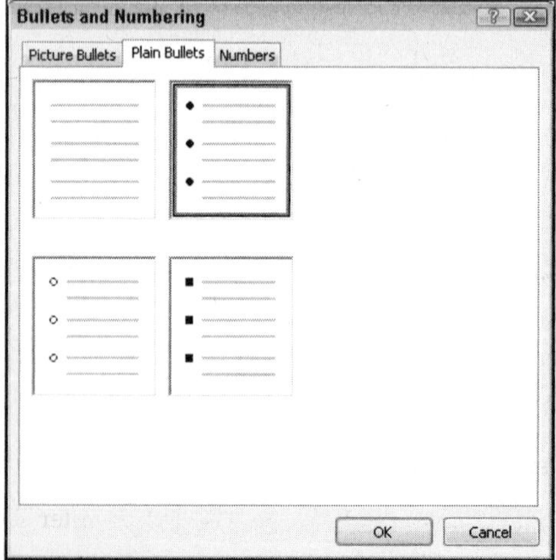

Figure 2-24

10. Type some text, like your favorite musical genre (Punk, Rock, Techno, and so on), and then press Enter. VWD inserts a new bullet for you automatically, so you can continue to add new items to the list. Add two more genres, so you end up with three bullets.

11. Repeat steps 7 through 10, but this time create a numbered list. First, type **Numbered List** in the first cell of the second row, then position your cursor in the second cell of the same row, and choose Format ➪ Bullets and Numbering. Switch to the Numbers tab (visible in Figure 2-24 behind the Plain Bullets tab) and click the second picture in the first row, which shows a standard numbered list, and click OK. Type a few items for the list, pressing Enter after each item.

12. Open the page in the browser by pressing Ctrl+F5. You should see a screen similar to Figure 2-25.

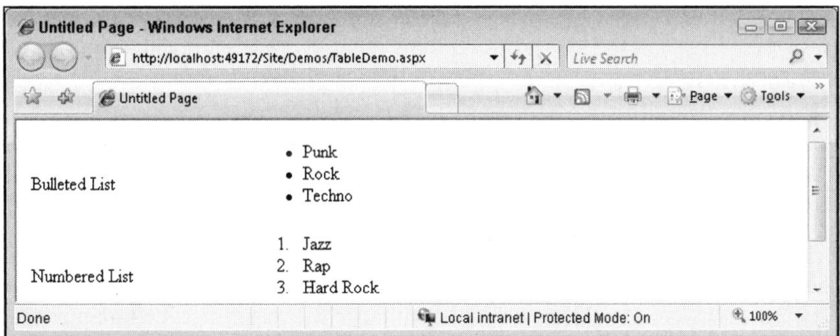

Figure 2-25

How It Works

When you visually insert page elements like tables or lists through the available menus, VWD inserts the required markup for you in Markup View. When you insert a table, VWD adds a `<table>` tag and a number of `<tr>` and `<td>` tags to define rows and cells, respectively. It also applies a `style` attribute to the table to control the table's width. It created another style for the `<td>` elements when you dragged the column width to be 200 pixels. Similarly, when you insert a list, VWD inserts a `<ol>` tag for numbered or *ordered lists* and a `<ul>` tag for *unordered* or bulleted lists. Within these tags, `<li>` elements are used to define each item in the list.

Besides the HTML tags you have seen thus far, there is another important tag you need to look at: the `<a>` tag, which is used to create links between pages.

Connecting Pages

An important part of any web site are the links that connect the pages in your site. Links allow your visitors to go from one page to another, in the same site, or to a completely different site on the Internet. There are a few ways to create links between pages, including:

- The HTML `<a>` element, explained in this chapter.
- Using the `<asp:HyperLink>` control, discussed in Chapter 7.
- Programmatically through code. This is discussed later in the book.

The following exercise shows you how easy it is to link from one page to another.

Try It Out Linking Pages

In this Try It Out, you'll modify the page TableDemo.aspx you created earlier by adding text that links to another page. Once you run the page in the browser and click that link, the new page will replace the old one.

1. Open the page TableDemo.aspx from the Demos folder.
2. If necessary, switch to Design View.
3. In the first cell of the third row, type the text **Link**.
4. In the second cell of the same row, type the text **Go to the Homepage** and highlight it with your mouse.
5. On the Formatting toolbar, click the Convert to HyperLink button. It's the last button on the toolbar with a green globe on it. If you don't see this button because it's obscured by other toolbars, either drag the formatting toolbar to a new location, or choose Format ➪ Convert to Hyperlink to bring up the same dialog box.
6. In the dialog box that appears, click the Browse button and browse to the Default.aspx page in the root of your site and click OK. Next, click OK again to dismiss the Hyperlink dialog box. The Design View of your page should look similar to the one displayed in Figure 2-26.

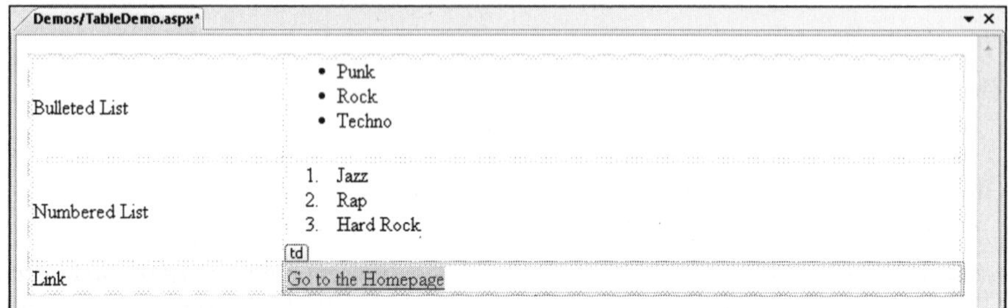

Figure 2-26

7. Switch to Markup View and notice how the HTML for the link has been inserted:

```
<a href="../Default.aspx">Go to the Homepage</a>
```

   Note that the `href` attribute points to the page you want to link to.

8. If you want to change the page being linked to from the code window, click somewhere between the opening and closing quote of the `href` attribute and press Ctrl+Spacebar. A dialog box pops up that allows you to select another page. Alternatively, you can click the Pick URL option and browse for the new page somewhere in your site.
9. Right-click the page TableDemo.aspx in the Solution Explorer and choose View in browser. When the page has finished loading, click the Go to the Homepage link. The request is sent to the web server and, as a response, you now get the home page of the web site.

How It Works

Links between pages are likely one of the most important elements in a web page, because they allow you to create a connection between a page in your site and another page, whether that page lives in your own site, or on a completely different server somewhere on the Internet. For simple links that should appear somewhere in your page, the HTML `<a>` tag with a `href` attribute set is the easiest to set up. When the user clicks such a link, the browser requests the new page from the server and displays it. Note that you're not limited to linking to pages in your own site. If you want to link to external pages instead, simply replace the `href` attribute value with the full address of the page as shown in the following example:

```
<a href="http://www.wrox.com ">Go to the Wrox Homepage</a>
```

It's important to include the `http://` prefix; otherwise, the browser goes out looking for a file or folder called `www.wrox.com` on your web site.

You'll use the things you learned in this chapter about page creation and formatting in the next chapter, which deals with designing your web pages using CSS.

Practical Tips on Working with Web Forms

Here are some tips for working with Web Forms:

- Always try to favor Web Forms with Code Behind over those with inline code. Although at first you may not notice a big difference in working with them, as your site and pages start to grow, you'll find that it's easier to work with a page where the code is separated from the markup. Also, when you're working with a team on a web site, Code Behind allows you to work with more than one person on the same file: one developer can work on the design in the `.aspx` file, while another developer can add code to the aspx.vb or aspx.cs file.
- Spend some time familiarizing yourself with the different menu items of the Format and Table menus. Most of them generate HTML tags that are inserted into your page. Take a look at the HTML tags and attributes that have been generated for you, and try to change them directly in the code, and through the menus and toolbars. This way, you get a good feel for the various tags available and how they behave.
- Experiment with links to connect pages in your site. Notice how VWD creates different links depending on the location of the page you are linking to. Chapter 7 deals with linking and the various ways to address pages in your site in much more detail.

Summary

This chapter introduced you to some important topics that help you build maintainable and structured ASP.NET web applications. Understanding the differences between the different project types and templates enables you to kick-start a web project with just the files you need.

The same applies to the different file types you can add to your site. Since each file type serves a specific purpose, it's important to realize what that purpose is and how you can use the file. You used some of the files in this chapter (a Web Form and its Code Behind class file); the remainder of this book will show you how to use the other file types that are introduced in this chapter.

Another important decision you need to make when building web sites is whether you build web pages with Code Behind or with inline code. Fortunately, this decision does not impact the entire site, and you'll need to reconsider it again for every file you add. So if you started out with inline code but find it harder to work with when your pages and site grow, you can start adding pages with Code Behind from that point.

One common activity that you'll perform when building ASP.NET web pages is adding markup to the page. As you saw in this and the previous chapter, markup comes in a few flavors, including plain HTML and ASP.NET Server Controls. Knowing how to add this markup to your page using the numerous menu options and toolbars that VWD offers is critical in building good-looking web pages.

Now that you have a solid understanding of creating and modifying Web Forms, it's time to look at how you can turn those dull looking black-and-white pages with a few controls into attractive web pages. The next chapter shows you how to work with the many CSS tools found in VWD to create the desired effect.

Exercises

1. Name three important files in the Web Files category and that you can add to your site. Describe the purpose of each file.
2. What do you need to do to make a piece of text both bold and italicized in your web page? What will the resulting HTML look like?
3. Name three different ways to add existing files to an ASP.NET web site in VWD.
4. What are the different views that VWD offers you for your ASPX pages? Does VWD offer other views as well?

Designing Your Web Pages

The pages you created in the previous two chapters look pretty plain and dull. That's because they lack styling information and therefore default to the standard layout that the browser applies. To spruce up your pages, you need a way to change their presentation in the browser. The most common way to do this is by using the *Cascading Style Sheets* (CSS) language. CSS is the de facto language for formatting and designing information on the Web, including ASP.NET web pages. With CSS you can quickly change the appearance of your web pages, giving them that great look that your design or corporate identity dictates.

Although earlier versions of Visual Web Developer lacked good tools for working with CSS, the IDE of Visual Web Developer 2008 has great support for CSS and is able to render pages much closer to how they'll eventually end up in the browser. The new tools enable you to visually create CSS, making it much easier to style your pages without the need to know or remember every little detail of CSS.

In this chapter, you'll learn more about the following topics:

- What CSS is and why you need it
- What the CSS language looks like and how to write it.
- The different ways to add CSS code to your ASP.NET pages and to external files.
- The numerous tools that VWD offers you to quickly write CSS.

To understand the relevance of and need for CSS in your ASP.NET projects, you need to understand the shortcomings of HTML first. The next section gives you a look at the problems that plain HTML presents, and how CSS is able to overcome these issues.

Why Do You Need CSS?

In the early days of the Internet, web pages consisted mostly of text and images. The text was formatted using plain HTML, using tags like `<b>` to make the text bold, and the `<font>` tag to influence the font family, size, and color. Web developers soon realized that they needed more power to format their pages, so CSS was created to address some of HTML's styling shortcomings.

Problems of HTML Formatting

One of the problems with using HTML for formatting is that it only offers a limited set of options to style your pages. You can use tags like `<i>`, `<b>`, and `<font>` to change the appearance of text and use attributes like `bgcolor` to change the background color of HTML elements. You also have a number of attributes at your disposal for changing the way links appear in your page.

Obviously, this feature set isn't rich enough to create the attractive web pages that your users expect and demand.

Another problem of HTML with a lot more impact on how you build your web pages is the way the styling information is applied to the page. By design, HTML forces you to embed your formatting in your HTML document, making it harder to reuse or change the design later. Consider the following example:

```
<p><font face="Arial" color="red" size="+1">
  This is red text, in an Arial type face and slightly larger than the default text
</font></p>
```

The problem with this code snippet is that the actual *data* (the text in the `<p>` element) is mixed with the *presentation* (the formatting of the text with the `<font>` tag in this example). Ideally, the two should be separated, so each of them is easier to change without affecting the other.

Imagine you used the `<p>` and `<font>` tags as the first paragraph in each of the pages in your web site. Clearly, this code is difficult to maintain. What happens when you decide to change the color of the font from red to dark blue? Or what if your corporate identity dictates a Verdana font instead of Arial? You would need to visit each and every page in your site, making the required changes.

Besides maintainability, another problem with HTML formatting is the fact that you can't easily change the formatting at runtime, in the user's browser. With the HTML from the previous code snippet, there is no way to let your visitor change things like the font size or color, a common request to help people who are visually impaired. If you want to offer your visitors an alternative version of the page with a larger font size or a different color, you'd need to create a copy of the original page and make the necessary changes.

The final problem with HTML formatting is that all the additional markup in your page adds considerably to the size of the page. This makes it slower to download and display as the information needs to be downloaded with each page in your web site. It also makes it harder to maintain your pages as you'd need to scroll through large HTML files to find the content you need.

To summarize, formatting with HTML suffers from the following problems:

- Its feature set severely limits the formatting possibilities that your pages require.
- Data and presentation are mixed within the same file.
- HTML doesn't allow you to easily switch formatting at runtime in the browser.
- The required formatting tags and attributes make your pages larger and thus slower to load and display.

Fortunately, CSS allows you to overcome all of these problems.

How CSS Fixes Formatting Problems

CSS is designed to format your web pages in almost every possible way. It offers a rich set of options to change every little aspect of your web page, including fonts (size, color, family, and so on), colors and background colors, borders around HTML elements, positioning of elements in your page, and much more. CSS is widely understood by all major browsers today, so it's *the* language for visual presentation of web pages and very popular among web developers.

CSS overcomes the problem of mixed data and presentation by allowing you to define all formatting information in external files. Your ASPX or HTML pages can then reference these files and the browser will apply the correct styles for you. With this separation, the HTML document contains *what* you want to display, while the CSS file defines *how* you want to display it, enabling you to change or switch one of the two documents, leaving the other unmodified. You'll see how this works in the next section. In addition, CSS can be placed directly in an HTML or ASPX page, which gives you a chance to add small snippets of CSS exactly where you need them. You should be cautious when placing CSS directly in an HTML or ASPX page, as you can then no longer control style information from a single, central location.

Since all CSS code can be placed in a separate file, it's easy to offer the user a choice between different styles — for example, one with a larger font size. You can create a copy of the external style sheet, make the necessary changes, and then offer this alternative style sheet to the user. You'll see how this works in Chapter 6 when ASP.NET themes are discussed.

Another benefit of a separate style sheet file is the decrease in bandwidth that is required for your site. Style sheets don't change with each request, so a browser saves a local copy of the style sheet the first time it downloads it. From then on, it uses this *cached* copy instead of requesting it from the server over and over again. Sometimes this caching can work against you when the browser doesn't download the latest CSS files with your changes. If you find that the browser is not picking up the changes you made to a CSS file, use Ctrl+F5 in the browser (not VWD) to get a fresh copy from the server.

Now that you have seen why CSS is so important, it's time to find out how it looks and how to use it.

An Introduction to CSS

In terms of syntax, CSS is an easy language to learn. Its "grammar" consists of only a few concepts. That makes it relatively easy to get started with. What makes CSS a bit more difficult is the way all major browsers render a page. While virtually every modern desktop browser understands CSS, they all have their quirks when it comes to displaying a page according to the CSS standard. This standard, maintained by the same organization that maintains the HTML standard, the World Wide Web Consortium, or W3C for short, comes in three different versions: 1.0, 2.1, and 3.0. From these three versions, 2.1 is the most applicable today. It contains everything that version 1.0 contained but also adds a lot of possibilities on top of that. It's also the version that VWD uses and generates by default. Version 3.0 is currently under development and it's expected to take some time before the major browsers have solid support for it.

Before you look at the actual syntax of CSS, it's a good idea to see an example first. In the next exercise, you'll write a simple ASPX page that contains some CSS to format the contents of the page. This helps in understanding the CSS language, which is discussed in full detail in the section that follows.

Try It Out Writing Your First CSS

In this Try It Out you'll write some CSS that changes the appearance of a header and two paragraphs. You'll hand code the page for now; the second half of this chapter shows you how to use the CSS tools available in VWD that make writing CSS easy.

1. In the Planet Wrox project, create a new file called CssDemo.aspx in the Demos folder. For this exercise, it doesn't matter if you choose inline code or code behind. The programming language for the page doesn't matter either, as you'll only use the markup part of the page.
2. Make sure the page is in Markup View and then locate the `</head>` tag in the source. Right before this tag, type the following highlighted code:

```
  <title>Untitled Page</title>
  <style type="text/css">

  </style>
</head>
```

   Note that as soon as you type the opening angle bracket (<), a list pops up that allows you to select the `<style>` tag. The same applies to the `type` attribute; simply type the letters `ty` and the `type` attribute is preselected in the list. All you need to do to complete the word is press the Tab or Enter key. And, once more, the same help is available for the attribute value `text/css`. Simply select it in the list and press Tab or Enter, and the value is inserted for you automatically, nicely surrounded by the double quotes.

3. Next, between the opening and closing `<style>` tags, type the following highlighted CSS code:

```
<style type="text/css">
  h1
  {
    font-size: 20px;
    color: Green;
  }

  p
  {
    color: Blue;
    font-style: italic;
  }

  .RightAligned
  {
    text-align: right;
  }
</style>
```

   Take great care when typing this code, as CSS is rather picky about syntax. The first item in the list is an `h1` tag to style a heading at the first level so it gets a size of 20 pixels and is displayed in a green font. Notice the colon between `font-size` and `20px` and that the line is closed with a semicolon.

The second item in the list simply contains the letter p and defines the look and feel for all <p> elements in the page.

The last item is prefixed with a period (.) followed by the text RightAligned. This item is used to right-align some text in the page.

4. Scroll down in the page a little until you see the opening <div> tag. Right after this tag, type the following highlighted code:

```
<div>
<h1>Welcome to this CSS Demo page</h1>
<p>CSS makes it super easy to style your pages.</p>
<p class="RightAligned">
    With very little code, you can quickly change the looks of a page.
</p>
</div>
```

Instead of typing in this code directly, you can also use the Formatting Toolbar while in Design View to create elements like <h1> and <p>. For now, you'll need to type class="RightAligned", but in later exercises in this chapter you'll see how you can have the IDE write this code for you.

5. If you switch to Design View (or Split View), you'll see that the designer shows your text with the formatting defined in the <style> element of the page. Figure 3-1 shows the page in Split View so you can see the code and the design at the same time.

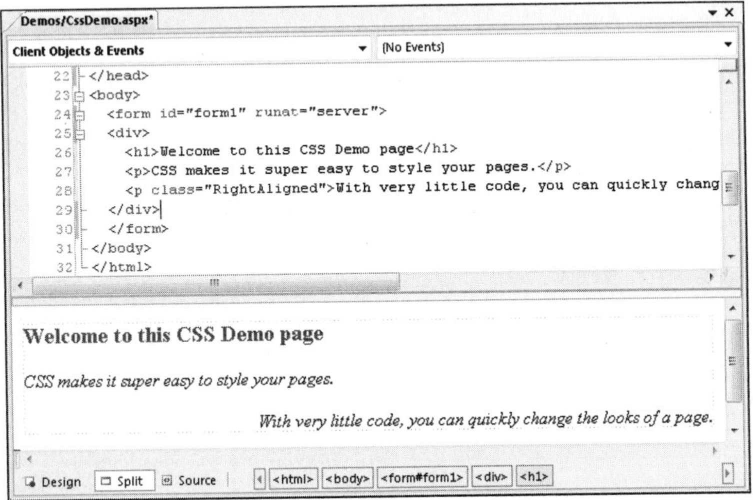

Figure 3-1

Although this black and white book makes it difficult to see different font colors, in Figure 3-1 you can clearly see that the <h1> has a larger font size. The figure also shows that all paragraphs (both the plain paragraph and the one with class="RightAligned") are now displayed with an italic font. Finally, you can see that the final paragraph is aligned to the right of the window, because the class attribute on the tag is set to RightAligned.

If you don't see the last paragraph glued to the right border of the Document Window, make sure you typed `RightAligned` exactly the same in the `<style>` tag and in the `class` attribute. Since CSS is case sensitive, there's a difference between `RightAligned` and `rightaligned`.

If you want to display the page in your browser, press Ctrl+F5. VWD spins up the built-in web server, then opens your default browser and sends it to the CssDemo.aspx page. The page you see in the browser is identical to the preview you got in the Design View of Visual Web Developer.

How It Works

Although the code you typed in this exercise is relatively simple, there's a lot going on under the hood of the browser (and the Design View) to make this possible. You started by adding some styles to the `<head>` section of the page:

```
<style type="text/css">
  h1
  {
    font-size: 20px;
    color: Green;
  }

  ...
</style>
```

The `<style>` tag is used to wrap a *style sheet* that is embedded in the page with its `type` attribute set to `text/css`. The code block from `h1` until the closing curly brace (`}`) between the `<style>` tags is called a *rule set* or simply a *rule*. The rule in this code snippet defines the appearance for all `<h1>` elements in your page. The `h1` at the top of the code block is called a *selector* and is used to indicate to what element the formatting should be applied. In this case, the selector maps directly to an HTML element, but there are many other selectors available, which you'll see later in this section. Figure 3-2 shows how the elements are related to each other.

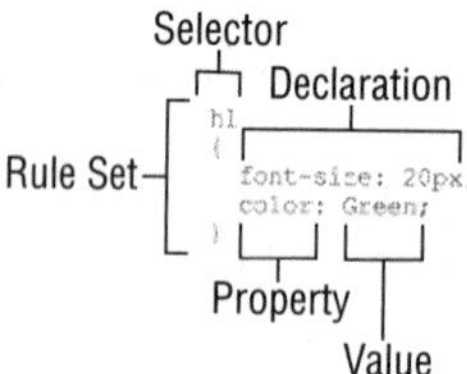

Figure 3-2

Between the curly braces you see the style information that should be applied to the heading. Each line between the curly braces is called a *declaration*. A declaration consists of a *property*, followed by a colon and then followed by a *value*. The semicolon (;) at the end of a declaration separates it from the next declaration and is required on all declarations except for the last one in the rule set. However, for consistency, it's a good idea to add it to all declarations, which is what I'll do in the remainder of this book.

When the browser loads this page, it also reads in the styles you defined between the `<style>` tags. Then, whenever it comes across an HTML element that matches the selector, it applies the CSS rules to that element. So, for the `<h1>` and `<p>` elements, their respective rules are applied. This causes the heading to turn green with a large font, while the paragraphs turn blue with an italic font.

But why does the last paragraph turn blue *and* get right-aligned? In CSS, you can have rules coming from different sources. The last `<p>` tag gets its style information from the standard `p` selector in the style definition. So, the `p` rule gives the paragraph a blue and italic font. However, it also has a *class* defined. This class, called `RightAligned` causes the text to be aligned to the right of the window. In the end, the last `<p>` element gets its rules from two selectors at the same time.

The next section digs a lot deeper in the syntax of CSS, giving you a much more detailed view on selectors, properties, and values.

CSS — The Language

As you saw in the previous Try It Out exercise, a cascading style sheet is actually a collection of rules. A rule is a combination of a selector and one or more declarations, which in turn can be broken down to a property and a value. You're probably getting a little dizzy from all the new terms that were introduced in the past few paragraphs, so in the next section, you'll see most of them again, with a detailed explanation and code examples that show you what they are used for and how they work.

The Style Sheet

The style sheet contains all the relevant style information that should be applied to page elements. In its simplest form, a style sheet looks like this:

```
h1
{
  color: Green;
}
```

A style sheet can also contain more than one rule as you saw in the previous exercise. At the same time, each rule can contain multiple declarations, allowing you to group them under a single selector, like this:

```
h1
{
  font-size: 20px;
  color: Green;
}
```

This code is functionally identical to this:

```
h1
{
  font-size: 20px;
}
h1
{
  color: Green;
}
```

The condensed form, where the two declarations are grouped under the same selector, is much easier to read and understand, so it's advisable to use this syntax as much as possible.

To be able to style an element on a page, a browser has to know three things:

- What element of the page must be styled?
- What part of that element must be styled?
- How do you want that part of the selected element to look?

The answers to these questions are given by selectors, properties, and values.

Selectors

As its name implies, a selector is used to select or point to a specific element within your page. A number of different selectors are available, giving you fine control over what element you want to style. The selector answers the first question: What element of the page must be styled? The next section shows you the four most important types of selectors.

The Universal Selector

The Universal selector, indicated by an asterisk (*) applies to all elements in your page. The Universal selector can be used to set global settings like a font family. The following rule set changes the font for all elements in your page to Arial:

```
*
{
  font-family: Arial;
}
```

The Type Selector

The Type selector allows you to point to a specific HTML element. With a Type selector, all HTML elements of that type will be styled accordingly.

```
h1
{
  color: Green;
}
```

This Type selector now applies to all `<h1>` tags in your code and gives them a green color. Type selectors are not case sensitive, so you can use both `h1` and `H1` to refer to the same heading.

The ID Selector

The ID selector is always prefixed by a hash symbol (#) and allows you to refer to a single element in the page. Within an HTML or ASPX page, you can give each element a unique ID using the `id` attribute. With the ID selector, you can change the behavior for that single element, like this:

```
#IntroText
{
  font-style: italic;
}
```

Since you can reuse this ID across multiple pages in your site (it only has to be unique within a single page), you can use this rule to quickly change the appearance of an element that you use more than once, for example with the following HTML code:

```
<p id="IntroText">I am italic because I have the right ID.</p>
<p id="BodyText">I am NOT italic because I have a different ID.</p>
```

In this example, the `#IntroText` selector changes the font of the first paragraph — which has the matching `id` attribute — but leaves the other paragraph unmodified.

The Class Selector

The Class selector enables you to style multiple HTML elements through the `class` attribute. This is handy when you want to give the same type of formatting to a number of unrelated HTML elements. The following rule changes the text to bold for all HTML elements that have their `class` attributes set to `Highlight`:

```
.Highlight
{
  font-weight: bold;
  color: Red;
}
```

The following code snippet uses the `Highlight` class to make the contents of a `<span>` element and a link (`<a>`) appear with a bold typeface:

```
This is normal text but <span class="Highlight">this is Red and Bold</span>
This is also normal text but
    <a href="CssDemo.aspx" class="Highlight">this link is Red and Bold as well</a>
```

Notice that the selector uses a period in its name, but you don't use this period when referring to the selector in the `class` attribute. The `class` attribute is very useful as it allows you to reuse a piece of CSS for many different purposes, regardless of the HTML element that uses the class.

CSS supports more types of selectors, giving you even more control over the elements you want to target, but the four different types you just saw are the most widely used.

Grouping and Combining Selectors

CSS also allows you to group multiple selectors, which is handy if you want to apply the same styles to different elements. The following rule turns all headings in the page to red:

```
h1, h2, h3, h4, h5, h6
{
  color: Red;
}
```

Moreover, with CSS you can also combine selectors, allowing you to hierarchically point to a specific element in a page. You can do this by separating the selectors with a space. The following example targets all `<p>` elements that fall within an element with an `id` of `MainContent`:

```
#MainContent p
{
```

```
    font-size: 18px;
  }
```

This rule affects only paragraphs that fall within the `MainContent` element, leaving all other paragraphs unmodified.

Note that combining is very different from grouping. Grouping is just a shortcut to avoid typing the same declarations over and over again, while combining allows you to target specific elements in your document.

With combining, you're not limited to ID and Type selectors; you can also use it with the other selectors, as is demonstrated with the following example:

```
#MainContent p.Highlight
{
  font-size: 18px;
  font-weight: bold;
}
```

This rule changes all paragraphs with the class `Highlight` within an element with its `id` set to `MainContent` and leaves all others untouched. The following HTML snippet uses this rule to show the effect:

```
<div id="MainContent">
  <p class="Highlight">Because I have a class called Highlight, my text appears in bold</p>
  <p>This text is not bold, as it lacks the Highlight class</p>
</div>
<p class="Highlight">I am NOT bold because I don't fall within MainContent</p>
```

The second question that needs to be answered to apply a certain style in your page is about what part of the element must be styled. This is done with properties.

Properties

Properties are the part of the element that you want to change with your style sheet. The CSS specification defines a long list of properties (VWD's IntelliSense list shows more than 100 items) although you won't use all of them in most web sites. The following table lists some of the most common CSS properties and describes where they are used.

Property	Description	Example
`background-color` `background-image`	Specifies the background color or image of an element.	`background-color: White;` `background-image: url(Image.jpg);`
`border`	Specifies the border of an element.	`border: 3px solid black;`
`color`	Changes the font color.	`color: Green;`

Property	Description	Example
`display`	Changes the way elements are displayed, allowing you to hide or show them.	`display: none;` This causes the element to be hidden, and not take up any screen space.
`float`	Allows you to "float" an element in the page using a left or right float. Other content is then placed on the opposite side.	`float: left;` This setting causes other content following a float to be placed on the top right corner of the element. You'll see how this works later in the chapter.

`font-family`
`font-size`
`font-style`
`font-weight`
	Changes the appearance of fonts used on your page.	`font-family: Arial;`
		`font-size: 18px;`
		`font-style: italic;`
		`font-weight: bold;`

`height` `width`	Sets the height or width of elements in your page.	`height: 100px;` `width: 200px;`
`margin` `padding`	Sets the amount of free space inside (padding) and outside (margin) of an element.	`padding: 0;` `margin: 20px;`
`visibility`	Controls whether an element is visible in the page or not. Invisible elements still take up screen space; you just don't see them.	`visibility: hidden;` This causes the element to be invisible. However, it still takes up its original space in the page. It's as if the element is still there, but completely transparent.

Fortunately, VWD helps you to find the right property with its many CSS tools, so you don't have to remember them all.

There are many more properties available in CSS than I have described here. For more detail on CSS, get yourself a copy of Beginning CSS: Cascading Style Sheets for Web Design, Second Edition *by Richard York (ISBN: 978-0-470-09697-0).*

For a property to be useful, you need to give it a value, which answers the third question: How do you want the part of the selected element to look?

Values

Just as with properties, values come in many flavors. The values you have available depend on the property. For example, the `color` attribute takes values that represent a color. This can be a named color (such as

White), or a hexadecimal number representing a red, green, and blue (RGB) component (such as #FF0000), or it can be set using the CSS RGB notation. The following examples are all functionally equivalent:

```
h1
{
  color: Red;
}

h1
{
  color: #FF0000;
}

h1
{
  color: rgb(100%, 0%, 0%);
}
```

The first declaration uses the named color Red, whereas the other two examples use an RGB value to specify the red color. Using named colors can increase the readability of your CSS code, but since you're limited to a relatively short list of named colors, you often need the hexadecimal notation to get the exact color you want.

There are many other values possible as well, including size units (px, em, and so on), font families, images (which take the form of url(SomeImage.jpg)), or so-called enumerations like the border-style, which allows you to set a border style to solid, dashed, double, and so on.

Using Shorthand

Many of the CSS properties allow you to write a shorthand version as well as a more expanded version. Take, for example, the border property. In its shortest form, the border property can be set like this:

```
border: 1px solid Black;
```

This border property applies a border to all four sides of an HTML element. The border size will be 1px, the style will be solid (some of the other options include dashed, dotted, and double), and the border color will be set to Black.

This is an easy way to quickly set all four borders of the HTML to the same values. However, if you want more control over the individual borders and their properties, you can use the expanded version, like this:

```
border-top-width: 1px;
border-top-style: solid;
border-top-color: Black;
border-right-width: 1px;
border-right-style: solid;
border-right-color: Black;
border-bottom-width: 1px;
border-bottom-style: solid;
border-bottom-color: Black;
border-left-width: 1px;
border-left-style: solid;
border-left-color: Black;
```

This long version causes the exact same style to be applied: a solid black border on all four sides with a thickness of 1 pixel. In most cases, you should favor shorthand notation over its expanded counterpart, as it's much easier to read and maintain. However, if you need absolute control over the border — for example, if you want a 2-pixel dashed border on the left and top sides, and a green, solid border on the right and bottom sides of the HTML element — it's good to know that you can set each `border` property of all four directions individually.

Other CSS properties that support shorthand include `font`, `background`, `list-style`, `margin`, and `padding`. If you're unsure whether a property supports shorthand, consult the IntelliSense pop-up list that appears by pressing Ctrl+Space when you're entering a value in a CSS file or `<style>` block in VWD.

In the next exercise, you'll modify the site's home page that you created in the previous chapter. You'll add the basic layout for the site which is then styled using a style sheet. In Chapter 6 you'll use this page again when you upgrade it to a master page.

Try It Out — Styling the Planet Wrox Homepage

In this exercise you'll modify two files: First, you'll add the basic layout elements to the Default.aspx page to create room for a header, a menu, the main content area, a sidebar, and a footer. Then you'll modify the Styles.css file from the Styles folder to change the size and location of these elements. Finally, you'll attach the style sheet to the page, so the style information is applied when the page is viewed in the designer or in a browser.

1. Open in Markup View the file Default.aspx from the root of your web site.
2. Right *before* the welcome text you created in the previous chapter, add the following highlighted HTML. Make sure you replace the existing HTML in the `<form>` element:

```
<form id="form1" runat="server">
  <div id="PageWrapper">
    <div id="Header">Header Goes Here</div>
    <div id="MenuWrapper">Menu Goes Here</div>
    <div id="MainContent">
    </div>
    <div id="Sidebar">Sidebar Goes Here</div>
    <div id="Footer">Footer Goes Here</div>
  </div>
  <h1>Hi there visitor and welcome to Planet Wrox</h1>
  ...
</form>
```

   This code uses `<div>` elements to identify important regions of the page, like the header, the menu, and the main content area.

3. Select the heading and the paragraphs (represented by the ellipsis (...) in the code snippet from step 2) you added to this page earlier, cut them to the clipboard, and then paste them between the opening and closing tags of the `MainContent` `<div>`. This moves your existing code into the main content block. You should end up with something like this:

```
<form id="form1" runat="server">
  <div id="PageWrapper">
```

```
      <div id="Header">Header Goes Here</div>
      <div id="MenuWrapper">Menu Goes Here</div>
      <div id="MainContent">
        <h1>Hi there visitor and welcome to Planet Wrox</h1>
        ...
      </div>
      <div id="Sidebar">Sidebar Goes Here</div>
      <div id="Footer">Footer Goes Here</div>
    </div>
  </form>
```

Make sure that the code in the page looks like the code from step 2. It's important that the various `<div>` elements and their IDs end up right, while the actual welcome text is less of a concern.

4. Open the file Styles.css from the Styles folder. If you added some code to this file during an earlier Try It Out, remove that code first.

5. At the top of the page, type the following code that uses an ID selector to select the `Header <div>`:

```
#Header
{

}
```

6. Position your mouse between the curly braces and then choose Styles ➪ Build Style from the main menu. Alternatively, you can choose the same item by right-clicking the ID selector, or clicking the Build Style button on the Styles toolbar. The Modify Style dialog box shown in Figure 3-3 appears.

7. In the Category list on the left, click Background and then open the drop-down list for the background color. From the color picker that appears, click the Silver color, as shown in Figure 3-4.

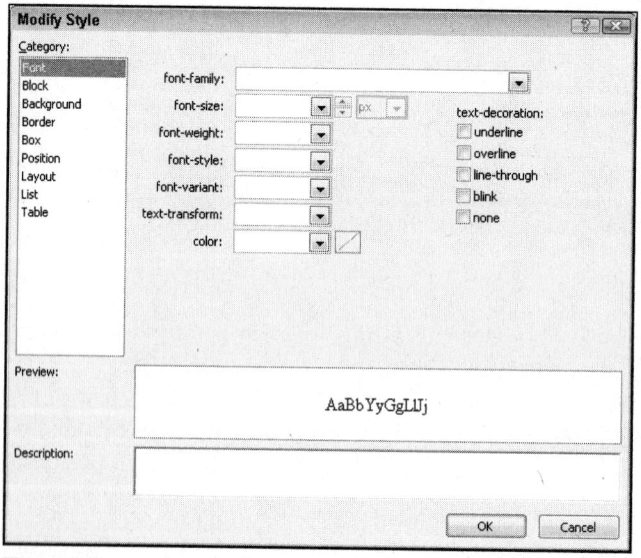

Figure 3-3

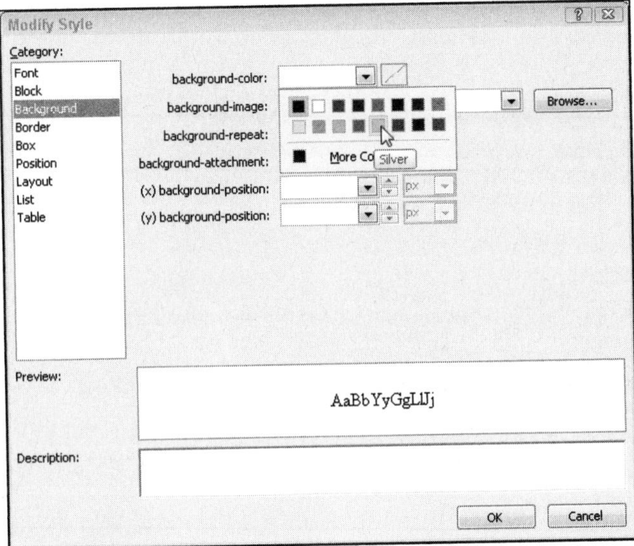

Figure 3-4

Alternatively, you can type the hexadecimal color code for Silver (`#C0C0C0`) in the background-color text box directly.

8. Switch to the Position category by clicking it in the list on the left. The panel that appears allows you to set position-related information, including the height and width. Under width, enter 844 and make sure that px is selected in the drop-down list at the right. For the height, enter 83. Click OK to dismiss the dialog box and to insert the declarations into your code, which now looks like this:

```
#Header
{
  background-color: #C0C0C0;
  width: 844px;
  height: 83px;
}
```

9. Repeat steps 5 through 8, this time creating the following rules:

```
*
{
  font-family: Arial;
}

h1
{
  font-size: 20px;
}

#PageWrapper
{
```

```
    width: 844px;
  }

  #MenuWrapper
  {
    width: 844px;
  }

  #MainContent
  {
    width: 644px;
    float: left;
  }

  #Sidebar
  {
    background-color: Gray;
    width: 200px;
    float: left;
  }

  #Footer
  {
    background-color: #C0C0C0;
    width: 844px;
    clear: both;
  }
```

You find the `float` and `clear` properties in the layout category of the Modify Style dialog box.

10. When you're done creating the rules, save and close the file Styles.css, as you're done with it for now.

11. Open the file Default.aspx again and switch to Design View. From the Solution Explorer, drag the file Styles.css from the Styles folder onto the page. VWD inserts code in the `head` section of the page in Markup View that attaches the style sheet to the document:

```
<head runat="server">
  <title>Untitled Page</title>
  <style type="text/css">
    .style1
    {
      color: #FF0000;
    }
  </style>
  <link href="Styles/Styles.css" rel="stylesheet" type="text/css" />
</head>
```

You can also drag an existing style sheet from the Solution Explorer directly in the `<head>` section of a page in Markup View. When you do that, VWD adds the same `<link>` element.

12. Finally, save the changes to all open documents (press Ctrl+Shift+S) and then request Default.aspx in your browser. Your screen should look similar to Figure 3-5, which shows the page in Mozilla Firefox.

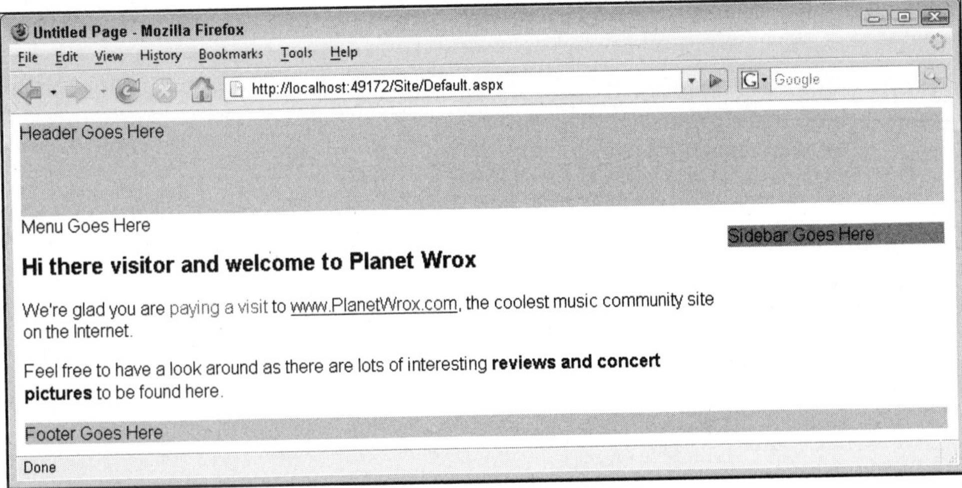

Figure 3-5

How It Works

The Style Builder makes it easy to select CSS properties and change their values. You don't need to memorize every little detail about CSS, but instead you can visually create your CSS code. Although the tool can do most of the work for you, it's still useful if you can read and understand the CSS code. Sometimes, when you need to make minor tweaks to your code, it's quicker to do it directly in the Document Window, instead of opening the Style Builder.

Note that the `Header`, `PageWrapper`, `MenuWrapper`, and `Footer` have an exact width of 844 pixels. This way, the site fits nicely on screens with a size of 1024 × 768 pixels, a common screen size for many of today's computers, without being squeezed between the Windows borders. Systems with bigger screens will simply expand the white background at the right of the page.

Note also that the `MainContent` area and the `Sidebar` are positioned next to each other. This is done with the CSS `float` property:

```
#MainContent
{
  width: 644px;
  float: left;
}

#Sidebar
{
  background-color: Gray;
  width: 200px;
  float: left;
}
```

This tells the `MainContent` to "float" on the left side of the `Sidebar`, effectively placing the `Sidebar` to the right of it. The combined width of the two elements adds up to 844 pixels, which is exactly the width of their parent element: the `PageWrapper`.

To end the float and tell the `Footer` element to be placed directly under the `MainContent` and `Sidebar` elements, the `clear` property is used to clear any float (left or right) that may be in effect:

```
#Footer
{
  background-color: #C0C0C0;
  width: 844px;
  clear: both;
}
```

The gray backgrounds are just temporarily added to the code, so it's easier to see what `<div>` ends up where. In future exercises, you'll modify the CSS file again to fit the scheme of the Planet Wrox web site.

To tell the browser what styles to apply, you link the style sheet in the head of the page:

```
<link href="Styles/Styles.css" rel="stylesheet" type="text/css" />
```

This tells the browser to look in the folder Styles for a file called Styles.css and apply all rules in that file to the current document. Once the browser has downloaded the CSS file, it applies all the styles it finds in there to your HTML elements, resulting in the layout shown in Figure 3-5.

In this exercise, you saw how to link a style sheet to a page using the `<link>` tag. There are, however, multiple ways to include style sheets in your web pages.

Adding CSS to Your Pages

The most useful way to add CSS styles to your web pages is through the `<link>` tag that points to an *external* CSS file, as you saw in the previous exercise. Take a look at the following `<link>` to see what options you have when embedding a style sheet in your page:

```
<link href="StyleSheet.css" rel="Stylesheet" type="text/css" media="screen" />
```

The `href` property points to a file within your site, just as you saw in the previous chapter when you created links between two pages. The `rel` and `type` attributes tell the browser that the linked file is in fact a cascading style sheet. The `media` attribute is quite interesting: it allows you to target different devices, including the screen, printer, handheld devices, and even Braille and aural support tools for visually impaired visitors. The default for the `media` attribute is `screen`, so it's OK to omit the attribute if you're targeting standard desktop browsers.

You briefly saw another way to include style sheets at the beginning of this chapter: using *embedded* `<style>` elements. The `<style>` tag should be placed at the top of your ASPX or HTML page, between the `<head>` tags. Within the `<style>` tags, you can write the exact same CSS you saw earlier. For example, to change the appearance of a `<h1>` element in the current page alone, you can add the following code to the `<head>` of your page:

```
<head runat="server">
  <title>Untitled Page</title>
```

```
  <style type="text/css">
    h1
    {
      color: Blue;
    }
  </style>
</head>
```

The final way to apply CSS to your HTML elements is to use *inline styles* with the style attribute that you saw in the previous chapter. Since the `style` attribute is already applied to a specific HTML element, you don't need a selector and you can write the declaration in the attribute directly:

```
<span style="background-color: Black; color: White;">
    This is white text on a black background
</span>
```

Choosing among External, Embedded, and Inline Style Sheets

Since you have so many options to add style sheets to your site, what's the best method to use? In general, you should preference external style sheets over embedded styles, which in turn are preferred over inline styles. External style sheets allow you to change the appearance of the entire site through a single file. Make one change to your external style sheet file, and all pages that use this style pick up the change automatically, instead of going through each page in your site and manually making the changes to embedded or inline style sheets.

However, it's perfectly acceptable to use embedded and inline styles as well in certain circumstances. If you want to change the look of a single page, without affecting other pages in your site, an embedded style sheet is your best choice. The same applies to inline styles: if you only want to change the behavior of a single element in a single page, and you're pretty sure you're not going to need the same declaration for other HTML elements, use an inline style.

An important thing to consider is the way that the various types of style sheets override each other. If you have multiple identical selectors with different property values, the one defined last takes precedence. For example, consider a rule defined in an external style sheet called Styles.css that sets the color of all `<h1>` tags to green:

```
h1
{
  color: Green;
}
```

Now imagine you're attaching this style sheet in a page that also has an embedded rule for the same `h1` but that sets a different color:

```
<link href="Styles/Styles.css" rel="stylesheet" type="text/css" />
<style type="text/css">
h1
{
  color: Blue;
}
</style>
```

With this code, the color of the actual `<h1>` tag in the page will be blue. This is because the embedded style sheet that sets the color to blue is defined later in the page and thus overrides the setting in the external file. This demonstrates the cascading part of *cascading style sheets*, where one style cascades down to the other. If you turn the styles around like this:

```
<style type="text/css">
h1
{
  color: Blue;
}
</style>
<link href="Styles/Styles.css" rel="stylesheet" type="text/css" />
```

The heading will be green, as the setting in the external style sheet now overrules that of the embedded style.

The same principle applies to inline style sheets. Since they're defined directly on the HTML elements, their settings take precedence over embedded and external style sheets.

> *There's a lot more to CSS than what is shown here. To learn more about CSS, pick up a copy of* Professional ASP.NET 2.0 Design: CSS, Themes, and Master Pages *by Jacob J. Sanford (ISBN: 978-0-470-12448-2) or a copy of* Beginning CSS: Cascading Style Sheets for Web Design, Second Edition *by Richard York (ISBN: 978-0-470-09697-0).*

In general, it's recommended that you attach external files at the top of the `<head>` section, followed by embedded style sheets. That way, the external file defines the global look of elements, and you can use embedded styles to overrule the external settings.

VWD makes it easy to move embedded style sheets to an external CSS file, something you'll learn how to do in the next section, which discusses the remainder of the CSS tools in VWD.

Working with CSS in Visual Web Developer

VWD has a number of handy tools on board for working with CSS. Most of them are new in the 2008 release of VWD, as good CSS support was one of the design goals of this latest release. The following tools are at your disposal:

- The **Style Sheet toolbar**, giving you quick access to creating new rules and styles.
- The **CSS Properties Grid**, which enables you to change property values.
- The **Manage Styles window**, enabling you to organize styles in your site, changing them from embedded to external style sheets and vice versa, reorder them, link existing style sheets to a document, and create new inline, embedded, or external style sheets.
- The **Apply Styles window**, which you can use to choose from all available styles in your site and quickly apply them to different elements in your page.
- The **Style Builder**, which you can use to visually create declarations.
- The **Add Style Rule window**, which helps in building more complex selectors.

Although you've already seen some of these tools in this chapter, the next sections give you a detailed look at the functionality they offer. You'll see how to carry out tasks, like creating new styles, modifying existing ones, and applying styles to existing elements. During the explanation, you get a good look at the tools mentioned here.

Creating New Styles in External Style Sheets

In an earlier Try It Out, you manually added selectors to the CSS file and then used the Style Builder to write the rules. However, you can also use the VWD tools to write the selectors for you. In the next Try It Out, you'll see how to use the Add Style Rule window to create a new rule in an external file. You'll then use the Style Builder to modify the rule.

Try It Out — Creating New Styles in an Existing Style Sheet

In this exercise, you'll create a new style that affects all the links in the `MainContent` area. By using combined selectors, you can target the links in the content area only, leaving the others unmodified.

1. Start by opening the file Styles.css from the Styles folder.
2. Scroll down in the file and position your cursor at the end, right below the `#Footer` rule.
3. Make sure the Style Sheet toolbar is visible and then click the first button, labeled Add Style Rule, or choose Styles ➪ Add Style Rule from the main menu. The dialog box shown in Figure 3-6 appears.

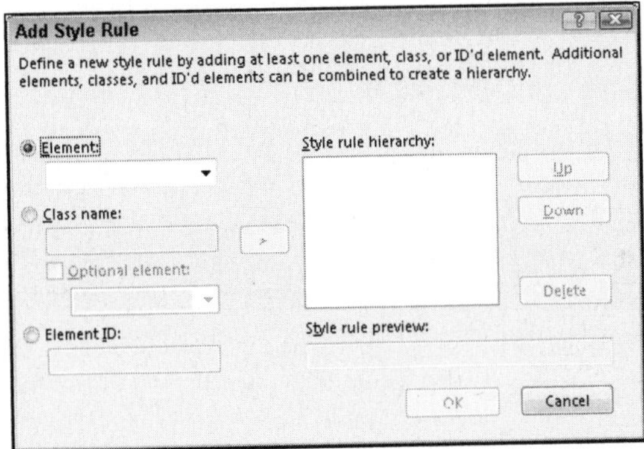

Figure 3-6

With this dialog box you can visually create a combined selector. In the left section of the dialog box, you can enter Type, Class, and ID selectors.

Select the last option, labeled Element ID, and then in its text box type `MainContent`. Click the button with the right arrow in the middle of the screen to add the selector to the Style rule hierarchy.

4. Next, select the Element radio button at the top of the dialog box and then from its drop-down list, choose `a` (for links) and click the arrow button once more. Your screen should now show a preview of the selector in the Style rule preview box, as in Figure 3-7.

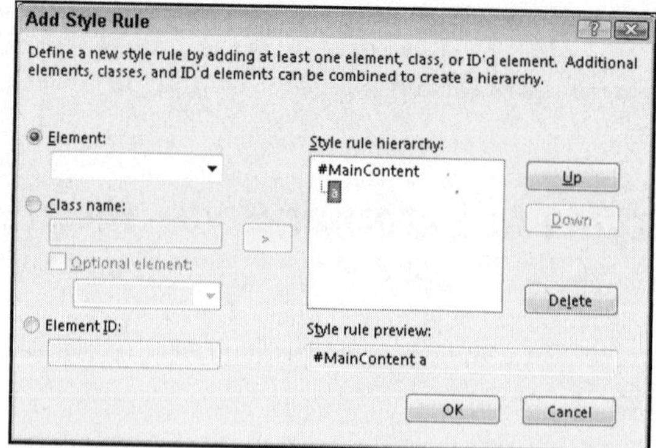

Figure 3-7

If you don't see the hash symbol (#) in front of `MainContent` in the Style rule hierarchy box, make sure you selected Element ID and not Element in step 3 of this exercise.

5. Click OK to add the selector to your style sheet file. You should end up with the following empty rule:

```
#MainContent a
{

}
```

6. Right-click between the curly braces of the rule you just inserted and choose Build Style.
7. In the Font Category, change the color property to `#008000` by clicking the arrow of the drop-down list box, and then clicking the green square on the top row.
8. In the text-decoration section at the right of the dialog box, place a check mark for the underline option. The Style dialog box should now look like the one shown in Figure 3-8.

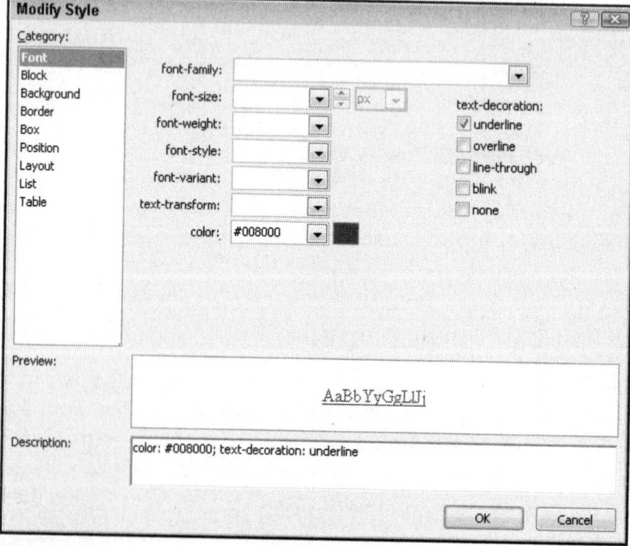

Figure 3-8

9. Click OK to dismiss the dialog box. Back in the CSS file, select the entire rule set you just created (including `#MainContent a` and both curly braces), copy it to the clipboard, and then paste it again *twice* below the original rule set.

10. Rename the first selector you just pasted from `#MainContent a` to `#MainContent a:visited`. This style is used for links that the user has already visited.

11. Right-click the new rule you just created and choose Build Style. In the Font category, change the color from green to red by typing `#FF0000` in the color text box, and then click OK.

12. Change the third selector in the file from `#MainContent a` to `#MainContent a:hover`. This style is applied to links when the user hovers over them with the mouse.

13. Once again, right-click the new style you just created and choose Build Style. In the Font category, change the color from green to orange by typing `#FFA500` in the color text box. Click OK to close the Modify Style dialog box.

    You should end up with the following three rules in your CSS file below the styles that were already present:

```
#MainContent a
{
  color: #008000;
  text-decoration: underline;
}

#MainContent a:visited
{
  color: #FF0000;
  text-decoration: underline;
}

#MainContent a:hover
{
  color: #FFA500;
  text-decoration: underline;
}
```

14. Save and close the Styles.css file as you're done with it for now.

How It Works

You started off by creating a new rule using the Add Style Rule dialog box. Quite often, you'll find it easier and quicker to type the rule directly in the code editor. However, when you're creating complex grouped rules, the Add Style Rule dialog box can help you understand and create the hierarchy of the rule.

The Modify Style dialog box is an excellent tool for creating new CSS declarations. Instead of memorizing all the different CSS properties and values, you can simply point and click them together in an organized dialog box. All the different CSS properties are grouped under logical categories, making it easy to find and change them.

The `:hover` and `:visited` parts on the `a` selector are probably new to you. These selectors are called *pseudo class selectors*. The `a:visited` selector is only applied for links that you have already visited in your browser. The `a:hover` selector is only applied to the <a> tag when the user hovers the mouse over the link. In the next Try It Out you'll see the effect of these two selectors in the browser.

With the style sheet created, the next thing you need to do is attach this style sheet to your document. There are a number of ways to do this, including typing in the code by hand or dropping the file in Markup or in Design View. The next Try It Out exercise shows you a third option: using the Manage Styles dialog box.

Try It Out — Attaching Your New Style Sheet to Your Document

In this exercise, you'll remove and reattach the style sheet called Styles.css to your Default.aspx page so you'll see another alternative to attaching a style sheet file to an ASPX page. You'll then add some text and links to this page so you can see the behavior of rule sets you created earlier.

1. Switch the page Default.aspx into Markup View and remove the `<link />` element from the `<head>` section that you added earlier in this chapter. Then switch to Design View and make sure the Manage Styles window is open. If it isn't, click somewhere in the Document Window to activate the Design View and then choose View ➪ Manage Styles from the main menu. The window shown in Figure 3-9 appears.

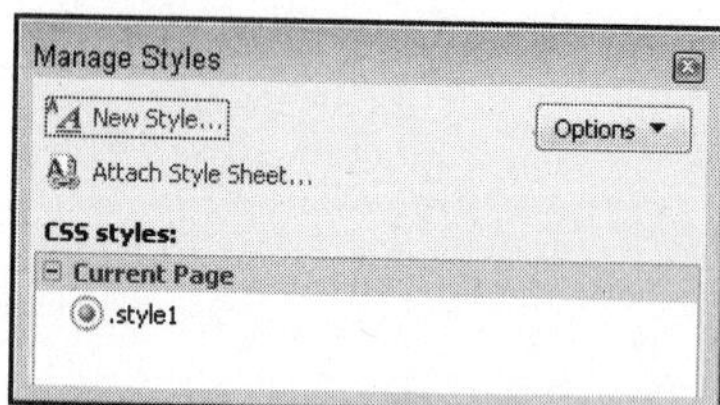

Figure 3-9

The Manage Styles window gives you an overview of all external and embedded style sheets that apply to the current document. Notice how VWD sees that the current document already contains an embedded style: `style1` that you created in the previous chapter.

2. Click the Attach Style Sheet link in the Manage Styles window, browse to your Styles folder in the root of the site, and select the Styles.css file. Click OK and the style sheet is inserted in your page again:

```
  </style>
  <link href="Styles/Styles.css" rel="stylesheet" type="text/css" />
</head>
```

3. When you attach the style sheet, the Manage Styles window (shown in Figure 3-10) is updated and now shows your newly attached style sheet.

4. With the page Default.aspx still open in Design View, select the text "look around" in the paragraph. If you typed something else in the earlier Try It Out, select that text instead. At this stage, all that's important is that you have some text to turn into a link.

5. On the Formatting toolbar, click the Convert to Hyperlink button (with the globe and link symbol on it), click the Browse button in the dialog box that appears, and select Default.aspx in the root of the site. This way, the link points to the same page it's defined in, which is fine for this exercise. Click OK twice to dismiss the dialog boxes.

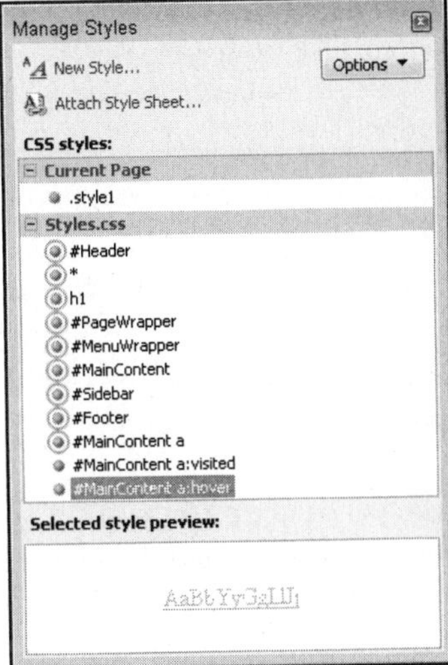

Figure 3-10

6. Save the changes to all open documents (choose File ➪ Save All from the main menu or press Ctrl+Shift+S) and then request Default.aspx in your browser by pressing Ctrl+F5. You should see the page appear with the "look around" link underlined, as shown in Figure 3-11.

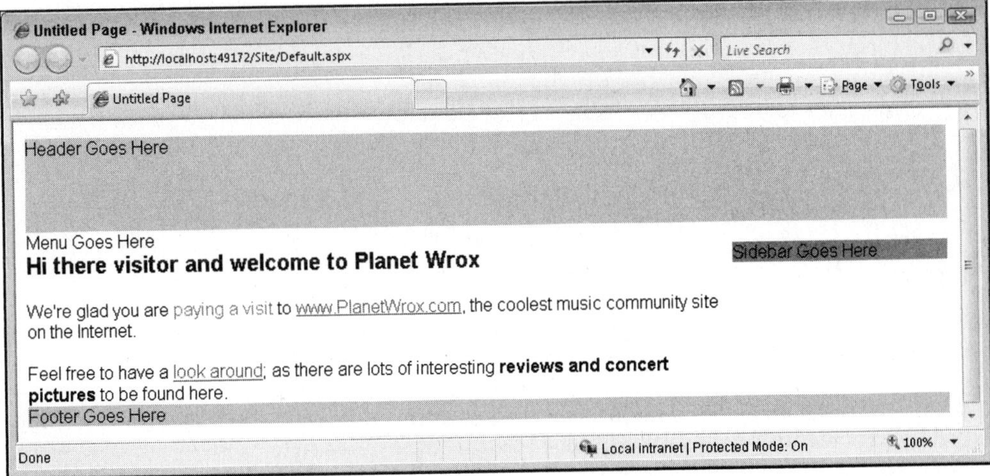

Figure 3-11

7. Hover your mouse over the "look around" link; note that it turns to orange.

8. Click the "look around" link, and the page will reload. The link has now turned to red. If the link was already red the first time you visited it, don't worry. You probably opened the page in your browser before, which caused the browser to mark the link as visited. The browser keeps track

of the pages you visit and then applies the correct style to new and visited links. If you want to see the desired behavior in Internet Explorer, open up the Internet Options by choosing Tools ➪ Internet Options. Then on the General tab, click the Delete button. In the dialog box that pops up, click the Delete History button. This clears your entire browsing history, so when you reload the page now by pressing Ctrl+F5 in your browser, the link should turn to green. Other browsers have similar options to clear the browser's history. For example, Firefox allows you to clear the history using the Tools ➪ Clear Private Data menu option. If you don't have this menu item, choose Tools ➪ Options and then switch to the Privacy tab, where you can delete the history as well.

Alternatively, you can open the page in a different browser. To select an alternate browser, right-click the page in VWD and choose Browse With from the context menu. If your alternate browser is listed there already, select it from the list and then click Browse. Optionally you can make this browser your default, by clicking the Set as Default button.

If your browser is not listed, click the Add button and then the ellipses next to the Program name box to search for your favorite browser. When the browser is displayed in the list, click it to select it and then click Browse to open the page in that browser.

The page should now appear in your alternate browser.

How It Works

The Manage Styles window gives you a quick overview of style sheets that are active for the current page, either as an external and attached style sheet, or as an embedded style sheet in the `<head>` section of the page. It's a very useful window to attach new styles to the current document, and to move styles from one location to another, which you'll see how to do in the next section. When you opened the page in the browser, the updated style sheet is downloaded and the browser then applies the `#MainContent a:visited` selector to all links to pages you visited before. When you hover your mouse over a link, the selector `#MainContent a:hover` is applied, causing the link to turn orange.

Useful as external style sheets may be, there are times where you really want to use embedded or inline styles instead. Creating and managing those styles, explained in the next section, is just as easy.

Creating Embedded and Inline Style Sheets

When you're working with a page in Design View, you often need to make minor tweaks to part of the page, like styling a piece of text, aligning an image, or applying a border to an element. At this stage, you need to make a decision about whether to create an inline, an embedded, or an external style sheet. As you saw earlier, you should opt for external or embedded style sheets if you envision you're going to reuse a style later. VWD doesn't care much, though. It allows you to create styles at all three levels. Even better, it allows you to easily upgrade an embedded style to an external one, or copy inline style information to a different location, giving you great flexibility and the option to change your mind later.

In the next exercise, you'll see how to create inline and embedded style sheets. You'll see later how to move those styles to an external style sheet, enabling other pages to reuse the same styles.

Try It Out Creating Embedded and Inline Styles in a Page

In this Try It Out, you'll add a style rule to the <h1> element of the page, to remove the default margin that a browser draws around the heading. In addition, you'll style the first paragraph using a class, giving it a different look to make it stand out from the other paragraphs on the page.

1. Go back to VWD and make sure that the page Default.aspx is open in Design View.
2. Click once on the `h1` element to select it and then choose Format ➪ New Style. The New Style dialog box appears (visible in Figure 3-12), which is pretty similar to the Modify Style dialog box you saw earlier.

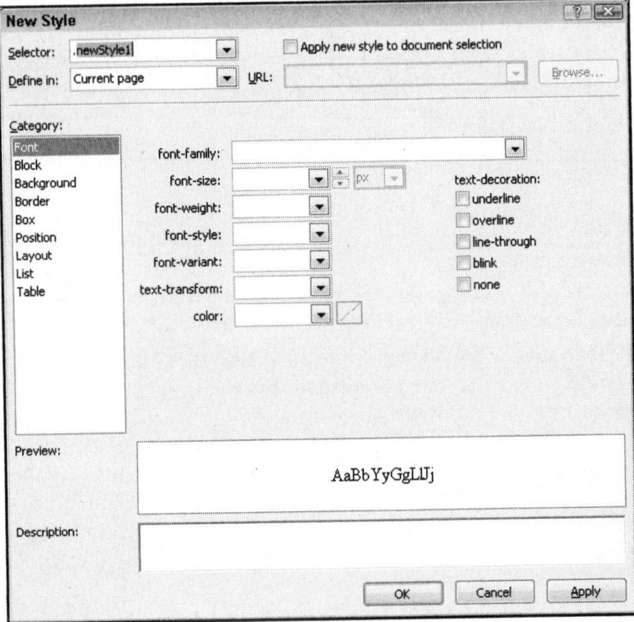

Figure 3-12

3. At the top of the screen, open the Selector drop-down list and choose (inline style). It's the first item in the list. This ensures that the new style is applied as an inline style to the <h1> element.
4. Switch to the Box category, shown in Figure 3-13.

   This dialog box has a handy diagram that shows you where CSS properties like `padding`, `border`, and `margin` end up. In the middle you see a blue rectangle that represents your element like <h1> or <body>. Around it, you see another rectangle that represents the padding. Around that, the border is applied. Finally, at the outer sides of the diagram you see margin that is applied *outside* the border of an element.

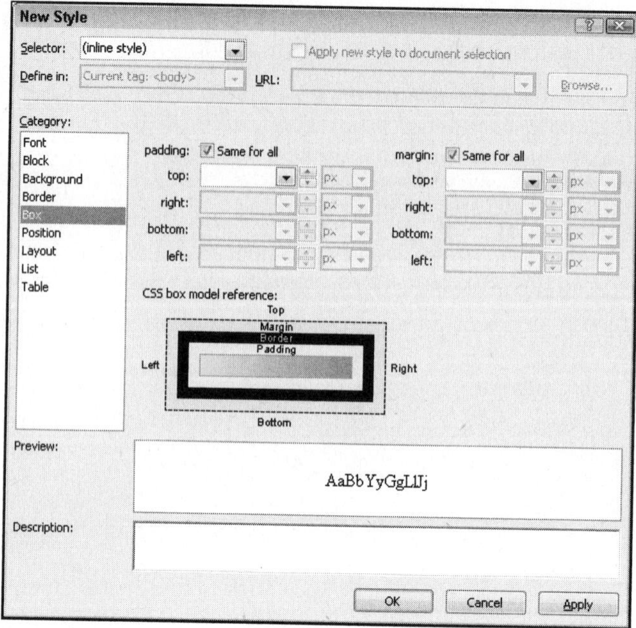

Figure 3-13

By default, browsers draw some white space above or below an `<h1>` element. To give each browser the same settings, you can reset the padding to 0 and then apply a little bit of margin at the bottom of the heading, which creates some distance to the elements following it. To do this, set padding to 0 in the top box. By leaving the Same for all option selected, VWD creates a shorthand declaration for you. Then uncheck Same for all for the margin section, enter 0 for the top, right, and left boxes and enter 10 for the bottom text box. Leave all drop-down lists set to px and click OK. You end up with the following `<h1>` element with an inline style in Markup View:

```
<h1 style="padding: 0px; margin: 0px 0px 10px 0px">
  Hi there visitor and welcome to Planet Wrox
</h1>
```

5. Next, in Design View, click the first paragraph by clicking on it. A small glyph appears to indicate you selected a `<p>` element, as visible in Figure 3-14. Also make sure the Tag Selector at the bottom of the Document Window highlights the `<p>` element, and not something else.

   If you don't see the glyph, you need to select Block Selection from the View ➪ Visual Aids menu in VWD.

6. With the paragraph still selected, choose Format ➪ New Style. This time, instead of creating an inline style, type the text `.Introduction` in the Selector box that is visible in Figure 3-15. Don't forget the dot (.) in front of the selector's name.

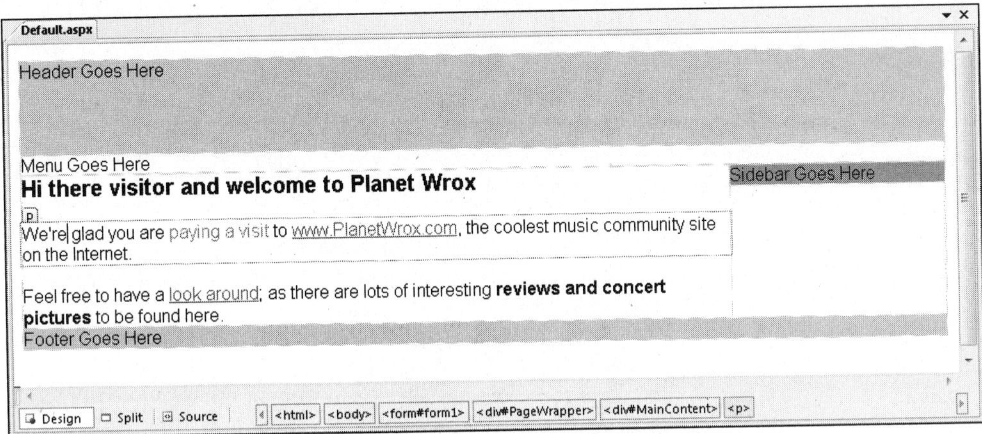

Figure 3-14

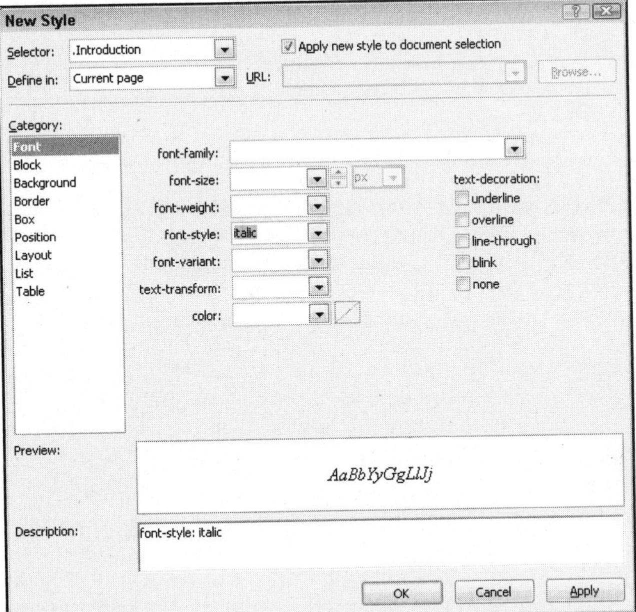

Figure 3-15

7. At the top of the screen, select the check box for Apply new style to document selection. With this setting on, the new class you're about to create is applied to the <p> tag.

8. From the font-style drop-down list, choose italic. Your New Style dialog box should now look like Figure 3-15.

9. Finally, click OK. Note that the entire paragraph is now displayed with an italic font.

10. With the <p> tag still selected, open the CSS Properties dialog box (see Figure 3-16) by choosing View ➪ CSS Properties. This dialog box gives you an overview of all the CSS properties and shows which ones are currently active for your page.

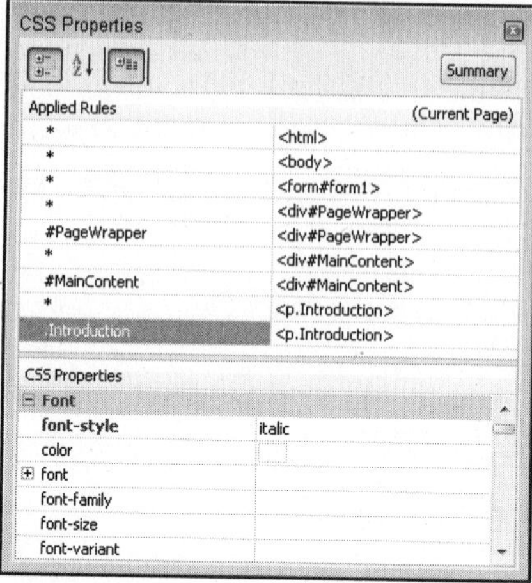

Figure 3-16

This dialog box shows a list of applied rules in the top half of the dialog box. The bottom half of the dialog box is used to show the CSS properties for those rules. In Figure 3-16 you see the rules that are applicable to the `.Introduction` selector. Properties that appear in blue and bold have their value set while others appear in a normal font. If you don't see these styles, click the third button on the toolbar of the CSS Properties dialog box, which moves the properties that are set up in the list.

11. In the CSS Properties list in the bottom half, locate the Color property and set it to a dark blue color, like `#003399`. To achieve this, open the drop-down list for the property value and choose a color from the color picker. If the color you're looking for is not available, click the More Colors button to bring up the extended color picker, shown in Figure 3-17.

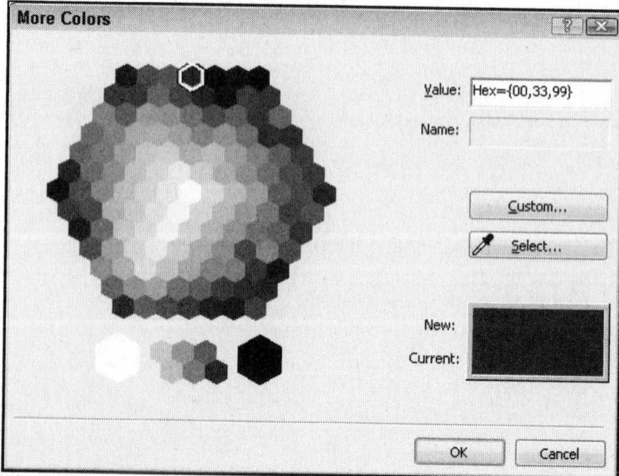

Figure 3-17

Instead of using the color picker, you can also type in a value in the Properties Grid directly. This is how all properties work in the CSS Properties Grid: They let you enter values directly or allow you to visually change the value using an arrow or a button with ellipses at the end of the property's value box. Figure 3-18 shows the different options you have for the font-style property in a convenient drop-down list.

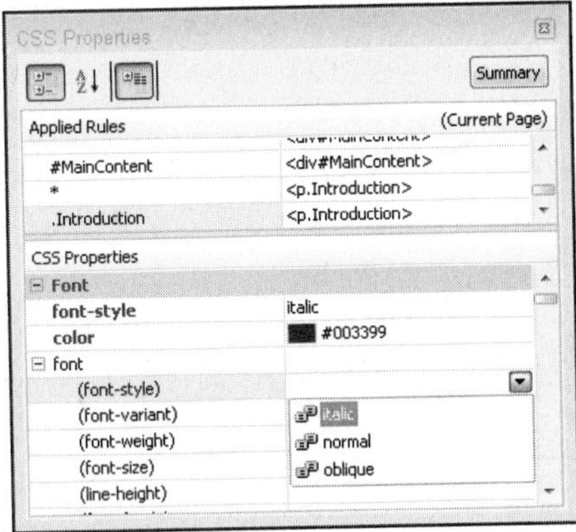

Figure 3-18

Take special note of the three buttons at the top of the window, as they house some useful functionality. The first two buttons allow you to switch between categorized mode and alphabetical mode, making it easier to find the right property. The third button enables you to display the selected properties at the top of the list (as is the case in Figure 3-18) or at their default location in the list.

12. Finally, save all changes and open Default.aspx in your browser (see Figure 3-19). You'll see that the first paragraph is now displayed with a blue and italic font except for the link in the text, which should be green. Additionally, if you followed all the instructions from the previous chapter, the text "paying a visit" is red, set by the embedded CSS class.

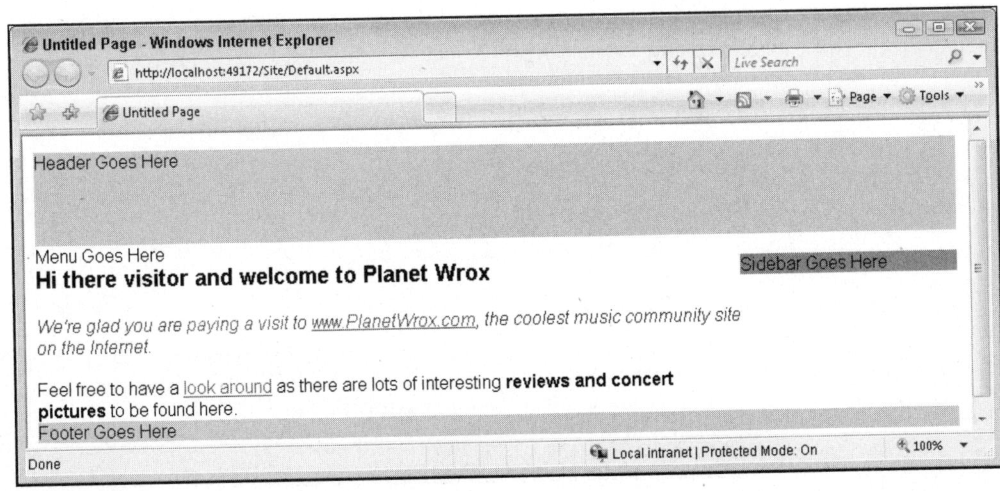

Figure 3-19

13. Switch back to VWD and look at your page in Markup View. In the <head> section of the page, you should see the following embedded style sheet:

```
    .Introduction
    {
      font-style: italic;
      color: #003399;
    }
  </style>
  <link href="Styles/Styles.css" rel="stylesheet" type="text/css" />
</head>
```

How It Works

The numerous tools that VWD offers make it easy to write CSS for your web site. You don't need to hand code anything, or remember all the different properties that the CSS standard supports. Instead, you can simply choose them from different lists on the CSS Properties Grid. This grid allows you to enter values manually but also offers handy tools to select colors, files, and items from drop-down lists.

All changes you make in the Properties Grid are applied to the relevant style sheet, whether you're working with an inline, embedded, or external style sheet. At the same time, the Design View is updated to reflect the new CSS options you have set.

When you look at the <h1> element, you can see that VWD created an inline style with a padding set to `0px` to affect all four sides at once and a margin set to `0px 0px 10px 0px` to control all four sides individually.

Once you have created a bunch of useful and reusable styles, you need a way to apply your existing styles to other pages or HTML elements. You'll see how this works next.

Applying Styles

If you have some experience with Microsoft Word, you may be used to the Styles dialog box, which lists all available styles and allows you to apply them to selected portions of text. This way, you can quickly apply identical formatting to blocks of text. This works similarly in VWD. With the Apply Styles panel — accessible by choosing View ➪ Apply Styles from the main menu — you can easily apply style rules to elements in the page.

Try It Out Applying Styles

In this exercise, you'll reuse the `.Introduction` class and apply it to the second paragraph of the page as well. That way, both paragraphs end up looking the same.

1. Still in Default.aspx, make sure you're in Design View and then select the second paragraph of the page by clicking it. Ensure that the Tag Selector at the bottom of the Document Window shows that the <p> tag is selected, and not another tag like <b> that may be part of the <p> element. If you have only one paragraph of text, create a new one first (by pressing Enter after the first paragraph in Design View), enter some text and then select that paragraph.

2. Open the Apply Styles dialog box by choosing View ➪ Apply Styles. This window shows all the selectors it finds in the current page and any attached style sheet. If you don't see all the styles shown in Figure 3-20, click the Options button and choose Show All Styles.

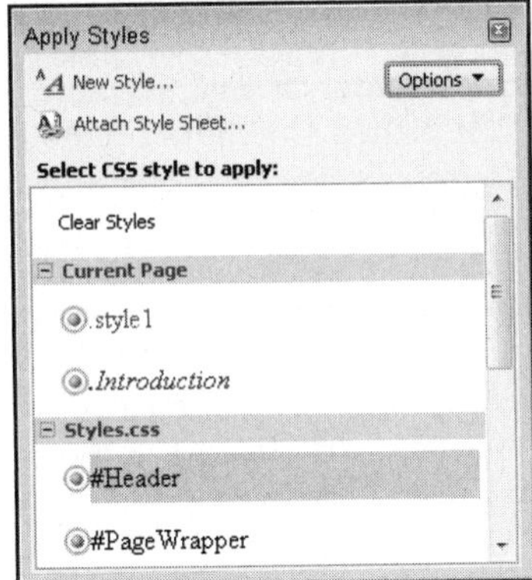

Figure 3-20

To help you find the right style, VWD uses a number of different visual cues. First of all, the Apply Styles dialog box uses red, green, and yellow dots to represent ID selectors, class selectors, and inline styles respectively. Figure 3-20 only shows red and green dots (you'll just have to trust me) because the `<p>` element doesn't have any inline styles applied. However, if you select the `<h1>` element, an inline style appears. If you do try this out, make sure you select the `<p>` element again afterward. Furthermore, styles that are currently used in the page are surrounded by an additional circle, as is the case with all selectors in Figure 3-20.

3. Click the `Introduction` class in the dialog box, and VWD adds a `class` attribute to the `<p>` tag:

```
<p class="Introduction">
  Feel free to have a <a href="Default.aspx">look around</a>; as there are lots of
  interesting <b>reviews and concert pictures</b> to be found here.
</p>
```

If you want to apply multiple classes, hold down the Ctrl key while clicking one of the other classes in the list. This applies a list of classes separated by a space to the element's `class` attribute. You can follow the same steps to apply the selected style in Markup View as well.

4. Using the Clear Styles button, you can quickly remove existing classes and inline styles from a tag. Consider the HTML fragment you saw in the previous chapter when you used the Formatting toolbar to format text in the page. If you used the Foreground Color button, you ended up with code similar to this:

```
We&#39;re glad you are <span class="style1">paying a visit</span>
```

To remove the `class` attribute, select the `<span>` tag in the tag selector, or simply click the `<span>` tag in Markup View and then click Clear Styles in the Apply Styles dialog box, which you can see at the top of Figure 3-20. You'll end up with this HTML:

```
We&#39;re glad you are paying a visit
```

Because an empty <span> around the text has no use, VWD removes it for you as well.

Removing style attributes from HTML elements works the same way.

How It Works

Once again, VWD is able to keep all relevant windows in sync: the Design View, Markup View, and the various CSS design tools. When you apply a class from the Apply Styles window, VWD adds the requested class to the selected HTML element in Markup View. It then also updates the Design View window. Similarly, when you remove a selector or a declaration from an embedded style in Design View, both the Design View and the CSS Tools windows are updated.

The final CSS functionality you need to look at in this chapter is located on the Manage Styles and Apply Styles windows. Besides helping you attach CSS files to your documents, these windows enable you to easily manage your styles.

Managing Styles

Especially since it's so easy to add new inline and embedded styles, your pages may quickly become messy. To achieve reusability, you should move as much of your inline and embedded styles as possible to an external style sheet. This is exactly what the Apply Styles and Manage Styles windows allow you to do.

Try It Out — Managing Styles

Earlier in this chapter, you modified the <h1> element and applied padding and margins to the heading. However, Default.aspx is not the only page that could benefit from this style, so it makes sense to move it to the Styles.css file. Similarly, the `Introduction` class seems reusable enough to include it in the Styles.css file so other pages can access it. This Try It Out shows you how to move styles around in your site.

1. Make sure that Default.aspx is still open and switch to Markup View if necessary.
2. Locate the <h1> tag and click it once. VWD makes the tag bold to indicate it's the active tag, as shown in Figure 3-21.

```
<div id="PageWrapper">
  <div id="Header">Header Goes Here</div>
  <div id="MenuWrapper">Menu Goes Here</div>
  <div id="MainContent">
    <h1 style="padding: 0px; margin: 0px 0px 10px 0px">Hi there visitor and we
    <p class="Introduction">We&#39;re glad you are paying a visit to <a href="
    <p class="Introduction">Feel free to have a <a href="Default.aspx">look ar
  </div>
  <div id="Sidebar">Sidebar Goes Here</div>
  <div id="Footer">Footer Goes Here</div>
```

Figure 3-21

3. Open the Apply Styles window by choosing View ➪ Apply Styles from the main menu. Alternatively, if you have the window docked with other windows, simply click its tab to make it active. At the bottom of the Apply Styles window, you'll see an inline style appear (see Figure 3-22).

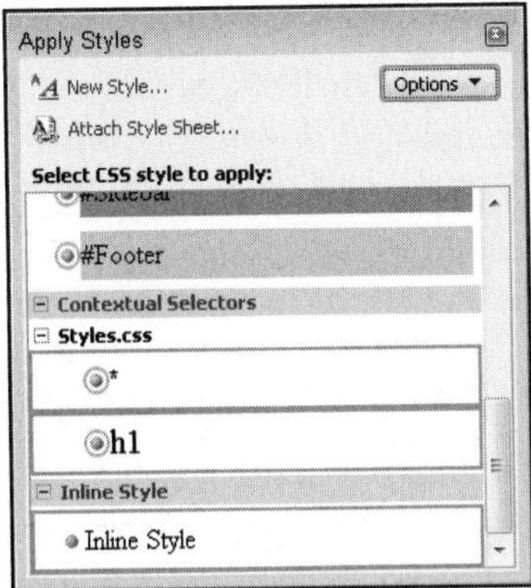

Figure 3-22

4. Right-click Inline Style and choose New Style Copy. The New Style dialog box appears, allowing you to create a new style based on the current selection. At the top of the window, choose `h1` from the Selector drop-down list, and from the Define in drop-down list choose Existing style sheet. From the URL drop-down list, choose Styles/Styles.css. If that item isn't available, click the Browse button to locate and select it. Your dialog box should end up like Figure 3-23.

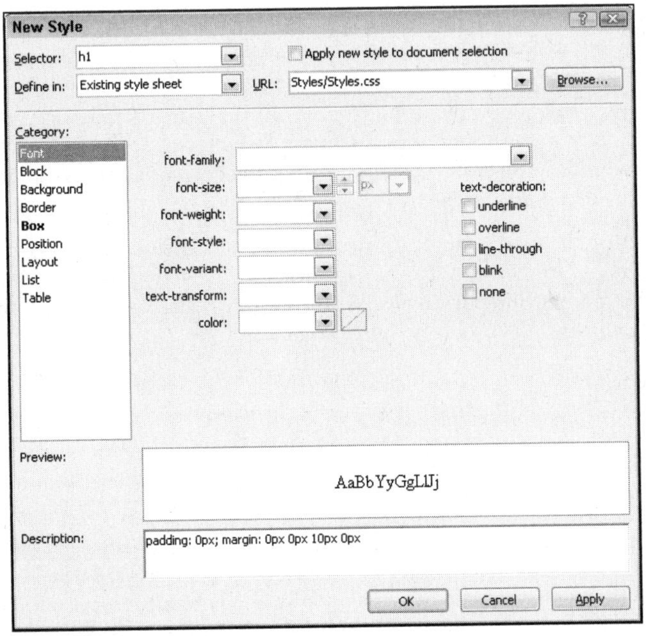

Figure 3-23

5. Click OK to dismiss the dialog box. VWD creates a copy of the `h1` style and places it in the file Styles.css. Notice that VWD creates a new selector for `h1` in the Styles.css file instead of adding the padding and margin info to the existing selector. If you want, you could combine the two selectors into one manually.

6. In the Apply Styles dialog box, right-click Inline Style again, and this time choose Remove Inline Style from the context menu. This removes the style attribute from the `h1` element.
7. Close the Apply Styles dialog box and open the Manage Styles window. Under the Current Page item, locate the `.Introduction` selector, visible in Figure 3-24.

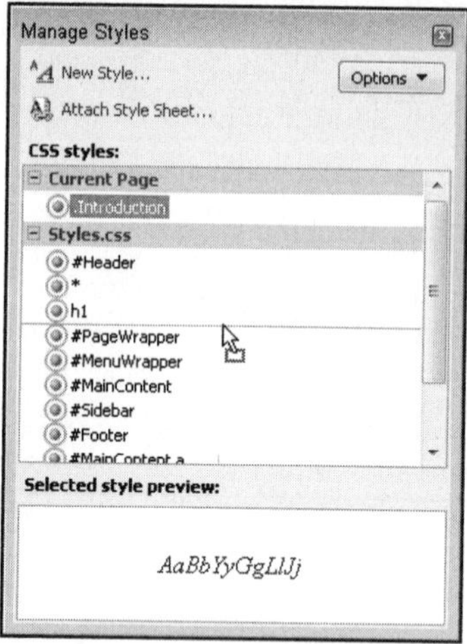

Figure 3-24

8. Click the `.Introduction` selector once, and then drag it into the area for Styles.css, for example dropping it after the `h1` selector. Note that VWD draws lines between the selectors as you hover over them to indicate the point where the selector will end up. Figure 3-24 shows how the `.Introduction` selector is dragged from the current page into Styles.css, between the `h1` and `#PageWrapper` selectors.
9. Once you drop the selector in the Styles.css section of the Manage Styles window, the associated style is removed from your current page, and then inserted in Styles.css. Since that CSS file is included in your current page using the `<link />` element, you won't see a difference in Design View. You can remove the empty `<style>` tag from Default.aspx, as it's not needed anymore.
10. Save any pending changes you may have and then open the Default.aspx page in your browser by pressing Ctrl+F5. Note that the paragraphs haven't changed and still use the same blue and italic font.

How It Works

Unfortunately, VWD doesn't allow you to move inline styles to external style sheet files. However, by creating a copy of the existing style, and then deleting the original inline style, you can achieve the same effect. Moving embedded or external style sheets between files is a lot easier. You can simply drag a style from one file to another, and VWD will automatically move the code for you. This makes it extremely easy to organize your CSS. Instead of leaving all your embedded CSS in your page because you're afraid to touch it, you can now simply drag and drop it into an external file. This makes it a lot easier to reuse those styles in other pages, decreasing page size and page bloat, and making your site a lot easier to manage. Obviously, it's important that the file you are moving your CSS to is attached to the pages you're working with.

Practical Tips on Working with CSS

Follow these tips to make the most of CSS:

- Take some time to familiarize yourself with the many properties that CSS supports. The best way to do this is to create a brand new page in your Demos folder, create a few HTML elements like `<div>` and `<p>` tags, and then simply experiment with all the different properties. By trying out many of the properties on the CSS Properties Grid, you get a feel for what options you have available. This makes it easier later if you want to apply a certain effect to some content.
- When creating custom CSS classes, try to come up with names that describe the behavior of the rule, rather than the look and feel. For example, a class called `.Introduction` to style the first paragraph of a page is a good description. It allows you to change the underlying values without affecting the actual meaning of the name. But classes with names like `.BlueAndItalic` are guaranteed to give you problems later. What if you decide to change the blue to black later? You either end up with a very odd class name not describing its own behavior, or you'll need to rename the class and then update the entire site, changing references to the old class to `.BlackAndItalic`.
- Try to create smaller and reusable rule sets that you can combine if required, rather than creating large, monolithic rules that can only be used on a single UI element. For example, instead of creating a style like this:

```
.ImportantHeading
{
  font-size: 20px;
  font-weight: bold;
  color: red;
}
```

You're better off creating a few lightweight styles that are easier to reuse:

```
h1
{
  font-size: 20px;
}

.Attention
{
  font-weight: bold;
  color: red;
}
```

When you apply the `.Attention` class to a heading like this: `<h1 class="Attention">` you get the exact same behavior you got when you gave it the `ImportantHeading` class. However, with the separate `Attention` class, you have created a reusable rule that you can apply to other elements that need the user's attention, like `<p>` or `<span>` tags.

Summary

This chapter gave you a good look at CSS, the most important language for styling your ASPX and HTML web pages.

CSS allows you to overcome the limitations of HTML with respect to styling your web pages as it is designed to minimize page bloat, give you greater control over the looks of your page, and generally help you create web sites that load quicker and that are easier to maintain.

Due to its simple set of grammar rules, CSS is relatively easy to learn. There is some important terminology that you need to be aware of before you can start using the full potential of CSS. First, you have to understand what a rule set or a rule is. A rule is a combination of a selector and one or more declarations that define the look of elements on your page. The selector is used to point to one or more elements in your page; the declaration determines how that element should look. The declaration itself can be split in two parts: the property and the value. The property determines what part of the element selected by the selector must be styled, while the value determines how it ends up.

When you have a good understanding of the CSS terminology, you'll find it's easier to work with the many CSS tools that VWD has on board. Tools like the Manage Styles and Apply Styles window, the Style Builder, and the smart IntelliSense in the code editor make writing CSS a breeze. Instead of remembering every little detail about CSS, you can rely on the built-in tools to write proper CSS for you.

At the end of the chapter, you saw how to use the Manage Styles window to move rules from an ASPX page to an external style sheet. This is extremely useful if you want to keep your pages tidy. You can start off by adding embedded style sheets in the document directly. When you're done with the page, you can move some or all of your rules to external style files, so that they can be used by the pages in your site as well. This dialog box is also useful if you want to reorder the different selectors in a single CSS file: You can just drag and drop them in a new location.

This chapter laid a good foundation for working with CSS in VWD 2008. The remainder of this book uses that knowledge to create good looking and well-organized web pages.

CSS can be applied not only to HTML as you've seen in this chapter, but to ASP.NET Server Controls as well. The CSS you apply to those controls eventually ends up in the browser as plain HTML where the same principles apply as those you've seen in this chapter. The next chapter gives you a detailed look at the many available ASP.NET Server Controls.

Exercises

1. What is the main benefit of using an external style over embedded style sheets?
2. Write a CSS rule that changes the appearance of all headings at level one (`h1`) in your page to the following:
    - The heading uses an Arial font face.
    - The heading should be blue.
    - The heading must have a font size if 18 pixels.
    - The heading has a blue, thin border at the top and left sides.

For the last requirement, check out VWD's IntelliSense list in a CSS file to discover another shorthand version for the border property.

3. Which of the two following rules is easier to reuse across pages in your web site? Can you explain why?

```
#MainContent
{
  border: 1px solid blue;
}

.BoxWithBorders
{
  border: 1px solid blue;
}
```

4. VWD allows you to attach an external style sheet to a page in a number of different ways. Can you name three different options to do this?

Working with ASP.NET Controls

ASP.NET Server Controls are the workhorses of ASP.NET. Almost all the pages you build in VWD will contain one or more server controls. These controls come in all sorts and sizes, ranging from simple controls like a `Button` and a `Label` to complex controls that are capable of displaying data from a database like the `TreeView` and the `GridView`, which you'll see in Chapters 7 and 12.

The architecture of ASP.NET Server Controls is deeply integrated into ASP.NET, giving the controls a feature set that is quite unique in today's technologies for building web sites.

This chapter shows you what server controls are, how they work, and which ones are available out of the box when you install Visual Web Developer.

In particular, this chapter teaches you the following topics:

- What ASP.NET Server Controls are
- The different kind of server controls you have at your disposal
- The common behavior shared among most of the server controls
- How the ASP.NET runtime processes the server controls on your page
- How server controls are able to maintain their state across postbacks

The chapter starts off with a general discussion of server controls. You'll see how to define them in your code by dragging them from the Toolbox into Design or Markup View.

The section that follows gives you a thorough look at the many controls that are available in the VWD Toolbox.

Introduction to Server Controls

It's important to understand how server controls operate and how they are completely different from the way you define controls in other languages like ASP or PHP, another popular programming language to create dynamic web sites.

For example, to influence the text in a text box in these languages, you would use plain HTML and mix it with server-side code. This works similar to the example in Chapter 2 where the current date and time are displayed on the page. For example, to create a text box with a message and the current time in it in classic ASP, you can use the following code:

```
<input type="text" value="Hello World, the time is now <%=Time()%>" />
```

As you can see, this code contains plain HTML, mixed with a server-side block, delimited by `<%` and `%>` that outputs the current time using the equals (=) symbol. This type of coding has a major disadvantage: the HTML and server-side code is mixed, making it difficult to write and manage your pages. Although this is a trivial example where it's still easy to understand the code, this type of programming can quickly result in very messy and complex pages.

Server controls work differently. In ASP.NET, the controls "live" on the server inside an ASPX page. When the page is requested in the browser, the server-side controls are processed by the ASP.NET runtime — the engine that is responsible for receiving and processing requests for ASPX pages. The controls then emit client-side HTML code that is appended to the final page output. It's this HTML code that eventually ends up in the browser, where it's used to build up the page.

So, instead of defining HTML controls in your pages directly, you define an ASP.NET Server Control with the following syntax where the italic parts differ for each control.

```
<asp:TypeOfControl ID="ControlName" Runat="Server" />
```

For example, to create a `TextBox` that can hold the same welcome message and current time, you can use the following syntax:

```
<asp:TextBox ID="txtMessage" Runat="Server" />
```

Note that the control has two attributes: an `ID` and a `Runat` attribute. The `ID` attribute is used to uniquely identify a control in the page, so you can program against it. It's important that each control on the page has a unique ID; otherwise the ASP.NET runtime won't understand what control you're referring to. If you accidentally type a duplicate control ID, VWD will signal the problem in the error list. The mandatory `Runat` attribute is used to indicate that this is a control that lives at the server. Without this attribute, the controls won't be processed and end up directly in the HTML source. If you ever feel you're missing a control in the final output in the HTML of the browser, ensure that the control has this required attribute. Note that for non-server elements, like plain HTML elements, the `Runat` attribute is optional. With this attribute on non-server controls, they can be reached by your programming code. You'll learn more about this later in the book.

You can program against this text box from code that is either placed inline with the page or in a separate Code Behind file, as you saw in Chapter 2. To set the welcome message and the time, you can use the following code:

VB.NET

```
txtMessage.Text = "Hello World, the time is now " & DateTime.Now.TimeOfDay.ToString()
```

C#

```
txtMessage.Text = "Hello World, the time is now " + DateTime.Now.TimeOfDay.ToString();
```

As you can see, the definition of the control in the markup section of the page is now separated from the actual code that defines the text displayed in the text box, making it easier to define and program the text box (or any other control) as it allows you to focus on one task at a time: either declaring the control and its visual appearance in the markup section of the page, or programming its behavior from a code block.

You'll see how server controls send their underlying HTML to the client in the next exercise.

Try It Out Working with Server Controls

In this exercise, you add a `TextBox` control, a `Label`, and a `Button` to a page. When you request the page in the browser, the server controls are transformed into HTML, which is then sent to the client. By looking at the final HTML for the page in the browser, you'll see how the HTML is completely different from the initial ASP.NET markup.

1. Open the Planet Wrox project in Visual Web Developer.

2. In the Demos folder in the Solution Explorer, create a new Web Form called ControlsDemo.aspx. Make sure it uses Code Behind and that the language drop-down list contains your programming language.

3. Switch to Design View. From the Toolbox, drag a `TextBox`, a `Button`, and a `Label` control onto the design surface within the dashed lines of the `<div>` tag that was added for you when you created the page.

   Type the text **Your Name** in front of the `TextBox` and add a line break between the `Button` and the `Label` by positioning your cursor between the two controls in Design View and then pressing Enter. If you're having trouble positioning the cursor between the controls, place it *after* the `Label` control and then press the left arrow key twice. The first time you press it, the `Label` will be selected; the second time, the cursor is placed between the two controls, allowing you to press Enter. Your Design View should now look like Figure 4-1.

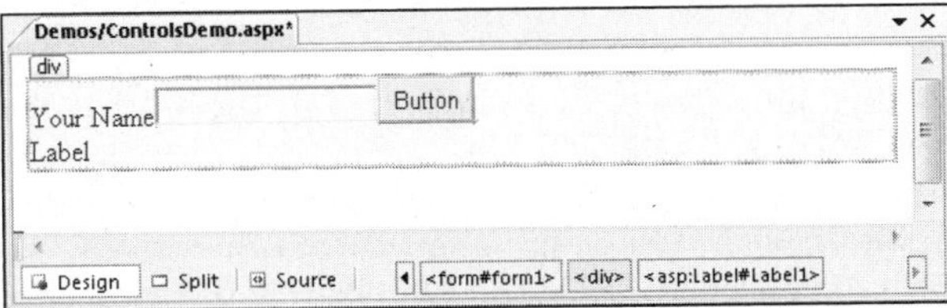

Figure 4-1

4. Right-click the `Button` and choose Properties to open up the Properties Grid for the control. Pressing F4 after selecting the `Button` does the same thing. The window that appears, shown in Figure 4-2, allows you to change the properties for the control, which in turn influence the way the control behaves at runtime.

5. Set the control's `Text` property to Submit Information and set its `ID` (which you'll find all the way down at the bottom of the list) to `btnSubmit`.

6. Change the `ID` of the `TextBox` to `txtName` using the Properties Grid.

7. Clear the `Text` property of the `Label` using the Properties Grid. You can leave its `ID` set to `Label1`.

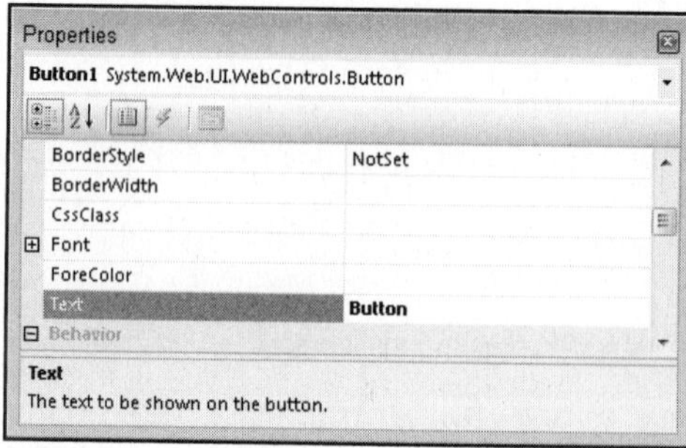

Figure 4-2

8. Still in Design View, double-click the button to have VWD add some code to the Code Behind of the page that will be fired when the button is clicked in the browser. Add the highlighted line of code to the code block that VWD inserted for you:

VB.NET

```
Protected Sub btnSubmit_Click(ByVal sender As Object, ByVal e As System.EventArgs) _
      Handles btnSubmit.Click
  Label1.Text = "Your name is " & txtName.Text
End Sub
```

C#

```
protected void btnSubmit_Click(object sender, EventArgs e)
{
  Label1.Text = "Your name is " + txtName.Text;
}
```

Note that the VB.NET example uses the underscore again to split the code over two lines. This is done only to be able to display the code within the boundaries of this book. In your own web page, you should see all the code on a single line, although you could add the underscore yourself if you wanted to.

9. Save the changes to the page and then open it in the browser by pressing Ctrl+F5. When it appears in the browser, don't click the button yet, but open up the source of the page by right-clicking the page in the browser and choosing View Source or View Page Source. You should see the following HTML code:

```
<div>
  Your Name<input name="txtName" type="text" id="txtName" />
  <input type="submit" name="btnSubmit" value="Submit Information" id="btnSubmit" />
  <br />
  <span id="Label1"></span>
</div>
```

10. Switch back to your browser, fill in your name in the text box, and then click the button. When the page is done reloading, open up the source for the page in the browser again using the browser's right-click menu. The code should now look like this:

```
<div>
  Your Name<input name="txtName" type="text" value="Imar" id="txtName" />
```

```
    <input type="submit" name="btnSubmit" value="Submit Information" id="btnSubmit" />
    <br />
    <span id="Label1">Your name is Imar</span>
  </div>
```

Note that the two highlighted lines have changed, and now show the name you entered in the text box.

How It Works

As its name implies, an ASP.NET Server Control lives at the server in your ASPX page where it can be processed by the ASP.NET runtime. When you request a page in the browser, the runtime creates an in-memory representation of the ASPX file with the controls you created. Once the runtime is about to send the HTML to the browser, it asks each of the controls in the page for their HTML which is then injected in the final result. For example, when the `Label` control is asked for its HTML the first time it loads, it returns the following:

```
<span id="Label1"></span>
```

As you can see, although you defined the `Label` control with the `<asp:Label>` syntax, it ends up as a simple `<span>` tag in the browser. Because the `Text` property of the `Label` control is empty, you don't see any text between the two `<span>` tags. The same applies to other controls; an `<asp:TextBox>` ends up as `<input type="text">` whereas the `<asp:Button>` ends up as `<input type="submit">`.

When you click the button, the control causes a *postback*, which sends the information for the controls in the page to the server, where the page is loaded again. Additionally, the code that you wrote to handle the button's `Click` event is executed. This code takes the name you entered in the text box and then assigns it to the `Label` control:

```
Label1.Text = "Your name is " + txtName.Text;
```

Don't worry about the syntax for the code that handles the button's `Click` event. In Chapter 5, you'll see how this works, and why you need this code.

At this stage, the `Label` control contains the text you entered in the text box, so when it is asked for its HTML, it now returns this:

```
<span id="Label1">Your name is Imar</span>
```

You get a good look at postbacks later in this chapter when the ASP.NET state engine is discussed.

A Closer Look at ASP.NET Server Controls

Since you'll be working with server controls for most of the time when building your ASP.NET web pages, you need to know in detail how they work and how to use them. In the next section, you'll see how to add the controls to your pages and change the way they behave in the browser. In the section that follows, you get an overview of the behavior that all server controls have in common. When you understand this shared behavior, you'll find it easy to apply it to other, new controls as well, enabling you to get up to speed with them very quickly.

Defining Controls in Your Pages

As demonstrated in the previous Try It Out, you can simply drag controls from the Toolbox onto the design surface of the page. This makes it very easy to add a bunch of controls to a page to get you started. However, because of the way the design surface works, it's sometimes difficult to add them exactly where you want them. For example, it can be difficult to drag a control between the opening and closing tags of an HTML element. Fortunately, you can just as easily drag a control from the Toolbox in Markup View. Additionally, you can also type the control's markup directly in Markup View, letting IntelliSense help you with the different tags and attributes. You'll also find that the Properties Grid works in Markup View. Simply click the relevant markup, and the Properties Grid will be updated to reflect the tag you clicked. This makes it easy to change the properties of the control, while you can still see exactly what markup gets generated for you.

If you look at the Properties Grid for some of the controls in a page, you'll notice that many of them have similar properties. In the next section, you'll see exactly what these properties are and what they are used for.

Common Properties for All Controls

Most of the server controls you find in the VWD Toolbox share some common behavior. For example, each control has an ID to uniquely identify it in the page, a `Runat` attribute that is always set to `Server` to indicate the control should be processed on the server, and a `ClientID` that contains the client-side ID attribute that will be assigned to the element in the final HTML. The `Runat` attribute does not really belong to the server control, but is necessary to indicate that the markup for the control should be processed as a server control and not end up as plain text or HTML in the browser.

Besides these properties, many of the server controls share more properties. The following table lists the most common ones and describes what they are used for.

Property	Description
`AccessKey`	Allows you to set a key with which a control can be accessed in the client by pressing the associated letter.
`BackColor` `ForeColor`	Allows you to change the color of the background (`BackColor`) and text (`ForeColor`) of the control in the browser.

`BorderColor`
`BorderStyle`
`BorderWidth`
	Changes the border of the control in the browser. The similarities with the CSS border properties you saw in the previous chapter are no coincidence. Each of these three ASP.NET properties maps directly to its CSS counterpart.

`CssClass`	Lets you define the HTML class attribute for the control in the browser.
`Enabled`	Determines whether the user can interact with the control in the browser. For example, with a disabled text box (`Enabled="false"`) you cannot change its text.
`Font`	Allows you to define different font-related settings, such as `Font-Size`, `Font-Names`, and `Font-Bold`.

Property	Description
`Height` `Width`	Determines the height and width of the control in the browser.
`TabIndex`	Sets the HTML `tabindex` attribute that determines the order in which users can move through the controls in the page by pressing the Tab key.
`ToolTip`	Allows you to set a tooltip for the control in the browser. This tooltip, rendered as a title attribute in the HTML is shown when the user hovers the mouse over the relevant HTML element.
`Visible`	Determines whether the control is sent to the browser or not. You should really see this as a server-side visibility setting because an invisible control is never sent to the browser at all. This means it's quite different from the CSS display and visibility properties you saw in the previous chapter that hide the element at the client.

To see how all these attributes end up in the browser, consider the following markup for a `TextBox` server control:

```
<asp:TextBox AccessKey="a" BackColor="Black" ForeColor="White" BorderColor="Blue"
 BorderStyle="Dashed" Font-Size="30px" BorderWidth="4" CssClass="TextBox"
 Enabled="true" Height="40" Width="200" TabIndex="1" ToolTip="Hover text here"
 Visible="true" ID="TextBox1" runat="server" Text="Hello World">
</asp:TextBox>
```

When you request the page with this control in the browser, you end up with the following HTML:

```
<input name="TextBox1" type="text" value="Hello World" id="TextBox1" accesskey="a"
  tabindex="1" title="Hover text here" class="TextBox" style="color:White;
  background-color:Black;border-color:Blue;border-width:4px;
  border-style:Dashed;font-size:30px;height:40px;width:200px;"
/>
```

This results in the text box in Figure 4-3 being displayed in the browser.

Note that most of the server-side control properties have been moved to CSS inline styles with the `style` attribute.

Figure 4-3

When building web sites, it's quite uncommon to define a `TextBox` in this manner. As you learned in the previous chapter, you should avoid inline styles as much as possible, and opt for external CSS style sheets instead. You can accomplish the exact same behavior with this server-side control:

```
<asp:TextBox ID="TextBox1" AccessKey="a" CssClass="TextBox" Enabled="true" TabIndex="1"
  ToolTip="Hover text here" Visible="true" runat="server" Text="Hello World">
</asp:TextBox>
```

And the following CSS class:

```
.TextBox
{
  color: White;
  background-color: Black;
  border-color: Blue;
  border-width: 4px;
  border-style: Dashed;
  font-size: 30px;
  height: 40px;
  width: 200px;
}
```

Obviously, the second example is much easier to read, reuse, and maintain. If you want another text box with the exact same look, you simply assign `TextBox` to the `CssClass` of that control.

Although it's recommended to use CSS classes instead of these inline styles, it's good to know about the server-side control properties in case you need fine control over them. If you programmatically change the control's properties (as you'll learn how to do later) they still end up as inline styles, and thus possibly override settings in embedded or external style sheets.

Now that you have seen the generic behavior that all server controls share, it's time to look at the large number of controls that ship with ASP.NET 3.5.

Types of Controls

Out of the box, ASP.NET 3.5 comes with a large number of server controls, supporting most of your web development needs. To make it easy for you to find the right controls, they have been placed in separate control categories in the Visual Web Developer Toolbox (accessible by pressing Ctrl+Alt+X). Figure 4-4 shows the Toolbox with all the available categories.

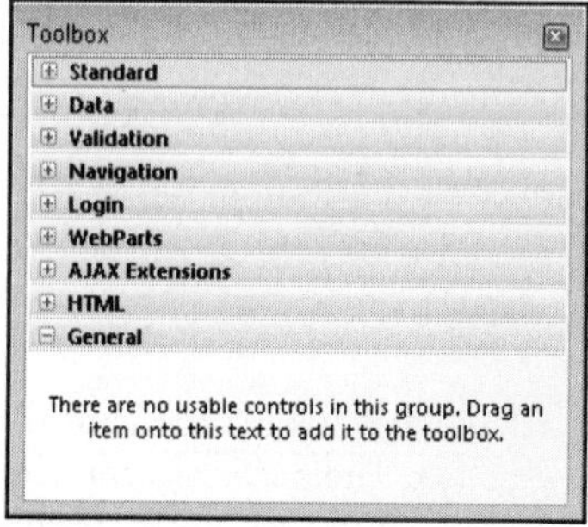

Figure 4-4

In the following sections, you'll see the controls each category contains, the tasks they are designed for, and how you can use them in your ASP.NET pages.

With the discussion of the various controls, you see a mention of the *properties* of a control. For example, a `TextBox` has a `Text` property (among many others), while a `ListBox` has a `SelectedItem` property. Some properties can only be set programmatically and not with the Properties Grid. Programmatically reading and changing control properties is discussed in detail in the next chapter.

Standard Controls

The Standard category contains many of the basic controls that almost any web page needs. You've already seen some of them, like the `TextBox`, `Button`, and `Label` controls earlier in this chapter. Figure 4-5 shows all the controls in the Standard category.

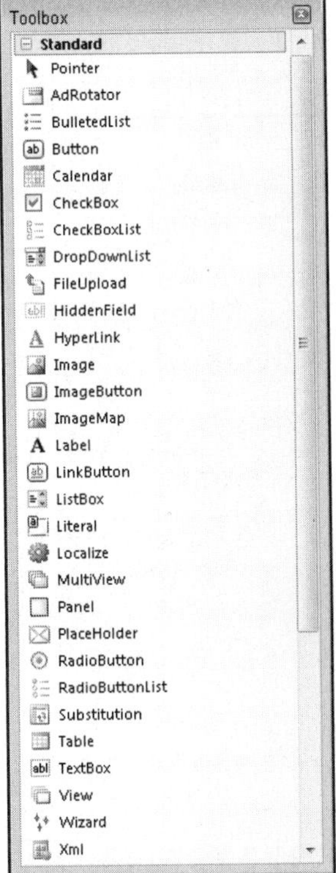

Figure 4-5

Many of the controls probably speak for themselves, so instead of giving you a detailed description of all these controls, the following sections briefly highlight a few important controls.

Simple Controls

The Toolbox contains a number of simple and straightforward controls, including `Button`, `Label`, `HyperLink`, `RadioButton`, and `CheckBox`. Their icons in the Toolbox give you a good clue of how they end up in the browser. In the remainder of this book, you'll see these controls used many times.

List Controls

The Toolbox contains a number of controls that present themselves as lists in the browser. These controls include `ListBox`, `DropDownList`, `CheckBoxList`, `RadioButtonList`, and `BulletedList`. To add items to the list, you define `<asp:ListItem>` elements between the opening and closing tags of the control, as shown in the following example:

```
<asp:DropDownList ID="lstFavoriteLanguage" runat="server">
  <asp:ListItem Value="C#">C#</asp:ListItem>
  <asp:ListItem Value="Visual Basic">Visual Basic</asp:ListItem>
  <asp:ListItem Value="CSS">CSS</asp:ListItem>
</asp:DropDownList>
```

To see the currently active and selected item of a list control programmatically, you can look at its `SelectedValue`, `SelectedItem`, or `SelectedIndex` properties. `SelectedValue` returns a string that contains the value for the selected item, like `C#` or `Visual Basic` in the example above. `SelectedIndex` returns the zero-based index of the item in the list. With the example above, if the user had chosen C#, then `SelectedIndex` would be 0. Similarly, when the user has chosen CSS, the index would be 2 (the third item in the list). The `BulletedList` control doesn't allow a user to make selections, and as such doesn't support these properties.

For controls that allow multiple selections (like `CheckBoxList` and `ListBox`), you can loop through the `Items` collection and see what items are selected. In this case, `SelectedItem` returns *only the first* selected item in the list; not all of them. You'll see how to access all the selected items in the next exercise.

To see how to add list items to your list control, and how to read the selected values, the following exercise guides you through creating a simple Web Form with the two list controls that ask users for their favorite programming language.

Try It Out Working with List Controls

In this exercise you'll add two list controls to a page. Additionally, you add a button that, when clicked, displays the selected items as text in a `Label` control.

1. In the Demos folder, create a new Web Form called ListControls.aspx. Make sure you create a Code Behind file by checking the Place Code in Separate File option.
2. Switch to Design View and then drag a `DropDownList` from the Toolbox onto the design surface of the page within the dashed border of the `<div>` element that is already present in your page.
3. Notice that as soon as you drop the `DropDownList` control on the page, a pop-up menu appears that is labeled DropDownList Tasks, as shown in Figure 4-6.

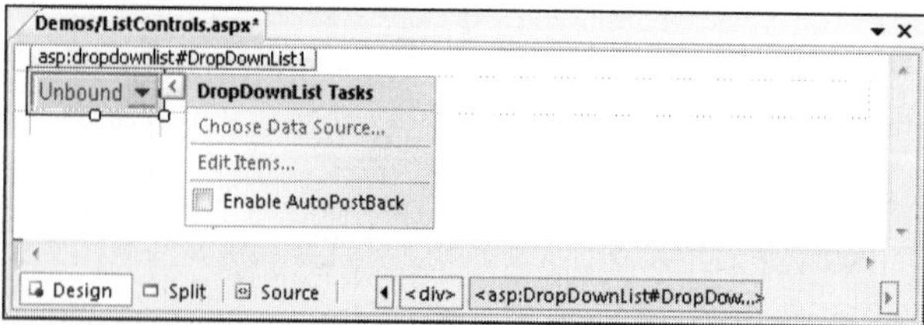

Figure 4-6

- ❑ This pop-up menu is called the Smart Tasks panel or menu. When it appears, it gives you access to the most common tasks of the control it belongs to. In the case of the `DropDownList`, you get three options. The first option allows you to bind the control to a data source, which is demonstrated in Chapter 12. The second item allows you to manually add items to the list, whereas the last option sets the `AutoPostBack` property of the control. With this option checked, the control will submit the page it's contained in back to the server as soon as the user chooses a new item from the list.
- ❑ The Smart Tasks panel only appears for the more complex controls that have a lot of features. You won't see it for simple controls like `Button` or `Label`. To reopen the Smart Tasks panel, right-click the control in the designer and choose Show Smart Tag. Alternatively, click the little arrow at the top-right corner of the control, visible in Figure 4-6.
- ❑ On the Smart Tasks panel of the `DropDownList`, click the Edit Items link to bring up the ListItem Collection Editor, shown in Figure 4-7.
- ❑ This dialog box allows you to add new items to the list control. The items you add through this window will be added as `<asp:ListItem>` elements between the tags for the control.

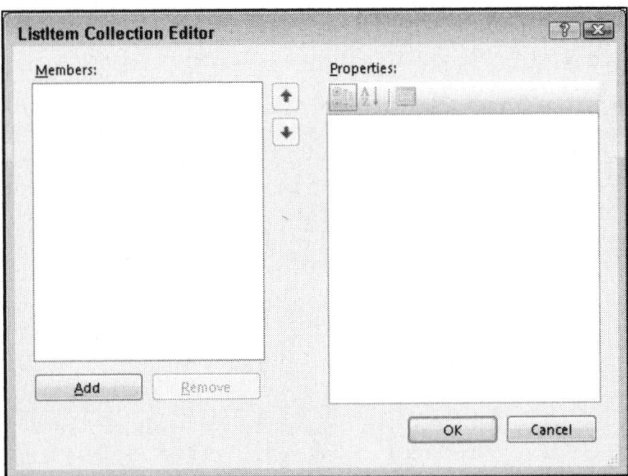

Figure 4-7

4. Click the Add button on the left side of the screen to insert a new list item. Then in the Properties Grid on the right, enter C# for the `Text` property and then press Tab. As soon as you tab away from the `Text` property, the value is copied to the `Value` property as well. This is convenient if you want both the `Text` and the `Value` property to be the same. However, it's perfectly OK (and quite common) to assign a different value to the `Value` property.
5. Repeat the previous step twice, this time creating list items for Visual Basic and CSS. You can use the up and down arrows in the middle of the dialog box to change the order of the items in the list. Finally, click OK to insert the items in the page. You should end up with the following code:

```
<asp:DropDownList ID="DropDownList1" runat="server">
  <asp:ListItem>C#</asp:ListItem>
  <asp:ListItem>Visual Basic</asp:ListItem>
```

```
    <asp:ListItem>CSS</asp:ListItem>
  </asp:DropDownList>
```

6. Switch to Markup View if necessary and then drag a `CheckBoxList` control from the Toolbox directly in the code window, right after the `DropDownList`.

7. Copy the three `<asp:ListItem>` elements from the `DropDownList` you created in steps 4 and 5 and paste them between the opening and closing tags of the `CheckBoxList`. You should end up with this code:

```
    <asp:ListItem>CSS</asp:ListItem>
  </asp:DropDownList>
  <asp:CheckBoxList ID="CheckBoxList1" runat="server">
    <asp:ListItem>C#</asp:ListItem>
    <asp:ListItem>Visual Basic</asp:ListItem>
    <asp:ListItem>CSS</asp:ListItem>
  </asp:CheckBoxList>
```

8. Switch to Design View and then drag a `Button` from the Toolbox in Design View to the right of the `CheckBoxList` control. The `Button` will be placed below the `CheckBoxList`. Next, drag a `Label` control and drop it next to the `Button`. Create some room between the `Button` and the `Label` by positioning your cursor between the controls and then pressing Enter twice. Double-click the `Button` to open the Code Behind of the page.

9. In the code block that VWD added for you, add the following highlighted code, which will be executed when the user clicks the button:

VB.NET

```
Protected Sub Button1_Click(ByVal sender As Object, ByVal e As System.EventArgs) _
          Handles Button1.Click
  Label1.Text = "In the DDL you selected " & DropDownList1.SelectedValue & "<br />"

  For Each item As ListItem In CheckBoxList1.Items
    If item.Selected Then
      Label1.Text &= "In the CBL you selected " & item.Value & "<br />"
    End If
  Next
End Sub
```

C#

```
protected void Button1_Click(object sender, EventArgs e)
{
  Label1.Text = "In the DDL you selected " + DropDownList1.SelectedValue + "<br />";

  foreach (ListItem item in CheckBoxList1.Items)
  {
    if (item.Selected == true)
    {
      Label1.Text += "In the CBL you selected " + item.Value + "<br />";
    }
  }
}
```

10. Save the changes to the page and then request it in the browser. Choose an item from the `DropDownList`, check one or more items in the `CheckBoxList`, and then click the button. You should see something similar to Figure 4-8, which shows the page in Firefox.

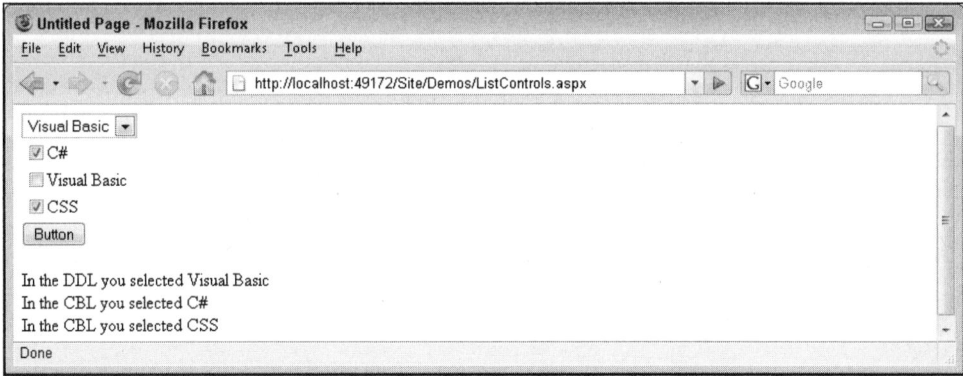

Figure 4-8

How It Works

The various list controls all use `<asp:ListItem>` elements. That makes it easy to reuse them by copying them from one control to another. Since the `DropDownList` supports only one selected item at a time, it's pretty easy to get the selected value. All it takes is a single line of code (shown in C#):

```
Label1.Text = "In the DDL you selected " + DropDownList1.SelectedValue + "<br />";
```

The `CheckBoxList` control allows a user to select multiple items at once. Therefore, you need a bit more code to *loop over the collection of items*, checking the `Selected` property of each item (again shown in C#):

```
foreach (ListItem item in CheckBoxList1.Items)
{
  if (item.Selected == true)
  {
    Label1.Text += "In the CBL you selected " + item.Value + "<br />";
  }
}
```

The `CheckBoxList` and the other list controls have an `Items` collection that contains all the items you defined in the code. So, given the code from this Try It Out, `CheckBoxList1` contains three items: for C#, Visual Basic, and CSS respectively. Each `ListItem` in turn contains a `Selected` property that determines whether the user has checked the item in the list or not.

Using a `foreach` loop (`For Each` in VB.NET), you can iterate over the collection of `ListItem` elements, checking the `Selected` property one by one. If the item was selected in the list, its `Selected` property is `true` and its `Value` is appended to the text of the `Label`. Notice the use of `+=` (`&=` in VB.NET) in the last code example to assign the `Value` of the list item together with the text `"In the CBL you selected "` to the `Text` property of the `Label`. The `+=` and `&=` syntax is shorthand for this:

```
Label1.Text = Label1.Text + "In the CBL you selected " + item.Value + "<br />";
```

This code takes the current text from the Label control, appends the string "In the CBL you selected " + item.Value + "<br />" to it, and then reassigns the entire string back to the Text property of the label. Using the += syntax is often a bit easier to write and understand, but the longer version is common as well.

Both VB.NET and C# have support for a For Each loop, although both languages use a slightly different syntax. In the next chapter you learn a lot more about looping and other language constructs.

Also of note is the way the ListItems are set up. In the first example, before the Try It Out, you saw ListItem elements with both a value and text:

```
<asp:ListItem Value="C#">C#</asp:ListItem>
<asp:ListItem Value="Visual Basic">Visual Basic</asp:ListItem>
<asp:ListItem Value="CSS">CSS</asp:ListItem>
```

When you add items to the list yourself with the ListItem Collection Editor, you don't get the Value attributes:

```
<asp:ListItem>C#</asp:ListItem>
<asp:ListItem>Visual Basic</asp:ListItem>
<asp:ListItem>CSS</asp:ListItem>
```

You didn't get the Value attribute, because you didn't supply an explicit value for the item in the ListItem Collection Editor. If you omit the Value, the text between the opening and closing tags of the ListItem is used implicitly as the value, which is fine in many cases. However, it's also quite common to have a different Value and Text property in the list. For example, when you have a list with countries, you could use the full name of the country as the Text (like Netherlands) and use the official country code (nl) as the Value for the drop-down list. You'll see the list controls at work in other chapters in this book.

Container Controls

Quite often it's desirable to have the ability to group related content and controls. This grouping can be done by putting the controls (and other markup) in one of the container controls, like the Panel, the PlaceHolder, the MultiView, or the Wizard. For example, you can use the PlaceHolder or the Panel control to hide or show a number of controls at the same time. Instead of hiding each control separately, you simply hide the entire container that contains all the individual controls and markup. Both of these controls have their own advantages and disadvantages. The good thing about the PlaceHolder control is that it emits no HTML of its own into the page, so you can use it as a container without any side effects in the final page. However, it lacks design-time support, making it hard to manage the controls inside the PlaceHolder at design time in VWD. In contrast, the Panel allows you to easily access all controls and other content it contains but renders itself as a <div> tag. In many cases this isn't a problem, so usually you're best off with the Panel control because of its design-time support.

The MultiView (which can contain one or more <asp:View> controls) and the Wizard are similar in that they allow you to split up a long page into multiple areas, making it easy to fill in a long form for example. The Wizard has built-in support for moving from page to page using Previous, Next, and Finish buttons, while the MultiView must be controlled programmatically.

A Closer Look at the Panel Control

In the following exercise, you'll use a Panel control to create a container for other controls and markup. You'll only add some text for now, but in a subsequent Try It Out exercise you'll add ASP.NET controls to the panel.

Try It Out Using the Panel Control

In this exercise you'll see how to use the Panel control as a container for some simple text. In addition, you'll use a simple CheckBox to control the visibility of the Panel at the server.

1. Start by creating a new Web Form with Code Behind called Containers.aspx in the Demos folder.
2. Switch the page into Design View and then drag a CheckBox and a Panel control from the Toolbox on the design surface into the dashed <div> element.
3. Give the CheckBox control a meaningful description by setting its Text property to Show Panel and set its AutoPostBack property to True using the Properties Grid.
4. Set the Visible property of the Panel control to False using the Properties Grid. This hides the Panel control when the page first loads.
5. Inside the Panel control, type some text (for example, **I am visible now**). Note that the panel behaves like the rest of VWD's design surface. You can simply add text to it, select and format it, and even add new controls to it by dragging them from the Toolbox. The code for the panel should end up like this:

```
<asp:Panel ID="Panel1" runat="server" Height="50px" Visible="False" Width="125px">
  I am visible now
</asp:Panel>
```

6. Double-click the CheckBox control in Design View and, inside the code that VWD added for you, enter the following highlighted line of code:

VB.NET

```
Protected Sub CheckBox1_CheckedChanged(ByVal sender As Object, _
               ByVal e As System.EventArgs) Handles CheckBox1.CheckedChanged
  Panel1.Visible = CheckBox1.Checked
End Sub
```

C#

```
protected void CheckBox1_CheckedChanged(object sender, EventArgs e)
{
  Panel1.Visible = CheckBox1.Checked;
}
```

7. Save all your changes and then request the page in the browser by pressing Ctrl+F5.
8. When the page first loads, all you see is the CheckBox and the text beside it. When you click the CheckBox control to place a checkmark in it, the page will reload and now shows the text you entered in step 5. If nothing happens, go back to the source of the page in VWD and ensure that AutoPostBack is set to True on the CheckBox control.

If you look at the HTML in the browser (right-click the page and choose View Source or View Page Source), you'll see that the text you typed in step 5 is surrounded with a `<div>` tag with an `id` of `Panel1`:

```
<div id="Panel1" style="height:50px;width:125px;">
  I am visible now
</div>
```

How It Works

In step 4 of this exercise you set the `Visible` property of the `Panel` control to `False`. This means that when the page loads, the control is not visible on the server and thus its HTML never makes it to the browser. When you then checked the `CheckBox`, a postback occurred, which sent the information contained in the form to the server. At the server, some code is run that is fired whenever the checkbox changes its state from checked to unchecked or vice versa. Inside that code block, the following code is executed (shown in C#):

```
Panel1.Visible = CheckBox1.Checked;
```

This means that the `Panel` is only visible when the checkbox is checked. When it isn't, the `Panel` is hidden automatically.

In the next chapter you'll learn much more about the code that makes this happen, and why you need code like the line with `CheckBox1_CheckedChanged`.

As you can see, it's easy to add text and other markup to the `Panel` control in Visual Web Developer. Right now, you only added some plain text but in the next section you'll see how to add a `Wizard` control and how to use it.

Magic with the Wizard Control

The `Wizard` control is a great tool for breaking apart large Web Forms and presenting them as bite-sized chunks of information to the user. Instead of confusing your user with one page with many controls and text on it, you can break the page apart and present each part on a separate wizard page. The wizard then handles all navigation issues by creating Next, Previous, and Finish buttons automatically. In the following exercise you'll use the wizard to ask a user for her name and favorite programming language. Although the example itself is pretty trivial, and you easily could have placed both questions on the same page without confusing the user, the example shows how the wizard works and why it's useful, so you can easily apply the same techniques to your own, and possibly larger, Web Forms.

Try It Out Using the Wizard to Create Easy-to-Use Forms

Inside the panel you created in the previous exercise, you will place a `Wizard` that allows a user to fill in a form that is spread over a couple of pages. The wizard will have two steps where a user can enter details and a results page that shows the data the user has provided.

1. Make sure you still have Containers.aspx page open in Design View. Remove the text "I am visible now" that you entered in the previous Try It Out, and then drag a `Wizard` control from the Toolbox

inside the `Panel`. Drag its right edge further to the right, increasing the total width of the control to `500px`. Switch to Markup View and remove the `Height` and `Width` attributes and their values from the `Panel` (leave the `Width` for the `Wizard` set to `500px`). When you switch back to Design View, your page looks similar to Figure 4-9.

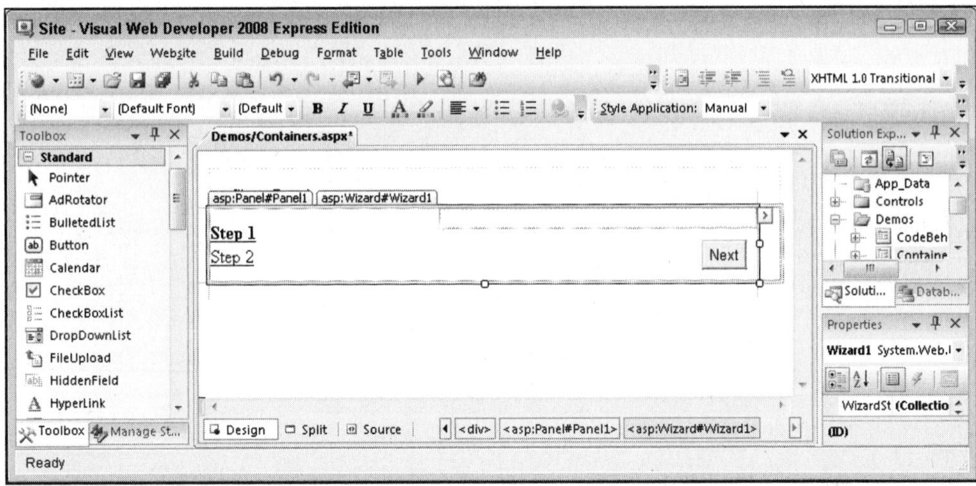

Figure 4-9

2. Right-click the `Wizard` in Design View and choose Add/Remove WizardSteps. In the dialog box that follows click the Add button to insert a third wizard step, shown in Figure 4-10.

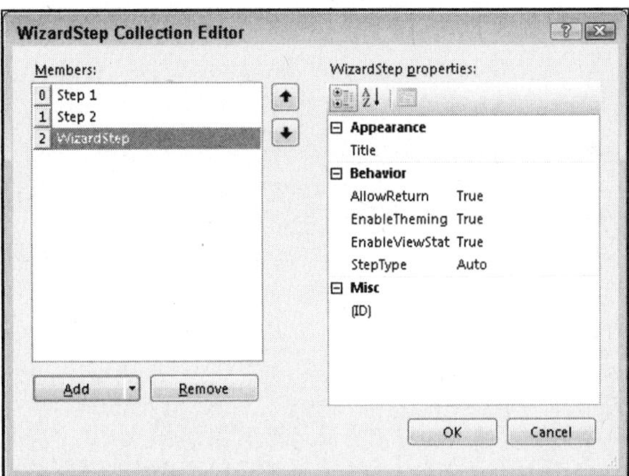

Figure 4-10

3. Click the first `WizardStep` labeled Step 1 in the Members list on the left and then change its `Title` from Step 1 to `About You`. Set the `Title` of the other two steps to `Favorite Language` and `Ready` respectively.

4. Change the `StepType` of the second step (now labeled Favorite Language) to `Finish` and of the last step to `Complete`. You can leave the `StepType` of the first step set to `Auto`. Click OK.

5. In Design View, click About You in the list at the left to make it the active step and then drag a `Label` and a `TextBox` to the right side of the `Wizard`. You need to drag them inside the blue rectangle that's in the upper-right corner of the `Wizard`, or the controls won't end up inside the `Wizard`. Set the `Text` of the `Label` to `Type your name` and then change the `ID` of the `TextBox` to `txtName`. When you're done, your `Wizard` looks like Figure 4-11.

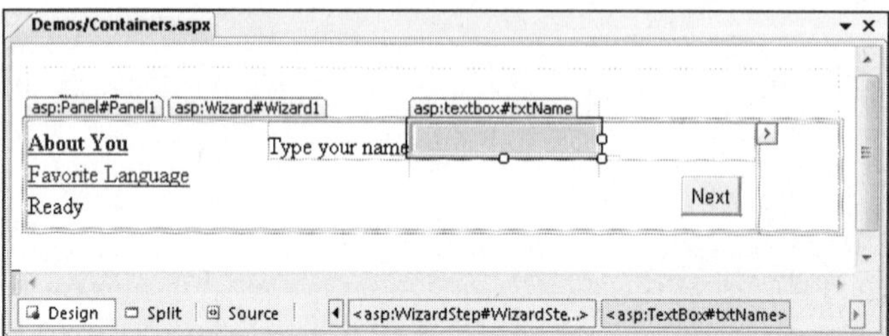

Figure 4-11

6. Click the Favorite Language item in the list on the left and then add a `DropDownList` to the rectangle with the blue border on the right part of the wizard step. Rename the list by setting its ID to `lstFavoriteLanguage`. Open the Smart Tasks panel of the `DropDownList` control and choose Edit Items. Add the same three items you added in an earlier Try It Out: for C#, Visual Basic, and CSS, respectively. If you want, you can copy the three items from the page ListControls.aspx and paste them between the `<asp:DropDownList>` tags inside the second step. You should end up with the following code for the second step:

```
</asp:WizardStep>
<asp:WizardStep ID="WizardStep2" runat="server" Title="Favorite Language"
          StepType="Finish">
  <asp:DropDownList ID="lstFavoriteLanguage" runat="server">
    <asp:ListItem>C#</asp:ListItem>
    <asp:ListItem>Visual Basic</asp:ListItem>
    <asp:ListItem>CSS</asp:ListItem>
  </asp:DropDownList>
</asp:WizardStep>
<asp:WizardStep runat="server" Title="Ready">
```

7. Switch to Markup View, and then inside the last `WizardStep` labeled Ready, drag a label control from the Toolbox and rename it by setting its `ID` to `lblResult`. If you try to switch to the last step in Design View, you may notice that the wizard disappears. If that happens, switch to Markup View and set `ActiveStepIndex` to `0` again.

8. Double-click the wizard in Design View and add the following highlighted code, which will be executed when the user clicks the Finish button on the last step of the wizard. If you're having problems getting VWD to create the correct code for you that you see in the next snippet, select the `Wizard`, press F4 to open up the control's Properties Grid, and then click the button with the lightning bolt on it (the fourth button from the left on the toolbar of the Properties Grid), shown in Figure 4-12.

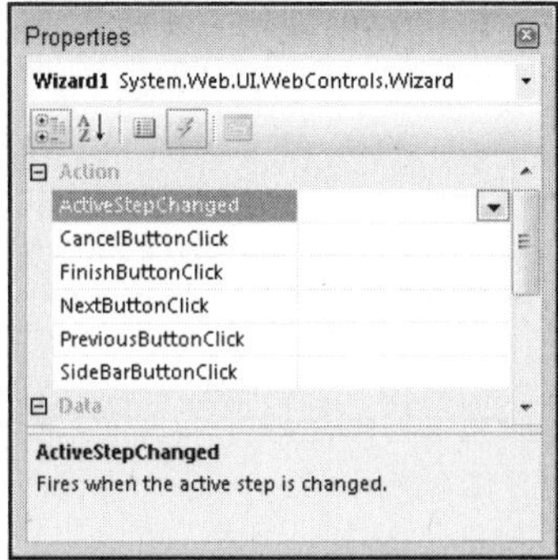

Figure 4-12

Locate and double-click `FinishButtonClick` in the Action category. With both methods, you should end up with some code for `Wizard1_FinishButtonClick` as shown below (the next chapter shows you what the lightning bolt does exactly and what it is used for):

VB.NET

```
Protected Sub Wizard1_FinishButtonClick(ByVal sender As Object, ByVal e As _
        System.Web.UI.WebControls.WizardNavigationEventArgs) _
        Handles Wizard1.FinishButtonClick
  lblResult.Text = "Your name is " & txtName.Text
  lblResult.Text &= "<br />Your favorite language is " & lstFavoriteLanguage.SelectedValue
End Sub
```

C#

```
protected void Wizard1_FinishButtonClick(object sender, WizardNavigationEventArgs e)
{
  lblResult.Text = "Your name is " + txtName.Text;
  lblResult.Text += "<br />Your favorite language is " + lstFavoriteLanguage.SelectedValue;
}
```

9. Switch back to Design View and open the Properties Grid for the `Wizard` and make sure its `ActiveStepIndex` is set to `0`. The designer remembers the last step you designed and stores the value in the `ActiveStepIndex` of the `Wizard` in Markup View. To make sure the wizard starts on the first page, you should always set the `ActiveStepIndex` back to `0` (or click the first step in the `Wizard` control in Design View) before you save your changes and run the page.

10. Press Ctrl+F5 to open the page in the browser. Select the `CheckBox` to make the `Panel` visible and then enter your name on the first wizard page. Click Next and choose your favorite programming language. Notice how there's now a Previous button available that allows you to go back to the first step of the wizard if you wanted to change your name. Instead of clicking the Next and Previous buttons, you can also click the links on the left of the wizard in the browser. When you click the Finish button, you'll see the results of the information you entered in the wizard (see Figure 4-13).

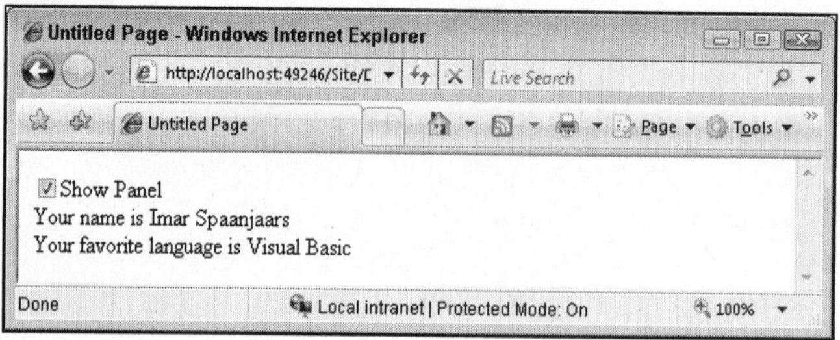

Figure 4-13

How It Works

The `Wizard` control takes care of most of the hard work for you. It handles the navigation, determines when to show the correct buttons (such as Next, Previous, and Finish), and ensures that in the resulting page the values for the controls you added in the wizard steps are still available so you can show them in the results label. It does this with a concept called view state, something you'll learn more about towards the end of this chapter.

All you have to do is define the steps and set their `StepType`. The `StepType` of the first step was set to `Auto`. With this setting, the wizard figures out what buttons to show. Since it's the first step in the `Wizard`, it leaves out the Previous button, as there's no previous step to go to. You set the `StepType` of the second step to `Finish`, which tells the wizard to draw a Previous button and a Finish button. When you click the Finish button, the wizard arrives at the last step with its `StepType` set to `Complete`. On this step, the navigation buttons are hidden, and all you see is the label with the result, which was assigned with the code in the Code Behind of the page. In Chapter 5, you'll learn the concepts of the code in the Code Behind that make this possible.

Besides the controls you have seen in the previous chapter there are a few other controls worth examining. Not all of them are discussed here in detail as they aren't used any further in this book. Consult the MSDN documentation that comes with VWD for a detailed description of these controls.

Other Standard Controls

This section briefly discusses the remainder of the controls in the Standard category of the Toolbox. You'll see many of them used in the sample application in the rest of the book.

LinkButton and ImageButton

The `LinkButton` and the `ImageButton` controls operate similarly to an ordinary `Button` control. Both of them cause a postback to the server when they are clicked. The `LinkButton` presents itself as a simple `<a>` element but posts back instead of requesting a new page. The `ImageButton` does the same, but displays an image that the user can click to trigger the postback.

Image and ImageMap

These controls are pretty similar in that they display an image in the browser. The `ImageMap` allows you to define *hotspots* on the image that when clicked either cause a postback to the server or navigate to a different page.

Calendar

The `Calendar` control presents a rich interface that allows a user to select a date. You'll see more of it toward the end of this chapter when the ASP.NET state engine is discussed.

FileUpload

The `FileUpload` control allows a user to upload files that can be stored on the server. You'll see more of this control later in this book.

Literal, Localize, and Substitute

All three controls look a little like the `Label` control as they can all display static text or HTML. The biggest advantage of the `Literal` is that it renders no additional tag itself; it only displays what you assign to its `Text` property and is thus very useful to display HTML or JavaScript that you build up in the Code Behind or that you retrieve from a database.

The `Localize` control is used in multilingual web sites and is able to retrieve its contents from translated resource files. The `Substitute` control is used in advanced caching scenarios and allows you to update only parts of a page that is otherwise cached completely.

Both of these controls fall outside the scope of this book, but for a good discussion of them you may want to get a copy of Wrox's *Professional ASP.NET 3.5: In C# and VB* (ISBN: 978-0-470-18757-9).

AdRotator

This control allows you to display random advertisements on your web site. The ads come from an XML file that you create on your server. Because it lacks advanced features like click tracking and logging that are required in most but the simplest scenarios, this control isn't used much in today's web sites.

HiddenField

The `HiddenField` control enables you to store data in the page that is submitted with each request. This is useful if you want the page to remember specific data without the user seeing it in the page. Because the field does show up in the HTML source of the page and is thus accessible to the end user, you should never store any sensitive data in it.

XML

The `XML` control allows you to transform data from the XML format to another format (like XHTML) for display on a page. Check out *Professional ASP.NET 3.5* for a detailed description.

Table

The `<asp:Table>` control is in many respects identical to its HTML `<table>` counterpart. However, since the control lives at the server, you can program against it, dynamically creating new columns and rows and adding dynamic data to it.

This concludes the discussion of the controls in the Standard category of the Toolbox. In most web pages, you'll be working with at least a few of these controls. The remainder of this section discusses the other categories of the toolbox. Since most of them are used in some form in the remainder of this book, this chapter just briefly describes their purpose so you get a rough idea what they are used for. You'll find cross-references to the other chapters to find out more information about them.

HTML Controls

The HTML category contains a number of HTML controls that look similar to the ones found in the Standard category. For example, you find the `Input (Button)` that looks like the `<asp:Button>`. Similarly, there is a `Select` control that has the `<asp:DropDownList>` and `<asp:ListBox>` as its counterparts.

In contrast to the ASP.NET Server Controls, the HTML controls are client-side controls and end up directly in the final HTML in the browser. You can expose them to server-side code by adding a `Runat="Server"` attribute to them. This allows you to program against them from the Code Behind of a Web Form, to influence things like their visibility.

The HTML controls have a lot less functionality than the ones in the Standard category. For example, the `Select` control lacks design-time support to add new items to the list with the ListItem Collection Editor. This forces you to write the items by hand in the Markup View of VWD.

Since the controls in the Standard and HTML category look quite like each other, the next section discusses their differences and gives you some idea when to favor one category over the other.

How to Choose between Standard and HTML Controls

There seems to be some overlap between the controls on the Standard and HTML categories of the Toolbox. So which ones should you choose and when? Generally, the true server controls in the Standard category offer you a lot more functionality, both in terms of design-time support in VWD and what they can do at runtime. But this functionality comes with a price. Because of their increased complexity, the server controls take a little more time to process. However, on most web sites you probably won't notice the difference. Only when you have a high-traffic web site with lots of controls on the page, the HTML controls give you a slightly better performance and consume less memory on the server when compared to the server controls.

In most scenarios, favor the server controls over their HTML counterparts. Because server controls offer more functionality, they give you more flexibility in your pages, allowing you to create a richer user experience. Also the better design-time support makes it worth choosing these controls.

Choose the HTML controls if you're really sure that you don't need the functionality that the server controls offer you.

The remainder of this section quickly guides you through the other categories in the Toolbox.

Data Controls

Data controls were introduced in ASP.NET 2.0, and offer a very easy way to access various data sources like databases, XML files, and objects. Instead of writing lots of code to access the data source as you had to do in earlier versions of ASP.NET, you simply point your data control to an appropriate data source, and the ASP.NET runtime takes care of most of the difficult issues for you. You'll see a lot more about these controls in the data-oriented chapters, starting with Chapter 12.

Validation Controls

Validation controls enable you to rapidly create Web Forms with validation that prohibit users from entering invalid data. For example, you can force users to enter values for required fields and check whether the entered data matches a specific format like a valid date or a number between 1 and 10. They even allow you to write custom code to create validation routines that are not covered by the standard controls. The beauty of the validation controls is that they can execute both on the client and the server, enabling you to create responsive and secure web applications. Chapter 9 digs much deeper into these controls.

Navigation Controls

The controls you find under the Navigation category of the Toolbox are used to let a user find their way through your site. The `TreeView` control presents a hierarchical display of data and can be used to show the structure of your site, giving easy access to all the pages in the site. The `Menu` control does a similar thing and provides options for horizontal and vertical fold-out menus.

The `SiteMapPath` control creates a "bread crumb trail" in your web pages that allows your users to easily find their way up in the hierarchy of pages in your site.

You'll see all of these controls in action in Chapter 7, which deals with navigation in web sites exclusively.

Login Controls

Just as the Data controls, the login controls were introduced in ASP.NET 2.0 and made it into ASP.NET 3.5. With very little effort, login controls enable you to create secure web sites where users need to sign up and log in before they can access specific parts of the web site (or even the entire web site). In addition, they provide the tools for users to change their password, or request a new password if they forget the old password, and allow you to display different data depending on the logged in status and role of the user. Chapter 15 provides more details about the security features and login controls of ASP.NET.

Ajax Extensions

More than a year after the official release of ASP.NET 2.0 in November 2005, Microsoft released the ASP.NET 2.0 Ajax Extensions 1.0 as an add-on for ASP.NET 2.0. These extensions enable you to create flicker-free web applications that are able to retrieve data from the server from client-side JavaScript without a full postback. Ever since Ajax became a hot technology in 2005, Microsoft has been working hard to get at the top of the Ajax implementers. The latest release of VWD is no exception: Ajax has now been fully integrated in the .NET Framework and the VWD IDE, giving you easy access to its rich feature set. Chapter 10 focuses on Ajax.

WebParts

ASP.NET WebParts are a set of controls that allows an end user of a web page to change the appearance and behavior of a web site. With a few simple actions, users can change the entire appearance of a web site by rearranging content, hiding or showing parts of the web page, and adding other content fragments to the page. The ASP.NET WebParts are outside the scope of this book as they deserve an entire book. If you want to learn more about WebParts, check out *Professional Web Parts and Custom Controls with ASP.NET 2.0* by Peter Vogel (ISBN: 978-0-7645-7860-1). Although the book is targeted at ASP.NET 2.0, you'll find that many of the concepts presented in the book still apply to ASP.NET 3.5.

Now that you have seen the large control set included with ASP.NET 3.5, there is another important topic you need to look at: the ASP.NET state engine. Although the behavior of some of the controls you have seen may appear to be pure magic, there is actually a technical and rational mechanism behind their functionality. The following section digs into the world of the ASP.NET state engine, explaining what it is, what view state is, how it works, and how you can put it to use.

The ASP.NET State Engine

In the previous chapter, you created a page with a `TextBox` and a `Button` control. In the Try It Out, you ran this page in the browser, typed some text, and clicked the button. The button caused a postback to the server, and when the page reloaded, the text was still present in the text box. You pretty much did the same thing with the `Wizard` control in this chapter, where the values from the text box and the drop-down list were maintained as well. If you're familiar with other web technologies like ASP or PHP, this probably surprised you. In those languages, you often need to write lots of code to make this happen. So why and how does this work automatically in ASP.NET?

The text in the text box is maintained by the ASP.NET state engine, a feature that is deeply integrated in the ASP.NET runtime. It enables controls to maintain their state across postbacks so their values and settings remain available after every postback of the page.

What Is State and Why Is It Important?

To understand state, it's important to realize that by design, HTTP — the protocol used to request and serve pages in a web browser — is *stateless*. What this means is that the web server does not keep track of requests that have been made from a specific browser. As far as the web server is concerned, each request you make to the server by browsing to a page and clicking links to other pages stands on its own. The web server has no recollection of pages you requested previously.

This poses some interesting problems. Consider, for example, a simple login page that allows you to log in to a web site, like your favorite web mail program. You can see a sample of the login box in Figure 4-14.

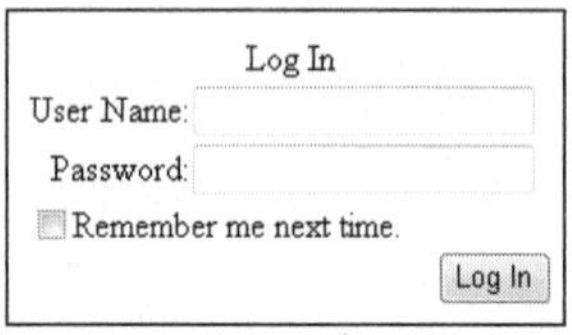

Log In
User Name:
Password:
Remember me next time.
Log In

Figure 4-14

Now imagine that you try to log in with a correct user name but with an incorrect password. The page will then inform you that your login attempt failed. Ideally, you would also want your user name to be filled in for you automatically, and you'd want the Remember me next time check box to retain its selection as well. That way, it's easy for the user to enter the correct password and click the Log In button again. This is just a trivial example but it's easy to come up with many more scenarios where it's useful if controls were able to maintain their own state.

However, by default, a web page or a control cannot do this on its own. Since each request is a standalone request, the server won't fill in the text boxes again after a postback, but will simply serve the page the same way it did when it first loaded it. In other web technologies, like classic ASP or PHP, you could work around this by manually writing code that prepopulates controls after a postback. Fortunately, ASP.NET makes this much easier for you by integrating this functionality in the ASP.NET feature set.

How the State Engine Works

The state engine in ASP.NET is capable of storing state for many controls. It can store state not only for user input controls like a `TextBox` and a `CheckBox` but for other controls like a `Label` and even a `Calendar`. This is best demonstrated by a demo. The following exercise shows you how to create a page with controls that are capable of maintaining their state. The sections that follow then explain how ASP.NET is able to do this.

Try It Out Examining the ASP.NET State Engine

In this exercise you'll add `Label`, `Button`, and `Calendar` controls to the page. These controls are used to demonstrate some of the inner workings of ASP.NET, including postbacks and the way ASP.NET maintains state.

1. Under the Demos folder, create a new page called State.aspx. Make sure it uses Code Behind, and don't forget to choose your preferred programming language from the drop-down list.
2. Switch the page to Design View, click inside the dashed `<div>` to put the focus on it, and then add a table with two rows and two columns by choosing Table ➪ Insert Table from the main menu.
3. In the first cell of the first row, drag a `Label` control from the Toolbox. In the first cell of the second row, drag a `Calendar` control. If you ordered the Toolbox alphabetically in an earlier Try It Out, the `Calendar` is the fourth control in the Standard category of the Toolbox. Otherwise, you'll find the calendar about two-thirds down in the Standard category.
4. Note that as soon as you drop the calendar in the cell, the Smart Tasks panel for the Calendar pops up as shown in Figure 4-15.

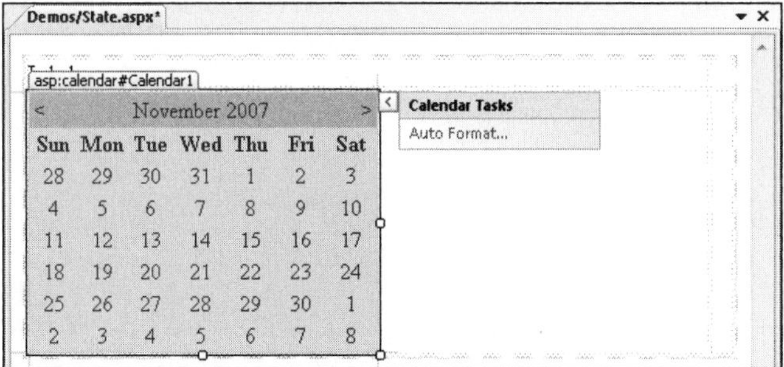

Figure 4-15

In the case of the `Calendar`, you only get one option on this panel, Auto Format, which allows you to change the appearance of the calendar. Click the link, choose from one of the predefined color schemes like Simple, and click OK.

5. Next, drag a `Button` control into each of the two cells of the right column of the table.

6. Click the `Button` in the first row and then press F4 to open the Properties Grid. Set the `Button`'s `ID` to `btnSetDate` and set its `Text` property to `Set Date`. You'll find the `ID` property all the way at the end of the list with properties or at the beginning if you have the list with properties sorted alphabetically.

7. Repeat the previous step for the other button but call it `btnPlainPostBack` and set its `Text` property to `Plain PostBack`. When you're done, the page should look like Figure 4-16 in Design View.

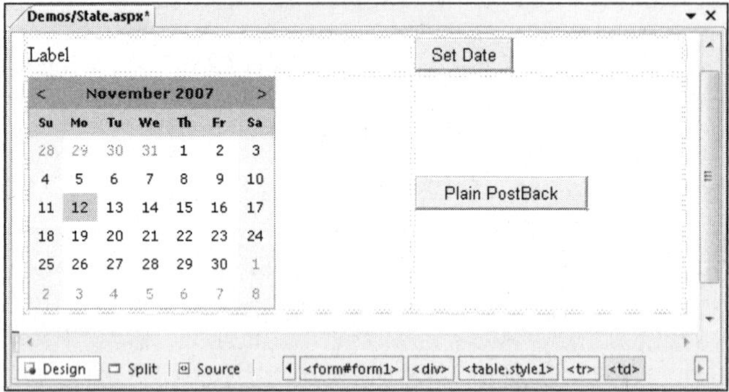

Figure 4-16

8. Double-click the Set Date button in Design View and add the following code on the empty line between the code lines that VWD inserted for you:

VB.NET

```
Protected Sub btnSetDate_Click(ByVal sender As Object, ByVal e As System.EventArgs) _
        Handles btnSetDate.Click
  Label1.Text = DateTime.Now.ToString()
End Sub
```

C#

```
protected void btnSetDate_Click(object sender, EventArgs e)
{
  Label1.Text = DateTime.Now.ToString();
}
```

9. Open the page in the browser by pressing Ctrl+F5. Select a date on the calendar by clicking one of the days. Notice that as soon as you click the date, the page seems to reload, caused by a post-back. You'll learn more about this in the How It Works section that follows this exercise.

10. Click the Set Date button a few times. Again, the page is posted back to the server and the `Label` is updated with today's date and time each time you click the button. Wait a few seconds, and then click the Plain PostBack button. Once again, a postback occurs and then the page reloads.

Now take a look at the text for the `Label`. It still contains the date and time that was displayed when you last clicked the Set Date button. Click the Plain PostBack button a few more times and notice that the `Label` doesn't change.

11. Go back to VWD and open the Properties Grid for the `Label` control in Design View. Locate the `EnableViewState` property and set it to `false` by selecting that value from the drop-down list.

12. Repeat steps 9 and 10 by reopening the page in the browser, and clicking the calendar and the buttons. This time when you click the Plain PostBack button, you'll see that the `Label` control defaults to its initial text: `Label`.

How It Works

To understand how this all works, there are a few important elements to look at. First, open up the page in the browser again and then view its HTML source. You can do this by right-clicking the page in the browser and then choosing the View Source or View Page Source menu item. Near the top of the window, you see the following `<form>` element:

```
<form name="form1" method="post" action="State.aspx" id="form1">
...
</form>
```

The HTML `<form>` element is used to allow a user to submit information from the browser to the server. A user can enter information using controls like text boxes, drop-down lists, check boxes, and so on. A form can be submitted in two ways: with `POST` (as shown in the previous `<form>` element) or with `GET`. In the former case, all data from the form is added to the body of the request and then sent to the server. In case of the `GET` method, all the data is appended to the actual address of the request. The intricacies of the differences are not that important right now; what's important to understand is what the `<form>` element is used for: it encapsulates form controls whose values are submitted back to the server en masse.

When a control like a `Button` is clicked, it causes a *postback* to the server. During this postback, all the relevant information in the form is submitted back to the server where it can be used to rebuild the page.

By default, all your ASP.NET Web Forms always use a `POST` method to send data to the server. Also, by default, an entire ASP.NET page always contains exactly one form. Since this is so common, and that is required for ASP.NET to operate correctly, a new page created in VWD already contains the `<form>` element so you don't have to add it yourself. Finally, it's important to understand that an ASP.NET Web Form by default always submits back to itself. In other web environments like classic ASP and PHP, it's not uncommon to set the action attribute of the page to a second page that then processes the data the user has submitted. However, with an ASP.NET page, you'll find that even if you set the action attribute in code explicitly, the ASP.NET runtime will revert it to the name of the current page.

The next thing to look at is the hidden `ViewState` field that you see in the HTML source highlighted in the following snippet:

```
<form name="form1" method="post" action="State.aspx" id="form1">
...
  <input type="hidden" name="__VIEWSTATE" id="__VIEWSTATE"
         value="/wEPDwULLTE5Njc4MzkzNDdkZI+lOWZMZpVv0hc7i/HFGMdOO8oc" />
</div>
```

Although at first the text appears to contain nothing more than random characters, it actually contains useful information. To protect the information stored in this field, and to decrease the size of it, ASP.NET has converted the page state in the string you see above. If you were able to look inside the value of the fields, you'd find a value for the `Label1` control with the current date and time.

When your ASP.NET page loads, the ASP.NET runtime fills this hidden field with information about the page. For example, it added the value for the `Text` property of the `Label1` control when you caused a postback by clicking the Set Date button. Similarly, it contains the selected date for the Calendar. When the page is then submitted back by a postback, the value in this hidden field is sent with the request. Then, when ASP.NET creates the new page on the server, the information from the `ViewState` field is read and applied to the controls. This way, a control like the `Label` is able to maintain its text even after the page has been posted back to the server.

To reiterate, here's a rundown of the process that took place in the previous Try It Out.

1. You requested the page in the browser by opening it from within VWD.
2. The browser got the page from the server by making a request for it.
3. The ASP.NET runtime read the page file from disk, processed it, and sent the resulting HTML to the browser. At this stage, all the controls were set to their default values that were defined in the markup of the page. For example, the `Text` of the `Label` control is set to Label.
4. When the page is displayed in the browser, you click the Set Date button. This causes a postback to the server.
5. At the server, the page is reconstructed again, similar to the first time it loads, described in step 3. At this stage, all the controls contain their default values. So, again, the `Label1` control has its `Text` property set to Label. Shortly after the defaults have been set, the runtime overrides these defaults for controls it finds in `ViewState`. However, since this is the first postback and the `Label` control's `Text` property hasn't changed yet, its value is not present in `ViewState` so the `Text` property just contains the default word Label.
6. While still processing the same request, the ASP.NET runtime fired the code in `btnSetDate_Click`. As you have seen, this code changed the `Text` property of the `Label` control to the current date and time. The ASP.NET runtime sees this change and stores this new value in `ViewState` as well, so it stays available for subsequent postbacks.
7. Next, you clicked the Plain PostBack button. Just as with the other button, this causes a postback to occur. The page is constructed again, and all defaults are set. Again, this means that the `Text` property of `Label1` control simply contains the word Label. However, shortly after that, during the same processing cycle, the ASP.NET runtime processes the view state, restoring controls it finds in the hidden `ViewState` field. In this example, it finds the `Text` property with the current date and time, and assigns it again to the `Label` control. Since the Plain PostBack button doesn't change the `Text` of the `Label` anymore, the `Text` property doesn't change: it contains the date and time from the previous postback. At the end, the entire page is sent to the browser, where the label correctly displays its previous value.
8. Finally, you turned off the `ViewState` for the `Label` control by setting `EnableViewState` to `false`. With this setting turned off, the ASP.NET runtime doesn't track the `Label` control anymore. So when you click the Plain PostBack button, the ASP.NET runtime doesn't find any information for the label in `ViewState`, which eventually results in the label displaying its own default text of the word Label.

Not All Controls Rely on ViewState

You have to understand that not all controls rely on view state all the time. There are a number of controls that are able to maintain their own state. These controls include the `TextBox`, `CheckBox`, `RadioButton`, and `DropDownList` controls. They are able to maintain their value, as they are rendered as standard HTML form controls in the browser. For example, a `TextBox` server control looks like this in the browser:

```
<input name="TextBox1" type="text" value="Initial Text" id="TextBox1" />
```

When a page with such a `TextBox` in it is posted back, the browser also sends the value of the control back to the server. The ASP.NET runtime can then simply look at that value to prepopulate the text box again, instead of getting the value from `ViewState`. Obviously, this is more efficient than storing the value in `ViewState` too. If that were the case, the value would get sent to the server twice: once in the text box, and once in `ViewState`. Especially with large values, this could quickly increase the page's size and thus its load time.

A Note About ViewState and Performance

Since the `ViewState` engine adds a considerable amount of information to the page, it's often a good idea to turn it off when you don't need it. This way, you can minimize the size of the hidden `ViewState` field, which means the page becomes smaller and thus loads faster in the browser. Turning off `ViewState` is easy, and can be done:

- **At the web site level.** You can do this in the web.config file by modifying the `<pages>` element, setting the `enableViewState` attribute to `false`:

```
<pages enableViewState="false">
  ...
</pages>
```

  This option is usually not recommended as it can severely impact the functionality of your site, breaking pages that reply on `ViewState`.

- **At the page level.** At the top of each page you find the page directive, a series of instructions that tell the ASP.NET runtime how the page should behave. In the page directive, you can set `EnableViewState` to `false`:

```
<%@ Page Language="VB" AutoEventWireup="false" CodeFile="State.aspx.vb"
           Inherits="Demos_State" EnableViewState="false" %>
```

  This option is useful for pages where you're sure you don't need `ViewState` at all.

- **At the control level.** Each ASP.NET Server Control allows you to set `EnableViewState` individually, giving you the option to turn it off for some controls, while leaving it on for others. Note that even if you set `EnableViewState` to `true` for some controls, if you have turned it off at the page level or the web site level, it remains turned off.

Considering the flexibility the last option gives you, it's recommended to use that most of the time. To create well-performing web pages, you should disable `ViewState` by default on each control whenever possible, and only enable it when you really need it. Later chapters in this book will revisit the `ViewState` of controls.

Practical Tips on Working with Controls

The following list presents some practical tips on working with controls.

- Spend some time trying out all the different controls. Although many of them are used and discussed throughout the book, it's good to know how you should use them and how they operate. By experimenting with them now in a few sample pages, you have a head start when the controls reappear in later chapters. Because of the complexity, ignore the controls in the categories other than the Standard one. For these controls, you'll need more background information that you'll be given throughout the remainder of this book.
- Seriously consider turning off `ViewState` for some of your controls. In many cases, you hardly notice the difference, but especially with the data-driven controls discussed in Chapter 12 and onward, disabling `ViewState` can seriously decrease the size of your web page, resulting in shorter load times and improved user experience.
- Before you design a complex Web Form with multiple controls to accept user input, step back from your computer and take a piece of paper and a pen to draw out the required functionality. By thinking about the (technical) design of your application before you start dragging and dropping or coding, it's much easier to create a consistent and well-thought-out user interface. Making considerable changes later in the page if you've taken a wrong route will always take more time than doing it (almost) right the first time.
- Experiment with the `ViewState` mechanism to get a better understanding of how it works. Create a couple of pages similar to the one you created in the last chapter. Then turn off `ViewState` at the page or control level and see how the page behaves. Take note of the controls, such as `TextBox`, that are capable of maintaining their value even with `ViewState` off.

Summary

This chapter gives you a good look at the large set of ASP.NET Server Controls. Since these controls are so important and used throughout every ASP.NET application, it's really critical that you understand what controls you have available in the Toolbox and what they are used for.

Many of the server controls share a large feature set. This makes it easy to understand new controls once you understand the basic set of rules and behaviors. This way, you can quickly familiarize yourself with third-party controls that you can download from the Internet as a ready-to-be-used component or as raw source.

Since server controls live at the server, you have to specify them in your ASP.NET pages with a `Runat` attribute set to `Server`. This way, the ASP.NET runtime knows how to deal with the control. During the processing of an ASP.NET page, the runtime asks each control for its HTML. The combined HTML for all controls in the page is eventually sent to the browser, where it's used to build up the user interface that the visitor sees.

Because there are so many ASP.NET Server Controls, they are logically grouped together in different categories in the Toolbox of VWD. The Standard category of the Toolbox contains the controls you're likely to use most. This category includes common controls like `Button`, `DropDownList`, `Label`, and `HyperLink`. With these controls, you can rapidly create fully functional Web Forms that allow a user to enter data in many different ways that can be submitted to the server where it can be processed further.

One of the biggest inventions in ASP.NET is the state engine that allows controls to maintain their state across postbacks. The state engine is a real time saver and frees you from writing loads of tedious and boring code in every single web page to replicate this behavior. Because of the state engine, controls like the `<asp:Wizard>` are a breeze to use. Just drag them on a page, define a number of wizard steps, and add controls to them and the ASP.NET runtime takes care of the rest. Obviously, this applies to all controls and not only to the `Wizard`.

This functionality comes with a price, however. Since all controls record their state in the hidden `ViewState` field, your page quickly increases in size. If you're not careful, you can easily create pages that are slow to load and consume more processing power of the web server than you want. Fortunately, it's easy to control the way `ViewState` is used. Of the three options to disable `ViewState` (at the application, page, or control level) the control-level option is usually your best bet. By disabling `ViewState` at the control level, you can determine precisely which controls attribute to `ViewState` and which controls don't, enabling you to turn it off for controls that don't really need it.

This chapter also introduced you to some server-side code in Visual Basic .NET and in C#. Because the examples were rather trivial, you were probably able to understand the code presented in this chapter pretty well. The next chapter will give you a much better understanding of programming in ASP.NET pages. You'll see how a programming language looks, what elements it contains, and how to write code yourself to use in your ASP.NET pages. And best of all, the examples are presented in Visual Basic .NET and C#, so you're not stuck with a language you may not like.

Exercises

1. Name the mechanism that enables server controls to maintain their state.
2. How is the ASP.NET runtime able to keep track of control state between postbacks?
3. Name a difference between an `<asp:DropDownList>` and an `<asp:ListBox>`.
4. What property do you need to cause a postback to the server when you change the checked state of a `CheckBox` in the browser?
5. Many server controls have a common set of properties that affects their looks at runtime. Name three properties that change styling elements such as color, borders, and size.
6. Instead of setting individual control properties like `BackColor` and `ForeColor`, it's better to set a single CSS-related property. What's the name of this property and what benefit does it give you?

5

Programming Your ASP.NET Web Pages

In the previous chapters, you created a number of Web Forms that contained mostly ASP.NET Server Controls and plain HTML. Only a few of the examples contained actual programming code, written in either C# or Visual Basic .NET (VB.NET), and most of that code was pretty straightforward. However, coding is an important part of any web site. Although the many smart server controls you have at your disposal minimize the amount of code you need to write compared to the older 1.*x* family of the .NET Framework or other web technologies like classic ASP or PHP, being able to read, understand, and write code is a critical asset in your web development toolkit.

This chapter teaches you the basics and beyond of programming for web applications. In particular, this chapter looks at:

- How to work with objects and collections in a programming environment
- Different ways to make decisions in your code
- The options available for creating repetitive blocks of functionality
- Different ways to write well-organized and documented code
- What object orientation is, and how you can use it in your applications

Best of all, just as with all the other samples in the book, this entire chapter covers both VB.NET and C# examples. For every concept or piece of theory introduced in this chapter, you see an example in both VB.NET and C# at the same time. The choice of your preferred language is really up to you.

To get the most out of this chapter, it's recommended to actually try out most of the code examples presented in this chapter. Reading and understanding code is one thing; actually seeing it at work is completely different. Most of the examples can be tested with a simple ASPX page. Drag a `Label` and a `Button` on your page, double-click the `Button` in Design View, and then type the relevant code on the open line of the code block that Visual Web Developer added for you.

Note that some of the examples call fictitious code that won't run correctly. They only serve to illustrate the topic being discussed.

Introduction to Programming

To get started with programming, it's critical to understand a common set of terminology shared by programmers in all types of languages and applications. The remainder of this chapter introduces you to a relatively large number of terms and concepts. Most of the terminology comes with code examples so you can see how they are used in real code.

It's also important to realize this is not a complete introduction to programming. Not every detail of a programming language is covered. Instead, this chapter focuses on the key concepts that you need to understand to successfully build day to day web sites. Once you get the hang of that you'll find it's easier to deepen your knowledge about programming by learning the more exotic features of your favorite programming language.

> *If you're interested in learning a lot more about programming VB.NET or C#, find* Beginning Microsoft Visual Basic 2008 *or* Beginning Microsoft Visual C# 2008, *both published by Wrox.*

The code you are going to write in this and coming chapters is either added to the Code Behind of a web page, or in a separate *class file* placed in the App_Code folder, which is discussed later in the chapter. When the ASP.NET runtime processes the request for a page containing code, it *compiles* any code it finds in the page, Code Behind, or class file first. When code is compiled, it is being transformed from a human readable programming language (like C# or VB.NET) into something that the computer can understand and is able to execute. The result of the compilation process of an ASP.NET web site is one or more files with a DLL extension in a temporary folder on your system. This compilation process only takes place the first time the page is requested after it has been changed. Subsequent requests to the same page result in the same DLL being reused for the request. Fortunately, in ASP.NET web sites, compilation takes place behind the scenes, so you usually don't have to worry about it.

The first concepts that you need to look at are data types and variables, as they are the building blocks of any programming language. Every .NET application makes use of a set of data types, which are often stored in variables. What these are is discussed in the next section.

Data Types and Variables

At first when you think about data, you may not realize that each piece of data has a data type. You may think that a computer would store the words *Hello World* in exactly the same way as today's date or the number 6. However, to be able to effectively work with data, many programming languages have different *data types*, where each data type is constrained to a specific type of information. Out of the box, the .NET Framework comes with a long list of data types that allows you to work with numbers (like `Integer`, `Short`, and `Double`), text strings (`Char` and `String`), dates (`DateTime`), true/false constructs (the `Boolean`), and more. A list with the most common types is described later in this section.

For each major type of data there is a special data type. To work with that type, you can store it in a *variable* that you need to *declare* first using the required data type. In VB.NET you use `Dim` *`myVariable`* `As`

DataType while in C# you use *DataType myVariable*. The following example shows you how to declare two variables: an `Integer` (`int` in C#) to hold a number and a `String` (`string` in C#) to hold a piece of text:

VB.NET

```
' Declare a variable of type Integer to hold medium sized whole numbers.
Dim distanceInMiles As Integer

' Declare a variable to hold some text like a first name.
Dim firstName As String
```

C#

```
// Declare a variable of type int to hold medium sized whole numbers.
int distanceInMiles;

// Declare a variable to hold some text like a first name.
string firstName;
```

After you have declared a variable, you can assign it a value. You can assign types like numbers and Booleans directly to a variable. To assign a `String` to a variable you need to enclose it in double quotes:

VB.NET

```
Dim distanceInMiles As Integer
distanceInMiles = 437

Dim firstName As String
firstName = "Imar"
```

C#

```
int distanceInMiles;
distanceInMiles = 437;

string firstName;
firstName = "Imar";
```

In addition to a single declaration, you can also declare and directly assign a value to the newly created variable in one fell swoop:

VB.NET

```
Dim distanceInMiles As Integer = 437
```

C#

```
int distanceInMiles = 437;
```

Although a variable name can be about anything you like, it's advised to give each variable a meaningful name that describes its purpose. For example, a string to hold a first name would be called `firstName` whereas a variable that holds someone's age would simply be called `age`. To help you find the type of the variable later in the code, VWD and all other products in Visual Studio show a useful tooltip when you hover over a variable in the code editor, making it super easy to find a variable's type. Figure 5-1 shows that the `distanceInMiles` variable in the C# example is of type `int`.

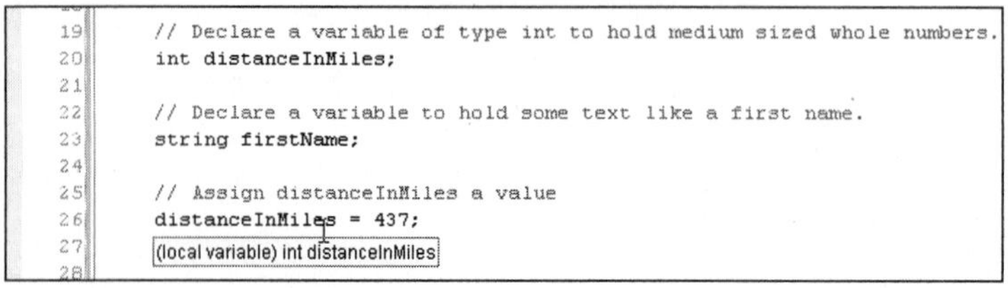

```
// Declare a variable of type int to hold medium sized whole numbers.
int distanceInMiles;

// Declare a variable to hold some text like a first name.
string firstName;

// Assign distanceInMiles a value
distanceInMiles = 437;
(local variable) int distanceInMiles
```

Figure 5-1

You're advised not to prefix your variables with a few letters to indicate the type. For example, write `firstName` and not `sFirstName` for a `String` holding someone's name. This type of notation, called *Hungarian Notation*, is considered outdated. IDEs like VWD, with their smart IntelliSense and other programming tools, don't really require this anymore. Without Hungarian Notation, your code becomes easier to read (`age` is more readable than `iAge`) and easier to maintain as you can change a variable's type without renaming it everywhere it's used.

Microsoft .NET (and thus the ASP.NET environment) supports a large number of different programming languages, including VB.NET, C#, and others. All these languages are able to communicate with each other. For example, you can write some code in C#, use Visual C# Express Edition to compile it to a .dll file (a file with reusable code that can be consumed in other .NET applications), and then use it in a web application that uses VB.NET as the primary language. Because of this interoperability, it's necessary to agree on some system that allows all .NET programming languages to understand each other. This system is called the *Common Type System* (CTS). It's the CTS that defines the data types that are accessible to all CTS-compliant languages. Each language is then free to define a set of *primitive types*, which are essentially shortcuts or aliases for the more complex type description in the .NET Framework. So, even if the CTS defines a type called `System.Int32`, a language like C# is free to alias this type as `int` to make it easier for a developer to work with it.

The following table lists the most common CTS types in the .NET Framework and their C# and VB.NET aliases. The table also lists the range of the variables and what they are used for.

.NET	C#	VB.NET	Description
System.Byte	byte	Byte	Used to store small, positive whole numbers from 0 to 255. Defaults to 0 when no value is assigned explicitly.
System.Int16	short	Short	Capable of storing whole numbers between –32,768 and 32,767. Defaults to 0.
System.Int32	int	Integer	Capable of storing whole numbers between –2,147,483,648 and 2,147,483,647. Defaults to 0.

.NET	C#	VB.NET	Description
System.Int64	long	Long	Holds large numbers between –9,223,372,036,854,775,808 and 9,223,372,036,854,775,807. Defaults to 0.
System.Single	float	Single	Stores large numbers with decimals between –3.4028235E+38 and 3.4028235E+38. Defaults to 0.0.
System.Double	double	Double	Can hold large fractional numbers. It's not as accurate as the Decimal when it comes to the fractional numbers but when extreme accuracy is not a requirement, you should prefer the Double over the Decimal, as Double is a little faster. Defaults to 0.0.
System.Decimal	decimal	Decimal	Stores extremely large fractional numbers with a high accuracy. Defaults to 0.
System.Boolean	bool	Boolean	Used to hold a simple boolean value: either True (in VB), true (in C#), False (in VB) or false (in C#). Defaults to False.
System.DateTime	n/a	Date	VB.NET has an alias for the System.DateTime data type to store date and time values. C# doesn't define an alias for this type, so you just use System.DateTime. Defaults to 1/1/0001: 12:00 am.
System.Char	char	Char	Holds a single character. Defaults to Nothing (null in C#).
System.String	string	String	Can hold text with a length of up to 2 billion characters. Defaults to Nothing (null in C#).
System.SByte	sbyte	SByte	Used to store small numbers from –128 to 127. Defaults to 0.
System.UInt16	ushort	UShort	Similar to a System.Int16, but this data type can only store unsigned whole numbers, between 0 and 65,535. Defaults to 0. The other data types prefixed with a U are all unsigned as well.
System.UInt32	uint	UInteger	Capable of storing whole numbers between 0 and 4,294,967,295. Defaults to 0.
System.UInt64	ulong	ULong	Capable of storing whole numbers between 0 and 18,446,744,073,709,551,615. Defaults to 0.
System.Object	object	Object	The parent of all data types in .NET, including the CTS types and types you may define yourself. Each data type is also an object as you'll learn later in the book. Defaults to Nothing (null in C#).

Sometimes you need to convert data from one type to another. For example, you may have an `Integer` from some source that you need to treat as a `Double`. You can do this in a number of different ways.

Converting Data Types

The most common way to convert a type is converting it into a `String`. Web applications use string types everywhere. For example, the `Text` returned from a `TextBox` is a `String`, and so is the `SelectedValue` of a `DropDownList`. To convert an `Object` to a `String`, you can simply call its `ToString()` method. Every object in the .NET world supports this method, although the exact behavior may differ from object to object. For now, it's important to understand that `ToString()` is a *method* — or an operation — on an object, like a `String` or a `Double` and even the parent `Object` itself. You'll learn more about methods and objects later in this chapter when *object-oriented programming* is discussed.

Using `ToString()` is easy, as the following example that outputs today's date and time on a Label demonstrates:

> *Remember, to try out the code examples simply create a new page in the Demos folder, add a* `Label` *and a* `Button` *to the page, double-click the button in Design View, add the following code, and then hit Ctrl+F5. After the page has finished loading, click the button and the code will be executed. You need the* `Label` *control as some code samples output some text to the page.*

VB.NET

```
Label1.Text = System.DateTime.Now.ToString()
```

C#

```
Label1.Text = System.DateTime.Now.ToString();
```

Another way to convert data types is using the `Convert` class. This class contains functionality to convert a lot of data types into another type. The following example shows a simple example of converting a `String` containing a value that looks like a Boolean into a true `Boolean` type:

VB.NET

```
Dim myBoolean1 As Boolean = Convert.ToBoolean("True")         ' Results in True
Dim myBoolean2 As Boolean = Convert.ToBoolean("False")        ' Results in False
```

C#

```
bool myBoolean1 = Convert.ToBoolean("True");                 // Results in true
bool myBoolean2 = Convert.ToBoolean("False");                // Results in false
```

Another way to convert one type into another is by using *casting*. With casting you actually force one type into another, which is different from converting, in which the underlying value of a data type is transformed into a new value.

Casting only works for compatible types. You can't, for example, cast a `DateTime` into an `Integer`. You can, however, cast similar types, like a `Double` to an `Integer` or a `String` to an `Object`. The reverse of the latter example isn't always true. Earlier I said that every data type in the .NET Framework is based on the `Object` data type. That means that, for example, a `String` is an `Object`. However, not every `Object` is also a `String`. When you try to cast one type into another and get a compilation error, keep this in mind. Later chapters in this book will show you how to cast compatible types into each other.

To cast one type into another using VB.NET, you have a few options. First, you can use `CType` and `DirectCast`. `CType` is a bit more flexible in that it allows you to cast between two objects that look similar. `DirectCast`, on the other hand, only allows you to convert between compatible types but performs slightly faster. The following VB.NET example shows how this works:

```
Dim o1 As Object = 1
Dim i1 As Integer = DirectCast(o1, Integer)       ' Works, because o1 is an Integer
Dim i2 As Integer = CType(o1, Integer)            ' Works, because o1 is an Integer

Dim o2 As Double = 1
Dim i3 As Integer = DirectCast(o2, Integer)       ' Fails, because o2 is not an Integer
Dim i4 As Integer = CType(o2, Integer)            ' Works, because 02 looks like an Integer
```

In the first part of the example, an object called `o1` is declared and assigned the `Integer` value of `1`. Although `o1` exposes itself to the outside world as an `Object`, its underlying value is still an `Integer`. When `DirectCast` is called, the cast succeeds because `o1` is, under the hood, an `Integer`.

In the second example, `o2` is declared as a `Double`, a numeric type that looks somewhat like an `Integer`, but isn't really one. Therefore, the call to `DirectCast` fails because a `Double` cannot be cast to an `Integer`. `CType` on the other hand works fine, because the underlying values of the variable `o2` *look* like an `Integer` and can therefore be casted to one.

The third option to cast in VB.NET is using the keyword `TryCast`, which is somewhat similar to the other two options. When an object cannot be casted correctly, `TryCast` returns `Nothing`, whereas `DirectCast` and `CType` result in a crash of the code.

In C# you have two options to cast objects. The most common way is to put the data type in parentheses in front of the expression you want to cast:

```
object o1 = 1;
int i1 = (int)o1;                        // Works

double o2 = 1;
int i2 = (int)o2;                        // Works
```

Alternatively, you can use the `as` keyword, which works similar to `TryCast` in VB.NET in that the code doesn't crash if the cast doesn't succeed. The following sample code shows that you cannot convert an `Integer` to an `ArrayList` (which you'll meet later in this chapter). Instead of crashing, the variable `myList` simply contains `null`.

```
object o1 = 1;
ArrayList myList = o1 as ArrayList;  // Doesn't convert, but doesn't crash either.
```

You'll see more about casting and converting in the remaining chapters in this book.

Using Arrays and Collections

So far the data types you have seen are relatively straightforward and singular objects. For example, you store a value of `True` or `False` in a `Boolean` type, and you store a number like `123` in an `Integer`. But what if you have the need to store lots of integers? You may have the need to do so if you want to store the points of a complex shape like a polygon. Or you may have the need to store all the roles that your application supports in a single variable so you can show them on a web page in the Management section for example. Here's where arrays and collections come to the rescue.

Defining and Working with Arrays

You can see an array as a big bag or list of the same type of things. You define the data type of the things in the array when you declare it. Each item in the array is identified by a sequential number (its so-called *index*) starting at 0, making arrays *zero-based*. When declaring and accessing an array in VB.NET you use parentheses, whereas in C# you use square brackets. After you have defined the array and populated its elements, you can access the elements by their zero-based element index (0, 1, 2, and so on).

The following code snippet defines an array called `roles` that can hold up to two roles at the same time:

VB.NET

```
Dim roles(1) As String
```

C#

```
string[] roles = new string[2];
```

See the difference between the VB.NET and C# examples? That's not a typo. In VB.NET you define an array's size by specifying the *upper bound*. The upper bound is the last element in the array that you can access. Since arrays are zero-based (that is, you address the first item in the array with an index of 0) it means that if you need room for two items, the upper bound is `1`, giving you the items `0` and `1`.

In C# on the other hand, you don't define the upper bound but instead you define the size. So in C#, you simply specify `2` to get an array with two elements.

Additionally, C# requires you to use the keyword `new`, which *instantiates* a new array for you. VB.NET does that for you automatically and raises an error if you add the `New` keyword as in the C# example. You'll see the `new` (`New` in VB) keyword again later in this chapter.

To enter the role names into the array you use the following syntax:

VB.NET

```
roles(0) = "Administrators"
roles(1) = "ContentManagers"
```

C#

```
roles[0] = "Administrators";
roles[1] = "ContentManagers";
```

Just as with the array's declaration, you use parentheses in VB.NET and square brackets in C# to address the elements in the array. Note that `roles[0]` refers to the first element in the array and `roles[1]` refers to the second.

By design, arrays have a fixed size. So, given the previous example that defines an array with room for two elements, the following code will throw an error:

VB.NET

```
roles(2) = "Members"      ' Throws an error
```

C#

```
roles[2] = "Members";     // Throws an error
```

This code tries to squeeze a third role into an array that has room for only two. Obviously, that doesn't fit and you'll get an error stating that the "Index was outside the bounds of the array." But what if you need to create more room in the array at a later stage in your code at runtime? In VB.NET this is pretty easy. You can use the `ReDim` statement:

```
ReDim Preserve roles(2)
roles(2) = "Members"      ' Works fine now
```

This line of code redimensions the array to its new size: an upper bound of two, thus creating room for three elements. The `Preserve` keyword is necessary to leave the current items in the array intact. Without it, the resized array will be empty.

In C#, you need to do a little more work. In that language, you need to create a new array of the desired size, and then copy over the elements from the old array into the new one. Then you can point your old variable to the new one and add the element:

```
string[] tempRoles = new string[3];             // Create new array with required size
Array.Copy(roles, tempRoles, roles.Length);     // Use Copy to copy the elements from the old
                                                // to the new array
roles = tempRoles;                              // Assign the new array to the old variable

roles[2] = "Members";                           // Works fine now
```

Instead of creating a new array and copying the elements, you can also use `Resize` with a concept called *generics*, which you'll learn about later in this chapter. For the brave of heart, here's some code that uses `Resize` and has the same effect as the previous code snippet:

```
Array.Resize<string>(ref roles, 3);      // Resize the array so it can hold three elements

roles[2] = "Members";                    // Works fine now
```

Don't worry about this odd-looking generics syntax right now; you probably won't need it very often, as the .NET Framework offers alternatives to fixed size arrays.

When you start working with arrays, you find that they are quick to use at runtime, but lack some useful functionality. For example, it's not so easy to add new elements or to remove existing items from the array. Fortunately, the .NET Framework offers a range of useful collections that do give you the feature set you need.

Defining and Working with Collections

Collections are similar to arrays in that they allow you to store more than one object in a single variable. The same bag analogy works for collections: you can simply drop a number of items in a bag, and it will hold them for you. What's different with collections is how they allow you to work with the data in the bag. Instead of simply accessing each item by its index, most collections expose an `Add` method that allows you to add an item to the collection. Similarly, they have `Remove` and `Clear` methods to remove one or all items from the collection. Just like arrays, they allow you to *iterate*, or loop, over them to get the items out of the collection again.

When collections were first introduced in the .NET Framework 1.0, the `ArrayList` and `Hashtable` became popular very quickly because they were so easy to use. The `ArrayList` allows you to add arbitrary objects that are then stored in the order you add them, while the `Hashtable` allows you to store objects referenced by a custom key. The main benefit of these collections over their array cousins is that they can grow on demand. Unlike the previous example where you needed to resize the array to create room for the third role, the `ArrayList` grows dynamically when required. The following example shows you how this works:

VB.NET

```
Dim roles As New ArrayList()               ' Create a new ArrayList. No need to set its size

roles.Add("Administrators")                ' Add the first role
roles.Add("ContentManagers")               ' Add the second role
roles.Add("Members")                       ' Keep adding roles and the ArrayList
                                           ' grows as necessary
```

C#

```
ArrayList roles = new ArrayList();         // Create a new ArrayList. No need to set its size

roles.Add("Administrators");               // Add the first role
roles.Add("ContentManagers");              // Add the second role
roles.Add("Members");                      // Keep adding roles and the ArrayList
                                           // grows as necessary
```

Because this code now calls a method (`Add`) rather than assigning an item to a predefined index in an array, you need parentheses (`()`) in both VB.NET and C#. The usage of methods is discussed later in this chapter.

Although collections solve some of the problems that arrays have, they introduce a few problems of their own. The biggest drawback of the `ArrayList` is that it isn't *strongly typed*. What this means is that you can add *any object* to the list using the `Add` method. This means that the `ArrayList` could hold objects that are of different types at the same time. This may not seem to be a big deal at first, but as soon as you start working with an `ArrayList` that contains multiple types of objects, you'll quickly see why this is problematic. Take the roles example again. With the array and the `ArrayList` versions, the code simply added a few strings containing role names. You can then use these three strings to, say, build up a drop-down list in a Web Form to allow a user to pick a role. So far so good. But what if one of the items in the list is not a string? What if another developer accidentally wrote some code that adds a `DropDownList` control to the `ArrayList`? Since the `ArrayList` accepts all objects, it won't complain. However, your code will crash if it expects a `String`, but gets a `DropDownList` control instead.

With .NET 2.0, Microsoft introduced a concept called *generics*. Generics are still strongly present in version 3.5 of .NET, helping you overcome the problems that weakly typed collections like the `ArrayList` introduced.

An Introduction to Generics

Since their introduction with .NET 2.0, generics pop up in many different locations in the .NET Framework. Although they are used often in situations where collections are used, generics are not limited to collections; you can also use them for singular type of objects.

Generics are to code what Microsoft Word templates are to word processing. They allow you to write a code *template* that can be used in different scenarios with different types. With generics, you can define a generic code template that doesn't explicitly specify a type. Only when that code is used do you define the type. The main benefit of this is that you can reuse the same template over and over again for multiple data types, without retyping and maintaining multiple versions of the code. Besides using generics in your own code definitions, you find a host of generics-enabled objects and collections in the .NET Framework ready to be used by your code.

To understand how you can take advantage of generics, take a look at the following example. It's essentially the same code you saw earlier where the `ArrayList` was used, but this time the type of the list is constrained so it only accepts strings:

VB.NET

```
Dim roles As New List(Of String)

roles.Add("Administrators")
roles.Add("ContentManagers")
roles.Add("Members")
```

C#

```
List<string> roles = new List<string>();

roles.Add("Administrators");
roles.Add("ContentManagers");
roles.Add("Members");
```

Not much code has changed to make the roles list *type safe*. However, with the definition of `List (Of String)` in VB.NET and `List<string>` the new list is now set up to only allow strings to be added through its `Add` method. This compiles fine:

```
roles.Add("Administrators");
```

The following will fail because 33 is not a String:

```
roles.Add(33);
```

Similar to a generics list of strings, you can also create lists to hold other types. For example:

VB.NET

```
Dim intList As New List(Of Integer)                ' Can only hold Integers
Dim boolList As New List(Of Boolean)               ' Can only hold Booleans
Dim buttonList As New List (Of Button)             ' Can only hold Button controls
```

C#

```
List<int> intList = new List<int>();               // Can only hold ints
List<bool> boolList = new List<bool>();            // Can only hold bools
List<Button> buttonList = new List<Button>();      // Can only hold Button controls
```

Since there's a lot more to generics than what is shown here, they deserve an entire book on their own. Wrox has released such a book: Professional .NET 2.0 Generics *by Tod Golding (ISBN: 978-0-7645-5988-4). Although it was originally written for .NET 2.0, you'll find that all the concepts and examples introduced in that book still apply.*

The generics examples you have seen barely scratch the surface of what is possible with generics. However, when building ASP.NET web sites, you often don't need all the advanced stuff that generics offer you. The List collection is so useful it had to be discussed here. Without a doubt, you'll use that collection in your own code one way or another.

Statements

To make a program or a web site do something useful, you need to provide it with statements that it can execute. Statements cover a wide range of actions, like: show this button, send this e-mail, execute this and that code when a user clicks that button, and so on. However, simply executing these actions is not enough. You often need to execute some code only when a certain *condition* is true. For example, if a visitor to an e-commerce web site is buying more than $100 of merchandise at one time, they might get a discount of 10 percent. Otherwise, they pay the full price. Conditions or decisions are therefore very important statements in a programming language. Another important set of statements is the *loops*. Loops allow you to repeat a certain piece of code a number of times. For example, you can have a loop that goes from 1 to 10, performing some action on each iteration. Or you can loop through the products in a shopping cart, summing up the total price for example.

The final important set of statements is the *operators*. Operators allow you to do something with your values; or, to be more exact, they allow you to *operate* on them. For example, you use operators to subtract values, concatenate (combine) them, or compare them to each other.

The following three sections dig deeper into operators, decision making, and loops.

Operators

The most important operators can be grouped logically into five different types. Of these five groups, the assignment operators are probably the easiest to understand and use.

Assignment Operators

The assignment operators are used to assign a value to a variable. This value can come from many sources: a constant value, like the number 6, the value of another variable, and the result of an expression or a function, which are discussed later. In its simplest form, an assignment looks like this:

VB.NET

```
Dim age As Integer = 36
```

C#

```
int age = 36;
```

What if the person this `age` variable is referring to just had his birthday? You'd need to add `1` to the age value. That's where arithmetic operators come into play.

Arithmetic Operators

Arithmetic operators allow you to perform most of the familiar calculations on variables and values, like adding, subtracting, and dividing. The following table lists the common arithmetic operators for both VB.NET and C#.

VB.NET	C#	Usage
+	+	Adds two values to each other. These values can be numeric types like `Int32`, but also `String`, in which case they are concatenated.
-	-	Subtracts one value from another.
*	*	Multiplies two values.
/	/	Divides two values.
\	n/a	Divides two values but always returns a rounded integer.
^	n/a	Raises one value to the power of another.
Mod	%	Divides two whole numbers and returns the remainder.

The first five operators probably look familiar, and their usage is pretty straightforward. The following code snippet shows the basic operations you can perform with these operators:

VB.NET

```
Dim firstNumber As Integer = 100
Dim secondNumber As Single = 23.5
Dim result As Double = 0

result = firstNumber + secondNumber     ' Results in 123.5
result = firstNumber - secondNumber     ' Results in 76.5
result = firstNumber * secondNumber     ' Results in 2350
result = firstNumber / secondNumber     ' Results in 4.25531914893617
result = firstNumber \ secondNumber     ' Results in 4
```

C#

```
int firstNumber = 100;
float secondNumber = 23.5F;
double result = 0;

result = firstNumber + secondNumber;     // Results in 123.5
result = firstNumber - secondNumber;     // Results in 76.5
result = firstNumber * secondNumber;     // Results in 2350
result = firstNumber / secondNumber;     // Results in 4.25531914893617
```

VB.NET supports the \ operator, which basically performs the division and then drops the remainder from the value, effectively rounding it down to the nearest integer. C# doesn't have a special operator for this. However, when you try to divide two integers, the result is always an integer as well. This means that 7 (stored as an `int`) divided by 2 (stored as an `int`) will be 3. It's important to realize that this rounding occurs or you may end up with unexpected results.

Note that in the C# example you need to add the letter `F` to the value of `23.5`. This tells the compiler you really want it to be a `float` rather than a `double`.

The final two operators need a bit more explanation. First, the ^ operator — for raising one number to the power of another — is only available in the VB.NET language:

VB.NET

```
Dim result As Double

result = 2 ^ 3             ' Results in 8
result = 3 ^ 2             ' Results in 9
```

C# doesn't support this operator, but you can easily replicate its behavior using `Math.Pow` that is made available by the .NET Framework. The following code snippet is functionally equivalent to the previous:

C#

```
result = Math.Pow(2, 3);     // Results in 8
result = Math.Pow(3, 2);     // Results in 9
```

Of course `Math.Pow` is available to VB.NET as well, so if you're using that language, you have two options to choose from.

The final operator is called the mod or the modulus operator. It returns the remainder of the division of two numbers, like this:

VB.NET

```
Dim firstNumber As Integer = 17
Dim secondNumber As Integer = 3
Dim result As Integer

result = firstNumber Mod secondNumber      ' Results in 2.
```

C#

```
int firstNumber = 17;
int secondNumber = 3;
int result;

result = firstNumber % secondNumber;      // Results in 2.
```

Simply put, the modulus operator tries to subtract the second number from the first as many times as possible and then returns the remainder. In the example above this will succeed five times, subtracting a total of fifteen, leaving a remainder of two, which is then returned and stored in the result.

Another common set of operators is the comparison operators, which allow you to compare values.

Comparison Operators

Just as with the arithmetic operators, VB.NET and C# each have their own set of comparison operators to compare one value to another. A comparison operator always compares two values or *expressions* and then returns a Boolean value as the result. The following table lists the most common comparison operators.

VB.NET	C#	Usage
=	==	Checks if two values are equal to each other.
<>	!=	Checks if two values are not equal.
<	<	Checks if the first value is less than the second.
>	>	Checks if the first value is greater than the second.
<=	<=	Checks if the first value is less than or equal to the second.
>=	>=	Checks if the first value is greater than or equal to the second.
Is	is	In VB.NET: Compares two objects. In C#: Checks if a variable is of a certain type.

The first thing you'll notice is that C# uses a double equals symbol (=) for the standard comparison operator. This clearly makes it different from the assignment operator. It's a common mistake in C# to use only a single equals symbol if you intend to compare two values. Consider the following example:

```
if (result = 4)
{
  // Do something here with result
}
```

The intention here is to see if `result` equals `4`. However, since the assignment operator is used instead of a proper comparison operator, you'll get the compile error that is displayed in Figure 5-2.

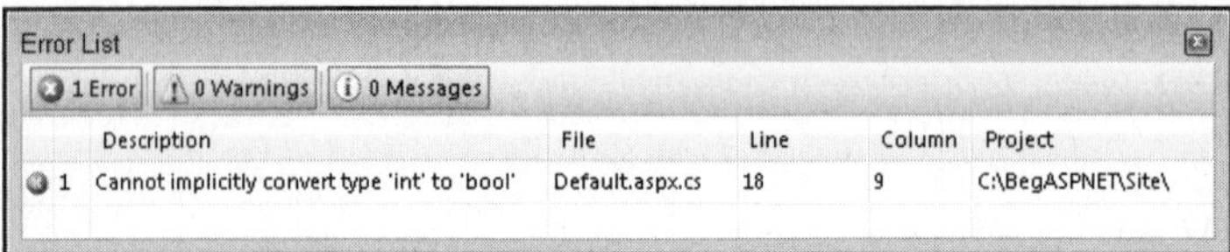

Figure 5-2

At first the error message may look a little strange. However, if you look at the code a little closer, it starts to make more sense. The assignment of `result = 4` results in the variable `result` getting an integer value of 4. The `if` statement on the other hand needs a Boolean value to determine whether it should run the code inside the `if` block or not. Since you can't convert an integer value to a Boolean like this, you get a compile error. The fix is easy though; just use the proper comparison operator instead:

```
if (result == 4)
{
  // Do something here with result
}
```

Similar to the simple comparison operator, you can use the other operators to compare values:

VB.NET

```
4 > 5         ' 4 is not greater than 5; evaluates to False
4 <> 5        ' 4 is not equal to 5; evaluates to True
5 >= 4        ' 5 is greater than or equal to 4; evaluates to True
```

C#

```
4 > 5         // 4 is not greater than 5; evaluates to false
4 != 5        // 4 is not equal to 5; evaluates to true
5 >= 4        // 5 is greater than or equal to 4; evaluates to true
```

The Is keyword in VB.NET and is in C# do something completely different. In VB.NET, Is compares two instances of objects, something you will learn more about in the second half of this chapter. In C#, you use is to find out if a certain variable is compatible with a certain type. You can accomplish that in VB.NET using the TypeOf operator. The following two examples are functionally equivalent:

VB.NET

```
Dim myTextBox As TextBox = New TextBox()

If TypeOf myTextBox Is TextBox Then
  ' Run some code when myTextBox is a TextBox
End If
```

C#

```
TextBox myTextBox = new TextBox();

if (myTextBox is TextBox)
{
  // Run some code when myTextBox is a TextBox
}
```

One of the arithmetic operators allows you to add two values to each other. That is, you use the plus (+) symbol to add two values together. But what if you want to combine two values, rather than adding them up? That's where the concatenation operators are used.

Concatenation Operators

To concatenate two strings, you use the + in C# and the & character in VB.NET. Additionally, you can use += and &= to combine the concatenation and assignment operators. Consider this example:

VB.NET

```
Dim firstString As String = "Hello "
Dim secondString As String = "World"
Dim result As String

' The following three blocks are all functionally equivalent
' and result in the value "Hello World"

result = firstString & secondString

result = firstString
result = result & secondString

result = firstString
result &= secondString
```

C#

```
string firstString = "Hello ";
string secondString = "World";
string result;

// The following three blocks are all functionally equivalent
// and result in the value "Hello World"

result = firstString + secondString;

result = firstString;
result = result + secondString;

result = firstString;
result += secondString;
```

In addition to the `&` and `&=` concatenation operators in VB.NET, you could use `+` and `+=` as well. However, depending on the data types of the expressions you're trying to concatenate, you may not get the result you'd expect. Take a look at this code snippet:

```
Dim firstNumber As String = "4"
Dim secondNumber As Integer = 5
Dim result As String = firstNumber + secondNumber
```

Since `firstNumber` is a `String`, you may expect the final result to be `45`, a concatenation of `4` and `5`. However, by default, the VB.NET compiler will silently convert the `String "4"` into the number `4`, after which addition and not concatenation takes place, giving `result` a value of `9`.

To avoid this ambiguity, always use the `&` and `&=` operators to concatenate values. Additionally, you can tell VB.NET to stop converting these values for you automatically by adding the following line to the top of your code files:

```
Option Strict On
```

This forces the compiler to generate errors when an implicit conversion is about to occur, as in the last example.

The final group of operators worth looking into is the logical operators, which are discussed in the next section.

Logical Operators

The logical operators are used to combine the results of multiple individual expressions, and to make sure that multiple conditions are true or false, for example. The following table lists the most common logical operators.

VB.NET	C#	Usage
And	&&	Returns True when both expressions result in a True value
Or	||	Returns True if at least one expression results in a True value.

VB.NET	C#	Usage
Not	!	Reverses the outcome of an expression.
AndAlso	&&	Allows you to short-circuit your logical condition checks.
OrElse	||	Allows you to short-circuit your logical condition checks.

The `And`, `Or`, and `Not` operators (`&&`, `||`, and `!` in C#) are pretty straightforward in their usage, demonstrated in the following code snippets:

VB.NET

```
Dim num1 As Integer = 3
Dim num2 As Integer = 7

If num1 = 3 And num2 = 7 Then       ' Evaluates to True because both expressions are True

If num1 = 2 And num2 = 7 Then       ' Evaluates to False because num1 is not 2

If num1 = 3 Or num2 = 11 Then       ' Evaluates to True because num1 is 3

If Not num1 = 5 Then                ' Evaluates to True because num1 is not 5
```

C#

```
int num1 = 3;
int num2 = 7;

if (num1 == 3 && num2 == 7)         // Evaluates to true because both expressions are true

if (num1 == 2 && num2 == 7)         // Evaluates to false because num1 is not 2

if (num1 == 3 || num2 == 11)        // Evaluates to true because num1 is 3

if (!(num1 == 5))                   // Evaluates to true because num1 is not 5
```

The `AndAlso` and `OrElse` in VB.NET operators work very similar to their `And` and `Or` counterparts. The difference is that with the `AndAlso` and `OrElse` operators, the second expression is never evaluated when the first one already determines the outcome of the entire expression. So with a simple `And` operator:

```
If num1 = 2 And num2 = 7 Then
```

both expressions are checked. This means that both `num1` and `num2` are asked for their value to see if they equal `2` and `7` respectively. However, since `num1` does not equal 2, there really isn't a point asking `num2` for its value anymore as the result of that expression will never change the final outcome of the combined expressions. This is where the `AndAlso` operator allows you to short-circuit your logic:

```
If num1 = 2 AndAlso num2 = 7 Then
```

With this code, the expression `num2 = 7` is never evaluated because `num1` already didn't meet the required criteria.

This may not seem like a big deal with these simple expressions, but it can be a real performance booster if one of the expressions is actually a slow and long-running operation. Consider this fictitious code:

```
If userName = "Administrator" And GetNumberOfRecordsFromDatabase() > 0 Then
```

The code for this `If` blocks only executes when the current user is called Administrator and the fictitious call to the database returns at least 1 record. Now, imagine that `GetNumberOfRecordsFromDatabase()` is a long-running operation. It would be a waste of time to execute it if the current user weren't Administrator. Again, `AndAlso` can fix this problem:

```
If userName = "Administrator" AndAlso GetNumberOfRecordsFromDatabase() > 0 Then
```

Now, `GetNumberOfRecordsFromDatabase()` will only be executed when the current user is Administrator. The code will be ignored for all other users, resulting in increased performance for them.

C# doesn't have an equivalent of the `AndAlso` and `OrElse` keywords. It doesn't need them because Boolean logic is by default already short-circuited in that language. This means that the second expression is never evaluated if the result of the first makes it unnecessary to evaluate the second.

Most of the previous examples used an `If` statement to demonstrate the logical operators. The `If` statement itself is a very important language construct as well. The `If` statement and other ways to make decisions in your code are discussed next.

Making Decisions

Making decisions in an application is one of the most common things you do as a developer. For example, you need to hide a button on a Web Form when a user is not an administrator. Or you need to display the even rows in a table with a light grey background while the odd rows get a white background. All these decisions can be made with a few different logic constructs: `If`, `If Else`, `ElseIf`, and `switch` or `Select Case` statements.

If, If Else, and ElseIf Constructs

The `If` statement is the simplest of all decision making statements. The `If` statement contains two relevant parts: the condition being tested and the code that is executed when the condition evaluates to `True`. For example:

VB.NET

```
If User.IsInRole("Administrators") Then
  btnDeleteArticle.Visible = True
End If
```

C#

```
if (User.IsInRole("Administrators"))
{
  btnDeleteArticle.Visible = true;
}
```

Note that VB.NET uses the `If` and `End If` keywords whereas C# uses `if` together with a pair of curly braces to indicate the code block that is being executed. Also, with C#, the parentheses around the condition being tested are required whereas VB.NET requires you to use the keyword `Then` after the condition.

Often you want to perform a different action if the condition is not `True`. Using the negation operator `Not` or `!` you could simply write another statement:

VB.NET

```
If User.IsInRole("Administrators") Then
  btnDeleteArticle.Visible = True
End If
If Not User.IsInRole("Administrators") Then
  btnDeleteArticle.Visible = False
End If
```

C#

```
if (User.IsInRole("Administrators"))
{
  btnDeleteArticle.Visible = true;
}
if (!User.IsInRole("Administrators"))
{
  btnDeleteArticle.Visible = false;
}
```

Clearly, this leads to messy code, as you need to repeat each expression evaluation twice: once for the `True` case and once for the `False` case. Fortunately, there is an easier solution: the `Else` block (`else` in C#):

VB.NET

```
If User.IsInRole("Administrators") Then
  btnDeleteArticle.Visible = True
Else
  btnDeleteArticle.Visible = False
End If
```

C#

```
if (User.IsInRole("Administrators"))
{
  btnDeleteArticle.Visible = true;
}
else
{
  btnDeleteArticle.Visible = false;
}
```

For simple conditions, this `If Else` construct works fine. But consider a scenario where you have more than two options. In those scenarios you can use `ElseIf` in VB.NET or the `else-if` ladder in C#.

Imagine that your site uses three different roles: administrators, content managers, and standard members. Administrators can create and delete content; content managers can only create new content, whereas members can't do either of the two. To show or hide the relevant buttons, you can use the following code:

VB.NET

```
If User.IsInRole("Administrators") Then
  btnCreateNewArticle.Visible = True
  btnDeleteArticle.Visible = True
ElseIf User.IsInRole("ContentManagers") Then
  btnCreateNewArticle.Visible = True
  btnDeleteArticle.Visible = False
ElseIf User.IsInRole("Members") Then
  btnCreateNewArticle.Visible = False
  btnDeleteArticle.Visible = False
End If
```

C#

```
if (User.IsInRole("Administrators"))
{
  btnCreateNewArticle.Visible = true;
  btnDeleteArticle.Visible = true;
}
else if (User.IsInRole("ContentManagers"))
{
  btnCreateNewArticle.Visible = true;
  btnDeleteArticle.Visible = false;
}
else if (User.IsInRole("Members"))
{
  btnCreateNewArticle.Visible = false;
  btnDeleteArticle.Visible = false;
}
```

Although the `ElseIf` or `else if` ladder helps to make the code more readable, you can still end up with difficult code when you have many expressions to test. If that's the case, you can use the `Select Case` (VB.NET) or `switch` (C#) statement.

Switches / Select Case Constructs

Imagine you're building a web site for a concert hall that has shows on Saturday. During the week, visitors can buy tickets online for Saturday's gig. To encourage visitors to buy tickets as early as possible, you decide to give them an early-bird discount. The earlier in the week they buy their tickets, the cheaper they are. Your code to calculate the discount rate can look like this, using `Select Case` / `switch` statement:

VB.NET

```
Dim today As DateTime = DateTime.Now
Dim discountRate As Double = 0

Select Case today.DayOfWeek
  Case DayOfWeek.Monday
    discountRate = 0.4
```

```
  Case DayOfWeek.Tuesday
    discountRate = 0.3
  Case DayOfWeek.Wednesday
    discountRate = 0.2
  Case DayOfWeek.Thursday
    discountRate = 0.1
  Case Else
    discountRate = 0
End Select
```

C#

```
DateTime today = DateTime.Now;
double discountRate = 0;

switch (today.DayOfWeek)
{
  case DayOfWeek.Monday:
    discountRate = 0.4;
    break;
  case DayOfWeek.Tuesday:
    discountRate = 0.3;
    break;
  case DayOfWeek.Wednesday:
    discountRate = 0.2;
    break;
  case DayOfWeek.Thursday:
    discountRate = 0.1;
    break;
  default:
    discountRate = 0;
    break;
}
```

For each day where the discount is applicable (Monday through Thursday) there is a `Case` block. The differences between VB.NET and C# syntax are quite small: C# uses a lowercase c for `case` and requires a colon after each case label. Additionally, you need to exit each block with a `break` statement. At runtime, the condition (`today.DayOfWeek`) is evaluated and the correct block is executed. It's important to understand that only the relevant block is executed, and nothing else. When no valid block is found (the code is executed on a day between Friday and Sunday) the code in the `Case Else` or `default` block fires. You're not required to write a `Case Else` or `default` block although it's recommended to do so, as it makes your code more explicit and easier to read. The examples above could have left it out, as `discountRate` already gets a default value of `0` at the top of the code block.

To get a feel for the statements you have seen so far, the following Try It Out exercise shows you how to use them in a small demo application.

Try It Out — Creating a Simple Web-Based Calculator

In this exercise you will create a simple calculator that is able to add, subtract, multiply, and divide values. It shows you how to use some of the logical and assignment operators and demonstrates the `If` and `Select Case` / `switch` constructs.

1. Start by creating a new file called CalculatorDemo.aspx under the Demos folder. Make sure you don't name the page Calculator or you'll run into troubles later in this chapter where you'll create a class by that name. Once again, make sure you're using the Code Behind model and select the correct language from the language drop-down list.
2. Switch the page in Design View, click in the dashed rectangle to put the focus on it, and add a table with three rows and three columns using Table ➪ Insert Table. Merge all three cells of the first row by selecting them, right-clicking the selection, and choosing Modify ➪ Merge Cells from the menu that appears.
3. Add the following controls to the page, set their ID and other properties as in the following table and arrange the controls as shown in Figure 5-3.

Control Type	Control ID	Property Settings
Label	lblResult	Clear its Text property. To do this, right-click the property Text in the Properties Grid and choose Reset.
TextBox	txtValue1	
DropDownList	lstOperator	Add four ListItems for the following arithmetic operators: + - * /
TextBox	txtValue2	
Button	btnCalculate	Set the Text property of the button to Calculate.

When you're done, your page should look like Figure 5-3 in Design View.

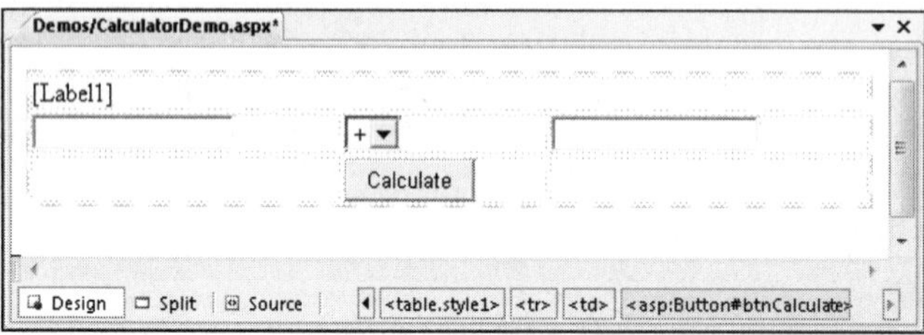

Figure 5-3

4. Double-click the Calculate button and add the following code in the code placeholder that Visual Web Developer added for you:

VB.NET

```
Protected Sub btnCalculate_Click(ByVal sender As Object, ByVal e As System.EventArgs) _
      Handles btnCalculate.Click
```

```
    If txtValue1.Text.Length > 0 AndAlso txtValue2.Text.Length > 0 Then

      Dim result As Double = 0
      Dim value1 As Double = Convert.ToDouble(txtValue1.Text)
      Dim value2 As Double = Convert.ToDouble(txtValue2.Text)

      Select Case lstOperator.SelectedValue
        Case "+"
          result = value1 + value2
        Case "-"
          result = value1 - value2
        Case "*"
          result = value1 * value2
        Case "/"
          result = value1 / value2
      End Select
      lblResult.Text = result.ToString()
    Else
      lblResult.Text = String.Empty
    End If
  End Sub
```

C#

```
protected void btnCalculate_Click(object sender, EventArgs e)
{
  if (txtValue1.Text.Length > 0 && txtValue2.Text.Length > 0)
  {
    double result = 0;
    double value1 = Convert.ToDouble(txtValue1.Text);
    double value2 = Convert.ToDouble(txtValue2.Text);

    switch (lstOperator.SelectedValue)
    {
      case "+":
        result = value1 + value2;
        break;
      case "-":
        result = value1 - value2;
        break;
      case "*":
        result = value1 * value2;
        break;
      case "/":
        result = value1 / value2;
        break;
    }
    lblResult.Text = result.ToString();
  }
  else
  {
    lblResult.Text = string.Empty;
  }
}
```

5. Save all changes and then press Ctrl+F5 to open the page in the browser. If you get an error instead of seeing the page, make sure you typed the code exactly as shown here, and that you named all controls according to the table you saw earlier.

6. Enter a number in the first and second text boxes, choose an operator from the drop-down list, and then click the Calculate button. The code in the Code Behind fires and then — based on the item you selected in the drop-down list — the correct calculation is performed and the label is updated with the result.

7. Go ahead and try some other numbers and operators; you'll see that the calculator carries out the right operation every time you click the Calculate button.

How It Works

When you enter two values and then click the Calculate button, the following code in the Code Behind fires:

VB.NET

```
If txtValue1.Text.Length > 0 AndAlso txtValue2.Text.Length > 0 Then
```

C#

```
if (txtValue1.Text.Length > 0 && txtValue2.Text.Length > 0)
```

This code is necessary to ensure that both text boxes contain a value. (In Chapter 9 you'll see a much cleaner way to perform this validation.) The code uses a simple `If` statement to ensure that both fields have a value. It also uses the VB.NET operator `AndAlso` to avoid checking the `Text` property of the second `TextBox` when the first is empty.

The code then declares a `Double` to hold the result of the calculation and then gets the values from the two text box controls, converts the values to a `Double` using the `ToDouble` method of the `Convert` class and then sets up a `Select Case` (`switch` in C#) block to handle the type of operator you have chosen in the drop-down list:

VB.NET

```
Select Case lstOperator.SelectedValue
  Case "+"
  result = value1 + value2
```

C#

```
switch (lstOperator.SelectedValue)
{
  case "+":
    result = value1 + value2;
    break;
```

For each item in the drop-down list, there is a case statement. When you have chosen the + operator from the list, the code in the first case block will fire, and `result` is assigned the sum of the number you entered in the two text boxes. Likewise, when you choose the subtraction operator, the two values are subtracted from each other.

At the end, the result is converted to a `String` and then displayed on the label called `lblResult`.

The `Select Case` / `switch` statements close off the discussion about making decisions in your code. There's one more group of statements left: Loops that allow you to loop over code or over objects in a collection.

Loops

Loops are extremely useful in many applications, as they allow you to execute code repetitively, without the need to write that code more than once. For example, if you have a web site that needs to send a newsletter by e-mail to its 20,000 subscribers, you write the code to send the newsletter once, and then use a loop that sends the newsletter to each subscriber the code finds in a database.

Loops come as a few different types, each with their own usage and advantages.

The For Loop

The `For` loop simply repeats its code a predefined number of times. You define the exact number of iterations when you set up the loop. The `For` loop takes the following format:

VB.NET

```
For counter [ As datatype ] = start To end [ Step step ]
   ' Code that must be executed for each iteration
Next [ counter ]
```

C#

```
for (startCondition; endCondition; step definition)
{
  // Code that must be executed for each iteration
}
```

This looks a little odd, but a concrete example makes this a lot easier to understand:

VB.NET

```
For loopCount As Integer = 1 To 10
  Label1.Text &= loopCount.ToString() & "<br />"
Next
```

C#

```
for (int loopCount = 1; loopCount <= 10; loopCount ++)
{
  Label1.Text += loopCount.ToString() + "<br />";
}
```

Although the syntax used in both languages is quite different, both code examples perform the same action: they write out numbers from 1 to 10 on a `Label` control. That is, the loop is started by the assignment of `1` to the variable `loopCount`. Next, the value is converted to a `String` and assigned to the `Label` control. Then `loopCount` is increased by 1, and the loop continues. This goes on until `loopCount` is `10` and then the loop ends. In this example, hardcoded numbers are used. However, you can replace the start and end conditions with dynamic values from variables or other objects. For example, if you're working with the roles array you saw earlier, you can write out each role in the array like this:

VB.NET

```
For loopCount As Integer = 0 To roles.Length - 1
  Label1.Text &= roles(loopCount) & "<br />"
Next
```

C#

```
for (int loopCount = 0; loopCount < roles.Length; loopCount ++ )
{
  Label1.Text += roles[loopCount] + "<br />";
}
```

Recall that arrays are zero-based. This means that you need to address the first item with `roles(0)` in VB.NET and `roles[0]` in C#. This also means that the loop needs to start at `0`. The `Length` property of an array returns the total number of items that the array contains. So when there are three roles in the array, `Length` returns 3 as well. Therefore, the code subtracts one from the `Length` and uses that value as the end condition of the loop, causing the loop to run from 0 to 2, accessing all three elements.

The C# example doesn't extract 1 from the `Length`, though. Instead it uses the expression:

```
loopCount < roles.Length;
```

So, as long as `loopCount` is less than the length of the array, the loop continues. Again, this causes the loop to access all three items, from 0 to 2.

If you are looping over an array or a collection of data, there's also another loop at your disposal that's a bit easier to read and work with: the `For Each` or `foreach` loop.

The For Each / foreach Loop

The `For Each` loop in VB.NET and the `foreach` in C# simply iterate over all the items in a collection. Taking the roles array as an example, you can execute the following code to print each role name on the `Label` control:

VB.NET

```
For Each role As String In roles
  Label1.Text &= role & "<br />"
Next
```

C#

```
foreach (string role in roles)
{
```

```
    Label1.Text += role + "<br />";
  }
```

Since the roles variable is an array of strings, you need to set up the loop with a `String` as well. Likewise, if the collection that is being looped over contained Integer or Boolean data types, you would set up the loop with an Integer or Boolean, respectively.

Besides the `For` and the `For Each` loops, there is one more loop that you need to look at: the `While` loop.

The While and Until Loops

As its name implies, the `While` loop is able to loop while a certain condition is true. Unlike the other two loops that usually end by themselves, the `While` loop could potentially loop forever if you're not careful. The following example shows how to use the `While` loop:

VB.NET

```
Dim success As Boolean = False
While Not success
  success = SendEmailMessage()
End While
```

C#

```
bool success = false;
while (!success)
{
  success = SendEmailMessage();
}
```

This code tries to send an e-mail message and will do so until it succeeds — that is, as long as the variable `success` contains the value `False` (`false` in C#). Note that `Not` and `!` are used to reverse the value of `success`. The `SendEmailMessage` method is supposed to return `True` when it succeeds and `False` when it doesn't. If everything works out as planned, the code enters the loop and calls `SendEmailMessage`. If it returns `True`, the loop condition is no longer met, and the loop will end. However, when `SendEmailMessage` returns `False`, for example, because the mail server is down, the loop will continue and `SendEmailMessage` is called again.

To avoid endless loops with the `While` loop, it's often a good idea to add a condition that terminates the loop after a certain number of tries. For example, the following code helps to avoid an infinite loop if the mail server is down:

VB.NET

```
Dim success As Boolean = False
Dim loopCount As Integer = 0
While Not success And loopCount < 3
  success = SendEmailMessage()
  loopCount = loopCount + 1
End While
```

C#

```
bool success = false;
int loopCount = 0;
while (!success && loopCount < 3)
{
  success = SendEmailMessage();
  loopCount = loopCount + 1;
}
```

With this code, the variable `loopCount` is responsible for exiting the loop after three tries to call `SendEmailMessage`. Instead of using `loopCount = loopCount + 1`, you can also use the combined concatenation and assignment operators, like this:

VB.NET

```
loopCount += 1
```

C#

```
loopCount += 1;

// Alternatively C# allows you to do this:
loopCount++;
```

All examples have the same result: the `loopCount` value is increased by one, after which the new total is assigned to `loopCount` again. The C# shortcut, `loopCount++`, is a very common way to increase a variable's value by 1. Similarly, you can use `loopCount--` or `loopCount -= 1` to decrease the value by 1.

Besides the `While` loop, there are a few other alternatives, like the `Do While` loop (that ensures that the code to be executed is always executed at least once) and the `Do Until` loop that goes on *until* a certain condition is true, as opposed to looping *while* a certain condition is true as is the case with the `While` loop.

So far, the code you've seen has been comprised of short and simple examples that can be placed directly in the Code Behind of a web page; for example, in `Page_Load` that you have seen before. However, in real-world web sites, you probably want to structure and organize your code a lot more. In the next section, you'll see different ways to accomplish this.

Organizing Code

When you start adding more than just a few pages to your web site, you're almost certain to end up with some code that you can reuse in multiple pages. For example, you may have some code that reads settings from the web.config file that you need in multiple files. Or you want to send an e-mail with user details from different pages. So you need to find a way to centralize your code. To accomplish this in an ASP.NET 3.5 web site, you can use functions and subroutines, discussed next. To make these functions and subroutines available to all the pages in your site, you need to create them in a special location, which is discussed afterward.

Methods: Functions and Subroutines

Functions and *subroutines* (subs) are very similar; both allow you to create a reusable block of code that you can call from other locations in your site. The difference between a function and a subroutine is that a function can return data while a sub doesn't. Together, functions and subroutines are referred to as *methods*. You'll see that term again in the final part of this chapter that deals with object orientation.

To make functions and subs more useful, they can be *parameterized*. That is, you can pass in additional information that can be used inside the function or subs. Functions and subs generally take the following format:

VB.NET

```
' Define a function
Public Function FunctionName ([parameterList]) As DataType

End Function

' Define a subroutine
Public Sub SubName ([parameterList])

End Sub
```

C#

```
// Define a function
public datatype FunctionName([parameterList])
{

}

// Define a subroutine
public void SubName([parameterList])
{

}
```

The complete first line, starting with `Public` is referred to as the *method signature* as it defines the look of the function, including its name and its parameters. The `Public` keyword (`public` in C#) is called an access modifier and defines to what extend other web pages or code files can see this method. This is discussed in detail later in the chapter. For now, you should realize that `Public` has the greatest visibility, so the method is visible to calling code from the outside.

The name of the function is followed by parentheses, which in turn can contain an optional parameter list. The italic parts in these code examples will be replaced with real values in your code. The parts between the square brackets (`[]`) are optional. To make it a little more concrete, here are some examples of functions and subs:

VB.NET

```
Public Function Add(ByVal a As Integer, ByVal b As Integer) As Integer
  Return a + b
End Function
```

```
Public Sub SendEmail(ByVal emailAddress As String)
  ' Code to send an e-mail goes here
End Sub
```

C#

```
public int Add(int a, int b)
{
  return a + b;
}

public void SendEmail(string emailAddress)
{
  // Code to send an e-mail goes here
}
```

In these code examples it's clear that functions return a value, and subs don't. So, the `Add` method uses the `Return` keyword (`return` in all lower case in C#) to return the total value of `a` and `b`. The `Sub` in VB.NET and the `void` method in C# don't require the `Return` keyword, although you can use it to exit the method prematurely.

Finally, both the function and subroutine have a parameter list. In the case of the `Add` method, there are two parameters: one for the left side of the addition and one for the right side. The `SendEmail` method only has a single parameter: a `String` holding the user's e-mail address.

In the VB.NET example you see the keyword `ByVal` in front of each parameter in the parameter list. This is the default type for all parameters and it will be added by the IDE for you automatically if you leave it out. The opposite of `ByVal` is `ByRef`. These keywords determine the way a value is sent to the function or subroutine. When you specify `ByVal`, a *copy* of the variable is made. Any changes made to that copy inside the method are lost as soon as the method finishes. In contrast, when you specify `ByRef`, a reference to the variable is sent to the method. Any changes made to the incoming variable reflect on the original variable as well. The following short example demonstrates how this works:

```
Public Sub ByValDemo(ByVal someValue As Integer)
  someValue = someValue + 20
End Sub

Public Sub ByRefDemo(ByRef someValue As Integer)
  someValue = someValue + 20
End Sub

Dim x As Integer = 0
ByValDemo(x)

Label1.Text = x.ToString()       ' Prints out 0; A copy of x is sent to ByValDemo,
                                 ' leaving the original value of x unmodified.

Dim y As Integer = 0
ByRefDemo(y)

Label2.Text = y.ToString()       ' Prints out 20; A reference to y is sent to ByRefDemo so
```

```
                                    ' when that method modified someValue, it also changed the
                                    ' variable y.
```

C# has a similar construct using the `ref` keyword. The biggest difference from VB.NET is that you don't need to specify anything when you don't want to use reference parameters, and that you need to specify the `ref` keyword in the call to the method as well:

```
public void ByRefDemo(ref int x)
{
  x = x + 20;
}

int y = 0;
ByRefDemo(ref y);                 // Just as in the VB example, y contains 20 after the call
                                  // to ByRefDemo
```

Be careful when using reference parameters like this; before you know it the method may change important variables in the calling code. This can lead to bugs that are hard to track down.

To make your site-wide methods accessible to pages in your web site, you should place them in a centralized location. The App_Code folder of your web site is a perfect location for your code.

The App_Code Folder

Just like the App_Data folder you saw in Chapters 1 and 2, the App_Code folder is a special ASP.NET 3.5 folder. It's designed specifically to hold code files, like classes that you'll use throughout the site. Code that only applies to one page (like the handler of a `Button` control's click) should remain in the page's Code Behind, as you have seen so far. To add the App_Code folder to your site, right-click the site's name in the Solution Explorer and choose Add ASP.NET Folder ➪ App_Code. The folder is added to the site and gets a special icon: a folder with a little code document on top of it, shown in Figure 5-4.

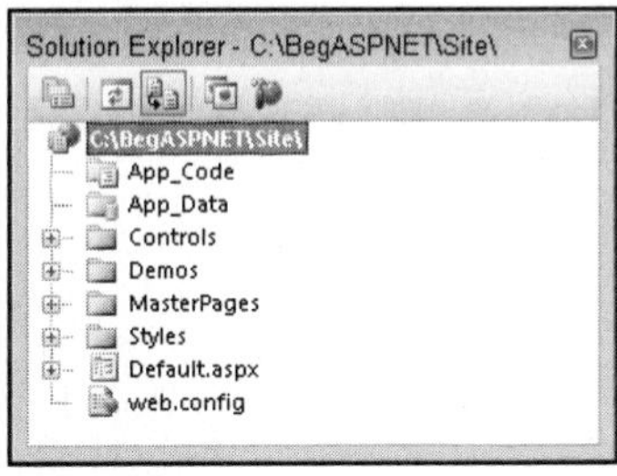

Figure 5-4

With the App_Code folder in place, you can start adding class files to it. Class files have an extension that matches the programming language you have chosen for the site: .cs for C# files and .vb for files containing VB.NET code. Inside these class files you can create classes that in turn contain methods (functions and subroutines) that can carry out common tasks. Classes are discussed in more detail in the final section of this chapter; for now, focus on the methods in the code file and how they are called, rather than on why you need to add the code to a class first.

The next exercise shows you how to use the App_Code folder to optimize the calculator you created in an earlier Try It Out.

Try It Out Optimizing the Calculator

In this exercise, you'll create a class called `Calculator` that exposes four methods: `Add`, `Subtract`, `Multiply`, and `Divide`. When the class is set up and is capable of performing the necessary computing actions, you'll modify the file CalculatorDemo.aspx so it uses your new `Calculator` class. Although this is a trivial example when it comes to the amount of code you need to write and the added flexibility you gain by moving your code from the ASPX page to the App_Code folder so it can be reused by other applications, this example helps you understand the general concept. It's comprehensive enough to show you the concept, yet short enough to allow you to understand the code.

1. If you haven't already done so, start by adding an App_Code folder to your site by right-clicking the site and choosing Add ASP.NET Folder ➪ App_Code.
2. Right-click the newly created App_Code folder and choose Add New Item.
3. In the dialog box that follows, click Class and then select the appropriate language from the Language drop-down list.
4. Type Calculator as the name of the file and click Add. This creates a class file that in turn contains a class called `Calculator`. Note that it's common practice to name classes using what's called Pascal Casing, where each word starts with a capital letter.
5. Right after the line of code that defines the `Calculator` class, add the following four methods:

VB.NET

```
Public Class Calculator

  Public Function Add(ByVal a As Double, ByVal b As Double) As Double
    Return a + b
  End Function

  Public Function Subtract(ByVal a As Double, ByVal b As Double) As Double
    Return a - b
  End Function

  Public Function Multiply(ByVal a As Double, ByVal b As Double) As Double
    Return a * b
  End Function

  Public Function Divide(ByVal a As Double, ByVal b As Double) As Double
    Return a / b
  End Function

End Class
```

C#

```
public class Calculator
{

  public double Add(double a, double b)
  {
    return a + b;
  }

  public double Subtract(double a, double b)
  {
    return a - b;
  }

  public double Multiply(double a, double b)
  {
    return a * b;
  }

  public double Divide(double a, double b)
  {
    return a / b;
  }

  public Calculator()
  {
    //
    // TODO: Add constructor logic here
    //
  }
}
```

6. Next, modify the Code Behind of the CalculatorDemo.aspx page so it uses the class you just created. You'll need to make two changes: first you need to add a line of code that creates an instance of the `Calculator` and then you need to modify each `Case` block to use the relevant calculation methods in the calculator:

VB.NET

```
Dim myCalculator As New Calculator()
Select Case lstOperator.SelectedValue
  Case "+"
    result = myCalculator.Add(value1, value2)
  Case "-"
    result = myCalculator.Subtract(value1, value2)
  Case "*"
    result = myCalculator.Multiply(value1, value2)
  Case "/"
    result = myCalculator.Divide(value1, value2)
End Select
```

C#

```
Calculator myCalculator = new Calculator();
switch (lstOperator.SelectedValue)
{
  case "+":
    result = myCalculator.Add(value1, value2);
    break;
  case "-":
    result = myCalculator.Subtract(value1, value2);
    break;
  case "*":
    result = myCalculator.Multiply(value1, value2);
    break;
  case "/":
    result = myCalculator.Divide(value1, value2);
    break;
}
```

7. Save all your changes and open the page in the browser. The calculator still works as before; only this time the calculations are not carried out in the page's Code Behind file, but by the `Calculator` class in the App_Code folder instead.

How It Works

The file you created in the App_Code folder contains a *class* called `Calculator`. You'll learn more about classes in the final section of this chapter, but for now it's important to know that a class is like a definition for an object that can expose methods you can call at runtime. In this case, the definition for the `Calculator` class contains four methods to perform arithmetic operations. These methods accept parameters for the left-hand and right-hand side of the calculations. Each method simply carries out the requested calculation (`Add`, `Subtract`, and so on) and returns the result to the calling code.

The code in the Code Behind of the CalculatorDemo.aspx page first creates an *instance* of the `Calculator` class. That is, it creates an object in the computer's memory based on the class definition. To do this, it uses the `New` (`new` in C#) keyword to create an instance of `Calculator`, which is then stored in the variable `myCalculator`. You'll learn more about the `New` keyword later in this chapter when objects are discussed. Note that the data type of this variable is `Calculator`: the name of the class.

VB.NET

```
Dim myCalculator As New Calculator()
```

C#

```
Calculator myCalculator = new Calculator();
```

Once the `Calculator` instance is created, you can call its methods. Just as you saw earlier with other methods, the methods of the `Calculator` class accept parameters that are passed in by the calling code:

VB.NET

```
  Case "+"
    result = myCalculator.Add(value1, value2)
```

C#

```
case "+":
  result = myCalculator.Add(value1, value2);
  break;
```

The `Add` method then adds the two values and returns the result as a `double`, which is stored in the variable `result`. Just as in the first version of the calculator, at the end the result is displayed on the page with a `Label` control.

Functions and subroutines are a great way to organize your web application. They allow you to create reusable blocks of code that you can easily call from other locations. Because code you need more than once is only defined once, it's much easier to maintain or extend the code. If you find a bug in a function, simply fix it in its definition in the App_Code folder and all pages using that function automatically benefit from the change. Besides the increased maintainability, functions and subs also make your code easier to read: Instead of wading through long lists of code in a page, you just call a single function and work with the return value (if any). This makes the code easier on your brain, minimizing the chance at bugs in your application.

Functions and subs are not the only way to organize code in your .NET projects. Another common way to organize things is to use namespaces.

Organizing Code with Namespaces

Namespaces seem to cause a lot of confusion with new developers. They think they're scary, they think there are way too many of them, or they don't see the need to use them. None of this is true, and with a short explanation of them, you'll understand and like namespaces.

Namespaces are intended to solve two major problems: to organize the enormous amount of functionality in the .NET Framework and in your own code, and to avoid *name collisions*, where two different data types share the same name.

To see what a namespace looks like, open one of the Code Behind files of the ASPX pages you've created so far. You'll see something similar to this:

VB.NET

```
Partial Class Demos_CalculatorDemo
    Inherits System.Web.UI.Page
```

C#

```
public partial class Demos_CalculatorDemo : System.Web.UI.Page
{
```

Note that the definition of the class name is followed by the `Inherits` keyword (a colon in C#), which in turn is followed by `System.Web.UI.Page`. You'll see later what this `Inherits` keyword is used for. In this code, `Page` is the name of a class (a data type), which is defined in the `System.Web.UI` namespace.

By placing the `Page` class in the `System.Web.UI` namespace, developers (and compilers) can see this class is about a web page. By contrast, imagine the following (fictitious) class name:

```
Microsoft.Word.Document.Page
```

This code also refers to a `Page` class. However, because it's placed in the (fictitious) `Microsoft.Word.Document` namespace, it's easy to see that it's referring to a page of a Word document, not a web page. This way there is no ambiguity between a web page and a Word document page. This in turn helps the compiler understand which class you are referring to.

Another benefit of namespaces is that they help you find the right data type. Instead of displaying thousands and thousands of items in the IntelliSense list, you get a few top-level namespaces. When you choose an item from that list and press the dot key (.) you get another relatively short list with types and other namespaces that live inside the chosen namespace.

Namespaces are nothing more than simple containers that you can refer to by name using the dot notation. They are used to prefix each data type that is available in your application. For example, the `Double` data type lives in the `System` namespace and thus its fully qualified name is `System.Double`. Likewise, the `Button` control you've added to your web pages lives in the `System.Web.UI.WebControls` namespace and thus its full name is `System.Web.UI.WebControls.Button`.

It's also easy to create your own namespaces. As long as they don't collide with an existing name, you can pretty much make up your own namespaces as you see fit. For example, you could wrap the `Calculator` class in the following namespace (in Calculator.vb or Calculator.cs in App_Code):

VB.NET

```
Namespace Wrox.Samples

  Public Class Calculator
    ...
  End Class

End Namespace
```

C#

```
namespace Wrox.Samples
{
  public class Calculator
  {
    ...
  }
}
```

With the calculator wrapped in this namespace, you could create a new instance of it like this:

VB.NET

```
Dim myCalculator As New Wrox.Samples.Calculator()
```

C#

```
Calculator myCalculator = new Wrox.Samples.Calculator();
```

Typing these long names becomes boring after a while. Fortunately, there's a fix for that as well.

Importing Namespaces

After you have created your own namespaces or you want to use existing ones, you need to make them available in your code. You do this with the keyword `Imports` (in VB.NET) or `using` (in C#). For example, to make your `Calculator` class available in the CalculatorDemo page, you can add the following namespace to your code:

VB.NET

```
Imports Wrox.Samples

Public Partial Class Demos_Calculator
  Inherits System.Web.UI.Page
```

C#

```
using Wrox.Samples;

public partial class Demos_Calculator : System.Web.UI.Page
{
```

If you are using C#, you'll see a number of `using` statements by default in the Code Behind of an ASPX page for namespaces like `System` and `System.Web.UI.WebControls`. If you're using VB.NET, you won't see these references. Instead, with a VB.NET web site, the default namespaces are included in the web.config file under the `<namespaces>` element.

Once you start writing lots of code, you may quickly forget where you declared what, or what a variable or method is used for. It's therefore wholeheartedly recommended to put comments in your code.

Writing Comments

No matter how clean a coder you are, it's likely that someday you will run into code that makes you raise your eyebrows and think, "What on earth is this code supposed to do?" Over the years, the way you program will change; you'll learn new stuff, optimize your coding standards and you find ways to code more efficiently. To make it easier for you to recognize and understand your code now and two years from now, it's a good idea to comment your code. There are two main ways to add comments in your code files: inline and as XML comments.

Commenting Inline Code

Inline comments are written directly in between your code statements. You can use them to comment on existing variables, difficult loops, and so on. In VB.NET, you can only comment out one line at a time using the tick (`'`) character that you place in front of the text that you want to use as a comment. To comment a single line in C#, you use two slashes (//). Additionally, you can use /* and */ to comment out an entire block of code in C#. The following examples show some different uses of comments:

VB.NET

```
' Usage: explains the purpose of variables, statements and so on.
' Used to store the number of miles the user has traveled last year.
Dim distanceInMiles As Integer

' Usage: comment out code that's not used (anymore).
' In this example, SomeUnfinishedFunction is commented out.
' to prevent it from being executed.
' SomeUnfinishedFunction()

' Usage: End of line comments.
If User.IsInRole("Administrators") Then  ' Only allow admins in this area
End If
```

C#

```
// Usage: explains the purpose of variables, statements and so on.
// Used to store the number of miles the user has traveled last year.
int distanceInMiles;

// Usage: comment out code that's not used (anymore).
// In this example, SomeUnfinishedFunction is commented out.
// to prevent it from being executed.
// SomeUnfinishedFunction();

// Usage: End of line comments.
if (User.IsInRole("Administrators")) // Only allow admins in this area
{ }

/*
 * This is a block of comments that is often used to add additional
 * information to your code for example to explain a difficult loop
*/
```

To comment out the code, simply type the code character (' or //) at the location where you want the comment to start. To comment out a block of code, select it in the text editor and then press Ctrl+K followed by Ctrl+C. Similarly, press Ctrl+K followed by Ctrl+U to uncomment a selected block of code.

Alternatively, you can choose Edit ➪ Advanced ➪ Comment Selection or Uncomment Selection from the main menu, or click the respective buttons on the Text Editor toolbar, shown in Figure 5-5.

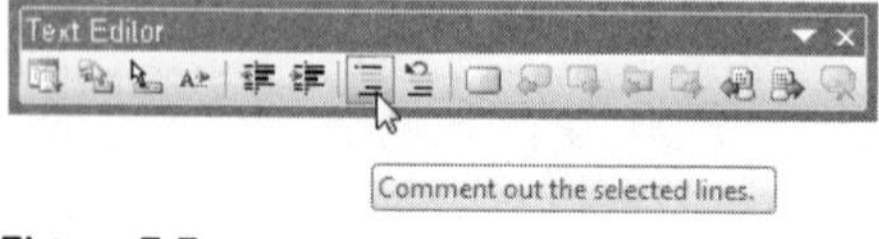

Figure 5-5

Inline comments are usually good for documenting small details of your code. However, it's also a good idea to provide a high-level overview of what your code does. For example, for a method called `SendEmail` it would be good to have a short description that explains what the method does and what the parameters are used for. This is exactly what XML comments are used for.

Writing XML Comments

XML comments are comments that are added as XML elements (using angle brackets < >) in your code to describe its purpose, parameters, return value, and so on. The VWD IDE helps you by writing these comments. All you need to do is position your cursor on the line just before a class or method and type `'''` (three tick characters) for VB or `///` (three forward slashes) for C#. As soon as you do that, the IDE inserts XML tags for the summary and optionally the parameters and return type of a method. Once again, consider the `SendEmail` method. It could have two parameters of type `String`: one for the e-mail address to send the message to, and one for the mail body. With the XML comments applied, the method could look like this:

VB.NET

```
''' <summary>
''' Sends out an e-mail to the address specified by emailAddress.
''' </summary>
''' <param name="emailAddress">The e-mail address of the addressee.</param>
''' <param name="mailBody">The body of the mail message.</param>
''' <returns>This method returns True when the message was sent successfully;
''' and False otherwise.</returns>
''' <remarks>Attention: this method assumes a valid mail server is available.</remarks>
Public Function SendEmail(ByVal emailAddress As String, ByVal mailBody As String) _
                 As Boolean
    ' Implementation goes here
End Function
```

C#

```
/// <summary>
/// Sends out an e-mail to the address specified by emailAddress.
/// </summary>
/// <param name="emailAddress">The e-mail address of the addressee.</param>
/// <param name="mailBody">The body of the mail message.</param>
/// <returns>This method returns true when the message was sent successfully;
/// and false otherwise.</returns>
/// <remarks>Attention: this method assumes a valid mail server is available.</remarks>
bool SendEmail(string emailAddress, string mailBody)
{
  // Implementation goes here
}
```

The cool thing about this type of commenting is that the comments you type here show up in IntelliSense in the code editor when you try to call the method (see Figure 5-6).

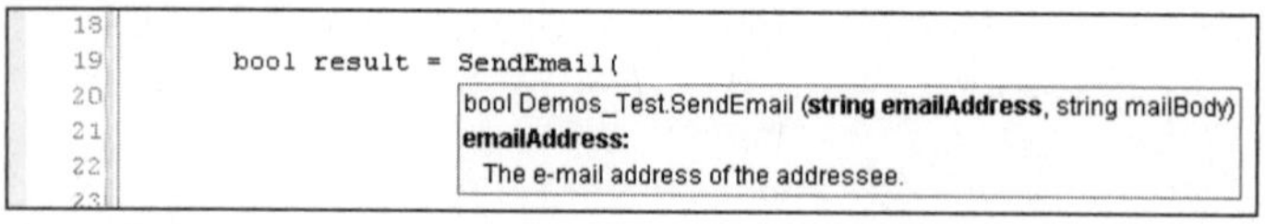

```
bool result = SendEmail(
                    bool Demos_Test.SendEmail (string emailAddress, string mailBody)
                    emailAddress:
                      The e-mail address of the addressee.
```

Figure 5-6

This makes it much easier for you and other developers to understand the purpose of the method and its parameters.

Besides aiding development in the code editor, the XML comments can also be used to create good looking, MSDN-like documentation. There are a number of third-party tools available that help you with this, including Microsoft's own Sandcastle (`http://msdn2.microsoft.com/en-us/vstudio/bb608422.aspx`) and Document! X from Innovasys (`www.innovasys.com/`).

Object Orientation Basics

A chapter about writing code in ASP.NET wouldn't be complete without a section on *object orientation*. Object orientation, or object-oriented programming (OO), is a highly popular style of programming where the software is modeled as a set of objects interacting with each other. Object orientation is at the heart of the .NET Framework. Literally everything inside the framework is an object, from simple things like integers to complex things like a `DropDownList` control, a connection to the database, or a data-driven control.

Since object orientation is such an important aspect of .NET, it's important to be familiar with the general concepts of object-oriented programming. At the same time, you don't have to be an expert on OO to be able to build web sites with ASP.NET. This section gives you a 10,000-foot overview of the most important terms and concepts. This helps you get started with object orientation in no time, so you can actually start building useful applications in the next chapter instead of keeping your nose in the books for the next three weeks.

Important OO Terminology

In object orientation, everything revolves around the concept of objects. In fact, in OO everything *is,* in fact, an object. But what exactly is an object? And what do classes have to do with them?

Objects

Objects are the basic building blocks of object-oriented programming languages. Just like in the real world, an object in OO-land is a thing. It can be an integer holding someone's age or an open database connection to a SQL Server located on the other side of the world, but it can also be something more conceptual, like a web page. In your applications, you create a new object with the `New` (`new` in C#) keyword, as you saw with the calculator example. This applies for complex or custom types like `Calculator` but even for simple types like `Integers` and `Strings`:

VB.NET

```
Dim myCalculator As New Calculator()

Dim age As Integer = New Integer()
```

C#

```
Calculator my Calculator = new Calculator()

int age = new int();
```

Because it's so common to create variables of simple types like `Integer` (`int` in C#) and `String` (`string` in C#), the compiler allows you to leave out the `new` keyword. Therefore, the following code is functionally equivalent to the previous `age` declaration:

VB.NET

```
Dim age As Integer
```

C#

```
int age;
```

All data types listed at the beginning of this chapter except `System.Object` can be created without the `New` keyword.

Once you have created an instance of an object, such as the `myCalculator` object, it's ready to be used. For example, you can access its methods and properties to do something useful with the object. But before you look at methods and properties, you need to understand classes first.

Classes

Classes are the blueprints of objects. Just as you can use a single blueprint to build a bunch of similar houses, you can use a single class to create multiple instances of that class. So the class acts as the definition of the objects that you use in your application. At its most basic form, a class looks like this:

VB.NET

```
Public Class ClassName

End Class
```

C#

```
public class ClassName
{
}
```

Since this code simply defines an empty class, it cannot do anything useful. To give it some behavior, you can give it properties, methods, and constructors. In addition, you can let the class inherit from an existing class to give it a head start in terms of functionality and behavior. You'll come to understand these terms in the next couple of sections.

Properties

Properties of an object are the characteristics the object has. Consider a `Person` object. What kind of properties does a `Person` have? It's easy to come up with many different characteristics, but the most common are:

- First name
- Last name
- Date of birth

You define a property in a class with the `Property` keyword (in VB.NET) or with a property header similar to a method in C#. In both languages, you use a `Set` block (`set` in C#) and a `Get` block (`get` in C#) to define the so-called setters and getters of the property. The getter is accessed when an object is asked for the value of a specific property while the setter is used to assign a value to the property. Properties only provide access to underlying data stored in the object; they don't contain the actual data. To store the data, you need what is called a *backing variable*. This is a simple variable defined in the class that is able to store the value for the external property. In the following example, the variable `_firstName` is the backing variable for the `FirstName` property:

VB.NET

```
Public Class Person
  Private _firstName As String
  Public Property FirstName() As String
    Get
      Return _firstName
    End Get
    Set(ByVal value As String)
      _firstName = value
    End Set
  End Property
End Class
```

C#

```
public class Person
{
  private string _firstName;
  public string FirstName
```

```
    {
      get { return _firstName; }
      set { _firstName = value; }
    }
  }
```

It is common to prefix the private backing variables with an underscore, followed by the first word in all lower case, optionally followed by more words that start with a capital again. So the `FirstName` property has a backing variable called `_firstName`, `LastName` has one called `_lastName`, and so on.

The main reason for a property in a class is to *encapsulate* data. The idea is that a property allows you to control the data that is being assigned to it. This way, you can perform validation or manipulation of the data before it's stored in the underlying backing variable. Imagine that one of the business rules of your application states that all first names must be written with the first letter as a capital. In non–object-oriented languages, the developer setting the name would have to keep this rule in mind every time a variable was filled with a first name. In an OO approach, you can make the `FirstName` property responsible for this rule so others don't have to worry about it anymore. You can do this type of data manipulation in the setter of the property:

VB.NET

```
Set(ByVal value As String)
  If Not String.IsNullOrEmpty(value) Then
    _firstName = value.Substring(0, 1).ToUpper() & value.Substring(1)
  End If
End Set
```

C#

```
set
{
  if (!string.IsNullOrEmpty(value))
  {
    _firstName = value.Substring(0, 1).ToUpper() + value.Substring(1);
  }
}
```

This code demonstrates that both in VB.NET as in C#, the `value` parameter is accessible, just as a parameter to a method. In VB.NET, the `value` parameter is defined explicitly in the property's setter. In C# it's not specified explicitly, but you can access it nonetheless.

The code first checks if the `value` that is being passed is not `Nothing` (`null` in C#) and that it doesn't contain an empty string using the handy `String.IsNullOrEmpty` method.

The code in the `If` block then takes the first letter of `value`, using the `SubString` method of the `String` class which it passes the values `0` and `1`. The `0` indicates the start of the substring while the `1` indicates the length of the string that must be returned. String indexing is zero-based as well, so a start of `0` and a length of `1` effectively returns the first character of the `value` parameter. This character is then changed to upper case using `ToUpper()`. Finally, the code takes the remainder of the `value` parameter using `SubString` again and assigns the combined name back to the backing variable.

You can now use code that sets the name with arbitrary casing. But, when you try to access the name again, the first name will always begin with a proper first character:

VB.NET

```
Dim myPerson As New Person()           ' Create a new instance of Person
myPerson.FirstName = "imar"            ' Accessing the setter that changes the value

Label1.Text = myPerson.FirstName       ' Accessing the getter that now returns Imar
```

C#

```
Person myPerson = new Person();     // Create a new instance of Person
myPerson.FirstName = "imar";        // Accessing the setter that changes the value

Label1.Text = myPerson.FirstName;   // Accessing the getter that now returns Imar
```

For simple properties that don't need any data manipulation or validation, you can use so-called *automatic properties* in C# only. With these properties, you can use a much more condensed syntax without the need for a private backing variable. When the code is compiled, the compiler will create the necessary backing variable for you, but you won't be able to access it in your code. Here's the `DateOfBirth` property of the `Person` in C# written as an automatic property:

```
public DateTime DateOfBirth { get; set; }
```

If you later decide you need to write code in the getter or the setter of the property, it's easy to extend the relevant code blocks without breaking your existing application. Until that time, you have nice, clean property definitions that don't clutter up your class.

Making Read-Only and Write-Only Properties

There are times where read-only or write-only properties make a lot of sense. For example, the ID of an object could be read-only if it assigned by the database automatically. When the object is constructed from the database, the ID is assigned to the private backing variable. The public `Id` property is then made read-only to stop calling code from accidentally changing it. Likewise, you can have a write-only property for security reasons. For example, you could have a `Password` property on a `Person` object that you can only assign to if you know it, but no longer read it afterward. Internally, code within the class can still access the backing variables to work with the password value.

Read-only or write-only properties in C# are simple: just leave out the setter (for a read-only property) or the getter (for a write-only property). VB.NET is a bit more verbose and wants you to specify the keyword `ReadOnly` or `WriteOnly` explicitly. The following code snippet shows a read-only `Id` property in both VB.NET and C#:

VB.NET

```
Private _id As Integer
Public ReadOnly Property Id() As Integer
  Get
    Return _id
```

```
  End Get
End Property
```

C#

```
private int _id;
public int Id
{
  get { return _id; }
}
```

When you try to assign a value to a read-only property, you'll get an error in VWD.

Similar to properties, objects can also have methods.

Methods

If properties are the things that a class has (its characteristics), then methods are the things a class can do. A car, for example, has characteristics such as `Brand`, `Model`, and `Color`. Its methods could be `Drive()`, `Brake()`, and `OpenDoors()`. Methods give objects the behavior that enables them to do something.

You have already seen methods at work earlier when this chapter discussed some ways to write organized code. All the rules you saw for functions and subroutines apply here as well. You simply add methods to a class by writing a function or a sub between the start and end elements of the class. For example, imagine the `Person` class has a `Save` method that enables the object to persist itself in the database. The method's signature could look like this:

VB.NET

```
Public Class Person
  Public Sub Save()
    ' Implementation goes here
  End Sub
End Class
```

C#

```
public class Person
{
  public void Save()
  {
    // Implementation goes here
  }
}
```

If you want to call the `Save` method to have the `Person` object save itself to the database, you'd create an instance of it, set the relevant properties like FirstName and then call `Save`:

VB.NET

```
Dim myPerson As New Person()
myPerson.FirstName = "Joop"
myPerson.Save()
```

C#

```
Person myPerson = new Person();
myPerson.FirstName = "Joop";
myPerson.Save();
```

The `Save` method would then know how to save the `Person` in the database.

Note that a new instance of the `Person` class is created with the `New` (`new` in C#) keyword followed by the class name. When this code fires, it calls the object's *constructor*, which is used to create instances of objects.

Constructors

Constructors are special methods in a class that help you create an instance of your object. They run as soon as you try to create an instance of a class, so they are a great place to initialize your objects to some default state. Earlier you learned that you create a new instance of an object using the `New` (`new` in C#) keyword:

VB.NET

```
Dim myCalculator As New Calculator()
```

C#

```
Calculator myCalculator = new Calculator();
```

The `New` keyword is followed by the object's constructor: the name of the class. By default, when you create a new class in Visual Web Developer, you get a default constructor for C# but not for VB.NET. That's not really a problem, though, as the compiler will generate a default constructor for you if you leave it out. A default constructor has no arguments and takes the name of the class in C# and the reserved keyword `New` in VB.NET:

VB.NET

```
Public Class Person
  Public Sub New()

  End Sub
End Class
```

C#

```
public class Person
{
  public Person()
  {

  }
}
```

Although this default constructor is nice for creating standard instances of your classes, there are also times when it is really useful to be able to send some information into the class up front, so it's readily available as soon as it is constructed. For example, with the `Person` class, it could be useful to pass in the first and last names and the date of birth to the constructor so that data is available immediately afterwards. To enable this scenario, you can create an *overloaded constructor*. An overloaded constructor or method is essentially a copy of an existing method with the exact same name, but with a different method signature. To have the constructor accept the names and the date of birth, you need the following code:

VB.NET

```
Public Sub New(ByVal firstName As String, ByVal lastName As String, _
                ByVal dateOfBirth As DateTime)
  _firstName = firstName
  _lastName = lastName
  _dateOfBirth = dateOfBirth
End Sub
```

C#

```
public Person(string firstName, string lastName, DateTime dateOfBirth)
{
  _firstName = firstName;
  _lastName = lastName;
  _dateOfBirth = dateOfBirth;
}
```

With this code, you can create a new `Person` object:

```
Person myPerson = new Person("Imar", "Spaanjaars", new DateTime(1971, 8, 9));
```

Right after this line of code, the `myPerson` object is fully initialized, and all of its properties now have a value.

In addition to overloaded constructors, .NET 3.5 offers another quick way to create an object and initialize a few properties: *object initializers*. With an object initializer, you provide the initial values for some of the properties at the same time you declare an instance of your objects. The following code creates a `Person` object and assigns it a default value for the `FirstName` and `LastName` properties:

VB.NET

```
Dim myPerson As New Person() With {.FirstName = "Imar", .LastName = "Spaanjaars"}
```

C#

```
Person myPerson = new Person() { FirstName = "Imar", LastName = "Spaanjaars" };
```

In VB.NET, you need the `With` keyword in front of the properties list. In addition, you need to prefix each property name with a dot (`.`). Other than that, the syntax is pretty much the same for both languages. Object initializers are great if you quickly need to set a bunch of properties on an object without forcing you to write specialized overloaded versions of the constructors.

Although it's useful to have this `Person` class in your application, there are times when you may need specialized versions of a `Person`. For example, your application may require classes like `Employee` and `Student`. What should you do in this case? Create two copies of the `Person` class and name them `Employee` and `Student`, respectively?

Although this approach certainly works, it has a few large drawbacks. The biggest problem is the duplicate code. If you decide to add a `SocialSecurityNumber` property, you now need to add it in multiple locations: in the general `Person` class and in the `Employee` and `Student` classes. Object inheritance, a major pillar of object orientation, is designed to solve problems of this kind.

Inheritance

Earlier you learned that `System.Object` is the parent of all other data types in .NET, including all the built-in types and types that you define yourself, meaning that each type in .NET (except `Object` itself) inherits from `Object`. One of the benefits of inheritance is that you can define a behavior at a high level (for example in the `Object` class) which is available to inheriting classes automatically without the need to duplicate that code. In the .NET Framework, the `Object` class defines a few members that all other objects inherit, including the `ToString()` method.

Think about the `Person` object shown in earlier examples. The class had a few properties such as `FirstName` and `LastName`, and a `Save` method. But, if it is inheriting from `Object`, does it also have a `ToString()` method? You bet it does. Figure 5-7 shows the relation between the `Object` class and the `Person` class that inherits from `Object`.

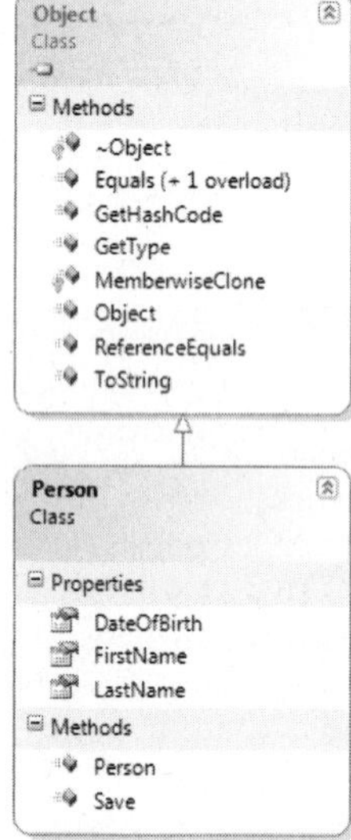

Figure 5-7

Figure 5-7 shows that Person inherits from Object (indicated by the line with a single arrow head pointing in the direction of the class that is begin inherited from) which in turn means that a Person instance can do whatever an Object can do. So, for example, you can call ToString() on your Person object:

```
Label1.Text = myPerson.ToString()                    ' Writes out Person
```

The default behavior of the ToString() method defined in Object is to say its own name. In the example above, it means that the Person class inherits this behavior and thus says Person as its name. Usually, this default behavior is not enough and it would be much more useful if the Person could return the full name of the person it is representing for example. You can easily do this by *overriding* the ToString() method. Overriding a method or property effectively redefines the behavior the class inherits from its parent class. To override a method you use the keyword Overrides in VB.NET and override in C#. The following snippet redefines the behavior of ToString in the Person class:

VB.NET

```
Public Overrides Function ToString() As String
  Return _firstName & " " & _lastName
End Function
```

C#

```
public override string ToString()
{
  return _firstName + " " + _lastName;
}
```

With this definition of ToString in the Person class, it no longer returns the word *Person*, but now returns the full name of the person it is representing:

```
Label1.Text = myPerson.ToString()                    ' Writes out Imar Spaanjaars
```

Object inheritance in .NET allows you to create a hierarchy of objects that enhance, or add functionality to, other objects. This allows you to start out with a generic base class (Object). Other classes can then inherit from this class, adding specialized behavior. If you need even more specialized classes, you can inherit again from the class that inherits from Object, thus creating a hierarchy of classes that keep getting more specialized. This principle works for many classes in the .NET Framework, including the Page class. You may not realize it, but every ASPX page you create in VWD is actually a class that inherits from the class System.Web.UI.Page. This Page class in turn inherits from TemplateControl, which inherits from Control, which inherits from Object. The entire hierarchy is shown in Figure 5-8. At the bottom you see the class MyWebPage, which could be a normal web page called MyWebPage.aspx in your web site.

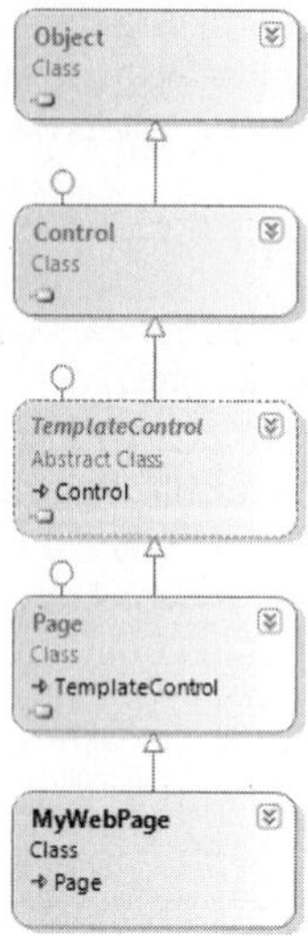

Figure 5-8

In Figure 5-8 you can see that `TemplateControl` is an *abstract class* — a class that cannot be instantiated; that is, you cannot use `New` (`new` in C#) to create a new instance of it. It serves solely as common base class for others (like `Page`) that can inherit from it. The exact classes between `Page` and `Object` are not really relevant at this stage. What is important is that your page inherits all the behavior that the `Page` class has. The fact that all your ASPX pages inherit from `Page` is more useful than you may think at first. Because it inherits from `Page`, you get loads of properties and methods defined in this class for free. For example, the `Page` class exposes a `Title` property that, when set, ends up as a `<title>` element in the page. Your page can simply set this property, and the parent `Page` class handles the rest for you:

VB.NET

```
Title = "Beginning ASP.NET 3.5 by Wrox"
```

C#

```
Title = "Beginning ASP.NET 3.5 by Wrox";
```

To create a class that inherits from another class you use the keyword `Inherits` in VB.NET and the colon (`:`) in C#. Take another look at the class definition you saw earlier when namespaces were discussed:

VB.NET

```
Partial Class Demos_CalculatorDemo
    Inherits System.Web.UI.Page
```

C#

```
public partial class Demos_CalculatorDemo : System.Web.UI.Page
```

This code defines a class called `Demos_CalculatorDemo` that inherits from `System.Web.UI.Page`. You can say that `Demos_CalculatorDemo` is a *specialized* version of `Page`, as it can do anything `Page` can but also adds its own behavior.

You'll use inheritance in the next chapter when you create a `BasePage` class that serves as the parent for all your Code Behind classes.

In earlier examples, including the override for the `ToString()` method, you have seen the keyword `Public`. Additionally, when creating backing variables, you saw the keyword `Private`. These keywords are called *access modifiers* and determine the visibility of your code.

Access Modifiers

Earlier in this chapter I mentioned that a core concept of OO is *encapsulation*. By creating members such as functions and properties, you make an object responsible for the implementation. Other objects interacting with this object consider those methods and properties as black boxes. That is, they pass some data in and optionally expect some result back. How the method performs its work is of no interest; it should just work as advertised. So to enable an object to shield some of its inner operations, you need a way to control access to types and members. You do this by specifying an access modifier in front of the class, property, or method name. The following table lists the available access modifiers for C# and VB.NET and explains their purpose.

C#	VB.NET	Description
public	Public	The class or member can be accessed from everywhere, including code outside the current application.
protected	Protected	Code with a protected access modifier is only available within the type that defines it or within types that inherit from it. For example, a protected member defined in the `Page` class is accessible to your ASPX page because it inherits from `Page`.
internal	Friend	Limits the accessibility of your code to other code within the same *assembly*. An assembly is a set of one or more compiled code files (either a .exe or a .dll file) containing reusable .NET code.
private	Private	A member that is only accessible within the type that defines it. For example, with the `Person` class, the `_firstName` variable is only accessible from within the `Person` class. Other code, like an ASPX page, cannot access this field in any way, and needs to access the public `FirstName` property to get or set the first name of a person.

Of these four access modifiers, only `protected` and `internal` (`Protected` and `Friend` in VB) can be combined. All the others must be used separately. By combining `protected` and `internal`, you can create members that are accessible by the current class and any class that inherits from it in the current assembly only.

As with some of the other OO concepts, you won't be spending half your day specifying access modifiers in your code. However, it's good to know that they exist and what they do. That way, you may have a clue why sometimes your classes don't show up in the IntelliSense list. There's a fair chance you forgot to specify the `Public` access modifier on the class in that case. The default is `internal` (Friend in VB.NET) which makes the class visible to other classes in the same assembly (a.DLL) but hides it from code outside the assembly) . Adding the keyword `Public` in front of the class definition should fix the problem.

Events

The final important topic that needs to be discussed in this chapter is events. ASP.NET is an *event driven* environment, which means that code can execute based on certain events that occur in your code. Events are *raised* by certain objects in the application and then *handled* by others. There are many objects in the .NET Framework capable of raising an event, and you can even add your own events to classes that you write.

To be able to handle an event raised by an object, you need to write an *event handler*, which is basically a normal method with a special signature. You can *wire up* this event handler to the event using event wiring syntax, although VWD takes care of that most of the time for you. When an object, such as a control in a web page, raises an event, it may have the need to pass additional information to the event handler, to inform it about relevant data that caused or influenced the event. You can send out this information using an *event arguments class*, which is the class `System.EventArgs` or any class that inherits from it.

To see how all these terms fit together, consider what happens when you click a button in a web page. When you click it, the client-side button in the browser causes a postback. At the server, the `Button` control sees it was clicked in the browser and then raises its `Click` event. It's as if the button says: "Oh, look everyone. I just got clicked. In case anyone is interested, here are some details." Usually, the code that is interested in the button's `Click` event is your own page that needs to have an event handler to handle the click. You can create an event handler for the `Button` by double-clicking it in the designer. Alternatively, you can double-click the relevant event on the Properties Grid of the control with the Events category listed (see Figure 5-9), which you can open by pressing the button with the lightning bolt on the toolbar.

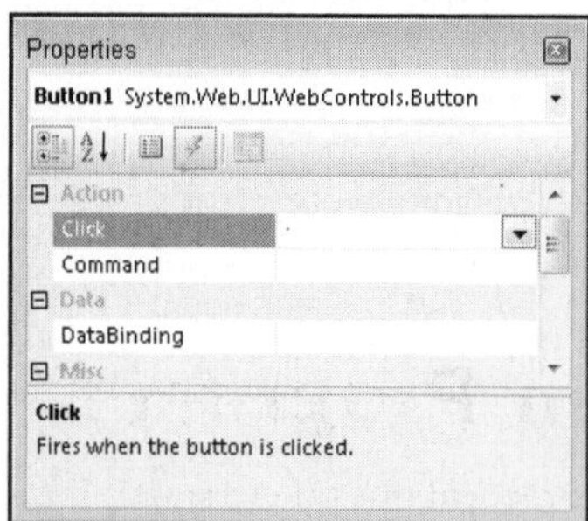

Figure 5-9

If you double-click the control in Design View or the event name in the Properties Grid, Visual Web Developer writes the code for the event handler for you. The following snippet shows the handler in VB.NET and C#:

VB.NET

```
Protected Sub Button1_Click(ByVal sender As Object, ByVal e As System.EventArgs) _
        Handles Button1.Click
End Sub
```

C#

```
protected void Button1_Click(object sender, EventArgs e)
{
}
```

In the VB.NET example, you see a standard method with some arguments, followed by `Handles Button1.Click`. This is the event wiring code that hooks up the `Button` control's `Click` event to the `Button1_Click` method. Now, whenever the button is clicked, the code inside `Button1_Click` is executed.

The C# version doesn't have this `Handles` keyword. Instead, with C# you'll find that VWD has added the following bold code to the `Button` control in the markup of the page:

```
<asp:Button ID="Button1" runat="server" Text="Button"
                OnClick="Button1_Click" />
```

With this piece of markup, the .NET runtime will generate the necessary code to link up the `Button1_Click` method to the `Click` event of the button. At runtime you'll see the exact same behavior: when you click the button, the code in `Button1_Click` is executed.

You can also see that this `Button1_Click` event handler has two parameters: an `Object` called `sender` and an `EventArgs` class called `e`. This is a standard .NET naming scheme and is followed by all objects that generate events. The sender parameter contains a reference to the object that triggered the event; `Button1` in this example. This allows you to find out who triggered an event in case you wired up the same event handler to multiple events.

The second parameter is an instance of the `EventArgs` class and supplies additional arguments to the event. With a button's click, there is no additional relevant data to submit, so the plain and empty `EventArgs` class is used. However, in later chapters (for example, Chapter 9, which deals with data-driven Web Forms), you'll see some examples of classes that fire events with richer information.

With the concepts of events, you have come to the end of the section on object orientation. This section should have familiarized you with the most important terms used in object-oriented programming. You'll see practical examples of these concepts in the remainder of this book.

Practical Tips on Programming

The following list presents some practical tips on programming:

- Always give your variables meaningful names. For simple loop counters, you can use `i` although `loopCount` probably describes the purpose of the variable much better. Don't prefix variables with the word `var`. All variables are variables, so adding `var` only adds noise to your code. Consider useful names such as `_firstName` and `_categoryId` as opposed to `strFName` or `catI` for private fields, and names like `FirstName` and `Person` for public properties and classes, respectively. The only exception to these rules is with the controls in your page — those are often prefixed with their type, like `lstOperator` to denote a list.
- Experiment and experiment. Even more so than with working with controls and ASPX pages, the best way to learn how to program is by actually doing it. Just type in some code and hit Ctrl+F5 to see how the code behaves. The compiler will bark at you when something is wrong,

providing you with useful hints on how to fix it. Don't be afraid to mess anything up; just keep trying variations until the code does what you want it to do.

- Whenever possible, try to program together with somebody else. Nothing beats a game of *pair programming* where one person programs and explains what he does, while the other gives comments and asks questions. Swap places regularly, to put yourself in the other's position.
- When writing functions or subroutines, try to minimize the number of lines of code. Usually, methods with more than 40 or 50 lines of code are a sign of bad design. When you see such code, consider the option to move certain parts to their own routine. This makes your code much easier to understand, leading to better code with fewer bugs. Even if a method is only used once, keeping a chunk of code in a separate method can significantly increase the readability and organization of your code.
- When writing comments in your code, try to describe the general purpose of the code instead of explaining obvious statements. For example, this comment (seen many times in real code) is completely useless:

```
Dim loopCount As Integer = 0      ' Declare variable loopCounter and initialize it to zero
```

Anyone with just a little bit of coding experience can see what this code does. Instead, describe in which loop the `loopCount` variable is used.

Summary

This chapter introduced you to the world of programming within the .NET Framework. Programming is a huge subject covered by literally thousands of books. Although programming can get really complex, the bare basics that you need to understand are relatively easy to grasp. The fun thing about programming is that you don't have to be an expert to make useful programs. You can simply start with a simple Hello World example and work from there, each time expanding your view on code a little.

To be able to write applications, each programming language defines data types. These are the building blocks of any application and are used to work with data that your application operates on. With variables you can store data with simple numeric types like `System.String` or `System.Boolean` or in other, more complex objects and collections that are defined in the .NET Framework and that you can define yourself. Arrays and collections allow you to group more than one object within a single variable, giving you easy access to them.

Besides data types, statements are another part of the grammar of a programming language. With statements you tell the program what you want it to do. The first group of statements is the operators, which enable you to work with data. For example, you can add two numeric values, concatenate two strings, or compare the result of an expression with a predefined value.

Making decisions in code is a common operation, so both VB.NET and C# offer a number of different ways to do this, including `If` and `If Else` statements and `Select Case` or `switch` blocks. To repeat a block of code or iterate over a collection you have various looping constructs at your disposal, including the `For` loop, the `For Each` / `foreach` loop, and various flavors of the `While` and `Do` loops.

To write code that is easy to read and maintain, you should try to write as structured as possible. Using functions and subroutines you can move repeating code to separate code files. With namespaces you can logically group your code, making it easier to find and navigate to. While you're coding, be sure to write inline and XML comments to describe the code. If you get into that habit early, you'll thank yourself two years from now if you need to maintain an old piece of code.

The final section of this chapter dealt with object orientation. While object orientation in itself is a very large subject, the basics are easy to pick up. In this chapter you learned about the basic elements of OO programming: classes, methods, properties, and constructors. You also learned a bit about inheritance, the driving force behind object-oriented design. With inheritance, you can define objects that inherit a lot of information from their parent classes, allowing you to create specialized classes that expose additional behavior without recoding the functionality that the class gets from its parent. This leads to cleaner code and objects that are easy to use by you and other programmers.

In the next chapter, which deals with creating consistent-looking web pages, you'll see inheritance again when you create a `BasePage` class that serves as the parent for all the Code Behind classes in the Planet Wrox project.

Exercises

1. Considering the fact that the oldest person in the world lived to be 122, what's the best numeric data type to store a person's age? There are bonus points to collect if you come up with an even better alternative to store someone's age.
2. What does the following code do?

VB.NET

```
DeleteButton.Visible = ShoppingCart.Items.Count > 0
```

C#

```
DeleteButton.Visible = ShoppingCart.Items.Count > 0;
```

3. Given the following class `Person`, what would the code look like for a new class `PersonWithPhoneNumber`? Make use of inheritance to create this new class.

VB.NET

```
Public Class Person
  Private _name As String
  Public Property Name() As String
    Get
      Return _name
    End Get
    Set(ByVal value As String)
      _name = value
    End Set
  End Property
End Class
```

C#

```
public class Person
{
  public string Name { get; set; }
}
```

Creating Consistent Looking Web Sites

When you're designing and building a web site you should always strive to make the layout and behavior as consistent as possible. Consistency gives your site a professional appearance and it helps your visitors to find their way around the site. Fortunately, ASP.NET 3.5 offers a number of great features to implement a consistent design. In addition, Visual Web Developer has a set of great tools and a rich Design View helping you create great-looking pages in no time.

In previous chapters you learned how to work with VWD, HTML, CSS, and server controls to create your web pages visually. Chapter 5 introduced you to programming in .NET. This chapter is the first that combines these concepts. You'll see how to write code that applies to all the pages in your site, creating a central location for shared behavior.

In particular, this chapter deals with the following topics that help you create well-designed and consistent web pages that are easy to maintain:

- Using master and content pages that allow you to define the global look of a web page
- Working with a centralized base page that allows you to define common behavior for all pages in your site
- Creating ASP.NET 3.5 themes to define the look and feel of your site with an option for the user to choose their favorite theme at runtime
- Creating skins to quickly make site-wide changes to control layout

The next section shows you how to create a master page that defines the general look and feel of a page. The ASPX pages in your site can then use this master page without the need to rewrite the layout. The remaining sections of this chapter build on top of the master page.

Consistent Page Layout with Master Pages

With most web sites, only part of the page changes when you go from one page to another. The parts that don't change usually include common regions like the header, a menu, and the footer. To create web pages with a consistent layout you need a way to define these relatively static regions in a single *template* file. Versions of ASP.NET prior to ASP.NET 2.0 did not have a template solution so you were forced to duplicate your page layout on every single page in the web site, or resort to weird programming tricks. Fortunately, this is no longer the case due to *master pages*. The biggest benefit of master pages is that they allow you to define the look and feel of all the pages in your site in a single location. This means that if you want to change the layout of your site — for instance if you want to move the menu from the left to the right — you only need to modify the master page and the pages based on this master will pick up the changes automatically.

When master pages were introduced in ASP.NET 2.0, they were quickly embraced by the developer community as *the* template solution for ASP.NET pages because they are very easy to use. Even better, VWD has great design-time support, as it allows you to create and view your pages at design time during development, rather than only in the browser at runtime.

To some extent, a master page looks like a normal ASPX page. It contains static HTML such as the `<html>`, `<head>`, and `<body>` tags, and it can also contain other HTML and ASP.NET Server Controls. Inside the master page, you set up the markup that you want to repeat on every page, like the general layout of the page and the menu.

However, a master page is not a true ASPX page and cannot be requested in the browser directly; it only serves as the template that real web pages — called *content pages* — are based on.

Instead of the `@ Page` directive that you have seen in previous chapters, a master page uses a `@ Master` directive that identifies the file as a master page:

VB.NET

```
<%@ Master Language="VB" %>
```

C#

```
<%@ Master Language="C#" %>
```

Just like a normal ASPX page, a master page can have a Code Behind file, identified by its `CodeFile` and `Inherits` attributes:

VB.NET

```
<%@ Master Language="VB" CodeFile="MasterPage.master.vb"
            Inherits="Masterpages_MasterPage" %>
```

C#

```
<%@ Master Language="C#" CodeFile="MasterPage.master.cs"
           Inherits="Masterpages_MasterPage" %>
```

To create regions that content pages can fill in, you need to define `ContentPlaceHolder` controls in your page like this:

```
<asp:ContentPlaceHolder ID="ContentPlaceHolder1" runat="server">
</asp:ContentPlaceHolder>
```

You can create as many placeholders as you like, although you'll usually limit their number to a maximum of four or five regions to keep the page manageable.

The content files, which are essentially normal ASPX files, but without the usual code you find in them like the `<html>`, `<head>`, `<body>`, and `<form>` tags, are connected to a master page using the `MasterPageFile` attribute of the `Page` directive:

VB.NET

```
<%@ Page Language="VB" MasterPageFile="~/Masterpages/MasterPage.master"
       AutoEventWireup="false" CodeFile="Default.aspx.vb" Inherits="_Default">
```

C#

```
<%@ Page Language="C#" MasterPageFile="~/Masterpages/MasterPage.master"
       AutoEventWireup="true" CodeFile="Default.aspx.cs" Inherits="_Default">
```

The page-specific content is then put inside an `<asp:Content>` control that points to the relevant `ContentPlaceHolder`:

```
<asp:Content ID="Content1" ContentPlaceHolderID="ContentPlaceHolder1" Runat="Server">
</asp:Content>
```

Note that the `ContentPlaceHolderID` attribute of the `Content` control points to the `ContentPlaceHolder` that is defined in the master page. Right now it points to the default name of `ContentPlaceHolder1`, but in a later exercise you'll see how to change this.

At runtime, when the page is requested, the markup from the master page and the content page are merged, processed, and sent to the browser. Figure 6-1 shows a diagram of the master page and the content page that result in the final page that is sent to the browser.

To see this process in action, the following sections guide you through creating master and content pages.

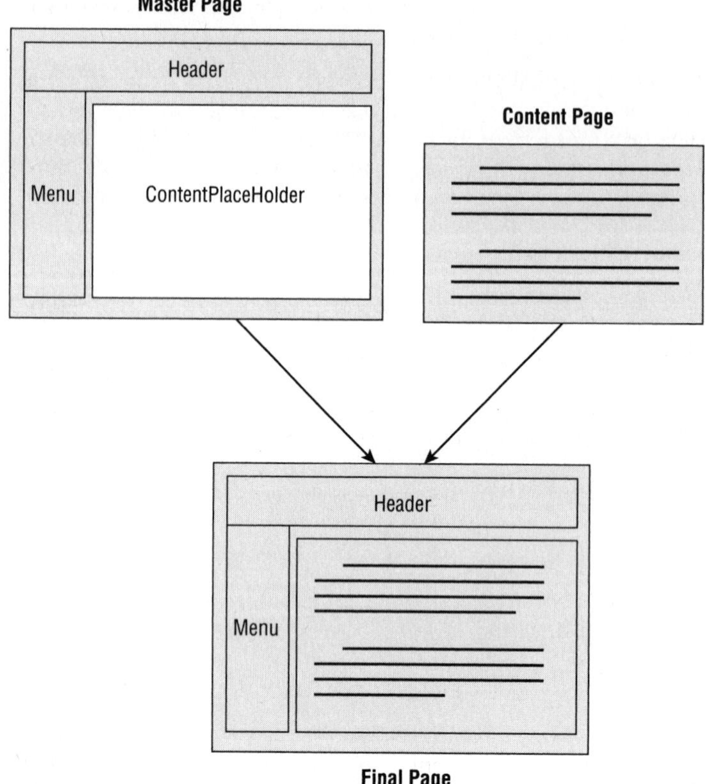

Figure 6-1

Creating Master Pages

Master pages are added to the site using the Add New Item dialog box. They can be placed anywhere in the site, including the root folder, but from an organizational point of view, it's often easier to store them in a separate folder. Just like normal ASPX pages, they support the inline code model as well as the Code Behind model. The master pages used in the Planet Wrox project use the Code Behind model exclusively. In the following exercise, you create a simple master page and add some HTML to it to define the general structure of the pages in your web site.

Try It Out — Creating a Master Page

1. If you don't have it open already, start by opening the Planet Wrox project.
2. In Chapter 2 you created a folder called MasterPages to hold your master pages and then added a single master page to that folder. If you didn't carry out that exercise, add the master page now. To do this, create the MasterPages folder, right-click the new folder, choose Add New Item, and

select Master Page. Make sure that the master page uses Code Behind and that it has your preferred programming language selected.

3. Add the following highlighted code between the `<form>` tags of the master page, replacing the `<div>` tags and the `ContentPlaceHolder` that VWD added for you when you created the master. Note that this is almost the same code you added to Default.aspx in Chapter 3, except for the `<asp:ContentPlaceHolder>` element and the `<a>` element within the `Header <div>`. The `<a>` element takes users back to the home page, and will be styled later.

```
<form id="form1" runat="server">
  <div id="PageWrapper">
    <div id="Header"><a class="HeaderLink" href="~/" runat="server">Header Goes
Here</a></div>
    <div id="MenuWrapper">Menu Goes Here</div>
    <div id="MainContent">
      <asp:ContentPlaceHolder ID="cpMainContent" runat="server">
      </asp:ContentPlaceHolder>
    </div>
    <div id="Sidebar">Sidebar Goes Here</div>
    <div id="Footer">Footer Goes Here</div>
  </div>
</form>
```

Make sure that you have the `ContentPlaceHolder` within the `MainContent <div>` tags. You can drag one from the Toolbox onto the page or enter the code directly, using IntelliSense's helpful hints. In both cases you should give the control an `ID` of `cpMainContent`.

4. Next, switch the master page into Design View and then drag the file Styles.css from the Styles folder in the Solution Explorer onto the master page. As soon as you drop the file, VWD updates the Design View and shows the layout for the site that you created in Chapter 3. If the design doesn't change, switch to Markup View and ensure there's a `<link>` tag in the head of the page pointing to your CSS file. If the link isn't there, you can add it manually:

```
  <asp:ContentPlaceHolder ID="head" runat="server">
  </asp:ContentPlaceHolder>
  <link href="../Styles/Styles.css" rel="stylesheet" type="text/css" />
</head>
```

The page should now look like Figure 6-2 in Design View.

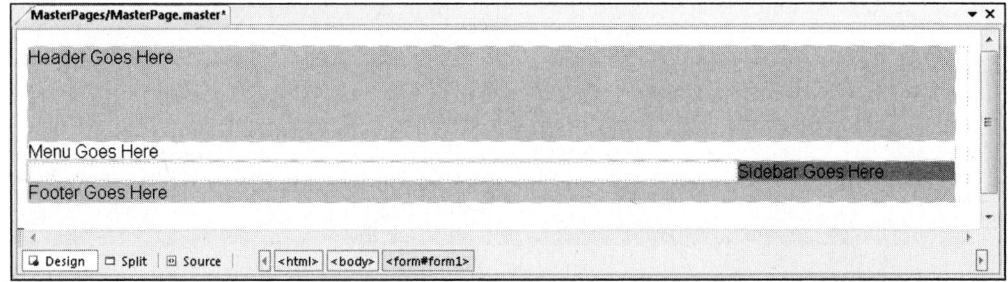

Figure 6-2

Note the area with the purple border around it between the menu and the footer region. This is the `ContentPlaceHolder` control that is used by the content pages. You'll see how this works after the explanation of the master page.

5. You can save and close the page as you're done with the master page for now.

How It Works

Within Visual Web Developer, master pages behave like normal pages. You can add HTML and server controls to them, and you can manage the page both in Markup and Design View. The big difference is, of course, that a master page isn't a true page itself; it only serves as a template for other pages in your site. How this works is discussed in the following section.

Creating Content Pages

A master page is useless without a content page that uses it. Generally, you'll only have a few master pages, while you can have many content pages. To base a content page on a master page, you can check the option Select Master Page at the bottom right of the Add New Item dialog box, which you can bring up by right-clicking your web site in the Solution Explorer and choosing Add New Item. Alternatively, you can set the `MasterPageFile` attribute on the page directly in the Markup View of the page. You saw this `@ Page` directive earlier in this chapter when master pages were introduced.

Content pages can only contain `<asp:Content>` controls that each map to a `<asp:ContentPlaceHolder>` control in the master page. These content controls in turn can contain standard markup like HTML and server control declarations. Because the entire markup in a content page needs to be wrapped by `<asp:Content>` tags, it's not easy to turn an existing ASPX page into a Content page. Usually the easiest thing to do is copy the content you want to keep to the clipboard, delete the old page and then add a new page based on the master page to the web site. Once the page is added, you can paste the markup within the `<asp:Content>` tags. You'll see how this works in the following exercise.

Try It Out — Adding a Content Page

In this Try It Out you'll see how to add a content page to the site that is based on the master page you created earlier. Once the page is added you can add content to the predefined `<asp:Content>` regions.

1. In previous exercises you added standard ASPX pages to your project, which should now be "upgraded" to make use of the new master page. Since VWD has no built-in support to change a standard page into a content page, you'll need to manually copy the content from the old ASPX page into the new one. If you want to keep the welcome text you added to Default.aspx earlier, copy all the HTML between the `MainContent <div>` tags to the clipboard (that is, the `<h1>` and the two `<p>` elements that you created earlier) and then delete the page Default.aspx from the Solution Explorer. Next, right-click the web site in the Solution Explorer and choose Add New Item. Choose Web Form, name the page Default.aspx, select the correct programming

language, and then, at the bottom of the dialog box, select the check boxes for Place Code In Separate File and Select Master Page, as shown in Figure 6-3.

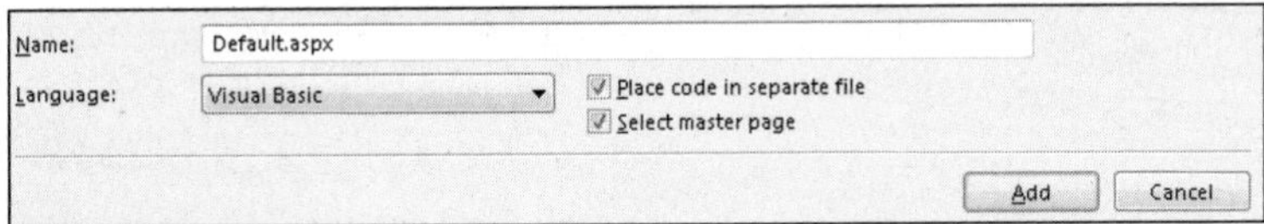

Figure 6-3

Finally, click the Add button.

2. In the Select a Master Page dialog box (see Figure 6-4), click the folder MasterPages in the left-hand pane, and then in the area at the right, click MasterPage.master.

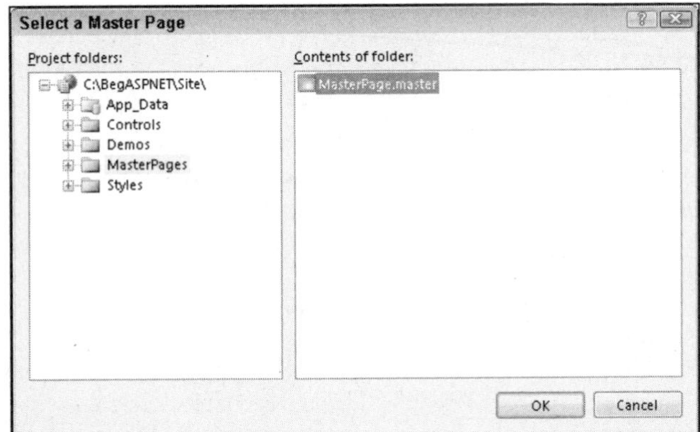

Figure 6-4

Click OK to add the page to your web site.

Instead of getting a full page with HTML as you got with standard ASPX pages, you now only get two `<asp:Content>` placeholders:

```
<%@ Page Language="VB" MasterPageFile="~/MasterPages/MasterPage.master"
    AutoEventWireup="false" CodeFile="Default.aspx.vb" Inherits="_Default"
    title="Untitled Page" %>
<asp:Content ID="Content1" ContentPlaceHolderID="head" Runat="Server">
</asp:Content>
<asp:Content ID="Content2" ContentPlaceHolderID="cpMainContent" Runat="Server">
</asp:Content>
```

3. Switch to Design View and note that everything is grayed out and read-only, except for the `<asp:Content>` region for `cpMainContent`. Figure 6-5 shows you how the page should look.

Figure 6-5

4. If you still have the old markup from the Default.aspx on the clipboard, click once inside the `cpMainContent` placeholder and press Ctrl+V. This adds the markup to the page, right between the `<asp:Content>` tags.

5. Save all pending changes by pressing Ctrl+Shift+S (or from the main menu choose File ➪ Save All) and press Ctrl+F5 to open the page in your browser. The browser should display the page very closely to what you saw in Design View (see Figure 6-5).

6. Now take a look at the HTML for the page in the browser. You can do this by right-clicking the page and choosing View Source. Note that the source of the final page in the browser is a combination of the source of the master page and the content page:

```
<div id="PageWrapper">
  <div id="Header"><a href="./" class="HeaderLink"></a></div>
  <div id="MenuWrapper">Menu Goes Here</div>
  <div id="MainContent">
    <h1>Hi there visitor and welcome to Planet Wrox</h1>
    <p class="Introduction">
      We&#39;re glad you are paying a visit to <a href="http://www.PlanetWrox.com">
      www.PlanetWrox.com</a>, the coolest music community site on the Internet.
    </p>
    ...
```

The first four lines come from the master page while the highlighted lines of HTML code come from the content page.

7. Switch back to VWD and create a new page, called Login.aspx. Make sure it's based on the master page again and that it uses Code Behind. There's no need to add any controls to this page just yet, but it serves as the basis for the login functionality you'll create in Chapter 15.

8. Go back to Default.aspx and switch to Design View. Below the welcome text with the header and two <p> elements, create a new paragraph and type some text (for example, You can log in here). Highlight the words *log in* and choose Format ➪ Convert to Hyperlink from the main menu. In the dialog box that follows, click the Browse button and select the page Login.aspx that you just created. Click OK twice.

9. Save all changes and press Ctrl+F5 again to View the Default.aspx page in the browser. Then click the link you created in the previous step. You should now be taken to Login.aspx. Note that the general layout, like the header and the sidebar, is maintained. The only thing that changes when you go from page to page is the content in the main content area.

How It Works

When a page based on a master page is requested in the browser, the server reads in both the content page and the master page, merges the two, processes them, and then sends the final result to the browser. In step 6 of this exercise you saw that the HTML in the browser for the requested page contained the markup from both files.

Master pages will save you from a lot of work when it comes to updating or radically changing the looks of your site. Since the entire design and layout of your site is defined in the master page, you only need to touch that single file when you want to make any changes. All content pages will pick up the changes automatically.

A Closer Look at Master Pages

So far you've seen a master page with a content placeholder for the main content. But if you look at the master page in Markup View, you'll find another `ContentPlaceHolder` in the head section of the page:

```
<head runat="server">
  <title>Untitled Page</title>
  <asp:ContentPlaceHolder id="head" runat="server">
  </asp:ContentPlaceHolder>
  ...
</head>
```

This placeholder is added for you automatically whenever you add a new master page to the site. You can use it in content pages to add page-specific content that belongs between the `<head>` tags of a page, like CSS (both embedded and external style sheets) and JavaScript. You'll learn more about JavaScript later in this book. You'll need to add content to this placeholder in Markup View, because it's not visible in Design View.

The `ContentPlaceHolder` called `cpMainContent` in the master page currently does not contain any markup itself. However, it doesn't have to be like this. You can easily add your own content there that will serve as the default in your content pages as long as it's not overridden by the content page. For example, you can have the following `<asp:ContentPlaceHolder>` in a master page:

```
<asp:ContentPlaceHolder ID="cpMainContent" runat="server">
  This is default text that shows up in content pages that don't
  explicitly override it.
</asp:ContentPlaceHolder>
```

When you base a new page on this master page, you won't see this default at first in Markup View. However, you can open the `Content` control's Smart Tasks panel, shown in Figure 6-6, and choose Default to Master's Content.

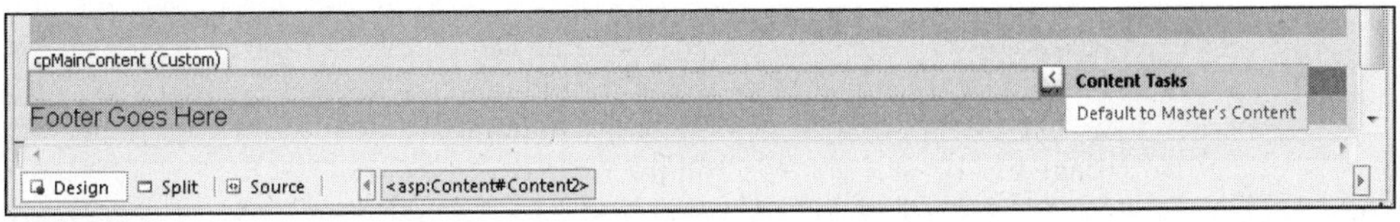

Figure 6-6

When you click Yes when asked if you want to default to the master page content, VWD removes the entire `<asp:Content>` block from the Markup View of the page. However, when you request the page in the browser you will still see the default content from the master page. In Design View, the content is still visible, now presented as a read-only area on the design surface. A master page with default content can be useful if you add a new `ContentPlaceHolder` at a later stage. Existing pages can simply display the default content, without the need for you to touch all these pages. New pages can define their own content.

Once you have defaulted to the master page's content, you can create custom content again by opening the Smart Tasks panel and choosing Create Custom Content. This will add an empty `<asp:Content>` control to the page that you can fill with your own content.

Nesting Master Pages

It is also possible to nest master pages. A nested master page is a master that is based on another master page. Content pages can then be based on the nested master page. This is useful if you have a web site that targets different areas that still need to share a common look and feel. For example, you can have a corporate web site that is separated by departments. The outer master page defines the global look and feel of the site, including corporate logo and other branding elements. You can then have different nested master pages for different departments. For example, the sales department's section could be based on a different master than the marketing department's, allowing each to add their own identity to their section of the site. Visual Web Developer 2008 has good design time support for nested maser pages in Design View, giving you a good look at how the final page will end up.

Creating a nested master page is easy: Check the Select Master Page check box when you add a master page just as you do when you add a normal content page to the site. Then add `<asp:ContentPlaceHolder>` controls to the `<asp:Content>` controls at locations that you want to override in the content pages.

Master Page Caveats

Although master pages are great and can save you from a lot of work, there are some caveats that you need to be aware of.

For starters, the ASP.NET runtime changes the *client ID* of your controls in the page. This is the `id` attribute that is used in client script to access controls from JavaScript in the browser. With normal ASPX pages, the server-side ID of a control is usually inserted one on one in the final HTML. For example, a `Button` control in a normal ASPX page defined with this code:

```
<asp:Button ID="Button1" runat="server" Text="Button" />
```

ends up like this in the HTML:

```
<input type="submit" name="Button1" value="Button" id="Button1" />
```

The server-side ID defined in the `Button` element is copied directly to the `id` attribute of the `<input>` element in the browser.

However, the same button inside an `<asp:Content>` control ends up like this:

```
<input type="submit" name="ctl00$cpMainContent$Button1" value="Button"
              id="ctl00_cpMainContent_Button1" />
```

Both the `name` and the `id` attributes have now been prefixed with the auto-generated ID of the master page (`ctl00`) and the ID of `ContentPlaceHolder` control (`cpMainContent`).

This means that any client-side code that refers to `Button1` should now refer to `ctl00_cpMainContent_Button1`.

Note that this is not just a master page problem; you'll also run into this behavior in other situations; for example, when working with User Controls (discussed in Chapter 8) and data-bound controls (discussed in Chapter 12 and onward).

The second caveat is related to the first. Because the `name` and `id` of the HTML elements are changed, they add considerably to the size of the page. This may not be problematic for a single control, but once you have pages with lots of controls, this could impact the performance of your site. The problem gets worse with nested master pages, where both content controls are appended to the ID. The same button inside a nested master page can end up like this:

```
<input type="submit" name="ctl00$ctl00$ContentPlaceHolder1$ContentPlaceHolder1$Button1"
   value="Button" id="ctl00_ctl00_ContentPlaceHolder1_ContentPlaceHolder1_Button1" />
```

To mitigate the problem, you should keep the IDs of your `ContentPlaceHolder` and `Content` controls as short as possible. To improve the readability, this book uses longer names, like `cpMainContent`. However, in your own sites, you can reduce this to `cpMC` or `cp1` in order to save some bandwidth on every request.

Master pages allow you to define the general look and feel of your site in a single location. This improves the consistency and maintainability of your site. However, there is another way to improve consistency: centralize the behavior of the pages in your web site. You can do this with a so-called base page, which is discussed next.

Using a Centralized Base Page

Chapter 5 states that by default all ASPX pages derive from a class called `System.Web.UI.Page`. This means all of your pages have at least the behavior defined in this class.

However, there are circumstances where this behavior is not enough and you need to add your own stuff to the mix. For example, you may have the need to add behavior that applies to all the pages in your site. Instead of adding this behavior to each and every individual page, you can create a common *base page*. All the pages in your site can then inherit from this intermediate page instead of from the standard `Page` class. The left half of Figure 6-7 shows how a default ASPX page called `MyWebPage` inherits from the `Page` class directly. The right half shows a situation where the ASPX page inherits from a class called `BasePage`, which in turn inherits from `Page`.

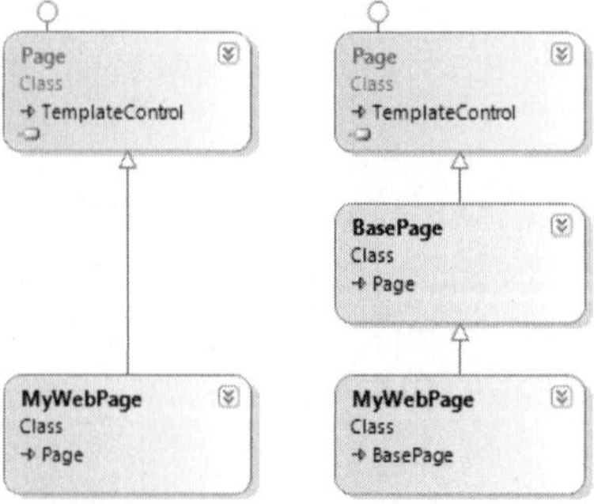

Figure 6-7

To be able to have your pages inherit from this base page, you need to do two things:

- Create a class that inherits from `System.Web.UI.Page` in the App_Code folder of your web site.
- Make the web pages in your site inherit from this base page instead of the standard `Page` class.

In the following exercise you create a new base page class inside the App_Code folder. For now, the sole purpose of this class is to check the `Title` of the page at runtime to avoid pages with the default name of Untitled Page that VWD assigns making it to the browser. This functionality is relatively easy to achieve, so you can focus on the concept of inheritance rather than on the actual code. In the section that discusses themes later in this chapter you'll modify the base page once more, this time to retrieve the user's preference for a theme.

However, before you can implement the base class, you need to know more about the *ASP.NET page life cycle*, another important concept that describes the process a web page goes through when requested by a browser.

An Introduction to the ASP.NET Page Life Cycle

When you think about how a page is served by a web server to the browser and think of this process as the life cycle of a page, you can probably come up with a few important moments in the page's life. For example, the initial request by the browser is the starting point for the page's "life." Similarly, when the page has sent its entire HTML to the browser, its life may seem to end. However, there are more interesting events going on in the page's life cycle. The following table describes eight broad phases the page goes through. Within each phase, at least one event is raised that allows a page developer to hook into the page's life cycle and perform actions at the right moment. You'll see an example of this in the next exercise.

Phase	Description
Page request	A request to an ASPX page starts the life cycle of that page. When the web server is able and allowed to return a cached copy of the page, then the entire life cycle is not executed. In all other situations, the page enters the start phase.
Start	The start phase for the page, where it gets access to properties like Request and Response, used to interact with the environment of the page. In addition, during this phase the `PreInit` event is raised to signal that the page is about to go into the initialization phase. You'll use this event later to set the theme of a page.
Page initialization	During this phase, the controls you have set up in your page or added programmatically become available. During this phase the `Page` class fires three events: `Init`, `InitComplete`, and `PreLoad`. Also during this phase, the control properties are loaded from ViewState again during a postback. So, when you changed the selected item in a `DropDownList` and then caused a postback, this is the moment where the correct items gets preselected in the drop-down list again.
Load	During this phase the page raises the `Load` event.
Validation	During the validation phase, the Validation controls used to validate user input are processed. You learn about validators in Chapter 9.
Postback event handling	During this phase, the controls in your page may raise their own events. For example, the `DropDownList` may raise a `SelectedIndexChanged` event when the user has chosen a different option in the list. Similarly, a `TextBox` may raise the `TextChanged` event when the user has changed the text before they posted back to the server. When all event processing is done, the page raises the `LoadComplete` event. During this phase the `PreRender` event is raised to signal that the page is about to render to the browser. Shortly after that, `SaveStateComplete` is raised to indicate that the page is done storing all the relevant data for the controls in ViewState.
Rendering	Rendering is the phase where the controls (and the page itself) output their HTML to the browser.
Unload	The Unload phase is really a clean-up phase. This is the moment where the page and controls can release resources like database connections. During this phase, the `Unload` event is raised so you can handle any cleanup you may need to do.

Now you may wonder why you need to know all of this. The biggest reason to have some understanding of the page life cycle is that certain actions can only be performed at specific stages in the page life cycle. For example, dynamically changing the theme has to take place early in the page's life cycle as you'll see later. To really understand the ASP.NET page life cycle, you need to know a little more about controls, state, events, and so on. Therefore, you'll revisit the page life cycle again in Chapter 14 where you get a good look at all the different events that fire, and in what order.

Since a page developer could set the page's title programmatically during many events, checking for a correct title should be done as late as possible in the page's life cycle. The next exercise shows you how this works.

Implementing the Base Page

Implementing a base page is pretty easy: all you need to do is add a class file to your App_Code folder, add some code to it, and you're done. What's often a bit more difficult is to make sure each page in your site inherits from this new base page instead of from the standard `System.Web.UI.Page` class. Unfortunately, there is no way to configure the application to do this for you automatically when using Code Behind, so you'll need to modify each page manually. Visual Web Developer makes it a little easier for you by allowing you to export a page template that already contains this code. After you have created the base page in the next exercise you will see how to export a page to a template so you can add files that use the base page in no time.

Try It Out — Creating a Base Page

1. Right-click the App_Code folder in the Solution Explorer and choose Add New Item. Select Class in the Templates list and name the file `BasePage`. You can choose any name you like but `BasePage` clearly describes the purpose of the class, making it easier to understand what it does. Just as with ASPX pages, you need to choose your preferred programming language from the drop-down list.

2. Clear the contents of the file, and then add the following code to this class file:

VB.NET

```
Public Class BasePage
  Inherits System.Web.UI.Page

  Private Sub Page_PreRender(ByVal sender As Object, ByVal e As System.EventArgs) _
          Handles Me.PreRender

    If Me.Title = "Untitled Page" Then
      Throw New Exception("Page title cannot be ""Untitled Page"".")
    End If
  End Sub

End Class
```

C#

```
using System;
using System.Web;

public class BasePage : System.Web.UI.Page
```

```
{
  private void Page_PreRender(object sender, EventArgs e)
  {
    if (this.Title == "Untitled Page")
    {
      throw new Exception("Page title cannot be \"Untitled Page\".");
    }
  }

  public BasePage()
  {
    this.PreRender += new EventHandler(Page_PreRender);
  }
}
```

3. Save the file and close it, and then open the Login.aspx page that you created earlier. Open its Code Behind file and then change the `Inherits` code (the colon [`:`] in C#) so the Login page inherits from the `BasePage` you created earlier:

VB.NET

```
Partial Class Login
    Inherits BasePage
  ...
End Class
```

C#

```
public partial class Login : BasePage
{
  ...
}
```

4. Save the page and then request it in the browser by pressing Ctrl+F5. If you haven't changed the title of the page earlier, you should get the error shown in Figure 6-8 in your browser.

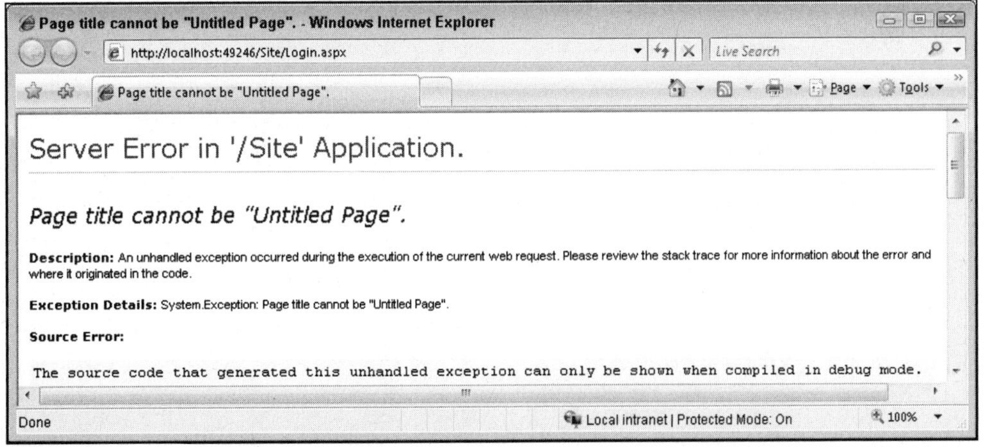

Figure 6-8

5. Go back to VWD and open the Login page in Markup View. Locate the `Title` attribute at the end of the `@ Page` directive and change it to Log in to Planet Wrox. The following snippet shows the Visual Basic version of the `@ Page` directive but the C# version is almost identical, except for the `Language` attribute:

```
<%@ Page Language="VB" MasterPageFile="~/MasterPages/MasterPage.master"
AutoEventWireup="false" CodeFile="Login.aspx.vb" Inherits="Login"
title="Log in to Planet Wrox" %>
```

6. Repeat steps 3 and 5 for all the pages in your site. To make this a bit quicker, you can use Find and Replace to quickly replace all the occurrences of `System.Web.UI.Page` with `BasePage`. Make sure you don't accidentally replace it in the BasePage file in the App_Code folder itself. To prevent this from happening, make sure you search only in Code Behind files, like this:

    - Open the Replace in Files dialog box (press Ctrl+Shift+H or select Edit ➪ Find and Replace ➪ Replace in Files).
    - In the Find What box enter System.Web.UI.Page. In the Replace With text box enter **BasePage**.
    - Expand the Find Options section and in the Look at These File Types text box enter ***.aspx.vb** or ***.aspx.cs** depending on the language you use. This leaves the BasePage file, which has a single extension of .vb or .cs alone.
    - Click Replace All and then click Yes to confirm the Replace operation.

7. Save the changes you made to any open page and then browse to Login.aspx again. If everything worked out as planned, the error should be gone and you now see the Login page.

    Remember, though, that all other pages in your site now throw an error when you try to access them. The fix is easy; just give them all a valid `Title`. If you don't like this behavior, simply comment out the line that starts with `Throw New Exception` in the `BasePage` class. Don't forget to give your pages a meaningful title, as you won't receive an alert anymore.

How It Works

By default, all pages in your web site inherit from the `Page` class defined in the `System.Web.UI` namespace. This gives them the behavior required to make them act as web pages that can be requested by the browser and processed by the server. Since the inheritance model in .NET allows you to create a chain of classes that inherit from each other, you can easily insert your own base page class between a web page and the standard `Page` class. You do this by changing the `Inherits` statement (the colon [`:`] in C#) to your new `BasePage`:

VB.NET

```
Partial Class Login
    Inherits BasePage
```

C#

```
public partial class Login : BasePage
```

Inside this new `BasePage` class you add an event handler that is fired when the class fires its `PreRender` event. As you learned earlier, this event is raised quite late in the page's life cycle, when the entire page has been set up and is ready to be rendered to the client:

VB.NET

```
Private Sub Page_PreRender(ByVal sender As Object, ByVal e As System.EventArgs) _
          Handles Me.PreRender

  ' Implementation here

End Sub
```

C#

```
private void Page_PreRender(object sender, EventArgs e)
{
  // Implementation here
}
```

Note that Visual Basic uses the `Handles` keyword to tell the compiler that the `Page_PreRender` method will be used to handle the event. In C#, you need to hook up this handler manually. A good place to do this is in the class's constructor:

```
public BasePage()
{
  this.PreRender += new EventHandler(Page_PreRender);
}
```

This highlighted line of code serves the same purpose as the `Handles` keyword in VB.NET: it tells the compiler what method to run when the page raises its `PreRender` event.

Inside the event handler, the code checks the current page title. If the page title is still `Untitled Page` (the default for any new page you add to your web project) it *throws an exception.*

VB.NET

```
If Me.Title = "Untitled Page" Then
  Throw New Exception("Page title cannot be ""Untitled Page"".")
End If
```

C#

```
if (this.Title == "Untitled Page")
{
  throw new Exception("Page title cannot be \"Untitled Page\".");
}
```

Notice how the keywords `Me` (in VB.NET) and `this` (in C#) are used. These keywords are context-sensitive and always refer to the class where it is used. In this example, `Me` (and `this`) refer to the current instance of the `Page` class. This `Page` instance has a `Title` property which can be checked for unwanted values. If it still contains the default title, the code raises (or throws) an exception. This immediately stops execution of the page so you as a page developer can fix the problem by providing a valid title before the page ends up in public. In Chapter 17 you'll learn more about exceptions and how to prevent and handle them.

To display a double quote (`"`) in the error message, both languages use a different format. In Visual Basic, you need to double the quotes. In C#, you need to prefix the double quote with a backslash (`\`) to *escape* the double quote. In both cases, the error message ends up in the browser with a single pair of double quotes around the error message:

```
Page title cannot be "Untitled Page".
```

This little bit of code in the `BasePage` prevents you from going live with your web site with web pages that still have the default and meaningless page title.

Because every page in the site should now inherit from this new base page, you should create a page template that already has the correct code in its Code Behind, making it easy to add the correct page to the site right from the start.

Creating Reusable Page Templates

Visual Web Developer comes with a great tool to export templates for a number of different file types including ASPX pages, class files, and even CSS files. By creating a custom template, you define the code or markup that you need in every file once and then create new files based on this template, giving you a jump start with the file and minimizing the code you need to type. The next exercise shows you how to create your own templates.

Try It Out Creating a Reusable Page Template

In this exercise you'll see how to create a template file for all new ASPX pages you will add to your site. To avoid conflicts with existing pages in your current site, you create a new temporary page and use that to create the template. Afterward you can delete the temporary file.

1. Add a new Web Form to the site and call it Template.aspx. Make sure it uses Code Behind, uses your programming language, and is based on the master page in the MasterPages folder.
2. Open the Code Behind of this new page and change the `Inherits` line (the colon in C#) so the page inherits from `BasePage` instead of from `System.Web.UI.Page`. Also rename the class from `Template` to `$safeitemname$`:

VB.NET

```
Partial Class $safeitemname$
        Inherits BasePage
  ...
End Class
```

C#

```
public partial class $safeitemname$ : BasePage
{
  ...
}
```

Make sure you don't remove any of the existing code, like the `using` statements or the `Page_Load` methods in the C# version.

Don't worry about any compile errors you may get about unexpected characters like `$`. Once you start adding pages based on this template, `$safeitemname$` will be replaced by the name of the page you're adding.

3. Switch to the Markup View of the page, and change the `Inherits` attribute from `Template` to `$safeitemname$`:

```
<%@ Page Language="C#" MasterPageFile="~/MasterPages/MasterPage.master"
    AutoEventWireup="true" CodeFile="Template.aspx.cs" Inherits="$safeitemname$"
    Title="Untitled Page" %>
```

You can leave the `CodeFile` attribute alone; VWD will change it to the right Code Behind file automatically whenever you add a new page to the site.

4. Optionally, add other code to the files you want to appear in your pages by default, like a comment block with a copyright notice.

5. Save the changes to the page and then choose File ➪ Export Template. In the dialog box that follows, select Item Template and choose your programming language from the drop-down list at the bottom of the screen, shown in Figure 6-9.

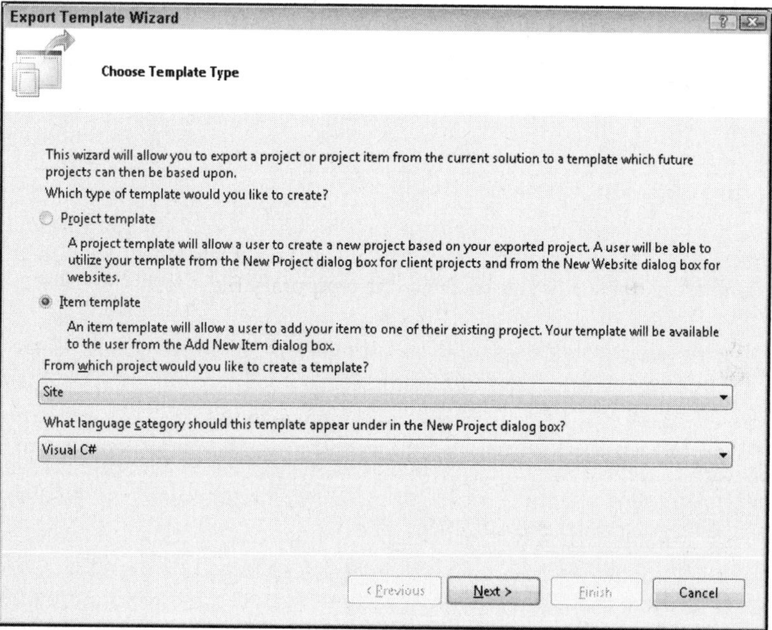

Figure 6-9

6. Click Next and place a check mark in front of Template.aspx that you find near the bottom of the list. Click Next again to go to the Select Item References dialog box.

7. There is no need to set anything in the Select Item References dialog box. If you had a web site referencing specific assemblies (.dll files) you could pick them here, so VWD adds the references for you automatically next time you add a file based on this template. In this case, click Next again to go to Select Template Options screen. Type **MyBasePage** as the new page name, and optionally type a short note describing the purpose of the template. Figure 6-10 shows the final dialog box.

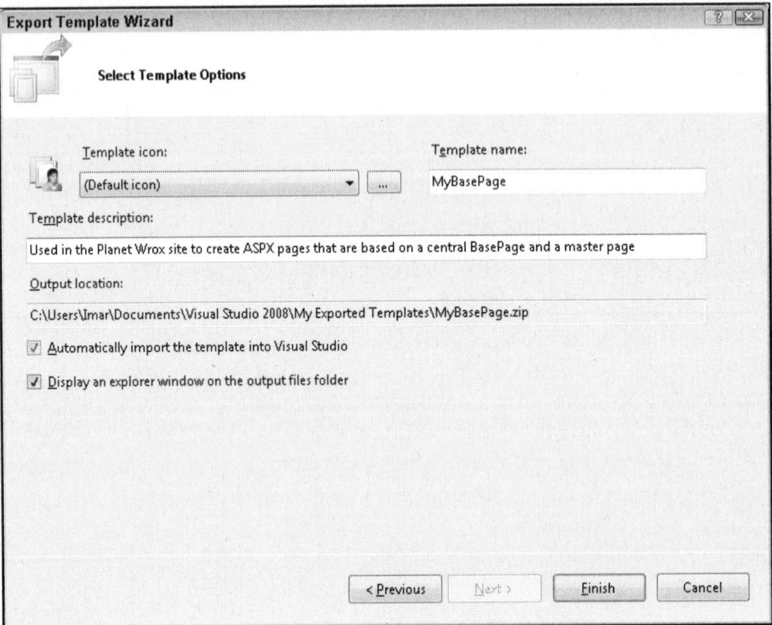

Figure 6-10

8. Click Finish to finish creating the template. VWD opens a Windows Explorer showing the new template as a ZIP file. You can close that window, as you don't need it.

   If you want to carry out this exercise for both VB.NET and C#, be sure to rename the resulting .zip file first before you make an export for the second language or otherwise it gets overwritten. To rename the file, open Windows Explorer, go to My Documents (just Documents in Vista) and then browse to Visual Studio 2008\Templates\ItemTemplates. You'll find a file called MyBasePage.zip, which you can rename to something like MyBasePageCS.zip. Note that the file's location is different from the one you see in Figure 6-10; the output location contains just a copy of the exported template that you can use as a backup.

9. Back in VWD, delete the temporary file Template.aspx you created. Then right-click the project in the Solution Explorer and choose Add New Item. Note that your custom template now shows up in the My Templates region at the bottom of the dialog box of Figure 6-11. If you click it, it even shows you the description you gave it earlier.

10. Type a new name for the page like TestPage.aspx and click Add to add it to your site. Look at the markup and the Code Behind of the file and verify that `$safeitemname$` has been

renamed to `TestPage` to reflect the new name of the page. If everything looks OK, you can delete TestPage.aspx as it's not used in the Planet Wrox web site.

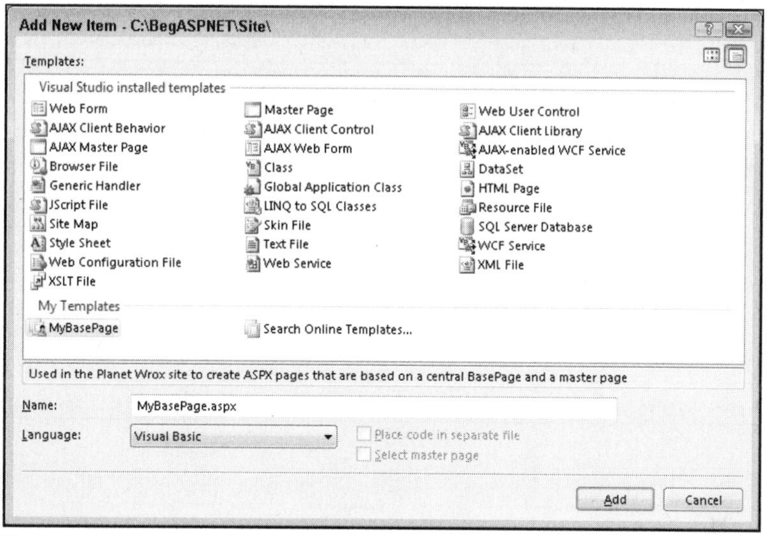

Figure 6-11

How It Works

When you export the template, Visual Web Developer creates a ZIP file with the necessary files — an ASPX file and a Code Behind file in this exercise. This template is then stored in the ItemTemplates subfolder of the Visual Studio 2008 folder under your Documents folder. Some of the files in the ZIP file contain the placeholder `$safeitemname$`. When you add a new file to the site that is based on your template using the Add New Item dialog box, VWD replaces `$safeitemname$` with the actual name of the page. In this exercise, you type TestPage.aspx as the new name for the page, so you end up with a class in the Code Behind called `TestPage` which in turn inherits from the global `BasePage`. In addition to `$safeitemname$`, there are a few other placeholders that you can use. Search the MSDN site at `http://msdn2.microsoft.com` for the term `$safeitemname$` to find the other template parameters.

If you need to make a change to the exported template, either redo the entire export process, or manually edit the files in the zip file.

With this exported template you now have a very quick way to add pages to your site that inherit from the `BasePage` class. You don't need to manually change the Code Behind of the class file or the markup of the page anymore.

Besides master pages and the central `BasePage` class there are more options to create consistent-looking web sites. One of them is themes.

Themes

So far you've seen how to create a master page to define the global look and feel of the pages in your site. You also saw how to centralize the behavior of your pages by using a central base page. There are, however, more ways to influence the look and feel of your site: themes and skins. Skins will be dealt with later in the chapter, as they are a part of themes, which need to be discussed first.

A *theme* is a collection of files that define the looks of a page. It can include skin files, CSS files, and images. You define themes in the special App_Themes folder in the root of your website. Within this folder you need to create one or more subfolders that define the actual themes. Inside each subfolder, you can have a number of files that make up the theme. Figure 6-12 shows the Solution Explorer for a web site that defines two themes: Monochrome and DarkGrey.

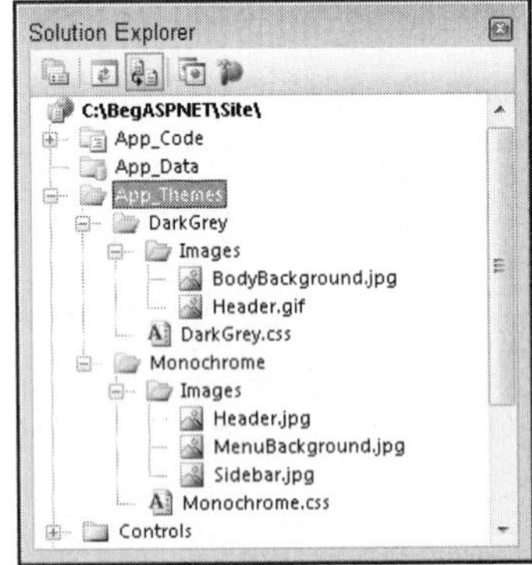

Figure 6-12

A link to each CSS file in the theme folder is added to your page's `<head>` section automatically whenever the theme is active. You'll see how this works later. The images in the themes folder are referenced from the CSS files. They can be used to change common elements of the web site, such as background images, or images used in bulleted lists or navigation lists.

To create a theme, you need to do the following:

- Create the special App_Themes folder if it isn't already present in your site.
- For each theme you want to create, create a subfolder with the theme's name, like Monochrome or DarkGrey in Figure 6-12.
- Optionally, create one or more CSS files that will be part of the theme. Although naming the CSS files after the theme helps in identifying the right files, this is not a requirement. Any CSS file you add to the theme's folder is added to the page at runtime automatically.
- Optionally, add one or more images to the theme folder. The CSS files should refer to these images with a relative path. Figure 6-12 shows how the DarkGrey theme has two images, used in the header and background of the site.
- Optionally, add one or more skin files to the themes folder. Skins allow you to define individual properties (like `ForeColor` and `BackColor`) for a specific control which are then applied at runtime.

After you have followed these steps, you can configure your site or an individual web page to make use of this theme. To be able to set up the right theme, you should be aware that there are two types of themes.

Different Types of Themes

An ASP.NET page has two different properties that allow you to set a theme: the `Theme` property and the `StyleSheetTheme`. Both of these properties use the themes that you define in the App_Themes folder. Although at first they seem very similar, it's their runtime behavior that makes the difference. The `StyleSheetTheme` is applied very early in the page's life cycle, shortly after the page instance has been created. This means that an individual page can override the settings from the theme by applying inline attributes on the controls. So, for example, a theme with a skin file that sets the `BackColor` of a button to green can be overridden by the following control declaration in the markup of the page:

```
<asp:Button ID="Button1" runat="server" Text="Button" BackColor="red" />
```

The `Theme` property on the other hand gets effective late in the page's life cycle, effectively overriding any customization you may have for individual controls.

Choosing Between Theme and StyleSheetTheme

Since properties of the `StyleSheetTheme` can be overridden by the page, while the `Theme` in turn can override these properties again, both serve a distinct purpose. You should set the `StyleSheetTheme` if you want to supply *default settings* for your controls. That is, the `StyleSheetTheme` can supply defaults for your controls which can then be overridden at the page level. You should use the `Theme` property instead if you want to *enforce* the look and feel of your controls. Because the settings from the `Theme` cannot be overridden anymore and effectively overwrite any customizations, you can be assured that your controls look the way you defined them in the theme.

With a theme, you can be sure that any changes you make to it are propagated to the controls in your web pages, unless the control disables theming by setting `EnableTheming` to `False`. You'll see how to set this property and its effect towards the end of the chapter.

Applying Themes

To apply a theme to your web site, you have three different options: at the page level in the `Page` directive, at the site level by modifying the web.config file, and programmatically.

- **Setting the theme at the page level:** Setting the `Theme` or `StyleSheetTheme` property at the page level is easy: just set the relevant attribute in the `Page` directive of the page:

```
<%@ Page Language="VB" AutoEventWireup="false" CodeFile="Default.aspx.vb"
        Inherits="_Default" Theme="DarkGrey" %>
```

  Replace `Theme` with `StyleSheetTheme` to apply a theme whose settings can be overridden by the individual pages. Figure 6-13 shows that as soon as you type `Theme="` VWD pops up with a list with all the themes it finds in the App_Themes folder.

```
Default.aspx*
Client Objects & Events                    (No Events)
aspx.vb" Inherits="_Default" title="Untitled Page" Theme=" %>
                                            DarkGrey
                                            Monochrome
```

Figure 6-13

- **Setting the theme at the site level:** To enforce a theme throughout the entire web site, you can set the theme in the web.config file. To do this, open the web.config file, locate the `<pages>` element, and add a `theme` attribute to it:

```
<pages theme="DarkGrey">
  ...
</pages>
```

  Make sure you type `theme` with all lower-case letters as the XML in the web.config file is case sensitive.

- **Setting themes programmatically:** The third and final way to set a theme is through code. Because of the way themes work, you need to do this early on in the page's life cycle. You'll see how this works in a later exercise.

The next Try It Out exercise shows you how themes work. You'll learn how to create a theme, add the necessary CSS, and then configure the application to use the new theme.

Try It Out — Creating a New Theme for Your Web Site

In this exercise you'll create two themes: Monochrome and DarkGrey. For each theme, you'll add the CSS layout, which is applied to the site automatically. You'll configure the application to use one of the themes and then switch to the other to see the differences.

1. Add the special App_Themes folder to your web site. To do this, right-click the project in the Solution Explorer and then choose Add ASP.NET Folder ➪ Theme. This not only creates the App_Themes folder, but immediately creates a subfolder for the theme called Theme1 by default. Type **Monochrome** as the new name instead. Your Solution Explorer should now look like Figure 6-14.

2. From the Styles folder, move the file Styles.css into this new Monochrome folder. You can either drag it directly into the new folder or use Ctrl+X to cut the file, then click the Monochrome folder, and press Ctrl+V to paste it again. You can leave the empty Styles folder as it's used later again.

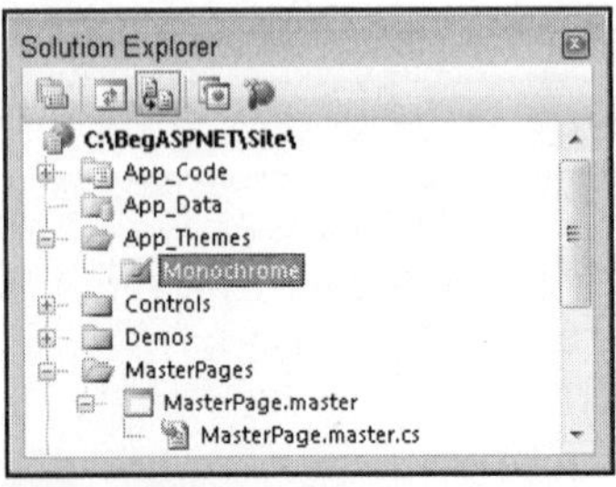

Figure 6-14

3. To make it clearer later to see where your CSS is coming from, rename the file from Styles.css to Monochrome.css.

4. Since the main layout is now going to be controlled by the theme, you no longer need the `<link>` element in the `<head>` section of the master page pointing to the old CSS file, so you can remove it. To this end, open the master page, switch to Markup View and remove the following highlighted line from the code:

```
<head runat="server">
  <title>Welcome to Planet Wrox</title>
  <asp:ContentPlaceHolder id="head" runat="server">
  </asp:ContentPlaceHolder>
  <link href="../Styles/Styles.css" rel="stylesheet" type="text/css" />
</head>
```

5. The next step is to apply the theme to the entire web site. To do this, open the web.config file from the root of the site, locate the `<pages>` element and add the `theme` attribute:

```
<pages theme="Monochrome">
```

6. To test the theme, save all your changes and then request the page Default.aspx in your browser. The design of the site should be identical to how it was. If you get an error about an invalid page title, go back to Visual Web Developer and change the `Title` attribute of the `Page` directive of Default.aspx to something like "Welcome to Planet Wrox."

    - Instead of linking to the CSS file from the master page, the CSS is now included in the page source through the theme set in the web.config file. To see how this works, open the HTML source of the page in the browser. At the top you should see the following code (the layout was altered for better readability).

```
<html xmlns="http://www.w3.org/1999/xhtml">
<head>
  <title>Untitled Page</title>
  <link href="App_Themes/Monochrome/Monochrome.css" type="text/css" rel="stylesheet" />
</head>
<body>
```

    - Note that a link to the style sheet from the Monochrome theme folder is injected in the `<head>` of the page. The ASP.NET runtime does this for *every* .css file it finds in the currently active theme folder, so be sure to keep your theme folder clean to avoid unnecessary files from being included and downloaded by the browser. Also note that the `<link>` is added just right before the closing `</head>` tag. This ensures that the theme file is included after all other files you may have added yourself (through the master page for example). This is in contrast to how the `styleSheetTheme` attribute works. Since this type of theme allows its settings to be overridden, it's imported at the top of the file, giving room for other CSS files that follow it to change the look and feel of the page.

7. Return to Visual Web Developer and open the master page file in Design View. Notice how all the design is gone and VWD now shows the basic layout of the page again. Unfortunately, VWD does not display the theme you've set using the theme attribute. However, you can overcome this limitation by setting the `styleSheetTheme` instead. To do this, open the web.config file again, locate the `<pages>` element and add the following attribute:

```
<pages theme="Monochrome" styleSheetTheme="Monochrome">
```

8. Save the changes to web.config, close and reopen the master page and switch to Design View. You'll see that VWD now applies the correct styling information to your pages.

9. To add another theme to the site, create a new folder under App_Themes and call it DarkGrey. Next, open the folder where you extracted the downloaded code that comes with this book. If you followed the instructions in the Introduction of this book, this folder is located at C:\BegASPNET\Resources. Open the Chapter 06 folder and then the DarkGrey folder. Drag the file DarkGrey.css from the Windows Explorer into the DarkGrey theme folder in VWD. Your Solution Explorer should now resemble Figure 6-15.

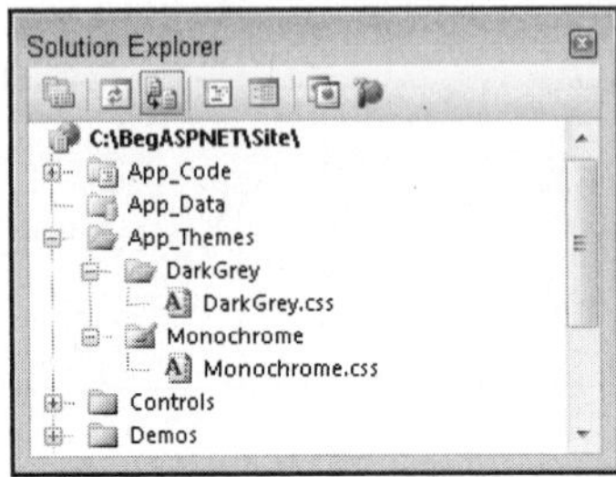

Figure 6-15

You'll add the images that the CSS file refers to in a later exercise.

10. Open the web.config file once more and change both occurrences of `Monochrome` to `DarkGrey` in the `<pages>` element. Save the changes again and then press Ctrl+F5. Instead of the greenish Monochrome theme, you'll now see the site with the DarkGrey theme applied as visible in Figure 6-16.

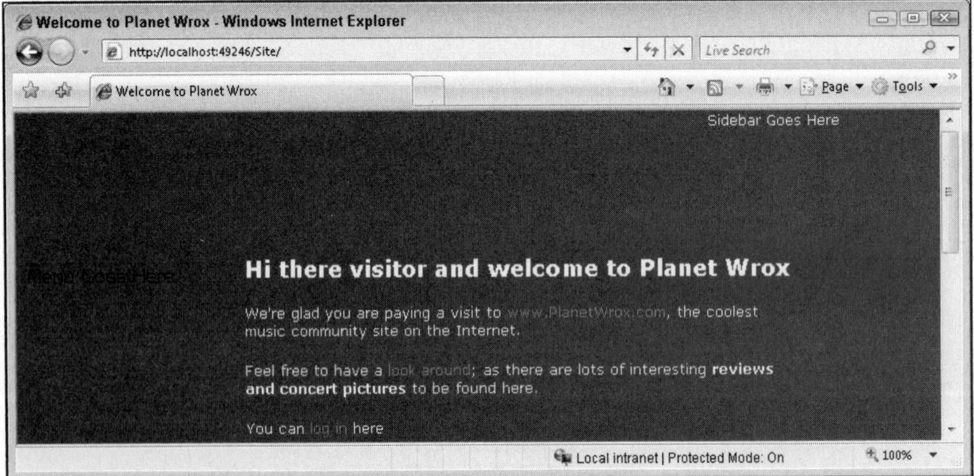

Figure 6-16

How It Works

In this exercise you applied the Monochrome theme by changing the `<pages>` element in the web.config file. When the runtime sees that a theme is active, it scans the associated theme folder for .css files and includes a link to all those files it finds in the page's `<head>` section. In the case of the Monochrome theme it finds the file Monochrome.css and adds it to the `<head>` section automatically. An identical process took place when you changed the theme to DarkGrey.

To enable design-time support in Visual Web Developer you need to change the `styleSheetTheme` in the web.config file as well. The only downside of this is that the relevant CSS file is now included *twice*: once for the theme and once for the `StyleSheetTheme`. Since the exact same file is included twice, it doesn't affect the layout of the site. All the selectors in the second file simply overrule those in the first. However, if you feel this duplication is a waste of CPU cycles, you should delete the `styleSheetTheme` attribute from the web.config file when you go live with the application.

The layout of the page is changed radically because of the CSS in the file DarkGrey.css. If you want to know what CSS the file contains and what elements of the page it changes, open it up in VWD. It has lots of comments describing each selector in detail.

Extending Themes

Besides .css files and skins (discussed toward the end of this chapter), a theme can also contain images. The most common use of theme images is by referring to them from the CSS. To put this to good use it's important to understand how CSS refers to images.

By design, an image referred to by a CSS selector will be searched for relative to the location of the CSS file, unless you give it a path that starts with a forward slash (/) to indicate the root of the site. Consider, for example, the App_Themes folder depicted in Figure 6-17.

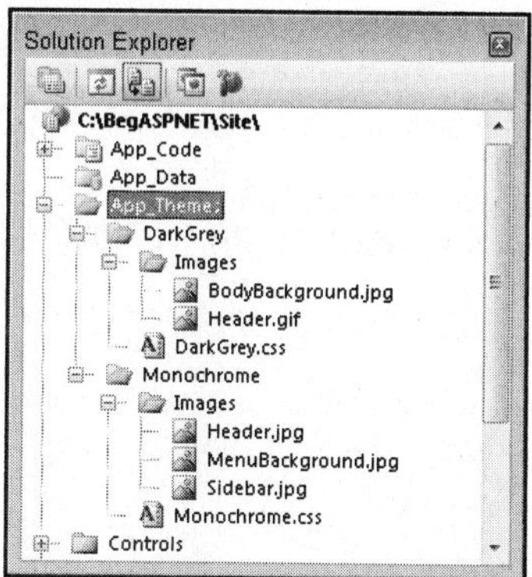

Figure 6-17

To refer to the MenuBackground.jpg file in the Images folder of the Monochrome theme, you can add the following CSS to Monochrome.css:

```
#MenuWrapper
{
  background-image: url(Images/MenuBackground.jpg);
}
```

If you wanted to refer to an image in the Images folder in the root of the site, you'd use this CSS:

```
background-image: url(/Images/MenuBackground.jpg);
```

Note the leading forward slash in front of the image path to indicate the root of the site. This latter syntax is useful if you want to share images between different themes. Simply put them in a folder outside a specific theme, like an Images folder at the root, and then use this root-based syntax to refer to them. The next chapter digs a lot deeper into the different forms a URL can take to refer to a resource like an image.

Try It Out Adding Images to Your Theme

In this Try It Out you'll add the images and CSS files to the site to complete both themes. The images and CSS files are available in the zip file that comes with this chapter's code download, found at `www.wrox.com`. You will overwrite the file Monochrome.css in the Monochrome theme, so if you made any customizations to that file, create a backup of it first.

1. Open Windows Explorer and navigate to the files you extracted from the zip file for this chapter (at C:\BegASPNET\Resources). If you didn't extract the files yet, check out the Introduction of this book for instructions on doing this. Open the Chapter 06 folder and then the Monochrome folder. Select the Images folder and the Monochrome.css file.
2. Next, arrange Visual Web Developer and the Windows Explorer so you can see both at the same time and then drag the selected folder and files from the Explorer window into the Monochrome theme folder in VWD. Click Yes when you're asked to overwrite Monochrome.css.
3. Repeat the previous two steps, but this time drag the file DarkGrey.css and the Images folder from the Windows Explorer's DarkGrey folder into the DarkGrey theme folder in VWD. Your Solution Explorer looks like Figure 6-17.
4. Request the Default.aspx page in your browser by right-clicking it and choosing View in Browser. You should now see the web page with images from the DarkGrey theme, shown in Figure 6-18.
5. Go back to VWD, open the web.config file and switch the two theme properties once more from DarkGrey to Monochrome. Refresh the page in the browser (or open it again) and you'll see the page with the new theme and images as shown in Figure 6-19.

Figure 6-18

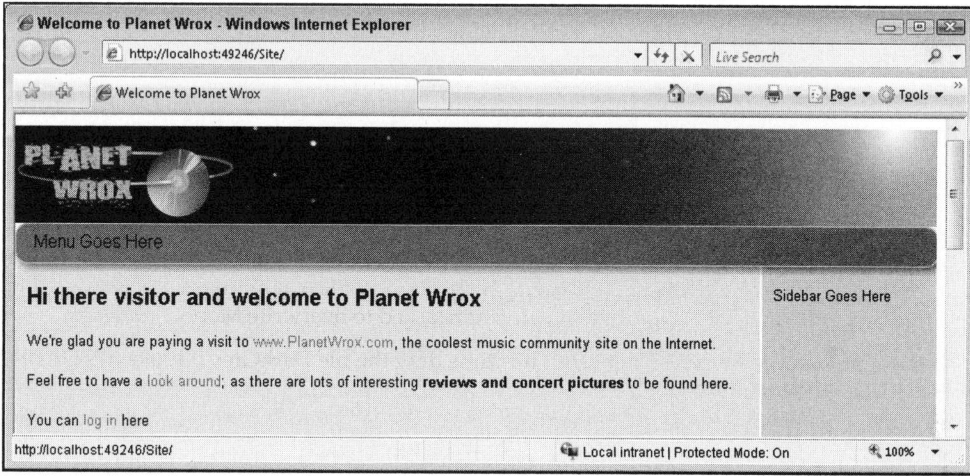

Figure 6-19

How It Works

From a theme point of view, not much has changed in the previous exercise. Just as you saw before, the theme is added to the head of the page. However, this time the style sheet in the theme points to images located in the Themes folder. The browser reads the CSS file, follows the link to the images, downloads them and then displays them at the right location as dictated by the various CSS selectors in the code file.

The CSS files you added for both themes contain a lot of comments, so if you want to know what the CSS does, check out the files in the two theme folders.

Useful as themes may be to allow you, the page developer, to quickly change the appearance and even the layout of the site, they become even more useful if you let your users switch them at runtime. This way, the user can customize the site to their liking. The next section shows you how to accomplish this.

Dynamically Switching Themes

Switching themes at runtime has a few benefits. For example, you can please your users by allowing them to choose a theme with colors and layout they like. Not everyone appreciates a dark background with white text, so the option to change that at runtime is something that many people like. However, you can also deploy themes to help visually impaired users. By creating a theme that has a high-contrast color scheme and a large font size, you make it much easier for people to see your site. The themes in the Planet Wrox web site only change screen elements like colors and layout, but it's easy to create a copy of one of those themes and then change the font size and the color scheme.

Because of the way themes are applied to a page at runtime, you need to set the theme early on in the page's life cycle, in the `PreInit` event to be precise. The base page of the web site is once again the ideal location to do this, as every page in the site inherits from this class.

To allow a user to change the theme you can offer them a drop-down menu that automatically posts back to the server when the user changes the active option in the list. At the server, you get the chosen theme from the list, apply it to the page and then store the selection in a *cookie* so it can be retrieved on subsequent visits to the web site.

Cookies are little pieces of text that you can store on the user's computer. The data you store in a cookie is only sent to the server that set it in the first place, so other sites can't read the cookie from yours. However, since cookies are stored on the user's computer as plain text, you should never store any sensitive data, such as a password, in a cookie. Storing harmless data like the preferred theme is an excellent use of cookies, though.

There has been a lot of debate about cookies and whether they can harm your privacy or not. Generally, cookies are safe, as they only store data that the server that sets it already has. They can't be used to steal sensitive data from your computer if you haven't given this data to the server yourself. In most scenarios, cookies improve the user's browsing experience by remembering little pieces of data instead of asking you every single time you visit a page. Unfortunately, some large corporations like advertising agencies use a unique cookie to track your trails on the web, giving them some global idea of the sites you visit. To ensure that visitors to your site understand what information you have and keep about them, it's usually a good idea to add a privacy statement to your site describing the intent and usage of cookies and any personal data you may keep.

In the following two exercises you'll see how to implement the functionality to switch themes dynamically. The first exercise guides you through modifying the master page to allow the user to select a theme. This exercise only retrieves the theme the user selects and stores it in a cookie. The second exercise then shows you how to apply that theme at runtime to every page that inherits from `BasePage`.

Try It Out — Letting the User Select a Theme

In this exercise you'll add a `DropDownList` control to the master page. This control contains the available themes so a user can choose one. The user's choice is stored in a cookie so it's available again later. The final step is to preselect the right theme in the drop-down list when the user revisits the page.

1. Open the master page in Markup View and locate the `<div>` called `Sidebar`. Remove the static text `Sidebar Goes Here` and replace it with a `DropDownList` control by dragging it from the Toolbox between the two `div` tags. Change the `ID` of the control from `DropDownList1` to `lstPreferredTheme`. Type some text (for example, Select a Theme) in front of the drop-down list to clarify the purpose of the list.
2. Switch to Design View, open the control's Smart Tasks panel, and select Enable AutoPostBack.
3. On the same Smart Tasks panel, click the Edit Items link and insert two items: one with the text Monochrome and one with DarkGrey.
4. Double-click the drop-down list to set up an event handler for the `SelectedIndexChanged` event. Alternatively, select the `DropDownList` control's Properties Grid and press F4, click the little lightning bolt to switch to the Events list, and then double-click `SelectedIndexChanged`. Figure 6-20 shows the Properties Grid in Events mode.

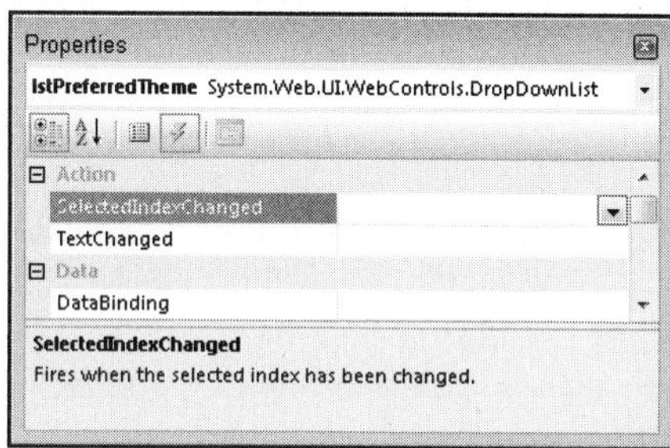

Figure 6-20

The code in the `SelectedIndexChanged` handler fires as soon as the user makes a new selection in the drop-down list. Within the handler block, add the following code that retrieves the selected theme from the list and stores it in a cookie:

VB.NET

```
Protected Sub DropDownList1_SelectedIndexChanged(ByVal sender As Object, _
          ByVal e As System.EventArgs) Handles lstPreferredTheme.SelectedIndexChanged
  Dim preferredTheme As HttpCookie = New HttpCookie("PreferredTheme")
  preferredTheme.Expires = DateTime.Now.AddMonths(3)
  preferredTheme.Value = lstPreferredTheme.SelectedValue
  Response.Cookies.Add(preferredTheme)
  Response.Redirect(Request.Url.ToString())
End Sub
```

C#

```
protected void lstPreferredTheme_SelectedIndexChanged(object sender, EventArgs e)
{
  HttpCookie preferredTheme = new HttpCookie("PreferredTheme");
  preferredTheme.Expires = DateTime.Now.AddMonths(3);
  preferredTheme.Value = lstPreferredTheme.SelectedValue;
  Response.Cookies.Add(preferredTheme);
  Response.Redirect(Request.Url.ToString());
}
```

5. Still in the Code Behind of the master page, you'll need to add some code that preselects the correct item in the list again when the page loads. The best place to do this is in the `Page` class' `Load` event. If you're using C#, the `Page_Load` handler should already be there. When you're using Visual Basic you can add one in two different ways: either double-click the page anywhere in Design View (this works in C# as well), or select (Page Events) from the left drop-down list just above the Document Window in the Code Behind (shown in Figure 6-21), and then choose `Load` from the second drop-down. This is a nice way to add handlers for other controls as well, like `Button` and `DropDownList` controls.

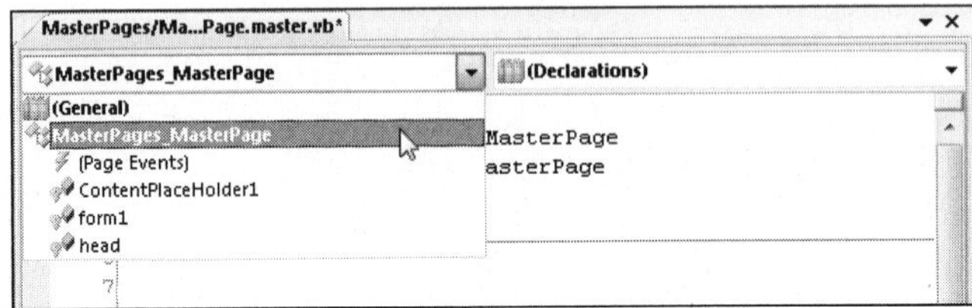

Figure 6-21

Within the handler block that VWD added for you, add the following code:

VB.NET

```
Protected Sub Page_Load(ByVal sender As Object, ByVal e As System.EventArgs) _
         Handles Me.Load
  If Not Page.IsPostBack Then
  Dim selectedTheme As String = Page.Theme
  Dim preferredTheme As HttpCookie = Request.Cookies.Get("PreferredTheme")
    If preferredTheme IsNot Nothing Then
      selectedTheme = preferredTheme.Value
    End If
    If lstPreferredTheme.Items.FindByValue(selectedTheme) IsNot Nothing Then
      lstPreferredTheme.Items.FindByValue(selectedTheme).Selected = True
    End If
  End If
End Sub
```

C#

```
protected void Page_Load(object sender, EventArgs e)
{
  if (!Page.IsPostBack)
  {
    string selectedTheme = Page.Theme;
    HttpCookie preferredTheme = Request.Cookies.Get("PreferredTheme");
    if (preferredTheme != null)
    {
      selectedTheme = preferredTheme.Value;
    }
    if (lstPreferredTheme.Items.FindByValue(selectedTheme) != null)
    {
```

```
            lstPreferredTheme.Items.FindByValue(selectedTheme).Selected = true;
        }
    }
}
```

6. Save all changes and then request Default.aspx in your browser. The drop-down list in the sidebar should display the first item in the list as selected. Select the other option from the list and the page will reload. Notice that you keep seeing the same theme because you haven't written any code yet that applies the selected theme. You'll see how to do that in a later exercise.

   The item you chose in the drop-down list last should be preselected in the drop-down list. If you get an error, make sure you have no typos in the code. If nothing seems to happen (for example, the page doesn't post back), check if you set the `AutoPostBack` attribute on the `DropDownList` control to `True`.

How It Works

You made three important changes to the master page. First, you added the drop-down list and set `AutoPostBack` to `true`. This causes the page to submit itself back to the server as soon as you choose a new item in the list. When that happens, the code in the `SelectedIndexChanged` handler fires. This code creates a cookie that can be stored on the user's browser. To make the cookie last between browser sessions, you need to set the `Expires` property. In the code example, the cookie is set to expire three months from now, which means the browser will discard it automatically after that period. However, whenever the user chooses a new theme, this date is extended, setting it for another three months:

VB.NET

```
Dim preferredTheme As HttpCookie = New HttpCookie("PreferredTheme")
preferredTheme.Expires = DateTime.Now.AddMonths(3)
```

C#

```
HttpCookie preferredTheme = new HttpCookie("PreferredTheme");
preferredTheme.Expires = DateTime.Now.AddMonths(3);
```

After the cookie has been created, you can set its `Value` property. In the example, the `SelectedValue` (containing the name of the theme) is stored in the cookie. The cookie is then added to the `Cookies` collection using `Response.Cookies.Add`:

VB.NET

```
preferredTheme.Value = lstPreferredTheme.SelectedValue
Response.Cookies.Add(preferredTheme)
```

C#

```
preferredTheme.Value = lstPreferredTheme.SelectedValue;
Response.Cookies.Add(preferredTheme);
```

Note that the cookie is added to the `Cookies` collection of the `Response` object that is associated with the response to the user. Later you'll see how to read this cookie again from the `Cookies` collection of the `Request` object that is associated with the request the user is making for a page.

The final step is to redirect the user to the same page:

VB.NET

```
Response.Redirect(Request.Url.ToString())
```

C#

```
Response.Redirect(Request.Url.ToString());
```

This is necessary because otherwise the new theme won't be applied immediately. Because the theme needs to be set early in the page's life cycle, it can no longer be set for the current request. By redirecting the user to the same page, a new request is made which can successfully apply the selected theme. The next exercise shows you how to do this.

The final change in the master page you made was modifying the `Page_Load` handler. Inside this method, a `String` variable is declared that holds the currently active theme by looking at `Page.Theme`. This will be the default theme that is preselected in the drop-down list if the user doesn't have a cookie holding their preferred theme. The code then sees if there is a cookie called `PreferredTheme`. If it exists, its value is used to give the string `selectedTheme` a new value. In the end, this `string` variable is then used to find the item in the drop-down list and preselect it.

This way, the drop-down list always displays the currently configured site theme or the item the user has chosen manually, even if she comes back to the site next week. Note the use of the `FindByValue` method on the `Items` collection of the `DropDownList` control. This method returns the item if it is found or `Nothing` (`null` in C#) when the item isn't there. This ensures that if the cookie contains a theme that no longer exists, the code doesn't try to preselect an item in the list that doesn't exist.

With the ability to let a user select a theme in place, the next step is to apply the chosen theme.

As you learned previously, the theme needs to be set in the `PreInit` event, which takes place early in the page's life cycle. Inside this event, you can see if the cookie with the selected theme exists. If it does, you can use its value to set the right theme.

Try It Out — Applying the User-Selected Theme

In this exercise, you'll modify the base page and add some code for the `PreInit` event to set the user's theme.

1. Open the BasePage file from the App_Code folder and add the following code that sets the selected theme during the `PreInit` event. You can add this code before or after the method that checks the page title.

VB.NET

```
Private Sub Page_PreInit(ByVal sender As Object, ByVal e As System.EventArgs) _
        Handles Me.PreInit
  Dim preferredTheme As HttpCookie = Request.Cookies.Get("PreferredTheme")
```

```
  If preferredTheme IsNot Nothing Then
    Page.Theme = preferredTheme.Value
  End If
End Sub
```

C#

```
private void Page_PreInit(object sender, EventArgs e)
{
  HttpCookie preferredTheme = Request.Cookies.Get("PreferredTheme");
  if (preferredTheme != null)
  {
    Page.Theme = preferredTheme.Value;
  }
}
```

2. If you're working with C#, you need to set up an event handler in the class's constructor for the `PreInit` event. Just as you did with the `PreRender` event handler in an earlier exercise, you need to add a line of code in the class constructor. This tells the ASP.NET runtime which method will handle the `PreInit` event:

```
public BasePage()
{
  this.PreRender += new EventHandler(Page_PreRender);
  this.PreInit += new EventHandler(Page_PreInit);
}
```

3. Save changes to all open documents and then request Default.aspx in the browser. The page should load with the theme you chose last in the drop-down list in the previous exercise.

4. Choose a new item from the list. The page should reload and should now show the other theme.

   If you find that the page in the browser is showing a combination of the two themes, go back to VWD, open web.config, and remove the `styleSheetTheme` attribute from the `<pages>` element.

How It Works

With the hard work of getting the user's favorite theme and storing it in a cookie already done, applying the theme is now very easy. The code in the `PreInit` event first verifies whether there is a cookie called `PreferredTheme`. It does this by comparing the return value of the `Get` method to `Nothing` (`null` in C#).

VB.NET

```
  Dim preferredTheme As HttpCookie = Request.Cookies.Get("PreferredTheme")
  If preferredTheme IsNot Nothing Then
```

C#

```
  HttpCookie preferredTheme = Request.Cookies.Get("PreferredTheme");
  if (preferredTheme != null)
```

Here, `Request.Cookies` is used to read from the cookies that the user's browser sent together with the request. If the cookie exists, its `Value` property is used to set the correct theme:

VB.NET

```
Page.Theme = preferredTheme.Value
```

C#

```
Page.Theme = preferredTheme.Value;
```

Because the theme is set early in the page's life cycle, this setting will carry through all the way to the end of the page, effectively giving the page the look and feel defined in it.

With the ability of setting the theme programmatically, you're offering your users a quick and easy way to change the page to their likings. The theme affects colors and layout throughout each page in the entire web site. Combined with master pages this gives you a flexible way to influence the look and feel of an entire page. It could also be useful if you were able to change certain controls on a page. For example, you may have the need to give each button in your site the exact same look. This is where the ASP.NET skins come into play.

Skins

Skins are simple text files that contain markup for controls. Placed in a theme folder under App_Themes, they are an integral part of the ASP.NET themes feature. A skin file (with a .skin extension) contains the server side presentational elements of a control. These settings are then applied to all the controls to which the skin applies. To see how this works, consider the following example that defines the skin or appearance of a `Button` control.

```
<asp:Button BackColor="#cccccc" ForeColor="#308462" runat="server" />
```

With this skin definition, all the buttons in your site will get a `BackColor` of `#cccccc` and a `ForeColor` of `#308462`. All you need to do is create a simple .skin file under your theme's folder, add this markup to it and that's it. From then on, all the buttons will be changed automatically. Just as with setting the properties on the controls directly as you saw earlier, these properties like `BackColor` and `ForeColor` are transformed into client-side HTML and CSS.

Note that this markup is similar to the markup of a button. There are a few differences though. First of all, the control in the .skin file cannot have an `ID` attribute. The `ID` is used to uniquely identify a control in a page, and since the skin is applied to all controls, there's no point in giving it an `ID`. Another difference is the number of attributes you can set in the markup. Not all properties of a control are skinnable. For example, you can't set the `Enabled` property of the `Button` through a .skin. Microsoft's MSDN documentation lists for each property whether they can be skinned or not. Another way to find out if you can skin a certain property is by simply trying it; just set the property in the skin and if you're not allowed to set it, you'll get an error at runtime.

Generally speaking, properties that influence the appearance (`BackColor`, `ForeColor`, `BorderColor`, and so on) can be skinned while properties that influence behavior (`Enabled`, `EnableViewState`, and more) cannot be set.

When you create a new skin file, using the Add New Item dialog box, you get a bunch of text wrapped in a server side comment block. You can safely remove these comments as they only give you a short example of how skins work. You can define multiple controls in a single skin file. However, from a maintainability point of view, it's often easier to name each skin file after the control it represents. For example, you have a file called Button.skin for buttons, Label.skin for labels, and so on.

Instead of applying formatting elements directly to the control's properties in the skin and thus to the final markup in the page, it's often better to use the `CssClass` property to point to a CSS class in one of your CSS files. That way, it's even easier to make site-wide changes and you avoid bloating the final HTML. Given the previous example, a file with the following skin definition and a class in the theme's CSS file would give the same effect:

```
<asp:Button CssClass="MyButton" runat="server" />

.MyButton
{
  color: #308462;
  background-color: #cccccc;
}
```

Creating a Skin File

Skin files must be created in the theme's folder directly. You can't store them in a subfolder like you do with the theme's images. In the following exercise you'll see how to create a simple skin file to change the look and feel of all button controls in the web site. Later chapters in this book will build on this knowledge by defining more complex skins for other controls like the `GridView`.

When you start typing in a skin file, you'll notice that the familiar IntelliSense doesn't kick in. This makes it difficult to define your controls and their attributes. However, there is a simple workaround:

1. Open VWD's Options dialog box by choosing Tools ➪ Options.
2. Make sure that Show All Settings at the bottom of the screen is selected.
3. Expand the Text Editor category and then click File Extension.
4. In the Extension box type skin and then from the Editor drop-down list choose User Control Editor.
5. Click the Add button and then click the OK button to dismiss the Options dialog box.

From now on, you'll get IntelliSense even in skin files, which you'll see in the next exercise. With this setting on, you may get an error in the Error List about build providers. You can safely ignore this error, as skins will work fine at runtime with this setting on.

Try It Out Creating a Skin for the Button Control

To effectively use skins, you should strive to use `CssClass` attributes as much as possible instead of applying inline attributes that all end up in the final HTML of the page, increasing its size and load time. However, to show you how it works in case you do have a special need to add inline attributes this exercise shows you how to apply both.

1. In the Monochrome theme folder, add a new .skin file and call it Button.skin. You add the file by right-clicking the Monochrome folder and choosing Add New Item. In the dialog box that follows select Skin File and then type Button as the file name.

2. Delete the entire contents from the file and then add the following code:

```
<asp:Button CssClass="MyButton" BackColor="#cccccc" runat="server" />
```

Note that this markup uses a combination of inline attributes for styling (the `BackColor`) and the `CssClass` to point to a selector in your CSS file.

3. Open the file Monochrome.css from the theme folder and add this CSS selector to the end of the file:

```
.MyButton
{
 color: #308462;
}
```

4. Create a new Web Form in the Demos folder and call it SkinsDemo.aspx. Make sure you base it on the exported template you created earlier. Give the page a `Title` of Skins Demo and then add a `Button` by dragging it from the Toolbox into the `cpMainContent` area of the page. You end up with this code:

```
<asp:Content ID="Content2" ContentPlaceHolderID="cpMainContent" Runat="Server">
  <asp:Button ID="Button1" runat="server" Text="Button" />
</asp:Content>
```

5. Save all changes and then request SkinsDemo.aspx in the browser. If necessary, switch to the Monochrome theme. The button you added in the last step should now have a grey background with light green text on it.

How It Works

To see how it works, you should take a look at the HTML for the page in the browser. The `<asp:Button>` control has been transformed in the following HTML:

```
<input type="submit" name="ctl00$cpMainContent$Button1" value="Button"
 id="ctl00_cpMainContent_Button1" class="MyButton" style="background-color:#CCCCCC;" />
```

Both the `CssClass` and the `BackColor` attributes in the skin have been added to the HTML. The former ended up as a `class` attribute on the button, while that latter has been transformed into a `style` attribute. The `MyButton` class in the CSS file gives the button its green text while the inline style determines the background color of the button.

As you can see, skins are extremely easy to use and allow you to radically change the look of specific controls in your site. But what if you don't want all your buttons to change green and grey at the same time? What if you need one special button that has a red background? You can do this with named skins.

Named Skins

Named skins are identical to normal skins with one exception: they have a `SkinID` set that allows you refer to that skin by name. Controls in your ASPX pages can then use that `SkinID` to apply that specific skin to the control. The next exercise shows you how this works.

Try It Out Creating a Named Skin for the Button Control

The easiest way to create a named skin is by copying the code for an existing one and then adding a `SkinID` attribute. Be aware that if you copy and paste a skin definition, Visual Web Developer automatically adds an `ID` attribute (that is, if you connected .skin files to the User Control Editor as described earlier). This `ID` is not allowed, so make sure you remove it.

1. Open `Button.skin` again, copy all the code, and then paste it below the existing markup.
2. If VWD added an `ID` attribute, remove it, together with its value (for example, remove `ID="Button1"`).
3. Remove the `CssClass` attribute and its value, change the `BackColor` of the button to `Red`, and then set the `ForeColor` to `Black`.
4. Add a `SkinID` of `RedButton`. You should end up with this code:

```
<asp:Button CssClass="MyButton" BackColor="#cccccc" runat="server" />
<asp:Button SkinID="RedButton" BackColor="Red" ForeColor="Black" runat="server" />
```

5. Save and close the skin file.
6. Open SkinsDemo.aspx and add a second button. Set the `SkinID` of this button to `RedButton`. The code for the two buttons should now look like this:

```
<asp:Button ID="Button1" runat="server" Text="Button" />
<asp:Button ID="Button2" runat="server" Text="Button" SkinID="RedButton" />
```

   Note that IntelliSense kicks in, helping you find the right `SkinID`.

7. Open SkinsDemo.aspx in the browser. You should now see two buttons with different colors.

How It Works

The named skin works almost exactly the same as normal skins. However, with a named skin a control can point to a specific skin in one of the skin files. In the Default.aspx page, the first button gets its settings from the default, unnamed skin, while the other now gets its settings from the skin with its `SkinID` set to `RedButton`.

With named skins, you have a very flexible solution at your disposal. With the normal skins, you can quickly change the appearance of all controls in your site. You can then use a named skin to override this behavior for a few controls that you want to look different.

A Final Note on Skins

If for some reason you don't want to apply a skin to a specific control you can disable the skin by setting the `EnableTheming` property of the control, like this:

```
<asp:Button ID="Button1" runat="server" EnableTheming="False" Text="Button" />
```

With `EnableTheming` set to `False`, the skin is not applied to the control. CSS settings from the theme's CSS file are still applied though.

Practical Tips on Creating Consistent Pages

The following list provides some practical tips on creating consistent pages.

- When you create a new web site, always start by adding a master page that you base all other pages on. Even if you think you have a site with only a few pages, a master page will help you ensure a consistent look across the entire site. Adding a master page at a later stage to the site means making a lot of manual changes to the existing pages, so adding one from the beginning saves you from having to do a lot of work later.
- As soon as you find yourself adding styling information to complex controls like the `TreeView` and `Menu` (discussed in the next chapter) or data-aware controls like the `GridView` (discussed in Chapter 12), consider creating a skin for them. The fact that you can control the layout of all similar controls from a single location makes it a lot easier to update your site. If you want to override the layout for a few controls, you can always use named skins with a `SkinID` or disable the skin entirely by setting `EnableTheming` to `False`.
- When creating skins or setting style properties directly on a control, consider using the `CssClass` property instead, and then moving all styling-related properties to the CSS for the site or theme. This decreases the page's size and makes it easier to make changes to the layout afterwards.
- The Export Template feature of Visual Web Developer is a great time saver. You can use it not only to create a template for an ASPX page and its Code Behind but also for other files like classes and CSS files. This allows you to jump-start the creation of new files, saving you from typing the same stuff over and over again.

Summary

ASP.NET 3.5 offers a number of great tools to aid you in creating a consistent looking web site. A consistent look and feel of all pages in your site is important to give your site a professional and attractive look. This in turn helps your visitors in finding the right information in your site, increasing the chances that they might visit your site again.

The best way to start creating consistent sites is by using a master page. With a master page, you can define the global look and feel of pages, adding relatively static items like a header and footer directly in it, and creating room with the `ContentPlaceHolder` controls for content pages to fill in.

A content page is then hooked up to this master page using the `MasterPageFile` attribute on the `@ Page` directive. The only thing that the content page needs to define is an `<asp:Content>` region for every `<asp:ContentPlaceHolder>` in the master page that it wants to override. There is no need to include repeating content like headers, footers, or menus in the content page, freeing you from making repetitious changes to all your content pages if you want to change the layout of your site.

Whereas master pages and content pages are used to define the global layout of a page in terms of the different content regions that your pages have, themes are used to change the look of these elements. Since themes can contain CSS files, images, and skins, you can change colors, fonts, positioning, and images simply by applying a theme. You can have as many themes as you want and you can switch between them by setting a single attribute in the web.config file or in an individual ASPX page. In addition, you can switch between themes programmatically, giving your users the option to select a theme that fits their preferences. Themes also allow you to improve the usability of your site by giving users with vision problems the option to select a high contrast theme with a large font size.

An important part of the Themes feature in ASP.NET 3.5 is skins. With a skin you can control the look of a control from a single location — a .skin file in the folder for the theme. Skins come in two flavors: a default skin that by design applies to all controls that the skin is targeting. The other is called a named skin, which you can refer to by its name. This gives you the possibility to change all similar controls in one fell swoop, while leaving in the option to change a single control on a page by page basis.

To take consistency one step further, you can create a base page for your site where all your ASPX pages inherit from. With this base page you can centralize the behavior of your pages, giving you an ideal location to check for things like invalid page titles or setting the user defined theme. When you use Visual Web Developer's Export Template feature, creating pages that inherit from this base page is as easy as adding a normal ASPX page.

The Planet Wrox web site is now starting to grow. This means it becomes more difficult for you and your visitors to find the right pages. The next chapter shows you a number of different ways for your users to navigate your site so they won't have any problems finding the page they are looking for.

Exercises

1. What's the difference between an `<asp:ContentPlaceHolder>` and an `<asp:Content>` control? In what type of page do you use which one?
2. How do you hook up an `<asp:Content>` control in a content page to the `<asp:ContentPlaceHolder>` in the master page?
3. Imagine you have created a skin that gets applied to all buttons in your site with the following skin definition:

```
<asp:Button runat="server" CssClass="MyButton" />
```

   The imaginary CSS class `MyButton` sets the background color of the button to white and the foreground color to black. To draw attention to a specific button in a page, you decide to give it a red background instead. Which options do you have to control the look of this single button?

4. Explain the differences between setting the `Theme` property and the `StyleSheetTheme` property for a page.
5. Name three different ways to set the `Theme` property for a page and explain the differences between the options.
6. What's the main reason for implementing a base page in your web site?

Navigation

When your site contains more than a handful of pages, it's important to have a solid and clear navigation structure that allows users to find their way around your site. By implementing a good navigation system, all the loosely coupled web pages in your project will form a complete and coherent web site.

When you think about important parts of a navigation system, the first thing that you may come up with is a menu. Menus come in all sorts and sizes, ranging from simple and static HTML links to complex, fold-out menus driven by CSS or JavaScript. But there's more to navigation than menus alone. ASP.NET comes with a number of useful navigation controls that allow you to set up a navigation system in no time. These controls include the `Menu`, `TreeView`, and `SiteMapPath`, which you'll learn about in this chapter.

Besides visual controls like `Menu`, navigation is also about *structure*. A well-organized site is easy for your users to navigate. The site map that is used by the navigation controls helps you define the logical structure of your site.

Another important part of navigation takes place at the server side. Sending a user from one page to another in Code Behind based on some condition is a very common scenario. For example, imagine an administrator entering a new CD or concert review in the Management section of the web site. When the review is done, you may want to show the administrator the full details of it on a new page.

In this chapter, you'll learn how to use the different navigation options you have at your disposal. In particular, this chapter looks at the following topics:

- How to move around your site using server controls and plain HTML
- How to address pages and other resources like images in your site
- How to use the ASP.NET `Menu`, `TreeView`, and `SiteMapPath` navigation controls
- How to send your user from one page to another through code

Before you look at the built-in navigation controls, you need to understand the different options you have to address the resources in your site like ASPX pages and images.

Different Ways to Move around Your Site

The most common way to let a user move from one page to another is by using the <a> element. This element has an href attribute that allows you to define the address of a page or other resource you want to link to. Between the tags you can place the content you want to link, such as text, an image, or other HTML. The following snippet shows a simple example of the <a> element:

```
<a href="Login.aspx">You can log in here</a>
```

With this code in a web page, users, after clicking the text "You can log in here," will be taken to the page Login.aspx that should be in the same folder as the page that contains the link.

The <a> element has a server-side counterpart called the HyperLink, which can be created in the markup using <asp:HyperLink>. It eventually ends up as an <a> element in the page. The NavigateUrl property of this control maps directly to the href attribute of the <a> element. For example, a server-side HyperLink like this:

```
<asp:HyperLink runat="server" id="lnkLogin" NavigateUrl="Login.aspx">
       You can log in here</asp:HyperLink>
```

produces the following HTML in the browser:

```
<a id="ctl00_cpMainContent_lnkLogin" href="Login.aspx">You can log in here</a>
```

Other than the long ID that is assigned by the ASP.NET runtime, this code is identical to the earlier example. In both cases, the href attribute points to the page Login.aspx using a *relative URL*. The next topic describes the differences between relative and *absolute* URLs.

Understanding Absolute and Relative URLs

Key to working with links in your site is a good understanding of the different forms a *Uniform Resource Locator* (URL) to a resource inside or outside your web site can take. A URL is used to uniquely identify a resource in your or another web site. These URLs are used in different places, including the href attribute of a hyperlink or a <link> element to point to a CSS file, the src attribute pointing to an image or a JavaScript source file and the url() value of a CSS property. These URLs can be expressed as a *relative URL* or as an *absolute URL*. Both have advantages and disadvantages that you should be aware of.

Relative URLs

In the previous examples you saw a relative URL that points to another resource relative to the location where the URL is used. This means that the page containing the <a> element and the Login.aspx page should both be placed in the same folder on disk. To refer to resources in other folders you can use the following URLs. All the examples are based on a site structure shown in Figure 7-1.

To link from Login.aspx page in the root to Default.aspx in the Management folder you can use this URL:

```
<a href="Management/Default.aspx">Management</a>
```

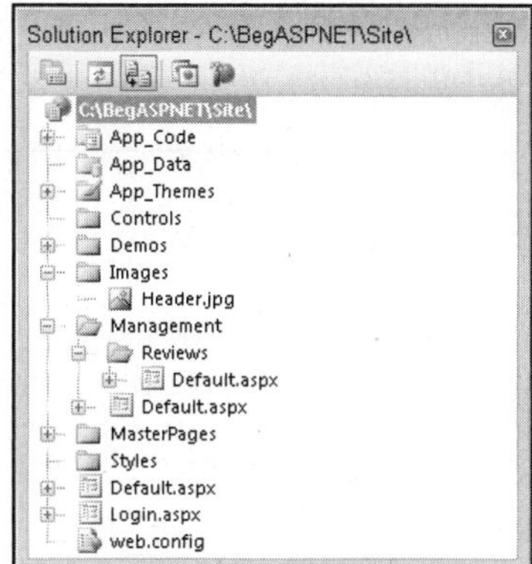

Figure 7-1

This points to Default.aspx in the Management folder which itself is located in the root, next to the Login.aspx page.

To refer to the image Header.jpg from the Default page in the Management folder you can use this URL:

```
<img src="../Images/Header.jpg" />
```

The two leading periods "navigate" one folder up to the root, and then back in the Images folder to point to Header.jpg.

For a deeper folder hierarchy, you can use multiple double periods, one for each folder you want to go upward in the site hierarchy, like this `<img>` element, which can be used to refer to the same image from pages in the Reviews folder, which is located under the Management folder:

```
<img src="../../Images/Header.jpg" />
```

One benefit of relative URLs is the fact you can move a set of files around to another directory at the same level without breaking their internal links. However, at the same time, they make it more difficult to move files to a different level in the site hierarchy. For example, if you moved the page Login.aspx to a separate folder like Members, the link to the Management folder would break. The new Members folder doesn't have Management as its subfolder so Management/Default.aspx is no longer a valid link.

To overcome this problem, you can use root-based relative URLs.

Root-Based Relative URLs

Root-based relative URLs always start with a leading forward slash to indicate the root of the site. If you take the link to the Management folder again, its root-based version looks like this:

```
<a href="/Management/Default.aspx">Management</a>
```

Note the leading forward slash in front of the Management folder. This link is unambiguous. It always points to the file Default.aspx in the Management folder in the root. With this link, moving the Login.aspx page to a subfolder doesn't break it; it will still point to the exact same file.

Relative URLs in Server Side Controls

With ASP.NET Server Controls you have another option at your disposal to refer to resources in your web site: you can use the tilde (~) character to point to the *current root of the site*. To understand what problems this tilde solves you need to be aware of the way Visual Web Developer creates new web sites and hooks them up to the built-in web server. When you create a new web site, VWD by default creates a site in a separate *application folder* under the built-in web server where all your pages are created. So, for example, when you create a new site and press Ctrl+F5 to open the default page in your browser you end up with an address similar to `http://localhost:23143/MyApplicationName`. Usually when you put your site live on a remote server, you don't want to have this application folder anymore. Instead, users browse to a URL such as `http://www.PlanetWrox.com` and expect to see the site. Fortunately, there's an easy way to stop VWD from creating this separate folder: you can set the Virtual Path property of the project to a forward slash (/) using the Properties Grid for the web site.

To see how this setting influences the way you refer to files, the following Try It Out shows you how to create a simple web site and add some images to it that use different URL naming schemes. You'll then set the virtual path property so you see what happens.

Try It Out — Investigating the Behavior of the Virtual Path Property

In this exercise, you'll create a brand new web site that is only used for this exercise. Afterward, you can delete the web site if you want. For this exercise, you also need an image file — for example, the Header.jpg from the previous chapter; any other image will do as well.

1. Choose File ➪ New Web Site to create a brand new web site.
2. Set the Location to File System and note that VWD offers a path that ends with WebSite1. If you've created other web sites before without giving them an explicit name, you may have a path that ends with WebSite2, WebSite3, and so on. The language doesn't matter in this exercise, so you can leave the Language drop-down list set to what it is. Click OK to create the site in VWD.
3. Add an image to the root of the site and call it Header.jpg. You can drop one of the images from the previous chapter in the root of the site, or you can use an existing image and add that to the site. If you don't rename the image to Header.jpg, make sure you adjust the code in the next step.
4. In Default.aspx, add the following code to the Markup View that inserts three ASP.NET Image controls using different ways to address the image. The images are separated by a line break:

```
<asp:Image ID="Image1" runat="server" ImageUrl="Header.jpg" /><br />
<asp:Image ID="Image2" runat="server" ImageUrl="/Header.jpg" /><br />
<asp:Image ID="Image3" runat="server" ImageUrl="~/Header.jpg" /><br />
```

5. Press Crlt+F5 to open the page in the browser. Note that the address bar of the browser reads something like `http://localhost:49198/WebSite1/Default.aspx`. Your port number and application name may be slightly different, but what's important to notice is that the web site is located in a folder called WebSite1 under the web server called localhost. You'll also find that the second image shows up broken. That's because the leading slash refers to the root of the web server, so the image is looked for at `http://localhost:49198/Header.jpg`, which doesn't exist since the image is located in the WebSite1 subfolder.

   Open up the source of the page in the browser and look at the three `<img>` elements:

```
<img id="Image1" src="Header.jpg" style="border-width:0px;" /><br />
```

```
<img id="Image2" src="/Header.jpg" style="border-width:0px;" /><br />
<img id="Image3" src="Header.jpg" style="border-width:0px;" /><br />
```

The first two URLs are identical to what you added to the ASPX page. However, the third one has been modified to refer to an image in the same document as the page that references the image.

6. Click the root of the web project in the Solution Explorer and press F4 to open up the web site's Properties Grid. Set the Virtual Path from /WebSite1 to / as shown in Figure 7-2.

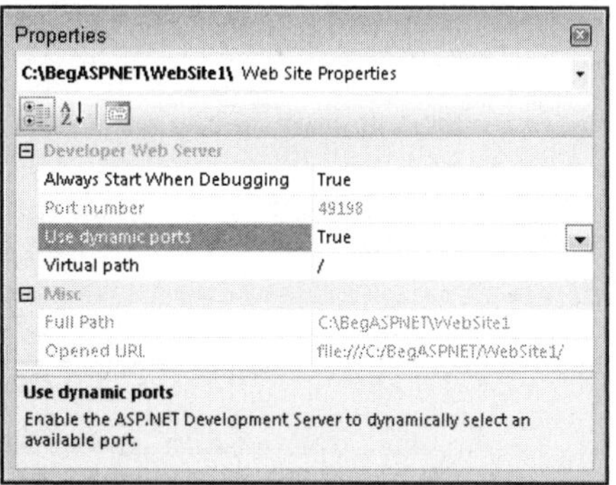

Figure 7-2

7. Press Ctrl+F5 again to reopen Default.aspx in the browser. The address bar now reads something like `http://localhost:49198/Default.aspx`. As you can see, the page Default.aspx is now located at the root of the server. Therefore, all three images show up correctly.

8. Go back to VWD and create a folder called Test. Drag the file Default.aspx from the root of the site into this new folder and then request the page in the browser. This time the first image will be broken. If you look at the HTML source, you'll see this:

```
<img id="Image1" src="Header.jpg" style="border-width:0px;" /><br />
<img id="Image2" src="/Header.jpg" style="border-width:0px;" /><br />
<img id="Image3" src="../Header.jpg" style="border-width:0px;" /><br />
```

The first `<img>` element tries to find an image relative to the current document. Since the current document lives in the Test folder and the image is located at the root of the site, this results in a broken image. The other two `src` attributes point to the correct image in the root of the site.

9. You can close the test project in VWD now, and delete it from disk because it is no longer needed.

How It Works

This example demonstrates that the ~ syntax to indicate the root of the site is often the most reliable way to refer to a resource like an image. In three different cases you saw in this exercise, only the third image showed up correctly every time. When a control like the `<asp:Image>` needs to render a path, it finds out what the current application root is and adjusts the path accordingly. This can be a real time saver when you decide to move around folders and files or develop your site using VWD's default setting of an additional application folder and then try to put your site on a production server that allows you to access files from the actual root of the server.

Plain HTML controls can also benefit from this syntax by changing them to server controls. You do this by adding a `runat="server"` attribute to the element. For example, the following `<img>` exhibits the same behavior as the third `<asp:Image>` from the previous example.

```
<img id="Image3" src="~/Header.jpg" runat="server" /><br />
```

The remainder of this book assumes you've set the virtual path property to a forward slash (/) which makes it easier to refer to your files using URLs without the ~ syntax. If you find that some resources don't show up correctly, check whether you set the virtual path property of your web site correctly.

Absolute URLs

In contrast to relative URLs that refer to a resource from a document or site root perspective, you can also use absolute URLs that refer to a resource by its full path. So instead of directly referring to an image and optionally specifying a folder, you include the full name of the domain and protocol information (the `http://` prefix). Here's an example that refers to the Wrox logo at the Wrox Programmer to Programmer site (`http://p2p.wrox.com`) where you go for questions regarding this and other Wrox books or for general questions regarding programming:

```
<img src="http://p2p.wrox.com/images/header/wrox_logo.gif" />
```

Absolute URLs are required if you want to refer to a resource outside your own web site. With such a URL, the `http://` prefix is important. If you leave it out, the browser will look for a folder called `p2p.wrox.com` inside your own web site.

Absolute URLs are unambiguous. They always refer to a fixed location, which helps you to make sure you're always referring to the exact same resource, no matter where the source document is located. This may make you think that they are ideal to use everywhere including references to resources within your own site. However, that's not the case. The extra protocol and domain information adds to the size of the page in the browser, making it unnecessarily slower to download. More importantly, it creates difficulties if you're changing your domain name, or if you want to reuse some functionality in a different web site. For example, if you previously had your site running on `www.mydomain.com` but you're moving it to `www.someotherdomain`, you will need to update all the absolute URLs in the entire web site.

You will also have trouble with absolute URLs during development. Quite often, you test your web site on a URL such as `http://localhost`. If you were to point all your images to that URL, they would all break as soon as you put your site on a production domain like `www.PlanetWrox.com`.

In short, use absolute URLs with caution. You always need them when referring to resources outside your web site, but you should give preference to relative URLs within your own projects wherever possible.

Understanding Default Documents

In the context of URLs you should also know about *default documents*. When you browse to a site like `http://www.domainname.com` you magically see a page appear. How does this work? Each web server has so-called default documents, a list of document names a browser can request when no explicit document name is supplied. So, when you browse to `http://www.domainname.com`, the web server scans the directory requested and processes the first file from the default document list it finds. In most ASP.NET scenarios, the web server is set up to use Default.aspx as the default document. So, when you browse to `http://www.domainname.com` on an ASP.NET web server, you are actually served the page `http://www.domainname.com/Default.aspx`.

In the links you create, you should generally leave out Default.aspx when it isn't needed. It decreases the page size, but more importantly, makes it easier for your users to type the address.

Some servers have set up Index.aspx as the default document. If you're finding that your pages don't load correctly with your ISP-hosted web sites, try renaming Default.aspx to Index.aspx.

Now that you have seen how you can use URLs to point to documents and other files, it's time to look at some higher-level controls that make use of these URLs: the ASP.NET navigation controls.

Using the Navigation Controls

ASP.NET 3.5 offers three useful navigation tools: `SiteMapPath`, `Menu`, and `TreeView`. Figure 7-3 shows basic examples of the three navigation controls, without any styling applied.

The `SiteMapPath` on the left shows the user the path to the current page. This helps if users want to go up one or more levels in the site hierarchy. It also helps them to understand where they are. The `TreeView` can display the structure of your site and allows you to expand and collapse the different nodes; in Figure 7-3 the entire tree is expanded. The `Menu` on the right displays Home only when the page first loads. However, as soon as you move the mouse over it, a submenu will appear showing the child nodes of the Home page element. In Figure 7-3 one of these child elements is the Reviews item, which in turn has child elements itself.

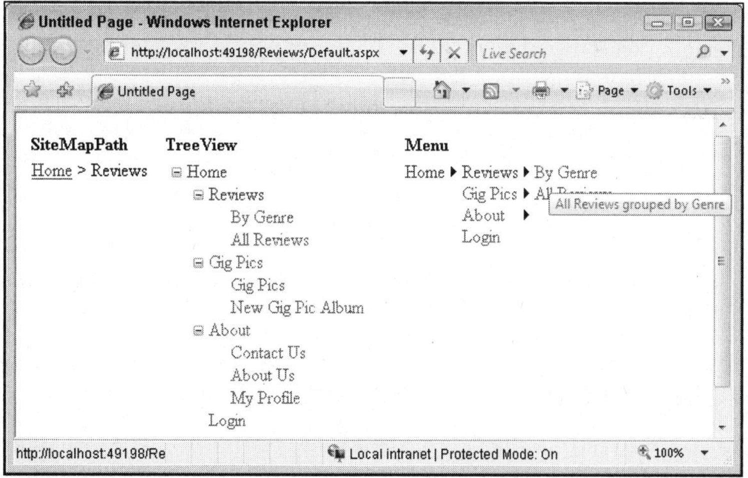

Figure 7-3

Architecture of the Navigation Controls

To make it easy to show relevant pages in your site using a `Menu`, a `TreeView`, or a `SiteMapPath`, ASP.NET uses an XML-based file that describes the *logical* structure of your web site. By default, this file is called Web.sitemap. This file is then used by the navigation controls in your site to present relevant links in an organized way. Simply by hooking up one of the navigation controls to the Web.sitemap file you can create complex user interface elements like fold-out menus or a `TreeView`.

Examining the Web.sitemap File

By default, you should call the site map file Web.sitemap. This allows the controls to find the right file automatically. For more advanced scenarios you can have multiple site map files with different names, with a configuration setting in the web.config that exposes these additional files to the system. In most cases, a single site map file will be sufficient. A basic version of the site map file can look like this:

```
<?xml version="1.0" encoding="utf-8" ?>
<siteMap xmlns="http://schemas.microsoft.com/AspNet/SiteMap-File-1.0" >
  <siteMapNode url="~/ " title="Home" description="Go to the homepage" />
    <siteMapNode url="~/Reviews" title="Reviews"
             description="Reviews published on this site" />
    <siteMapNode url="~/About" title="About"
             description="About this site" />
  </siteMapNode>
</siteMap>
```

The site map file contains `siteMapNode` elements that together form the logical structure of your site. In this example, there is a single root node called `Home`, which in turn contains two child elements, Reviews and About this site.

Key Elements of the Web.sitemap File

Each `siteMapNode` can have many child nodes, allowing you to create a site structure that can be both wide and deep at the same time. The `siteMapNode` elements in this example have three of their attributes set: `url`, `title`, and `description`. The `url` attribute should point to a valid page in your web site. You can use the ~ syntax you saw in the previous section to refer to application-root–based URLs. The ASP.NET runtime doesn't allow you to specify the same URL more than once, but you can work around that by making the URL unique by adding a query string. For example, `~/Login.aspx` and `~/Login.aspx?type=Admin` will be seen as two different pages. You'll see more of the query string later in this chapter.

The `title` attribute is used in the various navigation controls to display the name of the page. You'll see more about this later when you work with the `Menu` and `SiteMapPath` controls. The `description` attribute is used as a tooltip for the elements that appear in the browser.

The navigation controls work together with the ASP.NET security mechanism. That is, you can automatically hide elements from controls like the `Menu` that users don't have access to. Security is described in more detail in Chapter 15.

To be able to work with the Web.sitemap file, ASP.NET makes use of the `SiteMapDataSource` control which you'll find under the Data category of the Toolbox. When you use the `SiteMapPath` control to display a breadcrumb, ASP.NET will find the Web.sitemap file itself. With the other two navigation controls, you need to specify a `SiteMapDataSource` explicitly as an intermediate layer to the Web.sitemap file.

To create a useful Web.sitemap file, you need to add one to your site and then manually add the necessary `siteMapNode` elements to it. There is no automated way in Visual Web Developer to create a sitemap file based on the current site's structure, although there are third party solutions available that help you with this.

Try It Out Creating Your Web.sitemap File

In this exercise you add a new Web.sitemap file to the site and add a bunch of `siteMapNode` elements to it. This site map serves as the basis for the other navigation controls in the site.

1. Open the Planet Wrox project again in VWD and, in the Solution Explorer, click the project to select it. Press F4 to open the Properties Grid and then set the Virtual Path property to a forward slash (/) as shown in Figure 7-2. From now on, it's assumed that you always run the web site with this root-based URL.
2. Right-click the web site in the Solution Explorer and choose Add New Item to add a Web.sitemap file to the site and then click Site Map. Leave the default name set to Web.sitemap and click OK. You end up with one root element containing two child nodes.
3. Modify the Web.sitemap so it contains this code:

```
<?xml version="1.0" encoding="utf-8" ?>
<siteMap xmlns="http://schemas.microsoft.com/AspNet/SiteMap-File-1.0">
  <siteMapNode url="~/" title="Home" description="Home">
    <siteMapNode url="~/Default.aspx" title="Home" description="Go to the homepage" />
    <siteMapNode url="~/Reviews/Default.aspx" title="Reviews"
              description="Reviews published on this site">
      <siteMapNode url="~/Reviews/AllByGenre.aspx" title="By Genre"
                 description="All Reviews Grouped by Genre" />
      <siteMapNode url="~/Reviews/All.aspx" title="All Reviews"
                 description="All Reviews" />
    </siteMapNode>
    <siteMapNode url="~/About/Default.aspx" title="About" description="About this Site">
      <siteMapNode url="~/About/Contact.aspx" title="Contact Us"
                 description="Contact Us" />
      <siteMapNode url="~/About/AboutUs.aspx" title="About Us"
                 description="About Us" />
    </siteMapNode>
    <siteMapNode url="~/Login.aspx" title="Login" description="Log in to this web site" />
  </siteMapNode>
</siteMap>
```

Remember you don't have to type all this code yourself. You can find a copy of the file in this chapter's code file that you can download from the Wrox web site.

4. Save the file; you're done with it for now.

How It Works

Although you didn't add any spectacular code in the Web.sitemap file, there are a few things worth discussing. First of all, note that the site map only contains a single root node called `Home`. This is enforced by the Web.sitemap file, which doesn't allow more than one root element. The downside of this is that this single root element will also be the root item of your `Menu` and `TreeView` controls. In Figure 7-3 you can see how all submenus of the `TreeView` fall under the `Home` node. In most web sites, however, it's much more common to have the `Home` item on the same level as the others. Therefore, you added an additional `Home` node directly under the parent node to align it with the `Reviews` and `About` items. In a later exercise you'll see how to hide the root element from the controls, allowing you to only show the "first children" of the root node and their children. To overcome the problem that URLs in the `siteMapNode` elements need to be unique, you set one to `~/` and the other to `~/Default.aspx`. Because of the way web servers can handle default documents, this eventually points to the same file.

Also notice that some of the nodes specify a page called Default.aspx. Earlier you learned that you should try to leave out the name of the default documents to make the URLs shorter and easier to type. However, without an explicit document reference like Default.aspx, the site map and the navigation controls lose track of the page you are trying to refer to, so it's best to always add it explicitly. This isn't a real problem, however, as your users don't need to type these links themselves; they can simply click them in the relevant navigation control. They can still manually access the same page using its shorter notation.

A Web.sitemap file all by itself isn't very useful. You need to add navigation controls to your site to make use of the site map. In the next section you'll see how to use the `Menu` control, followed by the other controls.

Using the Menu Control

The `<asp:Menu>` control is very easy to use and tweak. To create a basic menu, all you need to do is add one to your page, hook it up to a `SiteMapDataSource` control and you're done. But at the same time, the control is quite flexible and has 80 public properties (including the ones shared by all controls) that allow you to tweak every visual aspect of the control. The following table lists the most common properties used with the menu. Refer to the VWD online help for a complete description of this control.

Property	Description
`CssClass`	Allows you to set a CSS class attribute that applies to the entire control.
`StaticEnableDefaultPopOutImage`	A Boolean that determines whether images are used to indicate submenus on the top-level menu items.
`DynamicEnableDefaultPopOutImage`	A Boolean that determines whether images are used to indicate submenus on submenu items.
`DisappearAfter`	Determines the time in milliseconds that menu items will remain visible after you move your mouse away from them.
`MaximumDynamicDisplayLevels`	Determines the number of levels of submenu items that the control can display. Useful with very large site maps to limit the number of items being sent to the browser.

Property	Description
`DataSourceID`	The ID of a `SiteMapDataSource` that supplies the data for the menu from the Web.sitemap file.
`Orientation`	Determines whether to use a horizontal menu with drop out submenus, or a vertical menu with fold out submenus.

The `Menu` control contains a few properties that start with `Static` or `Dynamic`. The `Static` properties are used to control the main menu items that appear when the page loads. Because they don't change or get hidden when you hover over them, they are considered static. The submenus are dynamic, as they appear only when you activate the relevant main menu items.

In addition to these properties, the menu also has a number of style properties that allow you to change the look and feel of the different parts of the menu. You'll see how to use some of these in a later exercise.

Things to Consider When Using the Menu

Although the `Menu` control is very easy to set up and use in a browser it has a few shortcomings you need to be aware of. For example, the control generates a lot of markup using HTML tables which adds to the size of the page.

Another problem with the generated code is that it is hard for non-desktop browsers to read. For example, blind people using a screen reader will have a hard time finding the right pages on your site.

To overcome these limitations, Microsoft released the ASP.NET CSS Friendly Control Adapters that alter the final markup of the menu control and deliver clean HTML instead that can be styled using CSS. You can find out more about the control adapters on the official ASP.NET web site `www.asp.net/CSSAdapters/Default.aspx`.

Creating a Basic Version of the Menu Control

To see how the `Menu` control operates, you're best off creating a very basic version first. Once you understand how it works and how it operates under the hood, you can style the menu to your likings so it blends in with the rest of the design of your site.

Try It Out Adding a Menu to the Site

In the next exercise, you'll see how to add a simple `Menu` control in the master page that uses the Web.sitemap file to build up the menu. The `Menu` is added to the `MenuWrapper` area in the master page and will present the menu items horizontally. Because of this orientation, this `Menu` is only suitable for the Monochrome theme. Later you will add a `TreeView` to represent the pages in the site, and write some code that shows the `Menu` for the Monochrome theme and the `TreeView` for the DarkGrey theme.

1. Open the master page in Markup View and locate the `<div>` called `MenuWrapper`. Remove the placeholder text `Menu Goes Here`. If you added some default text between the `ContentPlaceHolder` tags in an earlier exercise, now is a good place to remove that text again.

2. From the Navigation category of the Toolbox, drag a `Menu` and drop it between the `MenuWrapper` tags. Set the `CssClass` of the `Menu` control to `MainMenu`:

```
<div id="MenuWrapper">
  <asp:Menu ID="Menu1" runat="server" CssClass="MainMenu"></asp:Menu>
</div>
```

3. Switch to Design View. You may notice that the Design View doesn't look like the final page anymore. That's because you may have removed the `styleSheetTheme` attribute from the `<pages>` element in web.config. You can leave it like this for now. With much of the styling already done, this isn't so important. You can still see how the content inside the `cpMainContent` placeholder is going to end up in the browser.
4. Click the `Menu` control's grey arrow to open the Smart Tasks panel.
5. From the Choose Data Source drop-down list select `<New data source>`. In the dialog box that appears click the Site Map icon. Figure 7-4 shows what your screen should look like now.
6. Click OK to close the dialog box.
7. When you return to the page, the `Menu` control now shows the top-level element, Home (see Figure 7-5).

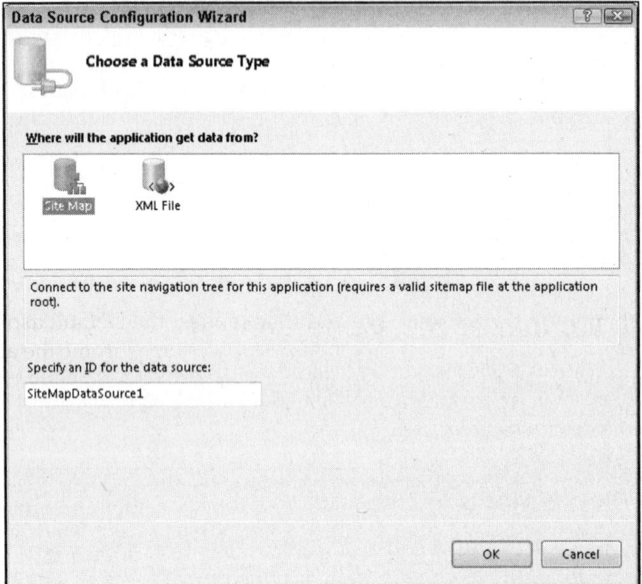

Figure 7-4

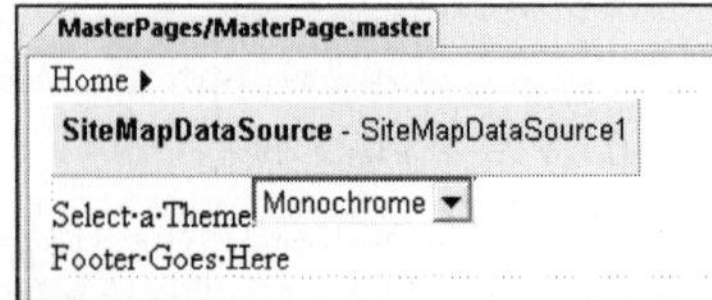

Figure 7-5

If your Design View doesn't look like this, but looks much closer to the final page, open the web.config file and remove the `styleSheetTheme` attribute from the `<page>` element.

8. Click the `SiteMapDataSource` once and then press F4 to open or activate the Properties Grid. Change the `ShowStartingNode` property from `True` to `False`. Note that as soon as you do this, the `Menu` control in the designer is updated and shows all direct child menus under the root element: Home, Reviews, About, and Login. Figure 7-6 shows how your menu should look now.

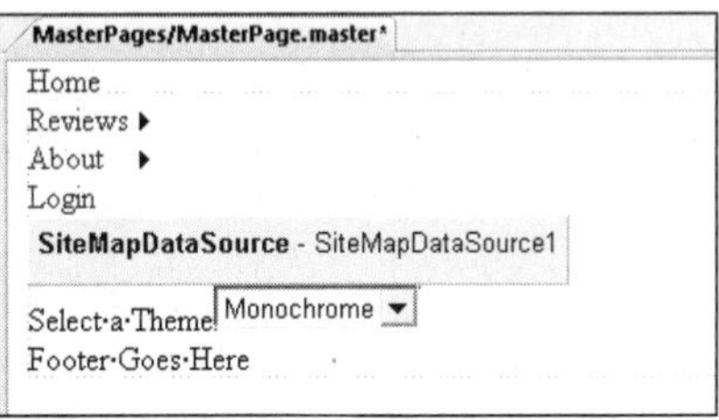

Figure 7-6

9. Click the `Menu` control once to select it and then make the following changes to the properties of the control using the Properties Grid:

Property	Value
`StaticEnableDefaultPopOutImage`	`False`
`Orientation`	`Horizontal`
`ItemSpacing` (a subproperty of `StaticMenuItemStyle` that you need to expand)	`10px`

10. Save the changes to the master page and then request the Default.aspx page in your browser. If necessary, use the Theme drop-down list to make Monochrome the active theme. You should now see the menu in the horizontal menu area. Hover your mouse over the items, and you'll see subitems appear (see Figure 7-7).

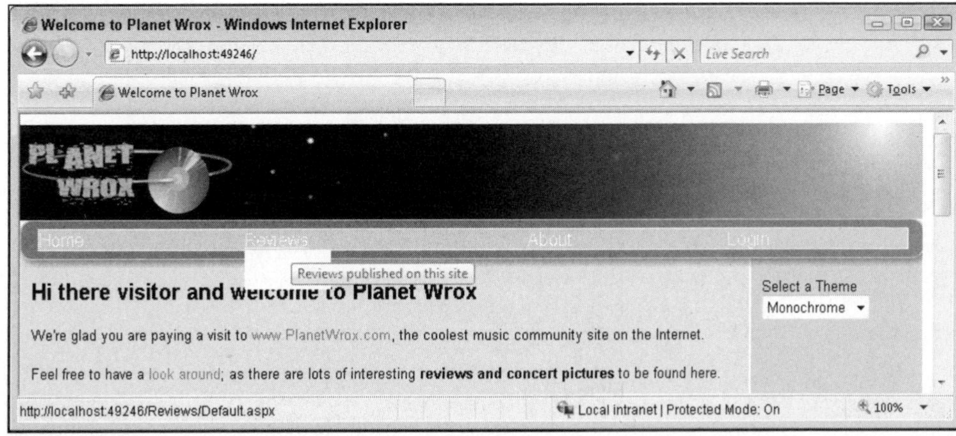

Figure 7-7

> Note that you can't read the text on the subitems. That's because the CSS from the Monochrome theme has changed the text of all anchors in the menu area to white. At the same time, the `Menu` control (not the theme's CSS file) has set the background color of the menu to white as well, effectively rendering the menus invisible. After you've seen how the `Menu` control works, you get a chance to fix its styling.

Don't worry if the menu doesn't look good in the DarkGrey theme. You'll see how to implement a different Navigation control for that theme later in this chapter.

How It Works

When a page with the menu is sent to the browser, the `Menu` control asks the `SiteMapDataSource`, defined in the same master page, for data. This data source control in turn reads the Web.sitemap file and then hands over the XML to the `Menu` control. Based on the hierarchical XML, the `Menu` is able to generate the necessary HTML and JavaScript. It generates a large HTML table with nested subtables, each containing one or more menu items. The `Menu` control hides the submenus through a CSS block that you find at the top of the page:

```
<style type="text/css">
  .ctl00_Menu1_0 { background-color:white;visibility:hidden;display:none;
            position:absolute;left:0px;top:0px; }
  .ctl00_Menu1_1 { text-decoration:none; }
  .ctl00_Menu1_2 {  }
  .ctl00_Menu1_3 {  }
  .ctl00_Menu1_4 {  }
</style>
```

All submenus have the class `ctl00_Menu1_0` when the page loads, making them hidden because the selector sets `visibility` to `hidden` and the `display` property to `none`.

When you hover your mouse over one of the main menu items, the submenu becomes visible. This is done with some JavaScript that is attached to the `<td>` tags of the menu like this:

```
<td onmouseover="Menu_HoverStatic(this)" onmouseout="Menu_Unhover(this)"
          onkeyup="Menu_Key(this)" title="Go to the homepage" id="ctl00_Menu1n0">
```

If you search the source of the page for the JavaScript that hides or shows the menu, you won't find any. So where is the JavaScript function that is used to show and hide the relevant menu items? The answer is in the cryptic `<script>` tag in the page that looks similar to this:

```
<script src="/WebResource.axd?d=7nGQ_0Tk41UEbNn9HVRm-
      A2&amp;t=633181994038144368" type="text/javascript"></script>
```

This `<script>` tag references a special ASP.NET *handler* called WebResource.axd. The seemingly random characters in the query string (the part of the URL after the question mark) tell the ASP.NET runtime to fetch a JavaScript file that contains the functionality for the menu. The file doesn't exist on your disk, but is returned by the WebResource.axd handler on the fly based on the query string. If you're brave, you can look at the file by requesting it in your browser by copying the value of the `src` attribute and pasting it right after the port number of your web site in the browser (for example, `http://localhost:50404`). You can safely ignore the file, as you don't need to make any changes to it for the menu to function correctly.

The WebResource.axd syntax is also used by other controls, like the `TreeView` that uses it to retrieve the images used in the `TreeView`.

To better integrate the `Menu` control with the existing design of the Monochrome theme, you can style it using inline style properties or with separate CSS classes.

Styling the Menu Control

The `Menu` control exposes a number of complex style properties that allow you to change the looks of items such as the main and submenu items. You can also define how these items look when they are active (selected) or when you hover your mouse over them. Each of these style properties has a number of subproperties for visual aspects, such as font, color, and spacing. Figure 7-8 shows the Properties Grid for the `StaticMenuItemStyle`, which defines the looks of the main menu items that are visible when the page first loads.

Most of the properties, like `BackColor`, `ForeColor`, and `Font` map directly to inline CSS styles. This makes it difficult to reuse the design in other pages or with other themes, so it's much better to use the `CssClass` instead and then define the necessary CSS classes in the theme's CSS file. You'll see how this works next.

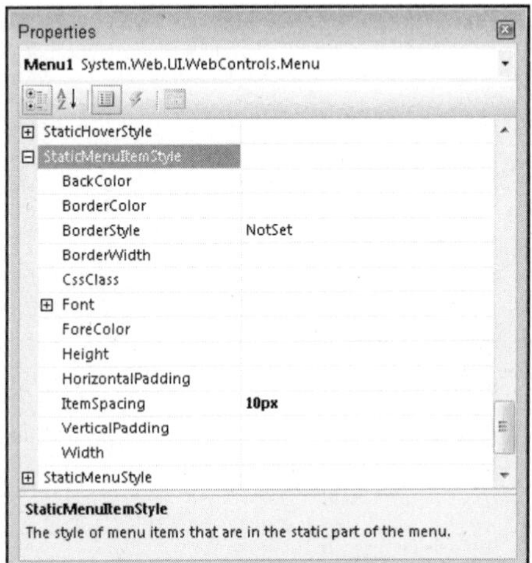

Figure 7-8

Try It Out: Styling the Menu Control

In this exercise you add CSS classes for items like `StaticMenuItemStyle`, `StaticHoverStyle`, and `DynamicMenuItemStyle`. You can then apply these classes to the relevant style properties of the `Menu` control.

1. Open Monochrome.css from the Monochrome theme folder and add the following CSS rules. You can leave out the comments placed between `/*` and `*/`, as they only serve to describe the

purpose of the selectors. If you don't feel like typing all this CSS, remember you can also get a copy of this file from the code download that comes with this book and copy it from that file into your file.

```
.StaticMenuItemStyle, .StaticMenuItemStyle a
{
 /* Defines the look of main menu items. */
 color: #707070;
 font-size: 14px;
 font-weight: bold;
 text-decoration: none;
 padding-left: 2px;
}

.StaticHoverStyle, .StaticSelectedStyle
{
 /* Defines the look of active and hover menu items */
 background-color: #c1e4ce;
}

.DynamicMenuItemStyle
{
 /* Defines the sub menu items */
 font-size: 14px;
 color: #707070;
 background-color: #cccccc;
 padding: 4px 2px 4px 3px;
}

.DynamicHoverStyle
{
 /* Defines the hover style of sub menus */
 background-color: #707070;
 color: White;
}

.DynamicHoverStyle a
{
 /* Removes the underline from links in the sub menus */
 text-decoration: none;
}
```

2. Save and close the file.

3. Open the master page, switch to Design View, and select the `Menu` control. Press F4 to open the Properties Grid and then set the `CssClass` of the following style properties:

Style Property	Set CssClass to	Explanation
`StaticMenuItemStyle`	`StaticMenuItemStyle`	Defines the look of main menu items.
`StaticHoverStyle`	`StaticHoverStyle`	Defines the style that is applied when you hover over the main menu items.

Style Property	Set CssClass to	Explanation
`StaticSelectedStyle`	`StaticSelectedStyle`	Defines the look of selected main menu items.
`DynamicMenuItemStyle`	`DynamicMenuItemStyle`	Defines the look of the submenu items.
`DynamicHoverStyle`	`DynamicHoverStyle`	Defines the style that is applied when you hover over the submenu items.

Note that the code uses the style property name as the `CssClass` to simplify things. This isn't required, but makes it much easier to find the relevant selectors in the CSS file.

4. Remove the `ItemSpacing` attribute from the `StaticMenuItemStyle` element in Markup View.

When you're ready, your `Menu` should look like this:

```
<asp:Menu ID="Menu1" runat="server" DataSourceID="SiteMapDataSource1" CssClass="MainMenu"
        Orientation="Horizontal" StaticEnableDefaultPopOutImage="False" >
  <StaticMenuItemStyle CssClass="StaticMenuItemStyle" />
  <StaticHoverStyle CssClass="StaticHoverStyle" />
  <StaticSelectedStyle CssClass="StaticSelectedStyle" />
  <DynamicMenuItemStyle CssClass="DynamicMenuItemStyle" />
  <DynamicHoverStyle CssClass="DynamicHoverStyle" />
</asp:Menu>
```

5. Next, create the following folders and files that you'll use in this and later chapters. Use the MyBasePage template to create the new files. Also, in Markup View, give each page a meaningful `Title` to avoid errors later.

Folder	File Name	Title
`/Reviews`	`Default.aspx`	`My Favorite Reviews`
`/Reviews`	`All.aspx`	`All Reviews`
`/Reviews`	`AllByGenre.aspx`	`Reviews Grouped by Genre`
`/About`	`Default.aspx`	`About this Site`
`/About`	`Contact.aspx`	`Contact Us`
`/About`	`AboutUs.aspx`	`About Us`

When you're working in Visual Basic, you'll get an error on the two Default.aspx pages. That's because with the template you created earlier, you end up with a class called `Default` for a file called Default.aspx. However, `Default` is also a reserved word in Visual Basic, leading to an error. This is an easy fix. Just prefix the `Default` class with an underscore in the Code Behind:

```
Partial Class _Default
Inherits BasePage
```

After you have changed the class name, you also need to change the `Inherits` attribute in the markup of the page:

```
<%@ Page Language="VB" MasterPageFile="~/MasterPages/MasterPage.master"
    AutoEventWireup="false" CodeFile="Default.aspx.vb" Inherits="_Default"
    title="My Favorite Reviews" %>
```

6. Save all changes and open the Default.aspx page from the root in your browser. Your site menu now looks a lot better and more in line with the rest of the Monochrome theme. When you hover the mouse over a main menu, the submenus appear showing the text on a light grey background. When you hover over a submenu, its background and foreground color change again. Figure 7-9 shows the expanded Reviews menu with the `hover` style applied to the By Genre menu item.

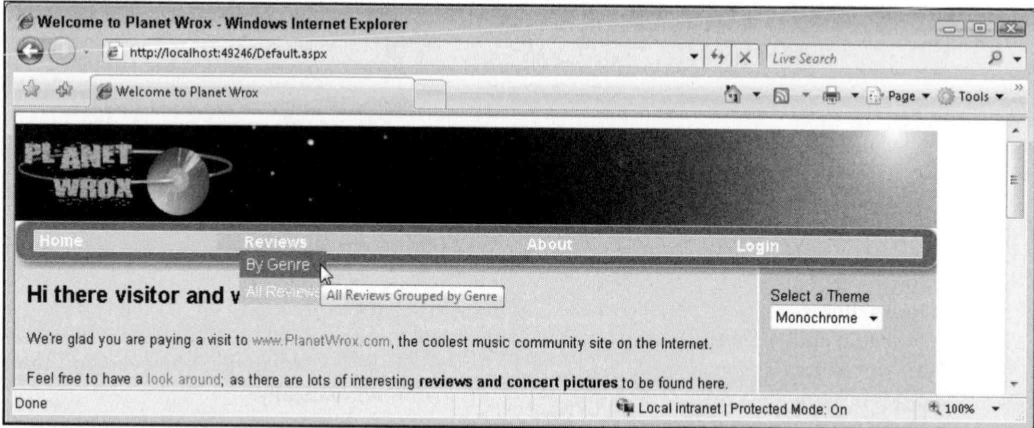

Figure 7-9

If you get an error when you navigate to one of the new pages you created, make sure you gave all of them a valid title. Since they all inherit from the base page, the title is checked when the page loads.

How It Works

The `Menu` control exposes style properties for all the relevant parts of the menu, including the main menu items (in normal, selected and hover state), and the various submenu items in different states. You can set individual styling properties for all the objects, but that results in a lot of HTML and CSS being sent to the browser. A cleaner solution is to apply CSS classes, which you can then manually manage in the CSS file of the theme.

When the Menu control creates its HTML, it applies the correct CSS class to parts of the menu. For example, the StaticHoverStyle is applied like this:

```
<table class="StaticMenuItemStyle ctl00_Menu1_4 StaticSelectedStyle ctl00_Menu1_9"
        cellpadding="0" cellspacing="0" border="0" width="100%">
<tr>
  <td style="white-space: nowrap;">
    ... Menu items go here; not shown
  </td>
</tr>
</table>
```

The table has the class StaticMenuItemStyle applied, which determines the font size and color of the menu items, removes the underline from the links in the menu, and adds a few pixels of padding to the item to create some room between the left border of the menu item and its text.

The other CSS classes work exactly the same way. Each of them serves a distinct purpose and is used to define the look of the element it's applied to.

The Menu control in horizontal mode is ideal for the Monochrome theme, as it features a horizontal navigation bar. For the DarkGrey theme you can use the same Menu and set its Orientation to Vertical. This creates a vertical menu with the main items stacked on top of each other, while the submenus will fold out to the right of the main menus. But instead of the Menu control, you can also use a TreeView control to display a hierarchical overview of the site map. This control is discussed next.

Using the TreeView Control

A TreeView is capable of displaying a hierarchical list of items, similar to how the tree in Windows Explorer looks. Items can be expanded and collapsed with the small plus and minus icons in front of items that contain child elements. As such, it's an ideal tool to display the site map of the web site as a means to navigate the site. The TreeView is not limited to the Web.sitemap file, however. You can also bind it to regular XML files and even create a TreeView programmatically.

The following table lists the most common properties of the TreeView. Again, the VWD online help is a good place to get a detailed overview of all the available properties and their descriptions.

Property	Description
CssClass	Allows you to set a CSS class attribute that applies to the entire control.
CollapseImageUrl	The image that collapses a part of the tree when clicked. The default is an icon with a minus symbol on it.
ExpandImageUrl	The image that expands a part of the tree when clicked. The default is an icon with a plus symbol on it.

Continued

Property	Description
`CollapseImageToolTip`	The tooltip that is shown when a user hovers over a collapsible menu item.
`ExpandImageToolTip`	The tooltip that is shown when a user hovers over an expandable menu item.
`ShowExpandCollapse`	Determines whether the items in the `TreeView` can be collapsed and expanded by clicking an image in front of them.
`ShowLines`	Determines whether lines are used to connect the individual items in the tree.
`ExpandDepth`	Determines the level at which items in the tree are expanded when the page first loads. The default setting is `FullyExpand`, which means all items in the tree are visible. Other allowed settings are numeric values to indicate the level to which to expand.

Just as with the `Menu` control, the `TreeView` control has a number of style properties that allow you to change the look and feel of the different parts of the tree. The way this works is identical to the `Menu` control.

To tell the `TreeView` which items to show, you bind it to a `SiteMapDataSource` control, which is demonstrated next.

Try It Out — Building a Navigation System with the TreeView Control

In this exercise, you add a `TreeView` control to the `MenuWrapper` `<div>` tag, right below the `Menu` you created earlier. The `TreeView` is then bound to the same data source as the `Menu`. Next, you'll write some code that either shows the `Menu` or the `TreeView`, depending on the active theme.

1. Open the master page and just below the `Menu` control, add a `TreeView` control by dragging it from the Toolbox into the page in Markup View.
2. Switch to Design View, click `TreeView` once, and click the little grey arrow to open the Smart Tasks panel. From the Choose Data Source drop down, select `SiteMapDataSource1`, the data source control you created for the `Menu` control (see Figure 7-10).

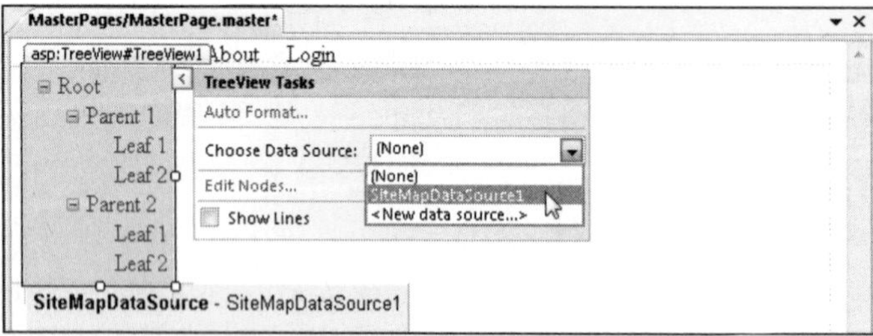

Figure 7-10

As soon as you select the data source, the `TreeView` is updated in Design View; it now shows the correct menu items from the sitemap file.

3. Open the Properties Grid for the `TreeView` control and set the `ShowExpandCollapse` property to `False`.

4. Click somewhere in the document to put the focus on it and then press F7 to open the Code Behind of the master page file and locate the `Page_Load` event that you used earlier to preselect the theme in the Theme list. Right below that code, and before the end of the method, add the following highlighted code that shows or hides the `TreeView` and `Menu` controls based on the currently active theme:

VB.NET

```
    End If
  End If
  Select Case Page.Theme.ToLower()
    Case "darkgrey"
      Menu1.Visible = False
      TreeView1.Visible = True
    Case Else
      Menu1.Visible = True
      TreeView1.Visible = False
  End Select
End Sub
```

C#

```
        lstPreferredTheme.Items.FindByValue(selectedTheme).Selected = true;
      }
    }
    switch (Page.Theme.ToLower())
    {
      case "darkgrey":
        Menu1.Visible = false;
        TreeView1.Visible = true;
        break;
      default:
        Menu1.Visible = true;
        TreeView1.Visible = false;
        break;
    }
}
```

5. Save all changes and open Default.aspx in the browser. Depending on your currently active theme, you should see either the `Menu` or the `TreeView` control. Select a different theme from the list and the page will reload, now showing the other control as the Navigation system of the web site (see Figure 7-11).

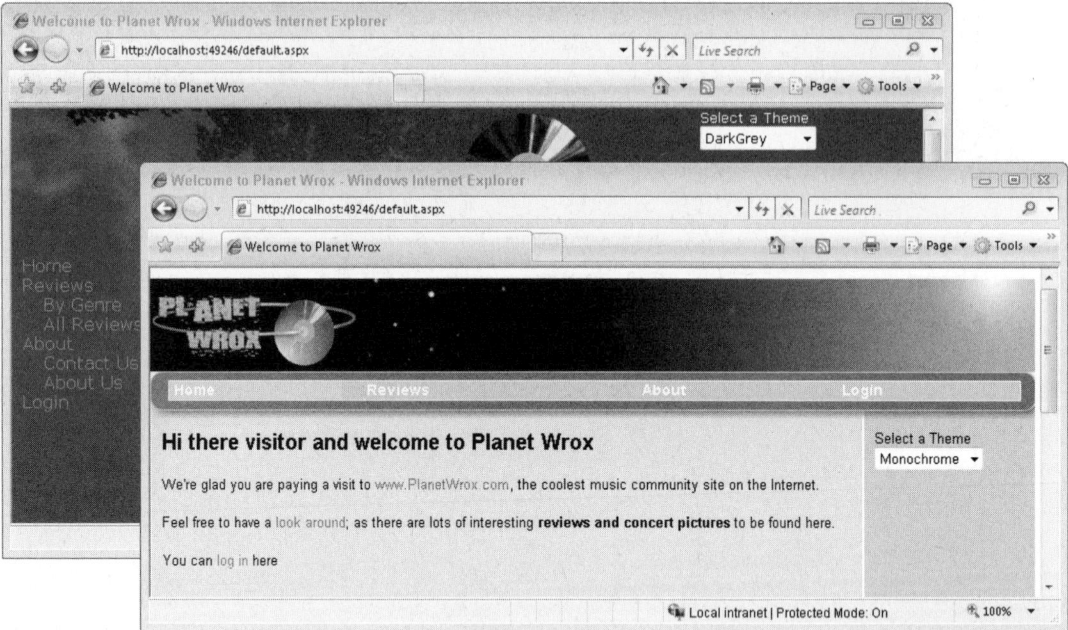

Figure 7-11

How It Works

Just as the `Menu` control, the `TreeView` control can get its data from a `SiteMapDataSource` control, which in turn gets its information from the Web.sitemap file. By default, the `TreeView` shows plus and minus signs to indicate that items can be collapsed and expanded. For a site menu this may not make much sense, so by setting `ShowExpandCollapse` to `False`, you effectively hide the images to expand and collapse.

The code in the Code Behind of the master page looks at the current theme by investigating the `Theme` property of the `Page`. When `DarkGrey` is the current theme, the code hides the `Menu` and then displays the `TreeView`. In the `Case Else` / `default` block the reverse is true. This means that for the Monochrome theme and all future themes you may add the `TreeView` is hidden and the `Menu` is used instead as the navigation system.

The `TreeView` suffers from the same problems as the `Menu` in that it generates a lot of bloated HTML. To have the `TreeView` generate a lot cleaner CSS-enabled code instead you can use the CSS Control Adapters mentioned earlier.

With two of the three navigation controls discussed, the final control you need to look at is the `SiteMapPath` control.

Using the SiteMapPath Control

The SiteMapPath control shows you where you are in the site's structure. It presents itself as a series of links, often referred to as a *breadcrumb*. It's a pretty simple yet powerful control with almost 50 public properties you can set through the Properties Grid to influence the way it looks. Just like the Menu and TreeView it has a number of style properties you use to change the look of elements like the current node, a normal node, and the path separator.

The following table lists a few of the most common properties of the SiteMapPath control.

Property	Description
PathDirection	Supports two values: RootToCurrent and CurrentToRoot. The first setting shows the root element on the left, intermediate levels in the middle, and the current page at the right of the path. The CurrentToRoot setting is the exact opposite where the current page is shown at the left of the breadcrumb path.
PathSeparator	Defines the symbol or text to show between the different elements of the path. The default is the greater than symbol (>) but you can change it to something like the pipe character (|).
RenderCurrentNodeAsLink	Determines whether the last element of the path (the current page) is rendered as a text link or as plain text. The default is False, which is usually fine, as you are already on the page that element is representing, so there's no real need for a link.
ShowToolTips	Determines whether the control displays tooltips (retrieved from the description attribute of the siteMapNode elements in the Web.sitemap file) when the user hovers over the elements in the path.

Depending on your personal preferences, you usually don't need to define any of the styles of the SiteMapPath control. In the final page in the browser, the SiteMapPath consists of mainly anchor tags (<a>) and plain text. If you have set up a specific selector for anchors in your CSS file, the SiteMapPath will automatically show itself in line with the other links in the page.

Try It Out — Creating a Breadcrumb with the SiteMapPath Control

A good location for the SiteMapPath is in the global master page of the site. That way it becomes visible in all your pages automatically.

1. Open the master page in Markup View and locate the opening tag of the MainContent <div>. Right after that tag, and before the <asp:ContentPlaceHolder> tag drag a SiteMapPath from the Toolbox. Right after the SiteMapPath add two line breaks (<br />). You should end up with code like this:

```
<div id="MainContent">
  <asp:SiteMapPath ID="SiteMapPath1" runat="server"></asp:SiteMapPath><br /><br />
  <asp:ContentPlaceHolder ID="cpMainContent" runat="server">
```

2. Save the changes and then request Default.aspx in the browser. Note that the page now shows the path from the root of the site (identified by the Home link) to the current page. Click a few of the items in the `Menu` or `TreeView` controls to navigate around the site and you'll see the breadcrumb change for each page. Figure 7-12 shows the breadcrumb for the All Reviews page that is a subelement of Reviews, which in turn falls under the Home root element.

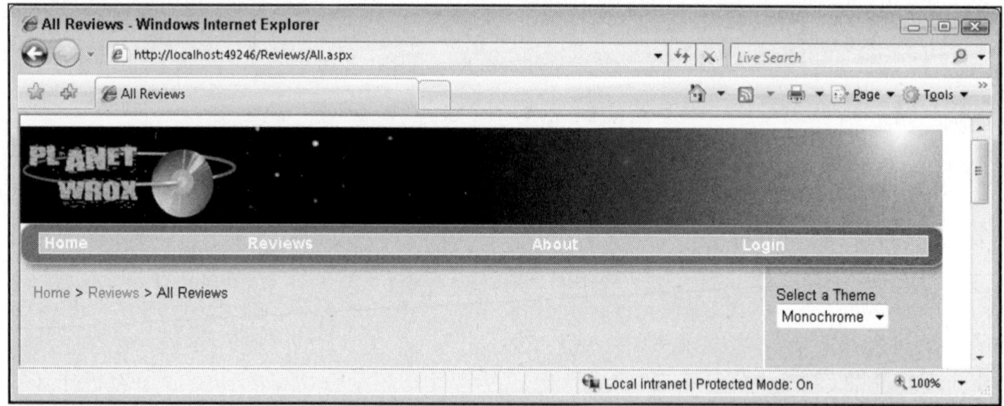

Figure 7-12

When you navigate to one of the subpages, you can click the elements of the path to go up one or more levels. Clicking Reviews in the page shown in Figure 7-12 takes you back to the main Reviews page, while clicking Home takes you back to the root of the site.

3. Using the Theme selector, switch to a different theme. Note that the `SiteMapPath` looks pretty much the same, except for the color of the links, which are defined in each of the theme's CSS file.

How It Works

The `SiteMapPath` renders as a series of `<span>` elements that either contain a link or plain text. Here's a part of the HTML code for the `SiteMapPath` from Figure 7-12:

```
<span><a title="Home" href="/">Home</a></span>
<span> &gt; </span>
<span><a title="Reviews published on this site"
      href="/Reviews/Default.aspx">Reviews</a></span>
<span> &gt; </span>
<span>All Reviews</span>
```

The first two elements (`Home` and `Reviews`) are represented by a link (`<a>`) to allow you to navigate to the pages defined in their `href` property. The final element — `All Reviews` — is just plain text. In between the elements you see a `<span>` with the character you set in the `PathSeparator` property.

If you look at the HTML for the page in your browser, you also see an `<a>` element that allows you to skip links. The `<a>` contains a small image with its `width` and `height` properties set to `0px` so it is invisible. This is used for screen readers that allow users to skip the navigation and directly go the content of the page. The `TreeView` and `Menu` controls use an identical approach to avoid a screen reader from reading out loud the entire site structure every time the page loads.

The three navigation controls give you a great feature set for a navigation system in your web site from the client side. Both the `Menu` and the `TreeView` controls allow you to quickly display the entire structure of the site so users can easily find their way. `SiteMapPath` helps users understand where they are in the site and gives them an easy way to navigate to pages higher up in the site hierarchy.

In addition to navigating from the client browser, it's also very common to navigate a user to a different page from the server side using code. How this works is discussed in the next section.

Programmatic Redirection

Programmatic redirection is very useful and common in ASP.NET pages. For example, imagine a page that allows users to enter a review into the database. As soon as they click the Save button, the review is saved and then users are taken to another page where they can see the entire review.

ASP.NET supports two major ways to redirect users to a new page programmatically: using `Response.Redirect` and `Server.Transfer`. Since both behave pretty differently, the following two sections describe their behavior in more detail.

Programmatically Redirecting the Client to a Different Page

Within each ASPX page you have access to a property called `Response` that you saw earlier when saving the cookie for the selected theme. The `Response` object gives you access to useful properties and methods that are all related to the response from the server to the user's browser. One of those methods is the `Redirect` method. This method sends an instruction to the browser to request a new page. This is useful if you want to redirect your user to another page in your site, or to a completely different web site. The `Redirect` method can be used in two different ways:

```
Response.Redirect(newUrl)
Response.Redirect(newUrl, endResponse)
```

The second version, which has an additional Boolean parameter called `endResponse`, allows you to execute any remaining code after the call to `Response.Redirect` when you pass `False` for the `endResponse` parameter. This is usually not necessary so you're better off calling the first version, which ends the response by default.

Quite often when you want to send the user to a different page, you want to send some additional information. You can do that by passing it in the *query string*, the part of the address that comes after the page name, separated by a question mark. Consider the following URL:

```
http://localhost:49246/Demos/Target.aspx?CategoryId=10&From=Home
```

The entire bold part (after the question mark) is considered the query string. It consists of name-value pairs, each separated from another by an ampersand (`&`). In this case, there are two pairs: `CategoryId` with a value of `10` and `From` with a value of the word `Home`. The page, Target.aspx in this example, is able to read these values using `Request.QueryString`. You'll see how to use the query string in the next exercise.

Try It Out — Redirecting the User to Another Page

To give you a closer look at how it works, this exercise shows you how to create a page that redirects from one page to another using `Response.Redirect`.

1. In the Demos folder, create two new Web Forms based on your exported template. Call them Source.aspx and Target.aspx. Set their `Title` to `Source` and `Target`.

2. Open Source.aspx in Design View and double-click somewhere in the grey, read-only area of the page outside the `ContentPlaceHolder` to set up a `Page_Load` handler. Inside this handler write the following code that redirects the user to the Target.aspx page. To show you how to pass additional data through the query string and how to read that information in the target page, the code passes a query string field called `Test` with `SomeValue` as the value:

VB.NET

```
Protected Sub Page_Load(ByVal sender As Object, ByVal e As System.EventArgs) _
          Handles Me.Load
  Response.Redirect("Target.aspx?Test=SomeValue")
End Sub
```

C#

```
protected void Page_Load(object sender, EventArgs e)
{
  Response.Redirect("Target.aspx?Test=SomeValue");
}
```

3. Open Target.aspx, switch to Design View, and add a `Label` control to the `cpMainContent` placeholder. Leave its `ID` set to `Label1`. Set up a `Page_Load` handler similar to the one you created in the previous step by double-clicking the grey, read-only area of the page and then add the following code:

VB.NET

```
Protected Sub Page_Load(ByVal sender As Object, ByVal e As System.EventArgs) _
          Handles Me.Load
  Label1.Text = Request.QueryString.ToString()
End Sub
```

C#

```
protected void Page_Load(object sender, EventArgs e)
{
  Label1.Text = Request.QueryString.ToString();
}
```

4. Go back to Source.aspx and press Ctrl+F5 to open it in the browser. Instead of seeing Source.aspx, you now see the page depicted in Figure 7-13.

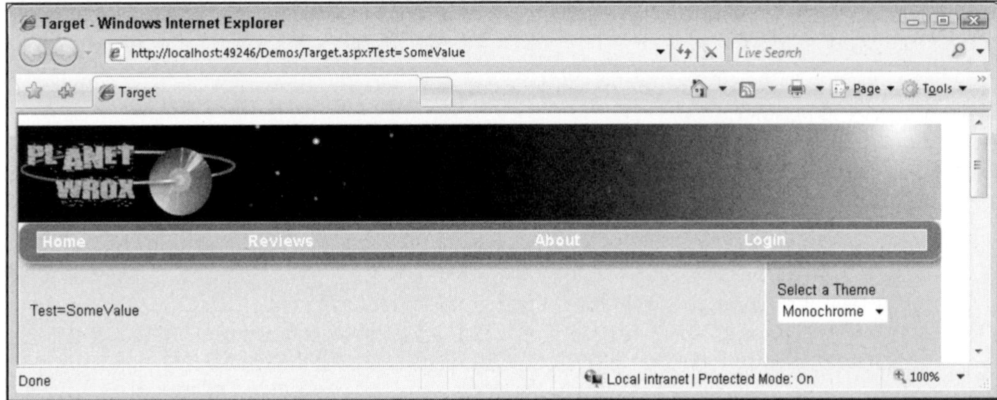

Figure 7-13

Note that the address bar now reads `Target.aspx?Test=SomeValue`, the page you redirected to in the `Page_Load` event handler of the source page. The `Label` in the target page correctly shows the query string that is passed to this page. Notice that `QueryString.ToString()` only contains `Test=SomeValue`. The address or even the question mark is not a part of the query string for the page.

How It Works

When you use `Response.Redirect`, ASP.NET sends an instruction to the browser to tell it to fetch a new page. In technical terms, it sends a "302" HTTP status code, which tells the browser the current page has moved to a new location. With this instruction it also sends the new URL so the browser understands what page to fetch next. In this exercise, the new page was `Target.aspx?Test=SomeValue`, which contains both the page name and a query string. The Target.aspx page is then requested by the browser, the `Page_Load` event fires and the query string is displayed on the label in the page. Because of this client redirect, the new page name and query string is fully exposed to the client.

In contrast to `Response.Redirect`, there is `Server.Transfer`, which redirects to another page at the server.

Server-Side Redirects

Server side redirects are great if you want to send out a different page without modifying the client's address bar. This allows you to hide details of page names and query string, which may lead to cleaner URLs from a user's point of view. This is often used in so-called URL-rewrite scenarios that are used to create pretty URLs. For example, a user may request a page like this:

```
http://www.domain.com/Cars/Volvo/850/T5/
```

Under the hood the server might transfer to:

```
http://www.domain.com/Cars/ShowCar.aspx?Make=843&Model=984&Type=7345
```

Clearly, the first URL is a lot easier to understand and type in a browser. It also allows a user to guess other URLs that match the same pattern. For example, there's a fair chance you can request a page like this:

```
http://www.domain.com/Cars/Volvo/V70/R/
```

and end up with the right page showing you the Volvo V70 R.

In addition to being easier to understand, server-side transfers may also speed up your site a little. Instead of sending a response to the browser to tell it to fetch a new page, which results in a new request for a page, you can directly transfer the user to a new page saving you from some network overhead.

Server-side transfers are carried out with the `Server` class. Just like the `Request` and `Response` objects you saw earlier give you information about the request and the response, so does the `Server` object provide you with information about the server the page is running on. You can use it to get information about the server name, its IP address, and so on. One of its methods is `Transfer`, which performs a server-side transfer.

`Server.Transfer` can only be used to redirect to other pages within your site. You cannot use it to send the user to pages on different domains. If you try to do so, the ASP.NET runtime throws an error.

To see the difference between `Response.Redirect` and `Server.Transfer`, the following exercise shows you how to change the Source page to perform a `Server.Transfer` action.

Try It Out Server-Side Redirecting

It's easy to change the redirect code so it transfers the user to another page. All you need to do is replace `Response.Redirect` with `Server.Transfer` as demonstrated in the next exercise.

1. Open the Code Behind of Source.aspx and replace the line with `Response.Redirect` with the following line:

VB.NET

```
Protected Sub Page_Load(ByVal sender As Object, ByVal e As System.EventArgs) _
          Handles Me.Load
  Server.Transfer("Target.aspx?Test=SomeValue")
End Sub
```

C#

```
protected void Page_Load(object sender, EventArgs e)
{
  Server.Transfer("Target.aspx?Test=SomeValue");
}
```

2. Save the changes and then press Ctrl+F5 to open Source.aspx in the browser (see Figure 7-14).

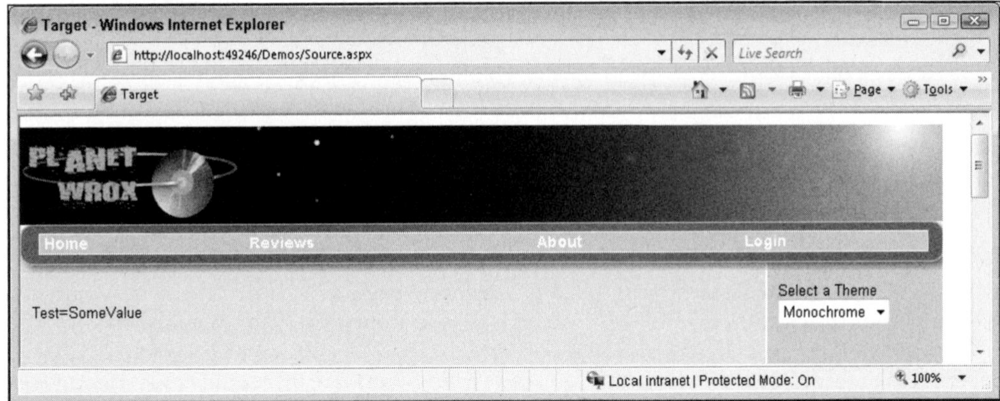

Figure 7-14

The `Label` control displays the query string values that were sent from Source.aspx to Target.aspx, demonstrating the fact that you are really viewing the output of the Target.aspx page. However, the browser's address bar is left unmodified and still shows Source.aspx, hiding the new page name and query string values from the user.

How It Works

Instead of instructing the browser to fetch a new page, `Server.Transfer` takes place completely at the server. The output of the old page is discarded and a new page life cycle is started for the page that is being transferred to. This page then generates its content and sends it back to the browser, while leaving the browser's address bar unmodified.

If you look at the emitted HTML in the browser, you'll see that the form action is set to the new page so any postback that occurs is executed against that page, which in turn will change the address in the address bar:

```
<form name="aspnetForm" method="post" action="Target.aspx?Test=SomeValue" id="aspnetForm">
...
</form>
```

With programmatic ways to send a user to another page, you have come to the end of this navigation chapter. With the concepts shown in this chapter, you have all the knowledge to create a highly effective navigation system in your site, from both the client's browser and your own server side code.

Practical Tips on Navigation

The following list presents some practical tips on navigation:

- When you start building a web site that you think will grow in the future, create a logical structure right away. Don't place all files in the root of your web site, but group logically related files in the same folder. Such logical grouping makes it easier for you to manage the site and for your users to find the pages they want. Although it's easy to move a page in a `Menu` or `TreeView` using the Web.sitemap file, it's more difficult if you are also using programmatic redirects or transfers, as you also need to update the server-side code to reflect the new site structure. To create a solid page structure, you can draw it out on paper before you start with the site, or use site map diagramming tools like Microsoft Visio.
- Try to limit the number of main and subitems that you display in your `Menu` or `TreeView` controls. Users tend to get lost or confused when they are presented with long lists of options to choose from.
- When creating folders to store your pages in, give them short and logical names. It's much more intuitive to navigate to a page using `http://www.PlanetWrox.com/Reviews` than it is to navigate to a folder with a long name including abbreviations and numbers.
- The CSS Control Adapters really offer a better alternative than the default controls such as the `TreeView` and the `Menu` in terms of the HTML they emit to the browser. Downloading, installing, and configuring the adapters is not very difficult, and the ASP.NET web site comes with many good examples and tutorials. They may not be suitable to start with right away, though. You probably want to get familiar with the standard behavior of the navigation controls before you make the jump to the CSS-enabled controls. Spend some time looking at the navigation controls and see how they behave. Try out different properties and styles and see how that affects the control in the browser. When you have a firm understanding of these controls, you find it easier to make the switch to the Control Adapters.

Summary

This chapter familiarized you with navigation in an ASP.NET web site. Users don't just type in the address of a web page directly, so it's important to offer them a clear and straightforward navigation system.

A critical foundation for a good navigation system is a good understanding of how URLs work. URLs come as two types: relative URLs and absolute URLs. Relative URLs have two subtypes: document relative and root relative. Document relative URLs point to another resource on the server relative to the document in which the URL is contained. This makes it easy to refer to other resources in the same folder without specifying a full path to it. This enables you to move a folder at the same level in the site without breaking links to other resources. The downside of relative URLs is that it's difficult to move folders to a different level, for example from the root to a subfolder. To overcome this problem, you can use root-based URLs that specify a path to a resource starting at the root of the site. Using ASP.NET's tilde (~) syntax to refer to the application root of the site makes this even easier.

Absolute URLs enable you to point to resources by their complete location, including protocol and domain information. Absolute URLs are mostly useful if you want to point to resources outside your own web site.

ASP.NET offers three navigation controls used in the user interface of a web site. These controls allow your users to visit the different pages in your site. The `Menu` control displays either as a vertical or a horizontal menu with submenus folding or dropping out. The `TreeView` control can show the complete structure of the site in a hierarchical way. And the `SiteMapPath` control displays a breadcrumb trail to give the user a visual cue as to where they are in the site.

All these controls can use the Web.sitemap file, an XML file that contains the logical structure of your web site. By using the site map as the source for your navigation controls, it's easy to move a menu item to a different location without affecting the physical location of the file. All you need to do is move the item in the Web.sitemap file to a different `siteMapNode` and you're done.

The chapter ended with a look at ways to programmatically send the user to a different page. ASP.NET supports two major ways to do this: `Response.Redirect` and `Server.Transfer`. The first option instructs the browser to fetch a new page from the server. This affects the address bar of the browser so the user can see where they are being redirected.

`Server.Transfer`, on the other hand, takes place at the server. As an advantage, this method doesn't change the client's address bar. As an additional advantage compared to `Response.Redirect`, `Server.Transfer` minimizes the network overhead of requesting a new page.

In Chapter 8 you will learn more about ASP.NET user controls, which enable you to reuse specific code and user interface elements in different pages in your web site.

Exercises

1. The `Menu` control exposes a number of style properties that allow you to change items in the menu. Which properties do you need to change if you want to influence the way the main and the submenu items are shown on screen?
2. What options do you have to redirect a user to another page programmatically? What's the difference between the two?
3. The `TreeView` controls can be used in two different ways: either as a list with items and subitems that can be collapsed and expanded by clicking them, or as a static list showing all the items with no way to collapse or expand. What property do you need to set on the control to prevent users from expanding or collapsing items in the tree?

User Controls

Besides the master pages, themes, and skins discussed in Chapter 6, ASP.NET 3.5 ships with another feature that allows you to create reusable and thus consistent blocks of information: *user controls*.

User controls allow you to group logically related content and controls together which can then be used as a single unit in content pages, master pages, and inside other user controls. A user control is actually a sort of mini ASPX page in that it has a markup section and optionally a Code Behind file in which you can write code for the control. Working with a user control is very similar to working with normal ASPX pages with a few minor differences.

In versions of ASP.NET before 2.0, user controls were used often to create blocks of reusable functionality that had to appear on every page in the site. For example, to create a menu, you would create a user control and then add that control to each and every page in the site. Due to the ASP.NET support for master pages, you don't need user controls for these scenarios anymore. This makes it easier to make changes to your site's structure. Despite the advantages that master pages bring, there is still room for user controls in your ASP.NET web sites as you'll discover in this chapter.

This chapter covers the following topics:

- What are user controls and how do they look?
- How do you create user controls?
- How do you consume user controls in your pages?
- How can you improve the usefulness of user controls by adding coding logic to them?

By the end of this chapter, you'll have a firm understanding of what user controls are and how they work, enabling you to create functional, reusable blocks of content.

Introduction to User Controls

User controls are great for encapsulating markup, controls, and code that you need repeatedly throughout your site. While master pages allow you to create content that is displayed in all pages in your site, it's common to have content that should only appear on some but not all pages. For example, you may want to display a banner on a few popular pages, but not on the home page or other common pages. Without user controls, you would add the code for the banner (an image, a link, and so on) to each page that needs it. When you want to update the banner (if you want to use a new image), you need to make changes to all pages that use it. If you move the banner to a user control and use that control in your content pages instead, all you need to change is the user control, and the pages that use it pick up the change automatically. This gives you a flexible way to create reusable content.

User controls have the following similarities with normal ASPX pages:

- They have a markup section where you can enter standard markup and server controls.
- They can be created and designed with Visual Web Developer in Markup and Design View.
- They can contain programming logic, either inline or with a Code Behind file.
- You have access to page-based information like `Request.QueryString`.
- They raise some (but not all) of the events that the `Page` class raises, including `Init`, `Load`, and `PreRender`.

You should also be aware of a few differences. User controls have an .ascx extension instead of the regular .aspx extension. In addition, user controls cannot be requested in the browser directly. Therefore, you can't link to them. The only way to use a user control in your site is by adding it to a page.

In the remainder of this chapter, you see how to create a user control that is capable of displaying banners. The user control is able to present itself as a horizontal or vertical banner to accommodate for differently sized regions in your pages. The next section shows you how to create a user control. The sections that follow show you how to use the control in an ASPX page.

Creating User Controls

User controls are added to the site like any other content type: through the Add New Item dialog box. Similar to pages, you get the option to choose the programming language and whether you want to place the code in a separate Code Behind file. Figure 8-1 shows the Add New Item dialog box for a user control.

Once you add a user control to the site, it is opened in the Document Window automatically. The first thing you may notice is that a user control doesn't have an `@ Page` directive, but an `@ Control` directive:

```
<%@ Control Language="C#" AutoEventWireup="true" CodeFile="Banner.ascx.cs"
      Inherits="Controls_Banner" %>
```

This marks the file as a user control, so the ASP.NET runtime knows how to deal with it. Other than that, the directive is identical to a standard ASPX page that doesn't use a master page.

With the user control open in the VWD Document Window, you can use all the tools you have used in the previous seven chapters to create pages. You can use the Toolbox to drag controls in Markup and Design View, the CSS windows to change the look and feel of the user control, and the Properties Grid to change the properties of controls in your pages. You can also write code that reacts to the events that the control raises.

To try this out yourself, the next exercise shows you how to create your first user control. In a later exercise you will see how to use the control in ASPX pages in your site.

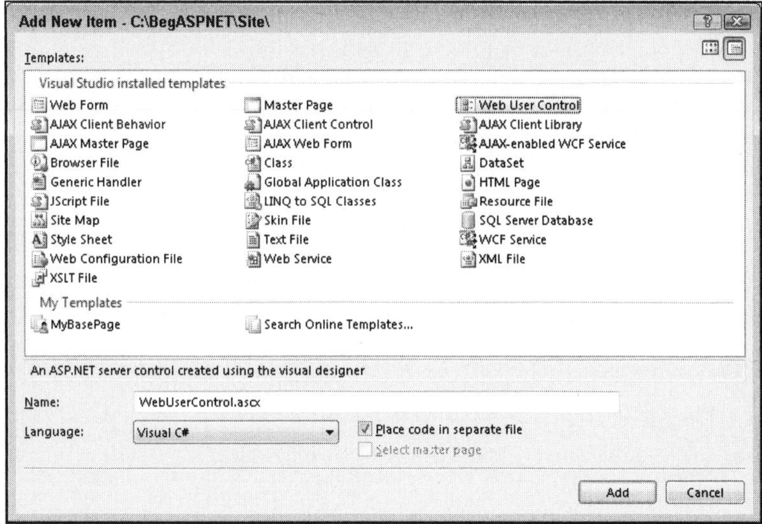

Figure 8-1

Try It Out — Creating a User Control

In this exercise, you create a basic user control that displays a single vertical banner using an `<asp:Image>` control. In later exercises in this chapter, you'll see how to use this control and how to add another (horizontal) image. You will then add some intelligence to the control so you can determine which of the two images to display at runtime.

For this exercise, you need two images that represent banners — one in portrait mode with dimensions of roughly 120 × 240 pixels and one in landscape mode with a size of around 486 × 60 pixels. The download that comes with this book has these two images, but you could also create your own. Don't worry about the exact size of the images; as long as they are close to these dimensions you should be fine.

1. Open the Planet Wrox site in VWD.
2. If you haven't done so already, create a new folder called Controls in the root of the site. While controls can be placed anywhere in the site hierarchy, placing them in a separate folder makes them easier to find and manage.
3. Repeat the previous step, but now create a folder called Images at the root of the site.
4. Using Windows Explorer, open up the Resources folder for this chapter (at `C:\BegASPNET\Resources\Chapter 08` if you followed the instructions in the Introduction of this book). If you haven't done so already, you can download it from `www.wrox.com`. Then drag the files Banner120x240.gif and Banner486x60.gif from the Explorer window into the Images folder you created in the previous step. If you're using your own images, drag them into the Images folder as well and give them the same names.
5. Right-click the Controls folder and choose Add New Item. In the dialog box that follows, click Web User Control as shown in Figure 8-1. Choose your programming language and make sure that Place Code In Separate File is selected. Name the file Banner.ascx and then click Add to add the control to the site. The control should open in Markup View in the Document Window. Your Solution Explorer should now look like Figure 8-2.

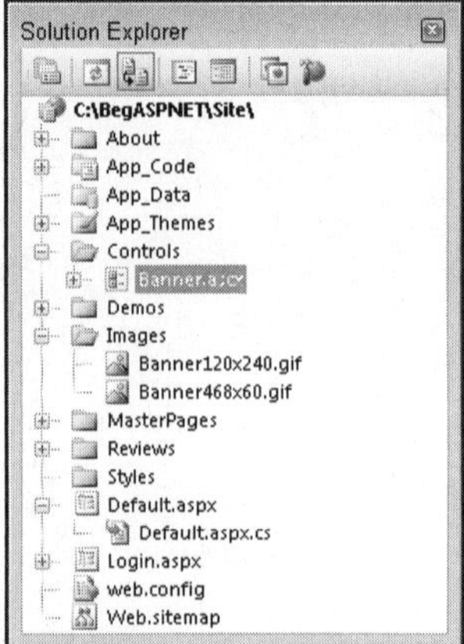

Figure 8-2

6. Switch the user control to Design View and then drag a `Panel` from the Standard category of the Toolbox onto the design surface. Using the Properties Grid, change the `ID` of the `Panel` to `pnlVertical`. You may briefly see a Refactoring dialog box that checks if there are any references to the old `ID` (`Panel1`) in your code and then updates them to `pnlVertical`. Since you just added the `Panel`, there's no code to update so you can ignore the dialog box.
7. From the Toolbox, drag an `Image` control into the `Panel`. Select the `Image` by clicking it once and then open the Properties Grid. Locate the `ImageUrl` property and click the ellipses button, shown in Figure 8-3.

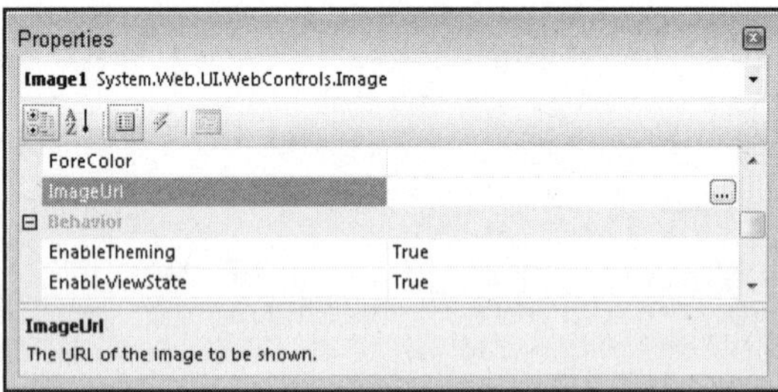

Figure 8-3

Browse to the Images folder, select the Banner120x240.gif image, and click OK to add it to the user control. Your Design View now looks like Figure 8-4.

8. Using the same Properties Grid, locate the `AlternateText` property and type **This is a sample banner**. Some browsers, like Firefox, display the alternate text only when the image cannot be displayed correctly. Other browsers like Internet Explorer show the alternate text as the tooltip for the image when you hover your mouse over it.
9. Switch to Markup View and if your `Panel` control has `Height` and `Width` attributes which were added by default when you dragged it on the page, remove both of them.

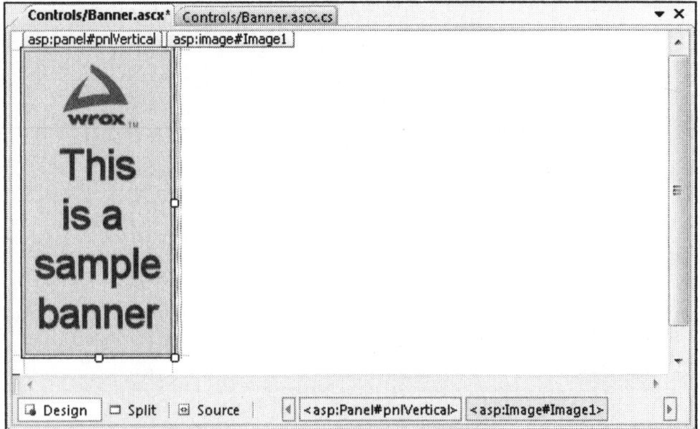

Figure 8-4

10. Wrap the `Image` in a standard `<a>` element and set its `src` attribute to `http://p2p.wrox.com`. Set the `target` of the anchor element to `_blank` to force the browser to open up the page in a new window when the image is clicked. When you're done, the code for the entire user control should look like the following code, except for the `Language` attribute you may have set to `VB` and the `AutoEventWireup` that is `False` by default in VB.NET:

```
<%@ Control Language="C#" AutoEventWireup="true" CodeFile="Banner.ascx.cs"
      Inherits="Controls_Banner" %>
<asp:Panel ID="pnlVertical" runat="server">
  <a href="http://p2p.wrox.com" target="_blank">
    <asp:Image ID="Image1" runat="server" AlternateText="This is a sample banner"
          ImageUrl="~/Images/Banner120x240.gif" />
  </a>
</asp:Panel>
```

11. Save the changes by pressing Ctrl+S and then close the user control file by pressing Ctrl+F4.

How It Works

The design experience of user controls in the Visual Web Developer IDE is identical to that of pages. You can use drag and drop, the Toolbox, the Markup and Design Views, and so on. This makes it easy to work with user controls because you can use all the familiar tools you also use for page development.

The control you just created displays a single image wrapped in an anchor element. In the next section you will see how to add the banner to the master page so it will be displayed in the sidebar `<div>` of every page in the site. Later sections in this chapter show you how to add the other image that can be used to display a horizontal banner in individual content pages.

Adding User Controls to a Content Page or Master Page

To be able to use a user control in a content or master page or in another user control, you need to perform two steps. First, you need to *register* the control by adding an `@ Register` directive to the page or control where you want the user control to appear. The second step involves adding the tags for the user control to the page and optionally setting some attributes on it.

A typical `@ Register` directive for a user control looks like this:

```
<%@ Register src="../Controls/Banner.ascx" tagname="Banner" tagprefix="uc1" %>
```

The directive contains three important attributes, described in the following table.

Attribute	Description
`src`	Points to the user control you want to use. To make it easier to move pages at a later stage, you can also use the tilde (~) syntax to point to the control from the application root.
`tagname`	The name for the tag that is used in the control declaration in the page. You're free to make up this name, but usually it is the same as the name of the control.
`tagprefix`	Holds the prefix of the `tagname` that is used in the control declaration. Just as ASP.NET uses the `asp` prefix to refer to its controls, you need to provide a prefix for your own user controls. By default, this prefix is `uc` followed by a sequential number, but you can also change it to your own liking — for example, to your own company name or a custom abbreviation.

When the control is registered, you can add it to the page using the `tagprefix:tagname` construct, similar to the way you add standard server controls to a page. Given the `@ Register` directive for the user control Banner.ascx you need the following markup to add the control to your page:

```
<uc1:Banner ID="Banner1" runat="server" />
```

This is the minimum code needed for a user control in a page. Note that the control is defined by a combination of the `tagprefix` and the `tagname`. The other two attributes — `ID` and `runat` — are standard attributes that most controls in an ASP.NET page have.

Fortunately, in most cases, you don't have to type all this code yourself. When you drag a user control from the Solution Explorer into a page in Design View, VWD adds the required code for you automatically. The following exercise demonstrates how this works.

Try It Out — Adding the User Control to Your Page

In this exercise you add the user control Banner.ascx to the master page, so it displays a banner on each page in the site in the sidebar area.

1. Open up MasterPage.master from the MasterPages folder and switch it into Design View.
2. Locate the drop-down list that allows you to select a theme, position your cursor right after the drop-down list, and press Enter three times to create some room.
3. From the Solution Explorer, drag the file Banner.ascx into the empty spot you just created. Design View is updated and now looks like Figure 8-5.

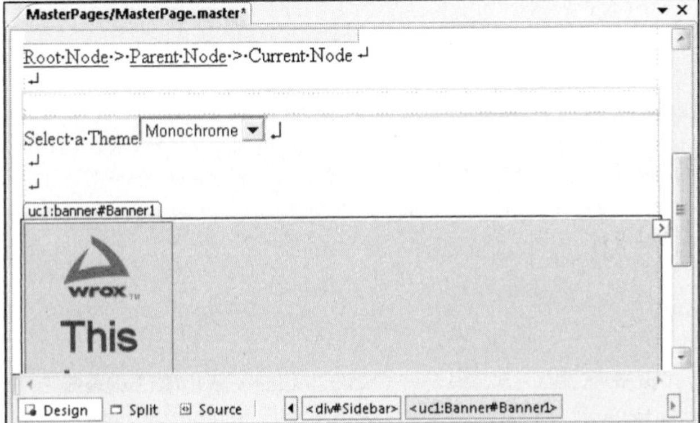

Figure 8-5

If your Design View doesn't look like this, but looks much closer to how the file ends up in the browser, you may still have the `styleSheetTheme` set in the web.config file. Alternatively, you may have more or fewer options selected in the View ➪ Visual Aids or View ➪ Formatting Marks menu.

4. Switch to Markup View and locate the `@ Register` directive at the top of the file. Change the two dots in the `src` attribute to a tilde (~):

```
<%@ Register src="~/Controls/Banner.ascx" tagname="Banner" tagprefix="uc1" %>
```

5. Save the changes to the master page, close it and then right-click the file Default.aspx in the root of your site and choose View in Browser.

6. The banner is now displayed below the drop-down list. Switch to the other theme and you'll see the same banner appear. When you click the banner, a new window is opened which takes you to the site you linked to in the previous exercise.

How It Works

When you dragged the user control onto the design surface of the master page, VWD performed two tasks: first it added the `@ Register` directive to tell the page where to look for the user control. It then added the control declaration right below the drop-down list.

When the page loads, the ASP.NET runtime sees the control declaration and injects the output of the control at the specified location. In this example, the `Panel`, the `<a>` element, and the `Image` are inserted in the sidebar region of the page. If you look at the HTML for the page in the browser, you see the following code:

```
</select>
<br /><br /><br />
<div id="ctl00_Banner1_pnlVertical">
  <a href="http://p2p.wrox.com" target="_blank">
    <img id="ctl00_Banner1_Image1" src="Images/Banner120x240.gif"
           alt="This is a sample banner" style="border-width:0px;" />
  </a>
</div>
```

The `<asp:Panel>` has been transformed into an HTML `<div>` element and the `<asp:Image>` into an `<img>` element. Since the anchor element was defined with plain HTML in the user control, it ends up exactly as you wrote it.

Notice how the `id` of the panel has been changed from `pnlVertical` to the client ID `ctl00_Banner1_pnlVertical`. This is necessary to give the `<div>` tag a unique client-side `id` attribute that is used in client-side scripting. The same has happened to the `id` of the `<img>` element. You'll see more about this in a later section of this chapter.

Normally when you put an `<img>` element inside an `<a>` element to link it, the browser draws a border around the image. The border is usually blue for unvisited links and purple for links you have visited before. With an `<asp:Image>` this isn't necessary as by default the image is rendered with an inline style that sets the border to `0` pixels. If you wanted to remove the border from linked images created with the `<img>` tag in other pages, you can use the following CSS:

```
img
{
  border: none;
}
```

This clears the border for all linked images in your site. When you add a user control to a page, VWD by default refers to the control using a relative path. In the previous exercise, this path first contained two dots (`..`) to indicate the parent folder, followed by the Controls folder, and finally by the name of the control:

```
<%@ Register src="../Controls/Banner.ascx" tagname="Banner" tagprefix="uc1" %>
```

By changing the two dots to the tilde symbol, it becomes easier to move your pages around in your site as the `src` attribute now always points to the Controls folder at the application's root, no matter where the page that consumes the control is located.

While the tilde syntax makes your pages with user controls a little easier to manage, there is an even easier way to register your user controls site-wide.

Site-Wide Registration of User Controls

If you have a control that you expect to use quite often on separate content pages in your site, like the banner in the previous examples, you can register the control globally in the web.config file. This way it becomes available throughout the entire site, without the need to register it on every page. The following exercise shows how to do this.

Try It Out — Registering User Controls in the web.config File

In this exercise you'll register the Banner.ascx user control in the web.config file. You can then remove the `@ Register` directive from the master page as it isn't needed anymore. After you have changed the web.config file, adding the same user control to other pages will no longer add the `@ Register` directive to the page.

1. Open the web.config file from the root of the site.

2. Scroll down a bit and locate the `<pages>` element that you used in Chapter 6 to apply the theme.
3. Add the following highlighted code as a child to the `<controls>` element that you find under `<pages>`:

```
<pages theme="Monochrome">
  ...
  <controls>
    <add tagPrefix="Wrox" tagName="Banner" src="~/Controls/Banner.ascx" />
```

4. Save the changes and close the file.
5. Open the master page again in Markup View and locate the `Banner` control in the sidebar area. Change `uc1` to `Wrox`:

```
<Wrox:Banner ID="Banner1" runat="server" />
```

   If the declaration for your user control has its own closing tag, be sure to update that as well:

```
<Wrox:Banner ID="Banner1" runat="server"></Wrox:Banner>
```

6. Scroll all the way up in the master page file and remove the entire line with the `@ Register` directive.
7. Save and close the master page.
8. Open Default.aspx again in your browser. Note that the banner is still present in the sidebar area. If you get an error, verify you added the correct code to the web.config file. Also make sure that you changed `uc1` to `Wrox` in the control declaration in the master page.

How It Works

Without the `@ Register` directive in the master page, the ASP.NET runtime scans the web.config file for controls that have been registered there. It then finds the registration of the `Wrox:Banner` control so it is able to successfully find the file using the `src` attribute and add its output to the page hierarchy.

When you add the control registration to the web.config file, it's much easier to move or rename the control. Instead of finding and replacing the `@ Register` directive in all pages that use it, the only thing you need to change is the registration in the web.config file. When you make a change there, all pages using the control will automatically find the new location or name of the user control.

User Control Caveats

Earlier you saw that the client `ID` of the `Panel` control you added to the page was modified by the ASP.NET runtime. Instead of getting a `<div>` element with its `id` set to `pnlVertical`, you got the following `id`:

```
<div id="ctl00_Banner1_pnlVertical">
  ...
</div>
```

In many cases, this isn't problematic as you often don't need the client `id`. However, if you need to access this control from client-side JavaScript or CSS, it's important to understand why this `id` is modified.

By design, all elements in an HTML page need to be unique. Giving them an id is not required, but if you do so, you have to make sure they are unique. To avoid conflicts in the final HTML code of the page, ASP.NET ensures that each client element gets a unique id by prefixing them with the name of their *naming container*. Within a naming container all elements should have unique IDs. The Visual Web Developer IDE warns you when you try to add a control that doesn't have a unique ID. For example, you get an error when you try to add a second panel with an ID of pnlVertical to the user control. But what if you place two Banner controls in the same page? Potentially, you could end up with two client <div> elements with an ID of pnlVertical. To avoid this problem, ASP.NET prefixes each element with the ID of its nearest naming container. For the Panel inside the user control it means it's prefixed with Banner1, the server-side ID of the user control in the master page. It then prefixes that new ID with the ID of the master page: ctl00. This ID is auto-generated by the ASP.NET runtime but you could override it by setting the ID explicitly in the Page_Load event of the master page:

VB.NET

```
Protected Sub Page_Load(ByVal sender As Object, ByVal e As System.EventArgs) _
          Handles Me.Load
  Me.ID = "Master"
```

C#

```
protected void Page_Load(object sender, EventArgs e)
{
  this.ID = "Master";
```

You can use the ClientID of a control to get its full client-side id. The following snippet shows how to display the ClientID of the Panel control on a Label control within the Banner.ascx user control:

VB.NET

```
  Label1.Text = pnlVertical.ClientID
```

C#

```
  Label1.Text = pnlVertical.ClientID;
```

With this code, the Label control's Text property will contain ctl00_Banner1_pnlVertical, the client-side id of the Panel if you didn't set the master ID explicitly. With an explicit ID as per the previous example, the Label displays: Master_Banner1_pnlVertical.

With an explicit ID, it's easier to predict the final id of a client-side HTML element, which in turn makes it easier to reference those elements in JavaScript or CSS. In later chapters you see how to make use of this.

> **Since the ASP.NET runtime can change the client id attributes of your HTML elements, you may have troubles using CSS ID selectors to refer to elements. The easiest way to fix this is to use class selectors instead of ID selectors. Alternatively, you can use the control's ClientID.**

Although the current user control makes it easy to display a banner at various locations in your site, it isn't very smart yet. All it can do is display a linked image and that's it. To improve its usability, you can add behavior to the control so it can behave differently on pages in your site.

Adding Logic to Your User Controls

Although using controls for repeating content is already quite useful, they become even more useful when you add custom logic to them. By adding public properties or methods to a user control, you can influence its behavior at runtime. When you add a property to a user control, it becomes available automatically in IntelliSense and in the Properties Grid for the control in the page you're working with, making it easy to change the behavior from an external file like a page.

To add properties or methods to a user control, you add them to the Code Behind of the control. The properties you add can take various forms. In its simplest form, a property looks exactly like the properties you saw in Chapter 5. For more advanced scenarios you need to add *ViewState properties* that are able to maintain their state across postbacks. In the next two exercises you see how to create both types of properties.

Creating Your Own Data Types for Properties

To make the banner control more useful, you can add a second image to it that displays as a horizontal banner. By adding a property to the user control you can then determine whether to display the vertical or horizontal image. You could do this by creating a numeric property of type `System.Byte`. Then `0` would be vertical and `1` would be horizontal for example. However, this makes it hard to remember what each number represents. You can make it a bit easier by creating a `String` property that accepts the values `Horizontal` and `Vertical`. However, strings cannot be checked at development time, so you may end up with a spelling mistake, resulting in an error or in the incorrect banner being displayed. Instead, you can create your own data type in the form of an *enumeration*. With an enumeration, or enum for short, you assign numbers to human friendly text strings. Developers then use this readable text, while under the hood the numeric value is used. The following snippet shows a basic example of an enum:

VB.NET

```
Public Enum Direction
  Horizontal
  Vertical
End Enum
```

C#

```
public enum Direction
{
  Horizontal,
  Vertical
}
```

With these enums, the compiler assigns numeric values to the `Horizontal` and `Vertical` members automatically, starting with `0` and counting upward. You can also explicitly define your numeric values if you want:

VB.NET

```
Public Enum Direction
  Horizontal = 0
  Vertical = 1
End Enum
```

C#

```
public enum Direction
{
  Horizontal = 0,
  Vertical = 1
}
```

The cool thing about enums is that you will get IntelliSense in code files, in the Properties Grid and even in the code editor for your user controls. Figure 8-6 shows how IntelliSense kicks in for VB.NET code file.

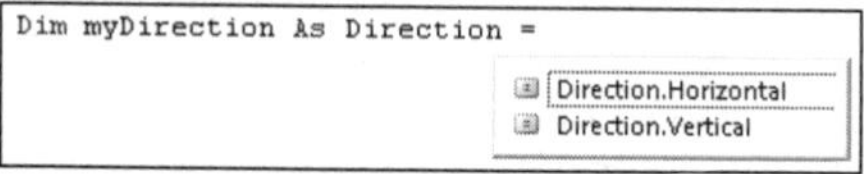

Figure 8-6

In Figure 8-7 you see the same list with values from the enum in the Properties Grid.

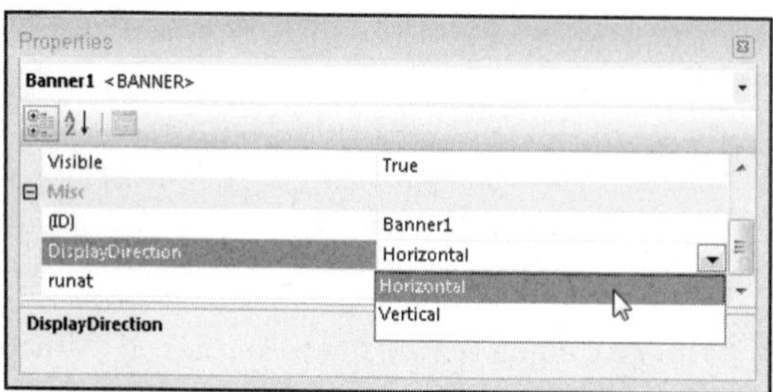

Figure 8-7

And in Figure 8-8 you see the same list appear for a property of a user control in Markup View.

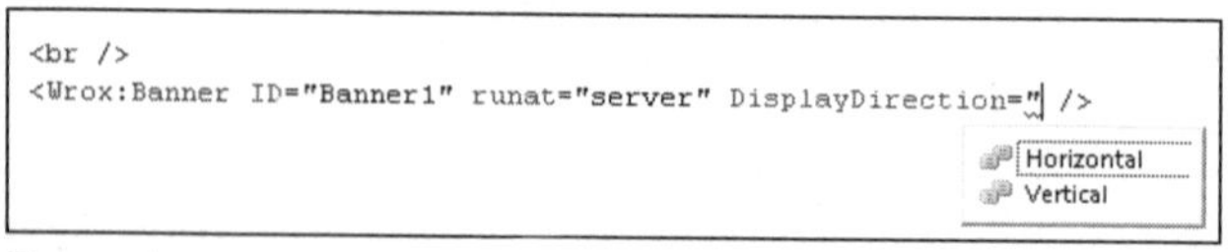

```
<br />
<Wrox:Banner ID="Banner1" runat="server" DisplayDirection="" />
                                                   Horizontal
                                                   Vertical
```

Figure 8-8

Just as with other code files like classes, you should put your enums in a file under the App_Code folder. If you have more than one of them you can store them all in the same file or create a separate file for each enum.

Enums are great for simple and short lists. They help you find the right item quickly without memorizing "magic numbers" like 0 or 1 but allow you to use human readable text strings instead.

In the next exercise, you see how to create an enum and use it in your `Banner` user control.

Try It Out — Creating Smarter User Controls

In this exercise, you add a second banner to the user control. This banner displays as a horizontal image inside its own panel. To avoid the two banners from showing up at the same time you will add a property that determines which banner to display. Pages that use the control can then define the correct banner.

1. Start by creating an enumeration that contains two members for the different directions: vertical and horizontal. To do this, right-click the App_Code folder and choose Add New Item. Add a class file called Direction and choose your programming language.
2. Once the file opens, clear its contents and add the following code to it:

VB.NET

```
Public Enum Direction
  Horizontal
  Vertical
End Enum
```

C#

```
public enum Direction
{
  Horizontal,
  Vertical
}
```

3. Save and close the file.
4. Open the Code Behind for the user control Banner.ascx and add the following property. To help you create this property, VWD comes with a handy code snippet. To activate the snippet in VB.NET, type `Property` (with no trailing space) and then press Tab. In C#, type `prop` and then press Tab twice. In both cases, VWD adds the code structure for a property for you; a normal property for VB.NET and an automatic property for C#. You can press Tab again to move from field to field, each time typing the right data type, variable, or property name. Complete the code so it looks like this:

VB.NET

```
Private _displayDirection As Direction = Direction.Vertical

Public Property DisplayDirection() As Direction
  Get
    Return _displayDirection
  End Get
  Set(ByVal value As Direction)
```

```
      _displayDirection = value
    End Set
  End Property
```

C#

```
public Direction DisplayDirection {get; set;}
```

Make sure you add the property outside the `Page_Load` method (when you're working with C#) but before the closing `End Class` (in VB.NET) or the curly brace for the class (in C#).

Note that the name of the property is `DisplayDirection` and its type is `Direction`. Also note that the C# example uses an automatic property, as you saw first in Chapter 5.

5. Open the Markup View of Banner.ascx, copy the entire `<asp:Panel>`, and paste it right below the existing `Panel`. Name the `Panel` `pnlHorizontal` and set the `src` of the image to `~/Images/Banner468x60.gif`. Your code should now look like this:

```
</asp:Panel>
<asp:Panel ID="pnlHorizontal" runat="server">
  <a href="http://p2p.wrox.com" target="_blank">
    <asp:Image ID="Image2" runat="server" AlternateText="This is a sample banner"
            ImageUrl="~/Images/Banner468x60.gif" />
  </a>
</asp:Panel>
```

6. Switch back to the Code Behind of the control and add the following code to the `Page_Load` handler. In C# the handler should already be there. In Visual Basic, you can choose (Page Events) from the left drop-down list at the top of the Document Window and Load from the right drop-down list to set up the handler or you can double-click the user control in Design View.

VB.NET

```
Protected Sub Page_Load(ByVal sender As Object, ByVal e As System.EventArgs) _
     Handles Me.Load
  pnlHorizontal.Visible = False
  pnlVertical.Visible = False

  Select Case DisplayDirection
    Case Direction.Horizontal
      pnlHorizontal.Visible = True
    Case Direction.Vertical
      pnlVertical.Visible = True
  End Select
End Sub
```

C#

```
protected void Page_Load(object sender, EventArgs e)
{
  pnlHorizontal.Visible = false;
  pnlVertical.Visible = false;

  switch (DisplayDirection)
  {
```

```
      case Direction.Horizontal:
        pnlHorizontal.Visible = true;
        break;
      case Direction.Vertical:
        pnlVertical.Visible = true;
        break;
    }
  }
```

7. Save and close the two files that make up the user control as you're done with them for now.

8. Open up the master page file once more in Markup View and locate the user control declaration. Right after the `runat="server"` attribute add the following `DisplayDirection` attribute that sets the correct image type:

```
<Wrox:Banner ID="Banner1" runat="server" DisplayDirection="Horizontal"  />
```

   IntelliSense will help you pick the right `DisplayDirection` from the list. If you don't get IntelliSense, wait a few seconds until VWD has caught up with all the changes. Alternatively, close all files and then open the master page again.

9. Save all changes and request the page Default.aspx in the browser. Note that the right sidebar area now contains the horizontal image, breaking the layout a little because the image is too wide for the sidebar area.

10. Switch back to the master page and change the `DisplayDirection` from `Horizontal` to `Vertical`. Save your changes and refresh the page in the browser. The sidebar should now display the vertical banner, as shown in Figure 8-9.

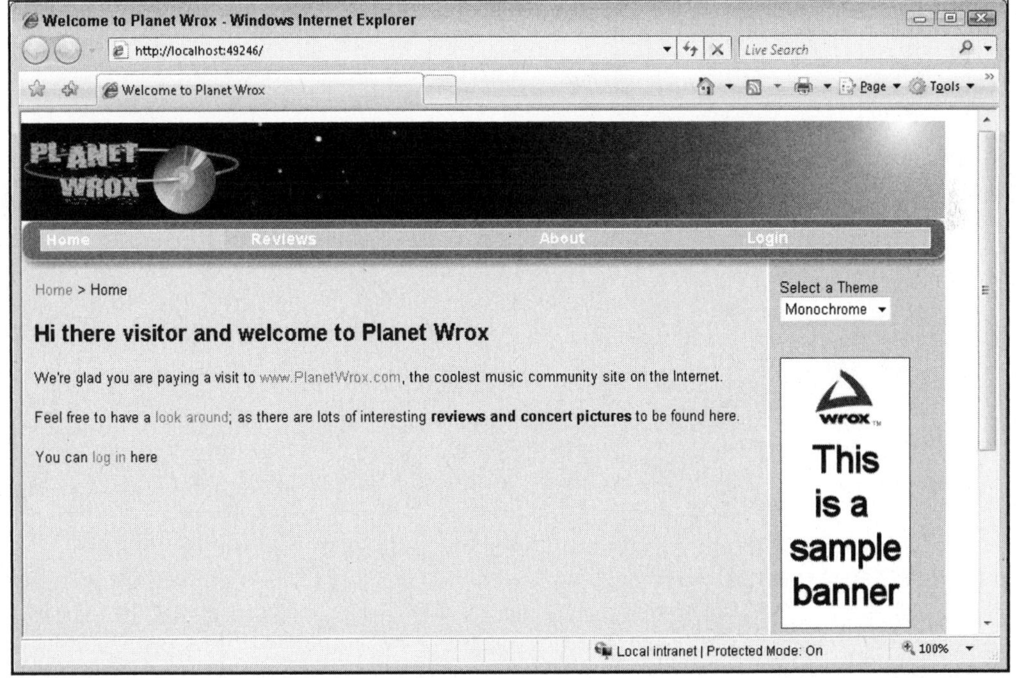

Figure 8-9

11. Open the page AboutUs.aspx from the About folder in Visual Web Developer in Markup View. If you don't have that file, create it first. In the `cpMainContent ContentPlaceHolder` add some text describing you or your organization and the reason you created the site. Switch to Design View and drop the Banner.ascx control from the Solution Explorer onto the design surface, right below the text you just added.

12. Select the control in Design View, open its Properties Grid and set the `DisplayDirection` to `Horizontal`.

13. Save all your changes and then press Ctrl+F5 to open the About Us page in your browser. Besides the banner in the right sidebar, you should now also see the horizontal banner appear in the Content area.

How It Works

The property called `DisplayDirection` gives your user control some extra behavior. Pages using the control should now set the `DisplayDirection` like this:

```
<Wrox:Banner ID="Banner1" runat="server" DisplayDirection="Horizontal" />
```

When the control instance is created by the ASP.NET runtime, the value you set in the control declaration is assigned to the property, which in turn stores it in the private field `_displayDirection` in VB.NET, or in the automatically generated backing variable in C#. Refer to Chapter 5 for more information on automatic properties.

When the page loads, the following code is executed:

VB.NET

```
pnlHorizontal.Visible = False
pnlVertical.Visible = False

Select Case DisplayDirection
  Case Direction.Horizontal
    pnlHorizontal.Visible = True
  Case Direction.Vertical
    pnlVertical.Visible = True
End Select
```

C#

```
pnlHorizontal.Visible = false;
pnlVertical.Visible = false;

switch (DisplayDirection)
{
  case Direction.Horizontal:
    pnlHorizontal.Visible = true;
    break;
  case Direction.Vertical:
    pnlVertical.Visible = true;
    break;
}
```

The first thing that this code does is hide both panels that contain the images. It then uses a `Select Case` / `switch` block to determine what image to show. When the `DisplayDirection` equals `Horizontal`, the `Visible` property of `pnlHorizontal` is set to `True`. The same principle is applied to the `Vertical` setting.

Implementing ViewState Properties

Besides the `DisplayDirection`, another useful property for the user control would be the URL that the banner links to. In the next section you will see how to implement this and learn how to create a `ViewState` property called `NavigateUrl` that is able to survive postbacks.

Try It Out — Implementing the NavigateUrl Property

To be able to set the URL that a user is taken to from code, you need to be able to access the anchor tag that is defined in the control's markup. To do this, you need to give it an `ID` and a `runat="server"` attribute. Alternatively, you could change the simple `<a>` tag to its server-side counterpart: the `<asp:HyperLink>`. To be able to set the new `NavigateUrl` property programmatically and to ensure it survives postbacks, you'll implement a `ViewState` property. To show you why you need a `ViewState` property, the first three steps of this exercise have you modify the About Us page so it sets the `DisplayDirection` of the `Banner` control programmatically. You'll then cause a postback to appear so you can see that the value for the direction gets lost because it doesn't maintain its state in `ViewState`. The second part of the exercise then shows you how to implement the `NavigateUrl` property that is able to maintain its state.

1. Open the Code Behind of AboutUs.aspx and add the following code to the `Page_Load` event. If the handler isn't there yet, switch to Design View and double-click somewhere on the grey area of the page.

VB.NET

```
Protected Sub Page_Load(ByVal sender As Object, ByVal e As System.EventArgs) _
       Handles Me.Load
  If Not Page.IsPostBack Then
    Banner1.DisplayDirection = Direction.Vertical
  End If
End Sub
```

C#

```
protected void Page_Load(object sender, EventArgs e)
{
  if (!Page.IsPostBack)
  {
    Banner1.DisplayDirection = Direction.Vertical;
  }
}
```

Verify that the Banner user control has an `ID` of `Banner1` in the Markup View of the page, or update your code accordingly.

2. Switch to Design View and add a `Button` control by dragging it from the Standard category of the Toolbox on top of the Banner.ascx control. It should end up above or below the banner. There's no need to write any code for the `Button` control's `Click` event.

3. Save the page and open it in your browser. Because of the code in `Page_Load`, the first time the page loads, the banner at the bottom of the screen displays the vertical banner. Now click the button so the page will reload. This time, the page displays the horizontal image. Because the `DisplayDirection` of the `Banner` control is only set in `Page_Load` when `Page.IsPostBack` is `False`, that setting is lost when you post back, causing the banner to revert to its default setting of `Horizontal`.

4. To avoid this problem with the `NavigateUrl`, you need to implement it as a `ViewState` property. Instead of a simple backing variable used with the `DisplayDirection` property (the field `_displayDirection` in VB.NET and the automatically generated property in C#), you use the `ViewState` collection as the backing store. That way, the value is stored in `ViewState` and sent to the browser and back to the server with every request. To implement the property, add the following code to the Code Behind of the Banner.ascx user control, right below the `DisplayDirection` property:

Remember, you don't have to type all this code manually. You can use the Property / prop code snippets as shown earlier. Alternatively, the download that comes with this book contains the code shown in this chapter.

VB.NET

```
Public Property NavigateUrl() As String
  Get
    Dim _navigateUrl As Object = ViewState("NavigateUrl")
    If _navigateUrl IsNot Nothing Then
      Return CType(_navigateUrl, String)
    Else
      Return "http://p2p.wrox.com"
    End If
  End Get
  Set(ByVal Value As String)
    ViewState("NavigateUrl") = Value
  End Set
End Property
```

C#

```
public string NavigateUrl
{
  get
  {
    object _navigateUrl = ViewState["NavigateUrl"];
    if (_navigateUrl != null)
    {
      return (string)_navigateUrl;
    }
    else
    {
```

```
        return "http://p2p.wrox.com";
      }
    }
    set
    {
      ViewState["NavigateUrl"] = value;
    }
  }
```

5. Switch to Markup View of the user control and add a `runat="server"` attribute to both the links. Give the link in the vertical panel an `ID` of `lnkVertical` and the other an `ID` of `lnkHorizontal`. They should end up looking like this:

```
<a href="http://p2p.wrox.com" target="_blank" runat="server" id="lnkVertical">
...
<a href="http://p2p.wrox.com" target="_blank" runat="server" id="lnkHorizontal">
```

6. Switch back to the Code Behind of the user control and modify the `Page_Load` handler of the user control so it also sets the `HRef` property of the anchor element:

VB.NET

```
Case Direction.Horizontal
  pnlHorizontal.Visible = True
  lnkHorizontal.HRef = NavigateUrl
Case Direction.Vertical
  pnlVertical.Visible = True
  lnkVertical.HRef = NavigateUrl
```

C#

```
case Direction.Horizontal:
  pnlHorizontal.Visible = true;
  lnkHorizontal.HRef = NavigateUrl;
  break;
case Direction.Vertical:
  pnlVertical.Visible = true;
  lnkVertical.HRef = NavigateUrl;
  break;
```

7. Save the changes and go back to the Code Behind of AboutUs.aspx. Modify the code so it sets the `NavigateUrl` property of the `Banner` control to a different URL. You should overwrite the code that sets the `DisplayDirection`.

VB.NET

```
Protected Sub Page_Load(ByVal sender As Object, ByVal e As System.EventArgs) _
       Handles Me.Load
  If Not Page.IsPostBack Then
    Banner1.NavigateUrl = "http://imar.spaanjaars.com"
  End If
End Sub
```

C#

```
protected void Page_Load(object sender, EventArgs e)
{
  if (!Page.IsPostBack)
  {
    Banner1.NavigateUrl = "http://imar.spaanjaars.com";
  }
}
```

8. Save all your changes and then request the AboutUs.aspx page in your browser. Make sure you get a fresh browser window, so close any windows you may have open first. Click the horizontal banner at the left side of the page. A new window will pop up, showing the URL you set in the previous step.

9. Close this new window and click the button you added to AboutUs.aspx earlier to cause the page to post back to the server. Once the page is reloaded, click the banner image again. You are taken to the same site as in step 8. This illustrates the point that the `NavigateUrl` property is now able to maintain its value across postbacks, unlike the `DisplayDirection` property you added to the user control earlier.

How It Works

In the first three steps you witnessed the behavior of non-ViewState properties. You started off by writing some code in the `Page_Load` event handler that sets the `DisplayDirection` programmatically:

VB.NET

```
If Not Page.IsPostBack Then
  Banner1.DisplayDirection = Direction.Vertical
End If
```

C#

```
if (!Page.IsPostBack)
{
  Banner1.DisplayDirection = Direction.Vertical;
}
```

Because of the check for `Page.IsPostBack`, this code only fires when the page loads the first time. It doesn't fire when the page is reloaded due to a postback. When it fires, it sets the `DisplayDirection` property of the `Banner` control so the banner displays the correct image. However, as soon as the page is posted back, this value is lost and the control reverts to its default `DisplayDirection` of `Horizontal`. One way to overcome this problem is to make sure the code fires both the first time and on subsequent postbacks. Removing the check for `Page.IsPostBack` is enough to accomplish this. However, this is not always a desired solution. Imagine you're getting the correct display direction from a database. Since fetching data from a database is a costly operation, you want to minimize the number of times you hit the database. In such scenarios, developers are likely to fetch the data only when the page loads the first time, and expect it to stay around on subsequent postbacks. That is exactly what the `NavigateUrl` property does. You set its value once and it stays available, even if you post the page back to the server. This is accomplished with a `ViewState` property.

To see how this works, take a look at the setter of that property first:

VB.NET

```
Public Property NavigateUrl() As String
  ...
  Set(ByVal Value As String)
    ViewState("NavigateUrl") = Value
  End Set
End Property
```

C#

```
public string NavigateUrl
{
  ...
  set
  {
    ViewState["NavigateUrl"] = value;
  }
}
```

When you assign a value to the `NavigateUrl` property, its value is stored in the ViewState collection. You can see the ViewState collection as a large bag that allows you to store data that you can retrieve again after a postback. You identify values in ViewState using a unique key. In the example the key equals the name of the property so it's easy to see they belong together. Once you assign a value to a `ViewState` property, it's stored in the page in the hidden `__VIEWSTATE` field that you learned about in Chapter 4. This means it gets sent to the browser when the page loads and it is sent back to the server when the page is posted back again.

When the postback occurs, the code in `Page_Load` in the user control fires again. Just as with the initial request, the code accesses the `NavigateUrl` property in the `Select Case` / `switch` block:

VB.NET

```
Case Direction.Horizontal
  ...
  lnkHorizontal.HRef = NavigateUrl
  ...
```

C#

```
case Direction.Horizontal:
  ...
  lnkHorizontal.HRef = NavigateUrl;
  ...
```

The value for NavigateUrl is returned by the getter of the property:

VB.NET

```
Public Property NavigateUrl() As String
  Get
    Dim _navigateUrl As Object = ViewState("NavigateUrl")
    If _navigateUrl IsNot Nothing Then
      Return CType(_navigateUrl, String)
    Else
      Return "http://p2p.wrox.com"
    End If
  End Get
  ...
End Property
```

C#

```
public string NavigateUrl
{
  get
  {
    object _navigateUrl = ViewState["NavigateUrl"];
    if (_navigateUrl != null)
    {
      return (string)_navigateUrl;
    }
    else
    {
      return "http://p2p.wrox.com";
    }
  }
  ...
}
```

This code first tries to get the value from ViewState using `ViewState("NavigateUrl")` in VB.NET or `ViewState["NavigateUrl"]` in C#, which uses square brackets to access items in a collection. If the value that is returned is `Nothing` or `null`, the getter returns the default value for the property: `http://p2p.wrox.com`.

However, if the value is not `Nothing`, it is converted to a string using `CType` in VB.NET and `(string)` in C# and eventually returned to the calling code. At the end, the `NavigateUrl` returned from the `ViewState` property is assigned to the `HRef` property of the anchor tag again, which is then used to set the correct URL for the image in the browser.

ViewState Considerations

Although ViewState is designed to overcome the problems of maintaining state as outlined in the previous exercise, you should carefully consider whether you use it or not. The values you store in ViewState are sent to the browser and back to the server on *every* request. When you store many or large values in ViewState, this increases the size of the page and thus negatively impacts performance. Never store large objects like database records in ViewState; it's often quicker to get the data fresh from the database on each request than passing it along in the hidden ViewState field.

Practical Tips on User Controls

The following list provides some practical tips on working with user controls.

- Don't overuse user controls. User controls are great for encapsulating repeating content, but they also make it a little harder to manage your site because code and logic is contained in multiple files. If you're not sure if some content will be reused in another part of the site, start by embedding it directly in the page. You can always move it to a separate user control later if the need arises.
- Keep user controls focused on a single task. Don't create a user control that is able to display five different types of unrelated content with a property that determines what to display. This makes the control difficult to maintain and use. Instead, create five lightweight controls and use them appropriately.
- When you create user controls that contain styled markup, don't hardcode style information like the `CssClass` for the server controls contained in the user control. Instead, consider creating separate `CssClass` properties on the user control which are then used to set the `CssClass` of your server controls. This improves the reusability of your user control, making it easier to incorporate the control in different designs.

Summary

User controls can greatly improve the maintainability of your site. Instead of repeating the same markup and code on many different pages in your site, you encapsulate the code in a single control, which can then be used in different areas of your site.

To incorporate a user control in a web page, you need to register it first. You can do this on a page-by-page basis using an `@ Register` directive at the top of the page that defines the `tagname`, the `tagprefix`, and the source of the user control. Alternatively, controls that are going to be used a lot can be registered in the web.config file in the `<controls>` element.

To improve the usefulness of your controls, you can add behavior to them. It's common to create controls with properties you can set in consuming pages allowing you to change the behavior of the control at runtime. You saw how to create a property that uses a custom enumeration to determine the type of banner to display. You also learned how to create an advanced `ViewState` property that is able to maintain its state across postbacks. With these kinds of properties it becomes much easier to programmatically change the behavior of the control.

Although `ViewState` properties can solve some of the state issues you may come across, you should carefully consider whether you really need them or not. Since these properties add to the size of the page, they can have a negative impact on your site's performance.

You can improve the `Banner` control by keeping track of the number of times each image has been clicked. The sample site for this book doesn't implement this, but with the knowledge you gain in the chapters about database interaction, this is easy to implement yourself.

In Chapter 9 you will create another user control that serves as a contact form. By building the form as a user control, it's easy to ask your users for feedback from different locations in the site.

Exercises

1. In this chapter you saw how to create a standard property and a `ViewState` property. What is the main difference between the two? And what are the disadvantages of each of them?
2. Currently, the `DisplayDirection` property of the `Banner` control doesn't maintain its state across postbacks. Change the code for the property so it is able to maintain its state using the ViewState collection, similar to how `NavigateUrl` maintains its value.
3. What are the two main benefits of using a custom enumeration like `Direction` over built-in types like `System.Byte` or `String`?

Validating User Input

So far you have been creating a fairly static site where you control the layout and content. At development time, you create your pages and add them to the menu so your users can reach them. You can make your site a lot more attractive by incorporating dynamic data. This data usually flows in two directions: it either comes from the server and is sent to the end user's browser, or the data is entered by the user and sent to the server to be processed or stored.

Data coming from the server can be retrieved from many different data sources, including files and databases, and is often presented with the ASP.NET data controls. You see how to access databases in Chapter 11 and onward.

The other flow of data comes from the user and is sent to the server. The scope of this information is quite broad, ranging from simple page requests and contact forms to complex shopping cart scenarios and wizard-like user interfaces. The underlying principle of this data flow is basically the same in all scenarios — users enter data in a Web Form and then submit it to the server.

To prevent your system from receiving invalid data, it's important to validate this data before you allow your system to work with it. Fortunately, ASP.NET 3.5 comes with a bag of tools to make data validation a simple task.

The first part of this chapter gives you a good look at the validation controls that ASP.NET supports. You see what controls are available, how to use and customize them, and in what scenarios they are applicable.

The second half of this chapter shows you how to work with data in other ways. You see how to send the information a user submits to your system by e-mail and how to customize the mail body using text-based templates.

This chapter covers the following important topics:

- What is user input and why is it important to validate it?
- What does ASP.NET 3.5 have to offer to aid you in validating user input?
- How do you work with the built-in validation controls and how do you create solutions that are not supported with the standard tools?

- How do you send e-mail using ASP.NET?
- How do you read text files?

By the end of the chapter, you will have a good understanding of the flow of information to an ASP.NET web application and the various techniques you have at your disposal to validate this data.

Gathering Data from the User

Literally every web site on the Internet has to deal with input from the user. Generally, this input can be sent to the web server with two different techniques, `GET` and `POST`. In Chapter 4 you briefly saw the difference between these two methods and saw that `GET` data is appended to the actual address of the page being requested whereas with the `POST` method the data is sent in the body of the request for the page.

With the `GET` method, data is added to the query string of a page. You can retrieve it using the `QueryString` property of the `Request` object as discussed in Chapter 7. Imagine you are requesting the following page:

```
http://www.PlanetWrox.com/Reviews/ViewDetails.aspx?id=34&catId=3
```

With this example, the query string is `id=34&catId=3`. The question mark is used to separate the query string from the rest of the address. To access individual items in the query string, you can use the `Get` method of the `QueryString` collection:

VB.NET

```
Dim id As Integer = Convert.ToInt32(Request.QueryString.Get("id"))        ' id is now 34
Dim catId As Integer = Convert.ToInt32(Request.QueryString.Get("catId")) ' catId is now 3
```

C#

```
int id = Convert.ToInt32(Request.QueryString.Get("id"));                  // id is now 34
int catId = Convert.ToInt32(Request.QueryString.Get("catId"));            // catId is now 3
```

The `POST` method on the other hand gets its data from a form with controls that have been submitted to the server. Imagine you have a form with two controls: a `TextBox` called `txtAge` to hold the user's age and a `Button` to submit that age to the server. In the `Button` control's `Click` event you could write the following code to convert the user's input to an integer:

VB.NET

```
Dim age As Integer = Convert.ToInt32(txtAge.Text)          ' age now holds the user's age
```

C#

```
int age = Convert.ToInt32(txtAge.Text);                    // age now holds the user's age
```

Note that in this case, there is no need to access a collection like `Post` as you saw with the `QueryString` earlier. ASP.NET shields you from the complexity of manually retrieving data from the submitted form, and instead populates the various controls in your page with the data from the form.

All is well as long as users enter a value that looks like an age in the text box. But what happens when a user submits invalid data, either deliberately or by accident? What if a user sends the text *I am 36* instead of just the number 36? When that happens, the code will crash. The `ToInt32` method of the `Convert` class *throws an exception* (an error) when you pass it something that cannot be represented as a number.

To avoid these problems, you need to validate all the data that is being sent to the server. When it doesn't look valid, you need to reject it and make sure your application deals with it gracefully.

Validating User Input in Web Forms

People concerned with validating user input often use the mantra: *Never trust user input*. Although this may seem like paranoia at first, it is really important in any open system. Even if you think you know who your users are and even if you trust them completely, they are often not the only users that can access your system. As soon as your site is out on the Internet, it's a potential target for malicious users and hackers that will try to find a way into your system. In addition to these evil visitors, even your trustworthy users may send incorrect data to your server by accident.

To help you overcome this problem as well as possible, ASP.NET ships with a range of *validation controls* that help you validate your data, before it is used in your application. In the following sections, you see how to use the standard validation controls to ensure the user submits valid data into the system.

The ASP.NET Validation Controls

ASP.NET 3.5 comes with six useful controls to perform validation in your web site. Five of them are used to perform the actual validation whereas the final control — the `ValidationSummary` — is used to provide feedback to the user about any errors made in the page. Figure 9-1 shows the available controls in the Validation category of the Toolbox.

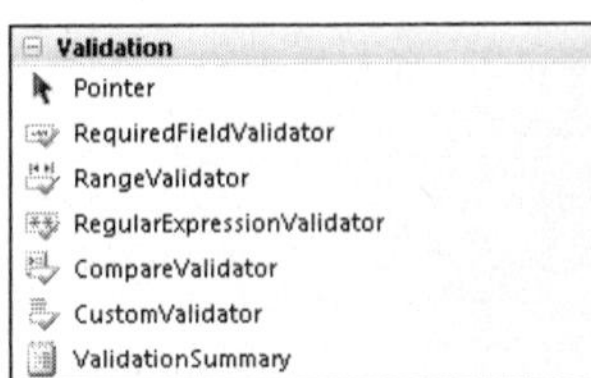

Figure 9-1

The validation controls are extremely helpful in validating the data that a user enters in the system. They can easily be hooked to other controls like the `TextBox` or a `DropDownList`; however, they also support custom validation scenarios. Figure 9-2 demonstrates two of the validation controls — `RequiredFieldValidator` and `RangeValidator` — at work to prevent a user from submitting the form without entering required and valid data.

The great thing about the validation controls is that they can check the input at the client and at the server. When you add a validation control to a web page, the control renders JavaScript that validates the associated control at the client. This client-side validation works on most modern web browsers with JavaScript enabled, including Microsoft Internet Explorer, Firefox, and Safari. At the same time, the validation is also carried out at the server automatically. This makes it easy to provide your user with immediate feedback about the data using client-side script, while your web pages are safe from bogus data at the server.

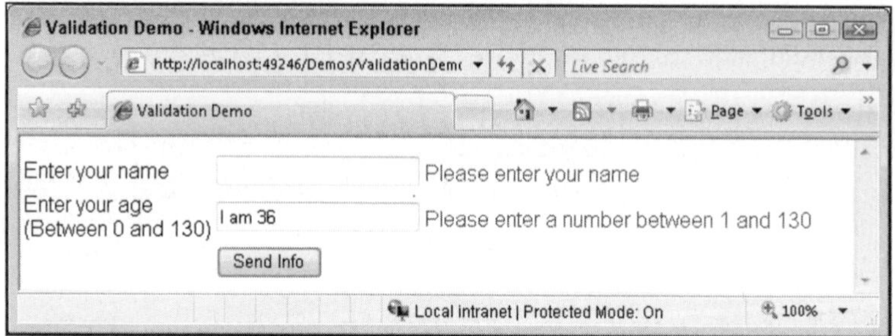

Figure 9-2

A Warning on Client-Side Validation

Although client-side validation may seem enough to prevent users from sending invalid data to your system, you should never rely on it as the only solution to validation. It's easy to disable JavaScript in the browser, rendering the client-side validation routines useless. In addition, a malicious user can easily bypass the entire page in the browser and send information directly to the server, which will happily accept and process it if you don't take countermeasures.

In general, you should see client-side validation as a courtesy to your users. It gives them immediate feedback so they know they forgot to enter a required field, or entered incorrect data without a full postback to the server. Server-side validation, on the other hand, is the only real means of validation. It's effectively the only way to prevent invalid data from entering your system.

The following section discusses how you can employ the validation controls to protect your data.

Using the Validation Controls

To declare a validation control in your ASPX page, you use the familiar declarative syntax. For example, to create the `RequiredFieldValidator` control used in Figure 9-2, you need the following code:

```
<asp:RequiredFieldValidator ID="ReqVal1" runat="server" ControlToValidate="TextBox1"
    Display="Dynamic" ErrorMessage="Please enter your name"></asp:RequiredFieldValidator>
```

To give you an idea of how they work, the following exercise guides you through the process of using the `RequiredFieldValidator` in a contact form that is placed in a user control.

Try It Out Using the RequiredFieldValidator

In this exercise you will create a user control called ContactForm.ascx. It can be placed in a web page so visitors to your site can leave some feedback. In later exercises you will extend the control by sending the response by e-mail to your e-mail account.

1. Open the Planet Wrox project and add a new user control in the Controls folder. Call the control ContactForm.ascx. Make sure it uses your programming language and a Code Behind file.
2. Switch to Design View and insert a table by choosing Table ➪ Insert Table. Create a table with eight rows and three columns.
3. Merge the three cells of the first row. To do this, select all three cells, right-click the selection, and choose Modify ➪ Merge Cells.

4. In the merged cell, type some text that tells your users they can use the contact form to get in touch with you.

5. In the first cell of the second row type the text **Your name**. Into the second cell of the same row, drag a textbox and call it `txtName`. Into the last cell of the second row, drag a `RequiredFieldValidator` from the Validation category of the Toolbox. Finally, into the second cell of the last row, drag a `Button`. Rename the button to `btnSend` by setting its `ID` and set its `Text` property to `Send`. When you're done, your Design View looks like Figure 9-3.

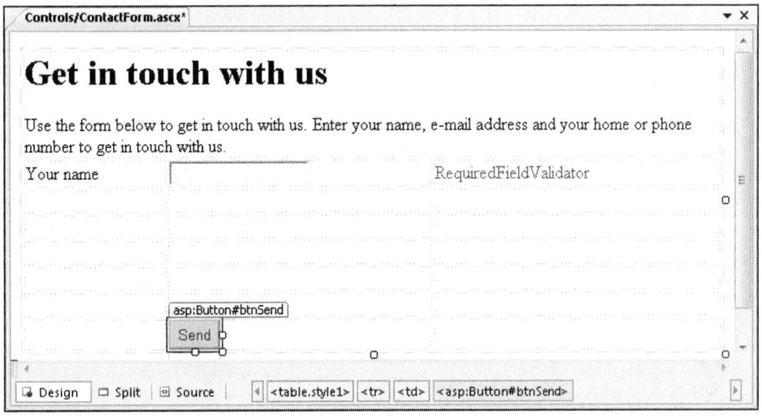

Figure 9-3

6. Click the `RequiredFieldValidator` once in Design View and then open up its Properties Grid by pressing F4. Set the following properties on the control.

Property	Value
`ErrorMessage`	Please enter your name
`Text`	*
`ControlToValidate`	txtName

7. Save the changes to the user control and then close it as you're done with it for now.

8. Open Contact.aspx from the About folder and switch to Design View.

9. From the Solution Explorer, drag the user control ContactForm.ascx into the main content area of the page, identified by the purple border. Switch back to Markup View, and you see this control declaration:

```
<asp:Content ID="Content2" ContentPlaceHolderID="cpMainContent" Runat="Server">
  <uc1:ContactForm ID="ContactForm1" runat="server" />
</asp:Content>
```

10. Save the page and then press Ctrl+F5 to open it in your browser. If you get an error, make sure you renamed the text box to `txtName` and that you set `ControlToValidate` on the `RequiredFieldValidator` to the same control ID.

11. Leave the Name text box empty and click the Send button. Note that the page is not submitted to the server. Instead, you should see a red asterisk appear in the row for the name field to indicate an error.

12. Enter your name and click Send again. The page now successfully posts back to the server.

How It Works

With the `RequiredFieldValidator` attached to the `TextBox` through the `ControlToValidate` property, JavaScript is sent to the browser that validates the control at the client. The `RequiredFieldValidator` control is able to validate another control like a `TextBox`. It does this by comparing the value of the other control with its own `InitialValue` property and making sure that the other control's value is different. By default, this property is an empty string, which means that anything except an empty string is considered a valid value. Whenever the user tries to submit the form to the server by clicking the Send button, the validation control checks the control it is attached to. When the text box is still empty, the red asterisk from its `Text` property is shown, and the form is not submitted. When the user enters something in the Name text box, validation succeeds and the page submits to the server successfully.

Besides the `RequiredFieldValidator` control, the Validation category of the Toolbox contains a number of other controls that are discussed next.

The Standard Validation Controls

The five validation controls ultimately all inherit from the same base class, and thus share some common behavior. Four of the five validation controls operate in the same way, and contain built-in behavior that allows you to validate associated controls. The last control, the `CustomValidator` allows you write custom functionality that is not supported out of the box.

The following table lists the properties that are shared by the validation controls and that you commonly use when working with validation controls.

Property	Description
`Display`	This property determines whether the hidden error message takes up space or not. With the `Display` set to `Static`, the error message takes up screen estate, even when it is hidden. This is similar to the CSS setting `visibility: hidden` you saw in earlier chapters. The `Dynamic` setting is similar to the CSS setting `display: none`. With a setting of `None`, the error message is not visible at all. Hiding the actual error message can be useful if you are using a `ValidationSummary`, which you'll see later in this chapter.
`CssClass`	This property allows you to set the CSS class that is applied to the error message text.
`ErrorMessage`	This property refers to the error message for the validation control used in the `ValidationSummary` control. When the `Text` property is empty, the `ErrorMessage` value is also used as the text that appears on the page.

Property	Description
`Text`	The `Text` property is used as the text that the validation control displays on the page. This could be an asterisk (*) to indicate an error or a required field, or text like "Please enter your name."
`ControlToValidate`	This property contains the ID of the control that needs to be validated.
`EnableClientScript`	This property gets or sets a setting that determines whether the control provides validation at the client. The default is `True`.
`SetFocusOnError`	This property determines whether client-side script gives the focus to the first control that generated an error. This setting is `False` by default.
`ValidationGroup`	Validation controls can be grouped together, allowing you to perform validation against a selection of controls. All controls with the same `ValidationGroup` are checked at the same time, which means that controls that are not part of that group are not checked. Consider, for example, a login page with a Login button and fields for a user name and password. The same page may also contain a search box that allows you to search the site. With the `ValidationGroup`, you can have the Login button validate the username and password boxes, whereas the search button triggers validation for just the search box.
`IsValid`	You don't typically set this property at design time, but at runtime it provides information about whether the validation test has passed.

The Difference between the Text and ErrorMessage Properties

At first glance, these two properties seem to serve the same purpose. Both of them can be used to provide feedback to the user in the form of an error message. But when used in combination with a `ValidationSummary` control, there's a subtle difference between the two. When you set both the properties at the same time, the `Validation` control displays the `Text` property, whereas the `ValidationSummary` displays the `ErrorMessage`. Figure 9-4 shows a sample Login page with two `RequiredFieldValidator` controls. Both the validation controls have their `Text` property set to an asterisk (`*`) to give the user a visual cue there is a problem. The `ValidationSummary` below the control then displays the full `ErrorMessage` properties.

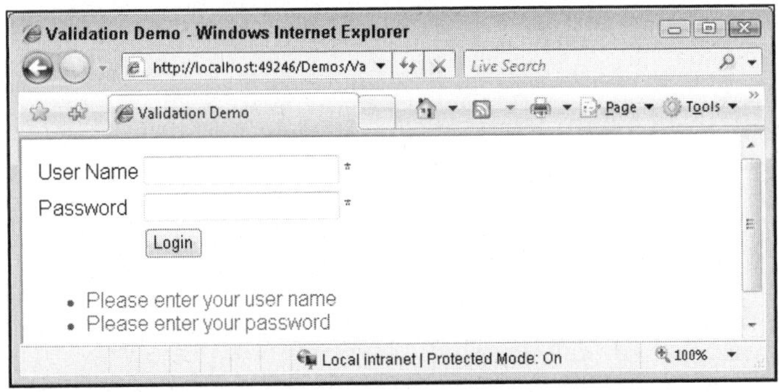

Figure 9-4

In the next sections, you get a good look at the three remaining standard validation controls. In the exercise that follows you see them at work. A later section then shows you how to use the `CustomValidator` and the `ValidationSummary` controls.

RangeValidator

The `RangeValidator` control enables you to check whether a value falls within a certain range. The control is able to check data types like strings, numbers, dates, and currencies. For example, you can use it to make sure a number is between 1 and 10, or a selected date falls between today and the next two weeks. The following table lists its most important properties.

Property	Description
`MinimumValue`	This property determines the lowest acceptable value. For example, when checking an integer number between 1 and 10, you set this property to 1.
`MaximumValue`	This property determines the highest acceptable value. For example, when checking an integer number between 1 and 10, you set this property to 10.
`Type`	This property determines the data type that the validation control checks. This value can be set to `String`, `Integer`, `Double`, `Date`, or `Currency` to check the respective data types.

RegularExpressionValidator

The `RegularExpressionValidator` control allows you to check a value against a *regular expression*. Regular expressions offer a compact syntax that allows you to search for patterns in text strings. Regular expressions are a complex subject, but fortunately, Visual Web Developer comes with a few built-in expressions that make it easy to validate values like e-mail addresses and zip codes. If you want to learn more about regular expressions, pick up a copy of *Beginning Regular Expressions* by Andrew Watt (ISBN: 978-0-7645-7489-4).

You set the regular expression in the `ValidationExpression` property of the control.

CompareValidator

The `CompareValidator` can be used to compare the value of one control to another value. This is often used in sign-up forms where a user has to enter a password twice to make sure they type the same password both times. Alternatively, instead of comparing to another control, you can also compare against a constant value.

The following table lists the additional properties for the `CompareValidator` control.

Property	Description
`ControlToCompare`	This property contains the ID of the control that the validator compares against. When this property is set, `ValueToCompare` has no effect.

Property	Description
`Operator`	This property determines the type of compare operation. For example, when `Operator` is set to `Equal` both controls must contain the same value for the validator to be considered valid. Similarly, you have options like `NotEqual`, `GreaterThan`, and `GreaterThanEqual` to perform different validation operations.
`Type`	This property determines the data type that the validation control checks. This value can be set to `String`, `Integer`, `Double`, `Date`, or `Currency` to check the respective data types.
`ValueToCompare`	This property allows you to define a constant value to compare against. This is often used in agreements where you have to enter a word like Yes to indicate you agree to some condition. Simply set the `ValueToCompare` to the word `Yes` and the `ControlToValidate` to the control you want to validate and you're done. When this property is set, make sure you clear the `ControlToCompare` property as that will otherwise take precedence.

In the following exercise you will see most of these controls at work, except for the `RangeValidator`. However, its usage is similar to the other validation controls, so it's just as easy to add it to your web page or user control when you need it.

Try It Out Extending the Contact Form

In the previous Try It Out exercise you started with the basics for the contact form by creating a user control holding a table and a few controls to let users enter their names. In this exercise, you extend the form and add fields for an e-mail address, a home phone number, and a business phone number. You will use the validation controls to ensure the e-mail address is in a valid format, and that at least one of the two phone numbers is filled in. To make sure users enter a correct e-mail address, they are asked to enter it twice. If you don't like this behavior, you can simply delete the row with the text box for the second e-mail address and ignore the `CompareValidator`.

1. Open ContactForm.ascx from the Controls folder again and switch it to Design View.
2. In the second column, drag five additional text boxes in the empty table cells between the text box for the name and the Send button. From top to bottom, name the controls as follows:
    - `txtEmailAddress`
    - `txtEmailAddressConfirm`
    - `txtPhoneHome`
    - `txtPhoneBusiness`
    - `txtComments`
3. Set the `TextMode` property of `txtComments` to `MultiLine` and then make the control a little wider and taller in the designer so it's easier for a user to add a comment. You can also adjust the table's column width to align the error message closer to the text box controls.

4. In the first cell of the rows to which you added the `TextBox` controls, add the text as shown in Figure 9-5.

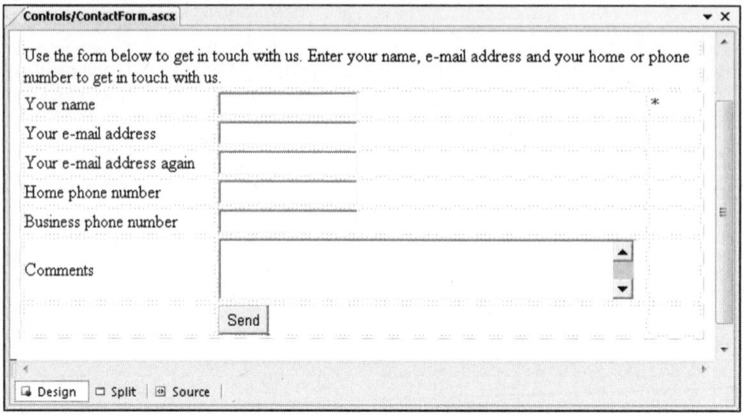

Figure 9-5

5. In the last column of the row for the first e-mail address, drag a `RequiredFieldValidator` and a `RegularExpressionValidator`. In the last column of the row for the second e-mail address, drag a `RequiredFieldValidator` and a `CompareValidator`. Finally, in the last cell for the Comments row, drag a `RequiredFieldValidator`. When you're done, your form looks as shown in Figure 9-6.

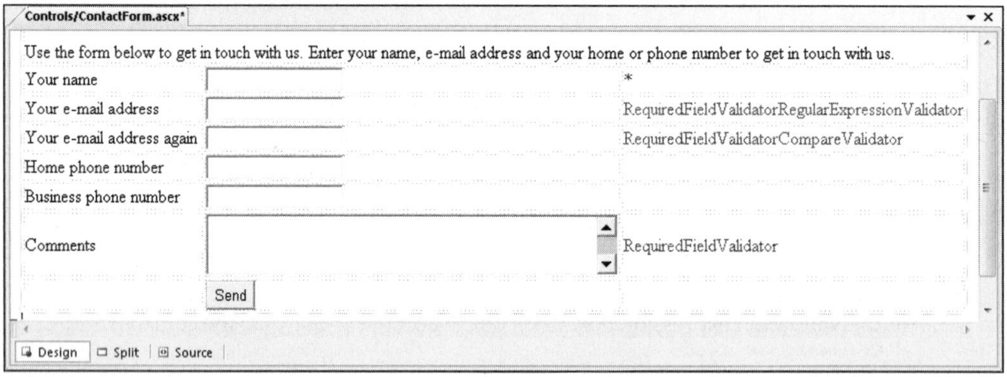

Figure 9-6

6. For each of the validation controls you added, open the Properties Grid and set the `Text` property to an asterisk (`*`) and the `Display` property to `Dynamic`. Then set the remaining properties for the controls as shown in the following table.

Control	Properties you need to set	
`RequiredFieldValidator` (for the first e-mail address)	`ErrorMessage:` `ControlToValidate:`	Please enter an e-mail address `txtEmailAddress`
`RegularExpressionValidator`	`ErrorMessage:` `ControlToValidate`	Please enter a valid e-mail address `txtEmailAddress`
`RequiredFieldValidator` (for the second e-mail address)	`ErrorMessage:` `ControlToValidate:`	Please confirm the e-mail address `txtEmailAddressConfirm`

`CompareValidator`	`ErrorMessage:`
	`ControlToValidate:`
	`ControlToCompare:`
		Please retype the e-mail address
		`txtEmailAddressConfirm`
		`txtEmailAddress`

`RequiredFieldValidator` (for the Comments field)	`ErrorMessage:` `ControlToValidate:`	Please enter a comment `txtComments`

7. Still in Design View, click the `RegularExpressionValidator` once, open its Properties Grid and locate the `ValidationExpression` property. When you click the property in the grid, the grid shows a button with ellipses. When you click that button you get a dialog box that allows you to select a regular expression, shown in Figure 9-7.

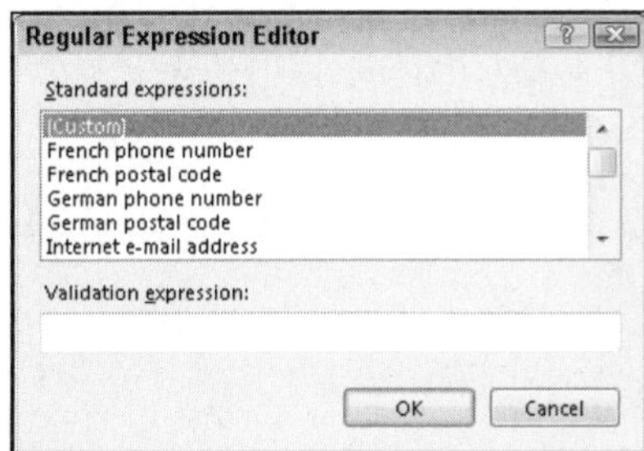

Figure 9-7

8. Click Internet e-mail address from the list and note that VWD inserts a long regular expression in the Validation expression box. Click OK to add the property to the control and dismiss the dialog box.

9. Save all the changes and then request Contact.aspx in your browser. Play around with the various validators by leaving out required data or by entering bogus data. Only when you have entered all required fields and typed the same e-mail addresses in both text boxes will the page submit to the server. At this stage, you will only see the red asterisks appear to give an indication of the problem. After you have seen how these validators work, you will see how to use the `ValidationSummary` to provide more detailed data to the user.

How It Works

Just like the RequiredFieldValidator control, the other validation controls emit JavaScript to the client, which is triggered when you click the Send button or when the value of one of the client controls is changed. The CompareValidator works by looking at the value of two different controls. Only when both contain the same data will it return true. It's important to realize that the CompareValidator control does not trigger its validation code when the text boxes are empty. Therefore, it's important to hook up a RequiredFieldValidator control as well. This control first makes sure the user entered at least some data and then the CompareValidator control ensures the text is the same in both text boxes.

The RegularExpressionValidator control works by checking the pattern of the data that it is validating. If you look at the ValidationExpression property of the control, you see a long, cryptic string. This pattern ensures that the e-mail address contains some text, optionally followed by some separation character like a dash (-) or period, followed by more text. It also ensures there's an @ symbol in the address, followed by a domain name, a period, and then at least one more character to represent the top-level domain like .com, .nl, or .co.uk. With this expression, you@yourprovider.com is considered a valid e-mail address. So is a@a.a, whereas you@you isn't.

Note that the RegularExpressionValidator control only roughly checks the syntax of the e-mail address. It's still perfectly possible to enter a non-existent e-mail address that just looks valid or even an invalid e-mail address as a@a.a. However, in many cases, this validator is good enough to filter out common typos that users make when entering e-mail addresses.

The CustomValidator and ValidationSummary Controls

The validation controls you have seen so far are very easy to use. You add them to a page, set a few properties, and then they'll do all the hard work for you. However, they do not support every possible validation scenario you may come up with. For example, what if you wanted to ensure that a user entered at least one of the two phone numbers? This is where the CustomValidator control comes in. This validator allows you to write custom validation functions for both the client (in JavaScript) and the server (using VB.NET or C#). This gives you great flexibility with regards to the data you want to validate.

The ValidationSummary provides the user with a list of errors that it retrieves from the individual validation control's ErrorMessage properties. It can display these errors in three different ways: using a list embedded in the page, using a JavaScript alert box, or using both at the same time. You control this setting with the ShowMessageBox and ShowSummary properties. Additionally, the DisplayMode property enables you to change the way the list of errors is presented. The default setting is BulletedList where each error is an item in a bulleted list, but other options are List (without bullets) and SingleParagraph.

You learn how to write client- and server-side validation methods and how to use the ValidationSummary control in the following exercise.

Try It Out — Writing Client- and Server-Side Validation Methods

In this exercise you see how to use the CustomValidator in your page to ensure at least one of the two phone numbers is entered. The validation is carried out at the client and at the server. Additionally, you see how to use the ValidationSummary control to provide feedback to the user.

1. Go back to the ContactForm.ascx control in VWD and switch it to Design View. Right-click the row with the `Button` control in it and choose Insert ➪ Row Below from the context menu to insert a new table row. Alternatively, you can press Ctrl+Alt+down arrow to have the row inserted for you as well.
2. Select the three cells of the row you just inserted, right-click them, and choose Modify ➪ Merge Cells to create a single cell that spans the entire three columns.
3. From the Validation category of the Toolbox, drag a `ValidationSummary` control into this newly created cell.
4. In the empty cell after the text box for the Home phone number, drag a `CustomValidator` control and set the following properties.

Property	Value
`Display`	Dynamic
`ErrorMessage`	Please enter your home or business phone number
`Text`	*
`ClientValidationFunction`	ValidatePhoneNumbers

5. Still on the Properties Grid for the `CustomValidator` control, click the button with the lightning bolt to switch to Events mode. Double-click the event `ServerValidate` to have VWD write an event handler for you. Add the following code to the handler:

VB.NET

```
Protected Sub CustomValidator1_ServerValidate(ByVal source As Object, _
         ByVal args As System.Web.UI.WebControls.ServerValidateEventArgs) _
         Handles CustomValidator1.ServerValidate
  If txtPhoneHome.Text IsNot String.Empty Or txtPhoneBusiness.Text IsNot String.Empty Then
    args.IsValid = True
  Else
    args.IsValid = False
  End If
End Sub
```

C#

```
protected void CustomValidator1_ServerValidate(object source, ServerValidateEventArgs args)
{
  if (txtPhoneHome.Text != string.Empty || txtPhoneBusiness.Text != string.Empty)
  {
    args.IsValid = true;
  }
  else
  {
    args.IsValid = false;
  }
}
```

6. Switch to Markup View of the user control and add the following block of JavaScript code right before the table with the controls:

```
<script type="text/javascript">
  function ValidatePhoneNumbers(source, args)
  {
    var txtPhoneHome = document.getElementById('<%= txtPhoneHome.ClientID %>');
    var txtPhoneBusiness = document.getElementById('<%= txtPhoneBusiness.ClientID %>');
    if (txtPhoneHome.value != '' || txtPhoneBusiness.value != '')
    {
      args.IsValid = true;
    }
    else
    {
      args.IsValid = false;
    }
  }
</script>
<table class="style1">
```

7. Save all the changes by pressing Ctrl+Shift+S and then request the page Contact.aspx in your browser. Note that you can't submit the form if you haven't at least entered one of the two phone numbers. Also note that the `ValidationSummary` control shows a list of all the problems with the data entered in the form. The client-side JavaScript function `ValidatePhoneNumbers` now ensures that you enter at least one phone number before you can submit the page back to the server. Figure 9-8 shows how the page ends up in Mozilla Firefox. 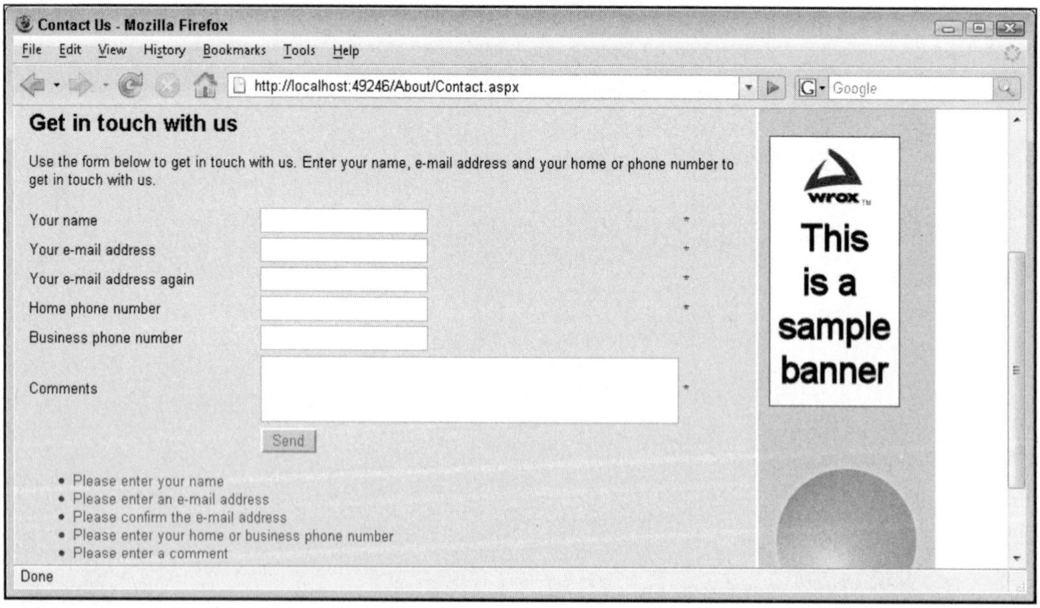

Figure 9-8

8. Go back to VWD and click the `ValidationSummary` control in Design View. On the Properties Grid, change `ShowMessageBox` to `True` and `ShowSummary` to `False`. Also, set its `HeaderText` property to: Please correct the following errors before you press the Send button.

9. Open the page in the browser again and click the Send button once more. Note that you now get a client-side alert instead of the inline list with errors, shown in Figure 9-9. The list of errors is preceded with the `HeaderText` of the `ValidationSummary`.

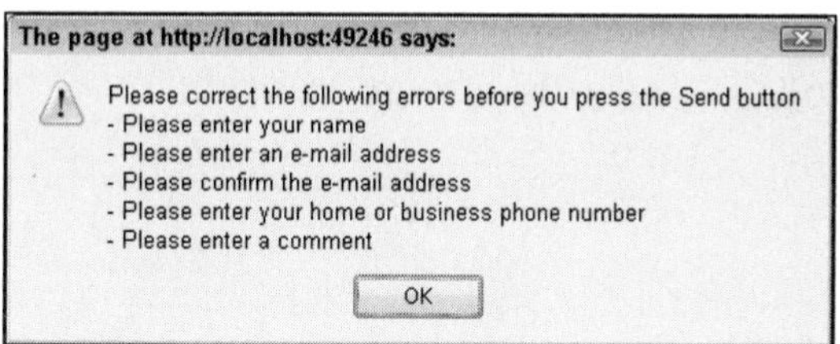

Figure 9-9

How It Works

When you added the `CustomValidator` control, you set up two event handlers: one for the client, and one for the server-side validation check, both in bold in the following snippet:

```
<asp:CustomValidator ID="CustomValidator1" runat="server" ErrorMessage="Please enter your
     home or business phone number" ClientValidationFunction="ValidatePhoneNumbers"
  OnServerValidate="CustomValidator1_ServerValidate"
  Display="Dynamic">*</asp:CustomValidator>
```

If you're using VB.NET, you won't see the `OnServerValidate` attribute as that is set up in the Code Behind using the `Handles` keyword.

The JavaScript function `ValidatePhoneNumbers` you set in the `ClientValidationFunction` is triggered at the client when you click the Send button. This function you defined in the markup section of the user control contains two references to the text boxes for the phone numbers:

```
var txtPhoneHome = document.getElementById('<%= txtPhoneHome.ClientID %>');
var txtPhoneBusiness = document.getElementById('<%= txtPhoneBusiness.ClientID %>');
```

Note that the `txtPhoneBusiness.ClientID` code is wrapped in a server-side `<%= %>` block. This code runs at the server, and then returns the `ClientID` of the control to the server. If you look at the HTML for the Contact page in the browser, you find the following code:

```
function ValidatePhoneNumbers(source, args)
{
  var txtPhoneHome =
        document.getElementById('ctl00_cpMainContent_ContactForm1_txtPhoneHome');
  var txtPhoneBusiness =
        document.getElementById('ctl00_cpMainContent_ContactForm1_txtPhoneBusiness');
  if (txtPhoneHome.value != '' || txtPhoneBusiness.value != '')
```

Here you can see how the server-side ClientID properties of the controls have been transformed into their client id properties. This is a much better solution than hard-coding the id attributes of the text boxes in the final HTML, as they can easily be changed by the ASP.NET runtime. You saw how and why this happened in the previous chapter. The code then calls the JavaScript function getElementById on the document object to get a reference to the text box in JavaScript. It then examines the value properties of these two text box controls. If one of them is not an empty string, the validation succeeds. But how does the ValidatePhoneNumbers method report back to the validation mechanism that the validation succeeded or not? When the ASP.NET validation mechanism calls the ValidatePhoneNumbers method it passes two arguments: source, which is a reference to the actual CustomValidator in the HTML, and args. The args object exposes an IsValid property that allows you to determine whether the validation succeeded or not:

```
if (txtPhoneHome.value != '' || txtPhoneBusiness.value != '')
{
  args.IsValid = true;
}
else
{
  args.IsValid = false;
}
```

With this code, if both text boxes are empty, IsValid is set to false, so validation won't succeed, stopping the form from being submitted. If one of the text boxes contains a value, IsValid is set to true. In this example, the source argument is not used, but you could use it to highlight or otherwise change the validation control based on whether it's valid or not.

At the server, the CustomValidator control calls the server-side validation method, which performs the same check:

VB.NET

```
If txtPhoneHome.Text IsNot String.Empty Or txtPhoneBusiness.Text IsNot String.Empty Then
  args.IsValid = True
Else
  args.IsValid = False
End If
```

C#

```
if (txtPhoneHome.Text != string.Empty || txtPhoneBusiness.Text != string.Empty)
{
  args.IsValid = true;
}
else
{
  args.IsValid = false;
}
```

By checking the data at the client and at the server, you ensure your system only accepts valid data. Even when the browser doesn't support JavaScript (possibly because the user turned it off deliberately) your data is still checked at the server. However, it's important to realize that you still need to check whether the page is valid before you work with the data submitted to it. You do this by checking the `IsValid` property of the page:

VB.NET

```
If Page.IsValid Then
  ' OK to proceed
End if
```

C#

```
if (Page.IsValid)
{
  // OK to proceed
}
```

The `IsValid` property returns `True` when all the controls in the page or in the active `ValidationGroup` are valid. By checking the `IsValid` property on the server before you work with the data, you can be sure that the data is valid according to your validation controls, even if the user turned off JavaScript in the browser, and sent the form to the server without any client-side checks. You see the `IsValid` property used again later in this chapter, when sending e-mail is discussed.

Processing Data at the Server

The information that a user inputs on your Web Forms is typically not the only data that makes your web site an interactive, data-driven system. In most web sites, you have information coming from other data sources as well, such as databases, text, XML files, and web services. In addition, there is also data going out of your system. You may want to send an e-mail to the owner of the web site whenever someone posted information through the contact page or you may want to notify people whenever you add a new feature or review to the web site. For these scenarios, it's important to understand how ASP.NET 3.5 allows you to send e-mail. This is discussed in the next section.

Sending E-mail from Your Web Site

Writing code that sends e-mail from an ASP.NET page is pretty straightforward. Inside the `System.Net.Mail` namespace you find a number of objects that make it very easy to create and send e-mail messages. These objects allow you to create new messages; add addressees in the To, CC, and Bcc fields; add attachments; and, of course, send the messages.

The following table describes four objects that you typically work with when sending e-mail from a .NET application.

Class	Description
MailMessage	This class represents the message you're going to send. It has properties such as Subject and Body to set the message contents; To, CC, and Bcc properties to set the addressees; and an Attachments collection to attach files to the message.
MailAddress	This class represents a sender or receiver address used in the e-mail. It has a few constructor overloads that allow you to set the e-mail address and display name.
Attachment	This class represents files you can attach to a MailMessage. When you construct an Attachment instance, you can pass in the name of the file you want to send. You then add the attachment to the MailMessage using the Add method of its Attachments collection.
SmtpClient	This class is used to send the actual message. By default, an instance of this class checks the web.config file for settings such as the SMTP server and a user name and password that is used for sending e-mail.

Configuring Your Web Site for Sending E-mail

Although the code to send e-mail is pretty easy, configuring your application and network can often be a bit trickier. The machine you are using to send e-mail must be able to access an SMTP server, either locally available in your network or over the Internet. In most cases, you should use the SMTP server that you also use in your e-mail client (for example, Microsoft Outlook). Contact your network administrator or your ISP if you are unsure about your SMTP server.

When you have the address of the SMTP server, you can configure it globally in the web.config file in the <system.net> element. When you are using the SMTP server from your ISP, the configuration setting looks like this:

```
  <system.net>
    <mailSettings>
      <smtp deliveryMethod="Network" from="Your Name &lt;you@yourprovider.Com&gt;">
        <network host="smtp.yourprovider.com" />
      </smtp>
    </mailSettings>
  </system.net>
</configuration>
```

The <system.net> element must be added as a direct child of the web.config file's root element <configuration>. Within <system.net> you add a <mailSettings> element, which in turn contains an <smtp> element. Finally, the <network> element has a host attribute that points to your SMTP server.

The <smtp> element accepts an optional from attribute that lets you set the name and e-mail address of the sender in the format Name <E-mail Address>. Because the < and > characters in XML have special meaning, you need to escape them with < and >. When you send e-mail programmatically, you can override this From address as you'll see in the next Try It Out exercise.

If your ISP requires you to authenticate before you can send the e-mail, you can also add user name and password attributes:

```
<smtp deliveryMethod="Network">
  <network host="smtp.yourprovider.com" userName="UserName" password="Password"/>
</smtp>
```

Refer to the online MSDN documentation for more information about the different settings that the `<system.net>` element takes.

Creating E-mail Messages

To create and send an e-mail message, you need to carry out four steps. First, you need to create an instance of the `MailMessage` class. You then configure the message by adding a body and a subject. The next step is to provide information about the sender and receivers of the message, and finally you need to create an instance of the `SmtpClient` class to send the message. The following exercise shows you how to code these four steps.

Try It Out Sending E-mail Messages

In this exercise, you create a simple page in the Demos folder. The code in this page creates an e-mail message that is sent when the page loads. In a later exercise you modify the contact form so it can send the user's response by e-mail.

1. Under the Demos folder create a new file called Email.aspx. Make sure it's based on your own base page template so that it has the right master page and inherits from `BasePage` automatically. Change the page's `Title` to E-mail Demo.

2. Switch to the Code Behind by pressing F7 and at the top of the file, before the class definition, add the following statement to make the classes in the `System.Net.Mail` namespace available to your code:

VB.NET

```
Imports System.Net.Mail
```

C#

```
using System.Net.Mail;
```

3. Add the following code to a `Page_Load` handler. If you're using VB.NET you need to set up the handler first using the two drop-down lists at the top of the Document Window:

VB.NET

```
Protected Sub Page_Load(ByVal sender As Object, ByVal e As System.EventArgs) _
        Handles Me.Load
  Dim myMessage As MailMessage = New MailMessage()
  myMessage.Subject = "Test Message"
  myMessage.Body = "Hello world, from Planet Wrox"
```

```
    myMessage.From = New MailAddress("you@yourprovider.com", "Sender Name Here")
    myMessage.To.Add(New MailAddress("you@yourprovider.com", "Receiver Name Here"))

    Dim mySmtpClient As SmtpClient = New SmtpClient()
    mySmtpClient.Send(myMessage)
  End Sub
```

C#

```
protected void Page_Load(object sender, EventArgs e)
{
  MailMessage myMessage = new MailMessage();
  myMessage.Subject = "Test Message";
  myMessage.Body = "Hello world, from Planet Wrox";

  myMessage.From = new MailAddress("you@yourprovider.com", "Sender Name Here");
  myMessage.To.Add(new MailAddress("you@yourprovider.com", "Receiver Name Here"));

  SmtpClient mySmtpClient = new SmtpClient();
  mySmtpClient.Send(myMessage);
}
```

Change the e-mail addresses and names in the two lines that set the `From` and `To` addresses to your own. If you have only one e-mail address, you can use the same address for the sender and the receiver.

4. Open web.config and scroll all the way down. Right before the closing `</configuration>` tag, add the following settings:

```
  <system.net>
    <mailSettings>
      <smtp deliveryMethod="Network" from="Your Name &lt;you@yourprovider.Com&gt;">
        <network host="smtp.yourprovider.com" />
      </smtp>
    </mailSettings>
  </system.net>
</configuration>
```

Don't forget to change `smtp.yourprovider.com` to the name of your SMTP server. Also, be sure to enter your name and e-mail address in the `from` attribute. If necessary, add the `userName` and `password` attributes to the `<network>` element as shown earlier.

5. Save all changes and then request the page Email.aspx in your browser by pressing Ctrl+F5. After a while, you should receive an e-mail message at the address you specified in step 3 of this exercise.

If you get an error, there are a couple of things you can check. First, make sure you entered the right SMTP server in web.config. You may need to talk to your Internet provider or network administrator to get the right address and optionally a user name and password. Also make sure that the mail server you are using actually allows you to send messages. Finally, if you get an error such as "The SMTP server requires a secure connection or the client was not authenticated," your provider may require you to use a secure connection. If that's the case, check the user name and password in web.config or try setting the `EnableSsl` *property of the* `mySmtpClient` *object to* `True` *in code like this:*

VB.NET

```
mySmtpClient.EnableSsl = True
```

C#

```
mySmtpClient.EnableSsl = true;
```

How It Works

You added the following `Imports` or `using` statement to the Code Behind file:

VB.NET

```
Imports System.Net.Mail
```

C#

```
using System.Net.Mail;
```

This statement is used to make the classes in this namespace available in your code without prefixing them with their full namespace. This allows you, for example, to create a `MailMessage` instance like this:

VB.NET

```
Dim myMessage As MailMessage = New MailMessage()
```

C#

```
MailMessage myMessage = new MailMessage();
```

Without the `Imports` or `using` statement, you would need this longer code instead:

VB.NET

```
Dim myMessage As System.Net.Mail.MailMessage = New System.Net.Mail.MailMessage()
```

C#

```
System.Net.Mail.MailMessage myMessage = new System.Net.Mail.MailMessage();
```

After the `Imports` / `using` statement, the code creates a new `MailMessage` object and sets its `Subject` and `Body` properties. The code then assigns addresses for the sender and recipient of the e-mail message:

VB.NET

```
myMessage.From = New MailAddress("you@yourprovider.com", "Sender Name Here")
myMessage.To.Add(New MailAddress("you@yourprovider.com", "Receiver Name Here"))
```

C#

```
myMessage.From = new MailAddress("you@yourprovider.com", "Sender Name Here");
myMessage.To.Add(new MailAddress("you@yourprovider.com", "Receiver Name Here"));
```

The From property of the MailMessage is of type MailAddress, so you can assign a new MailAddress directly. The constructor of the MailMessage class accepts the e-mail address and friendly name as strings so you can create and assign the From address with a single line of code.

The To property of the MailMessage class is a collection, so you cannot assign a MailAddress directly. Instead, you need to use the Add method to assign an address. This also allows you to add multiple recipients by calling To.Add multiple times, each time passing in a different MailAddress instance. You use the CC and Bcc properties in a similar way to assign e-mail addresses to the carbon copy and blind carbon copy fields of an e-mail message.

The final two lines of the code send out the actual message:

VB.NET

```
Dim mySmtpClient As SmtpClient = New SmtpClient()
mySmtpClient.Send(myMessage)
```

C#

```
SmtpClient mySmtpClient = new SmtpClient();
mySmtpClient.Send(myMessage);
```

When the Send method is called, the SmtpClient scans the web.config file for a configured SMTP server. It then contacts that server and delivers the message.

Besides the validation controls you have seen so far, ASP.NET comes with another validation mechanism, which is discussed next.

Understanding Request Validation

By design, an ASP.NET page throws an exception whenever one of the controls on a page contains content that looks like HTML tags. For example, you see the error shown in Figure 9-10 when you enter <h1>Hello World</h1> or <script type="text/javascript">alert('Hello World');</script> as the contents for the name text box in the contact form.

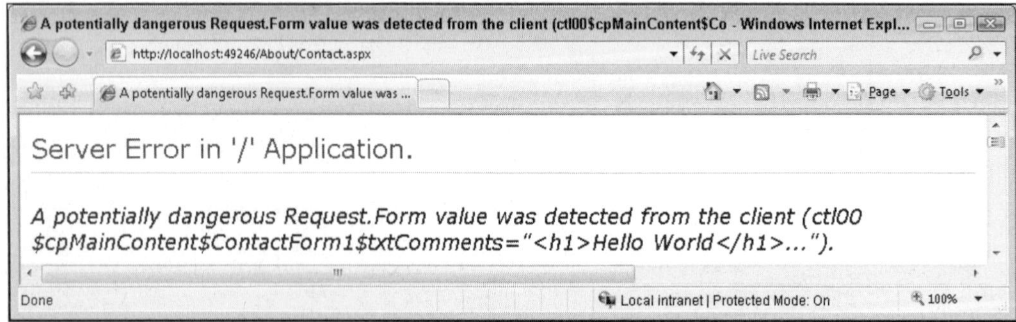

Figure 9-10

The ASP.NET runtime does this to prevent users from entering HTML or JavaScript that can potentially mess with the design or workings of your web site. If you're sure you want to allow your users to enter HTML, you can disable request validation by setting the `ValidateRequest` attribute in the `@ Page` directive to `False`:

```
<%@ Page .... Inherits="Contact" Title="Contact Us" ValidateRequest="False" %>
```

With this setting set to `False`, users can enter HTML without causing an error. Just make sure you really want to allow users to enter HTML when you set `ValidateRequest` to `False`.

In the previous Try It Out exercise, the body text for the e-mail message is hardcoded. This isn't always the best solution as it means you need to scan and change your code whenever you want to change the text. It's often better to use a text-based template instead. You see how this works in the next section.

Reading from Text Files

The .NET Framework comes with a few handy classes and methods that make working with files very easy. For example, the `File` class located in the `System.IO` namespace allows you to read to and write from files, create and delete files, and move files around. This class only contains static methods, which means you don't have to create an instance of the class first. Instead, you directly call methods on the `File` class. For example, to read the complete contents of a text file, you can use the following code:

VB.NET

```
Dim myContents As String = System.IO.File.ReadAllText("C:\MyFile.txt")
```

C#

```
string myContents = System.IO.File.ReadAllText(@"C:\MyFile.txt");
```

In this example, the file name in C# is prefixed with an `@` symbol, to avoid the need to prefix each backslash (\) with an additional backslash. In C#, the backslash has a special meaning, so to use it in a string you normally need to prefix it with another backslash. Using the `@` symbol tells the compiler that it should take each backslash it finds as a literal, ignoring the special meaning of the character.

The following table lists the most common methods of the `File` class that allow you to work with files.

Property	Value
`AppendAllText`	This property appends a specified string to a text file. If the file does not exist, it's created first.
`Copy`	This property copies a file from one location to another.
`Delete`	This property deletes the specified file from disk.
`Exists`	This property checks if the specified file exists on disk.
`Move`	This property moves the specified file to a different location.
`WriteAllText`	This property writes the contents of a string to a newly created file. If the target file already exists, it gets overwritten.

You can use these methods for all kinds of purposes. For example, when a user has uploaded a file, you can use the `Move` method to move it to a different folder. Additionally, when you want to get rid of uploaded files that you don't need anymore, you use the `Delete` method.

The `ReadAllText` method is useful to read the complete contents of a text file. For example, when sending text by e-mail, you could store the body text of the e-mail in a text file. When you're about to send the e-mail, you call `ReadAllText` and assign the contents that this method returns to the body of the e-mail. You see how this works in the following Try It Out.

Try It Out — Sending Mail from the ContactForm User Control

This exercise shows you how to use e-mail to send the user data from the contact form to your own inbox. As the body of the e-mail message, the code reads in a text file that contains placeholders. These placeholders are filled with the actual user data from the form and then sent by e-mail.

1. Start by creating a new text file to the App_Data folder in your web site. If you don't have the App_Data folder anymore, right-click the web site and choose Add ASP.NET Folder ⇨ App_Data. Create the text file by right-clicking the App_Data folder and choosing Add New Item. Name the text file ContactForm.txt.

2. Enter the following text in the text file, including the placeholders wrapped in a pair of double hash symbols:

```
Hi there,

A user has left the following feedback at the site:

Name:               ##Name##
E-mail address:     ##Email##
Home phone:         ##HomePhone##
Business phone:     ##BusinessPhone##
Comments:           ##Comments##
```

3. Open the Code Behind of the ContactForm.ascx user control and import the following namespace at the top of the file:

VB.NET

```
Imports System.Net.Mail

Partial Class Controls_ContactForm
  Inherits System.Web.UI.UserControl
```

C#

```
using System.Net.Mail;

public partial class Controls_ContactForm : System.Web.UI.UserControl
```

4. Switch to Markup View and add `runat="server"` and `id="FormTable"` attributes to the table with the server controls. This way you can hide the entire table when the form has been submitted. To do this, locate the opening table tag and modify it like this:

```
<table class="style1" runat="server" id="FormTable">
```

5. Scroll down to the end of the file and right after the closing `</table>` tag, add a label called `lblMessage`. Set its `Text` property to `Message Sent`. Hide the label by setting the `Visible` property to `false`:

```
</table>
<asp:Label ID="lblMessage" runat="server" Text="Message Sent" Visible="false"></asp:Label>
```

6. Switch the control into Design View and then set `ShowSummary` of the `ValidationSummary` back to `True` and `ShowMessageBox` to `False`. Next, double-click the Send button. Inside the event handler that VWD adds for you, add the following code:

VB.NET

```
Protected Sub btnSend_Click(sender As Object, e As EventArgs) Handles btnSend.Click
  If Page.IsValid Then
    Dim fileName As String = Server.MapPath("~/App_Data/ContactForm.txt")
    Dim mailBody As String = System.IO.File.ReadAllText(fileName)

    mailBody = mailBody.Replace("##Name##", txtName.Text)
    mailBody = mailBody.Replace("##Email##", txtEmailAddress.Text)
    mailBody = mailBody.Replace("##HomePhone##", txtPhoneHome.Text)
    mailBody = mailBody.Replace("##BusinessPhone##", txtPhoneBusiness.Text)
    mailBody = mailBody.Replace("##Comments##", txtComments.Text)

    Dim myMessage As MailMessage = New MailMessage()
    myMessage.Subject = "Response from web site"
    myMessage.Body = mailBody

    myMessage.From = New MailAddress("you@yourprovider.com", "Sender Name Here")
    myMessage.To.Add(New MailAddress("you@yourprovider.com", "Receiver Name Here"))

    Dim mySmtpClient As SmtpClient = New SmtpClient()
    mySmtpClient.Send(myMessage)

    lblMessage.Visible = True
    FormTable.Visible = False
  End If
End Sub
```

C#

```
protected void btnSend_Click(object sender, EventArgs e)
{
  if (Page.IsValid)
  {
    string fileName = Server.MapPath("~/App_Data/ContactForm.txt");
    string mailBody = System.IO.File.ReadAllText(fileName);

    mailBody = mailBody.Replace("##Name##", txtName.Text);
    mailBody = mailBody.Replace("##Email##", txtEmailAddress.Text);
    mailBody = mailBody.Replace("##HomePhone##", txtPhoneHome.Text);
    mailBody = mailBody.Replace("##BusinessPhone##", txtPhoneBusiness.Text);
    mailBody = mailBody.Replace("##Comments##", txtComments.Text);
```

```
        MailMessage myMessage = new MailMessage();
        myMessage.Subject = "Response from web site";
        myMessage.Body = mailBody;

        myMessage.From = new MailAddress("you@yourprovider.com", "Sender Name Here");
        myMessage.To.Add(new MailAddress("you@yourprovider.com", "Receiver Name Here"));

        SmtpClient mySmtpClient = new SmtpClient();
        mySmtpClient.Send(myMessage);

        lblMessage.Visible = true;
        FormTable.Visible = false;
    }
}
```

Again, make sure you replace the e-mail addresses for the `From` and `To` properties of the `MailMessage` with your own.

7. Save all your changes and once again request Contact.aspx in the browser. Enter your details and click the Send button. You'll see the text Message Sent appear.

8. Check the e-mail account you sent the e-mail to and after a while, you should receive an e-mail message, similar to Figure 9-11.

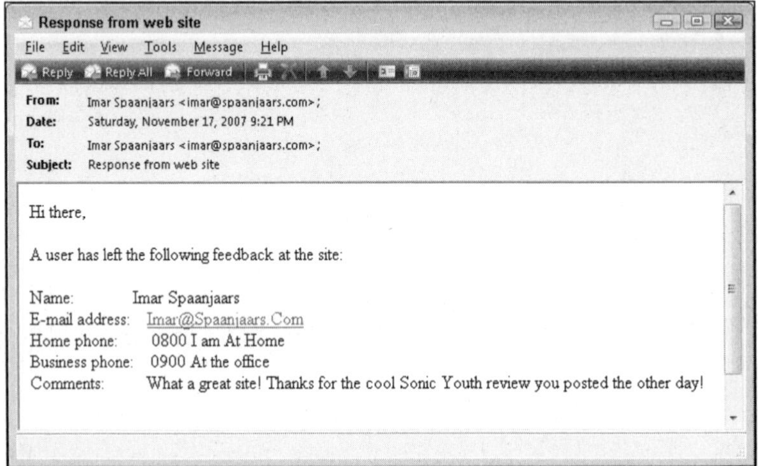

Figure 9-11

How It Works

The mail-sending part of this exercise is pretty similar to the demo page you created earlier. What's different, however, is where the body text for the mail message comes from. Instead of hardcoding the body in the Code Behind of the `ContactForm` control, you moved the text to a separate file. This file in turn contains a few placeholders that are replaced at runtime with the user's details. To read in the entire file at once, you use the following code:

VB.NET

```
Dim fileName As String = Server.MapPath("~/App_Data/ContactForm.txt")
Dim mailBody As String = System.IO.File.ReadAllText(fileName)
```

C#

```
string fileName = Server.MapPath("~/App_Data/ContactForm.txt");
string mailBody = System.IO.File.ReadAllText(fileName);
```

The first line uses `Server.MapPath` to translate a virtual path into its physical counterpart. By using the virtual path, it's easier to move your site to a different location as it doesn't depend on any hardcoded paths. `Server.MapPath("~/App_Data/ContactForm.txt")` returns a physical path such as `C:\BegASPNET\Site\App_Data\ContactForm.txt`. This path is then fed to the `ReadAllText` method of the `File` class, which opens the file and returns its contents, which are then assigned to the `mailBody` variable. The code then uses a number of calls to the `Replace` method to replace the static placeholders in the message body with the details the user entered in the contact form. The return value of the `Replace` method — the new text with the replaced strings — is reassigned to the `mailBody` variable. After the final call to `Replace`, the `mailBody` no longer contains the placeholders, but the user's details instead:

VB.NET

```
mailBody = mailBody.Replace("##Name##", txtName.Text)
...
mailBody = mailBody.Replace("##Comments##", txtComments.Text)
```

C#

```
mailBody = mailBody.Replace("##Name##", txtName.Text);
...
mailBody = mailBody.Replace("##Comments##", txtComments.Text);
```

The `Replace` method is case sensitive, so if you find that some placeholders are not replaced correctly, make sure you use the same capitalization in the code and in the message body.

The placeholders are wrapped in a pair of double hash symbols (`##`). The hash symbols are arbitrarily chosen, but help to identify the placeholders, minimizing the risk that you accidentally replace some text that is supposed to be in the actual message.

Once the message body is set up, it's assigned to the `MailMessage` object, which is then sent using the `SmtpClient`, identical to what you saw in an earlier exercise.

When you filled in your details in the contact form and clicked the Send button, you may have noticed some page flicker, as the page submits to the server and is then reloaded with the success message. This page flicker can easily be minimized or completely removed using Ajax technologies, which are discussed in the next chapter.

Practical Tips on Validating Data

The following list provides some practical tips on validating data.

- Always validate all user input. Whenever you have a public web site on the Internet, you lose the ability to control its users. To stop malicious users from entering bogus data in your system, always validate your users' input using the ASP.NET validation controls.
- Always provide useful error messages in your validation controls. Either assign the error message to the `ErrorMessage` property and leave the `Text` empty, or use a `ValidationSummary` control to show a list of error messages.
- Consider using the `CssClass` attribute of the validation controls to move the style definitions for the error messages to a separate CSS file. If you do use the `CssClass`, don't forget to clear the `ForeColor` property of the validator or the error message still appears in red.
- Whenever you are writing code that sends an e-mail message, consider moving the body of the e-mail to a separate text file. As you saw, reading in the file only takes a single line of code, and it makes your application much easier to maintain. Instead of wading through your code to find the body text, you simply change the template in the App_Data folder and the code picks up the changes automatically.
- When storing data in text or XML files, always store them in the App_Data folder that is designed specifically for this purpose. This way, all your data files are nicely packed together. More importantly, by default the web server blocks access to the files in this folder so a visitor to your site cannot directly request them.

Summary

User input is an important aspect of most interactive web sites. It comes from different sources in your web site: the contact form you created in this chapter, the query string, and other sources. To stop users from entering invalid or even dangerous content into your system, it's important to validate all input before you work with it.

The validation controls that ASP.NET supports make it easy to validate all data coming from form controls, such as `TextBox`, `DropDownList`, `Calendar`, and so on. The `RequiredFieldValidator` helps to ensure that a user has filled in a required field. The `RangeValidator`, `CompareValidator`, and `RegularExpressionValidator` are used to check the contents of the data against settings you define at design time. The `CustomValidator` allows you to write validation code that is not covered by the built-in validation controls, giving you maximum flexibility. The `ValidationSummary` control is used to give feedback about the errors that your users made while entering data. It can display these errors as a simple bulleted list in the page, or as a JavaScript alert window.

The biggest benefit of the validation controls is that they work at the client and at the server, enabling you to create responsive forms where a user gets immediate feedback about any errors they may have made, without the need for a full postback. At the same time, the data is validated at the server, ensuring that data coming from clients that don't support JavaScript is valid as well.

To store the information that users submit to your site, you have a couple of options. The data can be stored in a database or a text file or sent by e-mail. The latter option is particularly useful for contact forms, so you get an immediate alert when someone leaves a comment at your web site. Sending e-mail is a breeze with the classes in the `System.Net.Mail` namespace. These classes allow you to create an e-mail message, add subject, body, sender, and recipient information, and then send the message using the `SmtpClient` class.

To make the e-mail message easy to maintain, you're advised to store its contents in a separate text file, and not directly in the code. If you later decide to change the message, all you need to change is this single text file. Reading the file is done with the static methods on the `System.IO.File` class. This class allows you to do more with files than reading alone; you can also use its methods to create, copy, move, and delete files in your web site.

By adding placeholders in your text messages, you can easily fill them in the code that sends out the e-mail. By calling the `Replace` method on the body string, you can embed the information entered by the user in the message before you send it.

Exercises

1. To make the ContactForm.ascx user control even more reusable, you can create a string property such as `PageDescription` on it that allows you to set the name of the page that uses the control. You then add this string to the declaration of the control in the containing page. Finally, you can add the description to the subject of the message that you send. This way, you can see from what page the contact form was called. What code do you need to write to make this happen?
2. Why is it so important that you check the value of the `IsValid` property of the `Page` when processing data? What can happen if you forget to make this check?
3. What's the difference in behavior between the `To` and the `From` property of the `MailMessage` class?
4. When you use a `CustomValidator`, you can write validation code at the client and at the server. How do you tell the ASP.NET runtime what client-side validation method to call during the validation process?
5. How do you tell the validation mechanism that validation succeeded or failed in your `CustomValidator` routines?

ASP.NET AJAX

Without a doubt, the biggest hype in web development in the past few years is Ajax. Although the technologies that drive Ajax have been around for quite some time, it wasn't until the beginning of 2005 that it got an official name. Ajax, which stands for Asynchronous JavaScript And Xml, allows your client-side web pages to exchange data with the server through asynchronous calls. Probably the most popular feature driven by Ajax is the flicker-free page that allows you to perform a post-back to the server without refreshing the entire page.

To enhance your web site with Ajax features you can choose among different Ajax frameworks. Many of these frameworks offer you a set of features and tools including a client-side JavaScript framework to enable Ajax in the browser, JavaScript code for communication with the server, and server controls to integrate with your ASP.NET pages. Although there are a number of different Ajax frameworks available for ASP.NET, the most obvious one is *Microsoft ASP.NET AJAX*, as it comes with the .NET 3.5 Framework and Visual Web Developer.

Microsoft ASP.NET AJAX gives you a lot more than flicker-free postbacks alone. In addition to the controls that make flicker-free pages possible, Microsoft ASP.NET AJAX gives you a few more server controls to create rich, interactive, and responsive user interfaces.

In addition to the server control–based part of Ajax, the ASP.NET AJAX Framework also comes with a rich client-side framework. This framework enables your JavaScript to communicate with the server by means of Web Services. It also allows you to access the entire client-side page using an intuitive code model that works the same, regardless of the browser you're targeting.

In previous versions of ASP.NET and Visual Web Developer, Ajax was available as a separate download and add-on. Fortunately, Ajax is now fully integrated in VWD and ASP.NET, making it easy to get started with it.

This chapter looks at the following Ajax-related topics:

- Using the `UpdatePanel` control to avoid page flicker
- Understanding the `ScriptManager` control that enables the Ajax functionality

- Using the `UpdateProgress` control to notify users about progress of the Ajax operation
- Using triggers and the `Timer` control to trigger the update of `UpdatePanel` controls
- Creating Web Services that are accessible by your client-side script

By the end of the chapter, you should have a good understanding of the various server controls that the ASP.NET AJAX Framework has to offer. In addition, you should have a basic understanding of creating Web Services in the ASP.NET world and how you can call them from client-side JavaScript code using the client-side Ajax Framework.

Introducing Ajax

The concepts behind Ajax have been around for many years. Browsers since Internet Explorer 5 have shipped with the `XMLHttpRequest` object that allowed you to make calls to the server from JavaScript to send and receive data. However, people also used other techniques to emulate the behavior of what is now called Ajax, including Macromedia Flash, `iframe` elements, or hidden frames.

However, when the term *Ajax* was introduced, things really took off. In an attempt to stay ahead of the curve, Microsoft started building ASP.NET AJAX, the Ajax Framework that is now fully integrated in ASP.NET and Visual Web Developer 2008. This framework offers a number of benefits that you as a web developer can take advantage of to create responsive applications. In particular, ASP.NET AJAX enables you to:

- Create flicker-free pages that allow you to refresh portions of the page without a full reload and without affecting other parts of the page.
- Provide feedback to your users during these page refreshes.
- Update sections of a page and call server-side code on a scheduled basis.
- Access server-side Web Services and work with the data they return.
- Use the rich, client-side programming framework to access and modify elements in your page, and get access to a code model and type system that looks similar to that of the .NET Framework.

In the remainder of this chapter, you see how to use the ASP.NET AJAX Framework to create rich and interactive web applications. Note that Ajax itself is a broad subject that cannot be fully covered in a single chapter. If you want to learn more about ASP.NET AJAX, check out *Professional ASP.NET 2.0 Ajax*, by Matt Gibbs and Dan Wahlin (ISBN: 978-0-470-10962-5). Although the book covers the ASP.NET 2.0 Framework, many concepts carry over to ASP.NET 3.5 Ajax. Alternatively, pick up a copy of *ASP.NET AJAX Programmer's Reference: With ASP.NET 2.0 or ASP.NET 3.5* by Dr. Shahram Khosravi (ISBN: 978-0-470-10998-4).

The nice thing about ASP.NET AJAX is that it is very easy to get started with. Creating a flicker-free page is a matter of dragging and dropping a few controls from the Toolbox into your page. When you understand the basics of the Ajax Framework, you can extend your knowledge by looking at more advanced topics like calling Web Services and using the rich client-side framework to interact with the page.

Using ASP.NET AJAX in Your Projects

Prior versions of VWD and ASP.NET AJAX required you to modify the web.config file manually to enable Ajax for your ASP.NET application. If you worked with Ajax before in ASP.NET projects, you'll be happy to learn that this is no longer required. Whenever you create a new web site using the File ➪ New Web Site dialog box, it's already Ajax-enabled, meaning that you can start using Ajax right away. The Toolbox now contains an additional category with the available Ajax controls that you can use in your pages right from the start.

Creating Flicker-Free Pages

To avoid full postbacks in your ASPX pages and update only part of the page, you can use the `UpdatePanel` server control. For this control to operate correctly, you also need a `ScriptManager` control. If you're going to use Ajax functionality in many of your ASPX pages, you can place the `ScriptManager` in the master page, so it's available in all pages that are based on this master. You'll find these and other Ajax-related server controls in the AJAX Extensions category of the Toolbox, shown in Figure 10-1. Near the end of this chapter you get a closer look at the `ScriptManager` control, discovering what it does and what it is used for.

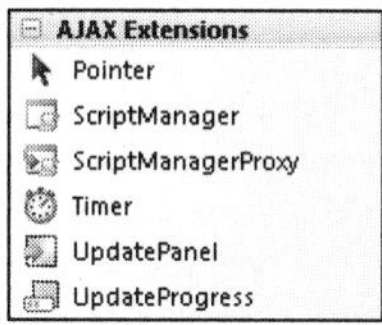

Figure 10-1

If you don't see the `ScriptManager` *and* `UpdatePanel` *controls in the Toolbox, right-click the AJAX Extensions category of the Toolbox and select Choose Items. Then select the two controls from the list on the .NET Framework Components tab.*

The following two sections introduce you to the `UpdatePanel` and `ScriptManager` controls. After that you see how to make use of these controls in your pages. Later sections introduce you to the `UpdateProgress`, `Timer`, and `ScriptManagerProxy` controls.

The UpdatePanel Control

The `UpdatePanel` control is a key component in creating flicker-free pages. In its most basic application, you simply wrap the control around content you want to update, add a `ScriptManager` to the page, and you're done. Whenever one of the controls within the `UpdatePanel` causes a postback to the server, only the content within that `UpdatePanel` is refreshed.

To see what problems the `UpdatePanel` control solves and how it behaves in a client page, the following Try It Out shows you a simple example that uses the panel to avoid page flicker during postbacks.

Try It Out Adding an UpdatePanel to a Page

In this exercise, you add a `Label` and a `Button` control to a page. Whenever you click the button in the browser, the `Text` property of the `Label` is updated with the current date and time at the server. To avoid the page flicker typically associated with postbacks, you then wrap the controls in an `UpdatePanel` to see how that control affects the behavior.

1. Open the Planet Wrox project from its location at C:\BegASPNET\Site in VWD.
2. In the Demos folder, create a new file called UpdatePanel.aspx. Make sure it's based on the central base page you created previously and that it uses your programming language. Give the page a `Title` of UpdatePanel Demo.
3. Switch the new page into Design View and drag a `Label` control and a `Button` control from the Toolbox into the `cpMainContent` placeholder. If the `ContentPlaceHolder` suddenly gets as small as the `Label`, simply drop the `Button` *on top* of the `Label`. The `Button` is then placed before the `Label` but if you now drag the `Label` on top of the `Button` again, the two change places. Alternatively, you can click the `Label` once to select it, then press the right arrow key once to position the cursor next to the `Label`. If you then press Enter a few times you can create some room in the `ContentPlaceHolder`.
4. Use the Properties Grid to clear the `Text` property of the `Label` control. To do this, right-click the Text property in the Properties Grid and choose Reset. You should end up with this markup:

```
<asp:Content ID="Content2" ContentPlaceHolderID="cpMainContent" runat="Server">
  <asp:Label ID="Label1" runat="server"></asp:Label>
  <asp:Button ID="Button1" runat="server" Text="Button" />
</asp:Content>
```

5. Double-click the grey and read-only area of the page in Design View to set up a handler for its `Load` event and add the following code to the handler that VWD added for you:

VB.NET

```
Protected Sub Page_Load(ByVal sender As Object, ByVal e As System.EventArgs) _
      Handles Me.Load
  Label1.Text = System.DateTime.Now.ToString()
End Sub
```

C#

```
protected void Page_Load(object sender, EventArgs e)
{
  Label1.Text = System.DateTime.Now.ToString();
}
```

6. Save all your changes and press Ctrl+F5 to open the page in your browser. The `Label` displays the current date and time. Click the `Button` control a few times. Note that each time you click the button, the page flickers and is then redrawn, displaying the updated date and time.

7. Close your browser and go back into VWD and switch the page UpdatePanel.aspx to Markup View. From the AJAX Extensions category of the Toolbox, drag an `UpdatePanel` into the code, right before the `Label` control you added in step 3.

8. Between the opening and closing tags of the `UpdatePanel`, add a `<ContentTemplate>` element. Note that IntelliSense kicks in as soon as you type the opening bracket, making it easy to complete the element. Next, cut both the closing `</ContentTemplate>` and the closing `</UpdatePanel>` tags and paste them below the button you created in step 3. You should end up with this markup:

```
<asp:UpdatePanel ID="UpdatePanel1" runat="server">
  <ContentTemplate>
    <asp:Label ID="Label1" runat="server"></asp:Label>
    <asp:Button ID="Button1" runat="server" Text="Button" />
  </ContentTemplate>
</asp:UpdatePanel>
```

9. Right before the opening tag of the `UpdatePanel`, drag a `ScriptManager` from the AJAX Extensions category of the Toolbox:

```
<asp:Content ID="Content2" ContentPlaceHolderID="cpMainContent" runat="Server">
  <asp:ScriptManager ID="ScriptManager1" runat="server"></asp:ScriptManager>
  <asp:UpdatePanel ID="UpdatePanel1" runat="server">
```

10. Save your changes and then request the page in the browser again. Click the button a few times to update the label with the current date and time. Note that there is no page flicker now. It's as if only the label is updated on the page.

How It Works

By wrapping the content in an `UpdatePanel` you define a region in your page that you want to refresh without affecting the entire page. In the previous example, the `Button` control inside the `UpdatePanel` caused a postback and thus a refresh of the region. Only the part of the page that is wrapped in the `UpdatePanel` is refreshed, causing a flicker-free reload of the page. It's also possible to update a region from controls that are placed outside the `UpdatePanel` as you'll see later.

The `ScriptManager` you placed in the master page is a requirement for most Ajax functionality to operate correctly. It serves as the bridge between the client page and the Ajax Framework and takes care of things like registering the correct JavaScript files that are used in the browser. You'll see both controls in more detail in the following sections.

A Closer Look at the UpdatePanel

The `UpdatePanel` and its content is the only part of the page that is updated when you press a button (as discussed in the previous exercise). This is the default behavior of an `UpdatePanel`, where only its inner contents are refreshed by other server controls defined within the `<ContentTemplate>` element. However, the `UpdatePanel` can do more than this. The following table lists some of the important properties of the `UpdatePanel` that allow you to influence its behavior.

Property	Value
ChildrenAsTriggers	This property determines whether controls located within the UpdatePanel can cause a refresh of the UpdatePanel. The default value is True, as you have seen in the previous exercise. When you set this value to False, you have to set the UpdateMode to Conditional. Note that controls defined within the UpdatePanel still cause a postback to the server with this set to False; they just don't update the panel anymore automatically.
Triggers	The Triggers collection contains PostBackTrigger and AsyncPostBackTrigger elements. The first is useful if you want to force a complete page refresh, whereas the latter is useful if you want to update an UpdatePanel with a control that is defined outside the panel.
RenderMode	This property can be set to Block or Inline to indicate whether the UpdatePanel renders itself as a <div> or <span> element.
UpdateMode	This property determines whether the control is always refreshed (the UpdateMode is set to Always) or only under certain conditions, for example, when one of controls defined in the <Triggers> element is causing a postback (the UpdateMode is set to Conditional).
ContentTemplate	Although not visible in the Properties Grid for the UpdatePanel, the <ContentTemplate> is an important property of the UpdatePanel. It's the container in which you place controls as children of the UpdatePanel. If you forget this required ContentTemplate, VWD gives you a warning.

As demonstrated in the previous exercise, UpdatePanel is capable of refreshing parts of a page. Controls that are defined either inside the UpdatePanel or outside of it can cause a refresh of the UpdatePanel. However, in order to function, the UpdatePanel needs a ScriptManager control that manages the client-side JavaScript, among other things.

The ScriptManager Control

The ScriptManager control serves as the bridge between the client page and the server. It manages script resources (the JavaScript files used at the client), takes care of partial-page updates as shown earlier and handles interaction with your web site for things like Web Services and the *ASP.NET application services* like membership, roles, and profile. Chapters 15 and 16 dig deeper into these services from a server perspective. For an in-depth look at accessing these services from client-side code using Microsoft ASP.NET AJAX, refer to *Professional ASP.NET 2.0 Ajax* by Matt Gibbs and Dan Wahlin.

You usually place the ScriptManager control directly in a content page if you think you need Ajax capabilities on only a handful of pages. You briefly saw how this worked in the previous Try It Out exercise.

However, you can also place the ScriptManager in a master page so it becomes available throughout the entire site. You'll do this in a later exercise in this chapter.

The ScriptManager class has a number of properties of which most are used in advanced scenarios. In many situations, like updating sections of a page using the UpdatePanel as you just saw, you don't need to change any of the properties of the ScriptManager class. In other scenarios, you may need to change or set some of its properties. The following table lists some of the more common properties of the ScriptManager control.

Property	Value
AllowCustomErrorsRedirect	This property determines whether errors that occur during an Ajax operation cause the customized error page to be loaded. The default is True; with a setting of False the error is shown as a JavaScript alert window in the browser or is hidden from the client when debugging is disabled. Note that if you haven't configured any customized error page, the error is always shown as a JavaScript alert, regardless of the value of this setting. Chapter 17 discusses more about setting up customized error pages and debugging your application.
AsyncPostBackErrorMessage	When you're not using customized error pages, this property allows you to customize the error message that users see when an Ajax error occurs. It allows you to hide the dirty details from the user and instead present them a more friendly error message.
EnablePageMethods	This property determines whether client code is allowed to call methods defined in the page. You see how this works later.
EnablePartialRendering	This property determines whether the ScriptManager supports the partial rendering of the page using UpdatePanel controls. You should leave this setting to True, unless you want to block the partial updates for the entire page.
Scripts	The <Scripts> child element of the ScriptManager control enables you to add additional JavaScript files that must be downloaded by the client at runtime.
Services	The <Services> element allows you to define Web Services that are accessible by your client side pages. You'll see how to use Web Services in the second half of this chapter.

Although the UpdatePanel and the ScriptManager together are all you need to create flicker-free pages, ASP.NET AJAX offers more to enhance the user's experience in an Ajax-enabled web site. One way to improve the user's experience is by using the UpdateProgress control, discussed next. Another option is to use the Timer control, which is discussed later in this chapter.

Providing Feedback to Users

Despite the visual problems that postbacks usually cause, they have one big advantage: the user can see something is happening. The UpdatePanel makes this a little more difficult. Users have no visual cue that something is happening until it has happened. To tell your users to hold on for a few seconds while their request is being processed, you can use the UpdateProgress control.

The UpdateProgress Control

You connect the UpdateProgress control to an UpdatePanel using the AssociatedUpdatePanelID property. Its contents, defined in the <ProgressTemplate> element, are then displayed whenever the associated UpdatePanel is busy refreshing. You usually put text like "Please wait" or an animated image in this template to let the user know something is happening, although any other markup is acceptable as well.

In addition to the AssociatedUpdatePanelID and <ProgressTemplate> properties, the UpdateProgress control features the following properties you typically use:

Property	Value
DisplayAfter	This property determines the time in milliseconds that the control waits before it displays its contents. This is useful when the refresh period is so short, that a notification message would be overkill. The default is 500 milliseconds, which is half a second.
DynamicLayout	This property determines whether the control takes up screen real estate when hidden. This again maps directly to the CSS display: none; or visibility: hidden; properties that you have seen before.

In the following exercise, you see how to combine the UpdatePanel, the ScriptManager, and the UpdateProgress to make the ContactForm user control flicker-free.

Try It Out Flicker-free Pages — Putting It All Together

In this exercise, you modify the user control ContactForm.ascx that you created earlier, wrapping the entire control in an UpdatePanel so the page doesn't perform a full postback when you enter a message and click the Send button. To help users understand the page is busy when the message is being sent, you add an UpdateProgress panel to the control. Inside this control you place an animated GIF image that is available in the code download from this book. Alternatively, you can go to www.ajaxload.info and create your own animated image.

1. Open the user control ContactForm.ascx from the Controls folder and in Markup View wrap the entire <table> element and the Label at the bottom of the control in an UpdatePanel with a <ContentTemplate>. You can do this by typing the code directly in Markup View, or by dragging the control from the AJAX Extensions category of the Toolbox. You should end up with the following code:

```
<asp:UpdatePanel ID="UpdatePanel1" runat="server">
  <ContentTemplate>
    <table class="style1" runat="server" id="FormTable">
      ....
```

```
    </table>
    <asp:Label ID="lblMessage" runat="server" Text="Message Sent"
            Visible="false"></asp:Label>
  </ContentTemplate>
</asp:UpdatePanel>
```

2. Save the changes to the control and then open the file MasterPage.master from the MasterPages folder. Between the opening `<form>` tag and the `<div>` for the `PageWrapper`, add a `ScriptManager` control by dragging it from the Toolbox into the source of the page. You should end up with this code:

```
<body>
  <form id="form1" runat="server">
    <asp:ScriptManager ID="ScriptManager1" runat="server"></asp:ScriptManager>
    <div id="PageWrapper">
```

3. Save the changes to the master page and then close it.

4. Open the UpdatePanel.aspx page you created in an earlier Try It Out and remove the `ScriptManager` element. Since this control is now declared in the master page, you can no longer redefine it in pages that are based on that master. Save the changes and close the page.

5. Open the Contact.aspx page from the About folder in your browser and then fill in the contact form. Note that as soon as you click the Send button, the form disappears and is replaced with the label stating that the message is sent. Just as with the earlier example, you'll notice no page flicker when the page reloads and displays the text *Message Sent*.

6. To keep the user updated on the progress while the message is delivered to the mail server, you should add an `UpdateProgress` control to the page. Inside this control, you add an animated image and some text informing the user the message is being sent. To add the image, locate the folder where you extracted the files that come with this book (at C:\BegASPNET\Resources) with Windows Explorer. Open the Chapter 10 folder and then the Monochrome folder. Drag the file PleaseWait.gif from Windows Explorer into the Images folder of the Monochrome theme under App_Themes. Repeat this process, but now drag PleaseWait.gif from the DarkGrey folder into its respective theme's Images folder. Figure 10-2 shows how both images should end up.

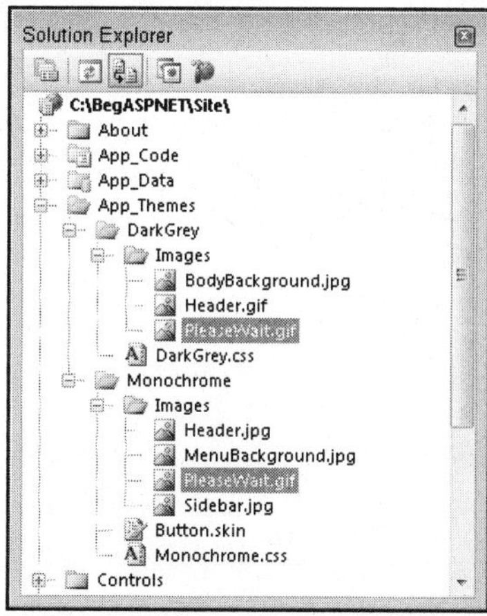

Figure 10-2

7. Open the Monochrome.css file, scroll all the way down to the end, and add the following rule:

```
.PleaseWait
{
  height: 32px;
  width: 500px;
  background-image: url(Images/PleaseWait.gif);
  background-repeat: no-repeat;
  padding-left: 40px;
  line-height: 32px;
}
```

8. Copy the exact same rule into the DarkGrey.css file for the DarkGrey theme.

9. Switch back to the ContactForm.ascx user control and below the closing tag of the `UpdatePanel` at the end of the file, drag an `UpdateProgress` control. Set its `AssociatedUpdatePanelID` to `UpdatePanel1`.

10. Between the `<UpdateProgress>` tags create a `<ProgressTemplate>`, and within this template, create a `<div>` element with its `class` attribute set to `PleaseWait`, the CSS class you created in step 7. Inside the `<div>` element, type some text to inform your users that they should hold on for a while. You should end up with this code:

```
</asp:UpdatePanel>
<asp:UpdateProgress ID="UpdateProgress1" runat="server"
               AssociatedUpdatePanelID="UpdatePanel1">
  <ProgressTemplate>
    <div class="PleaseWait">
      Please Wait...
    </div>
  </ProgressTemplate>
</asp:UpdateProgress>
```

11. To emulate a long delay while sending out the message so you can see the `UpdateProgress` control, add the following line of code to the Code Behind of the control, just after the lines that change the visibility of the controls in the method that sends out the e-mail:

VB.NET

```
          lblMessage.Visible = True
          FormTable.Visible = False
          System.Threading.Thread.Sleep(5000)
```

C#

```
          lblMessage.Visible = true;
          FormTable.Visible = false;
          System.Threading.Thread.Sleep(5000);
```

12. Save all your changes and open the page Contact.aspx from the About folder once again. Fill in the required details and click the Send button. Shortly after you press the button, you should see the `UpdateProgress` control appear that displays text and an animated image below the form, shown in Figure 10-3.

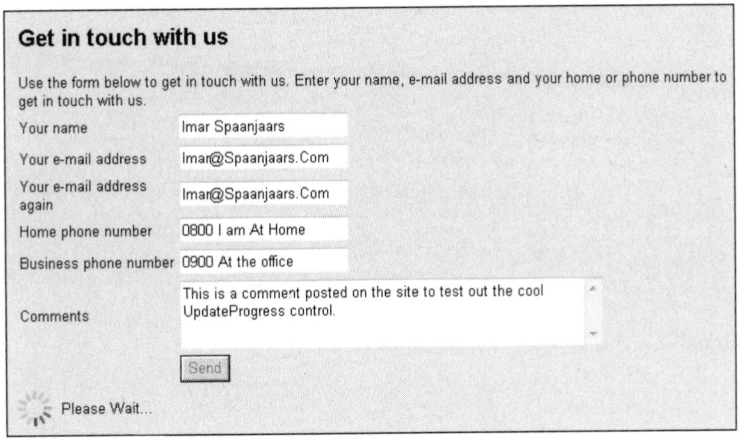

Figure 10-3

How It Works

With the UpdatePanel in the user control, everything that falls within the ContentTemplate of the UpdatePanel will be updated upon postback, without affecting other parts of the page. This way, you can hide the form with the server controls and replace it with the *Message sent* label without causing any page flicker.

To inform the user that his or her message is being sent, you also added an UpdateProgress control to the site. By default, this control will be shown when the update of the Ajax UpdatePanel it is attached to takes longer than 500 milliseconds (half a second) to refresh. The <ProgressTemplate> element for the control contained a simple <div> element with its class set to PleaseWait. You added the following CSS rule to the two CSS files for the themes:

```
.PleaseWait
{
  height: 32px;
  width: 500px;
  background-image: url(Images/PleaseWait.gif);
  background-repeat: no-repeat;
  padding-left: 40px;
  line-height: 32px;
}
```

This code first sets the dimensions of the Update message to be 500 pixels wide and 32 pixels high. This is enough to roughly span the width of the content block, giving you enough room for a longer message.

The code then adds the animated image as a background image. To prevent the image from being repeated in the background, the repeat property is set to no-repeat. Then the left padding is set to 40 pixels. This moves the text in the <div> to the right, so it appears next to the animated image. Finally, the line-height of the text is set to 32 pixels, the same height as the entire <div>. This centers the entire text block vertically within the <div> element.

Finally, you added the following line of code to the handler that sends the message:

```
System.Threading.Thread.Sleep(5000);
```

This code halts the execution of the page for 5 seconds (the number you pass to the `Sleep` method is expressed in milliseconds) so you can get a good look at the message in the `UpdateProgress` control. In production code, you should remove this line, as it slows down the page considerably without adding any value to the page.

In addition to user-triggered page updates as you saw with the Send button, you can also trigger page refreshes programmatically at a specified interval, as discussed in the following section.

Using the Timer Control

The `Timer` control that you find in the AJAX Extensions category of the Toolbox is great for executing server-side code on a repetitive basis. For example, you can use it to update the contents of an `UpdatePanel` every 5 seconds. The contents of this `UpdatePanel` could come from a variety of sources, such as a database to show new content added to the site, the membership services to display the number of users that are currently online, or even external Web Services with information like stock quotes or the lowest prices for specific products your users may be interested in.

The `Timer` control is pretty simple to use. At a specified interval, the control fires its `Tick` event. Inside an event handler for this event you can execute any code you see fit. If you hook up the `Timer` to the `UpdatePanel` using its `Triggers` collection, you can update a single region of a page whenever the `Timer` control ticks — that is, when it fires its `Tick` event.

In addition to the standard properties that most controls have, such as `ID` and `EnableViewState`, the control has two properties you're likely to use, as shown in the following table.

Property	Value
`Enabled`	This property determines whether the `Timer` control currently ticks. When `Enabled` is `True`, the control raises its `Tick` event at the interval specified in the `Interval` property. When `Enabled` is `False`, the control does nothing and raises no events.
`Interval`	This property determines the interval in milliseconds between the `Tick` events that the control raises. For example, if you want the control to fire an event every minute, set this property to 60,000.

To see the `Timer` control at work, the following exercise shows you how to create a page that is continuously updated without a full postback. You could use the same principles to show any type of dynamic data you like.

Try It Out Using the Timer Control in an ASPX Page

In this exercise, you see how to use the `Timer` control to update a region of the page. The `Timer` will tick every 5 seconds and then update a label. Besides the `Timer`, the page also has a regular button that when clicked allows you to refresh the screen on demand. This is a common scenario with automatically updating data, as it allows your users to force a refresh if they don't want to wait for the next automatic update.

1. Create a new page under the Demos folder based on your custom template and call it Timer.aspx. Give the page a `Title` of Timer Demo.
2. From the page UpdatePanel.aspx you created earlier, copy the markup of the entire `UpdatePanel` control and then paste it within the `Content` control for the `cpMainContent` block of the Timer.aspx page you just created. Remove the button from the `ContentTemplate`. Finally, add three line breaks (`<br />` elements) after the `UpdatePanel` to create some room. You should end up with this code:

```
<asp:Content ID="Content2" ContentPlaceHolderID="cpMainContent" Runat="Server">
  <asp:UpdatePanel ID="UpdatePanel1" runat="server">
    <ContentTemplate>
      <asp:Label ID="Label1" runat="server"></asp:Label>
    </ContentTemplate>
  </asp:UpdatePanel>
  <br /><br /><br />
</asp:Content>
```

3. Still in Markup View, drag a `Timer` control from the AJAX Extensions category of the Toolbox right below the `UpdatePanel` and the line breaks.
4. Drag a `Button` control below the `Timer`. Make sure both the `Timer` and the `Button` end up outside the `UpdatePanel` control by checking that the code looks like this:

```
</asp:UpdatePanel>
  <br /><br /><br />
  <asp:Timer ID="Timer1" runat="server"></asp:Timer>
  <asp:Button ID="Button1" runat="server" Text="Button" />
</asp:Content>
```

5. Switch to Design View, bring up the Properties Grid for the `Timer` control and set its `Interval` property to 5000 so it ticks every 5 seconds.
6. Switch the Properties Grid to the Events category. Double-click the `Tick` event, shown in Figure 10-4.

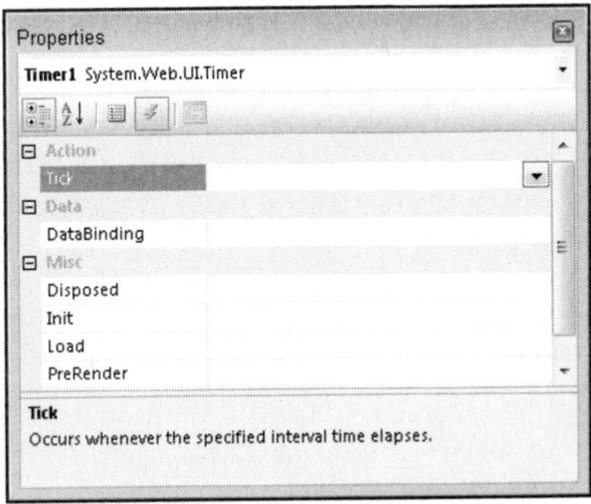

Figure 10-4

7. In the Code Behind, create a method (a `Sub` in VB.NET; a `void` method in C#) called `UpdateLabel` that sets the `Text` of `Label1` equal to the current date and time. From the event handler that was inserted by VWD for you in the previous step, call this new method. You should end up with the following code:

VB.NET

```
Protected Sub Timer1_Tick(ByVal sender As Object, ByVal e As System.EventArgs) _
                    Handles Timer1.Tick
  UpdateLabel()
End Sub

Private Sub UpdateLabel()
  Label1.Text = DateTime.Now.ToString()
End Sub
```

C#

```
protected void Timer1_Tick(object sender, EventArgs e)
{
  UpdateLabel();
}

private void UpdateLabel()
{
  Label1.Text = System.DateTime.Now.ToString();
}
```

8. Go back into Design View, and double-click the Button to set up its `Click` handler. Inside this handler, call the same `UpdateLabel` method:

VB.NET

```
Protected Sub Button1_Click(ByVal sender As Object, ByVal e As System.EventArgs) _
                    Handles Button1.Click
  UpdateLabel()
End Sub
```

C#

```
protected void Button1_Click(object sender, EventArgs e)
{
  UpdateLabel();
}
```

9. Return to Design View once more and select the `UpdatePanel`. Then open its Properties Grid (F4) and click the button with the ellipses for the `Triggers` property, shown in Figure 10-5.

10. In the dialog box that follows, click the Add button to insert a new `AsyncPostBack` trigger. Set its `ControlID` to `Timer1` and the `EventName` to `Tick` by choosing the right items from the drop-down lists of the Properties Grid. Repeat this step, but now add a trigger on `Button1` for its `Click` event. When you're done, your dialog box should look like Figure 10-6.

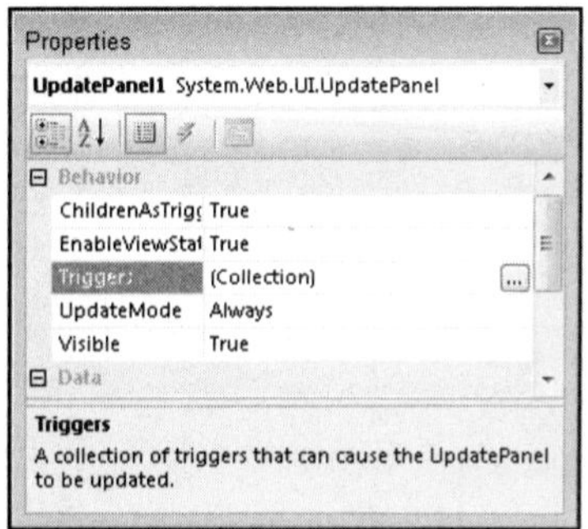

Figure 10-5

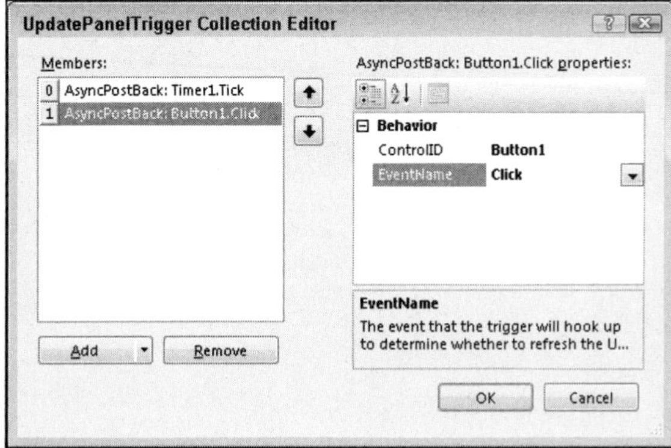

Figure 10-6

11. Click OK to dismiss the dialog box and switch back to Markup View and verify that your code looks like this:

```
<asp:Content ID="Content2" ContentPlaceHolderID="cpMainContent" runat="Server">
  <asp:UpdatePanel ID="UpdatePanel1" runat="server">
    <ContentTemplate>
      <asp:Label ID="Label1" runat="server"></asp:Label>
    </ContentTemplate>
    <Triggers>
      <asp:AsyncPostBackTrigger ControlID="Timer1" EventName="Tick" />
      <asp:AsyncPostBackTrigger ControlID="Button1" EventName="Click" />
    </Triggers>
  </asp:UpdatePanel>
  <br />
  <br />
  <br />
  <asp:Timer ID="Timer1" runat="server" OnTick="Timer1_Tick" Interval="5000"></asp:Timer>
  <asp:Button ID="Button1" runat="server" Text="Button" OnClick="Button1_Click" />
</asp:Content>
```

If you're using VB.NET, you won't see the handler code for `OnTick` and `OnClick`. Instead, Visual Basic uses the `Handles` keyword to hook up the methods to the events in the code behind.

12. Save all your changes and then request Timer.aspx in your browser. Note that the label is updated with the current date and time every 5 seconds. When you click the button, you'll see that the `Label` control is updated immediately, instead of waiting for the next `Tick` event on the `Timer` control to occur.

How It Works

In this exercise, you added a `Timer` control and a `Button` control outside the `UpdatePanel` that you copied from an earlier page. The `Timer` control has its `Interval` property set to `5000` which means it ticks every 5 seconds. When the `Timer` controls raises its `Tick` event, the code in the Code Behind of the Timer.aspx page runs the `UpdateLabel` method:

VB.NET

```
Protected Sub Timer1_Tick(ByVal sender As Object, ByVal e As System.EventArgs) _
         Handles Timer1.Tick
  UpdateLabel()
End Sub
```

C#

```
protected void Timer1_Tick(object sender, EventArgs e)
{
  UpdateLabel();
}
```

The `UpdateLabel` method in turn updates the `Label` inside the `UpdatePanel` by setting its `Text` property to the current date and time.

To have the `Timer` control update only the contents of the `UpdatePanel` and not cause a complete refresh of the page, it's important to register it in the `<Triggers>` element of the `UpdatePanel`, like this:

```
<Triggers>
  <asp:AsyncPostBackTrigger ControlID="Timer1" EventName="Tick" />
  <asp:AsyncPostBackTrigger ControlID="Button1" EventName="Click" />
</Triggers>
```

This code registers both the `Timer` and the `Button` control as controls that can force a partial update on the `UpdatePanel`.

Because of the `Interval` of 5,000 milliseconds on the `Timer` control, it automatically updates your screen every 5 seconds. If you can't wait that long, you can also click the `Button` you added to the page. When the button is clicked, it causes a postback to the server where the `Button` control's `Click` handler calls the same `UpdateLabel` method. Since the `Button` control is registered as a trigger for the `UpdatePanel`, the `Label` is updated without fully reloading the page. If you want to use the `Button` control to update the entire page and ignore the Ajax partial-page updates, simply remove the `AsyncPostBackTrigger` from the `<Triggers>` element. Then, when you click the `Button` control, a normal postback occurs and the entire page is updated.

This scenario with an auto-updating panel and the ability to refresh the content with a button click is quite common. The auto-refreshing panel is a non-intrusive way to feed the user the most up to date information from the server. At the same time, if users want to refresh the data at any moment they choose, all they need to do is click a button. From a coding perspective, there isn't much difference. In both cases, it all comes down to calling a single method: `UpdateLabel`.

The `Trigger` control concludes the discussion of the server-side controls that the ASP.NET AJAX Framework has to offer. What's left is a discussion of using Web Services in your Ajax-enabled web pages and an introduction of the client-side JavaScript framework that you have at your disposal. During the discussion of Web Services and the client framework, you also see how to use the `ScriptManagerProxy`, the final control in the Ajax Extensions category of the Toolbox.

Using Web Services in Ajax Web Sites

The ability to call Web Services from any Ajax-enabled ASP.NET web site is a great addition to your web development toolkit. Being able to call arbitrary Web Services accessible over the Internet means it's now much easier to access data at the client from other sources, such as your own web site, or external web sites that enable you to access their data through public Web Services, such as Google Search, Google Maps, Amazon, and Microsoft's Virtual Earth.

Before you can create and consume Web Services in your own application, it's important to understand what a Web Service is, and how you define one in your ASP.NET project.

What Are Web Services?

Web Services are essentially methods that you can call over the Internet and that can optionally return data to the calling code. This makes them ideal for exchanging data between different systems. Because Web Services are based on solid and well-understood standards, they make it easy to exchange data between different types of platforms. For example, with a Web Service it's easy to exchange data between an ASP.NET web site running on Microsoft Windows and a PHP-based site running on Linux. But at the same time, it's also possible to exchange data between an ASP.NET web site and a client browser using JavaScript.

The Web Services in the Planet Wrox project will only be used to have a client page in the browser talk to the server and exchange data. So, in this site, both the server and the client are in the same web project — one executes at the client (the JavaScript that calls the web server), the other lives at the server (the Web Service itself). From a security point of view, this is the easiest solution as both parts trust each other.

If you want your client-side pages to talk to a Web Service on a different domain, you need to set up security in the browser to allow this. Additionally, you can also use Web Services to have two servers or other applications (desktop applications for example) communicate with each other. In that case, one application (a Windows desktop application, a PHP or classic ASP web application, or even another ASP.NET Web Service) interacts with an ASP.NET Web Service over the network to exchange data. Both these scenarios fall outside the scope of this chapter though.

The Web Services you will create in the Planet Wrox projects look similar to ordinary methods you have created already. What's different is that you need to decorate each method with a `WebMethod` *attribute*. An attribute is like a little tag or label that you can stick on code, like methods, properties, and so on to mark that piece of code as something special. Other code interacting with the attributed code can then see what attributes that code contains and make decisions based on that information. Don't worry about that too much as you don't have to read those attributes yourself when working with Web Services. All you need to do is stick the attribute on a method to turn it into a `WebMethod` and you're good to go. For example, to change a standard method that returns a string into a `WebMethod`, you would apply the following attribute:

VB.NET

```
<WebMethod()> _
Public Function HelloWorld(ByVal yourName As String) As String
  Return String.Format("Hello {0}", yourName)
End Function
```

C#

```
[WebMethod]
public string HelloWorld(string yourName)
{
  return string.Format("Hello {0}", yourName);
}
```

Note that in the VB.NET example, angle brackets are used to wrap the attribute. In addition, the code uses an underscore (_) as the line-continuation character. In C# you use square brackets and you can place the attribute on its own line.

With this attribute in place, you signal to the ASP.NET runtime that you really want to expose this method as a Web Method. This also allows you to create other methods in the same class that are not exposed as Web Services automatically, giving you flexibility in determining what to open up for the outside world.

Besides the `WebMethod` attribute to mark the method as a Web Method, you generally place this method in a file with an .asmx extension and inside a class that inherits from `System.Web.Services.WebService`. You'll see how this works in the following section.

Creating Web Services

Creating Web Services with VWD is very easy. Just as with all the other document types, VWD comes with a template for a Web Service. You add a Web Service to the site using the Add New Item dialog box. You can then modify the service and test it out in a web browser using the standard test page that the ASP.NET runtime creates for you automatically. When the Web Service functions correctly, you can use it from your client-side JavaScript code, as you will see after the following exercise.

Try It Out Creating a Web Service

In this exercise you will create a simple Hello World Web Service. This service accepts your name as an input parameter and returns a friendly, personalized greeting. There's not much real world usage for this exact Web Service. However, because of the simplicity in the service itself, it's easier for you to focus on the underlying concepts.

1. Create a new folder called WebServices in the root of your site to group all Web Services in the site in a single folder.
2. Next, right-click this new folder and choose Add New Item. Click the Web Service item, call the service NameService.asmx, and make sure that your preferred programming language and Place Code in Separate File are selected, as shown in Figure 10-7.
3. Click Add to add the service to the site. Notice how the .asmx file is added to the WebServices folder while the Code Behind file is placed in the site's App_Code folder shown in Figure 10-8.

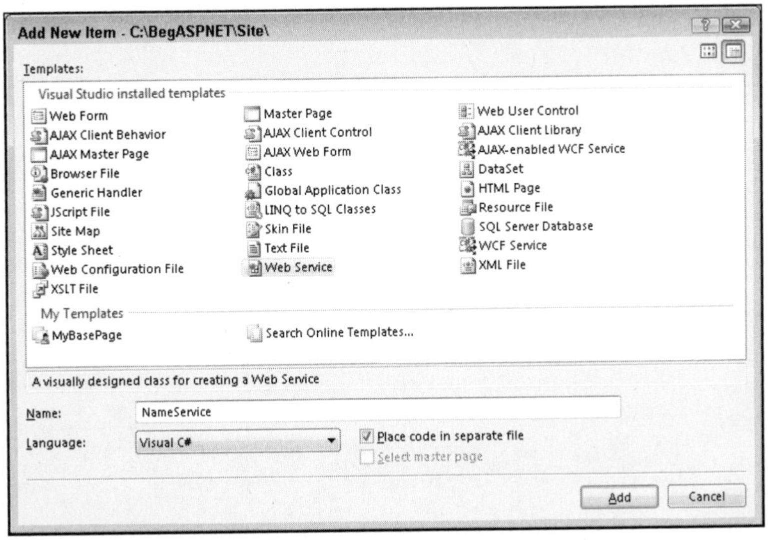

Figure 10-7

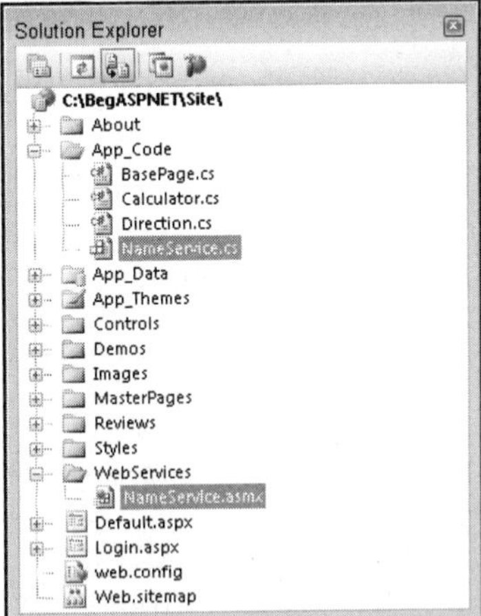

Figure 10-8

4. Open the NameService file in the App_Code folder and change the code for the `HelloWorld` method so it accepts a string and returns a personalized greeting. You should end up with code like this:

VB.NET

```
<WebMethod()> _
Public Function HelloWorld(ByVal yourName As String) As String
  Return String.Format("Hello {0}", yourName)
End Function
```

C#

```
[WebMethod]
public string HelloWorld(string yourName)
{
  return string.Format("Hello {0}", yourName);
}
```

5. Save all your changes, right-click NameService.asmx in the Solution Explorer, and choose View in Browser. Once the browser is done loading, you get a page that lists all the public Web Services defined in the NameService.asmx service. In this exercise, you should only see `HelloWorld`, shown in Figure 10-9.

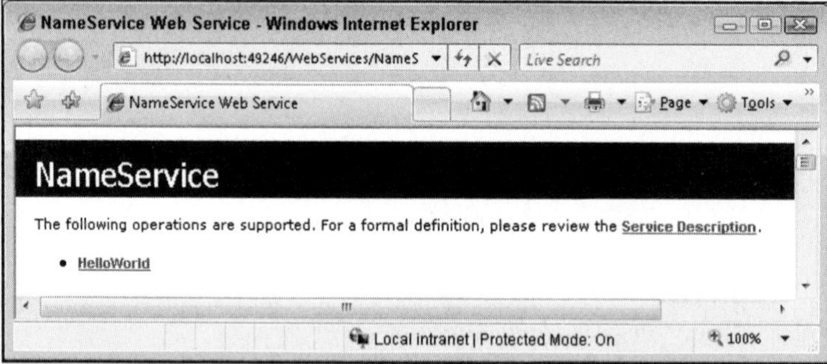

Figure 10-9

6. Click the `HelloWorld` link and you'll be taken to a page where you can test out the service. Type your name in the `yourName` field and then click Invoke. A new window opens (see Figure 10-10), showing the XML that has been returned by the Web Service.

Figure 10-10

How It Works

Web Services are essentially methods that can be called over the network, like the Internet or your local network. They are designed to enable applications to communicate and exchange data with each other. The underlying message format is XML, as you can see in Figure 10-10 that displays the result of the `HelloWorld` method.

When you add a Web Service to your projects, not all methods in this file become web-callable methods automatically. To expose a method as a service, you need to apply the `WebMethod` attribute:

VB.NET

```
<WebMethod()> _
Public Function HelloWorld(ByVal yourName As String) As String
```

C#

```
[WebMethod]
public string HelloWorld(string yourName)
```

With this attribute, the method is visible for the outside world, and can thus be accessed by external systems. When you open an .asmx file in the browser, you automatically get a test page that lets you try out your services. In the case of the HelloWorld service, you submitted your name and clicked the Invoke button to send this name as a parameter to the service. The service responded by adding your name to the welcome message and then returned it as a string using `String.Format`:

VB.NET

```
Public Function HelloWorld(ByVal yourName As String) As String
  Return String.Format("Hello {0}", yourName)
End Function
```

C#

```
public string HelloWorld(string yourName)
{
  return string.Format("Hello {0}", yourName);
}
```

As a first argument, the `String.Format` method takes a string that can contain numeric placeholders wrapped in a pair of curly braces (`{}`). Then for each numeric value, you supply a string value as subsequent parameters. In the previous example there is only one placeholder, but you can easily extend the call to the `Format` method with more parameters. For example, if you wanted to format a string with a first and last name, you'd use this code:

VB.NET

```
Return String.Format("Hello {0} {1}", firstName, lastName)
```

C#

```
return string.Format("Hello {0} {1}", firstName, lastName);
```

The `String.Format` method is great to make your strings much more readable. Instead of messy string concatenation using `&` or `+`, you simply define placeholders in the string, and then supply the values at runtime.

Finally, the Web Service method returns the welcome message as a string. The Web Service runtime then takes care of sending this return value to the calling code; the test page in this example shows the return value as a raw XML string.

Although this is a trivial example, the concepts you have seen here also work for complex Web Services that exchange extensive data that goes beyond simple strings. Obviously, the test page is only used to test whether your service operates correctly. In real Web Services the data is usually consumed by other code, like a web application or client-side JavaScript. You'll see how the latter works in the following section.

Using Web Services in Your Ajax Web Site

Before ASP.NET AJAX, calling Web Services from a client browser and working with the data they return involved writing a lot of code; especially if you wanted it to work in all major browsers like Internet Explorer and Firefox. Fortunately, the Ajax Framework shields you from all the complexity and code that is needed to consume a Web Service. All you need to do is add an attribute to the Web Service to mark it as a service that can be called by a script. Then you register the service in the `ScriptManager` and write a few lines of JavaScript to invoke the service and receive its return value. This only works for services that are defined within your own web site as you'll see next. If you want to call services that are not on the same domain as the page that calls them, you need to write additional code. This falls outside the scope of this book, but *Professional ASP.NET 3.5: in C# and VB* (ISBN: 978-0470187579) shows you more about calling external web services.

In the following section you'll see how to configure your Web Services so they can be called by client-side script. In the Try It Out that follows you see how to use this knowledge and call a Web Service from a client page.

Configuring the Web Service

Earlier you saw how to mark a method as a Web Method by adding an attribute. This exposes the method to the outside world. To make a Web Service visible by client-side script also, you need to add an attribute to the *service class*. If you look at the `NameService` class in the App_Code, you see that the template already added the attribute for you, but commented it out:

VB.NET

```
' <System.Web.Script.Services.ScriptService()> _
```

C#

```
// [System.Web.Script.Services.ScriptService]
```

Simply remove the comment tags to expose the entire service as a client-script service.

Configuring the ScriptManager

Recall from an earlier section in this chapter that the ScriptManager control is a required component in almost all Ajax-related operations. It registers client-side JavaScript files (those used by the Ajax framework and optionally your own), takes care of partial-page updates with the UpdatePanel, and handles interaction with the Web Services you have defined in your web site. You can add a ScriptManager to an individual page or to the master page so it becomes available throughout your site.

After you add the ScriptManager, the next thing you need to do is tell the ScriptManager that you want to expose your Web Service to a client script. There are two ways to do this:

- In the ScriptManager in the master page
- In a content page that uses the Web Service, using the ScriptManagerProxy class

When you are going to use the Web Service in all or in most pages, you're best off declaring the Web Service in the master page's ScriptManager. You do this by giving the ScriptManager control a <Services> element that in turn contains a ServiceReference control that points to your public service. For example, to make the NameService.asmx service you created available in all pages in your site, you'd add the following highlighted code to the master page:

```
<asp:ScriptManager ID="ScriptManager1" runat="server">
  <Services>
    <asp:ServiceReference Path="~/WebServices/NameService.asmx" />
  </Services>
</asp:ScriptManager>
```

By referencing the service in the master page, it becomes available to all pages based on that master. This also means that each page will download the JavaScript files needed to run this service. This is a waste of bandwidth and resources if your page is not using the Web Service at all. So, for services that you use on only a few pages, you're better off referencing the service in the page itself. On a normal page that doesn't use a master page with its own ScriptManager you can simply add a ScriptManager to the Web Form directly. However, if you are using a master page that has its own ScriptManager (as is the case with the pages in the Planet Wrox web site) you need to use a ScriptManagerProxy control. Since you can only have one ScriptManager in a page, you can't add another one in a content page that uses your master page with the ScriptManager. Therefore you need the ScriptManagerProxy to serve as a bridge between the content page and the ScriptManager in the master page, giving you great flexibility as to where you register your services.

When you have the ScriptManagerProxy in place, you add the exact same <Services> element to it as you saw with the ScriptManager itself:

```
<asp:ScriptManagerProxy ID="ScriptManagerProxy1" runat="server">
  <Services>
    <asp:ServiceReference path="~/WebServices/NameService.asmx" />
  </Services>
</asp:ScriptManagerProxy>
```

The ScriptManagerProxy control makes it easy to register Web Services and JavaScript files that are used in just a few content pages only.

The following exercise demonstrates how to register and access your Web Service from client-side code using the ScriptManagerProxy.

Try It Out Calling Web Services from Client Code

In this exercise you register your Web Service in a ScriptManagerProxy control so it becomes available in one page only. In addition, you modify the service so its methods are accessible by script. Finally, you write some client-side JavaScript code that accesses the service and then displays its return value.

1. The first thing you need to do is add the ScriptService attribute to your service class to mark it as callable by client-side script. To do this, open the file NameService.vb or NameService.cs from the App_Code folder and uncomment the line that defines the attribute. You should end up with this code:

VB.NET

```
<System.Web.Script.Services.ScriptService> _
<WebService(Namespace:="http://tempuri.org/")> _
<WebServiceBinding(ConformsTo:=WsiProfiles.BasicProfile1_1)> _
<Global.Microsoft.VisualBasic.CompilerServices.DesignerGenerated()> _
Public Class NameService
  Inherits System.Web.Services.WebService
```

C#

```
[System.Web.Script.Services.ScriptService]
public class NameService : System.Web.Services.WebService
{
```

2. While you're at it, change the Namespace property of the WebService attribute. By default, the namespace looks like this:

VB.NET

```
<WebService(Namespace:="http://tempuri.org/")> _
```

C#

```
[WebService(Namespace = "http://tempuri.org/")]
```

Although this name is fine during development of your Web Services, it should really reflect the unique name of your service once you put it in a production environment. If you have your own domain name, you can change the namespace to something like http://www.yourdomain.com/. If you don't have your own domain, don't worry about it. Even with the Namespace set to the default value of http://tempuri.org/, things will work fine.

3. The next step is creating a page that uses the service and then registers it using a ScriptManagerProxy control. Add a new page in the Demos folder and call it WebServices.aspx. Make sure you base this page on your central BasePage template, so it has the correct master page set and inherits from the BasePage class in the App_Code

folder and then give it a `Title` like Web Services Demo. Once you add the page, drag a `ScriptManagerProxy` control from the Toolbox into the markup of the `cpMainContent` placeholder.

4. Within the `ScriptManagerProxy` element, add a `<Services>` element that in turn contains a `ServiceReference` with its `Path` set to the NameService you created earlier. Note that IntelliSense helps you pick the right file as soon as you type `Path="` by showing you a list with files. Click Pick URL at the bottom of the list and browse to the service file in the WebServices folder. You should end up with this code in the WebServices.aspx page:

```
<asp:Content ID="Content2" ContentPlaceHolderID="cpMainContent" runat="Server">
  <asp:ScriptManagerProxy ID="ScriptManagerProxy1" runat="server">
    <Services>
      <asp:ServiceReference Path="~/WebServices/NameService.asmx" />
    </Services>
  </asp:ScriptManagerProxy>
</asp:Content>
```

5. Right below the closing tag of the `<ScriptManagerProxy>`, add an `Input (Text)` and an `Input (Button)` by dragging them from the HTML category of the Toolbox. By using plain HTML elements and not ASP.NET Server Controls, you can see that the code you are going to write really executes at the client. Set the `id` of the text box to `txtYourName` and the `id` of the button to `btnSayHello`. Set the `value` of the button to `Say Hello`. You should end up with this markup:

```
</asp:ScriptManagerProxy>
<input id="txtYourName" type="text" />
<input id="btnSayHello" type="button" value="Say Hello" />
```

6. Below these two lines, add a client-side JavaScript block with the following code:

```
<input id="btnSayHello" type="button" value="Say Hello" />
<script type="text/javascript">
  function HelloWorld()
  {
    var yourName = $get('txtYourName').value;
    NameService.HelloWorld(yourName, HelloWorldCallback);
  }

  function HelloWorldCallback(result)
  {
    alert(result);
  }

  $addHandler($get('btnSayHello'), 'click', HelloWorld);
</script>
```

7. Save all your changes by pressing Ctrl+Shift+S, and then request the page WebServices.aspx in your browser. Enter your name and then click the Say Hello button. If everything turned out well, you should be greeted with a message from the Web Service, repeating your name. Figure 10-11 shows the alert window in Mozilla Firefox.

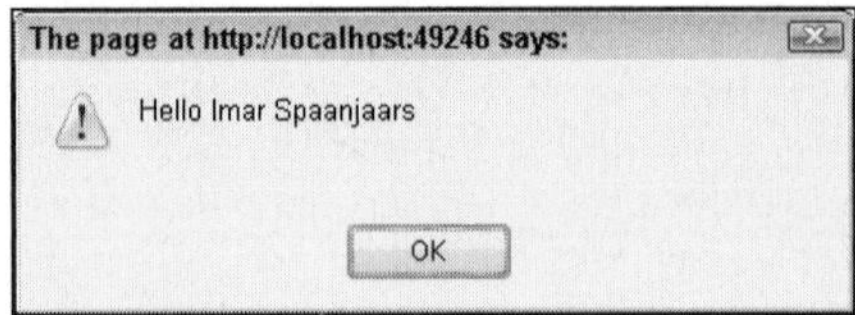

Figure 10-11

If you get an error instead of this message box, or you see a small yellow triangle in the bottom-left corner of the screen, make sure you typed the JavaScript exactly as in the code snippet. JavaScript is case sensitive, so make sure you get all the capitalization right. Also make sure that the JavaScript block you added in step 6 comes after the input box and button that you defined earlier. Finally, make sure that the path to your Web Service matches the actual path of your .asmx service file.

How It Works

The Web Service you used in this example is almost identical to the one you used in the test page in an earlier exercise. The only difference is the `ScriptService` attribute that marks the service as accessible by client-side script code.

To expose the service to the client-side script in your application, you need to register it. You can do this in the `<Services>` element of the `<ScriptManager>` in the master page. The downside of registering the Web Service in the master page is that its client JavaScript is referenced in each and every page in your site. For a service you only use once or twice, it's much better to add a `ScriptManagerProxy` to the specific page(s) and register the service there:

```
<asp:ScriptManagerProxy ID="ScriptManagerProxy1" runat="server">
  <Services>
    <asp:ServiceReference path="~/WebServices/NameService.asmx" />
  </Services>
</asp:ScriptManagerProxy>
```

All you need to do is refer to the service by setting the `Path` property. Just as with other server-side URLs you have seen in this book so far, you can use the tilde (~) syntax to refer to the application's root.

Once you have registered the service it becomes available in your client-side code. Note that IntelliSense in VWD is smart enough to discover the Web Services you have defined and registered. As soon as you type `NameService` followed by a dot in a client-side script block, IntelliSense kicks in again and shows the public methods it has found. Figure 10-12 shows the HelloWorld method highlighted in the IntelliSense list.

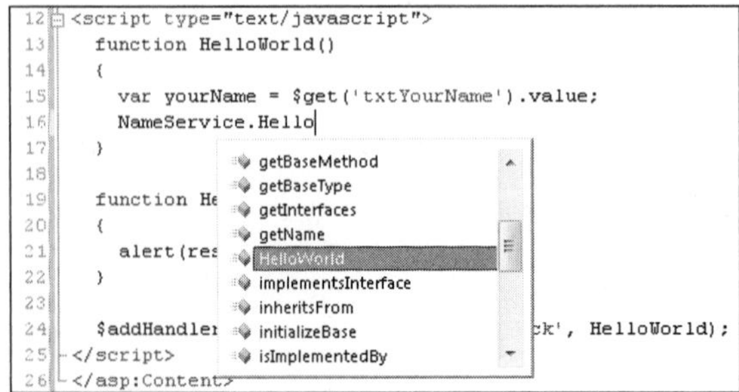

Figure 10-12

This makes it extremely easy to find the correct services you have defined in your site. This is a huge improvement over previous versions of Visual Studio that only had a fixed number of JavaScript-related items in the IntelliSense list. With Visual Web Developer 2008, IntelliSense is now actually able to look at your code and fill the IntelliSense list with the right variable names, methods, services, and so on that it finds in your code.

To see how the actual page works, and access the Web Service, take a look at the code in the `<script>` block.

The first code you need to look at is the `HelloWorld` method:

```
function HelloWorld()
{
  var yourName = $get('txtYourName').value;
  NameService.HelloWorld(yourName, HelloWorldCallback);
}
```

First, this code gets a reference to the text box you created earlier. Normally, with plain JavaScript you would use `document.getElementById('txtYourName')` to get at the text box. However, the client-side Ajax Framework offers a shortcut called `$get` that essentially performs the same function. Once you have a reference to the text box, you can access its value property to get the name the user entered.

This name is then sent to the Web Service method `HelloWorld` with the following code:

```
NameService.HelloWorld(yourName, HelloWorldCallback);
```

The first argument of the call to `HelloWorld` is the argument that the Web Service method expects: a string holding your name. The second argument, `HelloWorldCallback`, is a reference to a method that is triggered when the service gives back its result. This is called the callback method as it's the one called after the service has returned its information.

By design, the call to the Web Service is made *asynchronously*. This means the call to the service is made in a separate thread and the `HelloWorld` method exits shortly afterward. Because it can potentially take a long time for the Web Service to respond, you need to designate a method that is responsible for handling the response when it comes back from the service. In this case, this responsible method is called `HelloWorldCallback` although you could give the method any name you like.

In addition to this success callback, you could add another one that is triggered when the Web Service somehow fails, for example because the network connection is down or because the service threw an exception. In that case, the call to `HelloWorld` would look like this:

```
NameService.HelloWorld(yourName, HelloWorldCallback, ErrorCallback);
```

The `ErrorCallback` function could then look like this:

```
function ErrorCallback(error)
{
  alert(error.get_message());
}
```

The error object that is passed to this method has convenient methods and properties to display information about the exception. As in the example, you use `get_message()` to get at the original exception that occurred at the server.

If everything goes according to plan, the call to `HelloWorld` triggers the Web Service method `HelloWorld`. This method receives the name and returns a friendly welcome message, as you have seen before. When the Web Service returns its value, the `HelloWorldCallback` method is invoked. This method has a `result` parameter that holds the return value of the Web Service:

```
function HelloWorldCallback(result)
{
  alert(result);
}
```

In the previous exercise the `result` is a simple string. So you can use `alert(result)` to directly display the result in a JavaScript alert window.

In other situations the result parameter could hold more complex objects that provide access to its properties. The cool thing about the ASP.NET AJAX Framework is that most of the work to handle these complex objects is done for you transparently. If you return a complex object like a `Person`, an `Order`, or a `Review` from a Web Service, the ASP.NET AJAX Framework makes this object available in a client-side script automatically, without the need to write custom code to transform the object from a server-site instance to something that your client-side JavaScript understands.

The final thing you need to look at is how everything started in the first place. When you clicked the button, the client-side `HelloWorld` function was triggered automatically. But how is this possible? The answer is in the mysterious call to `$addHandler`:

```
$addHandler($get('btnSayHello'), 'click', HelloWorld);
```

The `$addHandler` is actually a shortcut to the `addHandler` method of the `Sys.UI.DomEvent` class defined in the Ajax Framework. You can use it to register event handlers for specific events of the objects in your pages. This is similar to the event handlers you have seen so far in VB.NET and C# server-side code.

In this example, `$get` is used again to get a reference to the button. Its `click` event is then hooked to the `HelloWorld` method. This means that whenever you click the button, the code in the `HelloWorld` function is executed.

Just like `$get`, the `$addHandler` method is a convenient shortcut that works cross-browser to register events. While it is possible to register events for events like a `Button`'s `click` without the client-side Ajax Framework, the `$addHandler` method makes it very easy to register events in a clear, concise, and cross-browser way, which also gives you some IntelliSense as an added bonus.

The cool thing about `$get` and `$addHandler` is that you can use them in any site. All you need to do is include the `ScriptManager` control in a master or content page and you're ready to use the client-side framework. You don't need to use Web Services or other Ajax-related controls in your page to make this work. This makes it very easy to write advanced JavaScript functionality with the least amount of code.

Obviously, the `NameService` you saw in this chapter has little real-world usage. However, the principles of Web Services you learned in this chapter are easily applied by more complex services as well, allowing you to access data on the server from client-side JavaScript with just a few lines of code.

You'll see the `NameService` again in Chapter 17 when debugging is discussed. In that chapter you'll step through the code line by line so you can see what code executes and in what order.

This Is Just the Beginning

So far you have seen a few of the methods and objects that the client-side Ajax Framework has to offer. However, `$get` and `$addHandler` are just the tip of the iceberg. The client-side framework contains six namespaces and a global namespace that in turn give you access to over 30 classes with hundreds of useful methods that help you in building rich, client-side web interfaces.

You can use the client-side framework to set up and handle page events like `load` and `unload`, make requests to other web pages using the `WebRequest` class, present data in different formats respecting the client's cultural settings with code in the `CultureInfo` class, and work with many of the extension methods for standard JavaScript types such as `startsWith` and `endsWith` for string variables.

For a detailed reference of the entire client-side Ajax Framework, check out the official documentation at `www.asp.net/AJAX/Documentation/Live/ClientReference/`. In addition, check out *Professional ASP.NET 2.0 Ajax* by Matt Gibb and Dan Wahlin.

Practical Ajax Tips

Remember these tips to help you create better user experiences:

- Since the content for the `UpdateProgress` panels is only visible during an Ajax page update, you'll find that it's hard to design its contents. You only see the content for a few seconds or less and only after you cause a postback to the server. To make it easier to design the `UpdateProgress` panels, you should first design the message outside of the `UpdateProgress` panel. For example, in the exercise from this chapter, you should move the `<div id="PleaseWait">` outside any other controls so it's always visible. You can then change the HTML and the CSS for the `<div>` until it looks exactly right. Then you can move the `<div>` back into the `UpdateProgress` panel so it's shown only during a partial page update.
- Whenever you are using an `UpdatePanel`, consider adding an associated `UpdateProgress` control as well. Even if you don't see the need because the `UpdatePanel` refreshes really fast, it may be worth adding the `UpdateProgress` for people on slow computers or slow networks. Or better yet: add an `UpdateProgress` to the master page in a convenient and visible area of the page (in the Footer region for example). Don't set `AssociatedUpdatePanelID` to anything so the progress panel will show on any Ajax callback. This way, you don't need lots of different waiting indicators in different areas of the page.
- Don't overuse `UpdatePanel` controls. In many situations, the *perceived* performance of an application increases when using `UpdatePanel` controls even if the true performance is the same. This is a good thing, as your users think your application is faster than without an `UpdatePanel`. However, using too many `UpdatePanel` controls may confuse your users, especially when they are not bound to an `UpdateProgress` control that tells them something is going on.

Summary

Ajax is a broad and very interesting technology that can really add a lot of value to your site. It can be divided in two different areas: the server-side controls and the client-side JavaScript Framework.

To start with, the `UpdatePanel` control enables you to create flicker-free pages in no time. All you need to do is wrap some content in an `UpdatePanel` control, add a `ScriptManager`, and you're done. To avoid adding the `ScriptManager` to every single page that needs it, you can add it to the master page for the site so it becomes available throughout the site.

Although the `UpdatePanel` solves some problems related to ugly page refreshes, it also comes with its own issues. Because the page no longer really reloads, the user may be unaware of the fact the page is busy processing and may start clicking buttons again, causing problems at the server, like the same e-mail message being sent more than once. To overcome this problem, you should consider attaching an `UpdateProgress` control to every `UpdatePanel` you use. The contents of the `UpdateProgress` control are shown during an Ajax page refresh, so the user gets a visual cue something is going on. To stop the `UpdateProgress` from showing up during very short page refreshes, you set the `DisplayAfter` property, which postpones the display of the `UpdateProgress` for the specified amount of time.

Besides these very useful server-side controls, the ASP.NET AJAX Framework also comes with a rich client-side framework that enables you to access Web Services in your site with just a few lines of code. The Web Services you create often look similar to other methods you have created so far. The biggest difference is that you define them within a class that inherits from `System.Web.Services.WebService` in an ASMX file with a separate Code Behind file in the App_Code folder.

After you have created the Web Service, you mark individual methods with the `WebMethod` attribute so they become available to calling code.

You can then call the Web Service using the format `ServiceName.MethodName`. Since Web Services are called asynchronously, you need to specify a method that is designed to handle the response from the Web Service. In the examples you saw, this was the `HelloWorldCallback` method. Inside this method, you can access the `result` parameter that is passed from the web method to the client code.

To work with controls in the page, for example, to gather user input or to display results from a Web Service, you have the rich client-side Ajax Framework at your disposal. This framework gives you hundreds of useful methods to work with almost every aspect of your page in the browser. All you need to do is include a `ScriptManager` control in your master or content page and you can use the entire client-side Ajax framework in your own web pages.

Although Ajax itself is a very compelling technology, it becomes even more useful in richer, data-driven scenarios. For example, using an `UpdatePanel` control around the records returned from a database to avoid page flicker when sorting, filtering, or paging your data greatly enhances the user's browsing experience. You learn how to work with databases in Chapter 11. With the knowledge about Ajax you gained from this chapter, you will quickly create flicker-free database-driven web pages.

Exercises

1. The AJAX Extensions category of the Toolkit defines a `ScriptManager` and a `ScriptManagerProxy`. Explain the difference between these two controls, and explain when you should use the `ScriptManager` and when the `ScriptManagerProxy`.
2. How can you let your users know a partial page update is in progress?
3. To expose a method in your site as a web method that can be called by client-side script, you need to create a special class and apply two attributes. What class do you need to create, and what attributes do you need to apply?

Introduction to Databases

Being able to use a database in your ASP.NET 3.5 web sites is just as critical as understanding HTML and CSS: it's almost impossible to build a modern, full-featured web site without it. Databases are useful because they allow you to store data in a structured way and enable you to retrieve that data in a structured way again. The biggest benefit of databases is that they can be accessed at runtime, which means you are no longer limited to just the relatively static files you create at design time in Visual Web Developer. You can use a database to store reviews, musical genres, pictures, information about users (user names, e-mail addresses, passwords, and so on), log information about who reads your reviews, and much more, and then access that data from your ASPX pages.

This gives you great flexibility in the data you present, and the way you present it, enabling you to create highly dynamic web sites that can adapt to your visitor's preferences, to the content your site has to offer, or even to the roles or access rights that your users have.

To successfully work with a database in an ASPX page, this chapter teaches you how to access databases using a query language called *SQL* — or *Structured Query Language*. This language allows you to retrieve and manipulate data stored in a database. You will also see how to use the database tools in VWD to create tables and queries.

Although ASP.NET and the .NET Framework offer you many tools and technologies that allow you to work with databases without having a firm knowledge of the underlying concepts like SQL, it's still important to understand them. Once you know how to access a database, you'll find it easier to understand other technologies, like LINQ to SQL, which provides easier access to database operations directly from code.

This chapter serves as an introduction to working with databases. In particular, it looks at:

- What is a database, and what databases are usually used with ASP.NET pages?
- What is SQL, how does it look, and how do you use it?
- How do you retrieve data from a database using the `SELECT` statement?
- How do you manipulate data in a database using other SQL constructs?

- ❑ What are database relations and why are they important?
- ❑ What tools do you have available in VWD to manage objects like tables and queries, and how do you use these tools?

In the chapters that follow, you apply the things you learn in this chapter. In Chapter 12, you'll see how to use built-in controls to work with data in your database. In Chapter 13, you see how to use LINQ as an additional layer on top of your database to access data in an object-oriented way with minimal code.

In the following sections, you see what a database is, and what different kinds of databases are available to you.

What Is a Database?

By its simplest definition, a database is a collection of data that is arranged so it can easily be accessed, managed, and updated. For the purpose of this book, and the web sites you will build, it's also safe to assume that the data in the database is stored in an electronic format.

The most popular type of database is the *relational database*. It's the type of database that is frequently used in web sites and is also the type of database that is used in the remainder of the book. However, the relational database is not the only one. Other types exist, including flat-file, object-relational, and object-oriented databases, but these are less common in Internet applications.

A relational database has the notion of *tables* where data is stored in rows and columns, rather like a spreadsheet. Each row in a table contains the complete information about an item that is stored in the table. Each column, on the other hand, contains information about a specific property of that record.

The term relational refers to the way the different tables in the database can be related to each other. Instead of duplicating the same data over and over again, you store repeating data in its own table and then create a relationship to that data from other tables. Consider the simple table called `Review` in Figure 11-1. This table could store the CD or concert reviews that are presented on the Planet Wrox web site.

As you can see in Figure 11-1, each review is assigned to a musical genre like Grunge, Rock, and Techno. But what if you wanted to rename the genre Techno to something like Hardcore Techno? You would need to update all the records that have this genre assigned. If you had other tables that stored a genre, you would need to visit those tables as well and manually make the changes.

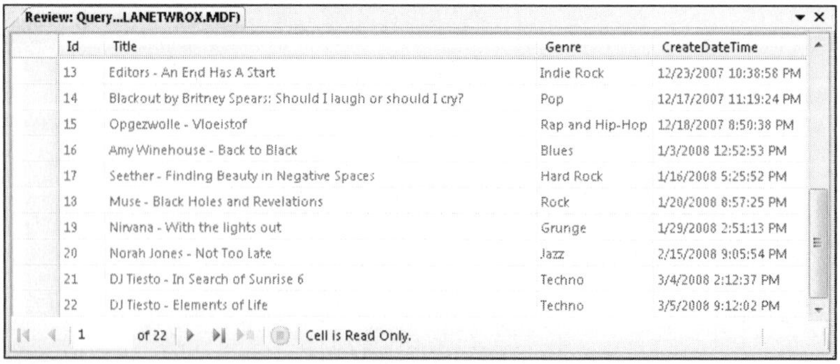

Review: Query...LANETWROX.MDF)

Id	Title	Genre	CreateDateTime
13	Editors - An End Has A Start	Indie Rock	12/23/2007 10:38:58 PM
14	Blackout by Britney Spears: Should I laugh or should I cry?	Pop	12/17/2007 11:19:24 PM
15	Opgezwolle - Vloeistof	Rap and Hip-Hop	12/18/2007 8:50:38 PM
16	Amy Winehouse - Back to Black	Blues	1/3/2008 12:52:53 PM
17	Seether - Finding Beauty in Negative Spaces	Hard Rock	1/16/2008 5:25:52 PM
18	Muse - Black Holes and Revelations	Rock	1/20/2008 8:57:25 PM
19	Nirvana - With the lights out	Grunge	1/29/2008 2:51:13 PM
20	Norah Jones - Not Too Late	Jazz	2/15/2008 9:05:54 PM
21	DJ Tiesto - In Search of Sunrise 6	Techno	3/4/2008 2:12:37 PM
22	DJ Tiesto - Elements of Life	Techno	3/5/2008 9:12:02 PM

1 of 22 Cell is Read Only.

Figure 11-1

A much better solution would be to use a separate table and call it `Genre`, for example. This table could store the name of a genre and an ID that uniquely identifies each genre. The `Review` table then gets a relation to the `Genre` table and only stores its ID instead of the entire name. Figure 11-2 shows the conceptual model for this change.

With just the ID of the genre now stored in the `Review` table, it's easy to rename a genre. All you need to do is change the name of the genre in the `Genre` table, and all tables with a relation to that genre pick up the change automatically. Later in this chapter, you'll see how to create and make use of relations in your relational database.

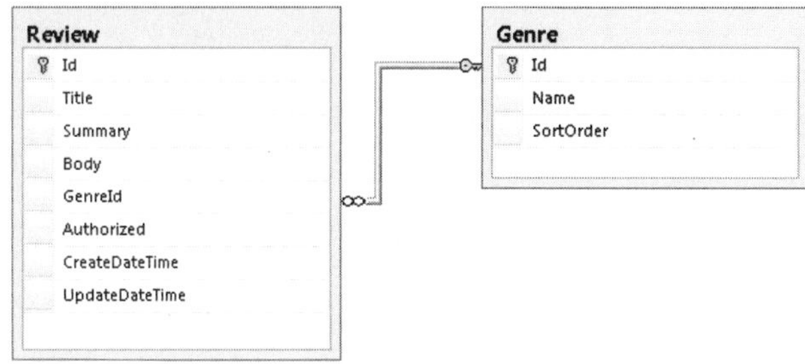

Figure 11-2

Different Kinds of Relational Databases

You can use many different kinds of databases in your ASP.NET projects, including Microsoft Access, SQL Server, Oracle, and MySQL. However, the most commonly used database in ASP.NET 3.5 web sites is probably SQL Server from Microsoft. This book focuses on using Microsoft SQL Server 2005 Express Edition, as it comes for free with VWD and has a lot to offer out of the box. Also, since the database engine is identical to that of the commercial versions of SQL Server, it's easy to upgrade to those versions at a later stage in the development cycle. This upgrade path is described in more detail in Appendix B.

To work with the data in the database, SQL Server (and all other relational database systems) supports a query language called SQL.

Using SQL to Work with Database Data

To get data in and out of a database, you need to use *Structured Query Language* (SQL). This is the de facto language for querying relational databases that almost all relational database systems understand. There are a number of clear standards, with the most popular one being the ANSI 92 SQL standard. Besides the grammar that this standard supports, many database vendors have added their own extensions to the language, giving it a lot more flexibility and power on their own system, at the cost of decreased interoperability with other systems.

Microsoft SQL Server 2005 database is no exception, and supports most of the grammar that has been defined in the ANSI 92 SQL Standard. On top of this standard, Microsoft has added some proprietary extensions. Collectively, the two are referred to as T-SQL, or Transact SQL. I'll stick to the term SQL for the remainder of this book.

In the following sections, you see how to use SQL against a SQL Server 2005 database to retrieve and manipulate data in your database. However, before you can write your first SQL statement, you need to know how to connect to your database first. The following exercise shows you how to connect to the sample database that comes with the downloadable code for this book.

Try It Out Connecting to the SQL Server Sample Database

In this exercise you learn how to connect to and work with a database from within VWD. To give you something to work with, the code download for this chapter comes with a sample database that contains a few tables. To be able to access the database from within VWD, the account that you use to log on to your Windows machine needs at least read and write permissions to the folder where the database resides. If you are logged on as an Administrator, there's a fair chance this is already the case. When you get errors while accessing the database in the next exercise, refer to Chapter 18, section "Understanding Security in IIS" for detailed instructions about setting up the proper permissions.

1. For this Try It Out exercise you need a clean, empty web site, which you can create by choosing File ➪ New Web Site (or File ➪ New ➪ Web Site) in Visual Web Developer. Don't follow this exercise with the Planet Wrox web site you've been working on so far or you'll get in trouble later when a database with the same name is used. Remember the location where you save the new web site; you'll need it in the next step.

2. After you have created the new web site, ensure that your account has sufficient permissions to write to its App_Data folder. Since Visual Web Developer, and thus the built-in web server, runs under the account that you use to log in to Windows, you need to make sure that your account has the correct permissions. To this end, locate the folder App_Data of the web site you created in step 1 using Windows Explorer, right-click it, and choose Properties. Switch to the Security tab, and ensure that your account (or a group you have been assigned to) has at least the Modify permission, as shown in Figure 11-3.

   If you don't have a Security tab, or your account is not listed, refer to the section titled "Configuring the File System" in Chapter 18 for detailed instructions on adding your own account to this list.

3. Open the Resources folder at `C:\BegASPNET\Resources`. If you don't have this folder, refer to the instructions in the Introduction of this book. Then open the Chapter 11 folder and select the files PlanetWrox.mdf and PlanetWrox_log.ldf. Arrange VWD and the Windows Explorer side by side and then drag the two selected files into the App_Data folder of your web site in Visual Web Developer. Click Yes when you're asked whether you want to overwrite the .ldf file that VWD created automatically as soon as you dropped the .mdf file in the App_Data folder. The .mdf file is the actual database and contains the actual tables and records, while the .ldf file is used to keep track of changes made to the database.

4. Double-click the database file in the Solution Explorer. Doing so opens the database in the Database Explorer (called the Server Explorer in the commercial versions of Visual Studio).

5. You can now expand the connected database to access its objects like the tables it contains, shown in Figure 11-4.

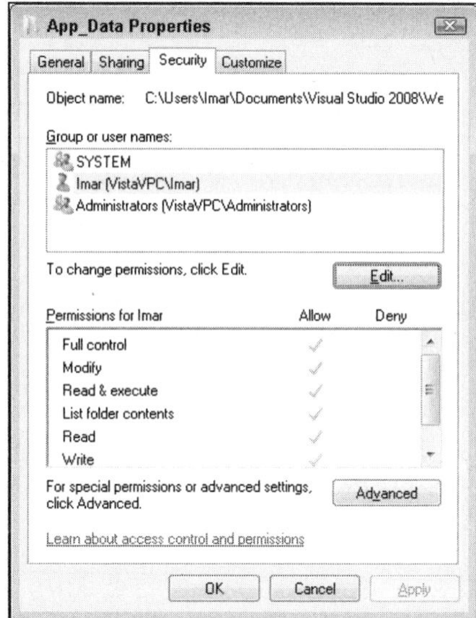

Figure 11-3

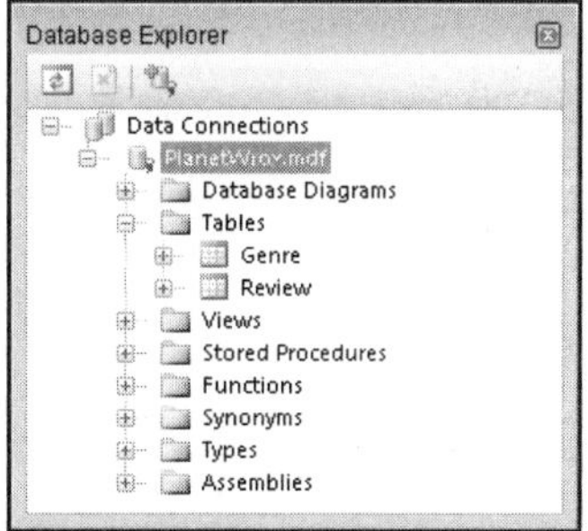

Figure 11-4

How It Works

To be able to access a database from within VWD, it needs to be registered in the Database Explorer window under Data Connections. In most cases, adding a database is as simple as adding the database to your App_Data folder and double-clicking it. However, when security on your system is tight, or you are not connecting to a physical SQL Server data file located in your web site, connecting to a database may be a bit trickier. In those cases, refer to the section "Understanding Security in IIS" in Chapter 18 and Appendix B for more details about configuring your system. You should use the App_Data folder only for data that is used at server, like databases and text files. Because the web server blocks access to this folder for remote browsers, you can't use it to store images that must be downloaded by the client.

When you have a connection to your database in the Database Explorer you can work with the objects in the database. Note that the previous Try It Out didn't make any changes to the web site. In a later exercise you see how to store the information about the connection to the database (called the *connection string*) in the web.config file.

However, first you need to understand how you can access and change the data in your database.

Retrieving and Manipulating Data

When interacting with databases, you'll spend a good deal of time retrieving and manipulating data. Most of it comes down to four distinct types of operations, grouped under the *CRUD* acronym: *Create, Read, Update,* and *Delete.*

Since these data operations are so crucial, the next couple of sections show you how to use them in detail.

Reading Data

To read data from a database, you typically use a few different concepts. First, you need the ability to indicate the columns that you want to retrieve from the table you are querying. That is done with the `SELECT` statement. You need to indicate the table(s) you want to select the data from using the `FROM` keyword. Then you need a way to filter the data, making sure only the records you're interested in are returned. You can filter the data using the `WHERE` clause in the SQL statement. Finally, you can order your results using the `ORDER BY` clause.

Selecting Data

To read data from one or more database tables, you use the `SELECT` statement. In its most basic form, the `SELECT` statement looks like this:

```
SELECT ColumnName [, AnotherColumnName] FROM TableName
```

Here, the parts between the square brackets are considered optional. For example, to retrieve all rows from the `Genre` table and only select their `Id` and `Name` columns you use this SQL statement:

```
SELECT Id, Name FROM Genre
```

Right after the `SELECT` statement comes a comma-separated list of column names. You can have only one or as many columns as you like here. Instead of explicitly specifying the column names, you can also use the asterisk (*) character to indicate you want all columns to be returned. However, using `SELECT *` is usually considered a poor programming practice so it's better to explicitly define each column you want to retrieve.

Right after the `FROM` keyword you specify the name of the table from which you want to retrieve data. The previous example showed only one table (the `Genre` table), but you'll see later that you can also specify multiple tables using joins.

Although the SQL language is not case sensitive, it's common practice to write all keywords like `SELECT` *and* `FROM` *in all caps. Additionally, in this book I use Pascal Casing — where each new word is capitalized — for names of tables, columns, and so on. For example, the date and time a certain review is created are stored in a column called* `CreateDateTime` *in the* `Review` *table.*

Filtering Data

To filter data, you use the `WHERE` clause with which you indicate the criteria that you want your data to match. For example, to retrieve the ID of the Grunge genre you use the following SQL statement:

```
SELECT Id FROM Genre WHERE Name = 'Grunge'
```

Note that the word Grunge is wrapped in single quotes. This is required for text data types and dates when you filter data or want to send values to an `INSERT` or `UPDATE` statement that allows you to create new or change existing records as explained later. You can't use them for numeric or Boolean types, though, so to get the name of the genre with an ID of 8 you would use the following statement:

```
SELECT Name FROM Genre WHERE Id = 8
```

The previous two examples show a `WHERE` clause that uses the equals symbol for an exact match. However, you can also use other operators for different criteria. The following table lists a few popular comparison operators you can use in your `WHERE` clauses.

Operator	Description
=	The *equals* operator matches only when the left side and the right side of the comparison are identical.
>	The *greater than* operator matches when the left side of the comparison represents a larger value than the right side.
>=	The *greater than or equal* operator matches when the left side of the comparison is equal to or larger than the right side.
<	The *less than* operator matches when the left side of the comparison represents a smaller value than the right side.
<=	The *less than or equal* operator matches when the left side of the comparison is equal to or smaller than the right side.
<>	The *not equals* operator does the reverse of the equals operator and matches when the left side and the right side of the comparison are different.

To combine multiple `WHERE` criteria, the SQL language supports a number of logical operators like `AND` and `OR`. In addition, it supports other operators to search for text and to specify ranges. The following table lists a few of the operators and describes what they are used for.

Operator	Description
AND	Allows you to join two expressions. For example the WHERE clause: `... WHERE Id > 20 AND Id < 30` gives you all records with IDs that fall between 20 and 30 (with 20 and 30 themselves not included).
OR	Allows you to define multiple criteria of which only one has to match (although more matches are allowed). For example, this WHERE clause: `... WHERE Id = 12 OR Id = 27` gives you all the records with an ID of 12 or 27.
BETWEEN	Allows you to specify a range of values that you want to match with a lower and upper bound. For example: `... WHERE Id BETWEEN 10 AND 35` gives you all records whose IDs are between 10 and 35 (including 10 and 35 themselves if they exist in the database).
LIKE	Used to determine if a value matches a specific pattern. You can use wild cards like % (any string of zero or more characters) and the underscore ([_]; any single character) to match specific parts of the value. For example, the following WHERE clause: `... WHERE Name LIKE '%rock%'` returns all genres that have rock in their name, including Indie Rock, Hard Rock and so on.

After you have defined your filtering requirements with the WHERE clause, you may want to change the order in which the results are returned from the database. You do this with the ORDER BY clause.

Ordering Data

The ORDER BY clause comes at the end of the SQL statement and can contain one or more column names or expressions which can optionally include ASC or DESC to determine if items are sorted in ascending order (with ASC, which is the default if you leave out the keyword) or in descending order (using DESC).

For example, to retrieve all genres from the Genre table and sort them alphabetically by their name in ascending order, you can use this SQL statement:

```
SELECT Id, Name FROM Genre ORDER BY Name
```

Since ascending is the default order, you don't need to specify the ASC keyword explicitly, although you could if you wanted to. The next example is functionally equivalent to the previous example:

```
SELECT Id, Name FROM Genre ORDER BY Name ASC
```

If you wanted to return the same records but sort them in reversed order on their SortOrder column, you use this syntax:

```
SELECT Id, Name FROM Genre ORDER BY SortOrder DESC
```

Notice how you can order by columns in the `ORDER BY` statement that are not part of the `SELECT` statement as is the case with the `SortOrder` column. So, even though a specific column is not part of the final result set, you can still use it to order on.

In the next exercise, you see how to perform a number of queries against the sample database, giving you a good idea of how different queries affect the results returned from the database.

Try It Out Selecting Data from the Sample Database

In this exercise you use the database that you connected to in an earlier exercise. This database is only used for the samples in this chapter, so don't worry if you mess things up.

1. Open the Database Explorer (or the Server Explorer in the paid versions of Visual Studio), locate the Data Connection that you added earlier, expand it, and then expand the Tables node. You should see two tables, `Genre` and `Review`, as shown in Figure 11-5.

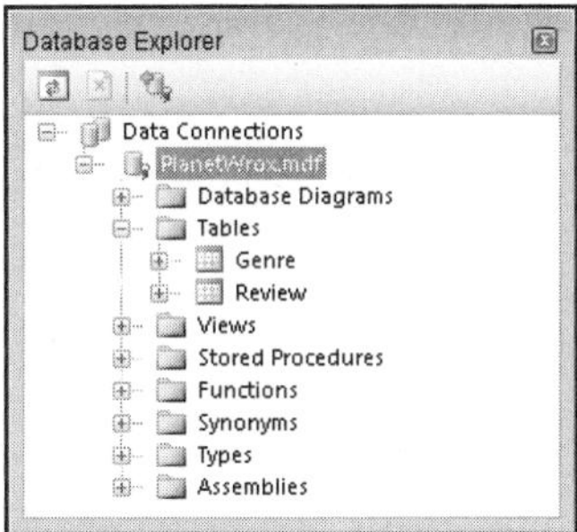

Figure 11-5

2. Right-click the `Genre` table and choose Show Table Data. In the main editor window you should now see a list with all the available genres in the `Genre` table, shown in Figure 11-6.

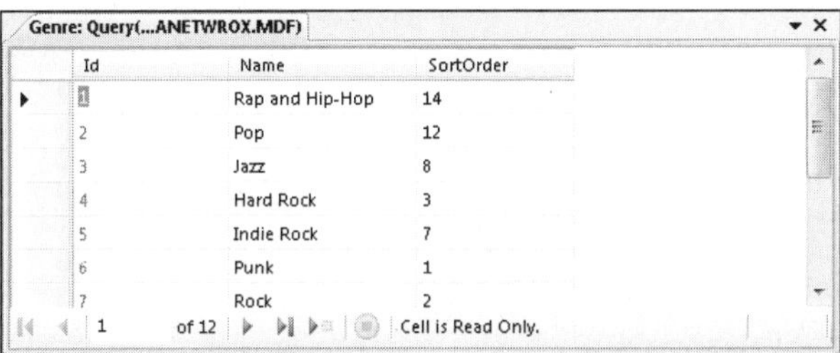

Figure 11-6

- Note that this is not just a list with all the records in the `Genre` table. It's actually the result of a SQL `SELECT` query that is executed when you opened the window. To see the query behind this list, ensure that the Query Designer toolbar, shown in Figure 11-7, is displayed on screen. If the toolbar isn't visible, right-click an existing toolbar and click Query Designer.

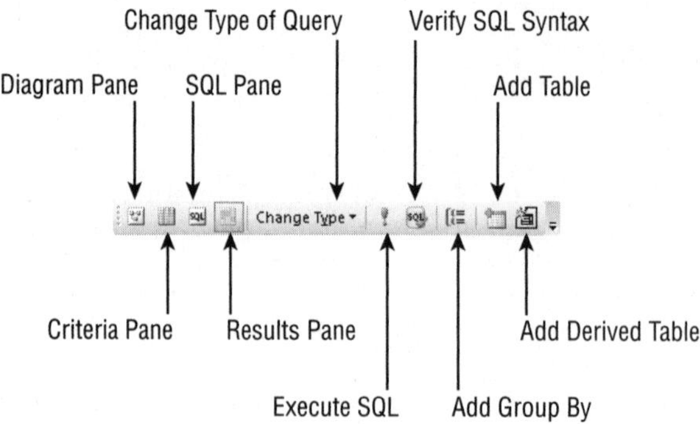

Figure 11-7

- On the toolbar, click the Criteria pane, the Diagram pane, and the SQL pane buttons to open their respective windows. Note that they are displayed in the Document Window in a stacked order. The first four buttons on the toolbar should now be in a pressed state and the Document Window is split in four regions, with each region corresponding to one of the buttons on the toolbar. Figure 11-8 shows the entire Document Window with the four panes.

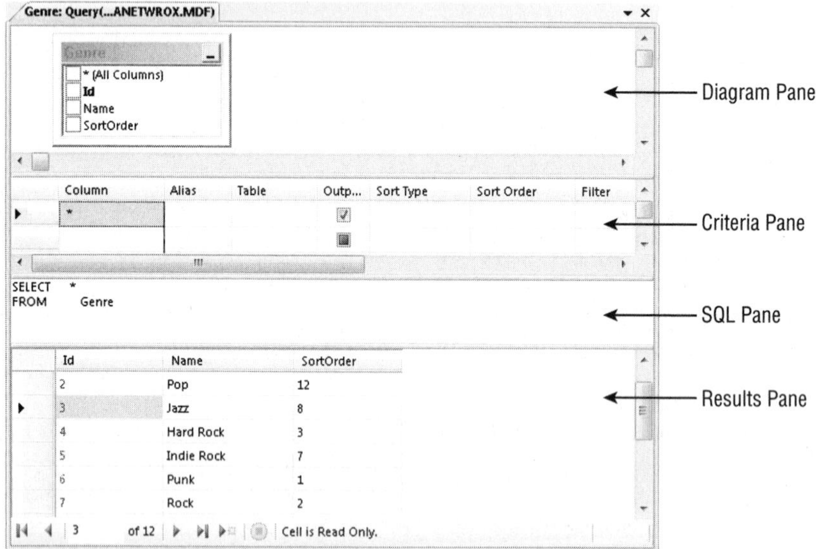

Figure 11-8

The SQL pane displays the SQL statement that is used to retrieve the genres displayed at the bottom of the screen. In this case, the SQL statement reads `SELECT * FROM Genre` to retrieve all columns and records from the table, but you can easily change that.

3. In the SQL pane, position your cursor right after the word `Genre`, press Enter once and then type `WHERE Id > 4`. Your complete SQL statement should end up like this:

```
SELECT * FROM Genre WHERE Id > 4
```

In your SQL pane, the query is split over multiple lines. That's fine, as SQL allows you to spread your statements over multiple lines without the need for a line continuation character.

4. To make sure the SQL statement is valid, click the Verify SQL Syntax button on the toolbar and then fix any errors your SQL statement may contain. Next, click the Execute SQL button (the one with the red exclamation mark on it) or press Ctrl+R. In both cases, the SQL statement is executed and the Results pane is updated to show all genres with an ID larger than 4.

5. Besides showing the results, VWD also changed your query. Instead of `SELECT *`, it has listed each column in your table explicitly. Now take a look at the Diagram pane; the top part of the dialog box in Figure 11-8 that shows your entire table. In the Diagram pane you can check and uncheck column names to determine whether they end up in the query. De-select the `SortOrder` column (don't accidentally change the checkmark of the Output column in the Criteria pane instead). Note that it also gets removed from the Criteria pane (visible in Figure 11-9) and the SQL statement in the SQL pane.

6. Take a look at the Criteria pane. It shows the two columns you are selecting. In the Filter column it shows the expression that filters all genres with an ID larger than 4, shown in Figure 11-9.

Column	Alias	Table	Output	Sort Type	Sort Order	Filter	Or...	Or...	Or...
Id		Genre	✓			> 4			
Name		Genre	✓						

Figure 11-9

In this pane you can modify the query without manually writing a lot of code. To see how you can apply an additional filter, type `LIKE '%rock%'` in the Filter cell for the `Name` row. This limits the results to all genres that contain the word `rock` and that have an ID that is larger than 4.

7. To determine the sort order, you can use the Sort Type column. You can do this for visible columns (for example, those that have their Output checkbox checked and end up in the final result set) but also for other columns. To order by the `SortOrder` column, click the cell under `Name` once. It changes and now shows a drop-down list instead. Choose `SortOrder` from the drop-down list. When you click or tab away from the field, VWD places a checkmark in the Output column. You can click that checkmark to remove the column again from the output so it remains available for ordering and filtering, but won't show up in the query results. However, for this exercise it's OK to leave the column selected.

8. Then in the Sort Type column choose Descending from the drop-down list for the `SortOrder`. Your final Criteria pane now looks like Figure 11-10.

Column	Alias	Table	Output	Sort Type	Sort Order	Filter	Or...	Or...	Or...
Id		Genre	✓			> 4			
Name		Genre	✓			LIKE '%rock%'			
SortOrder		Genre	✓	Descendi...	1				

Figure 11-10

While you make your changes using the Diagram and Criteria panes, VWD continuously updates the SQL pane. Your final SQL statement should now include the extra `WHERE` clause and the `ORDER BY` statement:

```
SELECT Id, Name, SortOrder
FROM Genre
WHERE (Id > 4) AND (Name LIKE '%rock%')
ORDER BY SortOrder DESC
```

9. Press Ctrl+R again (or click the Execute SQL button on the toolbar) and the Results pane will show the records from the `Genre` table that match your criteria, visible in Figure 11-11.

	Id	Name	SortOrder
▶	5	Indie Rock	7
	7	Rock	2
*	NULL	NULL	NULL

Figure 11-11

Note that the records are now sorted in descending order based on the `SortOrder` column.

How It Works

The Query Designer in VWD is a very helpful tool to create new queries against your database. Instead of hand coding the entire SQL statement in the SQL pane, you use the Diagram and Criteria panes to create your queries visually. Of course, you can still use the SQL pane to make manual tweaks to the SQL code that VWD generates for you.

The final query you executed returned all the records that contained the word *rock* and that had an ID larger than 4. The query shown in step 9 has a `WHERE` clause that consists of two parts: the first part limits the records returned to those with an ID larger than 4. The second part filtered the records to those that contain the text *rock*. The two criteria are both applied at the same time using the `AND` keyword, so only records with an ID larger than 4 *and* the word *rock* in their name are returned. Effectively, this returns the Indie Rock and Rock genres, while leaving out the Hard Rock genre because it has an ID of 4.

At the end, the result set is sorted in descending order on the `SortOrder` column using the syntax `ORDER BY SortOrder DESC`. Notice that `SortOrder` is an arbitrarily chosen name. You can easily give this column a different name, or order on a different column like the `Name` column to retrieve the genres in alphabetical order.

In this example, you saw how to retrieve data from a single table. However, in most real-world applications you get your data from multiple tables that are somehow related to each other. You define this relationship in your SQL syntax using the `JOIN` keyword.

Joining Data

A `JOIN` in your query allows you to express a relationship between one or more tables. For example, you can use a `JOIN` to find all the reviews from the `Review` table that have been published in a specific genre and then select some columns from the `Review` table together with the `Name` of the genre.

The basic syntax for a JOIN looks like the highlighted code:

```
SELECT
  SomeColumn
FROM
  LeftTable
INNER JOIN RightTable ON LeftTable.SomeColumn = RightTable.SomeColumn
```

The first part is the standard SELECT part of the query that you saw earlier while the second part introduces the keywords INNER JOIN to express the relationship between the two tables. This query only returns the records in the table LeftTable with a corresponding record in RightTable. For example, to return the Id and the Title of a review together with the name of the genre it belongs to, you use this SQL statement:

```
SELECT
  Review.Id, Review.Title, Genre.Name
FROM
  Review
INNER JOIN Genre ON Review.GenreId = Genre.Id
```

Note that in the SELECT statement each column is prefixed with the table name. This makes it clear what table you are referring to and avoids conflicts when multiple tables have similar column names (like the Id column that exists in both tables).

In addition to an INNER JOIN that only returns matching records, you can also use an OUTER JOIN. The OUTER JOIN allows you to retrieve records from one table regardless of whether they have a matching record in another table. The following example returns a list with all the genres in the system together with the reviews in each genre:

```
SELECT
  Genre.Id, Genre.Name, Review.Title
FROM
  Genre
LEFT OUTER JOIN Review ON Genre.Id = Review.GenreId
```

For each review assigned to a genre, a unique row is returned that contains the review's Title. However, even if a genre has no reviews assigned, the row is still returned.

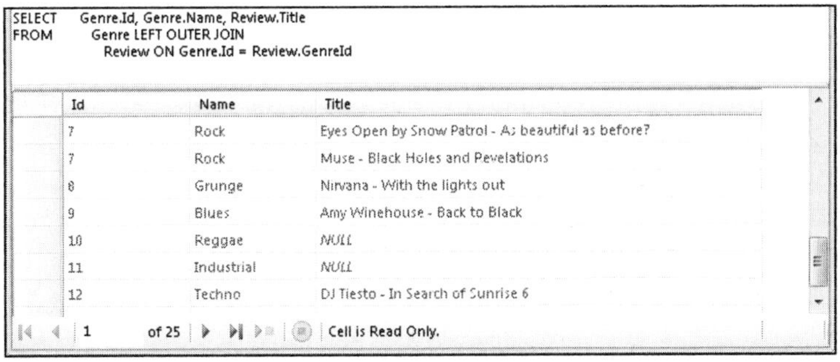

```
SELECT    Genre.Id, Genre.Name, Review.Title
FROM        Genre LEFT OUTER JOIN
              Review ON Genre.Id = Review.GenreId
```

Id	Name	Title
7	Rock	Eyes Open by Snow Patrol - As beautiful as before?
7	Rock	Muse - Black Holes and Revelations
8	Grunge	Nirvana - With the lights out
9	Blues	Amy Winehouse - Back to Black
10	Reggae	NULL
11	Industrial	NULL
12	Techno	DJ Tiesto - In Search of Sunrise 6

1 of 25 Cell is Read Only.

Figure 11-12

In Figure 11-12 you can see that the genre Rock is repeated multiple times, for each review in the `Review` table that has been assigned to that genre. Genres like Grunge and Blues have only one review attached to them, so they're listed only once. Finally, the Reggae and Industrial genres have no reviews associated with them. However, because the SQL statement uses a `LEFT OUTER JOIN`, those two genres (listed on the left side of the `JOIN`) are still returned. Instead of the Title of a review, that column now contains a `NULL` value to indicate there is no associated review.

Besides the `LEFT OUTER JOIN`, there is also a `RIGHT OUTER JOIN` that returns all the records from the table listed at the right side of the `JOIN`. `LEFT` and `RIGHT OUTER JOIN` statements are very similar, and in most cases you'll see the `LEFT OUTER JOIN`.

In addition, there are other joins including cross joins and self joins. For a detailed description of these types of joins, pick up a copy of the book *Beginning SQL Server 2005 Programming* by Robert Vieira (ISBN: 978-0-7645-8433-6).

You'll see how to use a very common type of join, the `INNER JOIN`, in the next Try It Out exercise.

Try It Out Joining Data

To join data from two tables, you need to write a `JOIN` statement in your code. To help you write the code, VWD tries to add a `JOIN` for you whenever you add a table to the Diagram pane. However, in most cases this `JOIN` is not correct, so you'll need to modify it manually.

1. In the Database Explorer (or Server Explorer) window, right-click the `Review` table and choose Show Table Data. You'll see all the reviews in the table appear. Next, enable the Diagram, Criteria, and SQL panes by clicking their respective buttons on the Query Designer toolbar.
2. Right-click an open spot of the Diagram pane next to the `Review` table and choose Add Table. Alternatively, choose Query Designer ➪ Add Table from the main menu.
3. In the dialog box that follows, click the `Genre` table and then click the Add button. Finally, click Close.
4. Look at the SQL statement that VWD generated. It didn't see the relationship between the `GenreId` column of the `Review` table and the `Id` column of the `Genre` table, so instead it joined both tables on their respective `Id` fields:

```
SELECT * FROM Review
INNER JOIN Genre ON Review.Id = Genre.Id
```

5. To correct this error, right-click the line that is drawn between the two tables and choose Remove.
6. Next, click the `GenreId` column of the `Review` table in the Diagram pane once and then drag it onto the `Id` column of the `Genre` table. As soon as you release the mouse, VWD creates a new `JOIN` in the SQL pane for you:

```
SELECT * FROM Review
INNER JOIN Genre ON Review.GenreId = Genre.Id
```

7. In the Criteria pane, click the left margin of the first row that contains the asterisk symbol to select the entire row and then press the Delete key or right-click the left margin and choose Delete. This removes the asterisk from the SQL statement. Alternatively, you can delete the asterisk from the SQL pane directly.

8. In the Diagram pane place a checkmark in front of the `Id` and `Title` columns of the `Review` table and in front of the `Name` column of the `Genre` table.

9. Finally, press Ctrl+R to execute the query. Your Document Window should now look like Figure 11-13, showing the results of the query at the bottom of the screen in the Results pane.

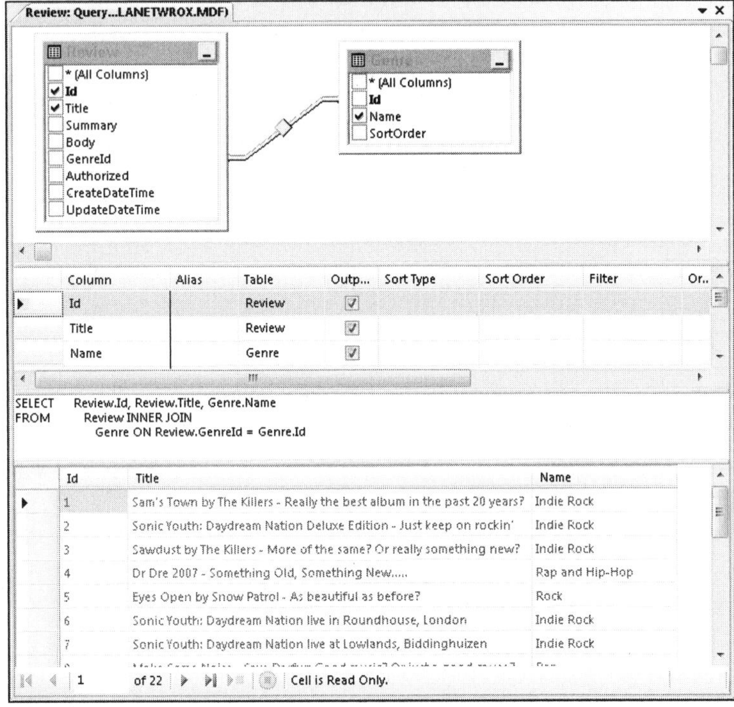

Figure 11-13

How It Works

By using a `JOIN` in your SQL statement, you tell the database how to relate records to each other. In the previous example, you created a relationship between the `GenreId` column of the review and the actual `Id` of the `Genre` table:

```
SELECT
  Review.Id, Review.Title, Genre.Name
FROM
  Review
INNER JOIN Genre ON Review.GenreId = Genre.Id
```

With this `JOIN`, you can retrieve data from multiple tables and present them in a single result set. The query processor of SQL Server returns the correct genre name for each review, as is shown in Figure 11-13.

Besides selecting data, you also need to be able to insert data into the database. This is done with the `INSERT` statement.

Creating Data

To insert new records in a SQL Server table, you use the `INSERT` statement. It comes in a few different flavors, but in its simplest form it looks like this:

```
INSERT INTO TableName (Column1 [, Column2]) VALUES (Value1 [, Value2])
```

Just as with the `WHERE` clause, you need to enclose string and date values in single quotes, while you can enter numbers and Boolean values directly in your SQL statement. The following snippet shows how to insert a new row in the `Genre` table:

```
INSERT INTO Genre (Name, SortOrder) VALUES ('Tribal House', 20)
```

After you have created data, you may want to edit it again. You do this with the `UPDATE` statement.

Updating Data

To update data in a table, you use the `UPDATE` statement:

```
UPDATE TableName SET Column1 = NewValue1 [, Column2 = NewValue2] WHERE Column3 = Value3
```

With the `UPDATE` statement, you use `Column = Value` constructs to indicate the new value of the specified column. You can have as many of these constructs as you want, with a maximum of one per column in the table. To limit the number of items that get updated, you use the `WHERE` clause, just as with selecting data as you saw earlier.

The following example updates the record that was inserted with the `INSERT` statement you saw earlier. It sets the `Name` to `Trance` and updates the `SortOrder` to `5` to move up the item a little in sorted lists. It also uses the unique ID of the new record (`13` in this example) in the `WHERE` clause to limit the number of records that get affected with the `UPDATE` statement.

```
UPDATE Genre SET Name = 'Trance', SortOrder = 5 WHERE Id = 13
```

Obviously, you may also have the need to delete existing records. It should come as no surprise that the SQL language uses the `DELETE` statement for this.

Deleting Data

Just as with the `SELECT` and `UPDATE` statements, you can use the `WHERE` clause in a `DELETE` statement to limit the number of records that get deleted. This `WHERE` clause is often very important, as you will otherwise wipe out the entire table instead of just deleting a few records.

When you write a `DELETE` statement, you don't need to specify any column names. All you need to do is indicate the table that you want to delete records from and an (optional) `WHERE` clause to limit the number of records that get deleted. The following example deletes the record that was inserted and updated in the previous two examples:

```
DELETE FROM Genre WHERE Id = 13
```

You'll see these SQL statements at work in the next exercise.

Try It Out Working with Data in the Sample Database

In this exercise, you put everything you learned so far in practice. In a series of steps, you'll see how to create a new record in the `Genre` table, select it again to find out its new ID, update it using the `UPDATE` statement, and finally delete the genre from the database. Although the examples themselves may seem pretty trivial, they are at the core of how SQL works. If you understand the examples from this section, you'll be able to work with the remaining SQL statements in this and coming chapters.

1. Open the Database Explorer window in your temporary test site and locate the `Genre` table in the database. Right-click it and choose Show Table Data. If the table was already open with an old query, you need to close it first by pressing Ctrl+F4. This gets rid of the existing SQL statement.
2. Click the first three buttons on the Query Designer toolbar (Diagram, Criteria, and SQL pane) to open up their respective panes.
3. In the Diagram pane, check the columns `Name` and `SortOrder`. Make sure you leave `Id` unchecked, as shown in Figure 11-14.

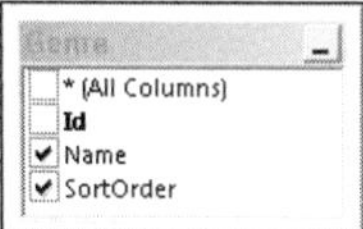

Figure 11-14

4. On the Query Designer toolbar click the Change Type button and then choose the third option: Insert Values. The query in the SQL pane is updated and now contains a template for the `INSERT` statement:

```
INSERT INTO Genre (Name, SortOrder) VALUES (,)
```

5. Between the parentheses for the `VALUES`, enter a name (between apostrophes) and a sort order for your genre separated by a comma:

```
VALUES ('Folk', 15)
```

6. Press Ctrl+R to execute the query. You should get a dialog box that tells you that your action caused one row to be affected as shown in Figure 11-15.

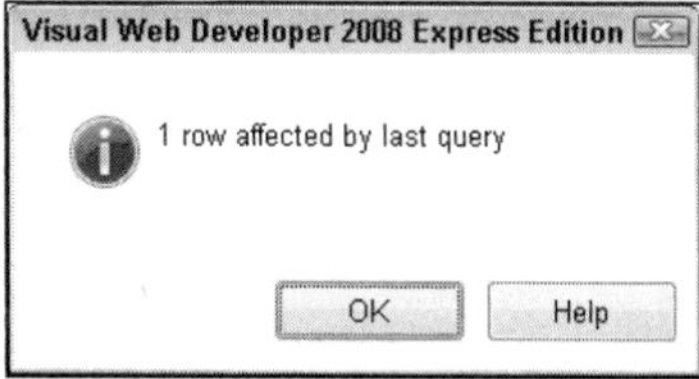

Figure 11-15

7. Click OK to dismiss the dialog box.
8. Clear out the entire SQL statement from the SQL pane (you can use Ctrl+A to select the entire SQL statement and then press the Delete key to delete it) and replace it with this code that selects all the genres and sorts them in descending order:

```
SELECT Id, Name FROM Genre ORDER BY Id DESC
```

9. Press Ctrl+R to execute this `SELECT` statement. The Results pane shows a list of genres with the one you just inserted at the top of the list. Note the ID of the newly inserted record. It should be 13 if you haven't inserted any record before although it's OK if you have a different ID.
10. Click the Change Type button on the toolbar again, this time choosing Update. Complete the SQL statement that VWD created for you so it looks like this:

```
UPDATE
  Genre
SET
  Name = 'British Folk',
  SortOrder = 5
WHERE
  Id = 13
```

11. Don't forget to replace the number 13 in the SQL statement with the ID you determined in step 9. Press Ctrl+R again to execute the query and you'll get a dialog box informing you that one record has been modified.
12. Once again, clear the SQL pane and then enter and execute the following query by pressing Ctrl+R:

```
SELECT Id, Name FROM Genre WHERE Id = 13
```

Replace the `Id` in the `WHERE` clause with the ID of the record you determined in step 9. You should see the updated record appear.

13. On the Query Designer toolbar, click the Change Type button and choose Delete. VWD changes the SQL statement so it is now set up to delete the record with an ID of 13:

```
DELETE FROM Genre WHERE (Id = 13)
```

14. Press Ctrl+R to execute the query and delete the record from the database.
15. To confirm that the record is really deleted, click the Change Type button once more and choose Select. Then choose one or more columns of the `Genre` table in the Diagram pane and press Ctrl+R again. You'll see that this time no records are returned, confirming the newly inserted genre has indeed been deleted from the database.

How It Works

In this short exercise, you carried out all four parts of the CRUD acronym, which gave you a look at the life cycle of data in a SQL Server database from creation to deletion.

You started off with an `INSERT` statement:

```
INSERT INTO Genre (Name, SortOrder) VALUES ('Folk', 15)
```

This creates a new record in the `Genre` table. As you will see in the next section, the `Id` column of the `Genre` table is an *identity column*, which means that each new record gets a new, sequential ID assigned automatically.

To retrieve that ID, you used a `SELECT` statement with an `ORDER BY` clause that orders the IDs in descending order, so the most recent ID was put on top of the list. Retrieving the new ID like this in a busy application is not reliable as you may end up with someone else's ID. You'll see later in the book how to retrieve the ID in a reliable way, but for the purpose of this exercise, the `ORDER BY` method works well enough.

Armed with the new ID, you executed an `UPDATE` statement to change the `Name` and `SortOrder` of the newly inserted genre. If you only want to update a single column with the `UPDATE` statement — say you want to change only the `Name` — you can simply leave out the other columns. For example, the following `UPDATE` statement changes only the `Name`, leaving all other columns at their original values:

```
UPDATE
  Genre
SET
  Name = 'British Folk'
WHERE
  Id = 13
```

Finally, at the end of the exercise, you executed a `DELETE` statement to get rid of the new record. It's always important to specify a `WHERE` clause when executing a `DELETE` or an `UPDATE` statement to stop you from clearing the entire table or from setting the names of all records to the same value.

```
DELETE FROM Genre WHERE (Id = 13)
```

This SQL statement simply deletes the record with an ID of 13. If the record exists, it gets deleted. If the record does not exist, no error is raised, but the dialog box in VWD shows you that zero records have been affected.

Up to this point, you have seen how to work with existing tables in a database. However, it's also important to understand how to create new tables with relationships yourself. This is discussed in the next section.

Creating Your Own Tables

Creating tables in a SQL Server 2005 database is easy using the built-in database tools that are part of VWD. You'll see how you can create your own tables in the database after the next section that briefly introduces you to the data types you have at your disposal in SQL Server 2005 and up.

Data Types in SQL Server

Just as with programming languages like Visual Basic .NET and C#, a SQL Server database uses different data types to store its data. SQL Server 2005 supports almost 30 different data types, most of which look similar to the types used in .NET. The following table lists the most common SQL Server data types together with a description and their .NET counter parts.

SQL 2005 Data Type	Description	.NET Data Type
`bit`	Stores Boolean values in a 0 / 1 format	`System.Boolean`
`char / nchar`	Contains fixed-length text. When you store text shorter than the defined length, the text is padded with spaces. The `nchar` stores the data in Unicode format, which allows you to store data for many foreign languages.	`System.String`
`datetime`	Stores a date and a time.	`System.DateTime`
`decimal`	Allows you to store large, fractional numbers.	`System.Decimal`
`float`	Allows you to store large, fractional numbers.	`System.Double`
`image`	Allows you to store large binary objects such as files. Although the name suggests that you can only use it to store images, this is not the case. You can use it to store any kind of document or other binary object.	`System.Byte[]`
`tinyint`	Used to store integer numbers ranging from 0 to 255.	`System.Byte`
`smallint`	Used to store integer numbers ranging from -32,768 to 32,767.	`System.Int16`
`int`	Used to store integer numbers ranging from -2,147,483,648 to 2,147,483,647	`System.Int32`
`bigint`	Used to store large integer numbers ranging from -9,223,372,036,854,775,808 to 9,223,372,036,854,775,807.	`System.Int64`
`text / ntext`	Used to store large amounts of text.	`System.String`
`varchar / nvarchar`	Used to store text with a variable length. The `nvarchar` stores the data in Unicode format, which allows you to store data for many foreign languages.	`System.String`
`uniqueidentifier`	Stores globally unique identifiers.	`System.Guid`

Some of these data types allow you to specify the maximum length. When you define a column of type `char`, `nchar`, `varchar`, or `nvarchar` you need to specify the length in characters. For example, an `nvarchar(10)` allows you to store a maximum of 10 characters. Starting with SQL Server 2005, these data types also allow you to specify `MAX` as the maximum size. With the `MAX` specifier, you can store data up to 2GB in a single column. For large pieces of text, like the body of a review, you should consider the `nvarchar(max)` data type. If you have a clear idea about the maximum length for a column (like a zip code or a phone number) or you want to explicitly limit the length of it, you should specify that length instead. For example, the title of a review could be stored in a `nvarchar(200)` column to allow up to 200 characters.

Understanding Primary Keys and Identities

To uniquely identify a record in a table, you can set up a *primary key*. A primary key consists of one or more columns in a table that contains a value that is unique across all records. When you identify a column as a primary key, the database engine will ensure that no two records can end up with the same value. A primary key can consist of just a single column (for example, a numeric column called `Id` that contains unique numbers for each record in the table) or it can span multiple columns, where the columns together form a unique ID for the entire record.

SQL Server also supports *identity columns*. An identity column is a numeric column whose values are generated automatically whenever a new record is inserted. They are often used as the primary key for a table. You see how this works in the next section when you create your own tables.

It's not a requirement to give each table a primary key, but it makes your life as a database programmer a lot easier, so it's recommended to always add one to your tables.

Creating primary keys and identity columns is really easy with Visual Web Developer's database tools as you'll see in the next Try It Out exercise.

Try It Out — Creating Tables in the Table Designer

In this exercise you will add two tables to a new database that you add to the Planet Wrox project. In a later exercise you learn how to create a relationship between the two tables in the database. Note that you should carry out the exercises in the Planet Wrox web site you have been building so far. You can close and delete the test site you created at the beginning of this chapter because you don't need it anymore.

1. Right-click the App_Data folder and choose Add New Item. In the dialog box that follows, click SQL Server Database, type **PlanetWrox.mdf** as the name, and then click Add to add the database to your site. The Database Explorer (or Server Explorer) should open automatically showing you the new database. If it doesn't, double-click PlanetWrox.mdf in the Solution Explorer.
2. On the Database Explorer, right-click the Tables node and choose Add New Table, as shown in Figure 11-16.

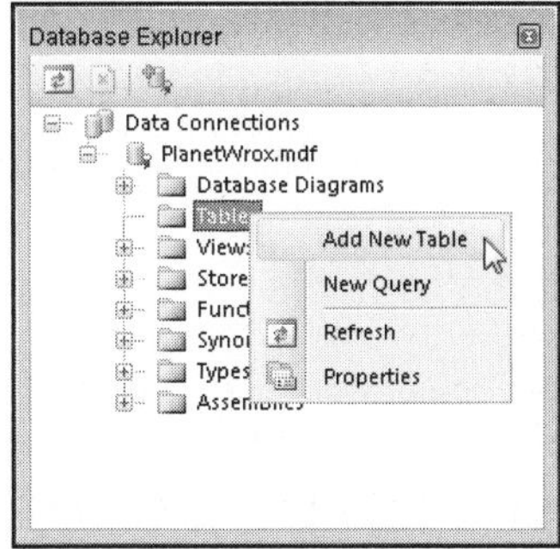

Figure 11-16

3. In the dialog box that follows, you can enter column names and data types that together make up the table definition. Create three columns for the `Id`, `Name`, and `SortOrder` of the `Genre` table so the dialog box ends up as shown in Figure 11-17.

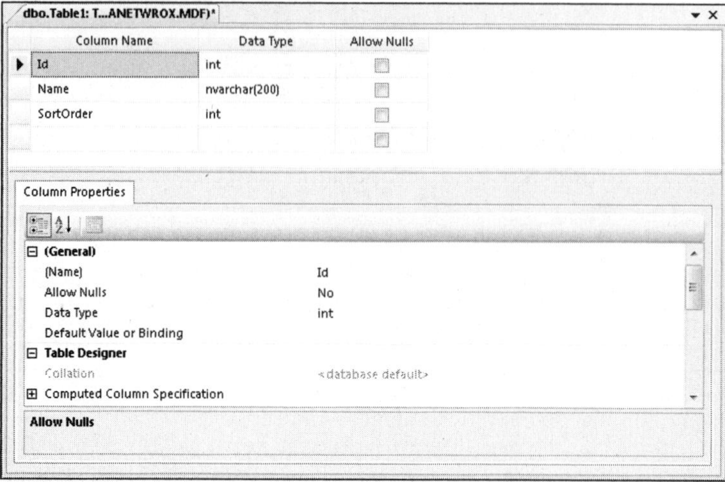

Figure 11-17

Make sure you clear the checkbox for all three items in the Allow Nulls column. This column determines if fields are optional or required. In the case of the `Genre` table, all three columns are required, so you need to clear the Allow Nulls column.

4. Next, select the entire row for the `Id` by clicking in the margin on the left (identified by the black arrow in Figure 11-17) and then on the Table Designer toolbar, visible in Figure 11-18, click the second button from the left (with the yellow key on it) to turn the `Id` column into a primary key.

Figure 11-18

5. Below the table definition you see the Column Properties, a panel that looks similar to the Properties Grid in VWD. With the `Id` column still selected, scroll down a bit on the Column Properties Grid until you see Identity Specification. Expand the item and then set (Is Identity) to Yes, as shown in Figure 11-19.

6. Press Ctrl+S to save your changes. A dialog box pops up that allows you to provide a name for the table. Type `Genre` as the name and click OK to apply your changes.

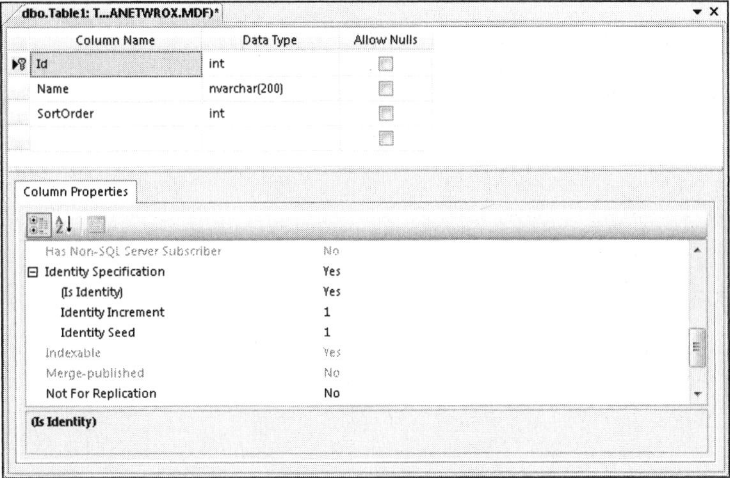

Figure 11-19

7. Create another table by following steps 2 through 6, but this time create a table with the following specifications to hold the CD and concert reviews for the Planet Wrox web site.

Column Name	Data Type	Allow Nulls	Description
`Id`	`int`	No	The primary key and identity of the table.
`Title`	`nvarchar(200)`	No	Contains the title of the review.
`Summary`	`nvarchar(max)`	No	Contains a short summary or teaser text for the review.
`Body`	`nvarchar(max)`	Yes	Contains the full body text of the review.
`GenreId`	`int`	No	Contains the ID of a genre that the review belongs to.
`Authorized`	`bit`	No	Determines whether the review is authorized for publication by an administrator. Unauthorized reviews will not be visible on the web site.
`CreateDateTime`	`datetime`	No	The date and time the review is created.
`UpdateDateTime`	`datetime`	No	The date and time the review is last updated.

8. Make the `Id` column the primary key again, and set its (Is Identity) property to Yes.
9. Click the CreateDateTime column once and then on the Column Properties Grid, type `GetDate()` in the field for the Default Value or Binding property, as shown in Figure 11-20.

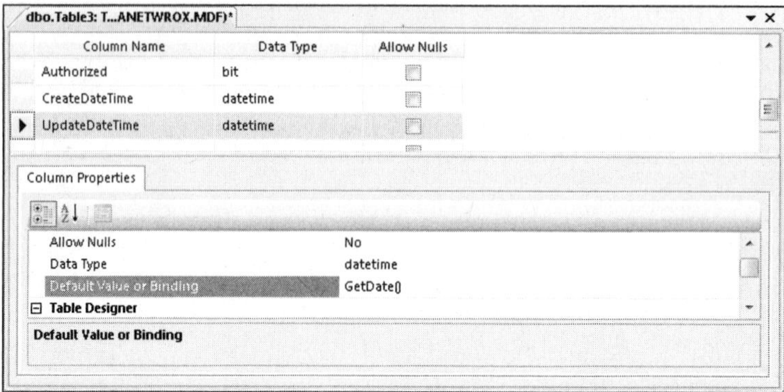

Figure 11-20

10. Repeat the previous step for the UpdateDateTime column.
11. When you're done, press Ctrl+S to save the table and call it Review.

How It Works

The Table Designer in VWD is pretty straightforward. You simply type new column names and define a data type for the column, and you're pretty much done. Some columns, such as the `Id` column in the `Genre` and `Review` tables, require a bit more work. For those columns, you set the Identity to Yes. This means that SQL Server automatically assigns a new sequential number to each new record that you insert. By default, the first record in the table gets an ID of 1 while subsequent records get an ID increased by one. You can change the default behavior by setting the Identity Increment and Identity Seed in the Identity Specification element for the column.

You also assigned a *default value* to the `CreateDateTime` and `UpdateDateTime` columns. Default values are inserted by the database when you don't supply one explicitly. This means that if your `INSERT` statement does not contain a value for the `CreateDateTime` or `UpdateDateTime` column, the database will insert a default value for you automatically. In the previous Try It Out, this default value was `GetDate()`, which inserts today's date and time automatically.

If you're unsure if you followed all the steps correctly, take a look at the database that comes with the source for this chapter. It contains the correct tables that already have a few records in them. To look at the database, create a new temporary web site in VWD and then drag the database files into the App_Data folder. You can then access the database using the Database Explorer.

In addition to relationships that are only defined in your own SQL queries as you saw before with the `SELECT` and `JOIN` statements, you can also create relations in the database. The benefits of relations and how you can create them in your database are discussed in the next topic.

Creating Relationships Between Tables

Consider the tables you have created so far. You created a `Genre` table with an `Id` column to uniquely identify a genre record. You also created a `Review` table with a `GenreId` column. Clearly, this column should contain an `Id` that points to a record in the `Genre` table so you know to which genre a review belongs. Now imagine that you delete a record from the `Genre` table that has reviews attached to it. Without a relationship, the database will let you do that. However, this is causing a great deal of troubles. If you now try to display the genre together with a review, it will fail because there is no longer a matching genre. Similarly, if you want to list all the reviews in your system grouped by genre, you'll miss the ones that belong to the deleted genre.

To avoid these kinds of problems and keep your database in a healthy and consistent state, you can create a relationship between two tables. With a proper relationship set up, the database will stop you from deleting records in one table that still have other records attached to it.

Besides the protection of data, relations also make your data model clearer. If you look at the database through a diagram (which you'll use in the next exercise) you'll find that relations between tables help you better understand how tables are connected, and what data they represent.

You can define a relationship by creating a relationship between the primary key of one table, and a column in another table. The column in this second table is often referred to as a *foreign key*. In the case of the `Review` and `Genre` tables, the `GenreId` column of the `Review` table points to the primary key column `Id` of the `Genre` table, thus making `GenreId` a foreign key. In the next section, you see how to create a relationship between two tables and then execute a SQL statement that shows how the relationship is helping you to protect your data.

Try It Out — Creating a Relationship Between Two Tables

Before you can add a relationship between two tables, you need to add a diagram to your database. A diagram is a visual tool that helps you understand and define your database. On the diagram, you can drag a column from one table to another to create the relationship. In this exercise, you will create a relationship between the `Review` and `Genre` tables.

1. Open up the Database Explorer again for the Planet Wrox site. Right-click the Database Diagrams element (visible in Figure 11-16) and click Add New Diagram. If this is the first time you are adding a diagram to the database, you may get a dialog box asking if you want VWD to make you the owner of the database. Click Yes to proceed. This prompt may be followed by another that indicates that in order to work with diagrams, VWD needs to create a few required objects. Again, click Yes to proceed.
2. In the Add Table dialog box that follows, select both tables you created in the previous Try It Out (hold down the Ctrl key while you click each item), click Add to add the tables to the diagram, and then click Close to dismiss the Add Table dialog box.
3. Arrange the tables in the diagram using drag and drop so they are positioned next to each other.

4. On the `Genre` table, click the left margin of the `Id` column (it should contain the yellow key to indicate this is the primary key of the table) and then drag it onto the `GenreId` column of the `Review` table and release your mouse.

5. Two dialog boxes pop up that allow you to customize the defaults for the relation. Click OK to dismiss the top window. In the dialog box that remains, visible in Figure 11-21, notice how Enforce Foreign Key Constraint is set to Yes. This property ensures that you cannot delete a record from the `Genre` table if it still has reviews attached to it. Click OK to dismiss this dialog box as well.

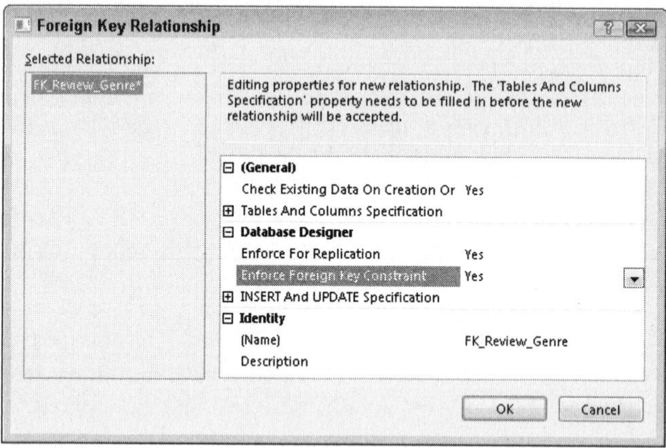

Figure 11-21

6. The diagram window should now show a line between the two tables. At the side of the `Genre` table you should see a yellow key to indicate this table contains the primary key for the relationship. At the other end you should see the infinity symbol (the number 8 character turned 90 degrees) to indicate that the `Review` table can have many records that use the same `GenreId`. You see the diagram in Figure 11-22.

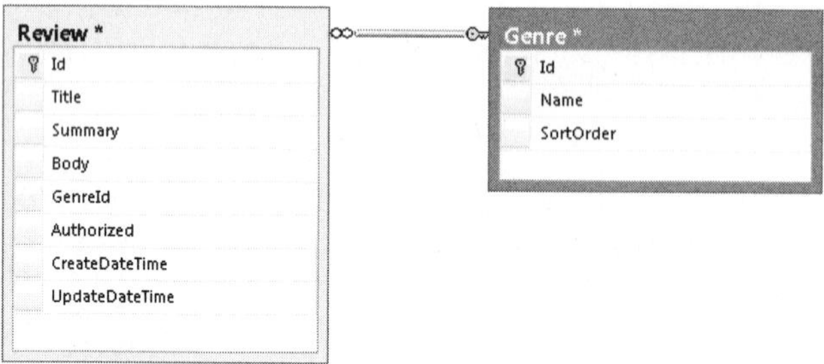

Figure 11-22

7. Press Ctrl+S to save the changes to the diagram. You can leave the name set to its default of Diagram1 or you can enter a more descriptive name like `Reviews and Genres` and click OK. You'll get another warning that states that you are about to make changes to the `Review` and `Genre` tables. Click Yes to apply the changes.

8. Go back to the Database Explorer, right-click the `Genre` table and choose Show Table Data. Enter a few different genres by typing a `Name` and a `SortOrder`. When you press tab in the `SortOrder` field to tab away from the current row, the row is inserted in the database, and the `Id` column is filled with a unique, sequential number. You should end up with a list similar to the one shown in Figure 11-23.

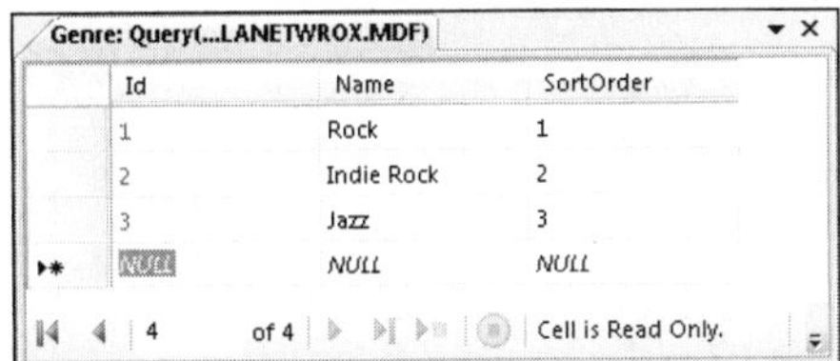

Genre: Query(...LANETWROX.MDF)

	Id	Name	SortOrder
	1	Rock	1
	2	Indie Rock	2
	3	Jazz	3
▸*	NULL	NULL	NULL

4 of 4 | Cell is Read Only.

Figure 11-23

9. Open the `Review` table and enter a few fake reviews. For the `GenreId`, supply some of the new IDs you got when you inserted records in the `Genre` table. You can just make up the Title, Summary, and Body fields for now and set Authorized to True. Remember you don't have to enter a value for the date columns. If you leave them out, the database will insert the default value for you. Notice that you can't insert a value in the `Id` column yourself. Since this column is an Identity field, the database supplies values for you automatically. If you get an error about missing values for the date columns, ensure that you entered a proper default value in the previous exercise. When you're done entering a row, click outside the row (on the new, empty row below it, for example), and then press Ctrl+R to insert the row in the table. Your list of records should look similar to Figure 11-24, although your content, of course, for the columns may be different.

Review: Query...ANETWROX.MDF)

	Id	Title	Summary	Body	GenreId	Authorized
▸	2	Editors - An End Has A Start	Discusses the new Editors CD	NULL	2	True
	4	Sonic Youth - Daydream Nation Live	A review of the concert that Sonic Youth ga...	NULL	2	True
*	NULL	NULL	NULL	NULL	NULL	NULL

1 of 2 | Cell is Read Only.

Figure 11-24

10. Right-click the `Genre` table again and choose Show Table Data. Click the SQL pane button on the Query Designer toolbar and then use the Change Type button on the same toolbar to create a delete query. Modify the query so it looks like this:

```
DELETE FROM Genre WHERE Id = 2
```

Make sure that the `Id` in the `WHERE` clause matches one of the genre IDs you used in step 9 to link the reviews to. Press Ctrl+R to execute the query. Instead of deleting the record from the `Genre` table, VWD now shows you the dialog box in Figure 11-25.

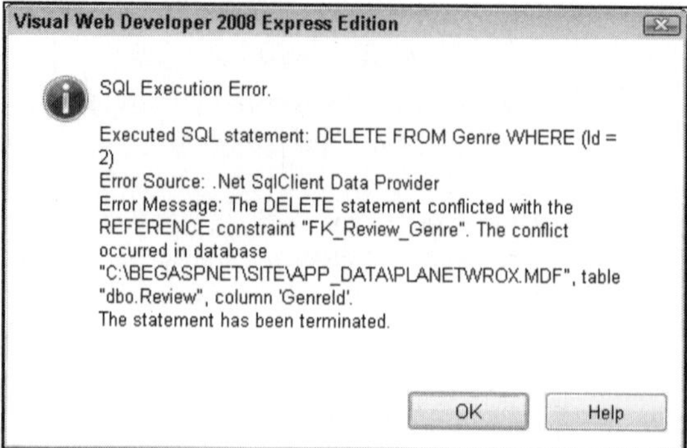

Figure 11-25

How It Works

When you create a relationship between two tables, the database will enforce this relationship when you try to insert, update, or delete data. In the previous example, there are records in the `Review` table that have a genre that exists in the `Genre` table. When you try to delete a record from the `Genre` table, the database sees that the genre is used by a record in the `Review` table and cancels the delete operation.

Practical Database Tips

The following list provides some practical tips on working with databases.

- Since the database is often at the heart of a web site, you need to carefully consider its design. It's especially important to think of a good design up front, before you start building your site on top of it. When you have a number of pages that access your database, it will become harder to make changes, such as removing tables or renaming columns, to the data model.
- Always consider the primary key for your table. I prefer to give each table a column called `Id`. The underlying data type is then an `int` and an identity, which gives each record a unique ID automatically. Instead of an `int`, you can also consider the `uniqueidentifier` data type, which ensures uniqueness even across database or application boundaries.
- Give your database objects like tables and columns logical names. Avoid characters like spaces, underscores, and dashes. A name like `GenreId` is much easier to read than `colGen_ID_3`.
- Don't use `SELECT *` to get all columns from a database. By using `SELECT *` you may be selecting more columns that you actually need. By explicitly defining the columns you want to retrieve, you make your intentions to others clearer and increase the performance of your queries at the same time.
- Always create relationships between tables when appropriate. Although querying for the reviews and genres you saw in this chapter without a relationship between the two tables works just fine, it's relationships that help you enforce the quality of your data. With proper relationships, you minimize the chance of ending up with orphaned or incorrect data.

Summary

The ability to work with databases is a good addition to your set of web development skills. Most of today's modern dynamic web sites use a database, so it's important to understand how to work with them.

Although databases come in many different forms, including flat-file, object-relational, and object-oriented databases, the relational database is the most popular form of databases used today. Microsoft SQL Server is a relational database and naturally blends in with the ASP.NET programming environment, making it easy to retrieve and manipulate data that is stored in the database. Because SQL Server 2005 Express Edition ships with Visual Web Developer 2008 for free and because this database can be upgraded easily to the full and commercial versions of SQL Server, this database is the natural choice for your ASP.NET 3.5 web sites.

To access and manipulate data in a relational database, you use a language called Structured Query Language, SQL for short. Among other elements, this language defines four important keywords that allow you to perform CRUD — Create Read Update Delete — operations against a database.

The `SELECT` statement allows you to retrieve data from one or more tables. To access more than one table you can use one of the available `JOIN` types to define a relationship between the tables. To limit the number of records returned by a query, you can use a `WHERE` clause. To order the items in the result set returned by your query, you use the `ORDER BY` clause.

To create new records in your database you use the `INSERT` statement, while you need an `UPDATE` statement to change existing records. With both statements, you define values for the columns that you want to insert or change. Text and date values need to be enclosed in quotes, while you can add numeric and Boolean (bit) values directly to your query.

To delete records that you no longer need, you use the `DELETE` statement. Just like the `SELECT` and `UPDATE` statements, `DELETE` takes an optional `WHERE` clause that allows you to limit the number of records that get deleted.

The second half of this chapter showed you how to use the built-in database tools to create new tables and create relations between them. Additionally, you saw how a relationship between two tables enables you to protect your data from becoming corrupt or orphaned.

Although this chapter had a strong focus on the SQL that you need to write to access a database, you'll see in the next chapter that in many cases VWD makes accessing databases pretty easy by generating most of the code for you. However, a solid knowledge of SQL helps you in understanding and tweaking the code that VWD writes for you.

Exercises

1. If you try to delete a record from the `Genre` table that has matching records in the `Review` table, the `DELETE` statement fails. How is this possible?

2. If you try to delete a record from the `Review` table that has its `GenreId` set to the `Id` of an existing genre in the `Genre` table, the `DELETE` statement succeeds. Why?

3. Imagine you want to clean up your database and decide to delete all records from the `Review` table that have an `Id` of 100 or less. What does your SQL statement look like?

4. Imagine you want to delete the genre with an ID of 4. But before you delete the genre, you want to reassign reviews assigned to this genre to another genre with an ID of 11. What SQL statements do you need to accomplish this?

Displaying and Updating Data

Now that you have seen how to interact with databases using SQL it's time to put that knowledge into practice and start building some useful pages that allow you to manage the data in your web site.

In this chapter you learn how to display, insert, update, and delete data using the popular data controls that ship with ASP.NET. Besides working with the visual controls that are used to display and edit data in a web page, you also learn how to work with the `SqlDataSource` control that acts as the bridge between the database and your ASPX pages.

In particular, this chapter gives you a good look at the following topics:

- Controls that display and maintain data in your web site
- How to display data using the `GridView` control
- How to access the database to retrieve and update data using a `SqlDataSource` control
- How to insert, edit, and delete data using the data controls like the `GridView` and the `DetailsView`
- How to create a rich interface that allows a user to insert and edit data while maintaining data integrity with the ASP.NET validation controls
- The best way to store your connection strings in your application so they are easily updateable

The first things you need to look at are the available data controls, discussed in the next section.

Data Controls

To enable you to work efficiently with the data in your system, ASP.NET offers two sets of data-aware controls: the *data-bound controls* and the *data source controls*.

The first group contains controls that you use to display and edit data, like the `GridView`, `Repeater`, and the new `ListView` control. The data source controls are used to retrieve data from a data source, like a database or an XML file, and then offer this data to the data-bound controls. Figure 12-1 shows you the complete list of available data controls in the Data category of the Toolbox.

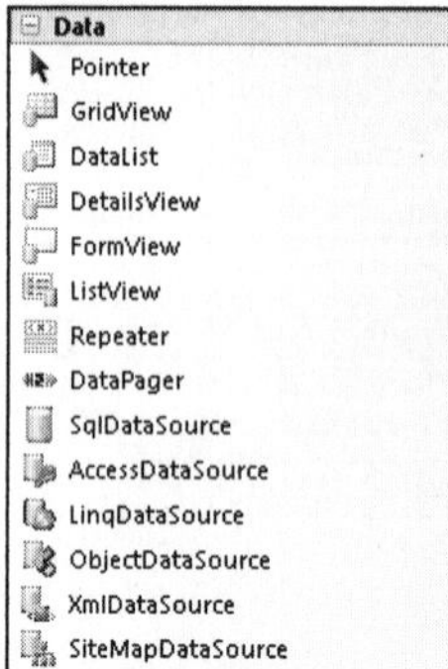

Figure 12-1

The following two sections provide a quick overview of all the controls in the data category. In the remainder of this chapter you get a much more detailed look at some of these controls and how to use them.

Data-Bound Controls

The first seven controls in the Toolbox depicted in Figure 12-1 are the so-called data-bound controls. You use them to display and edit data on your web pages. The `GridView`, `DataList`, `ListView`, and `Repeater` are all able to display multiple records at the same time, whereas the `DetailsView` and the `FormView` are designed to show a single record at a time. The `DataPager` is used to provide paging capabilities to the `ListView` controls and is, just like the `ListView`, new in ASP.NET 3.5.

List Controls

Since ASP.NET offers multiple controls to display lists of records, you may be wondering when to choose what control. The `GridView` is a very versatile control that supports automatic paging, sorting, editing, deleting, and selecting. It renders its data like a spreadsheet with rows and columns. Although there are many possibilities to style the looks of these rows and controls (you'll learn more about this in Chapter 14), you cannot radically change the way the data is presented. Additionally, the `GridView` does not allow you to insert records in the underlying data source directly.

Figure 12-2 shows a typical `GridView`.

	Id	Title	Date Created
Edit Delete Select	9	The National - Boxer	11/29/2007 10:10 PM
Edit Delete Select	10	P.J. Harvey - White Chalk: Wow: really something new...	12/12/2007 1:08 PM
Edit Delete Select	11	Interpol - Our Love to Admire	12/12/2007 1:29 PM
Edit Delete Select	12	Yeah Yeah Yeahs - The Is Is EP	12/20/2007 10:36 PM
1 2 3 4 5 6			

Figure 12-2

The GridView is often used for complex lists of data, such as a list of reviews in the management section of the Planet Wrox web site, items in a shopping cart, and so on.

The DataList control allows you to present your data not only in rows as with the GridView, but in columns as well, allowing you to create a matrix-like presentation of data. Additionally, the control allows you to define the look and feel of the data through a set of templates. As a downside, the control does not support paging and sorting natively, and doesn't allow you to insert new records or update or delete existing ones.

The DataList is often used to display repeating data in rows and columns — for example, pictures in a photo album or products in a product catalog.

The Repeater gives you the greatest flexibility in terms of the HTML that you output to the browser as the control by itself does not add any HTML to the page output. You define the entire client markup through the numerous templates the control exposes. However, this flexibility comes at a price: the control has no built-in capabilities for the paging, sorting, and modification of data.

The Repeater is extremely useful in situations where you need precise control over the markup that is generated by the control. As such, it's often used for HTML ordered or unordered lists (<ol> and <ul>) and other lists where you can't afford to have unwanted HTML mixed with your own. You'll see more of the Repeater control in the next chapter.

The ListView is new in ASP.NET 3.5 and is a best-of-all-worlds combination of the GridView, the DataList, and the Repeater. It supports editing, deleting, and paging of data, similar to the GridView. It supports multi-column and multi-row layouts like the DataList offers, and it allows you to completely control the markup generated by the control, just as the Repeater does. In Chapter 13, you'll see a lot more of the ListView control.

Single Item Controls

The DetailsView and FormView controls are somewhat similar in that both of them can display a single record at a time. The DetailsView uses a built-in tabular format to display the data, whereas the FormView uses templates to let you define the look and feel of your data. A simple, template-based FormView could look like the one shown in Figure 12-3.

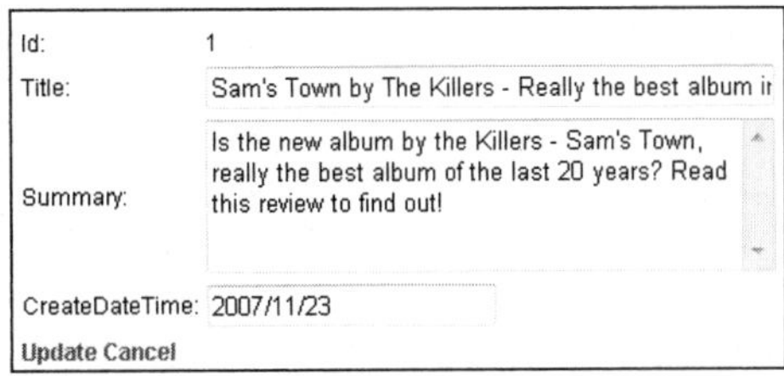

Figure 12-3

Both controls allow you to define the templates for different situations, like a read-only display of data, and inserting and updating of data. You'll see how to customize these templates in the second half of this chapter.

Paging Controls

New in the ASP.NET control Toolbox is the `DataPager` control, a simple yet useful control that enables paging on other controls. For the time being, it can only be used to extend the `ListView` control, but that might change with future versions of the .NET Framework. The `ListView` and `DataPager` controls are discussed in Chapter 13.

For the data-bound controls to display something useful, you need to assign them a *data source*. To bind this data source to the controls, you have two main methods available: You can assign data to the control's `DataSource` property, or you can use one of the separate data source controls. In later chapters, you see how to use the `DataSource` property; the different data source controls are the topic of the following section.

Data Source Controls

The Data category of the Toolbox contains six different data source controls that you can use to bind data to your data-bound controls. The last two in the group, `XmlDataSource` and `SiteMapDataSource`, are used to bind hierarchical, XML-based data to these controls. You have seen `SiteMapDataSource` at work when you created the site map in Chapter 7.

The `AccessDataSource` control is used to display data from a Microsoft Access database in your web pages. It's pretty straightforward, and to some extent it's similar to the `SqlDataSource` control in that it allows you to work with data from a database. However, it differs in that it's optimized (and only works with) Microsoft Access databases.

The `ObjectDataSource` control allows you to connect your data-bound controls to separate objects in your application. Instead of tying your data-aware controls directly to a database, you bind data from a separate layer with custom objects to them. Get yourself a copy of *Professional ASP.NET 3.5* (ISBN 978-0-470-18757-9) if you want to find out more about the `ObjectDataSource` control.

The other two controls, `SqlDataSource` and `LinqDataSource`, are covered in this chapter and Chapter 13, respectively.

Data Source and Data-Bound Controls Working Together

The `SqlDataSource` control allows you to quickly create functional, database-driven web pages. Without writing a whole lot of code, you can create web pages that allow you to perform all four operations of the CRUD acronym: create, read, update, and delete data. Although its name may seem to imply that the control can only access Microsoft's SQL Server, that's not the case. The control can access other databases, such as Oracle or MySQL as well.

Displaying and Editing Data with GridView

To give you an idea of how the `SqlDataSource` control works in conjunction with the data-bound controls, the next Try It Out lets you create a very simple data-driven web page that allows you to manage the records that are stored in the `Genre` table in the database. This chapter assumes you have the PlanetWrox.mdf database with the `Genre` and `Review` tables in your App_Data folder. It's also assumed that these tables each contain at least a few records. If you didn't follow the steps in the previous chapter, or you're not sure you followed them correctly, be sure to grab a copy of the files PlanetWrox.mdf and PlanetWrox_log.ldf from the Resources folder in the code download for this chapter (at `C:\BegASPNET\Resources\Chapter 12`) and drop them in the App_Data folder of the Planet Wrox web site, overwriting the existing database if you had one. It's also a good idea to get a copy of the PlanetWrox.mdf database from the Resources folder if your own copy doesn't contain a lot of review and genre records. That way, you have a good set of sample records to work with.

Try It Out Using the GridView and SqlDataSource Controls

In this exercise you start building the Management section of the web site that will be your main entry point to manage things like reviews and genres in your site. For now, the pages you create in this section are accessible to all users of your site, but Chapter 15 shows you how to block access to this folder to any user that is not an administrator.

You'll see how to drag a table from the Database Explorer (the Server Explorer in the commercial version of Visual Studio) onto the page and have VWD create a web user interface to manage items in the database for you by automatically generating the necessary code for a `GridView` and a `SqlDataSource`. In later exercises in this book you'll see how to reproduce this behavior manually, giving you more control over the generated code.

1. Open the Planet Wrox project from its location at `C:\BegASPNET\Site` in VWD.
2. Right-click the MasterPages folder, choose Add New Item, and add a new Master Page called ManagementMaster.master to the site. Make sure it uses your programming language and that it's not based on an existing master page.
3. Change the HTML inside the `<form>` element to the following code that creates two `<div>` elements floating next to each other. The first contains a simple list-based menu for the Management section whereas the second `<div>` contains the `ContentPlaceHolder` control that allows content pages to provide custom content:

```
<form id="form1" runat="server">
<div>
  <div style="width: 200px; float: left;">
    <ul>
      <li><a href="~/Management/Default.aspx" runat="server">Management Home</a></li>
      <li><a href="~/Management/Genres.aspx" runat="server">Manage Genres</a></li>
    </ul>
  </div>
  <div style="width: 750px; float: left;">
    <asp:ContentPlaceHolder ID="cpMainContent" runat="server"></asp:ContentPlaceHolder>
  </div>
</div>
</form>
```

   You can ignore the warnings that VWD shows you for the missing pages as they'll be added later. Save and close the master page.

4. Add a new folder to the root of the site and call it Management. Right-click this new folder, choose Add New Item, and create a new page called Default.aspx. Make sure the page is based on the new ManagementMaster.master file; there's no need to base it on the central `BasePage` class in the App_Code folder. As soon as the file opens in the Document Window, add some

text to the `cpMainContent` content block that welcomes the user to the Management section of the web site:

```
<asp:Content ID="Content2" ContentPlaceHolderID="cpMainContent" runat="Server">
  <h1>Planet Wrox Management Section</h1>
  <p>Welcome to the Management section of this web site. Please choose an item from the
      menu on the left to continue.</p>
</asp:Content>
```

Give the page a `Title` of Planet Wrox – Management - Home.

5. Create another page in the Management folder and call it Genres.aspx. Base it on the same master page and then change its `Title` to Planet Wrox - Management - Genres.

6. Switch the page into Design View and make sure the Database Explorer window is open. If you don't see the Planet Wrox database listed here, refer to the first Try It Out of the previous chapter that explains how to set up the connection. Remember there's a database in the resources folder for this chapter that contains the tables you'll work with in this chapter.

7. Expand the PlanetWrox.mdf database, then the Tables node, and then drag the `Genre` table from the Database Explorer and drop it in the `cpMainContent` area of the Genres page. VWD creates a `GridView` and a `SqlDataSource` for you automatically.

8. On the Smart Tasks panel for the `GridView` control that should open automatically (if it doesn't, click the grey arrow on the upper-right corner of the control or right-click the control and choose Show Smart Tag), select all the available options, shown in Figure 12-4.

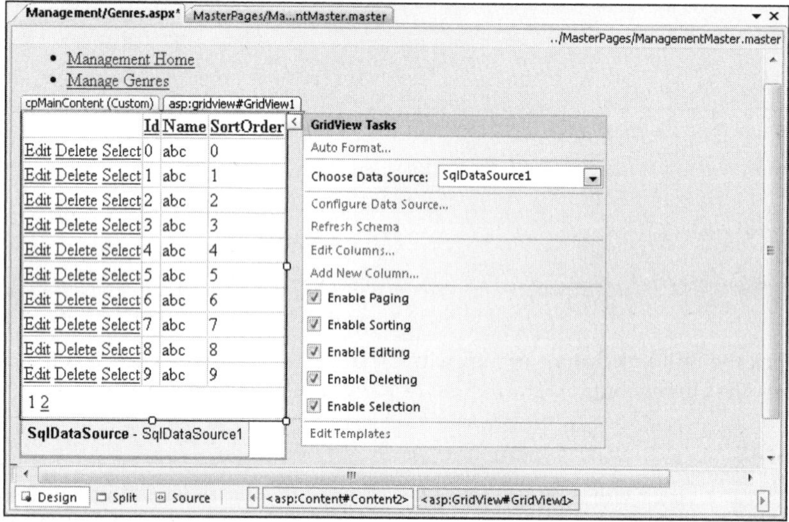

Figure 12-4

9. Right-click the Management folder in the Solution Explorer and choose Add New Item. Click Web Configuration File once and then click Add to add a web.config file that applies to the Management folder only. In the file that opens, add a `<pages>` element that sets the `theme` to an empty string:

```
<configuration>
  <appSettings/>
```

```
    <connectionStrings/>
    <system.web>
      <pages theme=""></pages>
    </system.web>
  </configuration>
```

10. Save all your changes and then request Genres.aspx from the Management folder in your browser (see Figure 12-5). You should see a grid with the genres from the `Genre` table. The links in the left columns allow you to edit, delete, and select the relevant genres. Note that you can't delete genres that have one or more reviews attached to them. If you try, you'll get an error instead. Chapter 14 digs much deeper into changing the user interface (UI) to disable the Delete links so users can no longer accidentally click them.

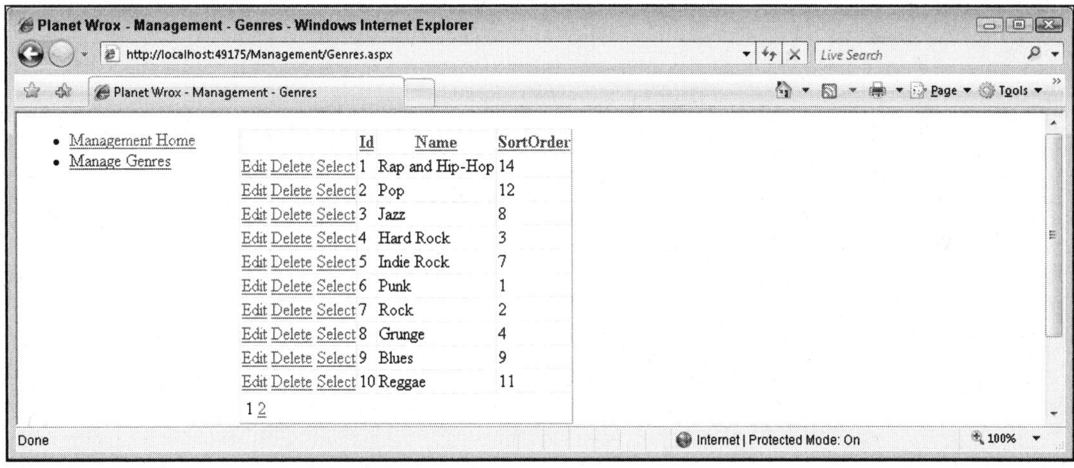

Figure 12-5

If the list with reviews ends up below the menu on the left, you may need to make your browser window a little wider.

11. You can click the column headers visible in Figure 12-5 to sort the data in the grid on that column. If you click the same header again, the data is sorted in reversed order.

12. Click the Edit link for one of the genres, change the name in the text box that has appeared and click the Update button. The `GridView` should now display the new name.

How It Works

You didn't write much code in this exercise, but you got a lot of functionality simply by dragging and dropping a database table. To see how it works, take a look at the source that VWD generated. First, look at the markup for the `SqlDataSource` control:

```
<asp:SqlDataSource ID="SqlDataSource1" runat="server"
    ConnectionString="<%$ ConnectionStrings:PlanetWroxConnectionString1 %>"
    ProviderName="<%$ ConnectionStrings:PlanetWroxConnectionString1.ProviderName %>"
    DeleteCommand="DELETE FROM [Genre] WHERE [Id] = @Id"
    InsertCommand="INSERT INTO [Genre] ([Name], [SortOrder]) VALUES (@Name, @SortOrder)"
    SelectCommand="SELECT [Id], [Name], [SortOrder] FROM [Genre]"
```

```
    UpdateCommand="UPDATE [Genre] SET [Name] = @Name, [SortOrder] = @SortOrder
        WHERE [Id] = @Id">
  <DeleteParameters>
    <asp:Parameter Name="Id" Type="Int32" />
  </DeleteParameters>
  <InsertParameters>
    <asp:Parameter Name="Name" Type="String" />
    <asp:Parameter Name="SortOrder" Type="Int32" />
  </InsertParameters>
  <UpdateParameters>
    <asp:Parameter Name="Name" Type="String" />
    <asp:Parameter Name="SortOrder" Type="Int32" />
    <asp:Parameter Name="Id" Type="Int32" />
  </UpdateParameters>
</asp:SqlDataSource>
```

A couple of interesting things are worth examining. First, note that the `ConnectionString` and `ProviderName` attributes point to a connection string that has been defined in the web.config file. You'll see more of this in the next section, including an explanation of the `<%$ %>` syntax used for the connection string and `ProviderName` attribute.

You then see four commands, each one of them containing a SQL statement that is used for one of the four operations of the CRUD acronym: The `INSERT`, `UPDATE`, and `DELETE` commands contain *parameters*, identified by the at symbol (`@`) prefix. At run time, when the control is asked to perform the relevant data operation, these parameters are substituted by run-time values. The `SqlDataSource` control keeps track of the relevant parameters in the `*Parameters` collections. For example, the `<DeleteParameters>` element contains a single parameter for the `Id` (the primary key) of the genre:

```
<DeleteParameters>
  <asp:parameter Name="Id" Type="Int32" />
</DeleteParameters>
```

Note that the `Name` of the parameter lines up with the parameter in the SQL statement:

```
  DeleteCommand="DELETE FROM [Genre] WHERE [Id] = @Id">
```

All by itself, the `SqlDataSource` control can't do much at this stage. It needs a data-bound control that tells it what data operations to execute. In this Try It Out exercise the data-bound control is the `GridView` that is defined with this code:

```
<asp:GridView ID="GridView1" runat="server" AllowPaging="True" AllowSorting="True"
     AutoGenerateColumns="False" DataKeyNames="Id" DataSourceID="SqlDataSource1"
     EmptyDataText="There are no data records to display.">
  <Columns>
    <asp:CommandField ShowDeleteButton="True" ShowEditButton="True"
        ShowSelectButton="True" />
    <asp:BoundField DataField="Id" HeaderText="Id" ReadOnly="True" SortExpression="Id" />
    <asp:BoundField DataField="Name" HeaderText="Name" SortExpression="Name" />
    <asp:BoundField DataField="SortOrder" HeaderText="SortOrder"
        SortExpression="SortOrder" />
  </Columns>
</asp:GridView>
```

The GridView contains a few important attributes. First, the DataKeyNames attribute tells the GridView what the primary key of the record in the database is. It needs this to be able to uniquely identify records in the grid.

The DataSourceID attribute points to the SqlDataSource control that you saw earlier, whereas AllowPaging and AllowSorting enable their associated features on the GridView.

Under the <Columns> element you see a number of fields set up. First, you see a CommandField. A CommandField is a column in the GridView that enables a user to execute one or more actions for the row that the CommandField applies to. It ends up in the browser as one or more text links or buttons. In this example, ShowDeleteButton, ShowEditButton, and ShowSelectButton have all been set to true. This gives the grid the functionality you see in Figure 12-5. When you click one of the links that have been created by the CommandField, they'll trigger a command at the server. For example, clicking the Edit link puts the GridView in Edit mode so you can edit the selected record. Notice how clicking the Select link doesn't seem to change the GridView at all. In Chapter 14 you'll see how to create styles for the GridView so you can radically change the appearance of the control, including visually distinguishing a selected row from the others.

If you want the GridView to render buttons instead of links you need to set ButtonType to Button:

```
<asp:CommandField ShowDeleteButton="True" ShowEditButton="True" ShowSelectButton="True"
    ButtonType="Button"></asp:CommandField>
```

The other three fields are so-called *bound fields* and map directly to the columns of the Genre table in the database with their DataField attribute so the GridView knows what data to display where.

The GridView and SqlDataSource controls work together closely to retrieve and modify the data in the underlying data source. To give you an idea of how this works, here's a rundown of the events that took place when you requested the Genres page in the browser and then edited a single genre:

1. You request the page in your browser and the page begins its page life cycle.
2. The GridView knows it's set up to retrieve and display data because it has its DataSourceID attribute set up. It contacts the SqlDataSource identified in the DataSourceID attribute and asks it for its data. The SqlDataSource in turn contacts the database and then fires its SelectCommand, the SQL statement that selects the Id, Name, and SortOrder from the Genre table in the database:

```
SelectCommand="SELECT [Id], [Name], [SortOrder] FROM [Genre]"
```

3. When the SqlDataSource receives the requested records from the database it hands them over to the GridView, which creates an HTML table out of them using the bound fields that have been set up in the <Columns> element. For each Edit, Delete, and Select link in the CommandField column, the GridView keeps track of the unique ID for each record that is displayed in the page by storing it in ViewState.
4. As soon as you click the Edit button, the page posts back. The GridView is able to see what row you clicked by looking at the associated DataKeyName. It then gets the latest results from the database by asking the SqlDataSource again to fire its SelectCommand and then puts the selected row in edit mode so you can change the relevant details. When you click the Update link, the GridView collects the new values from the TextBox controls and then contacts the SqlDataSource again.

5. For each of the parameters in the `<UpdateParameters>` element of the `SqlDataSource`, the `GridView` supplies a value. It retrieves the `Id` of the genre from the selected row, and then retrieves the new `Name` and `SortOrder` values from the `TextBox` controls in the page.

6. Armed with the relevant data for the `Id`, `Name`, and `SortOrder`, the `SqlDataSource` then executes its `UpdateCommand` against the database:

```
UpdateCommand="UPDATE [Genre] SET [Name] = @Name, [SortOrder] =
    @SortOrder WHERE [Id] = @Id"
```

- Each of the parameters prefixed with the at (`@`) symbol is filled with the values that the `GridView` supplied. The SQL statement that gets sent to the database may end up looking like this:

```
UPDATE [Genre] SET [Name] = 'New Name', [SortOrder] = 1 WHERE [Id] = 1
```

- The table names and column names have been wrapped in a pair of square brackets (`[]`). This isn't needed in this scenario, but it's useful in cases where the column name contains a space, or where the table or column name matches a reserved word.

7. Finally, the `GridView` refreshes the data on the page by once again asking the `SqlDataSource` to execute its `SelectCommand`. This way, the `GridView` now displays the latest data with the update you made.

   The other commands work in a similar way and send their own SQL commands to the database.

At the end of the exercise, you added a new web.config file to the Management folder and reset the theme that is applied to all pages in the Management section. With the theme removed, it's easier to focus on the functionality of the Management section, rather than be distracted by layout issues. In Chapter 14 you will create a third theme specifically for the Management folder and apply that theme in the web.config file in the Management folder. That way, your management pages will have a different look and feel than the pages in the front end. Chapter 14 digs much deeper into changing the appearance of the data controls in the Planet Wrox web site.

Inserting Data with DetailsView

Just as displaying, updating, and deleting data with the `GridView` are pretty easy, so is inserting data with the `DetailsView` control. As with the `GridView`, the `DetailsView` supports a number of templates that allow you to customize the look and feel of the control in different states. For example, the control has a `<FooterTemplate>`, a `<HeaderTemplate>`, and a `<PagerTemplate>` element that enable you to define the looks of the top and bottom parts of the control. In addition, the control has a `<Fields>` element that allows you to define the rows that should appear in the control, much like the `<Columns>` element of the `GridView`.

The `DetailsView` is able to display data in a few different modes. First of all, it can display an existing record in read-only mode. In addition, the control can be used to insert brand new records and to update existing ones. You control the mode of the `DetailsView` with the `DefaultMode` property that you can set to `ReadOnly`, `Insert`, and `Edit` respectively. You see how to configure the `DetailsView` and set the `DefaultMode` property next.

Try It Out Inserting Data with the DetailsView Control

In this exercise, you see how to use the `DetailsView` to let your users insert new records into the `Genre` table. As with the `GridView` example, the next exercise requires no coding from your side. All you need to do is drag and drop a few controls, set a few properties, and you're done. Obviously, these code-free pages have limitations that make them less useful in more advanced scenarios. Therefore, later in this chapter, you'll see how to extend and customize these controls.

1. Go back to the Genres.aspx page in VWD and make sure it's in Design View.
2. Drag and drop a `DetailsView` from the Data category of the Toolbox immediately below the `GridView`. If you have trouble dropping the control below the `GridView` but above the `SqlDataSource` control, you can simply drop it *on* the `SqlDataSource`; VWD then adds the markup of the dropped control before the one you drop it on.
3. Open the control's Smart Tasks panel (which should open automatically) and then hook it up to `SqlDataSource1` by selecting that name from the Choose Data Source drop-down list.
4. On the same Smart Tasks panel, select the item Enable Inserting.
5. Open the control's Properties Grid by pressing F4 and then locate the `DefaultMode` property in the Behavior category. Set the `DefaultMode` to `Insert`. The code for the `DetailsView` should now look like this:

```
<asp:DetailsView ID="DetailsView1" runat="server" AutoGenerateRows="False"
    DataKeyNames="Id" DataSourceID="SqlDataSource1" DefaultMode="Insert" Height="50px"
    Width="125px">
  <Fields>
    <asp:BoundField DataField="Id" HeaderText="Id" InsertVisible="False" ReadOnly="True"
                SortExpression="Id" />
    <asp:BoundField DataField="Name" HeaderText="Name" SortExpression="Name" />
    <asp:BoundField DataField="SortOrder" HeaderText="SortOrder"
                SortExpression="SortOrder" />
    <asp:CommandField ShowInsertButton="True" />
  </Fields>
</asp:DetailsView>
```

6. Save the changes to the page, and press Ctrl+F5 to open it up in your browser. Below the `GridView` you should now see the controls that enable you to insert a new genre (see Figure 12-6).
7. Insert a new genre. Make sure you enter both a name and a sort order and then click the Insert link.
8. Close your browser and go back to VWD and switch the page into Markup View. Wrap the markup inside the `cpMainContent Content` block inside an Ajax `UpdatePanel` that you can drag from the Toolbox into the code editor. Don't forget to also add a `ContentTemplate`:

```
<asp:Content ID="Content2" ContentPlaceHolderID="cpMainContent" runat="Server">
  <asp:UpdatePanel ID="UpdatePanel1" runat="server">
    <ContentTemplate>
      <asp:GridView ID="GridView1" runat="server" AutoGenerateColumns="False"
           DataKeyNames="Id" DataSourceID="SqlDataSource1" EmptyDataText="There are no data
           records to display." AllowPaging="True" AllowSorting="True">
      ...
      </asp:SqlDataSource>
```

```
    </ContentTemplate>
  </asp:UpdatePanel>
</asp:Content>
```

9. Open up the master page for the Management section (ManagementMaster.master) and add a `ScriptManager` right after the opening `<form>` tag:

```
<form id="form1" runat="server">
  <asp:ScriptManager ID="ScriptManager1" runat="server"></asp:ScriptManager>
  <div>
```

10. Save all your changes and open Genres.aspx again. Enter a few more genres. Notice how the addition of the `UpdatePanel` made the insert operation flicker-free.

11. If you click one of the numbers at the bottom of the screen in the Pager bar, the `GridView` switches to that page showing the next set of records. Notice how this page switching (called paging), sorting, and editing now all occurs within the `UpdatePanel`, causing the page to refresh without a full postback.

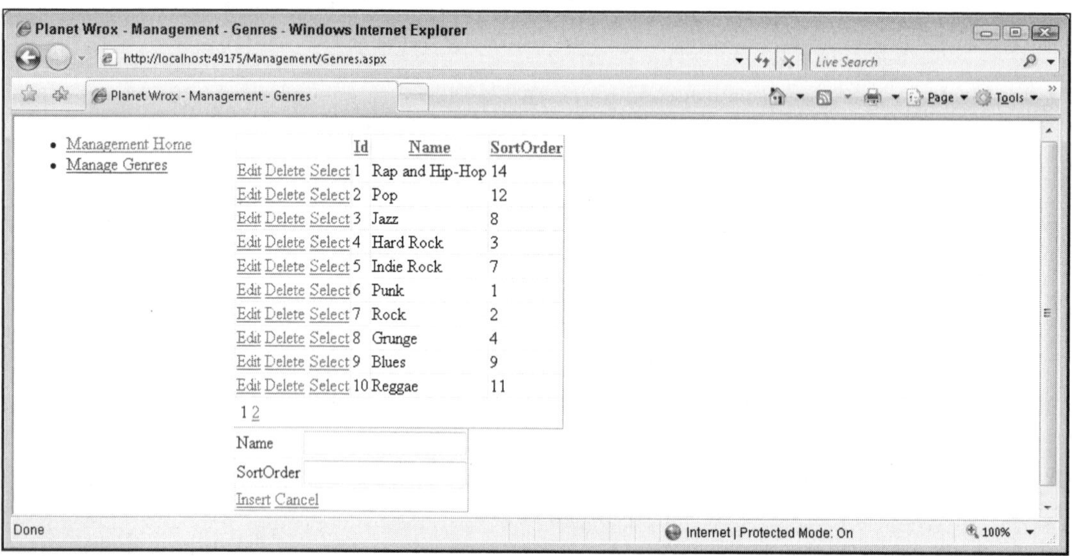

Figure 12-6

How It Works

Identical to the other data-bound controls, you hook up the `DetailsView` to a data source control by setting the `DataSourceID` property. Since you already have a working `SqlDataSource` control on the page, you can simply reuse that. The `DetailsView` exposes different views, for read-only, insert, and edit modes. By setting the `DefaultMode` to `Insert`, you force the control to switch to `Insert` mode, which means you automatically get a UI for entering details for the genre, and Insert and Cancel links.

The `DetailsView` control is actually pretty smart. When you point it to the `SqlDataSource` control, it is able to figure out the `DataKeyNames` property, which it set to `Id`:

```
<asp:DetailsView ID="DetailsView1" runat="server" AutoGenerateRows="False"
    DataKeyNames="Id" DataSourceID="SqlDataSource1" DefaultMode="Insert" Height="50px"
```

It also understands that the `Id` column is an identity column in the database and therefore hides it in the Insert screen in Figure 12-6 by setting `InsertVisible` to `False`. Since the database generates this ID automatically, there is no point in letting the user enter a value for it.

When you enter some values and click the Insert link, a process similar to updating with the `GridView` takes place. The `DetailsView` collects the relevant information from the page's controls (the `Name` and the `SortOrder`) and forwards them to the `SqlDataSource`. This control in turn pushes the new values in the parameters for the `INSERT` statement and then sends the command off to the database, which inserts the new record in the `Genre` table.

At the end of the exercise, you wrapped the page content inside an `UpdatePanel`. With just minimal effort, you improved the perceived quality and speed of the page in the browser. By eliminating post-backs, the page appears to behave faster, giving the user a much better impression.

Storing Your Connection Strings in web.config

The first time you drop the `Genre` table on your page, VWD creates a `SqlDataSource` control for you. To tell this control what database to access, it also creates a connection string in the web.config file under the `<connectionStrings>` element and points the `SqlDataSource` to this connection string. The setting in web.config looks like this:

```
<connectionStrings>
  <add name="PlanetWroxConnectionString1" connectionString="
          Data Source=.\SQLEXPRESS;AttachDbFilename=|DataDirectory|\PlanetWrox.mdf;
          Integrated Security=True;User Instance=True"
      providerName="System.Data.SqlClient" />
</connectionStrings>
```

The `SqlDataSource` then accesses this connection string:

```
<asp:SqlDataSource ID="SqlDataSource1" runat="server"
  ConnectionString="<%$ ConnectionStrings:PlanetWroxConnectionString1 %>"
```

This code uses *expression binding syntax* to refer to the connection string in the web.config. It effectively asks the web.config file for the connection string that listens to the name `PlanetWroxConnectionString1`.

In addition to the expression binding syntax that uses `<%$ %>` to bind control values to resources like values from the connection string, you also come across similar syntax that uses `<%# %>`. This is called the *data-binding expression syntax* and it allows you to bind control values to data that comes from data sources like a database. You'll see more about data-binding expression syntax in this and the next two chapters.

Storing your connection strings in web.config is always considered a very good practice. This way, you centralize your connection strings in a single location, making it much easier to modify them when your database changes (for example, when you switch from a development environment to a production server). Never store your connection strings directly in Code Behind files or in the markup section of the page. You'll seriously regret the day you have to change your connection string and have to wade through all the pages in your site looking for connection strings.

The Express Edition of SQL Server that you have used so far allows you to work with databases that are *attached* to SQL Server on the fly when you need them. Take a look at the actual connection string to see how this works:

```
Data Source=.\SQLEXPRESS;
AttachDbFilename=|DataDirectory|\PlanetWrox.mdf;
Integrated Security=True;
User Instance=True"
```

This connection string consists of four parts. The first contains the data source to identify the SQL Server that is targeted and can be split in two parts of its own. The part before the backslash (the dot in this example) identifies the server. The dot refers to the local machine although you could also use `(local)`. Additionally, you can enter the server's name here instead of the dot. The part after the dot is optional and is referred to as the *instance name* or simply the *instance*. Since you can install multiple instances of SQL Server side by side on the same machine, the instance name is used to refer to a unique SQL Server instance. When you install SQL Server Express Edition 2005, it gets a default instance name of `SqlExpress`. Therefore, to refer to your SQL Server 2005 Express Edition instance on your local machine you need to refer to it as `.\SqlExpress` or `(local)\SqlExpress`.

`AttachDbFileName` contains a path to your SQL Server Express database. The `|DataDirectory|` placeholder is expanded to the full path of the App_Data folder at run time. So, when your pages load and the `SqlDataSource` needs to connect to the database, it will open the file PlanetWrox.mdf in `C:\BegASPNET\Site\App_Data\`. As an alternative to `AttachDbFileName` you'll also come across `Initial Catalog` in other connection strings. The `Initial Catalog` simply points to a database available on the SQL Server you are using, like PlanetWrox. You'll see more of this in Appendix B.

The last two parts of the connection string have to do with security. With Integrated Security, the account used by the web server is used to connect to the database. In the case of VWD and the built-in web server, this account is the one you use to log on to your machine. In case you're using IIS, this account is a special ASP.NET account. Chapter 18 that deals with deployment, and Appendix B that explains how to connect to SQL Server dig deeper into security related issues.

So far you have seen most of the database concepts that were introduced in the previous chapter. You saw creating (with the `DetailsView` in Insert mode), reading (with the `SelectCommand` and the `GridView`), updating (inline within the `GridView` and an `UpdateCommand`), and deleting (also with the delete option in the `GridView` and a `DeleteCommand`). Moreover, you saw sorting that can be enabled in the `GridView` with just a single property. What you haven't seen is *filtering*, a way to limit the data that is presented in the page. In the next section you will see how to create a filter that allows you to display reviews that belong to a certain genre. You do this in the Management section in a new page called Reviews.aspx that will be your main entry point for managing the reviews in your web site. Subsequent sections build on top of this, gradually expanding the Reviews page with more useful features.

Filtering Data

As you learned in the previous chapter, filtering your data is done with a `WHERE` clause. Fortunately, VWD and ASP.NET come with a bunch of tools that make creating filters very easy. To filter data, the `SqlDataSource` control (and other data source controls) has a `<SelectParameters>` element that enables you to supply values at run time that are used for filtering. These values can come from a few different sources, described in the following table.

With a	The value is retrieved from
`ControlParameter`	A control in the page, such as a `DropDownList` or a `TextBox`.
`CookieParameter`	A cookie that is stored on the user's computer and that is sent to the server with each request.
`FormParameter`	A value posted in the form that has been submitted to the server.
`Parameter`	A variety of sources. With this parameter, you typically set the value through code.
`ProfileParameter`	A property on the user's profile. The ASP.NET Profile is discussed in full detail in Chapter 16.
`QueryStringParameter`	A query string field.
`SessionParameter`	A value that is stored in a session, which is a user-specific store of data that exists during a user's visit to a site.

Because these parameters all behave more or less the same, it's easy to use them in your own code. Once you understand how to use one of them, you'll quickly be able to use the others as well. You'll see the `ControlParameter` at work in the next exercise where you use a `DropDownList` with all the genres to filter a list of reviews that belong to the chosen genre.

Try It Out Setting Up the Filter

To make long lists of data easier to manage, it's a good idea to offer them to the user in smaller, bite-size blocks. For example, when you need to present a list with reviews in your database, it's a good idea to allow your users to filter them by genre. A `DropDownList` with the genres right above the `GridView` with reviews would be the perfect solution for that. You'll see how to build this next.

1. Create a new page called Reviews.aspx in the Management folder and make sure it's based on the Management master page. Change the `Title` of the page to Planet Wrox - Management - Reviews.
2. Add a link to this page in the master page for the Management section:

```
  <li><a href="~/Management/Genres.aspx" runat="server">Manage Genres</a></li>
  <li><a href="~/Management/Reviews.aspx" runat="server">Manage Reviews</a></li>
</ul>
```

3. Go back to Reviews.aspx and switch the page into Design View. From the Standard category of the Toolbox, drag a `DropDownList` control into the page. On its Smart Tasks panel, select Enable AutoPostBack and then click the Edit Items link. Insert an item with its `Text` set to `Please make a selection`, and then clear its `Value` that was inserted for you automatically.

4. Once you return from the ListItem Collection Editor dialog box, the Smart Tasks panel for the drop-down list is still open. Click the Choose Data Source dialog box and choose `<New data source>` from the drop-down list at the top of the screen. The Data Source Configuration Wizard, shown in Figure 12-7, appears.

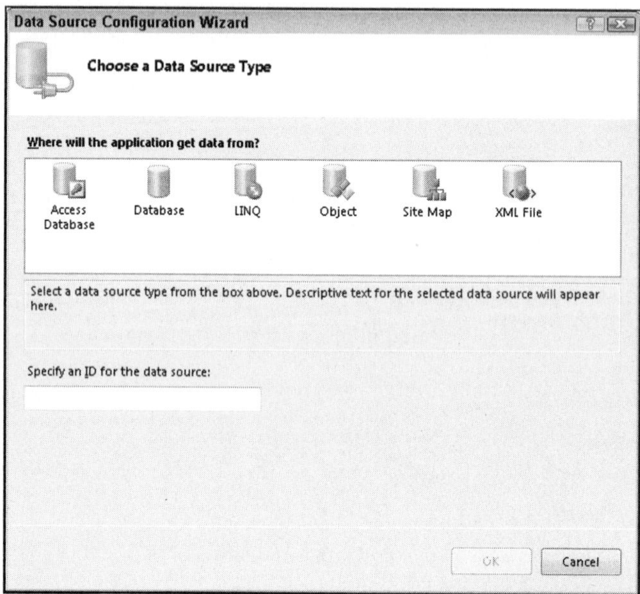

Figure 12-7

5. Click Database, leave the ID set to `SqlDataSource1`, and click OK.

6. In the dialog box that follows, select the connection string called `PlanetWroxConnectionString1` from the drop-down list and click Next.

7. Verify that the radio button for Specify Columns from a Table or View is selected. Also ensure that Genre is selected in the drop-down list with table names and then select the `Id` and `Name` columns in the Columns section. Click the ORDER BY button and choose SortOrder from the Sort by drop-down list and click OK. When you're done, your Configure Data Source Wizard should look like Figure 12-8.

8. Click Next and then Finish to have VWD create the right `SqlDataSource` for you. You return to the Data Source Configuration Wizard for the drop-down list where you can now set up a field that is displayed in the drop-down list for the genres and a field that serves as the underlying value in the list. Choose Name from the first drop-down list that is used to set the data field that is being displayed in the drop-down list. Leave the second drop-down list — used for the underlying value of the items in the drop-down list — set to Id. You should end up with the screen shown in Figure 12-9.

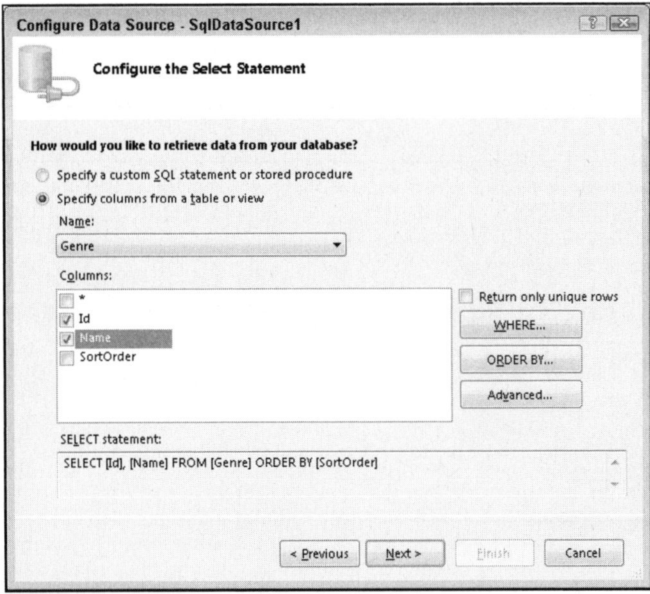

Figure 12-8

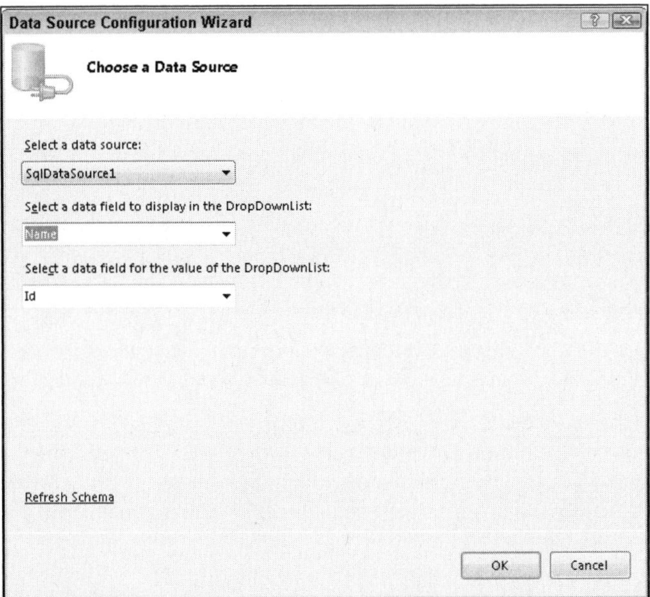

Figure 12-9

9. Click OK to close the dialog box and finish setting up the data source for the drop-down list.

10. With the DropDownList control still selected in Design View, press F4 to open up its Properties Grid and set the property AppendDataBoundItems to True. Switch to Markup View and if the static ListItem that instructs your users to select an item does not have a Value attribute, add it manually and set it to an empty string. Your final code should look like this:

```
<asp:DropDownList ID="DropDownList1" runat="server" DataSourceID="SqlDataSource1"
      DataTextField="Name" DataValueField="Id" AppendDataBoundItems="true"
      AutoPostBack="True">
   <asp:ListItem Value="">Please make a selection</asp:ListItem>
</asp:DropDownList>

<asp:SqlDataSource ID="SqlDataSource1" runat="server"
      ConnectionString="<%$ ConnectionStrings:PlanetWroxConnectionString1 %>"
      SelectCommand="SELECT [Id], [Name] FROM [Genre] ORDER BY [Name]">
</asp:SqlDataSource>
```

11. Save all your changes and then press Ctrl+F5 to open the page in the browser. You should now see a drop-down list with all the genres in the database. Once you choose a new genre from the list, the page posts back to the server. Nothing else happens because you didn't tie any logic to the DropDownList control but you'll see how to do this in the next exercise.

How It Works

At the end of this exercise you end up with code similar to what VWD created automatically when you dropped a GridView on the page in an earlier exercise. You have a data-bound control (the DropDownList) that gets its data from a data source control (the SqlDataSource control). What's different is that the way you set things up gave you a lot more flexibility with regards to the code that is generated. Instead of relying on VWD to generate a SQL statement for all the columns in the database, you now choose only the two columns that you need. Additionally, since the SqlDataSource doesn't require any updates to the data source, you only needed to provide a SelectCommand. You also used the ORDER BY button to control the order in which the items are added to the list.

With the SqlDataSource control set up, displaying the data it returns in a DropDownList control is pretty easy. You start by pointing the DropDownList to the correct data source using the DataSourceID attribute, and then set up the DataTextField and DataValueField to tell the control what columns to use for the text displayed in the control and the underlying value. By setting AppendDataBoundItems to true, you can preserve the item that you add in your code manually. With this setting turned off, the static field Please make a selection would have been cleared as soon as the data-bound items were added.

With the filter set up, the next step is to create the GridView that displays reviews for the selected genre. You'll see how to do this in the next exercise.

Try It Out Applying the Filter

In this Try It Out exercise you add another SqlDataSource that gets its data from the Review table. By creating a filter (the WHERE clause in the SQL statement) you can limit the number of items displayed in the grid to those that belong to a specific genre. The genre chosen in the drop-down list you created in the previous section is sent into the SqlDataSource control's SelectParameters collection using an <asp:ControlParameter>.

1. Switch the page Reviews.aspx to Design View and drag a `GridView` from the Toolbox on top of the existing `SqlDataSource` control. The `GridView` is added right above it and the Smart Tasks panel opens.
2. In the Choose Data Source drop-down list, choose <New data source>. In the Data Source Configuration Wizard, click Database (just as with the wizard for the genres that is shown in Figure 12-7) and click OK.
3. In the dialog box that follows, select the Planet Wrox connection string from the drop-down list and click Next again.
4. Select the `Review` table in the Name drop-down list and then click the asterisk (*) in the Columns list to select all columns.
5. Click the WHERE button that allows you to set up a `WHERE` clause using the `SelectParameters`. In the dialog box that follows, enter the details so the screen ends up like Figure 12-10.

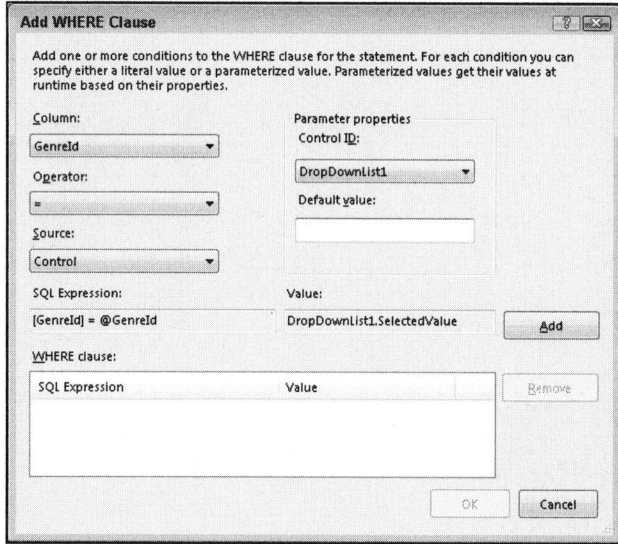

Figure 12-10

For some reason, each of your controls may show up twice in the Control ID drop-down list. It doesn't matter which of the DropDownList1 options you choose.

6. Click the Add button to add the selection to the `WHERE` clause list at the bottom the screen and then click OK.
7. Back in the Configure Data Source wizard, click Next. To test the query, click the Test Query button. If you set up the parameter correctly, a dialog box pops up allowing you to enter a value. Enter a number that you know exists in the `Genre` table and click OK. If there are records in the `Review` table for the chosen genre, they are displayed in the Test Query window. Finally, click Finish to finalize the wizard. If you get a dialog box about refreshing parameters, click Yes to have the code in Markup View updated for you.

8. Just like you did with the genres page, wrap the content inside the `cpMainContent` block in an `UpdatePanel` with a `ContentTemplate` to make refreshing the page when a new genre is chosen as smooth as possible.

9. Save all your changes and open Reviews.aspx in your browser. If you get an error, ensure that you set the `Value` of the static `ListItem` in the drop-down list to an empty string (`""`).

10. Select a new item in the drop-down list. The page refreshes, and now shows the reviews that belong to the chosen genre. If the page doesn't refresh, ensure that you set `AutoPostBack` to true in the previous exercise. At this stage the page looks rather messy as the `GridView` contains many columns, some of which can be very wide (like the `Body` column). In the next Try It Out exercise you see how to fix this.

How It Works

For a large part, this exercise works the same as a previous exercise where you displayed a list with the available genres. What's different this time is the way the `SqlDataSource` is able to filter the records from the `Review` table based on the selection you made in the drop-down list. Take a look at the code for the `SqlDataSource` to see how this works:

```
<asp:SqlDataSource ID="SqlDataSource2" runat="server"
      ConnectionString="<%$ ConnectionStrings:PlanetWroxConnectionString1 %>"
      SelectCommand="SELECT * FROM [Review] WHERE ([GenreId] = @GenreId)">
  <SelectParameters>
    <asp:ControlParameter ControlID="DropDownList1" Name="GenreId"
        PropertyName="SelectedValue" Type="Int32" />
  </SelectParameters>
</asp:SqlDataSource>
```

The SQL statement for the `SelectCommand` contains a parameter for the `GenreId`. That means that the SQL statement only returns records from the `Review` table for a specific genre. At run time, the value for this parameter is retrieved from the control defined in the `ControlParameter` element. In this example, the code is set up to get the value from the `DropDownList1` control. VWD knows that in order to get the selected value from the `DropDownList` it should access its `SelectedValue` property so it adds that as the `PropertyName` for the `ControlParameter`. If you have the need to use a different property, you can simply change it in the `ControlParameter` element's declaration.

With this code set up, the `GridView` asks the `SqlDataSource` for its data. This data source in turn asks the `DropDownList` for the item that the user has selected in the list. This value is inserted in the SQL statement, which is sent to the database. The results that are returned from the database are sent back through the data source to the `GridView`, which uses them to create the HTML table in the browser.

When you choose the Please Make a Selection Item from the drop-down list, you get an empty page with no records. In this case, the `DropDownList` returns an empty string as its value (defined in the `Value` property), which is converted to `null`, the database equivalent of nothing. This in turn causes the query to return no records from the `Review` table.

Until now, you've relied on the code generation tools of VWD to set up the `GridView` and the `DetailsView`. By default, VWD creates a column (for the `GridView`) or a field (for the `DetailsView`) for each column that it finds in the data source. It's smart enough to recognize some of the underlying types of the data in the data source so you get a nice `asp:CheckBoxField` for Boolean (bit) fields in the database, but that's about it. To further customize the look and feel of these data controls, you need to customize their `Columns` and `Fields` collections.

Customizing the Appearance of the Data Controls

By default, the `GridView` and `DetailsView` render columns or rows automatically based on the data they receive. Alternatively, you can have VWD create a number of fields or columns for you when you attach the control to a data source. But, more often than not, you want to change what you see on screen, be it fewer columns, different column headings, or different controls to display data. Fortunately, this is really easy to do with the Fields editor in VWD. In the next section you see how to use this editor to create and modify the different types of built-in columns and fields. In the section that follows, you see how to customize the fields even further with user-defined templates.

Configuring Columns or Fields of Data-Bound Controls

Within the `<Columns>` or `<Fields>` element of the `GridView` and the `DetailsView`, you can add the types of fields shown in the following table.

Field Type	Description
`BoundField`	This is the default field for most data base types. It renders as simple text in read-only mode, and as a `TextBox` in edit mode.
`ButtonField`	This type renders as a link or a button allowing you to execute a command on the server.
`CheckBoxField`	This type renders as a read-only checkbox in read-only mode, and as an editable checkbox in edit mode.
`CommandField`	This type enables you to set up various commands, including editing, inserting, updating, and deleting.
`HyperLinkField`	This type renders as a link (an <a> element). You can set properties like `DataNavigateUrlFields`, `DataNavigateUrlFormatString`, and `DataTextField` to influence the behavior of the hyperlink. You'll see more of this in the next exercise.
`ImageField`	This type renders as an `<img>` element in the browser.
`TemplateField`	This type allows you to define your own look and feel for various templates, like `ItemTemplate`, `InsertItemTemplate`, and `EditItemTemplate`.

Clearly, each Field type serves a distinct purpose so you can choose the one that best fits your needs. You'll see some of these Field types in more detail in the next exercise.

In the next exercise, you'll see how to do the following in the Reviews.aspx page:

- Use the Fields editor to customize the fields for the `GridView` with reviews.
- Use a `HyperLink` column to create a link to a details page that allows you to manage the details of a review.
- Format the output of the existing `BoundField` columns.
- Use a custom function in the Code Behind to have full control over the output in a `TemplateField`.

A later exercise then shows you how to create the details page to insert new and edit existing reviews.

Try It Out — Customizing GridView Columns

1. In Reviews.aspx, open the Smart Tasks panel for the `SqlDataSource2` control and click Configure Data Source. Click Next to skip the connection string screen and then complete the screen as shown in Figure 12-11 by selecting the `Id`, `Title`, `Authorized`, and `CreateDateTime` columns from the Review table. Then click the WHERE button and set up a `WHERE` clause for the `GenreId` column that gets its value from the DropDownList1 control, just as in Figure 12-10.

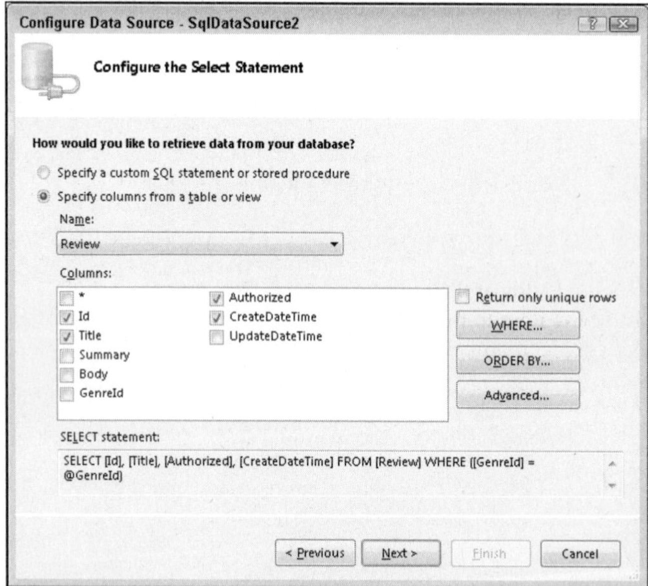

Figure 12-11

Click the Advanced button and have VWD generate commands for the INSERT, UPDATE, and DELETE statements. You can leave the Optimistic Concurrency check box — which deals with detecting changes to the record since it was last loaded from the data source — cleared. Click OK to close the Advanced SQL Generation Options dialog box, then click Next and finally Finish to update the SQL statement in the source for the page. When asked whether you want to reset the fields and keys for the `GridView`, click Yes.

2. At this stage, VWD hasn't created the columns for the `GridView` in Markup View. To do this, open the Smart Tasks panel for the `GridView` and click Edit Columns. This brings up the Fields dialog box. If the Selected Fields list already contains items, use the Delete button (with the big red X) to clear the list first.

3. In the Available Fields list, select Authorized and then click the Add button to copy the item to the Selected Fields list. Repeat this step for the CreateDateTime field. Your dialog box now looks like Figure 12-12.

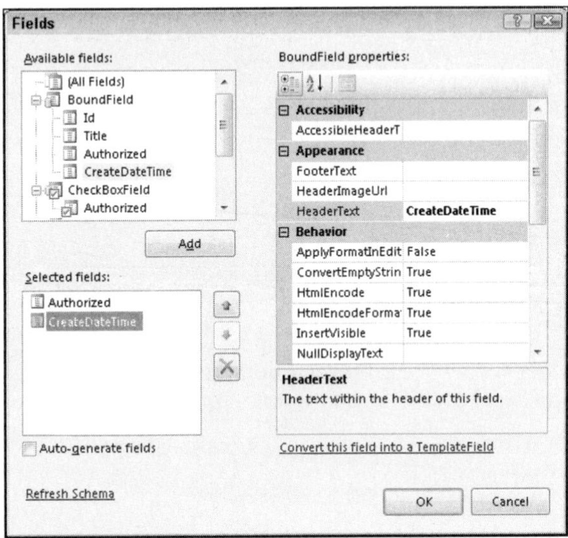

Figure 12-12

4. In the Available Fields at the top of the screen, select `HyperLinkField` and then click the Add button to add the item to the Selected Fields list as well. Move the `HyperLinkField` to the top of the list by clicking the button with the up arrow twice. Then, using the Properties Grid on the right, set the following properties on the `HyperLinkField`.

Property	Set Its Value To
`HeaderText`	`Title`
`DataNavigateUrlFields`	`Id`
`DataNavigateUrlFormatString`	`AddEditReview.aspx?Id={0}`
`DataTextField`	`Title`

5. In the list with Available Fields, click `CommandField` and click the Add button again. Then set the `HeaderText` of the item you just inserted to `Delete` and `ShowDeleteButton` to `True` using the Properties Grid. This allows you to delete reviews from the database using the `GridView` later.

   The Fields dialog box should now look like Figure 12-13.

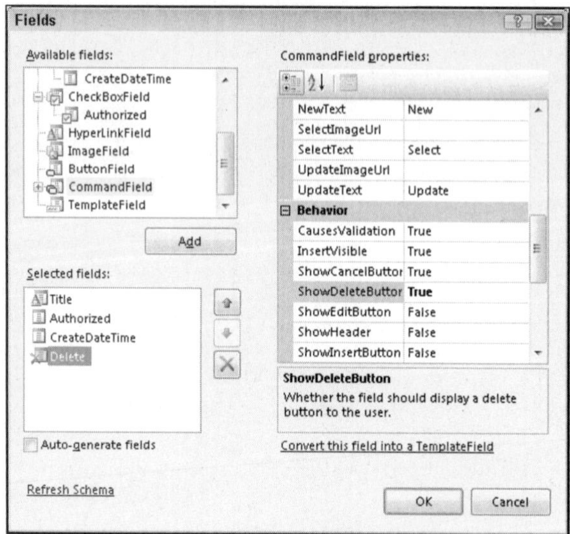

Figure 12-13

6. Click the Authorized column in the Selected Fields list and then click the blue "Convert This Field into a TemplateField" link at the bottom right of the dialog box.
7. Click the CreateDateTime column on the left and set its `DataFormatString` to `{0:g}`.
8. Click OK to apply the changes to the source code.
9. Switch to Markup View and then remove the `<EditItemTemplate>` for the `Authorized` field. The `GridView` displays reviews only in read-only mode, so you don't need this template.
10. Modify the `Label` control in the `ItemTemplate` of the Authorized field so it ends up like this:

```
<asp:Label ID="lblAuthorized" runat="server"
    Text='<%# GetBooleanText(Eval("Authorized")) %>' />
```

11. Switch to the Code Behind of the page and add the following function that returns the text Yes or No depending on the Boolean value that you pass to the top of the class file, right after the `Inherits` line in VB.NET and after the opening curly brace in C#:

VB.NET

```
Protected Function GetBooleanText(ByVal booleanValue As Object) As String
  Dim authorized As Boolean = CType(booleanValue, Boolean)
  If authorized Then
    Return "Yes"
  Else
    Return "No"
  End If
End Function
```

C#

```
protected string GetBooleanText(object booleanValue)
{
```

```
    bool authorized = (bool)booleanValue;
    if (authorized)
    {
      return "Yes";
    }
    else
    {
      return "No";
    }
  }
```

12. Save all your changes (press Ctrl+Shift+S) and then press Ctrl+F5 to open Reviews.aspx in the browser. Choose a genre from the drop-down list and you'll see a list of reviews appear. Note that the Authorized column now shows the text Yes or No. The `CreateDateTime` column shows the date and time in a short format. Figure 12-14 shows the result for the Indie Rock genre.

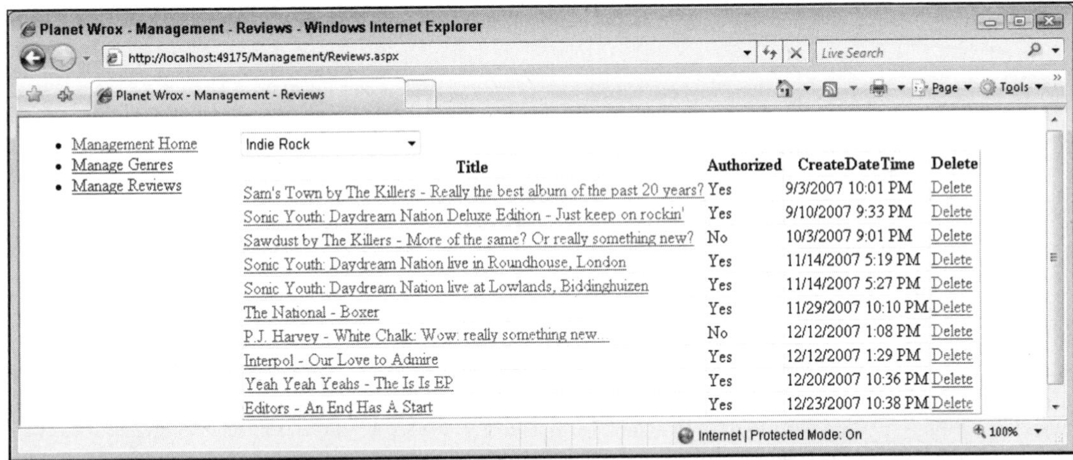

Figure 12-14

Note that the title in the first column of the `GridView` now links to a page where the ID of the review is passed in the query string field `Id`:

```
http://localhost:49394/Management/AddEditReview.aspx?Id=10
```

You'll create this page later in this chapter. You will finish the Delete behavior to delete Reviews from the system in Chapter 14.

How It Works

You started off by modifying the `SelectCommand` for the `SqlDataSource`. Instead of selecting all columns using `SELECT *`, the SQL statement now contains a subset of the columns, making the page load slightly faster:

```
<asp:SqlDataSource ID="SqlDataSource2" runat="server"
    ConnectionString="<%$ ConnectionStrings:PlanetWroxConnectionString1 %>"
    SelectCommand="SELECT [Id], [Title], [Authorized], [CreateDateTime] FROM [Review]
            WHERE ([GenreId] = @GenreId)">
  ...
</asp:SqlDataSource>
```

You then used the Fields dialog box to modify the different fields that are displayed by the `GridView`. You created the Title column using a `HyperLinkField`:

```
<asp:HyperLinkField DataNavigateUrlFields="Id" DataTextField="Title"
     DataNavigateUrlFormatString="AddEditReview.aspx?Id={0}" HeaderText="Title">
</asp:HyperLinkField>
```

The `DataNavigateUrlFields` contains a comma-separated list of fields you want to use in the `DataNavigateUrlFormatString` property. In this case, only one field is used. To display the value of this field you use placeholders such as `{0}` in the `DataNavigateUrlFormatString` property. For example, a review with an ID of 10 will end up with a `HyperLink` column having this `NavigateUrl`: `AddEditReview.aspx?Id=10`. With this setup, the `{0}` is replaced with the value for the first field in the `DataNavigateUrlFields` property. If you defined more fields separated by a comma, you would access them with `{1}`, `{2}`, and so on.

The `DataTextField` is set to the column `Title`. This causes the `HyperLink` to render its `Text` attribute with the title of the review, as shown in Figure 12-14.

You also set the `DataFormatString` property of the bound field for the `CreateDateTime` column:

```
<asp:BoundField DataField="CreateDateTime" HeaderText="CreateDateTime"
     SortExpression="CreateDateTime" DataFormatString="{0:g}"></asp:BoundField>
```

The `DataFormatString` allows you to define the format in which the underlying data is displayed. In this case, the lowercase letter `g` is used to display both the date and the time in short format (without seconds). You'll find more information about the different format strings in the MSDN documentation at `http://msdn2.microsoft.com/en-us/library/97x6twsz(VS.90).aspx`.

You then converted the `Authorized` column to a template column. A template column gives you full freedom with regard to the content you are presenting. Essentially, you can add almost anything you see fit as content for the column, including HTML and ASPX controls. In the previous exercise, you changed the `Label` so that it gets its text from a custom function using the data binding expression syntax `<%# %>`:

```
<asp:Label ID="lblAuthorized" runat="server"
      Text='<%# GetBooleanText(Eval("Authorized")) %>'></asp:Label>
```

Two things are used here to make this work. First, look at the `Eval("Authorized")` statement. This is called a *one-way data binding expression* and results in the value of the `Authorized` column being passed as an object to the custom `GetBooleanText` method. This method in turn converts the incoming value to a `Boolean` and then returns `Yes` or `No`, depending on the value of the `Authorized` column in the database. This is just a simple example to demonstrate how to call custom methods in your Code Behind during data binding. However, the principle remains the same for more complex methods: you pass one or more arguments to a Code Behind method using `Eval("ColumnName")`. The method in the Code Behind accepts these arguments as objects, casts them to an appropriate type, and then uses them as appropriate. In the end, the method can return a string with any text or HTML you see fit.

The `HyperLink` for the Title column that you set up points to a page called AddEditReview.aspx. This page allows you to create new and update existing reviews. You see how to create this page in the following section.

Updating and Inserting Data

Earlier in this chapter I discussed how to do simple updates with the `GridView` and the `SqlDataSource` controls. Although this built-in update behavior is fine in many circumstances, it is not always extensive enough to meet all your demands.

Fortunately, controls like `FormView` and `DetailsView` enable you to tweak their look and feel, giving you a lot more flexibility in the way your end users work with their data. In the next section you see how to use the `DetailsView` to give the user a much easier interface to insert and edit reviews in the database.

Using DetailsView to Insert and Update Data

Earlier in this chapter you learned how to set up a simple `DetailsView` control and fully rely on VWD and the control itself to render the relevant user interface in the browser. Obviously, this default behavior is often not enough. What if you wanted to influence the controls used in the interface? For example, what if you wanted to use a `DropDownList` instead of a simple `TextBox` for the genre? And what if you wanted to add one or more validation controls that you learned about in Chapter 9? Or what if you wanted to manage some of the data being sent to the database programmatically? All of this is possible with the `DetailsView` control, its template-based columns, and the numerous events that the control fires at various stages in its life cycle.

You'll see the template-based columns in the exercise for this section. First, however, you need to learn a bit more about the different events that the data-bound and data source controls fire. The following table lists some of the events that the `DetailsView`, the `FormView`, and the `ListView` expose and raise during their lifetime. The `GridView` has similar events, but they start with `Row` instead of `Item`. Since the `DataList` and `Repeater` controls do not natively support editing of data, they do not have any of these events.

Event	Description
`ItemInserting`	This event fires right before the `Insert` command is executed against the data source. This is an ideal location to change the data that is about to be sent to the database.
`ItemInserted`	This event fires right after the `Insert` command has been executed against the data source.
`ItemUpdating`	This event fires right before the `Update` command is executed against the data source. This is an ideal location to change the data that is about to be sent to the database.
`ItemUpdated`	This event fires right after the `Update` command has been executed against the data source.
`ItemDeleting`	This event fires right before the `Delete` command is executed against the data source.
`ItemDeleted`	This event fires right after the `Delete` command has been executed against the data source.

These six events fire at very convenient moments in the life of the control: right before and right after the data for the operation is sent to the database. You'll see how to use them in the next Try It Out exercise.

Try It Out Managing Data with the DetailsView Control

In this exercise you create the AddEditReview.aspx page that you created a link for earlier in the Reviews page. In this page you create a `DetailsView`, customize most of its fields by implementing template fields, and then handle some of the events of the control to change its behavior. After you're done, you have everything you need to create, list, update, and delete reviews in your web site.

1. In the Management folder, create a new Web Form and call it AddEditReview.aspx. Again, base it on the master page for the Management section and select your programming language. Give it a `Title` of Planet Wrox - Management - Insert and Update Reviews.
2. Switch the page to Design View and drop a `DetailsView` control on the page. In the Smart Tasks panel that opens automatically, choose <New data source> from the Choose Data Source drop-down list. Click the Database icon and then click OK. In the dialog box that follows, choose the connection string from the drop-down list and click Next.
3. Enter the details as displayed in Figure 12-15.

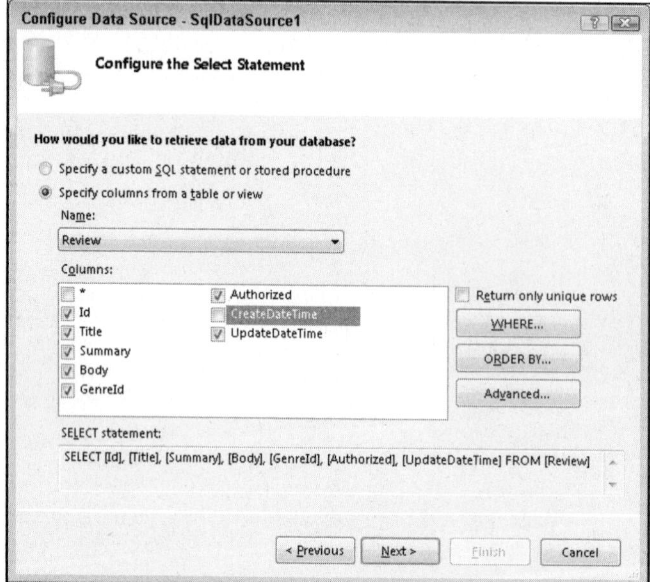

Figure 12-15

Note that all fields of the `Review` are selected explicitly, except for the `CreateDateTime` field.

4. Click the WHERE button to set up a `SelectParameter` that retrieves the review ID from the query string by completing the dialog box as shown in Figure 12-16.

   Don't forget to type **Id** in the QueryString field.
5. Click the Add button to add the parameter and then click OK to close the dialog box.

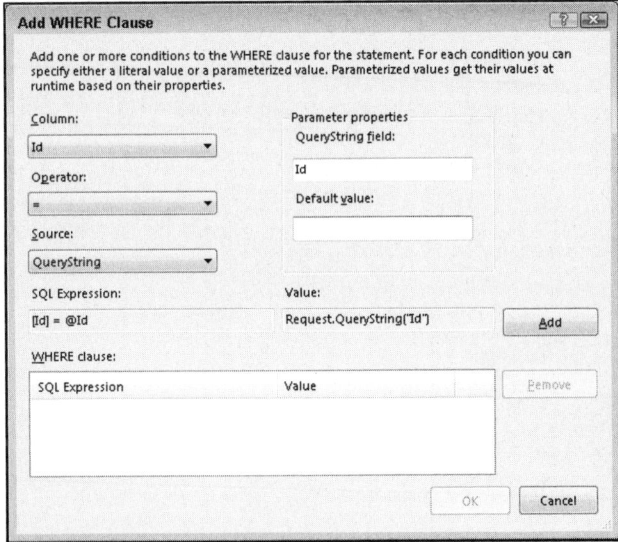

Figure 12-16

6. Back in the Configure Data Source wizard (shown in Figure 12-15), click the Advanced button, select the option to generate `INSERT`, `UPDATE`, and `DELETE` statements, and then click OK to close the dialog box. Finally, click Next and then Finish to finalize the data source wizard.

7. On the Smart Tasks panel for the `DetailsView`, depicted in Figure 12-17, select the options for Inserting and Editing.

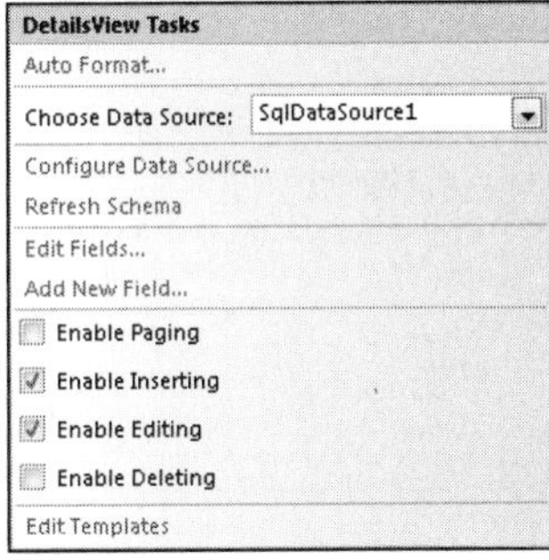

Figure 12-17

8. On the Properties Grid for the `DetailsView`, set `DefaultMode` to `Insert`.

9. Double-click an empty spot of the page in Design View to set up a `Page_Load` handler and enter the following code:

VB.NET

```
Protected Sub Page_Load(ByVal sender As Object, ByVal e As System.EventArgs) _
           Handles Me.Load
  If Request.QueryString.Get("Id") IsNot Nothing Then
```

```
      DetailsView1.DefaultMode = DetailsViewMode.Edit
    End If
End Sub
```

C#

```
protected void Page_Load(object sender, EventArgs e)
{
    if (Request.QueryString.Get("Id") != null)
    {
      DetailsView1.DefaultMode = DetailsViewMode.Edit;
    }
}
```

10. Open the page Reviews.aspx in Design View and drag the page AddEditReview.aspx from the Solution Explorer onto the page below the `GridView`. This creates a link to this page so you can insert new reviews. Switch to Markup View and then change the text between the `<a>` tags to Insert New Review:

```
<a href="AddEditReview.aspx">Insert New Review</a>
```

11. Save all your changes and then open AddEditReview.aspx in your browser. You should get the default layout for the control, with simple text boxes for all the columns in the data source. If you get an empty screen, make sure you set `DefaultMode` to `Insert`. Fill in the fields as shown in Figure 12-18. (The order in which the fields appear may be slightly different in your page.)

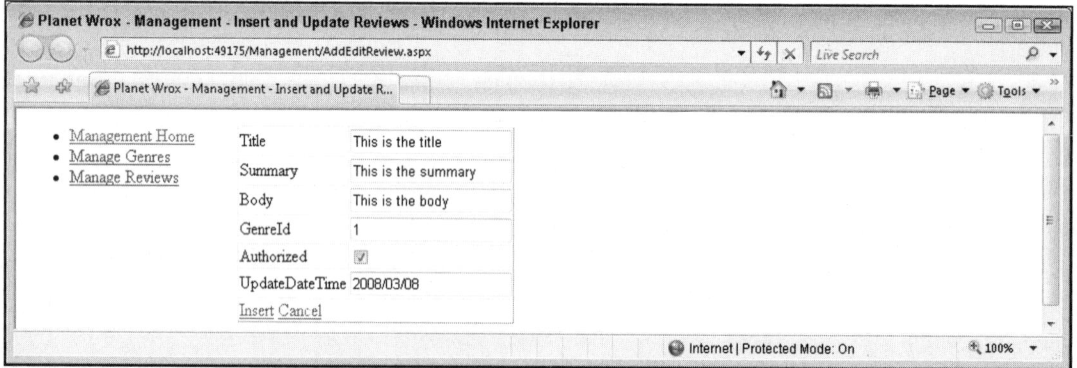

Figure 12-18

Be sure the `GenreId` that you enter matches one of the genres in the `Genre` table in the database or you'll get an error when you try to insert the item. Also be sure you enter a valid date.

Click Insert to insert the item in the database. At first, not much seems to happen, but you can locate the new review through the Reviews.aspx by following these two steps:

- ❑ Click the Manage Reviews link in the menu on the left.

- Select the right genre from the drop-down list at the top of the page. If you are using the database that comes with the download for this chapter and you entered `1` for the `GenreId` when inserting the Review, the genre is Rap and Hip-Hop.

When you have found your review, you can click its title and you'll be taken to AddEditReview.aspx where you can change the review's details again.

How It Works

Most of this exercise should be familiar by now. The `DetailsView` works the same for inserting as the `DetailsView` for genres you saw earlier. What's different is how updates are handled. The code in the Code Behind looks at the query string and if it finds an `Id` query string parameter, it flips the `DetailsView` into Edit mode:

VB.NET

```
If Request.QueryString.Get("Id") IsNot Nothing Then
  DetailsView1.DefaultMode = DetailsViewMode.Edit
End If
```

C#

```
if (Request.QueryString.Get("Id") != null)
{
  DetailsView1.DefaultMode = DetailsViewMode.Edit;
}
```

When the control is in Edit mode, it knows what to do. It calls the `SqlDataSource` and requests its data. The `SqlDataSource` in turn retrieves the ID of the review from the query string, accesses the database, and then returns the right review, which is displayed on the page. When you subsequently click the Update link, the `SqlDataSource` fires its `UpdateCommand` to send the changes to the database.

This exercise provides a nice foundation for the following exercise, where you'll extend the `DetailsView` by implementing custom templates with validation controls and set up various event handlers to respond to the control's events.

Try It Out — Customizing the DetailsView and Handling Its Events

Right now, the page with the `DetailsView` looks quite dull. It would look a lot better and be easier to use if it had the following features:

- A text area instead of a single line text box for the Summary and Body fields
- A drop-down list for the genre filled with the available genres from the database
- Automatic updating of the `UpdateDateTime` column

- Validation controls to stop you from leaving required fields empty
- Automatic redirection to the Reviews.aspx page after an item has been inserted or updated.

This exercise shows you how to implement all of these features.

1. Make sure AddEditReview.aspx is in Design View and bring up the Fields editor for the `DetailsView` control by clicking Edit Fields on its Smart Tasks panel. Locate the `UpdateDateTime` column and set its `Visible` property to `False`.
2. Click the Title column in the Selected Fields list and then click the blue link with the text Convert This Field into a TemplateField. Repeat this for the `Summary`, `Body`, and `GenreId` fields and then close the Fields dialog box by pressing OK.
3. Switch to Markup View and then add a `TextMode` attribute with its value set to `MultiLine` for the four text box controls for the Summary and Body fields. In addition, set their `Width` and `Height` properties to 500 and 100 pixels, respectively. Make sure you do this for both the `EditItemTemplate` and the `InsertItemTemplate`. You should end up with the following code that shows the `Summary` field:

```
<asp:TemplateField HeaderText="Summary" SortExpression="Summary">
  <ItemTemplate>
    <asp:Label ID="Label2" runat="server" Text='<%# Bind("Summary") %>'></asp:Label>
  </ItemTemplate>
  <EditItemTemplate>
    <asp:TextBox ID="TextBox2" TextMode="MultiLine" Width="500" Height="100" runat="server"
           Text='<%# Bind("Summary") %>'></asp:TextBox>
  </EditItemTemplate>
  <InsertItemTemplate>
    <asp:TextBox ID="TextBox2" TextMode="MultiLine" Width="500" Height="100" runat="server"
           Text='<%# Bind("Summary") %>'></asp:TextBox>
  </InsertItemTemplate>
</asp:TemplateField>
```

4. Add a `RequiredFieldValidator` in the `EditItemTemplate` and the `InsertItemTemplate` of both the `Title` and the `Summary` rows. You can enter the code directly, or you can drag and drop it from the Toolbox directly in Markup View. Hook the controls up to the `TextBox` controls in the template by setting the `ControlToValidate` property and provide a useful error message. Give all four `RequiredFieldValidator` controls unique names by setting their `ID` to `reqVal1`, `reqVal2`, and so on.

   - When you're done, the summary field should look like this:

```
<asp:TemplateField HeaderText="Summary" SortExpression="Summary">
  <ItemTemplate>
    <asp:Label ID="Label2" runat="server" Text='<%# Bind("Summary") %>'></asp:Label>
  </ItemTemplate>
  <EditItemTemplate>
    <asp:TextBox ID="TextBox2" TextMode="MultiLine" Width="500" Height="100" runat="server"
            Text='<%# Bind("Summary") %>'></asp:TextBox>
    <asp:RequiredFieldValidator ID="reqVal3" ControlToValidate="TextBox2"
         runat="server" ErrorMessage="Please enter a summary">
    </asp:RequiredFieldValidator>
```

```
  </EditItemTemplate>
  <InsertItemTemplate>
    <asp:TextBox ID="TextBox2" TextMode="MultiLine" Width="500" Height="100" runat="server"
                Text='<%# Bind("Summary") %>'></asp:TextBox>
    <asp:RequiredFieldValidator ID="reqVal4" ControlToValidate="TextBox2"
           runat="server" ErrorMessage="Please enter a summary">
    </asp:RequiredFieldValidator>
  </InsertItemTemplate>
</asp:templatefield>
```

- The Title and Body fields should look similar to this. The TextBox for the Title field doesn't have the TextMode, Width, and Height properties applied whereas the Body field is missing the RequiredFieldValidator. Other than that, the fields should look pretty similar to the Summary field.

5. Switch to Design View and drag a new SqlDataSource control next to SqlDataSource1 that is already on the page. Open its Smart Tasks panel and click Configure Data Source. Select the Planet Wrox connection string from the drop-down list and click Next. Select the Id and Name columns from the Genre table and set up an ORDER BY clause on the SortOrder column by clicking the ORDER BY button and choosing SortOrder from the sort by drop-down list. When you click OK, the Configure Data Source screen looks like Figure 12-19.

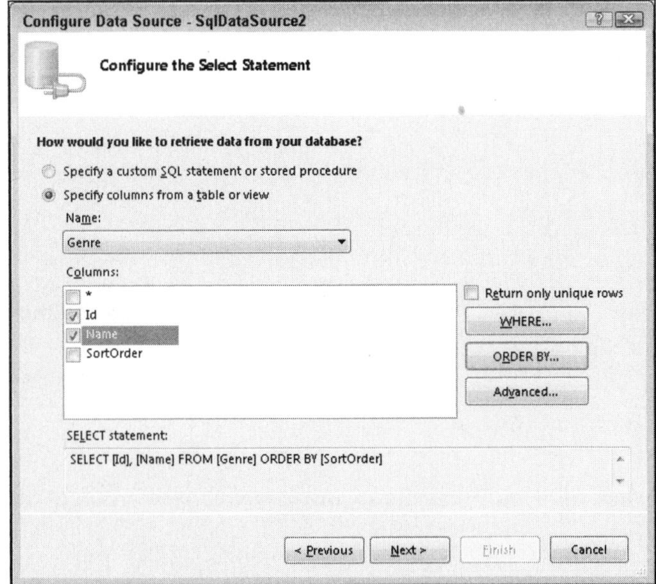

Figure 12-19

6. Click Next and then Finish to finalize the Configure Data Source wizard.

7. Select the new SqlDataSource (called SqlDataSource2) in Design View and change its ID to sdsGenres using the Properties Grid.

8. Switch to Markup View, locate the `InsertItemTemplate` for the `GenreId` of the `DetailsView`, and remove all content (the `TextBox` control). At the place where you removed the `TextBox`, add a `DropDownList` by dragging it from the Toolbox into Markup View. Your code looks like this:

```
<asp:DetailsView ID="DetailsView1" runat="server" AutoGenerateRows="False"
    DataKeyNames="Id" DataSourceID="SqlDataSource1" DefaultMode="Insert" Height="50px"
    Width="125px">
  <Fields>
    ...
    <asp:TemplateField HeaderText="GenreId" SortExpression="GenreId">
      ...
      <EditItemTemplate>
        <asp:TextBox ID="TextBox4" runat="server"
                 Text='<%# Bind("GenreId") %>'></asp:TextBox>
      </EditItemTemplate>
      <InsertItemTemplate>
        <asp:DropDownList ID="DropDownList1" runat="server">
        </asp:DropDownList>
      </InsertItemTemplate>
    ...
  </Fields>
</asp:DetailsView>
```

9. Switch to Design View, click the `DetailsView` once to select it, then right-click the `DetailsView`, and choose Edit Template ➪ Field[4] - GenreId, as shown in Figure 12-20.

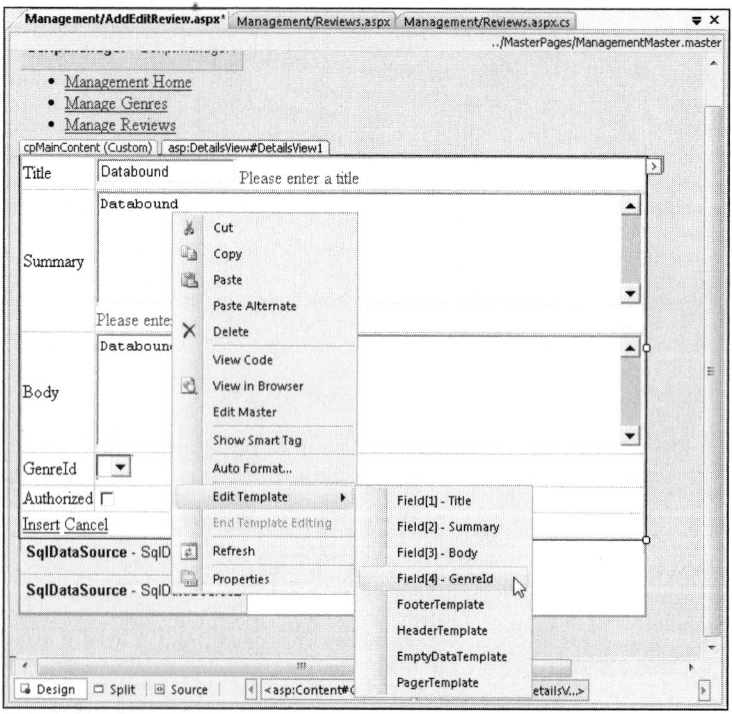

Figure 12-20

10. When the control is in template editing mode, you can directly access the `DropDownList`. Open the `DropDownList` control's Smart Tasks panel and select Choose Data Source. In the Data Source Configuration Wizard choose `sdsGenres` from the data source drop-down list and `Name` and `Id` from the other two drop-down lists (see Figure 12-21).

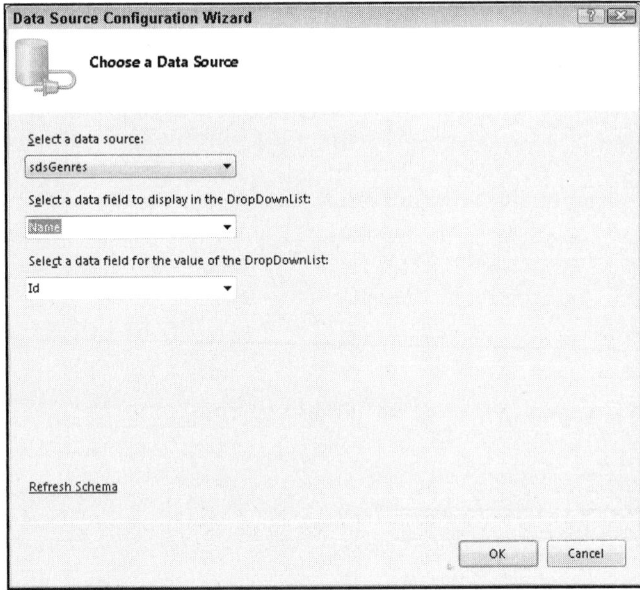

Figure 12-21

11. Click OK to close the Data Source Configuration Wizard.

12. Back on the Smart Tasks panel of the `DropDownList` control-click Edit DataBindings. In the dialog box that follows, click `SelectedValue` in the list on the left and then choose `GenreId` from the Bound To drop-down list on the right, as shown in Figure 12-22.

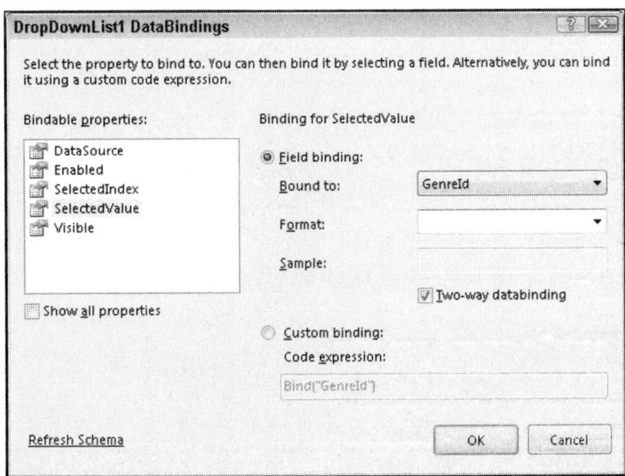

Figure 12-22

13. Click OK to close the dialog box. The code for the `InsertItemTemplate` now looks like this in Markup View:

```
<InsertItemTemplate>
  <asp:DropDownList ID="DropDownList1" runat="server" DataSourceID="sdsGenres"
      DataTextField="Name" DataValueField="Id" SelectedValue='<%# Bind("GenreId") %>'>
  </asp:DropDownList>
</InsertItemTemplate>
```

14. Copy the contents of the `InsertItemTemplate` (the highlighted code in the previous step) and paste it in the `EditItemTemplate`, overwriting the existing `TextBox` control. This adds the same drop-down list to the `DetailsView` in Edit mode.

15. Switch back to Design View, click the `DetailsView`, and then press F4 to open up the Properties Grid. Switch to the Events category of the Properties Grid and double-click the following events. VWD switches to the Code Behind for the page every time you double-click an event, so you need to switch back to the page (using Ctrl+Tab) to add the other events:

    - `ItemInserted`
    - `ItemInserting`
    - `ItemUpdated`
    - `ItemUpdating`

    When you're done, the event category of the Properties Grid should look like Figure 12-23.

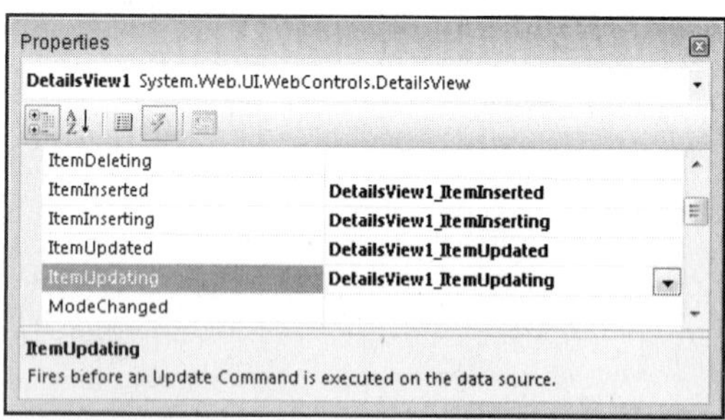

Figure 12-23

16. Go into the Code Behind and modify the code as follows. Note that the `ItemInserted` and `ItemUpdated` handlers call the `EndEditing` method (that you also need to add to the code), whereas `ItemInserting` and `ItemUpdating` both set the `UpdateDateTime` value:

VB.NET

```
Protected Sub DetailsView1_ItemInserted(ByVal sender As Object, _
     ByVal e As System.Web.UI.WebControls.DetailsViewInsertedEventArgs) _
     Handles DetailsView1.ItemInserted
  EndEditing()
End Sub

Protected Sub DetailsView1_ItemInserting(ByVal sender As Object, _
```

```
    ByVal e As System.Web.UI.WebControls.DetailsViewInsertEventArgs) _
    Handles DetailsView1.ItemInserting
  e.Values("UpdateDateTime") = DateTime.Now
End Sub

Protected Sub DetailsView1_ItemUpdated(ByVal sender As Object, _
    ByVal e As System.Web.UI.WebControls.DetailsViewUpdatedEventArgs) _
    Handles DetailsView1.ItemUpdated
  EndEditing()
End Sub

Protected Sub DetailsView1_ItemUpdating(ByVal sender As Object, _
    ByVal e As System.Web.UI.WebControls.DetailsViewUpdateEventArgs) _
    Handles DetailsView1.ItemUpdating
  e.NewValues("UpdateDateTime") = DateTime.Now
End Sub

Private Sub EndEditing()
  Response.Redirect("Reviews.aspx")
End Sub
```

C#

```
protected void DetailsView1_ItemInserted(object sender, DetailsViewInsertedEventArgs e)
{
  EndEditing();
}

protected void DetailsView1_ItemInserting(object sender, DetailsViewInsertEventArgs e)
{
  e.Values["UpdateDateTime"] = DateTime.Now;
}

protected void DetailsView1_ItemUpdated(object sender, DetailsViewUpdatedEventArgs e)
{
  EndEditing();
}

protected void DetailsView1_ItemUpdating(object sender, DetailsViewUpdateEventArgs e)
{
  e.NewValues["UpdateDateTime"] = DateTime.Now;
}

private void EndEditing()
{
  Response.Redirect("Reviews.aspx");
}
```

17. Finally, save all your changes and open AddEditReview.aspx in your browser. Leave all fields empty and click the Insert link. Note that the validation controls kick in, preventing you from sending empty values to the server. Next, fill in valid values and click Insert again. You're now taken to Reviews.aspx. Locate your review by choosing its genre and then click its title to edit it. The `DetailsView` should now display all the values you entered previously (see Figure 12-24).

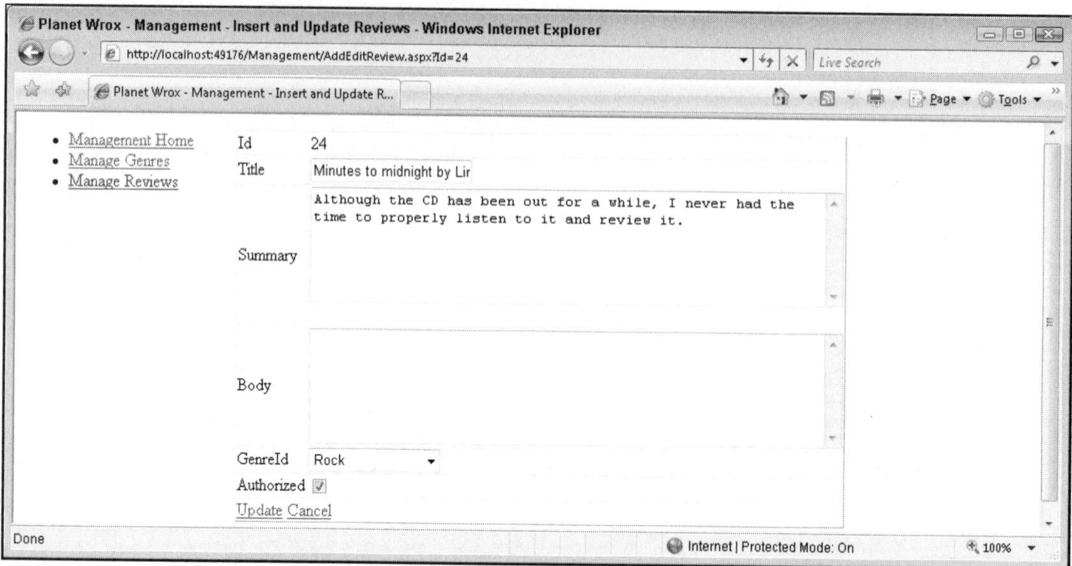

Figure 12-24

How It Works

The DetailsView and the SqlDataSource controls take care of most of the hard work for you. You set up different templates that allow a user to insert new records and update existing records and then the two controls take care of the rest. There are a few interesting things to look at to help you understand how all of this works. Take a look at the InsertItemTemplate for the Title column first:

```
<InsertItemTemplate>
  <asp:TextBox ID="TextBox1" runat="server" Text='<%# Bind("Title") %>'></asp:TextBox>
  <asp:RequiredFieldValidator ID="RequiredFieldValidator2" ControlToValidate="TextBox1"
     runat="server" ErrorMessage="Please enter a title"></asp:RequiredFieldValidator>
</InsertItemTemplate>
```

The most important piece of code in this snippet is the way the Text property of the TextBox is bound. Earlier you saw the one-way binding syntax using Eval that basically outputs the value of a bound column. With Bind, however, something much more powerful occurs. Basically, Bind allows you to express a data binding between a column from the SqlDataSource and a control in the page in *two directions*. In this example, the Title column of a review is bound to the TextBox. This means that when the control must display its data (for example, when updating an existing record) it knows that it must display the Title of a review. But more importantly, on postback, after you click the Update link, the control still understands the relationship between the TextBox control and the Title column. So, when you click Update after making changes to the review in the page, the DetailsView collects all the bound data from the form (the Title, Summary, Body, GenreId, and whether the item is authorized) and then sends it to the SqlDataSource control that has parameters set up for each of the relevant columns of the Review table:

```
<asp:SqlDataSource ID="SqlDataSource1" runat="server"
  ...
  <UpdateParameters>
    <asp:Parameter Name="Title" Type="String" />
    <asp:Parameter Name="Summary" Type="String" />
```

```
      <asp:Parameter Name="Body" Type="String" />
      <asp:Parameter Name="GenreId" Type="Int32" />
      <asp:Parameter Name="Authorized" Type="Boolean" />
      <asp:Parameter Name="UpdateDateTime" Type="DateTime" />
      <asp:Parameter Name="Id" Type="Int32" />
    </UpdateParameters>
  </asp:SqlDataSource>
```

Eventually, the SqlDataSource grabs all the parameter values, injects them in the UpdateCommand, and then sends them to the database.

This all works nice for all columns of the Review table that have a form control attached to them, but what about the other columns? You may have noticed that the CreateDateTime was not a part of any of the SqlDataSource commands. Since the database is set up to insert today's date and time automatically, there's no need to include it in the code. The UpdateDateTime column is a different story. Obviously, you don't want your users to enter the value for this column manually. Instead, the system should keep track of it automatically. That's why you hid the control from the user interface by setting its Visible property to False. However, since the Insert and Update commands still expect a value for this column, you need to find a different way to insert it. Here's where the Inserting and Updating events come into play. Take a look at the ItemInserting event to get a general understanding of how this works:

VB.NET

```
Protected Sub DetailsView1_ItemInserting(ByVal sender As Object, _
     ByVal e As System.Web.UI.WebControls.DetailsViewInsertEventArgs) _
     Handles DetailsView1.ItemInserting
  e.Values("UpdateDateTime") = DateTime.Now
End Sub
```

C#

```
protected void DetailsView1_ItemInserting(object sender, DetailsViewInsertEventArgs e)
{
  e.Values["UpdateDateTime"] = DateTime.Now;
}
```

As you saw earlier, ItemInserting fires right before the InsertCommand is sent to the database. This is a perfect location to supply (default) values for the columns in your table that have no corresponding control in the user interface, as is the case with the UpdateDateTime. This code simply sets the UpdateDateTime value to today's date and time. This value is then sent to the database where it is used to update the Review table's UpdateDateTime value.

The same principle applies to the ItemUpdating command. Within that event, you need to index the NewValues collection instead of the Values collection, but the principle is the same.

If you paid close attention, you may argue that in the case of an Insert command, you don't need to set the UpdateDateTime. After all, the database inserts a value for you automatically when you insert a new record. However, to make the distinction between inserting and updating, you need to do a lot more manual work. You have to remove the column from the InsertCommand and then remove the column from the <InsertParameters> collection as well. Although in itself this is not a lot of work, you get into trouble when you later try to modify the SQL commands for the SqlDataSource, as the Insert and Update commands are now out of sync. Simply setting the UpdateDateTime through code, as in this case, solves many of these problems.

When the `SqlDataSource` control is done with inserting or updating, it fires its `ItemInserted` or `ItemUpdated` events, respectively. Inside these events, the `EndEditing` method is called, which simply takes the user back to the Reviews.aspx page:

VB.NET

```
Private Sub EndEditing()
  Response.Redirect("Reviews.aspx")
End Sub
```

C#

```
private void EndEditing()
{
  Response.Redirect("Reviews.aspx");
}
```

With the discussion of the various events that the `DetailsView` control fires, you have come to the end of this chapter. By now, you should have a reasonably good understanding of how to perform CRUD operations using the `GridView`, `DetailsView`, and `SqlDataSource` controls. The following chapter shows you how to use the `LinqDataSource` control and the `ListView` and `DataPager` controls to perform similar actions without the need to write embedded SQL statements in your code.

Practical Tips for Displaying and Updating Data

The following list provides some practical tips for displaying and updating data.

- Always store your connection strings in the web.config file. Although it may seem easy to store them directly in the `SqlDataSource` in a page, you'll get in trouble when you need to make changes to your connection string later.
- Always consider adding validation controls to your data entry pages. It makes it a lot easier for your users to find out what data is required, and in what format they should deliver it, while you protect your system from receiving and processing invalid or incorrect data.
- If you have long lists of data to present, always consider turning paging on for controls like the `GridView`. Users tend to get lost if you present them with lists of over 50 items. Generally, a page size of somewhere between 10 and 20 items is best.
- Consider renaming the controls in the page to something other than their default values. For example, in the previous Try It Out exercise you renamed `SqlDataSource2` to `sdsGenres`. This makes it much easier to see which data source is needed to get information about the genres. With only a few controls in a page this isn't really an issue, but as soon as your page grows, it is increasingly important to choose distinguishing names for your controls.

Summary

This chapter built on the general knowledge you gained in the previous chapter about accessing a database through SQL. It started off with a discussion of the numerous controls in the Data category of the Toolbox in Visual Web Developer.

These controls can be split in two groups: data-bound controls and data source controls. The first group of controls — including the `GridView`, the `DetailsView`, and the `ListView` — is used to display data in a web page. Most, but not all of them allow you to maintain your data as well, by exposing inserting, updating, and deleting capabilities.

The other group, the data source controls, have no visual appearance themselves. They serve as a bridge between the user interface and the database. There are a number of different data source controls, each providing access to a specific kind of data store. In this chapter you saw the `SqlDataSource` control, which allows you to retrieve data from many different kinds of relational databases.

To offer your users an easy way to manage simple data, like the `Genre` table in the system, you can use the `GridView` in conjunction with a `DetailsView`. Hooked up to a `SqlDataSource`, the `GridView` offers you advanced features like data display, sorting, paging, updating, and deleting with little to no code. The `DetailsView` then allows your users to insert new records, as the `GridView` does not natively support inserting.

To filter data that you display in your web pages, you need to set up a `WHERE` clause in the SQL statement of the `SqlDataSource`. You then hook up the parameters for this `WHERE` clause to any of the available parameters, including the `ControlParameter` that gets its value from an existing control on the page, or the `QueryStringParameter` that gets its data from the query string.

Because it's unlikely that the inline editing capabilities of the `GridView` fit in all your data scenarios, you need to look at other ways to insert and update. One of those ways is the `DetailsView` together with the `SqlDataSource` control. The `DetailsView` allows you to customize the templates for the underlying columns in the data source, enabling you to create a rich user interface using more complex controls than the standard `TextBox`, while also giving you a chance to change the appearance of the controls, add validation controls, and so on.

The `SqlDataSource` control is certainly not the only way to get data in and out of your database. In Chapter 13, I'll introduce you to LINQ to SQL, a new Microsoft technology that allows you to access your database in a much more object-oriented way.

Exercises

1. If you need to create a user interface that allows a user to display, filter, edit, and delete data coming from a database, what is the best control to use? How do you hook up that control to the database?

2. Which control would you pick if you want to display a simple list of the genres in your database in the following format:

```
<ul>
  <li>Punk</li>
  <li>Hard Rock</li>
  <li>Jazz</li>
  <li>Techno</li>
</ul>
```

3. What's the difference between a `BoundField` and a `TemplateField`? When would you use which of the two?

4. What's the best place to store your connection strings? How do you access the connection strings from that location? And why shouldn't you store them in a page?

13

LINQ

If I had to choose my favorite new feature in .NET 3.5, I'd probably pick LINQ, the new query language that is tightly integrated with the programming languages used in the .NET Framework. LINQ stands for *language-integrated query* and enables you to query data from within .NET programming languages similar to how SQL allows you to query data in a database. In fact, the LINQ syntax has been modeled partially after the SQL language, making it easier for programmers familiar with SQL to get started with LINQ.

LINQ comes in a few different implementations, allowing you to access and query a wide variety of sources including collections in your own code, XML files, .NET DataSets, and SQL Server databases from your VB.NET or C# code. In the next section you get a brief overview of the main LINQ pillars while the remainder of the chapter focuses on that part of LINQ that enables you to query Microsoft SQL Server databases, called LINQ to SQL.

In addition to the LINQ syntax that is now part of the two most popular programming languages, C# and Visual Basic, the .NET 3.5 Framework ships with a few additional tools that make using LINQ in your projects a smooth experience.

Additionally, the new `LinqDataSource` control allows you to hook up data-bound controls to LINQ-compatible data sources directly. You'll see how to consume and configure this control in the second half of this chapter.

This chapter introduces you to both the LINQ language and its syntax, as well as to the numerous ways you can use LINQ data in your ASP.NET projects. In particular, this chapter examines the following topics:

- What is LINQ and what does its syntax look like?
- What different forms of LINQ are available and when are they appropriate?
- How do you create LINQ to SQL Classes and how can you query them in your ASPX pages?
- How do you configure and use the new `LinqDataSource` control to access LINQ data sources in your ASPX pages?
- How can you use the new `ListView` and `DataPager` controls together with LINQ to create flexible, data-driven web pages with little to no code.

Introducing LINQ

LINQ enables you to query data from a wide variety of data sources, directly from your programming code. LINQ is to your .NET application what SQL is to relational databases. With straightforward, declarative syntax you can query collections for objects that match your criteria.

LINQ is not just an add-on that is part of the .NET Framework. On the contrary, LINQ has been designed and implemented as a true part of the programming languages in .NET. This means that LINQ is truly integrated into .NET, giving you a unified way to query data, regardless of where that data comes from. In addition, because it is integrated into the language and not in a certain project type, LINQ is available in all kinds of projects including web applications, Windows Forms applications, Console applications, and so on. To help developers get familiar with LINQ, its syntax is closely modeled after SQL, the most popular query language for relational databases. This means that LINQ has keywords like `Select`, `From`, and `Where` to get data from a data source.

To give you an idea of what a LINQ query looks like, here's a quick example that shows a list of Wrox authors whose last names start with the letter S.

VB.NET

```
Imports System.Linq
...
Dim authors As String() = New String() {"Homer, Alex", "Sussman, Dave", _
          "Livermore, Shawn", "Bellinaso, Marco", "Spaanjaars, Imar"}
Dim result = From author In authors _
             Where author.StartsWith("S") _
             Select author
For Each author In result
  Label1.Text += author + "<br />"
Next
```

C#

```
using System.Linq;
...
string[] authors = new string[] { "Homer, Alex", "Sussman, Dave", "Livermore, Shawn",
          "Bellinaso, Marco", "Spaanjaars, Imar" };
var result = from author in authors
             where author.StartsWith("S")
             select author;

foreach (var author in result)
{
  Label1.Text += author + "<br />";
}
```

Although the syntax used in this example is probably quite easy to follow, the example itself is really powerful. Given an array of strings containing author names, you can simply select all the authors whose names start with the letter S. It should come as no surprise that in this example, the `Label` control displays the names of Dave Sussman and Imar Spaanjaars, as only those two names match the `Where` criterion. Of course this is only the beginning. The different types of LINQ allow you to create much more powerful queries against a wide variety of data sources.

Different Types of LINQ

Because LINQ is so powerful and has so much potential, it has been integrated into many different locations of the .NET Framework. The following sections introduce the different LINQ implementations.

LINQ to Objects

This is the purest form of language integration. With LINQ to Objects, you can query collections in your .NET applications as you saw in the previous example. You're not limited to arrays as LINQ allows you to query almost any kind of collection that exists in the .NET Framework.

LINQ to XML

LINQ to XML is the new .NET way to read and write XML. Instead of typical XML query languages like XSLT or XPath you can now write LINQ queries that target XML directly in your application.

LINQ to ADO.NET

ADO.NET is the part of the .NET Framework that enables you to access data and data services like SQL Server and many other different kinds of data sources. With LINQ to ADO.NET you can query database-related information sets, including LINQ to Entities, LINQ to DataSet, and LINQ to SQL. At the time of this writing, LINQ to Entities is still in beta and is expected to be released some time after the official release of Visual Studio 2008, and .NET 3.5. LINQ to Entities is a superset of LINQ to SQL and as such has a much richer feature set than LINQ to SQL alone. However, for many different types of applications, LINQ to SQL will be all you need.

LINQ to DataSet allows you to write queries against the `DataSet`, a class that represents an in-memory version of a database.

Finally, LINQ to SQL enables you to write object-oriented queries in your .NET projects that target Microsoft SQL Server databases. The LINQ to SQL implementation translates your queries into SQL statements, which are then sent to the database to perform typical CRUD operations.

This chapter discusses LINQ to SQL exclusively. For more information about the other types of implementations, check out the official LINQ home page at `http://msdn2.microsoft.com/en-us/netframework/aa904594.aspx`.

Introducing LINQ to SQL

LINQ to SQL is actually LINQ to Microsoft SQL Server. With the official RTM of .NET 3.5 only SQL Server 2000 and 2005 are supported, although it's expected that third parties will release implementations that target other databases.

With LINQ to SQL, you take a bunch of database objects like tables and turn them into .NET objects that you can access in your code. You can then use these objects in queries or use them directly in data binding scenarios.

Working with LINQ to SQL is pretty easy and quite flexible. Using a diagram designer, you drag and drop objects from your database into your LINQ to SQL model. These objects can be tables, views, stored procedures, and even user-defined functions, although this chapter only looks at using tables in your diagrams. The database tables you drop on the diagram become available as objects. For example, if you drop the `Review` table on the diagram, you end up with a strongly typed `Review` class. You can create instances of this class using LINQ queries and other means as you'll see later in this chapter.

When you drop more than one related database table on your diagram, the LINQ to SQL designer detects the relationships between the tables that you created in your database. The designer then replicates these relationships in your object model. For example, if you had a `Review` instance created in code using some LINQ query (as you'll see later), you could access its `Genre` property, which in turn gives you access to properties like `Name`:

VB.NET

```
Label1.Text = myReview.Genre.Name
```

C#

```
Label1.Text = myReview.Genre.Name;
```

Similarly, you can access the associated `Reviews` collection for a specific genre:

VB.NET

```
Repeater1.DataSource = myGenre.Reviews
```

C#

```
Repeater1.DataSource = myGenre.Reviews;
```

Don't worry about the actual syntax right now. You see a lot more of it in the remainder of this chapter. What's important to take away from this section is that LINQ to SQL creates a layer between your .NET application and your SQL Server database. The LINQ to SQL designer takes care of most of the work for you, providing access to a clean object model that you can use in your application.

Mapping Your Data Model to an Object Model

With LINQ to SQL, you map database items such as tables, columns, and relationships in the database, to objects and properties in an object model in your application. VWD comes with great tools to make this mapping as easy as possible as you see in the next exercise. Later sections and exercises in this chapter give you a deeper look at the way LINQ to SQL works.

Try It Out A Simple LINQ Example

In this exercise, you see how to add a LINQ to SQL Classes file to your project, add database tables to the model, and then write a simple LINQ query to access the data in the underlying tables.

1. Open the Planet Wrox project that you have been working on so far. Then right-click the App_Code folder, choose Add New Item, and click the LINQ to SQL Classes item. Type **PlanetWrox** as the name and choose your programming language. Finally, click Add to add the item to your project.
2. VWD adds a file called PlanetWrox.dbml to your site and then opens the Object Relational Designer for you in the main editor window, shown in Figure 13-1.

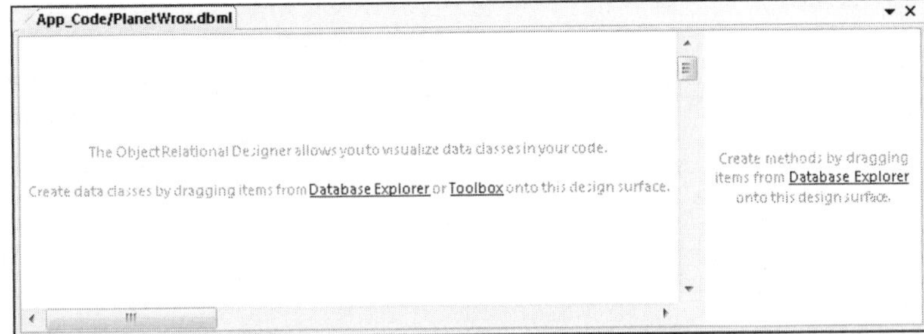

Figure 13-1

This window is split in two parts. In the left pane, you can drag and drop items like database tables or items from the Object Relational Designer Toolbox to create data classes for your application. In the right pane, you can drop items like functions and stored procedures from your database to create additional methods in your database classes.

3. Make sure the Database Explorer (the Server Explorer in the paid versions of Visual Studio) window is open (press Ctrl+Alt+S if it isn't) and then locate your database.

4. Expand the database in the Database Explorer, and then expand the Tables node. Drag the table `Review` from the explorer onto the left side of the diagram, followed by the `Genre` table. Note that VWD draws a line connecting the two tables, shown in Figure 13-2. This is to indicate it has picked up the relationship that you created between these two tables in Chapter 11.

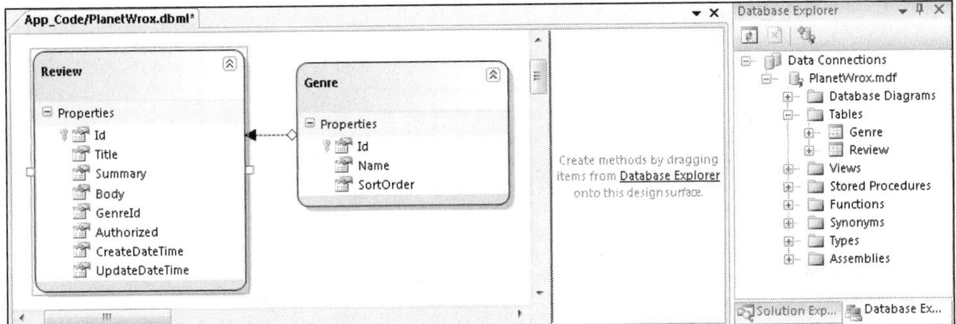

Figure 13-2

5. Save and close the diagram.

6. Switch to the Solution Explorer and open the file All.aspx from the Reviews folder. Switch the page to Design View and drag a `GridView` from the Toolbox onto the page.

7. Double-click the page in the grey, read-only area to have VWD set up a handler for the `Page_Load` event and add the following highlighted code:

VB.NET

```
Protected Sub Page_Load(ByVal sender As Object, ByVal e As System.EventArgs) _
        Handles Me.Load
  Using myDataContext As New PlanetWroxDataContext()
```

```
    Dim allReviews = From review In myDataContext.Reviews _
                     Where review.Authorized = True _
                     Order By review.CreateDateTime Descending _
                     Select review

    GridView1.DataSource = allReviews
    GridView1.DataBind()
  End Using
End Sub
```

C#

```
protected void Page_Load(object sender, EventArgs e)
{
  using (PlanetWroxDataContext myDataContext = new PlanetWroxDataContext())
  {
    var allReviews = from review in myDataContext.Reviews
                     where review.Authorized == true
                     orderby review.CreateDateTime descending
                     select review;

    GridView1.DataSource = allReviews;
    GridView1.DataBind();
  }
}
```

8. Save all your changes and then press Ctrl+F5 to open the page. You'll get a screen full of reviews that have been retrieved from the `Review` table in the database, as shown in Figure 13-3.

   The page looks rather messy because of the way the data is presented in the `GridView`, but in later exercises you'll see how to improve the layout of the grid and the data.

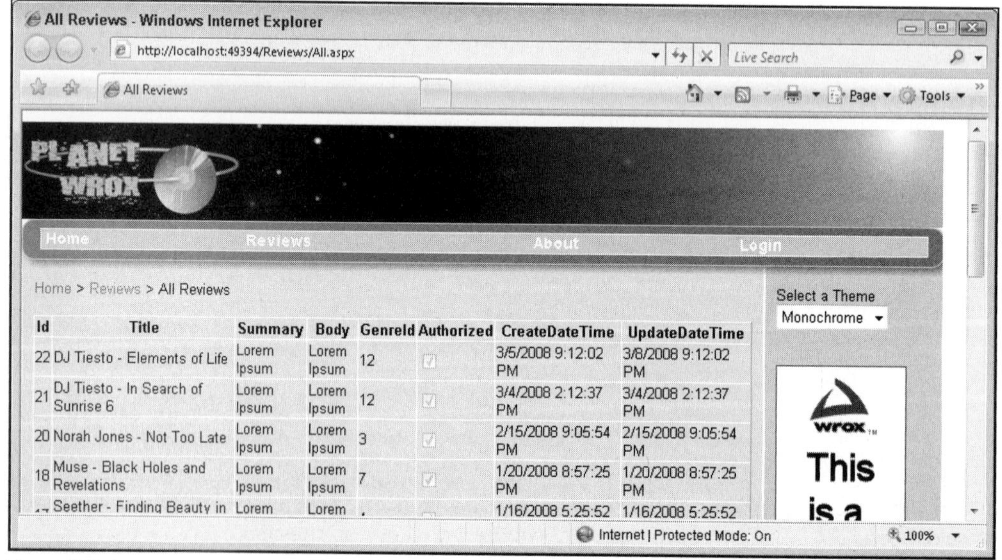

Figure 13-3

How It Works

VWD comes with an object-relational designer that allows you to create an object model that is accessible through code based on the tables in your database. Simply by dragging tables to this designer, VWD generates code for you that enables you to access the underlying data in the database without writing a lot of code. The classes you drag onto your designer are stored in the .dbml file and its Code Behind files. These files contain a class that inherits from `DataContext`, the main entity in LINQ to SQL that provides access to your database. In the previous example, this class is called `PlanetWroxDataContext` (named after the .dbml file) and you use it to access the data in the tables you added to the diagram. Although you normally don't need to look at the generated code, you can open the file PlanetWrox.designer.vb or PlanetWrox.designer.cs and see what code has been generated for you.

The designer is smart enough to detect the relationships in the database and is thus able to create the necessary relationships in code as well, as you saw in Figure 13-2. The model generates two main object types: `Review` and the `Genre`, both of which also have a collection counterpart called `Reviews` and `Genres`, respectively. Note that the designer has correctly pluralized the names of the `Review` and `Genre` tables (Reviews and Genres, respectively), making it easier to see what is a collection (`Reviews`) and what is a single instance of an object (`Review`).

After the model has been generated, you can execute *LINQ queries* against it to get data out of the underlying database. To access the data, you need an instance of the `DataContext` class, which is created inside the `Using` block in the code. A `Using` block (`using` in C#) is used to wrap code that creates a variable that must be disposed off (cleared from memory) as soon as you're done with it. Since the `myDataContext` variable holds a (scarce) connection to the SQL Server database, it's a good idea to wrap the code that uses it in a `Using` block, so the object is destroyed at the end of the block. This `myDataContext` object then exposes your data (like reviews and genres) that you can use in a query:

VB.NET

```
Using myDataContext As New PlanetWroxDataContext()
  Dim allReviews = From review In myDataContext.Reviews _
                   Where review.Authorized = True _
                   Order By review.CreateDateTime Descending _
                   Select review
  ...
End Using
```

C#

```
using (PlanetWroxDataContext myDataContext = new PlanetWroxDataContext())
{
  var allReviews = from review in myDataContext.Reviews
                   where review.Authorized == true
                   orderby review.CreateDateTime descending
                   select review;
  ...
}
```

Note that this query looks similar to the SQL that you learned in the previous chapters. This makes it pretty easy to get started with LINQ if you already understand SQL a little bit. Under the hood, the run time converts this LINQ query into its SQL counterpart, and executes it against the underlying database.

Within this query, the variable review in the From clause is used to refer to the review in the other parts of the query (Where, Order By, and Select), enabling you to specify the select, filter, and ordering criteria.

Besides the Reviews collection the model now also contains a Genres collection. When you want to select all the genres in the database, you can use this query:

VB.NET

```
Dim allGenres = From genre In myDataContext.Genres _
                Order By genre.Name _
                Select genre
```

C#

```
var allGenres = from genre in myDataContext.Genres
                orderby genre.Name
                select genre;
```

In addition to these two separate objects and their collections, both objects have properties that refer to each other's type. For example, a Review instance has a Genre property that provides additional information about the genre the review was assigned to. A Genre instance in turn has a Reviews collection property, giving you access to all reviews posted in that genre. You'll see later how to make use of these properties.

From the keywords used in the first query in this Try It Out exercise it's probably easy to see what the query does: it gets a list of all the reviews in the system that have been authorized and orders them in descending order on their creation date. The result of the query is then assigned to the allReviews variable. You may notice some strange syntax here. For example, the VB.NET example doesn't use an As clause to define the type of the variable. Similarly, the C# snippet uses the new var keyword, also without a type name. Although you may not conclude it from these code snippets, in both languages the variable allReviews is still *strongly typed* and not just a variable of type Object. This works through a concept called *type inference*, where the compiler is able to infer the type for a variable by looking at the right side of the assignment. In this case, the compiler sees that a list of Review objects will be returned from the query, and correctly types the allReviews variable as a *generics* type IQueryable(Of Review) in VB.NET syntax or IQueryable<Review> in C#. While this looks a little scary and incomprehensible at first, it becomes much easier to understand if you simply read it as "a bunch of Review objects that you can access in queries."

These Review objects are then assigned to the DataSource property of the GridView. In previous chapters you saw how to use the DataSourceID property to refer a control like the GridView to a data source control like the SqlDataSource. By using the DataSource property instead, you can assign the actual data, which the control then uses to build up the UI:

VB.NET

```
GridView1.DataSource = allReviews
GridView1.DataBind()
```

C#

```
GridView1.DataSource = allReviews;
GridView1.DataBind();
```

By calling `DataBind()` on the `GridView` you instruct the control to display the individual `Review` objects on the page. Since the `GridView` control's `AutoGenerateColumns` property is `true` by default, the control creates a column for each property it finds on the `Review` object. Later you'll see how to customize the control and the data that is being assigned to the `DataSource` property.

In the following section you learn more about the LINQ query syntax, the language that drives the querying capabilities of .NET 3.5.

Introducing Query Syntax

The query you saw in the previous example is quite simple; it requests all the authorized reviews from the system and returns them in a sorted order. However, the querying capabilities of LINQ are much more powerful than this. In this section you learn more about the LINQ query syntax that you use to query your object model.

Standard Query Operators

LINQ supports a large number of query operators — keywords that allow you to select, order, or filter data that is to be returned from the query. Although all of the examples in this chapter are discussed in the context of LINQ to SQL, you can easily apply them to the other LINQ implementations as well. In the following section you get an overview of the most important standard query operators followed by an example. Each of the examples uses the object model and the `DataContext` object called `myDataContext` you created earlier as the data source to query against.

Select

The `Select` keyword (`select` in C#) is used to retrieve objects from the source you are querying. In this example you see how to select an object of an existing type. Later in this chapter you see how to define new object shapes on the fly.

VB.NET

```
Dim allReviews = From r In myDataContext.Reviews _
                 Select r
```

C#

```
var allReviews = from r in myDataContext.Reviews
                 select r;
```

The `r` variable in this example is referred to as a *range variable* that is only available within the current query. You typically introduce the range variable in the `From` clause, and then use it again in the `Where` and `Select` clauses to filter the data, and to indicate the data you want to select. Although you can choose any name you like, you often see single letter variables like the `r` (for `Review`) or you see the singular form of the collection you are querying (`review` instead of `r` in the preceding examples).

From

Although not considered a standard query operator — since it doesn't operate on the data but rather points to the data — the `From` clause (`from` in C#) is an important element in a LINQ query, as it defines the collection or data source that the query must act upon. In the previous example, the `From` clause indicates that the query must be executed against the `Reviews` collection that is exposed by the `myDataContext` object.

Order By

With `Order By` (`orderby` in C#) you can sort the items in the result collection. `Order By` is followed by an optional `Ascending` or `Descending` (`ascending` and `descending` in C#) keyword to specify sort order. You can specify multiple criteria by separating them with a comma. The following query returns a list of genres first sorted by `SortOrder` in descending order, then sorted on their `Name` in ascending order (the default):

VB.NET

```
Dim allGenres = From g In myDataContext.Genres _
                Order By g.SortOrder Descending, g.Name _
                Select g
```

C#

```
var allGenres = from g in myDataContext.Genres
                orderby g.SortOrder descending, g.Name
                select g;
```

Where

Just like the `WHERE` clause in SQL, the `Where` clause in LINQ (`where` in C#) allows you to filter the objects returned by the query. The following query returns all authorized reviews:

VB.NET

```
Dim allReviews = From r In myDataContext.Reviews _
                 Where r.Authorized = True _
                 Select r
```

C#

```
var allReviews = from r in myDataContext.Reviews
                 where r.Authorized == true
                 select r;
```

Note that the `Where` clause uses the language's standard equality operator: a single equals sign (=) in VB.NET and two of them in C#.

Sum, Min, Max, Average, and Count

These aggregation operators allow you to perform mathematical calculations on the objects in the result set. For example, to retrieve the average `SortOrder` of all genres, you can execute this query:

VB.NET

```
Dim average = (From g In myDataContext.Genres _
               Select g.SortOrder).Average()
```

C#

```
var average = (from g in myDataContext.Genres
               select g.SortOrder).Average();
```

Note that the `Average` method is applied to the entire result set. Therefore, you need to wrap the entire statement in parentheses followed by a call to the `Average` method. Without the parentheses you'll get an error. The `average` variable in this example will be *inferred* as a `Double` and contain the average value of all the `SortOrder` values in the `Genre` table. Not a very useful thing to calculate in a real-world application, but good enough to serve as an example of the `Average` method here.

Similarly, you can retrieve the number of reviews like this:

VB.NET

```
Dim numberOfReviews = (From r In myDataContext.Reviews _
                       Select r).Count()
```

C#

```
var numberOfReviews = (from r in myDataContext.Reviews
                       select r).Count();
```

Take, Skip, TakeWhile, and SkipWhile

`Take` and `Skip` allow you to make sub-selections within the result set. This is ideal for paging scenarios where only the records for the current page are retrieved. `Take` gets the requested number of elements from the result set and then ignores the rest, while `Skip` ignores the requested number of elements and then returns the rest.

Within LINQ to SQL, the `Take` and `Skip` operators are translated to SQL statements as well. This means that paging takes place at the database level, and not in the ASP.NET page. This greatly enhances performance of the query, especially with large result sets since not all elements have to be transferred from the database to the ASP.NET page.

The following example shows you how to retrieve the second page of records, given a page size of 10:

VB.NET

```
Dim allReviews = (From r In myDataContext.Reviews _
                  Select r).Skip(10).Take(10)
```

C#

```
var allReviews = (from r in myDataContext.Reviews
                  select r).Skip(10).Take(10);
```

Just as with `Average`, the query is wrapped in a pair of parentheses, followed by the calls to `Skip` and `Take` to get the requested records.

The `TakeWhile` and `SkipWhile` query operators work in a similar fashion, but allow you to take or skip records while a specific condition is true.

Single and SingleOrDefault

The `Single` and `SingleOrDefault` operators allow you to return a single object as a strongly typed instance. This is useful if you know your query returns exactly one record; for example, when you retrieve it by its unique ID. The following example retrieves the review with an ID of 22 from the database:

VB.NET

```
Dim review22 = (From r In myDataContext.Reviews _
                Where r.Id = 22 _
                Select r).Single()
```

C#

```
var review22 = (from r in myDataContext.Reviews
                where r.Id == 22
                select r).Single();
```

The `Single` operator raises an exception when the requested item is not found or if the query returns more than one instance. If you want the method to return null (for example, for a `Review` or `Genre` that is not found) or the default value for the relevant data type (such as a 0 for an `Integer`, `False` for a `Boolean`, and so on) instead, use `SingleOrDefault`.

Even though there is only one `Review` with an `Id` of `22` in the database, you would still get a list of Reviews (holding only one element) if you omit the call to `Single`. By using `Single` you force the result set into a single instance of the type you are querying.

First, FirstOrDefault, Last, and LastOrDefault

These operators allow you to return the first or the last element in a specific sequence of objects. Just as with the `Single` method, `First` and `Last` throw an error when the collection is empty, whereas the other two operators return the default value for the relevant data types.

In contrast to `Single`, the `First`, `FirstOrDefault`, `Last`, and `LastOrDefault` operators don't throw an exception when the query returns more than one item.

Unfortunately, the `Last` and `LastOrDefault` queries are not supported in LINQ to SQL. However, you can easily accomplish the same behavior with `First` and a `descending` sort order. The following code snippet shows how to retrieve the oldest and the most recent review from the database:

VB.NET

```
Dim firstReview = (From r In myDataContext.Reviews _
                   Order By r.Id _
                   Select r).First()

Dim lastReview = (From r In myDataContext.Reviews _
                  Order By r.Id Descending _
                  Select r).First()
```

C#

```
var firstReview = (from r in myDataContext.Reviews
                   orderby r.Id
                   select r).First();

var lastReview = (from r in myDataContext.Reviews
                  orderby r.Id descending
                  select r).First();
```

Simply by reordering the result set before executing `First`, you actually get the last record in the sequence. Note that in both cases, the type returned by the query is a true `Review` object, allowing you to access its properties like `Id` and `Title` directly.

Shaping Data with Anonymous Types

So far, the queries you have seen in the previous sections returned full types. That is, the queries returned a list of `Review` instances (such as the `Select` method), a single instance of `Review` (`Single`, `First`, or `Last`), or a numeric value (like `Count` and `Average`).

Quite often, however, you don't need all the information from these objects. Figure 13-3 shows a `GridView` with all the properties from the `Review` object. To improve the presentation of this list, you usually want to skip properties like `Body` and `Authorized`, and instead of the genre ID you probably want to display the genre name instead. This is pretty easy to do with *anonymous types*, another feature that is new in the C# and VB.NET languages. An anonymous type is a type without a name that you don't define up front like you do with other types like classes. Instead, you construct the anonymous type by selecting data and then let the compiler infer the type for you.

If you don't define the actual type and give it a name, then how can you access the type and its properties? This is once again done with type inference, where the compiler can see what data is assigned to a variable.

Creating an anonymous type is easy; instead of selecting the actual object using something like `Select review`, you use the `new` keyword in C# and `New With` in Visual Basic and then define the properties you want to select between a pair of curly braces:

VB.NET

```
Dim allReviews = From myReview In myDataContext.Reviews _
                 Where myReview.Authorized = True _
                 Select New With {myReview.Id, myReview.Title, _
                     myReview.Genre.Name}
```

C#

```
var allReviews = from review in myDataContext.Reviews
                 where review.Authorized == true
                 select new { review.Id, review.Title, review.Genre.Name };
```

Although the type is anonymous and cannot be accessed by name directly, the compiler is still able to infer the type, giving you full IntelliSense for the new properties that were selected in the query. Figure 13-4 shows how you access the properties of the anonymous type in the `allReviews` variable, using the `var` keyword in C#.

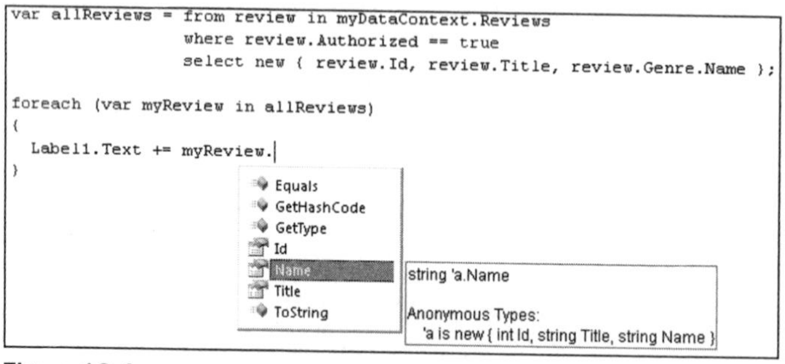

```
var allReviews = from review in myDataContext.Reviews
                 where review.Authorized == true
                 select new { review.Id, review.Title, review.Genre.Name };

foreach (var myReview in allReviews)
{
  Label1.Text += myReview.
}
```

Equals
GetHashCode
GetType
Id
Name
Title
ToString

string 'a.Name

Anonymous Types:
'a is new { int Id, string Title, string Name }

Figure 13-4

Note that the previous query accessed the actual `Genre` property of the `Review`. Besides its `GenreId` (defined as a column in the table `Review` in the database), the `Review` class now also has a strongly typed `Genre` property, giving you direct access to the genre's properties like the `Name` as the previous query demonstrates.

Besides directly selecting existing properties — as shown in the query that selected the `Id`, `Title`, and `Name` of the `Genre` — you can also make up property values and give them different names as you go. For example, the following query creates a new anonymous type that renames the `Id` as `Number`, limits the `Title` to the first 20 characters, and contains a Boolean value that determines whether the item has been updated in the database previously:

VB.NET

```
Dim allReviews = From myReview In myDataContext.Reviews _
                 Select New With {.Number = myReview.Id, _
                    .Title = myReview.Title.Substring(0, 20), _
                    myReview.Genre.Name, _
                    .HasBeenUpdated = (myReview.UpdateDateTime > myReview.CreateDateTime)}
```

C#

```
var allReviews = from myReview in myDataContext.Reviews
                 select new
                 {
                   Number = myReview.Id,
                   Title = myReview.Title.Substring(0, 20),
                   myReview.Genre.Name,
                   HasBeenUpdated = (myReview.UpdateDateTime > myReview.CreateDateTime)
                 };
```

Note the difference between VB.NET and C#; in the VB.NET example, the names of the new properties (`Number`, `Title`, and `HasBeenUpdated`) are prefixed with a period (.). C# doesn't have this requirement and lets you write new property names directly.

The ability to select extra properties that are not present in the original object gives you great flexibility in the data you display. This sample simply determines whether the current review has been updated by comparing the `CreateDateTime` and `UpdateDateTime` properties. The result of this comparison (a Boolean with the value `True` or `False`) is then stored in the property `HasBeenUpdated`. You can select nearly anything you want, including the current date and time, complex calculations, substrings or combinations of properties, and so on.

In the following exercise you see how to create a new anonymous type that has a `Reviews` collection as a property. You'll use this type to create a list of all the available genres in the database, and the reviews that each genre contains.

Try It Out Working with Queries and Anonymous Types

In this exercise you create a simple master detail page that lists all the available genres, each followed by the list of reviews that have been published in the genre. You'll use a `Repeater` control to display the list of genres and a nested `BulletedList` to display the inner reviews. When you're done, you should see a list similar to the one displayed in Figure 13-5.

1. Open the page AllByGenre.aspx from the Reviews folder. Make sure the page is in Markup View and then drag a `Repeater` from the Data category of the Toolbox into the `cpMainContent` content placeholder.
2. Between the opening and closing tags of the `Repeater`, create an `<ItemTemplate>` element. Inside the element create an `<h3>` element that in turn contains a `Literal`. You should end up with this code:

```
<asp:Repeater ID="Repeater1" runat="server">
  <ItemTemplate>
    <h3><asp:Literal ID="Literal1" runat="server"></asp:Literal></h3>
  </ItemTemplate>
</asp:Repeater>
```

3. Set the `Text` property of the `Literal` control to `<%# Eval("Name") %>`. Instead of double quotes, make sure you use single quotes to delimit the attribute's value:

```
<asp:Literal ID="Literal1" runat="server" Text='<%# Eval("Name") %>'></asp:Literal>
```

4. Below the `<h3>` element, drag and drop a `BulletedList` control from the Standard category and set the following properties on the control. You can either enter them directly in Markup View or use the Properties Grid.

Property Name	Value
ID	lstReviews
DataSource	<%# Eval("Reviews")%> (make sure you use single quotes again to wrap this attribute value as shown in the following code snippet)
DataTextField	Title
DisplayMode	Text

You should end up with the following control code:

```
<asp:BulletedList ID="lstReviews" runat="server" DataSource='<%# Eval("Reviews")%>'
    DataTextField="Title" DisplayMode="Text"></asp:BulletedList>
```

5. Switch to Design View and double-click the page somewhere in the read-only area defined by the master page to set up a handler for the `Load` event of the page. Within the handler, write the following code:

VB.NET

```
Protected Sub Page_Load(ByVal sender As Object, ByVal e As System.EventArgs) _
          Handles Me.Load
  Using myDataContext As New PlanetWroxDataContext()

    Dim allGenres = From genre In myDataContext.Genres _
                    Order By genre.Name _
                    Select New With {genre.Name, genre.Reviews}

    Repeater1.DataSource = allGenres
    Repeater1.DataBind()

  End Using
End Sub
```

C#

```
protected void Page_Load(object sender, EventArgs e)
{
  using (PlanetWroxDataContext myDataContext = new PlanetWroxDataContext())
  {
    var allGenres = from genre in myDataContext.Genres
                        orderby genre.Name
                        select new { genre.Name, genre.Reviews };

    Repeater1.DataSource = allGenres;
    Repeater1.DataBind();
  }
}
```

6. Save the changes to your page and then request it in the browser. You should see a similar result as shown in Figure 13-5 where each genre appears as a group header above the lists with reviews.

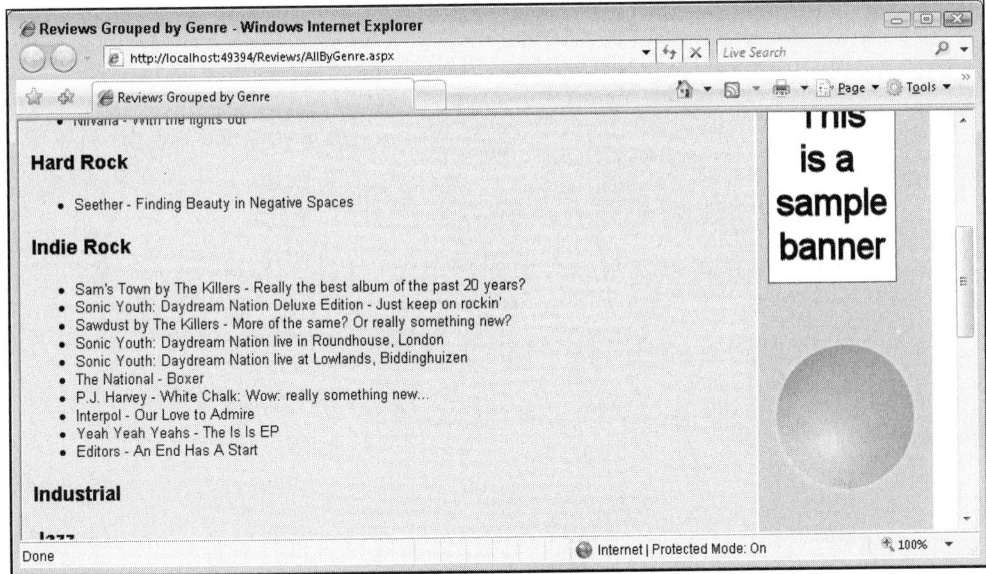

Figure 13-5

How It Works

There are two important things to look at in this exercise. First of all, there's the LINQ query that is used to get the genres and reviews from the database. This query creates a new anonymous type with two properties: the `Name` of the `Genre` as a `String` and a collection of `Review` objects called `Reviews`. The class diagram for the new anonymous type could look like Figure 13-6.

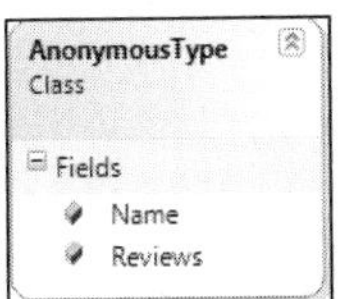

Figure 13-6

These `Name` and `Reviews` fields are then used in the second important part: the `Repeater` control with the nested bulleted list. First, take a look at the `Repeater`:

```
<asp:Repeater ID="Repeater1" runat="server">
  <ItemTemplate>
    <h3><asp:Literal ID="Literal1" runat="server"
         Text='<%# Eval("Name") %>'></asp:Literal></h3>
    <!-- BulletedList here -->
  </ItemTemplate>
</asp:Repeater>
```

Although you haven't worked with the Repeater control before, it may look familiar, as it works in a manner similar to the other data controls. Within the <ItemTemplate> you define the markup that you want repeated for each item in the data source. Using Eval you can get the value of the Title and assign it to the Literal which is wrapped in a pair of <h3> tags. A similar construct is used for the BulletedList to feed it a DataSource:

```
<asp:BulletedList ID="BulletedList1" runat="server" DataSource='<%# Eval("Reviews")%>'
    DataTextField="Title" DisplayMode="Text" />
```

In addition to assigning simple properties like the Text of the Literal from the Name of the underlying data item, you can also use Eval to get complex properties. In this example, Eval("Reviews") is used to get the collection of Reviews for the current Genre. The BulletedList control then understands how to handle this data source and retrieves the Title from each individual Review object and then displays that in the list. The diagram in Figure 13-7 shows you how each Genre contains one or more reviews whose titles are displayed below the name of the genre.

Name (from AnonymousType(0).Name)
Review Title (from AnonymousType(0).Reviews(0).Title)
Review Title (from AnonymousType(0).Reviews(1).Title)
Review Title (from AnonymousType(0).Reviews(2).Title)
Review Title (from AnonymousType(0).Reviews(3).Title)

Name (from AnonymousType(1).Name)
Review Title (from AnonymousType(1).Reviews(0).Title)
Review Title (from AnonymousType(1).Reviews(1).Title)

Name (from AnonymousType(2).Name)
Review Title (from AnonymousType(2).Reviews(0).Title)
Review Title (from AnonymousType(2).Reviews(1).Title)
Review Title (from AnonymousType(2).Reviews(2).Title)

Figure 13-7

After you have set up the Repeater and defined the query, you need to start the data binding process. You do this by assigning the results of the query to the DataSource property of the Repeater, followed by a call to DataBind():

```
        Repeater1.DataSource = allGenres;
        Repeater1.DataBind();
```

These two lines set things in motion: as soon as you call DataBind(), the query is executed and the relevant genres and reviews are retrieved from the database. In this example, the genres are sorted on their Name, but obviously you can order on other columns, like SortOrder, as well. The Repeater then loops through each item in the result set (this item is the anonymous type you just saw) and uses that item's Name to fill in the <h3> element with the genre name. The Repeater then assigns the Reviews collection to the inner BulletedList control's DataSource property. This control loops over the available Review instances, using their Title to build up the bulleted list.

Although it may take you some time to fully understand the principles behind these LINQ queries, I am sure you begin to appreciate their power and accessibility. With just a few lines of code and a few controls, you can create powerful data presentation pages.

However, it's possible to create LINQ queries and use them with the ASP.NET Server Controls with even fewer lines of code. You see how this works in the next section that deals with the new `LinqDataSource`, the `ListView`, and the `DataPager` controls.

Using Server Controls with LINQ Queries

So far you have seen one way to bind the results of a LINQ query to a control in your ASPX page: assign the data to the control's `DataSource` property and then call `DataBind`. This way of getting data into the controls has a few shortcomings. First of all, this method does not support the editing, updating, and deleting of data directly. Secondly, since you define the data source in the Code Behind, the `GridView` doesn't know what data you're feeding it until run time, so you get no tool support to set up its columns. These shortcomings are easy to overcome by using the new server controls, including the `ListView` and the `LinqDataSource` control.

New Controls Introduced in ASP.NET 3.5

Together with LINQ, Microsoft introduced three new controls in ASP.NET 3.5 that enable you to build rich web interfaces with little to no code in no time. Two of them provide a visual interface in your ASP.NET pages, while the third one works as a bridge between your data-bound controls and your underlying data sources. The following table briefly introduces you to these new controls.

Control	Description
`LinqDataSource`	As with the `SqlDataSource` that you saw in previous chapters, the `LinqDataSource` works as a bridge between your data-bound controls and your underlying data sources. This data source can be any of the types that LINQ supports, including SQL Server databases, XML documents, and even arrays and collections. This chapter looks at the `LinqDataSource` from a LINQ to SQL perspective only.
`ListView`	The `ListView` control provides a visual interface that allows you to display, insert, edit, and delete items in a database, providing full CRUD services.
`DataPager`	The `DataPager` is used together with the `ListView` and enables you to paginate the data in the data source, feeding data to users in bite-sized chunks instead of all records at once.

The next few sections provide you more detail about these new controls and show you how to use them in a few Try It Out exercises.

Introducing the LinqDataSource control

As its name implies, the `LinqDataSource` is a close relative of the `SqlDataSource` and other data source controls. The `LinqDataSource` control is to LINQ what the `SqlDataSource` control is to SQL-based data sources: it provides a declarative way to access LINQ-enabled data sources. Just like the `SqlDataSource` control, `LinqDataSource` gives you easy access to the CRUD operations and additionally makes sorting and filtering of data very easy. The following table describes the main properties of this new control. The descriptions should give you a good idea of the capabilities of the control.

Property	Description

`EnableDelete`
`EnableInsert`
`EnableUpdate`
	Whether the control provides automatic insert, update, and delete capabilities. When enabled, you can use the control together with data-bound controls like the `GridView` to support data management. You'll see this at work later.

`ContextTypeName`	The name of the `DataContext` class that the control should use. In the examples in this book, this type name is `PlanetWroxDataContext`.
`TableName`	The table from the LINQ to SQL diagram you want to use, like `Reviews`.

Together with a data-bound control, the `LinqDataSource` provides you full access to the underlying SQL server database through LINQ. The next exercise shows you how to use the control in your ASPX pages.

Try It Out A Simple LinqDataSource Application

In this exercise you start building the Gig Pics feature of Planet Wrox, a section of the web site where users can upload the photos they created during concerts of their favorite bands. You see how to let a user create a new photo album that acts as a placeholder for the pictures that are uploaded. You'll see how to use the `LinqDataSource` and a `DetailsView` to create a user interface that allows a user to enter a name for the photo album into the system. In later exercises you see how to add pictures to this photo album. The database will only contain a reference to the image; the actual picture will be stored on disk as you'll see later.

1. Add the following two tables to your database using the Database Explorer window. Refer to Chapter 11 for more details about creating tables, primary keys, and identity columns. If you don't want to create the tables by hand, you can also grab the database that comes with this chapter's code download.

PhotoAlbum

Column Name	Data Type	Allow Nulls?	Description
`Id`	int	No	The unique ID (identity and primary key) of the photo album.
`Name`	nvarchar(100)	No	The name of the photo album.

Picture

Column Name	Data Type	Allow Nulls?	Description
`Id`	int	No	The unique ID (identity and primary key) of the picture.
`Description`	nvarchar(300)	No	A short text describing the picture.
`Tooltip`	nvarchar(50)	No	A tooltip displayed when you hover over a picture.
`ImageUrl`	nvarchar(200)	No	The virtual path to the picture on disk.
`PhotoAlbumId`	int	No	The ID of the photo album this picture belongs to.

For both tables, make the `Id` column the primary key by clicking it once, and then clicking the yellow key icon on the Table Designer toolbar. Additionally, make this column the table's Identity column by setting the Is Identity property on the Column Properties Grid to Yes. Refer to Chapter 11 if you're not sure how to do this.

2. In the Database Explorer open the database diagram that you created in Chapter 11 and add the two new tables to it (to do this, right-click the diagram and choose Add Table). Then drag the `Id` column from the `PhotoAlbum` table onto the `PhotoAlbumId` column of the `Picture` table. Click OK twice to have the designer create a relationship between the `PhotoAlbum` and `Picture` tables, as shown in Figure 13-8.

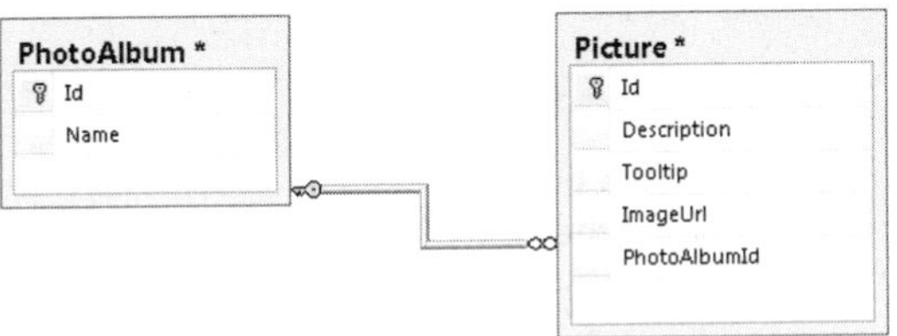

Figure 13-8

3. Save and close the diagram. Click OK to confirm the changes that are to be made to the `PhotoAlbum` and `Picture` tables.

4. Next, open the LINQ to SQL Classes file PlanetWrox.dbml from the App_Code folder. Then from the Database Explorer window drag the two new tables onto the diagram. Your diagram should end up like Figure 13-9.

   Save the changes and then close the diagram.

5. Create a new ASPX file in the root of the site. Call it NewPhotoAlbum.aspx and make sure it's based on your custom template that makes the Code Behind class inherit from your `BasePage` class. Give the page a title of Create New Photo Album.

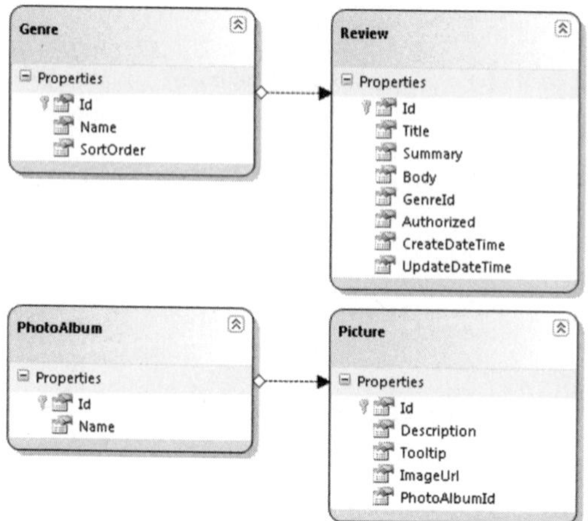

Figure 13-9

6. Switch the page into Design View and from the Data category of the Toolbox, drag a `DetailsView` control and drop it into the `cpMainContent` placeholder. Open the `DetailsView` control's Smart Tasks panel and from the Choose Data Source drop-down list choose <New data source>. In the Data Source Configuration Wizard dialog box, click the LINQ icon and click OK. In the Choose a Context Object dialog box, ensure that the `PlanetWroxDataContext` class is selected and click Next to go to the Configure Data Selection screen, shown in Figure 13-10. From the Table drop-down list, choose PhotoAlbums.

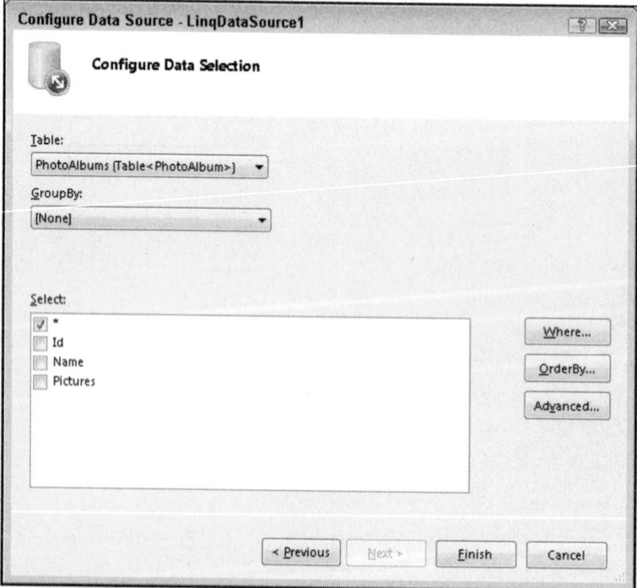

Figure 13-10

This dialog box works in a similar fashion to the `SqlDataSource` wizard you saw in earlier chapters. It allows you to select a table in the Table drop-down list. For this exercise, make sure you choose PhotoAlbums from the drop-down list. At the right-hand side you have buttons to create filters (using the Where button), determine sort order (using the OrderBy button), and tell the `LinqDataSource` whether or not to enable inserting, updating, and deleting.

- ❑ For this exercise, you need insert behavior, so click the Advanced button and then enable inserts, as shown in Figure 13-11.

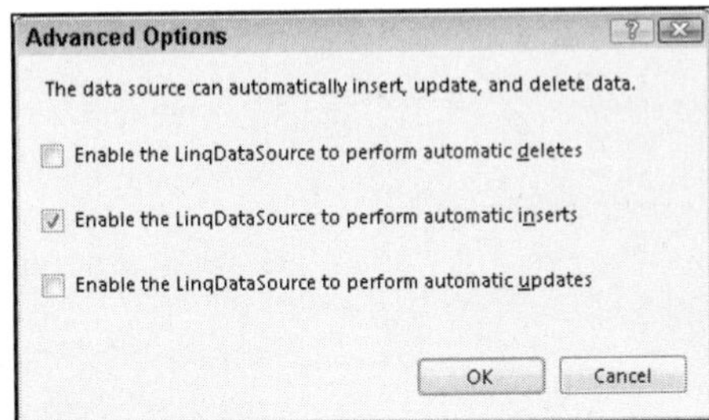

Figure 13-11

- ❑ Click OK to close the Advanced Options screen, and then click Finish to end the configuration wizard.

7. Enable inserting for the `DetailsView` control by checking the item Enable Inserting on the control's Smart Tasks panel.
8. Open the `DetailView` control's Properties Grid and change the `DefaultMode` from `ReadOnly` to `Insert`.
9. Select the `LinqDataSource` control in Design View, open its Properties Grid, and then switch to the Events category. Double-click the `Inserted` event, visible in Figure 13-12.

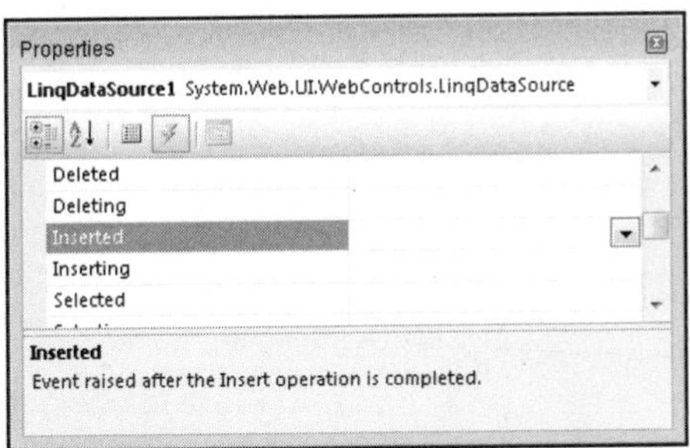

Figure 13-12

10. Inside the event handler, write the following code that redirects the user to a new page once the photo album has been inserted in the database:

VB.NET

```
Protected Sub LinqDataSource1_Inserted(ByVal sender As Object, _
     ByVal e As System.Web.UI.WebControls.LinqDataSourceStatusEventArgs) _
```

```
    Handles LinqDataSource1.Inserted
  Dim myPhotoAlbum As PhotoAlbum = CType(e.Result, PhotoAlbum)
  Response.Redirect(String.Format("ManagePhotoAlbum.aspx?PhotoAlbumId={0}", _
               myPhotoAlbum.Id.ToString()))
End Sub
```

C#

```
protected void LinqDataSource1_Inserted(object sender, LinqDataSourceStatusEventArgs e)
{
  PhotoAlbum myPhotoAlbum = (PhotoAlbum)e.Result;
  Response.Redirect(string.Format("ManagePhotoAlbum.aspx?PhotoAlbumId={0}",
               myPhotoAlbum.Id.ToString()));
}
```

11. Save all changes and then request NewPhotoAlbum.aspx in the browser. Enter a new name for the photo album like `Sonic Youth Playing Daydream Nation Live in London` and click the Insert button. You'll get a page not found error (because you haven't created ManagePhotoAlbum.aspx yet) but you can see the ID of the photo album in the address bar of the browser.

How It Works

You started this exercise by adding `Picture` and `PhotoAlbum` tables to both the database and the LINQ to SQL Classes diagram. These tables are used to store data about photo albums and the pictures they contain. Each individual picture belongs to a `PhotoAlbum` referred to by its `PhotoAlbumId` that points to the `Id` column of the `PhotoAlbum` table in the database. The `Picture` table is designed to only hold data *about* the picture; the actual picture file will be stored on disk as you'll see later.

To allow users to create a new photo album you add a `DetailsView` control to the page. To make sure the control can be used to insert new photo albums, you enable inserting and then set the `DefaultMode` to `Insert`. This forces the control to jump into insert mode, instead of the default read-only mode. You then hook up a `LinqDataSource` to the `DetailsView` which takes care of inserting the photo album in the `PhotoAlbum` table. The code for the `LinqDataSource` control looks like this:

```
<asp:LinqDataSource ID="LinqDataSource1" runat="server"
          ContextTypeName="PlanetWroxDataContext" EnableInsert="True"
          OnInserted="LinqDataSource1_Inserted" TableName="PhotoAlbums">
</asp:LinqDataSource>
```

If you are using Visual Basic.NET, your code won't have the `OnInserted` attribute set. Note how straightforward the `LinqDataSource` is in this scenario: you point it to a `DataContext`, the `PlanetWroxDataContext` in this example. You also turn on inserting by setting `EnableInsert` to `True`. Additionally, you set the `TableName`, so the control knows what table to use from the LINQ to SQL Classes diagram. For simple inserts, this is all you need to do. When the page loads in the browser, the `DetailsView` renders a user interface that allows you to enter a new name for the photo album. When you click Insert, the data you entered is assembled and forwarded to the `LinqDataSource`. This control in turn creates a new `PhotoAlbum` instance and then saves it in the database by sending the appropriate `INSERT` SQL statement to the database.

In many situations, this standard behavior is not enough. You may need to validate the data that is entered or you may have a need to change the actual data before it gets sent to the database. You'll see an example of the latter in a later Try It Out when you upload images to the server. Another common requirement is retrieving the ID of the newly created item, which is sent to the next page. The example uses the following code to accomplish that:

VB.NET

```
Dim myPhotoAlbum As PhotoAlbum = CType(e.Result, PhotoAlbum)
Response.Redirect(String.Format("ManagePhotoAlbum.aspx?PhotoAlbumId={0}", _
                myPhotoAlbum.Id.ToString()))
```

C#

```
PhotoAlbum myPhotoAlbum = (PhotoAlbum)e.Result;
Response.Redirect(string.Format("ManagePhotoAlbum.aspx?PhotoAlbumId={0}",
                myPhotoAlbum.Id.ToString()));
```

The cool thing about the `LinqDataSource` control is that it works with strongly typed objects, where the type maps to the tables you added to the LINQ to SQL Classes diagram. In this case, you are working with real instances of `PhotoAlbum`, the class that represents the photo albums in the web site. This allows you to retrieve the photo album you have inserted in the database in the `Inserted` event of the data source control. The `e` argument exposes a property called `Result` that contains a reference to the new photo album. Simply by casting it to a real `PhotoAlbum` (by using `CType` in VB.NET or putting the class name in parentheses before it), you can access the properties of the `PhotoAlbum`, including its new ID that has been generated by the database (through the Identity settings on the ID column) and then stored in the `Id` property of the `PhotoAlbum`. The final line in the event handler takes the user to the next page and sends the ID of the new photo album in the query string.

Now that you can insert new photo albums, the next logical step is to add pictures to the photo album. In the next exercise you see how to create a user interface with the `ListView` control that allows a user to upload new pictures in the photo album.

Introducing the ListView Control

Up until now, you have seen a few data-bound controls at work. You saw the `GridView`, which is quite powerful, as it supports updates, deletes, sorting, and paging of data, but lacks inserting and generates a lot of HTML markup. You also saw the `Repeater` control that gives you precise control over the generated HTML, but lacks most advanced features that the other data controls have, such as update and delete behaviors and sorting and filtering capabilities. You also saw the `DetailsView` that allows you to insert or update one record at a time.

The `ListView` is a "best of all worlds" control, combining the rich feature set of the `GridView` with the control over the markup that the `Repeater` gives you. The `ListView` enables you to display data in a variety of formats, including a grid (rows and columns like the `GridView`), as a bulleted list (similar to how you set up the `Repeater` earlier in this chapter), and in Flow format, where all the items are placed in the HTML after each other, leaving it up to you to write some CSS to format the data.

The ListView displays and manages its data through templates that allow you to control many of the different views that the ListView gives you on its underlying data. The following table describes all the available templates that you can add as direct children of the ListView control in the markup of the page.

Template	Description
<LayoutTemplate>	Serves as the container for the control. It enables you to define a location where all the individual data items (like Reviews) are placed. The data items, presented through the ItemTemplate and AlternatingItemTemplate are then added as children of this container. You'll see how this works later.
<ItemTemplate> <AlternatingItemTemplate>	Defines the read-only mode for the control. When used together, they allow you to create a "zebra effect," where odd and even rows have a different appearance (usually a different background color).
<SelectedItemTemplate>	Allows you to define the look and feel of the currently active, or selected item.
<InsertItemTemplate> <EditItemTemplate>	These two templates enable you to define the user interface for inserting and updating items in the list. You typically place controls like text boxes, drop-down lists, and other server controls in these templates and bind them to the underlying data source. You'll see how this works next.
<ItemSeparatorTemplate>	Defines the markup that is placed between the items in the list. Useful if you want to add a line, an image, or any other markup between the items.
<EmptyDataTemplate>	Displayed when the control has no data to display. You can add text or other markup and controls to it to tell your users there's no data to display.
<GroupTemplate> <GroupSeparatorTemplate> <EmptyItemTemplate	Used in advanced presentation scenarios where data can be presented in different groups.

Although this long list of templates seems to suggest you need to write a lot of code to work with the ListView, this is not the case. First of all, Visual Web Developer 2008 creates most of the code for you based on the data that is exposed by controls as the LinqDataSource. Secondly, you don't always need all templates, allowing you to minimize the code for the control.

Besides the numerous templates, the control has the following properties that you typically set to influence its behavior.

Property	Description
ItemPlaceholderID	The ID of a server-side control placed within the LayoutTemplate. The control referred to by this property is replaced by all the repeated data items when the control is displayed on-screen. It can be a true server control like an <asp:PlaceHolder> or a simple HTML element with a valid ID and its runat attribute set to server (for example, <ul runat="server" id="MainList"></ul>). If you don't set this property, ASP.NET tries to find a control with an ID of itemPlaceholder and use that control instead.
DataSourceID	The ID of a data source control on the page, like a LinqDataSource or a SqlDataSource control.
InsertItemPosition	The enumeration for this property contains three values — None, FirstItem, and LastItem — and allows you to determine the position of the InsertItemTemplate: either at the beginning or end of the list, or not visible at all.

Just like the other data-bound controls, the ListView has a number of events that fire at specific moments during the control's lifetime. For example, it has ItemInserting and ItemInserted events that fire right before and after an item has been inserted in the underlying data source. Similarly, it has events that trigger right before and after the updating and deleting of data. You'll see more about handling these kinds of events in the next chapter.

Besides the templates, properties, and events you just saw, the ListView has more to offer. For a detailed explanation of the ListView control and its behavior, check out the MSDN documentation or pick up a copy of the book *Professional ASP.NET 3.5*.

The next exercise shows you how to put all of this information together. You see how to define the various templates and set the relevant properties to control the look and feel of the ListView control.

Try It Out — Inserting and Deleting Data with the ListView Control

Inserting items with the ListView is just as easy as with the DetailsView: point the control to a data source and let VWD create the necessary templates for you. However, in many real-world web sites, these default templates won't cut it. You may want to display fewer fields than available in the data source, validate data before it gets sent to the database, or you may want to store data at a different location than the database. For example, you may want to store uploaded images on disk rather than in the database and then only store a reference to the file in the database table. Therefore, the next exercise shows you how to customize the ListView templates and handle the Inserting event of the LinqDataSource to grab the uploaded image and store it on disk.

This exercise has you work with a lot of code that is generated automatically by VWD. Most of what you need to do in this exercise is remove code instead of adding new code. If you get lost somewhere, or you feel your code does not look like it should, remember this chapter comes with the full source code that you can download from the Wrox web site.

1. In the root of the web site, create a new page called ManagePhotoAlbum.aspx and base it on your custom template. Set its `Title` to something like Manage Photo Album and switch into Design View.

2. From the Toolbox, drag a `ListView` control onto the page in the `cpMainContent` placeholder and then hook it up to a `LinqDataSource` control by choosing <New data source> in the Choose Data Source drop-down list on the Smart Tasks panel (just as you did with the `DetailsView` earlier). Make sure you choose `PlanetWroxDataContent` as the context object and in the Configure Data Selection, visible in Figure 13-10, choose the `Pictures` table from the Table drop-down list.

3. Click the Where button to set up a `Where` clause that limits the pictures in the list to those belonging to a specific photo album ID. You may recall that the page ManagePhotoAlbum.aspx receives the photo album ID through the query string so you'll set up a `QueryStringParameter` in this step. Fill in the Configure Where Expression dialog box as shown in Figure 13-13.

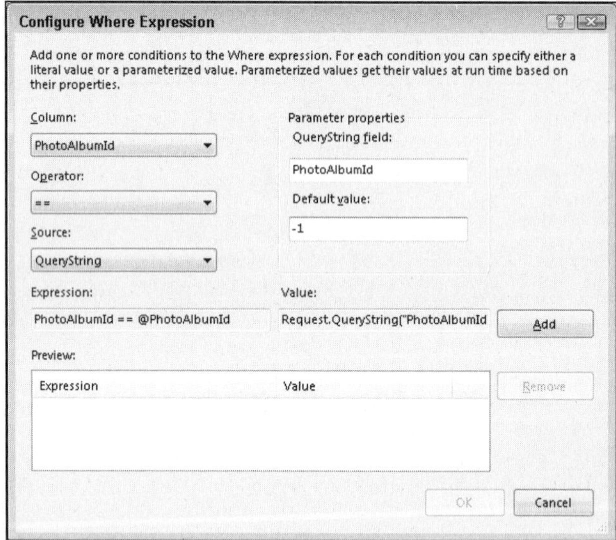

Figure 13-13

4. When you're done, click the Add button to add the parameter to the list at the bottom of the screen and then press OK to dismiss the dialog box.

5. Back in the Configure Data Selection screen, click the Advanced button and check the first two items that give the `LinqDataSource` delete and insert support and click OK. Finally, click Finish to close the Configure Data Source wizard. Back in the page, the `ListView` should appear as a plain rectangle, shown in Figure 13-14, because you haven't provided any template information yet.

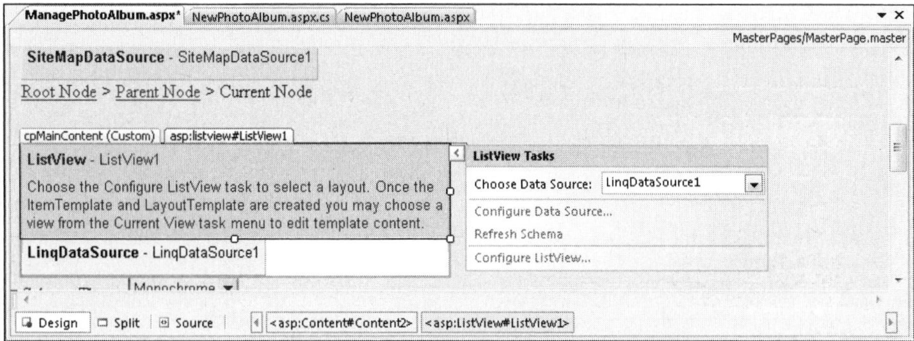

Figure 13-14

6. On the Smart Tasks panel of the `ListView` choose Configure ListView. A dialog box appears that allows you to choose the layout of the control, a style, and whether or not you want to enable operations like inserting and updating. Choose Bulleted List as the layout, and check the Enable Inserting and Enable Deleting items so your dialog box ends up as shown in Figure 13-15.

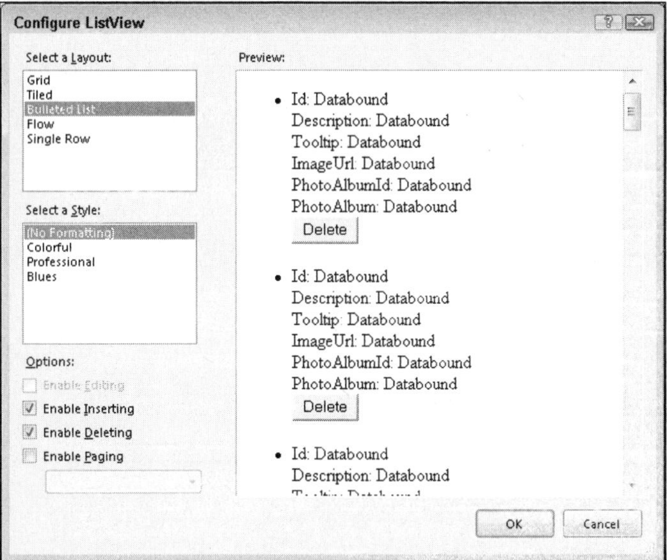

Figure 13-15

7. Click OK to close the dialog box. If you get a dialog box that asks if you want to regenerate the `ListView` control, click Yes.

8. Switch to Markup View and remove the code for the templates listed below. To make this as easy as possible, click the relevant opening tag once, then click the tag in the tag selector at the bottom of the Document Window to select the entire element and its content and then press the Delete key:

    - `<AlternatingItemTemplate>`
    - `<SelectedItemTemplate>`
    - `<EmptyDataTemplate>`
    - `<EditItemTemplate>`
    - `<ItemSeparatorTemplate>`

9. Locate the `<ul>` element in the `LayoutTemplate` and remove the `ID`, `runat`, and `style` attributes. Then add a `class` attribute and set it to `itemContainer`. You can also remove the empty `<div>` element that VWD added for you. Your `<LayoutTemplate>` now contains this code:

```
<LayoutTemplate>
  <ul class="itemContainer">
    <li ID="itemPlaceholder" runat="server" />
  </ul>
</LayoutTemplate>
```

10. Locate the `ItemTemplate` and *remove* the lines that make up the `Id`, `PhotoAlbumId`, and `PhotoAlbum` columns, highlighted in the following code snippet as you don't need them. Make sure you don't accidentally delete the opening `<li>` tag:

```
<li style="">
  Id:
  <asp:Label ID="IdLabel" runat="server" Text='<%# Eval("Id") %>' />
  <br />
  Description:
  <asp:Label ID="DescriptionLabel" runat="server" Text='<%# Eval("Description") %>' />
  <br />
  Tooltip:
  <asp:Label ID="TooltipLabel" runat="server" Text='<%# Eval("Tooltip") %>' /><br />
  ImageUrl:
  <asp:Label ID="ImageUrlLabel" runat="server" Text='<%# Eval("ImageUrl") %>' /><br />
  PhotoAlbumId:
  <asp:Label ID="PhotoAlbumIdLabel" runat="server" Text='<%# Eval("PhotoAlbumId") %>' />
  <br />
  PhotoAlbum:
  <asp:Label ID="PhotoAlbumLabel" runat="server" Text='<%# Eval("PhotoAlbum") %>' />
  <br />
  <asp:Button ID="DeleteButton" runat="server" CommandName="Delete" Text="Delete" />
</li>
```

11. Repeat the previous step for the `InsertItemTemplate` that is also part of the `ListView` control's markup. This template doesn't have an `ID` field, so all you need to remove is `PhotoAlbumId` and `PhotoAlbum`.

Your complete control should now look like this (after some formatting of the HTML source to improve the readability):

```
<asp:ListView ID="ListView1" runat="server" DataKeyNames="Id"
              DataSourceID="LinqDataSource1" InsertItemPosition="LastItem">
  <LayoutTemplate>
    <ul class="itemContainer">
      <li ID="itemPlaceholder" runat="server" />
    </ul>
  </LayoutTemplate>
  <InsertItemTemplate>
    <li style="">
      Description:
      <asp:TextBox ID="DescriptionTextBox" runat="server"
              Text='<%# Bind("Description") %>' /><br />
      Tooltip:
      <asp:TextBox ID="TooltipTextBox" runat="server" Text='<%# Bind("Tooltip") %>' />
      <br />
      ImageUrl:
      <asp:TextBox ID="ImageUrlTextBox" runat="server" Text='<%# Bind("ImageUrl") %>' />
      <br />
      <asp:Button ID="InsertButton" runat="server" CommandName="Insert" Text="Insert" />
      <asp:Button ID="CancelButton" runat="server" CommandName="Cancel" Text="Clear" />
    </li>
  </InsertItemTemplate>
  <ItemTemplate>
    <li style="">Description:
      <asp:Label ID="DescriptionLabel" runat="server" Text='<%# Eval("Description") %>' />
      <br />
      Tooltip:
      <asp:Label ID="TooltipLabel" runat="server" Text='<%# Eval("Tooltip") %>' />
      <br />
      ImageUrl:
      <asp:Label ID="ImageUrlLabel" runat="server" Text='<%# Eval("ImageUrl") %>' />
      <br />
      <asp:Button ID="DeleteButton" runat="server" CommandName="Delete" Text="Delete" />
    </li>
   </ItemTemplate>
</asp:ListView>
```

12. Switch back to Design View, select the `LinqDataSource` control, and open its Properties Grid. Switch to the Events category and double-click the `Inserting` event. In the event handler that VWD added for you, write the following code:

VB.NET

```
Protected Sub LinqDataSource1_Inserting(ByVal sender As Object, _
          ByVal e As System.Web.UI.WebControls.LinqDataSourceInsertEventArgs) _
          Handles LinqDataSource1.Inserting
  Dim myPicture As Picture = CType(e.NewObject, Picture)
  myPicture.PhotoAlbumId = Convert.ToInt32(Request.QueryString.Get("PhotoAlbumId"))
End Sub
```

C#

```
protected void LinqDataSource1_Inserting(object sender, LinqDataSourceInsertEventArgs e)
{
  Picture myPicture = (Picture)e.NewObject;
  myPicture.PhotoAlbumId = Convert.ToInt32(Request.QueryString.Get("PhotoAlbumId"));
}
```

13. Create a new Style Sheet file in the Styles folder and call it Styles.css. Replace the existing CSS in the file with this:

```
.itemContainer
{
  width: 600px;
  list-style-type: none;
}

.itemContainer li
{
  height: 280px;
  width: 200px;
  float: left;
}

.itemContainer li img
{
  width: 180px;
  margin: 10px 20px 10px 0;
}
```

14. Save and close the file.

15. Open the site's master page from the MasterPages folder. Make sure you open MasterPage.master and not the master page for the Management section of the site. Switch to Design View and drag the Styles.css file from the Solution Explorer onto the master page. This ensures that all pages in the site get a reference to this new style sheet, regardless of the theme that is being used.

16. Save all your changes, close all open files, and then request NewPhotoAlbum.aspx in your browser. Make sure you don't accidentally open ManagePhotoAlbum.aspx as it requires a query

string that is sent by NewPhotoAlbum.aspx. Enter a new name for the photo album and then click Insert. You're taken to ManagePhotoAlbum.aspx where you can enter new pictures. For now, all you can do is enter the description of the picture, the tooltip, and a fake URL of the image (just enter some text); you'll see later how to modify this and let a user upload real pictures to the web site. Once you click the Insert button, a new item appears in the list, next to the Insert controls. Add a few more items and you'll notice that the Insert controls move to a row below the others, as shown in Figure 13-16, that shows the Manage Photo Album page in Firefox.

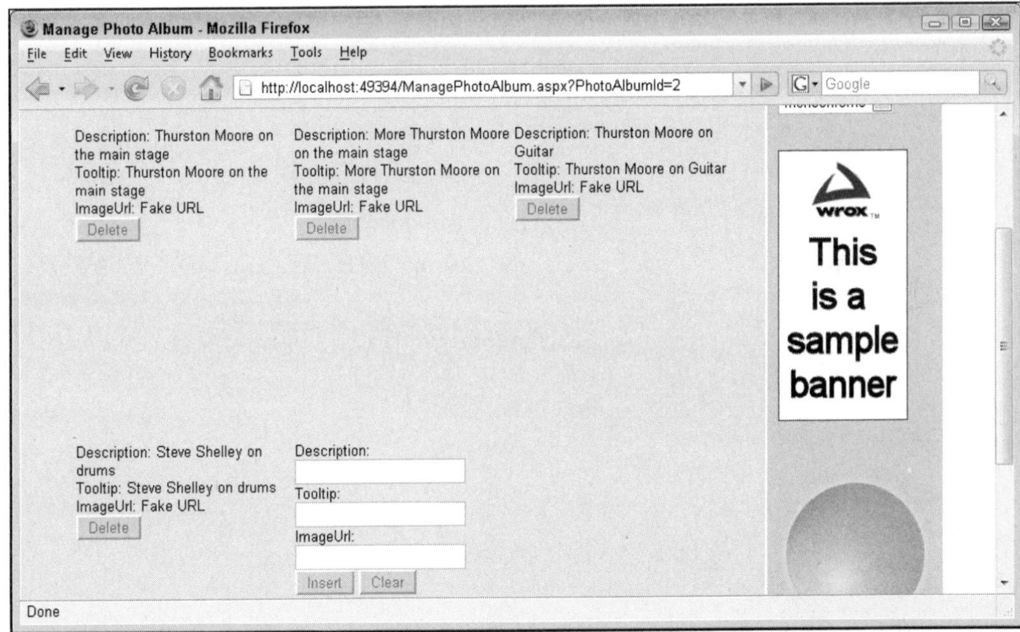

Figure 13-16

17. Click the Delete button for an item and see how the item is removed from the list automatically.

18. If you're currently watching the site in the Monochrome theme, use the drop-down list to switch to DarkGrey. Note that the layout is slightly messed up because there is not enough room to place three images side by side. The fix is easy though. Open up the DarkGrey.css file from the DarkGrey theme folder and add the following CSS to the end of the file:

```
.itemContainer
{
  width: 400px;
}
```

This changes the width for the picture list to 400 pixels, so only two columns of pictures are shown in this theme.

How It Works

You started this exercise by attaching a `LinqDataSource` control to the `ListView` control. The `LinqDataSource` is configured to work with the `Pictures` table. As you saw earlier, each picture is linked to a photo album by its `PhotoAlbumId`. To have the ManagePhotoAlbum.aspx page display only those pictures that belong to the current photo album (identified by the `PhotoAlbumId` query string) you set up a `WhereParameter`:

```
<asp:LinqDataSource ID="LinqDataSource1" runat="server"
    ContextTypeName="PlanetWroxDataContext" EnableDelete="True" EnableInsert="True"
    TableName="Pictures" Where="PhotoAlbumId == @PhotoAlbumId"
    OnInserting="LinqDataSource1_Inserting">
  <WhereParameters>
    <asp:QueryStringParameter DefaultValue="-1" Name="PhotoAlbumId"
          QueryStringField="PhotoAlbumId" Type="Int32" />
  </WhereParameters>
</asp:LinqDataSource>
```

You should take note of two important parts in this markup. First, there's the `WhereParameters` collection that contains a `QueryStringParameter` that looks at the `PhotoAlbumId` field in the query string. When the `LinqDataSource` is about to get its data, it retrieves the value for the parameter from the query string. If there is no value, it uses the `DefaultValue` of `-1` in this example.

The second important part is the `Where` attribute of the `LinqDataSource` control. It uses a `Where` clause to limit the items that are returned from the database:

```
Where="PhotoAlbumId == @PhotoAlbumId"
```

This gets all the `Pictures` from the `Picture` table that have the requested `PhotoAlbumId`. The first time the page loads after you created a new photo album, there won't be any pictures. However, as soon as you start adding items using the `InsertTemplate` of the `ListView` control, you'll see them appear in the list.

To display the pictures on the page, you used the `ListView` control. Just like other data-bound controls, the `ListView` is able to display repetitive data in a structured way. In this example, you set the `ListView` to bulleted list mode, so it presents its data as a set of `<li>` elements. To indicate the container of the items in the list, you use the `<LayoutTemplate>`:

```
<LayoutTemplate>
  <ul class="itemContainer">
    <li ID="itemPlaceholder" runat="server" />
  </ul>
</LayoutTemplate>
```

Note that this `<li>` has its `ID` set to `itemPlaceholder`. This tells the `ListView` control where to add the individual pictures. At run time, this element will be *replaced* by the actual items from the templates like `<ItemTemplate>`.

When the ListView control needs to display its data, it creates an item based on the <ItemTemplate> for each data item in the data source. In this example, each data item is a strongly typed Picture object that allows you to access properties like ToolTip and Description:

```
<ItemTemplate>
  <li>
    ...
    Tooltip:
    <asp:Label ID="TooltipLabel" runat="server" Text='<%# Eval("Tooltip") %>' />< />
    ...
    <asp:Button ID="DeleteButton" runat="server" CommandName="Delete" " />
  </li>
</ItemTemplate>
```

With this code in place, each item in the data source is presented as a series of labels that display relevant properties of the picture. Eval(*PropertyName*) is used to retrieve the requested value from the object, which is then displayed as the Label control's text. Note that at this stage, the <ItemTemplate> only displays data *about* the picture. You'll see how to upload and display real pictures later.

Note the CommandName of the Button control in the ItemTemplate. It's set to Delete which turns this button into a true Delete button. When you click it, the ListView figures out what picture you clicked the button for and then instructs the LinqDataSource control to delete the associated picture from the database.

The CSS you added to the Styles.css displays the items in an organized way. By setting the class attribute of the <ul> control to itemContainer, the following CSS is applied to that list:

```
.itemContainer
{
  width: 600px;
  list-style-type: none;
}
```

The first declaration sets the entire width of the list to 600 pixels while the second declaration removes the bullet from the items in the list. Each item in the list is then displayed within a <li> element, to which the following CSS is applied:

```
.itemContainer li
{
  height: 280px;
  width: 200px;
  float: left;
}
```

Each item gets a forced width of 200 pixels. The float property tells each <li> element to float next to each other. Within the parent area of 600 pixels you can fit three <li> elements of 200 pixels each, causing the fourth and further elements to be placed on their own line. This is a great alternative to presenting data with HTML tables, which generally needs a lot more markup to achieve the same effect.

Finally, each image within the <li> element gets a forced width of 180 pixels and 10 pixels of margin at the top and bottom, 20 pixels on the right (to create some room between the images) and none at the left side:

```
.itemContainer li img
{
  width: 180px;
  margin: 10px 20px 10px 0;
}
```

In the DarkGrey theme, the width of the itemContainer is overridden to only 400 pixels. This way, the <div> is just wide enough to display two images side by side.

In contrast to many of the other data-bound controls, the ListView also supports inserting. You define an InsertItemTemplate that contains one or more controls that are bound to properties in the underlying object. For example the Description property of the picture is bound like this:

```
<InsertItemTemplate>
  <li>
    Description:
    <asp:TextBox ID="DescriptionTextBox" runat="server"
                     Text='<%# Bind("Description") %>' /><br />
    ...
</InsertItemTemplate>
```

Instead of Eval(*ColumnName*), this code uses Bind(*ColumnName*) to set up a two-way binding mechanism. This ensures that the ASP.NET run time is able to figure out the relationship between the Description property of a Picture and the text box called DescriptionTextBox, even after a postback. So when you enter some details and press the special Insert button (with its CommandName set to Insert), a new Picture object is constructed, its properties like Description, Title, and ToolTip are filled with the values from the associated server controls in the InsertItemTemplate and then the picture is forwarded to the LinqDataSource control, which takes care of saving the item in the database and refreshing the list of pictures that are displayed on the page.

Obviously, it's not very user friendly to have the user enter the ImageUrl of an image directly. It would be much easier for them if they could pick an image from their local computer and upload it to the server. You'll see how to accomplish this in the next exercise.

Try It Out — Customizing Templates of the ListView Control

The default templates for the ListView control that VWD generates based on the information from the LinqDataSource are enough only in the most trivial situations. Usually, you need much more control. For example, in the ItemTemplate you may want to display an actual <asp:Image> control instead of the plain ImageUrl property as text. Likewise, in the InsertItemTemplate you may want to display a file upload control instead of a simple text box. In the next exercise, you see how to change the standard templates so you can incorporate both features in your page. Additionally, you see how to handle the Inserting event of the LinqDataSource control to save the uploaded file to disk, and update the database with the URL of the image.

For this example to work, the account used by the web server (the account you use to log on to your machine if you are using the built-in web server that comes with VWD) needs read and write permissions to the GigPics folder that you will create in this exercise. To configure the permissions, refer to the section "Understanding Security in IIS" in Chapter 18.

1. Create a new folder in the root of the web site called GigPics. This folder contains the uploaded images that users took at gigs they went to.

2. Open the page ManagePhotoAlbum.aspx in Markup View and locate the `<ItemTemplate>` element. Remove the `Label` that displays the `ImageUrl` and replace it with an `Image` control, with its `ImageUrl` set to the `ImageUrl` of the picture object.

```
<asp:Image ID="ImageUrl" runat="server" ImageUrl='<%# Eval("ImageUrl") %>' />
```

   Remove the text `ImageUrl:` that appears right above the image.

3. To allow users to upload images, you need to replace the `TextBox` for the `ImageUrl` property with a `FileUpload` control. You also need to remove the text `ImageUrl:` again. You do this in the `InsertItemTemplate`:

```
<asp:TextBox ID="TooltipTextBox" runat="server" Text='<%# Bind("Tooltip") %>' /><br />
<asp:FileUpload ID="FileUpload1" runat="server" /><br />
<asp:Button ID="InsertButton" runat="server" CommandName="Insert" Text="Insert" />
```

   Note that you don't need to bind the property to the control here. Because the uploaded image needs special treatment, you'll write some code in the Code Behind of the page instead of relying on the built-in data binding capabilities.

4. Set the `CausesValidation` property of the Cancel button in the `<InsertItemTemplate>` to `False`:

```
<asp:Button ID="CancelButton" runat="server" CommandName="Cancel" Text="Clear"
          CausesValidation="false" />
```

5. Similarly, set the `CausesValidation` property of the Delete button in the `<ItemTemplate>` to `False` as well.

6. Switch to the Code Behind of the page and then extend the `Inserting` event handler with the following code that saves the file to disk and then updates the `ImageUrl` property of the `Picture` instance with its new location:

VB.NET

```
myPicture.PhotoAlbumId = Convert.ToInt32(Request.QueryString.Get("PhotoAlbumId"))

Dim FileUpload1 As FileUpload = _
           CType(ListView1.InsertItem.FindControl("FileUpload1"), FileUpload)
Dim virtualFolder As String = "~/GigPics/"
Dim physicalFolder As String = Server.MapPath(virtualFolder)
Dim fileName As String = Guid.NewGuid().ToString()
Dim extension As String = System.IO.Path.GetExtension(FileUpload1.FileName)

FileUpload1.SaveAs(System.IO.Path.Combine(physicalFolder, fileName + extension))
myPicture.ImageUrl = virtualFolder + fileName + extension
```

C#

```
myPicture.PhotoAlbumId = Convert.ToInt32(Request.QueryString.Get("PhotoAlbumId"));

FileUpload FileUpload1 = (FileUpload)ListView1.InsertItem.FindControl("FileUpload1");
string virtualFolder = "~/GigPics/";
string physicalFolder = Server.MapPath(virtualFolder);
string fileName = Guid.NewGuid().ToString();
string extension = System.IO.Path.GetExtension(FileUpload1.FileName);

FileUpload1.SaveAs(System.IO.Path.Combine(physicalFolder, fileName + extension));
myPicture.ImageUrl = virtualFolder + fileName + extension;
```

7. Go back to Markup View and add three validation controls to the `InsertItemTemplate`: two `RequiredFieldValidator` controls hooked up to the text boxes for the `Description` and `Tooltip`, and one `CustomValidator` with its `ErrorMessage` set to `Please select a valid .jpg file`. Finally, set the `TextMode` property of the text box for the `Description` to `MultiLine`.

   You should end up with the following code:

```
<asp:TextBox ID="DescriptionTextBox" runat="server" TextMode="MultiLine"
        Text='<%# Bind("Description") %>' /><br />
<asp:RequiredFieldValidator ID="RequiredFieldValidator1"
      ControlToValidate="DescriptionTextBox" runat="server"
      ErrorMessage="Please enter a description."></asp:RequiredFieldValidator>
Tooltip:
<asp:TextBox ID="TooltipTextBox" runat="server" Text='<%# Bind("Tooltip") %>' /><br />
<asp:RequiredFieldValidator ID="RequiredFieldValidator2"
      ControlToValidate="ToolTipTextBox" runat="server"
      ErrorMessage="Please enter a tooltip."></asp:RequiredFieldValidator>
<asp:FileUpload ID="FileUpload1" runat="server" /><br />
<asp:CustomValidator ID="CustomValidator1" runat="server"
      ErrorMessage="Please select a valid .jpg file"></asp:CustomValidator>
<asp:Button ID="InsertButton" runat="server" CommandName="Insert" Text="Insert" />
```

8. Switch to Design View, select the `ListView` control, and then set up an event handler for its `ItemInserting` event by double-clicking the event in the Event category of the Properties Grid. Complete the event handler with the following code:

VB.NET

```
Protected Sub ListView1_ItemInserting(ByVal sender As Object, _
          ByVal e As System.Web.UI.WebControls.ListViewInsertEventArgs) _
          Handles ListView1.ItemInserting
  Dim FileUpload1 As FileUpload = _
               CType(ListView1.InsertItem.FindControl("FileUpload1"), FileUpload)
  If Not FileUpload1.HasFile OrElse _
             Not FileUpload1.FileName.ToLower().EndsWith(".jpg") Then
    Dim CustomValidator1 As CustomValidator = _
             CType(ListView1.InsertItem.FindControl("CustomValidator1"), CustomValidator)
    CustomValidator1.IsValid = False
```

```
    e.Cancel = True
  End If
End Sub
```

C#

```
protected void ListView1_ItemInserting(object sender, ListViewInsertEventArgs e)
{
  FileUpload FileUpload1 = (FileUpload)ListView1.InsertItem.FindControl("FileUpload1");
  if (!FileUpload1.HasFile || !FileUpload1.FileName.ToLower().EndsWith(".jpg"))
  {
    CustomValidator CustomValidator1 =
              (CustomValidator)ListView1.InsertItem.FindControl("CustomValidator1");
    CustomValidator1.IsValid = false;
    e.Cancel = true;
  }
}
```

9. Save all your changes, and then request NewPhotoAlbum.aspx in your browser. Enter a new name for the photo album and click the Insert link. Insert a few pictures by entering a description and a tooltip, selecting a .jpg picture from your hard drive, and clicking the Insert button. Then enter the description and tooltip of another image, but leave the File browse dialog box empty. When you click Insert, you get an error message indicating that you didn't upload a valid JPG file, as shown in Figure 13-17.

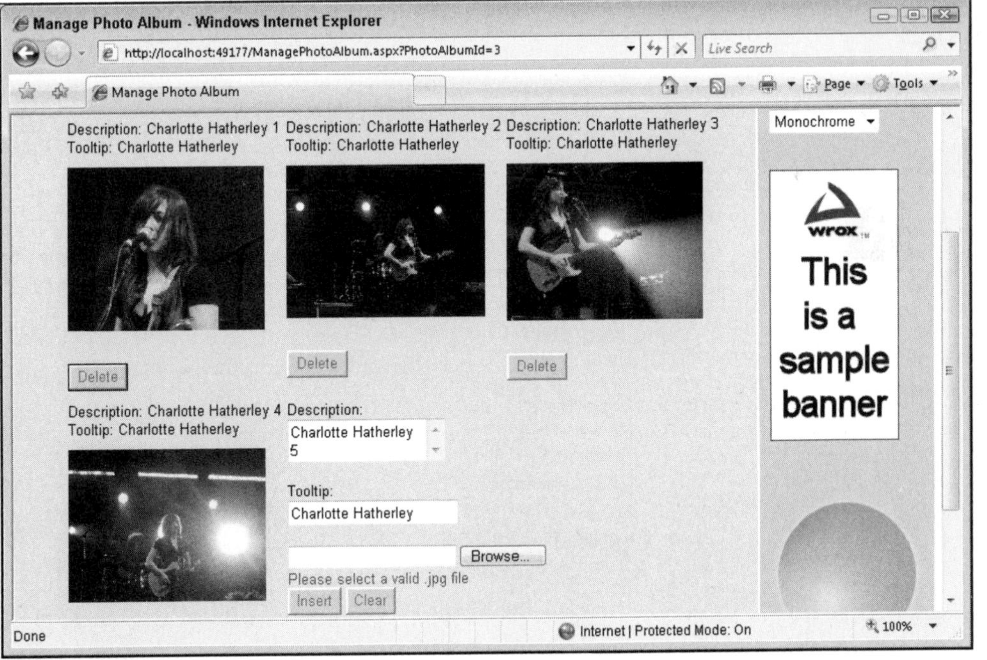

Figure 13-17

10. Click the Browse button of the File upload control, browse for a valid JPG file, and then click the Insert button once more. The file now gets uploaded successfully.

How It Works

You haven't changed much in the actual process of inserting the `Picture` into the database. The `ListView` control still collects all the relevant data from the page and then sends it to the `LinqDataSource` control, which then inserts the item in the `Picture` table in the database. What is different is the way you set up the templates and the way you handled the events of the `LinqDataSource` and `ListView` controls. Look at the templates first. Inside the `ItemTemplate` you added an `<asp:Image>` to take the place of the plain text label. As you can see in Figure 13-17 this displays the actual image, rather than just its URL.

To allow a user to upload the images, you replaced the `TextBox` control in the `InsertItemTemplate` with a `FileUpload` control. Additionally, you added a few validation controls to force the user to enter the required fields. As soon as you press the Insert button, the page posts back and the `ListView` control fires its `ItemInserting` event. This event is a good place to perform any custom validation. One of the arguments this event handler receives (the `e` argument) is of type `ListViewInsertEventArgs`, a class that provides context-sensitive information about the Insert operation of the `ListView` control. When you detect an error, you can set the `Cancel` property of the `e` argument that is passed to the event handler to `False` to tell the `ListView` control you want to cancel the insert operation. Inside this event handler you added some code that "finds" the upload control in the `InsertItem` template. Because you can potentially have multiple controls with the same name (for example, a `FileUpload` control in the `InsertItemTemplate` and `EditItemTemplate`) you cannot access the `FileUpload` control directly. Instead, you need to use `FindControl` on the `InsertItem` object to search for the control:

VB.NET

```
Dim FileUpload1 As FileUpload = _
         CType(ListView1.InsertItem.FindControl("FileUpload1"), FileUpload)
```

C#

```
FileUpload FileUpload1 = (FileUpload)ListView1.InsertItem.FindControl("FileUpload1");
```

When you have a reference to the `FileUpload` control you can check its `HasFile` property to see if a file has been uploaded. Additionally, you can check `FileUpload1.FileName.ToLower().EndsWith(".jpg")` to see if a file with a .jpg extension has been uploaded. To ensure that this test is only carried out when the user has uploaded a file, the code uses `OrElse` in VB to short-circuit the logic in the `If` statement, as explained in Chapter 5.

If the user doesn't upload a valid file, the code in the `If` block runs. It uses `FindControl` again to find the `CustomValidator` control and sets its `IsValid` property to `False`. This tells the control to display its `ErrorMessage` property when the page renders. Finally, to stop the `ListView` from continuing the insert operation you need to set the `Cancel` property of the `e` argument to `True`:

VB.NET

```
e.Cancel = True
```

C#

```
e.Cancel = true;
```

If the user uploaded a valid .jpg file, the `ListView` continues with its insert operation, which eventually results in an insert action against the `LinqDataSource` control. When that control is about to send the insert operation to the database, it fires its `Inserting` event, giving you a last chance to hook into the process and look at the data. Inside this event handler, you used similar code to find a reference to the `FileUpload` control inside the `InsertItem` template. You then used the following code to determine the physical and virtual folder for the file, its name, and its extension:

VB.NET

```
Dim virtualFolder As String = "~/GigPics/"
Dim physicalFolder As String = Server.MapPath(virtualFolder)
Dim fileName As String = Guid.NewGuid().ToString()
Dim extension As String = System.IO.Path.GetExtension(FileUpload1.FileName)
```

C#

```
string virtualFolder = "~/GigPics/";
string physicalFolder = Server.MapPath(virtualFolder);
string fileName = Guid.NewGuid().ToString();
string extension = System.IO.Path.GetExtension(FileUpload1.FileName);
```

The variable `virtualFolder` holds the virtual location of the folder where the uploaded images are stored. Using `Server.MapPath` you can turn this into a physical folder. Assuming you have your project in its default location of `C:\BegASPNET\Site`, the `physicalFolder` variable now contains `C:\BegASPNET\Site\GigPics`.

Next, a new, random file name is generated using `Guid.NewGuid()`. This assigns `fileName` something like `f6d8ed05-2dbe-4aed-868a-de045f9462e3` which guarantees a unique file name. Finally, the extension of the file is retrieved using the static `GetExtension` method of the `Path` class in the `System.IO` namespace.

At this stage, you have all the required information to store the file on disk, and then update the database. Storing the file on disk is easy using the `SaveAs` method of the `FileUpload` control:

VB.NET

```
FileUpload1.SaveAs(System.IO.Path.Combine(physicalFolder, fileName + extension))
```

C#

```
FileUpload1.SaveAs(System.IO.Path.Combine(physicalFolder, fileName + extension));
```

This code takes the physical folder, the file name, and the extension and passes it to the `SaveAs` method, which saves the file at the requested location.

Finally, the Picture instance is updated with the new ImageUrl:

VB.NET

```
myPicture.ImageUrl = virtualFolder + fileName + extension
```

C#

```
myPicture.ImageUrl = virtualFolder + fileName + extension;
```

This assigns something like ~/GigPics/f6d8ed05-2dbe-4aed-868a-de045f9462e3.jpg to the ImageUrl property which is the new virtual location of the uploaded image. Right after you insert the new image, the ListView is updated and now shows the new image using the Image control with its ImageUrl set to the image you just uploaded.

You can imagine that if you upload a large number of images for a single photo album, the page becomes more difficult to manage. This is especially true at the front end where users may be accessing your site over a slow network connection. Instead of presenting them all the images in the photo album on a single page, you can split up the photo album in multiple pages, allowing the user to go from page to page. You see how to do this in the next section that discusses the DataPager control.

Introducing the DataPager Control

The DataPager control is new in ASP.NET 3.5. In previous versions of ASP.NET paging was only possible using functionality built in directly to some controls, like the GridView and the DetailsView, or by manually writing code.

The DataPager is different in that it is a separate control that you can use to extend another, data-bound control. Currently, you can use the DataPager only to provide paging capabilities to the ListView controls, but it's expected that third-party controls or other future ASP.NET controls can be extended as well.

There are two ways to hook up the DataPager to the ListView control: you can either define it within the <LayoutTemplate> of the ListView control or you can define it entirely outside the ListView. In the first case the DataPager knows to what control it should provide paging capabilities. In the latter case, you need to set the PagedControlID property of the DataPager to the ID of a valid ListView control. You'll see how to configure and use the DataPager in conjunction with a ListView next. Being able to define the DataPager outside of the ListView control is useful if you want to place it at a different location of the page, in the Footer or SideBar area for example.

Try It Out — Paging Data with the ListView and DataPager Controls

In this exercise you create the front-end page of the Gig Pics feature. Users to your site can choose one of the available photo albums from a drop-down list and then view all the available pictures in a pageable list that is created by a ListView and a DataPager control. Figure 13-21 shows the final result of this exercise.

1. In the root of your site, create a new folder called PhotoAlbums. Inside this folder create a new Web Form, call it Default.aspx, and make sure it's based on your custom page template. Set the Title of the page to All Photo Albums. If you're using VB.NET, switch to the Code Behind and rename the class to _Default to avoid a conflict with the reserved keyword Default. Make the same change in the @ Page directive for this new page in Markup View.

2. Switch to Design View and drop a `DropDownList` control on the page. On the control's Smart Tasks panel enable `AutoPostBack` and then hook it up to a new `LinqDataSource` control by clicking Choose Data Source, and then choose New data source from the first drop-down list. Click the LINQ icon, click OK, and then make sure the `PlanetWroxDataContext` is selected in the drop-down list. Click Next and then on the Configure Data Selection dialog box choose PhotoAlbums from the Table drop-down list and select the fields `Id` and `Name` as shown in Figure 13-18.

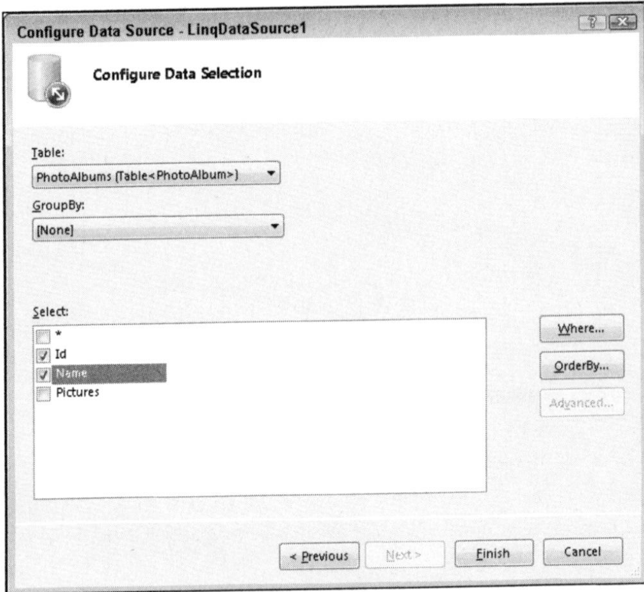

Figure 13-18

3. Click Finish to close the Data Source Wizard and then in the Choose Data Source dialog box select `Name` from the Data Field to Display drop-down list, and leave `Id` selected in the Data Field for the Value drop-down list, as depicted in Figure 13-19.

4. Click OK to close the Data Source Configuration wizard.

5. Below the `DropDownList` add a new `ListView` control and connect it to a new `LinqDataSource` by selecting <New data source> from the drop-down list on the control's Smart Tasks panel. Click the LINQ icon and click OK. Then ensure that `PlanetWroxDataContext` is selected and click Next. In the dialog box that follows, choose Pictures (Table<Picture>) from the Table drop-down list and then click the Where button. Fill in the resulting dialog box as shown in Figure 13-20 to set up a filter that limits the selected pictures to those belonging to the photo album selected in the `DropDownList`.

6. Click Add to create the parameter, and then click OK and Finish to insert the `LinqDataSource` control to your page.

7. On the `ListView` control's Smart Tasks panel, click Configure ListView. In the Select a Layout list in the dialog box that follows choose Bulleted List, and then in the Options area choose Enable Paging. The drop-down list below it should default to Next/Previous Pager which is fine for this exercise.

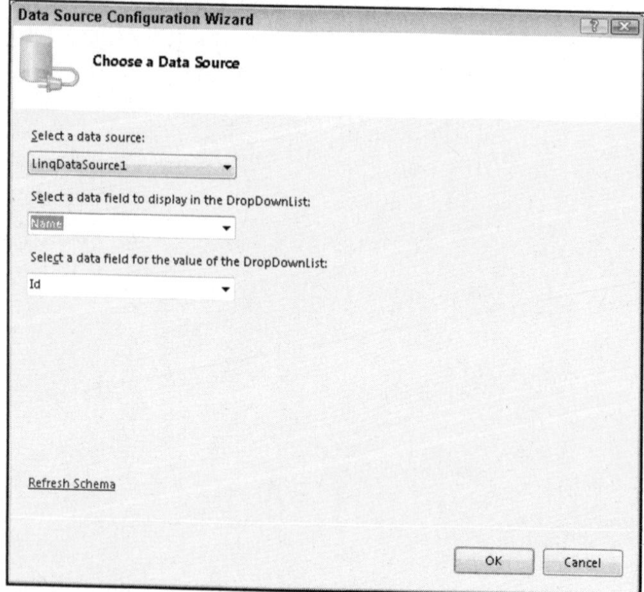

Figure 13-19

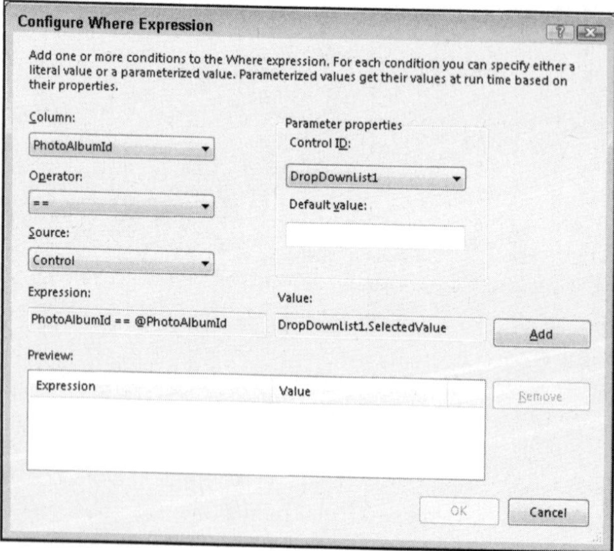

Figure 13-20

8. Click OK and VWD creates a couple of templates for you.
9. Switch to Markup View and remove the following templates and the code they contain:
    - `<AlternatingItemTemplate>`
    - `<InsertItemTemplate>`

- <SelectedItemTemplate>
- <EditItemTemplate>
- <ItemSeparatorTemplate>

10. Remove the ID, runat, and style attributes from the <ul> in the LayoutTemplate and then add a class attribute and set it to itemContainer. Locate the DataPager inside the LayoutTemplate and then add a PageSize attribute set to 3:

```
<LayoutTemplate>
  <ul class="itemContainer">
    <li id="itemPlaceholder" runat="server" />
  </ul>
  <div style="">
    <asp:DataPager ID="DataPager1" runat="server" PageSize="3">
      <Fields>
        <asp:NextPreviousPagerField ButtonType="Button" ShowFirstPageButton="True"
                ShowLastPageButton="True" />
      </Fields>
    </asp:DataPager>
  </div>
</LayoutTemplate>
```

11. Modify the code in the ItemTemplate so it ends up like this:

```
<ItemTemplate>
  <li>
    <asp:Image ID="Image1" runat="server" ImageUrl='<%# Eval("ImageUrl") %>'
          ToolTip='<%# Eval("ToolTip") %>' />
    <asp:Label ID="DescriptionLabel" runat="server" Text='<%# Eval("Description") %>' />
  </li>
</ItemTemplate>
```

This creates an Image control with its ImageUrl and ToolTip properties bound to the corresponding properties of the Picture object that you're binding to. The ToolTip appears when you hover your mouse over the image in the browser. Below the image, a simple Label control displays the Description of the image.

12. Next, wrap the entire code in the cpMainContent content block in an Ajax UpdatePanel with a ContentTemplate element to avoid page flicker when paging the list of pictures, or when choosing a new photo album from the list.

```
<asp:Content ID="Content2" ContentPlaceHolderID="cpMainContent" runat="Server">
  <asp:UpdatePanel ID="UpdatePanel1" runat="server">
    <ContentTemplate>
      <asp:DropDownList ID="DropDownList1" runat="server" AutoPostBack="True"
            DataSourceID="LinqDataSource1" DataTextField="Name" DataValueField="Id">
      ...
    </ContentTemplate>
  </asp:UpdatePanel>
</asp:Content>
```

13. Open the Web.sitemap file for the site and add a main menu and two submenu items for the PhotoAlbum section, between the Reviews and About sections:

```
</siteMapNode>
  <siteMapNode url="~/PhotoAlbums/" title="Gig Pics" description="All Gig Pics">
    <siteMapNode url="~/PhotoAlbums/Default.aspx" title="Gig Pics"
          description="All Gig Pics" />
    <siteMapNode url="~/NewPhotoAlbum.aspx" title="New Album"
          description="Create a new Photo Album with Gig Pics" />
  </siteMapNode>
<siteMapNode url="~/About/Default.aspx" title="About" description="About this site">
```

14. Save all your changes and then request Default.aspx from the PhotoAlbums folder in your browser. Choose a photo album from the drop-down list and the page reloads, showing you the relevant pictures in the photo album. If you don't have any pictures in a photo album, or not enough to fill an entire page, choose New Album from the Gig Pics menu, create a new photo album, and add at least four images to it. Then click the Gig Pics menu item and choose your new photo album from the drop-down list. Note that there is now a paging user interface, allowing you to move forward and backward through the list of pictures in the photo album using the First, Previous, Next, and Last buttons visible at the bottom of the screen in Figure 13-21.

    Note that because of the Ajax panel you added, the paging operations now occur completely flicker-free.

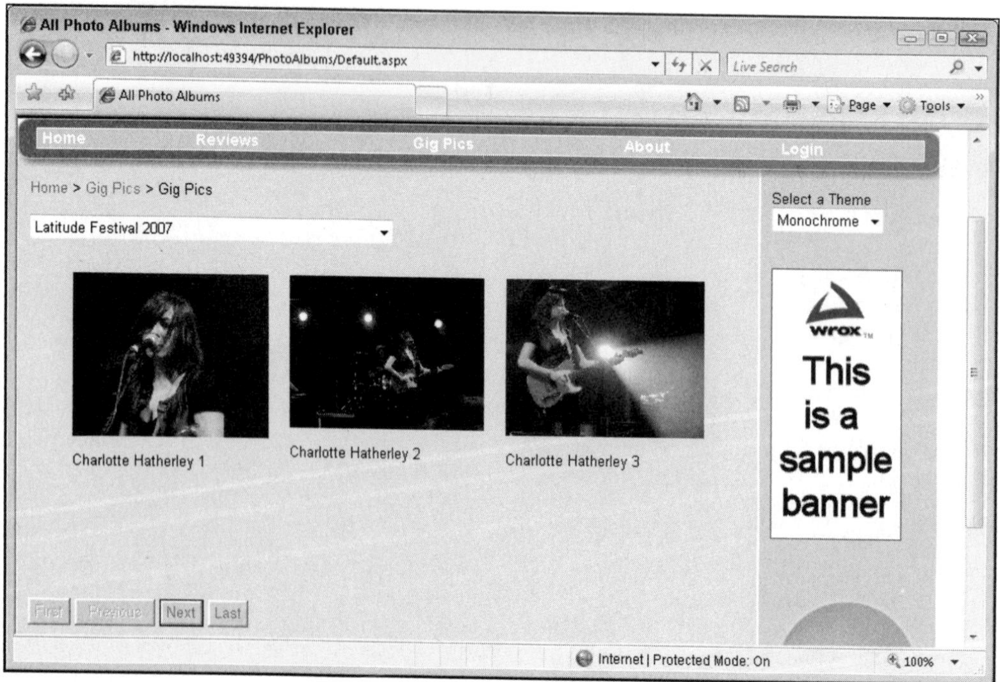

Figure 13-21

How It Works

Most of what you have seen in this exercise should be familiar. You connected a `DropDownList` to a `LinqDataSource` similar to how you created the Genres drop-down list in the previous chapter. The `ListView` and its associated `LinqDataSource` are also similar to what is discussed earlier in this chapter. However, instead of a `Where` parameter that looks at the query string, the code now uses a `Where` parameter that looks at the `DropDownList`:

```
<WhereParameters>
  <asp:ControlParameter ControlID="DropDownList1" Name="PhotoAlbumId"
          PropertyName="SelectedValue" Type="Int32" />
</WhereParameters>
```

When the `LinqDataSource` is about to get its data from the database, it looks at the `SelectedValue` property of the drop-down list and then only retrieves the pictures that match the requested `PhotoAlbumId`.

The biggest difference from previous examples is the addition of the `DataPager`. As demonstrated in this exercise, paging is handled for you automatically. All you need to do is embed a `DataPager` control somewhere in the `LayoutTemplate` of the `ListView` and the rest is taken care of automatically. If you place the `DataPager` outside the `ListView`, don't forget to hook it up to the `ListView` by setting the `PagedControlID` property. If you prefer links or images over buttons, you can set the `ButtonType` property of the `NextPreviousPagerField` element to `Link` or `Image` respectively. If you prefer a numeric pager, replace the `NextPreviousPagerField` item with a `NumericPagerField`:

```
<asp:NumericPagerField NextPageText="..." PreviousPageText="..." />
```

A Few Notes about Performance

This exercise has two known performance problems that you should be aware of. First, although the `ItemTemplate` of the `ListView` resizes the images to 180 pixels *in the browser* by setting their widths through CSS, the actual image is left unmodified. This means that if you upload a large image, the entire image is still downloaded, only to display as a small thumbnail image. It would be better to create a true thumbnail image at the server, and send that to the browser instead. The chapter "Greeting Cards" of my book *ASP.NET 2.0 Instant Results* has a number of examples on resizing images on the server.

The other potential performance problem lies in the way the data is paged. With the `DataPager` control, the data is paged inside the ASPX page. That means that all data is retrieved from the database and sent to the `LinqDataSource` control. The `DataPager` control then selects the right records to display on the current page. This works fine for result sets of up to hundreds of records. However, as soon as the number of items in a photo album or other collection grows above that number, you may find that your pages start to slow down. If that's the case you may want to look at paging at the database level. The LINQ to SQL Classes support this scenario using the `Skip()` and `Take()` methods. Pick up a copy of *Professional LINQ* by Scott Klein (ISBN: 978-0-470-04181-9) for more information about this.

Practical LINQ Tips

Here are some practical LINQ tips.

- In this chapter you saw how to create anonymous types to shape the data you want to return from your queries. The compiler and IntelliSense are invaluable tools in determining what data you can return and what properties you have available. Spend some time playing around with the anonymous types, looking at the different options that the IntelliSense lists give you.
- Just as with other data access methods like the `SqlDataSource` control you saw in the previous chapter, try to filter your data as much as possible. If you know you only need reviews in the Jazz genre, be explicit and incorporate a `Where` clause in your code that limits the list of reviews at the database level. This speeds up your queries and data retrieval, improving the overall speed of the application.
- Make use of anonymous types to decrease the memory consumption of your LINQ queries. Instead of retrieving the entire `Review` object, use the `New` keyword to create a new anonymous type on the fly. Since this new object only contains the properties you really need, you save yourself the overhead of bringing in the full object.

Summary

LINQ is a compelling and exciting new technology that ships with .NET 3.5. LINQ is going to take a big place in many data-access scenarios, including database access in ASP.NET web applications using LINQ to SQL.

Because LINQ is going to be so important, it has been integrated in many different places in .NET. LINQ is available for objects allowing you to query in-memory collections. Additionally, LINQ is available for XML, Entities, and DataSets, each type providing access to a different data store, but with the same, unified querying language. The final type of LINQ is LINQ to SQL that provides access to your SQL Server database.

To write LINQ queries, you use query operators that include keywords like `Select`, `From`, and `Where` and aggregation operators like `Sum` and `Count`. To get data out of a LINQ query you can use type inference to let the compiler determine the resulting type. This also allows you to create anonymous types, where the actual type returned by the query doesn't have a name, but its public interface is inferred by the compiler, giving you IntelliSense at compile time, and full access to the object at run time.

To work with LINQ to SQL in your ASP.NET web applications you have a couple of different options. First, you can write queries in the Code Behind of a page and then bind the results to a data-bound control using the `DataSource` property and `DataBind` method of the control. Although this method gives you a lot of flexibility in terms of the queries you can execute, it also means you need to write a lot of code manually.

To minimize the code you need to write, the other option to work with LINQ in your ASP.NET pages is using the `LinqDataSource` control, the bridge between your data-bound controls and your LINQ model. Combined with the new `ListView` and `DataPager` controls, the `LinqDataSource` gives you the ability to create fully functional CRUD pages, enabling you to create, read, update, and delete data in your database with as little code as possible.

Until now, the database-driven pages you have seen look quite dull. You haven't applied any styling, or provided any conditional formatting, where data is presented differently based on its intrinsic values. This can be accomplished through control styles and the many events of the data-bound and data source controls. Chapter 14 shows you how to make use of these styles and events.

Exercises

1. Imagine you have a page in the Reviews folder called MostRecent.aspx. This page shows the 10 reviews most recently added to the database. What would your LINQ query look like if you only wanted to show the review's `Title` property and the name of the genre it belongs to? You should use the `Take` method to limit the result set to 10. If you're having trouble writing the code to get the last reviews, look at the section titled "First, FirstOrDefault, Last, and LastOrDefault," which shows you how to get the last review in the database.
2. What is the major benefit of the new `ListView` control over other data controls like `GridView` and `Repeater`?
3. Currently the Default.aspx page from the PhotoAlbums folder just shows the thumbnails of the pictures. What would you need to do to display the full-size picture on its own page using a LINQ query?

Presenting Data — Advanced Topics

In the previous three chapters you have been introduced to a lot of new concepts. Chapter 11 discusses databases in general and SQL Server 2005 Express Edition in particular. The chapter also covers the basic CRUD operations to create, read, update, and delete data that is stored in a database. Chapter 12 focuses mostly on working with the `SqlDataSource` control and the different data-bound controls that you have at your disposal. Finally, the previous chapter explores the world of LINQ, Microsoft's latest data access strategy designed to speed up the way you write data access code.

To help you really understand the core concepts of data access, those three chapters focus mainly on the data source controls and the principles behind them, and much less on the presentation of data with the data-bound controls. Obviously, in a real-world application this is not enough and you need a way to present data in a clear and attractive way.

The data-bound controls that ship with ASP.NET 3.5 provide the necessary options to change the way data is presented. They allow you to completely change the design (font, colors, spacing, and so on) of the data they are presenting. Additionally, you can tweak these controls to hide specific columns, modify column headers, or even colorize odd rows differently from even rows. Finally, because of the rich event model that drives the data-bound and data source controls, you can change the look and feel of the controls conditionally. For example, you can hide the Delete link on the Genres management page for those genres that still have reviews attached to them.

Besides pages that look good, your application can also benefit from speed to make a good impression on your users. Good performance is always a welcome ingredient of any popular web site. ASP.NET comes with great caching capabilities that help you speed up the application.

This chapter shows you how to implement these concepts in your own web site. In particular, you see how to do the following:

- Change formatting of the various data-bound controls using styles
- Combine styles, themes, and skins to create good-looking and easy-to-maintain web sites

- Use the various events that are fired by the data controls to change the appearance of your data controls conditionally — for example, to hide or disable certain controls in the user interface when it doesn't make sense to have them visible or enabled
- Use the built-in caching mechanisms to improve the speed of your web site

Formatting Your Controls Using Styles

Chapters 12 and 13 explain how to work with the numerous data-bound ASP.NET 3.5 controls. You learned how to display and edit lists of data with controls like `GridView`, `Repeater`, and `ListView`, as well as how to work with single record controls like `DetailsView`.

So far, you've relied on the built-in look and feel of the controls, which results in dull and plain-looking HTML. Figure 14-1 shows the `GridView` that you created in Chapter 12 to manage the genres in the Planet Wrox database.

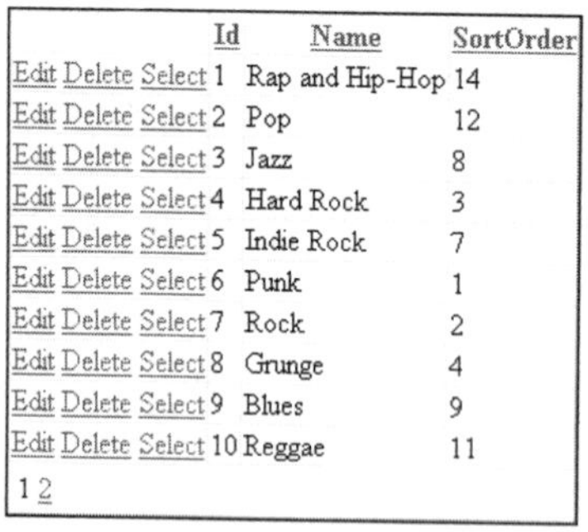

	Id	Name	SortOrder
Edit Delete Select	1	Rap and Hip-Hop	14
Edit Delete Select	2	Pop	12
Edit Delete Select	3	Jazz	8
Edit Delete Select	4	Hard Rock	3
Edit Delete Select	5	Indie Rock	7
Edit Delete Select	6	Punk	1
Edit Delete Select	7	Rock	2
Edit Delete Select	8	Grunge	4
Edit Delete Select	9	Blues	9
Edit Delete Select	10	Reggae	11
1 2			

Figure 14-1

This control relies on the default settings of the browser to display text and links, which usually results in purple and blue links with the default font, like Times New Roman. Additionally, the columns in the grid are just as wide as necessary to display the text they contain. It would be a lot easier on the eyes if you could present the `GridView` as in Figure 14-2 instead.

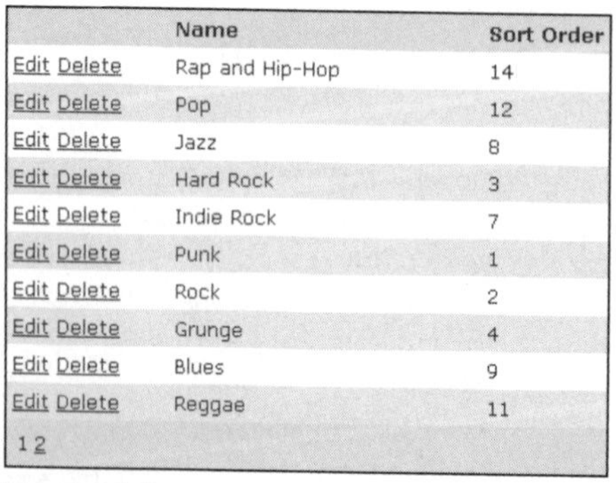

	Name	Sort Order
Edit Delete	Rap and Hip-Hop	14
Edit Delete	Pop	12
Edit Delete	Jazz	8
Edit Delete	Hard Rock	3
Edit Delete	Indie Rock	7
Edit Delete	Punk	1
Edit Delete	Rock	2
Edit Delete	Grunge	4
Edit Delete	Blues	9
Edit Delete	Reggae	11
1 2		

Figure 14-2

The column for the Edit and Delete links is now a little wider, separating it clearly from the actual content in the grid. The `Id` column has been hidden and the `Name` column has been made wider as well. The different colors for the header, footer, items, and alternating items make the data in the grid a lot easier to read.

Changing the dull-looking `GridView` from Figure 14-1 into the snazzier one shown in Figure 14-2 can easily be accomplished with the use of *ASP.NET styles*. In the next section you see how to apply these styles to a single control in a page. In the section that follows you see how to apply the styles to a theme, so styles can be reused more easily by all controls in a section of your site. You have already seen some styles at work in Chapter 7, where you used them to style the `Menu` and the `TreeView` controls. However, because styles are used so much for formatting data-bound controls, they really deserve their own topic.

An Introduction to Styles

Many of the data-bound and navigation controls have a number of style properties that allow you to modify the look and feel of the control. For example, the `GridView` control has a `RowStyle` property that allows you to customize the look of an individual row in the grid. Likewise, the `DetailsView` has a `CommandRowStyle` property that is used to control the appearance of the command row that holds commands such as `Insert`, `Delete`, `Cancel`, and so on.

Ultimately, each style property inherits from the `Style` class that lives in the `System.Web.UI.WebControls` namespace. Figure 14-3 shows you a filtered view of the diagram for this class with its most common properties visible.

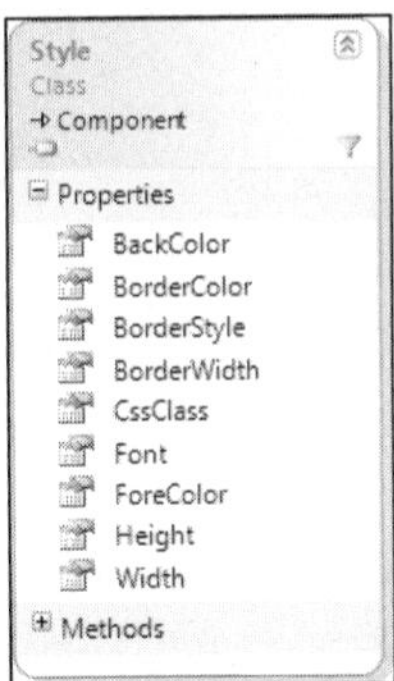

Figure 14-3

As you can see from their names, the properties of the `Style` class are used to change style-related information on the objects to which this class is applied. Each of these properties is eventually converted to a CSS property or an HTML attribute, like `background-color`, `color`, and so on. Other styles, like the styles for the `GridView` control, add various layout-related properties, such as different options to control alignment. The following table lists the most important properties of the various `Style`-derived classes that are available. Note that not every property is available for every style. IntelliSense shows you exactly what properties you can use in a certain style.

Property	Description
`BackColor` `ForeColor`	This property allows you to change the background and text color of the elements. They map to the CSS properties `background-color` and `color`, respectively.

`BorderColor`
`BorderStyle`
`BorderWidth`
	These properties enable you to change the border of the element to which the style is applied. They map directly to their CSS counterparts `border-color`, `border-style`, and `border-width`.

`CssClass`	This property enables you to assign a CSS class instead of inline style information. You'll see how to use `CssClass` in a later exercise. You should try to give preference to the `CssClass` property over the individual style properties because they minimize page bloat, as you'll see later.
`Font`	This property allows you to set the font for the element through the various subproperties like `Font-Names`, `Font-Size`, and `Font-Bold`. These properties end up as various CSS font properties, such as `font-family`, `font-size`, and `font-weight`.
`HorizontalAlign` `VerticalAlign`	These properties end up as `align` and `valign` attributes on the HTML element to which they are applied and allow you to control the alignment of the contents of the element. For example, you use `HorizontalAlign` to left-, center-, or right-align the text of the column headers of a `GridView`.
`Wrap`	The `Wrap` property ends up as a `white-space: nowrap;` CSS declaration when set to `False` and determines whether a table cell allows wrapping of its contents to a new line.
`Height` `Width`	These properties allow you to control the width and height of the elements to which they are applied. They map directly to their CSS height and width counterparts.

The different data-bound controls all have a different set of styles, although they do share a number of styles. The following table lists the available styles for the `GridView` and the `DataList` classes, and describes their purpose. The other data-bound controls have slightly different styles, but from their names you should be able to see what they do and determine what they are used for. Check out the MSDN documentation for the data-bound controls for a full description of all their style properties. Another good way to learn more about the different styles that are available is by using Visual Web Developer's Auto Format that inserts a number of styles for you. You see later how to use and improve the styles that are generated by the Auto Format feature.

Style	Description
RowStyle AlternatingRowStyle	These styles control the looks of a single row in the GridView. By default, the RowStyle affects all rows while the AlternatingRowStyle can override the RowStyle on only even rows when it's set. Since the DataList doesn't work with rows, but with more generic data items, it has ItemStyle and AlternatingItemStyle properties instead, but their behavior is more or less the same.
SelectedRowStyle	This style can be applied to selected rows, and gives you the opportunity to visually present selected rows differently from unselected rows. The DataList control has a SelectedItemStyle that serves the same purpose.
EditRowStyle	This style can be applied to rows that are currently in edit mode. For example, when you click the Edit link for a row in the GridView on the Genres page in the management section, the row switches to edit mode and this EditRowStyle is applied. To define the layout of an editable item in the DataList, you use the EditItemStyle instead.
EmptyDataRowStyle	This style allows you to define the look of the row that is displayed when the grid is bound to an empty data source. This style works together with the EmptyDataText property of the grid that contains the text displayed when there are no records, or with the EmptyDataTemplate that allows you to define your own custom template to be displayed when an empty data source is used. The DataList has no support for an EmptyDataRowStyle.
HeaderStyle FooterStyle	These styles control the appearance of the header and footer of the GridView.
PagerStyle	This style allows you to influence the look of the pager bar displayed in the GridView when paging is enabled. The DataList does not support paging all by itself, and as such has no PagerStyle.

Some controls, like Repeater and ListView, have no built-in styles. Since these controls do not contribute any HTML to the page all by themselves and leave it up to you to define the look and feel in the numerous templates these controls have, there is no point in having separate styles.

To show you how to use these styles with your controls, the next exercise guides you through the process of enhancing the GridView control in the Genres page of the Management section. In a later exercise, you see how to move the style-related information to a theme and CSS file to improve the reusability of the formatting code and to reduce the amount of HTML sent to the browser on each request.

Try It Out Applying Styles

In this exercise, you use the built-in formatting capabilities of VWD to change the appearance of the `GridView` control. You see how VWD creates the necessary styles for you, each with their relevant styling properties set. In a later exercise you see how to modify these styles to use the `CssClass` properties instead, resulting in a much easier to manage style set.

1. Open Genres.aspx from the Management folder of the main Planet Wrox application that you have been working on so far.
2. Switch the page into Design View and open the `GridView` control's Smart Tasks panel.
3. At the top of the panel, click the Auto Format link.
4. From the list of format schemes on the left, choose Classic. The Preview window on the right is updated and now looks like Figure 14-4.

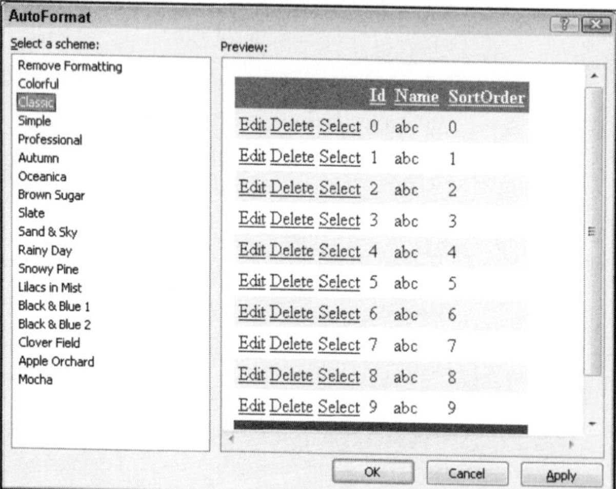

Figure 14-4

5. Click OK to have VWD generate the necessary templates for you. The `GridView` is updated in Design View immediately, showing the selected format scheme.
6. Switch back to Markup View and inspect the various styles that have been generated. You should see the following styles, some placed before and others placed below the `<Columns>` element:

```
<FooterStyle BackColor="#507CD1" Font-Bold="True" ForeColor="White" />
<RowStyle BackColor="#EFF3FB" />
<PagerStyle BackColor="#2461BF" ForeColor="White" HorizontalAlign="Center" />
<SelectedRowStyle BackColor="#D1DDF1" Font-Bold="True" ForeColor="#333333" />
<HeaderStyle BackColor="#507CD1" Font-Bold="True" ForeColor="White" />
<EditRowStyle BackColor="#2461BF" />
<AlternatingRowStyle BackColor="White" />
```

7. Save the changes to the page and request it in the browser by pressing Ctrl+F5. You should see the list of genres with the selected formatting scheme applied.

8. Open the HTML source for the page by right-clicking the page in the browser and choosing the View Source or View Page Source command. Scroll down a bit until you see an HTML table with its `id` set to `ctl00_cpMainContent_GridView1`. You'll see that the table itself has a `style` attribute that sets text color and border properties:

```
<table cellspacing="0" cellpadding="4" border="0" id="ctl00_cpMainContent_GridView1"
          style="color:#333333;border-collapse:collapse;">
```

   Additionally, you see that the numerous child elements of the table (table rows and anchor elements) all have different style settings applied. For example, odd and even rows now have the following style applied:

```
<tr style="background-color:#EFF3FB;"> ... </tr>
<tr style="background-color:White;"> ... </tr>
```

How It Works

The different style elements you created in step 5 are converted into their CSS and HTML equivalents. For example, `RowStyle` and `AlternatingRowStyle` have their `BackColor` set to a different background color:

```
<RowStyle BackColor="#EFF3FB" />
<AlternatingRowStyle BackColor="White" />
```

When the control renders its HTML it applies these backgrounds to the table row of the items and alternating items:

```
<tr style="background-color:#EFF3FB;"> ... </tr>
<tr style="background-color:White;"> ... </tr>
```

The same principle is applied to the other styles in the `GridView`. Each style is applied to a different area of the `GridView` and each style property is either rendered in an inline `style` attribute or as an HTML attribute directly on an element.

If you look at the source of the page in the browser, you see a lot of page bloat, as each individual row has its properties set. This increases the page size, especially with larger results displayed in the `GridView`. To minimize the page size and improve the performance of the page, you should move the style definitions to a page theme and then use a CSS file and the `CssClass` properties instead. You see how to do this next.

Combining Styles, Themes, and Skins

Chapter 6 discusses how to create consistent-looking web pages using master pages, themes, and skins. With the basic theme infrastructure set up, it's now easy to add a new theme that applies to the entire management section. That allows you to create a consistent look for the entire management section with little to no effort. Earlier you saw how to create a .skin file to change the appearance of a button; in the following exercise you see how to reuse this concept to create a .skin file for the `GridView`, enabling you to style all `GridView` controls in the Management folder in one fell swoop.

Try It Out — Creating Advanced Style Solutions

In this exercise you move the various `Style` properties from the Genres.aspx page into a separate .skin file. Additionally, you replace all the inline properties like `BackColor`, `ForeColor`, and so on with a single `CssClass` attribute and move all formatting-related information to a CSS file for the theme.

1. On the Solution Explorer, right-click the App_Themes folder, choose Add ASP.NET Folder ➪ Theme, and then type **Management** as the new theme.
2. Right-click this new folder and choose Add New Item. Add a skin file called GridView.skin. Next, add a Style Sheet and call it Management.css. You should end up with a Solution Explorer looking like Figure 14-5.

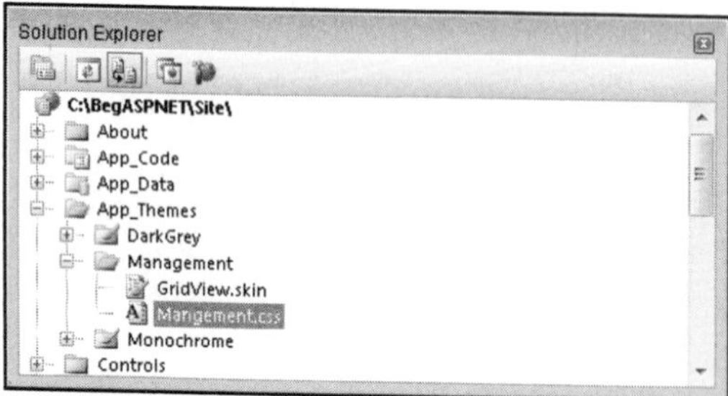

Figure 14-5

3. Open the Genres.aspx page in Markup View and then delete the styles for `FooterStyle`, `RowStyle`, and `SelectedRowStyle` as you don't need them for this exercise. For the remaining four styles, remove all attributes and replace them with a single `CssClass` attribute named after the style and prefixed with `GridView`. You should end up with the following styles:

```
<AlternatingRowStyle CssClass="GridViewAlternatingRowStyle" />
<HeaderStyle CssClass="GridViewHeaderStyle" />
<PagerStyle CssClass="GridViewPagerStyle" />
<EditRowStyle CssClass="GridViewEditRowStyle" />
```

   Don't worry if VWD adds red error lines under the CSS class names. Since the CSS classes aren't defined yet, it can't find them. Later you will add them to the theme's CSS file, where VWD still can't find them. They'll work fine at run time, though, so don't worry.

4. Select all four styles in the code editor and then cut them to the clipboard using Ctrl+X. Switch to the file GridView.skin, delete all existing code (the comment text you saw earlier), and paste the four styles.
5. Wrap the four styles in an `<asp:GridView>` element with its `runat` attribute set to `server` and its `CssClass` attribute set to `GridView`. Don't add an `ID` attribute, as skin files don't need this. You should end up with this code:

```
<asp:GridView runat="server" CssClass="GridView">
  <AlternatingRowStyle CssClass="GridViewAlternatingRowStyle"  />
  <!-- Other three styles go here -->
</asp:GridView>
```

6. Open the file Management.css and add the following CSS. The `body` selector should already be there, so you can reuse it.

```
*
{
  font-family: Verdana, Arial, Sans-Serif;
}

body
{
  font-size: 80%;
}

.GridView, .GridView a
{
  color: #000;
}

.GridViewHeaderStyle, .GridViewPagerStyle, .GridViewEditRowStyle
{
  background-color: #bee4cf;
}

.GridViewAlternatingRowStyle
{
  background-color: #e1e1e1;
}

.GridViewHeaderStyle
{
  text-align: left;
}

.GridViewHeaderStyle a
{
  text-decoration: none;
}
```

7. Open the web.config file for the Management folder that you added earlier and set the `theme` to `Management`:

```
<system.web>
  <pages theme="Management"></pages>
</system.web>
```

8. Go back to Genres.aspx and in Markup View under the `Columns` element of the `GridView` control, delete the bound column for the `Id`. Users typically don't need to see the ID of items in the user interface as they are often meaningless to them. By removing the `Id` column, you reduce the noise in the page. Set the `ItemStyle-Width` for the `CommandField` to `100px` and for the `Name` column to `200px`. Finally, set `ShowSelectButton` of the `CommandField` to `False`. You should end up with this `GridView`:

```
<asp:GridView ID="GridView1" runat="server" AllowPaging="True"
    AllowSorting="True" AutoGenerateColumns="False" DataKeyNames="Id"
```

```
    DataSourceID="SqlDataSource1" GridLines="None" CellPadding="4" ForeColor="#333333"
    EmptyDataText="There are no data records to display.">
  <Columns>
    <asp:CommandField ShowDeleteButton="True" ShowEditButton="True"
            ShowSelectButton="False" ItemStyle-Width="100px"></asp:CommandField>
    <asp:BoundField DataField="Name" HeaderText="Name"
            SortExpression="Name" ItemStyle-Width="200px"></asp:BoundField>
    <asp:BoundField DataField="SortOrder" HeaderText="Sort Order"
            SortExpression="SortOrder"></asp:BoundField>
  </Columns>
</asp:GridView>
```

9. Save all your changes and then open Genres.aspx in the browser. You should now see the list of genres that was presented in Figure 14-2.

10. Click Manage Reviews in the main Management menu to open the Reviews page. Select a genre from the drop-down list to display a list of reviews. Note that the Reviews list — visible in Figure 14-6 — now also has the same styles applied as the Genres list you saw earlier.

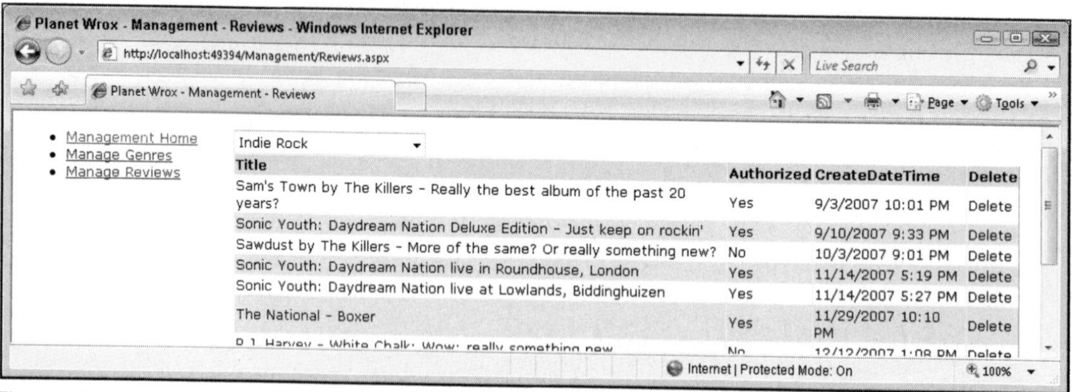

Figure 14-6

Obviously you can still tweak the controls at the page level. While the skin defines the global look and feel of the `GridView`, you can still set individual properties on columns as you did with the `ItemStyle-Width` in the Genres page.

How It Works

The concepts from this exercise should be familiar by now. You have seen how to create and apply themes and skins in Chapter 6, and how to use the various control styles in the previous exercise. The only thing that is really new in this exercise is the way these concepts are combined. By moving your control style declarations to a separate skin file that in turn is part of a theme, you have created a very flexible, maintainable solution. If you want to change the layout of all the `GridView` controls in the Management section, all you need to do now is modify the relevant CSS in the file Management.css. If you need to make changes to other styles, don't forget to add them to the GridView.skin file first. If you want to see how the new styles are applied, open the source of the page in the browser using its View Source command. Instead of inline styles the relevant `class` attributes are applied.

Although styles, skins, and themes are powerful tools to style your web pages, you'll find that they are often an all-or-nothing solution. For example, when you create `ItemStyle` and `AlternatingItemStyle` elements, they are applied to each and every row in the grid. What if you wanted to change the look and feel of just a few rows? Or what if you wanted to change some rows based on the actual data that the row is holding? You'll see how to accomplish conditional formatting and much more using custom events in the following section.

Handling Events

Most chapters so far have covered how the ASP.NET controls trigger events. You learned how to handle these events with event handler code that you typically add to the page's Code Behind file. For example, you wrote code to handle a `Button` control's `Click` event. Additionally, in the previous chapter, you learned how to react to various events — such as `Inserting` and `Inserted` — that happen just prior to and after an insert operation in the database. However, most controls expose a lot more events, enabling you to hook into the life cycle of your page and controls at different stages.

A solid understanding of the various events that fire during a control's life cycle and the order in which they fire is important knowledge for an ASP.NET developer. Being able to hook into the control's life cycle, tweaking parts of the output as you go enables you to create flexible, dynamic web pages that do exactly what you want.

To gain an understanding of the various events and the order in which they fire, the next section explains the basic steps in the ASP.NET control pipeline. You won't see every event that is fired in the process, but instead you see the ones you are most likely to use. Later sections then show you how to make use of these events to change the behavior of your web pages.

The ASP.NET Page and Controls Life Cycles Revisited

In Chapter 6 you learned about the different stages in a page's life. You learned about different events like `PreInit`, `Load`, `PreRender`, and `Unload`. Besides these events that are raised by the ASPX page, all the other controls in your ASPX pages can raise their own events. These events can be as simple as a `Button` control's `Click` event (triggered by a user action) or be more complex events, such as `Inserting`, which is raised by controls like the `LinqDataSource` and the `SqlDataSource`, or the `DataBound` event that is raised by various data-bound controls.

To give you an idea of the different events that you can hook into during a page or control's life cycle and the order in which they fire, the next exercise shows you how to set up a page that displays some data from the `Genres` table using a `LinqDataSource`. Additionally, you place a button on the page that you can use to trigger a postback to see how that influences things. You then hook up a number of event handlers to a few interesting events of the controls on the page. Inside each event handler, you update a `Label` control so you can see in what order things are called.

Try It Out — Seeing the Page and Controls Life Cycles at Work

1. Inside the Demos folder create a new file called Events.aspx. Make sure it's based on your custom page template so it inherits from `BasePage`. Set the page's `Title` to Events Demo.
2. Switch the page to Design View, drop a `GridView` into the `cpMainContent` placeholder, and then hook up the `GridView` to a new `LinqDataSource` control using the `GridView's` Smart Tasks

panel. Bind the `LinqDataSource` control to the `Genres` table. There's no need to set up any `Where` clause or `Order By` clause or set any of the advanced properties of the data source.

3. Back on the `GridView` control's Smart Tasks panel, enable sorting by selecting the second check-box. When you're done, you should have this code in your ASPX page:

```
<asp:GridView ID="GridView1" runat="server" AutoGenerateColumns="False"
            DataKeyNames="Id" DataSourceID="LinqDataSource1" AllowSorting="True">
  <Columns>
    <asp:BoundField DataField="Id" HeaderText="Id" InsertVisible="False"
              ReadOnly="True" SortExpression="Id" />
    <asp:BoundField DataField="Name" HeaderText="Name"
              SortExpression="Name" />
    <asp:BoundField DataField="SortOrder" HeaderText="SortOrder"
              SortExpression="SortOrder" />
  </Columns>
</asp:GridView>
<asp:LinqDataSource ID="LinqDataSource1" runat="server"
            ContextTypeName="PlanetWroxDataContext" TableName="Genres">
</asp:LinqDataSource>
```

4. Make sure you're in Markup View and then, from the Toolbox, drag two `Label` controls, drop them before the `GridView` control in the markup, and then delete their `Text` attributes. Set the `ID` of the labels to `lblNoPostback` and `lblPostback` respectively.

5. Wrap the two labels in a `<table>` element with a single row and two cells so the labels end up side by side. Since you only need a few tags, you can type them in Markup View directly instead of using the Table menu that only works in Design View. Finally, above each label, add an `<h1>` element with either "Postback" or "No Postback" as text. You end up with this code:

```
<table>
  <tr>
    <td>
      <h1>No Postback</h1><asp:Label ID="lblNoPostback" runat="server"></asp:Label>
    </td>
    <td>
      <h1>Postback</h1><asp:Label ID="lblPostback" runat="server"></asp:Label>
    </td>
  </tr>
</table>
```

6. Switch to Design View and below the `GridView` drop a `Button` control and double-click it in Design View to set up an event handler for its `Click` event in the Code Behind.

7. Switch back to Design View and double-click the page to set up a handler for the `Page` control's `Load` event that ends up in the Code Behind of the Events.aspx page again.

8. Switch back to Design View again, click the `GridView`, and open its Properties Grid by pressing F4. Switch to the Events category and then double-click the following events to set up handlers

for them in the Code Behind. After each handler, switch back to Design View so you can add the next event.

By pressing Ctrl+Tab you can quickly switch back to the previous document.

- `Sorted`
- `Sorting`
- `RowCreated`
- `DataBinding`
- `DataBound`
- `RowDataBound`

9. Repeat the previous step, but now set up the following events for the `LinqDataSource` control:
    - `ContextCreating`
    - `Selecting`

10. Make sure you are in the Code Behind of the page and below the last event handler (but still within the class definition), add the following method that writes some text to one of the two labels depending on whether the current page request is the result of a postback:

VB.NET

```
Private Sub WriteMessage(ByVal handlerName As String)
  If Page.IsPostBack Then
    lblPostback.Text &= handlerName & "<br />"
  Else
    lblNoPostback.Text &= handlerName & "<br />"
  End If
End Sub
```

C#

```
private void WriteMessage(string handlerName)
{
  if (Page.IsPostBack)
  {
    lblPostback.Text += handlerName + "<br />";
  }
  else
  {
    lblNoPostback.Text += handlerName + "<br />";
  }
}
```

11. To each of the event handlers that you have set up, add the following code that calls your custom method and sends it the name of the event, which is then added to the two `Label` controls by the

WriteMessage method. Don't forget to replace the name of the event in the text with the actual event name:

VB.NET

```
Protected Sub Page_Load(ByVal sender As Object, ByVal e As System.EventArgs) _
            Handles Me.Load
  WriteMessage("Page_Load")
End Sub
```

C#

```
protected void Page_Load(object sender, EventArgs e)
{
  WriteMessage("Page_Load");
}
```

12. Finally, add the following event handler to the page manually:

VB.NET

```
Protected Sub Page_PreRenderComplete(ByVal sender As Object, ByVal e As System.EventArgs) _
            Handles Me.PreRenderComplete
  WriteMessage("Page_PreRenderComplete<br />-----------------")
End Sub
```

C#

```
protected void Page_PreRenderComplete(object sender, EventArgs e)
{
  WriteMessage("Page_PreRenderComplete<br />-----------------");
}
```

The PreRenderComplete event fires very late in the Page control's life cycle, making it an ideal place to put a line at the bottom of the event list. That way you can clearly see what set of events belong to each other which in turn helps to figure out what events are triggered during which postback.

13. Save all your changes and open the page in the browser. Besides the GridView with the available genres, you should also see a list with event names under the No Postback heading:

```
Page_Load
LinqDataSource1_Selecting
LinqDataSource1_ContextCreating
GridView1_DataBinding
GridView1_RowCreated
GridView1_RowDataBound
GridView1_RowCreated
GridView1_RowDataBound
...
GridView1_DataBound
Page_PreRenderComplete
-----------------
```

- Note that the RowCreated and RowDataBound events are repeated multiple times — once for each record in the data source.
- Click the button to cause a postback. The No Postback label won't change, but the Postback label now shows the following list of event names:

```
...
GridView1_RowCreated
GridView1_RowCreated
GridView1_RowCreated
GridView1_RowCreated
Page_Load
Button1_Click
Page_PreRenderComplete
-----------------
```

Click one of the column headers of the GridView to order the data it is displaying. Notice that the second label's text is extended with a second set of event names.

How It Works

Technically, this exercise isn't complicated. You set up a bunch of event handlers for the various controls in your page. Inside the event handler you call a method that checks whether the page is currently loading for the first time or is loading due to a postback. Finally, the code updates one of the two Label controls with the name of the event that triggered the event handler.

What's interesting about this exercise is the order in which the events occur. Take a look at the first list, displayed when the page first loads:

```
Page_Load
LinqDataSource1_Selecting
LinqDataSource1_ContextCreating
GridView1_DataBinding
GridView1_RowCreated
GridView1_RowDataBound
GridView1_RowCreated
GridView1_RowDataBound
...
GridView1_DataBound
Page_PreRenderComplete
-----------------
```

First Page_Load is triggered. Then the GridView sees that it's hooked up to a LinqDataSource and asks for that control for its data. This causes the Selecting and ContextCreating events to be triggered. When the GridView receives the data from the LinqDataSource, it fires its DataBinding event to signal it's about to bind the data to the control. The GridView then starts to create rows. For each item in the data source, it creates a row, fires RowCreated, binds the item's data to the row, and finally calls RowDataBound. If you carefully count the number of times that RowCreated and RowDataBound are called, you'll notice that it's being called two times more than the actual number of items that are in the data source. This is because the same event is also raised when the control creates its Header and Footer rows. You see how to distinguish between these rows inside an event handler in a later exercise.

Finally, when the GridView is done creating and binding all the rows in the data source, it fires its DataBound event.

On postback, the story looks quite different. When you click the button to cause a postback, the following events are raised:

```
...
GridView1_RowCreated
GridView1_RowCreated
GridView1_RowCreated
GridView1_RowCreated
Page_Load
Button1_Click
Page_PreRenderComplete
-----------------
```

Note that there are no RowDataBound or DataBound events in this list and the LinqDataSource is also nowhere to be seen. The GridView is able to reconstruct the entire control from ViewState, eliminating the need to access the database again. While getting the data from ViewState, the GridView still needs to recreate each row in the grid, so you still see the RowCreated events. Toward the end of the list you see the Page_Load event followed by the Button control's Click event. It's important to understand and remember that user-triggered control events like a Button control's Click or a SelectedIndexChanged of a DropDownList occur *after* the Load event of the Page. Note that this Load event isn't the start of the Page control's life cycle. Before the Load event, the Page is already instantiated and has fired its Init event.

At the end of the exercise, you clicked a column header to sort the data in the grid. This time, the GridView knows it must sort the data that is being displayed. It cannot do that itself, so instead it asks the LinqDataSource for a fresh copy of the data in the order the user requested. Just as the first time the page loaded, you see the various RowCreated and DataBound events appear.

If you want to see other events at work, simply repeat steps 8 and 11 of the previous exercise, setting up handlers for the various events. To see the effect of ViewState, try disabling ViewState either at the control level (for example for the GridView) or at the page level.

Although the previous exercise should help you gain an understanding of the various control events and the order in which they fire, the example itself is quite useless in a real-world application. However, you can use the exact same principle to hook into the page and make modifications to the page itself, or to any of the controls in the page. In the next exercise you see how to change the appearance of rows in the data source, depending on the data that you are displaying.

The ASP.NET Page Life Cycle and Events in Data Controls

As discussed earlier, the GridView raises its RowCreated and RowDataBound events for each row it adds to its output. These events are ideal to peek into the data and then, based on the data, take appropriate action. For example, you can use these events to verify whether a review that is being displayed is authorized. If it's not (it means it won't be visible in the front-end web site) you can change its appearance to draw attention to it. You see what code you need to write to accomplish this in the next exercise.

Try It Out Hooking into RowDataBound

In this exercise you write an event handler for the `RowDataBound` event of the `GridView` control in the Reviews page of the Management section. Within this event, you can diagnose the data item that is being bound to the `GridView` row, allowing you to see if the item is authorized or not. If it's not, you apply a different CSS class to make the row stand out from the others.

1. Open the page Reviews.aspx from the Management folder and switch to Design View. Locate the `GridView`, open its Properties Grid and then set the `DataKeyNames` property of the `GridView` to `Id`. This tells the `GridView` the primary key of the review in the database, which is necessary to support the delete behavior to delete reviews from the `GridView`.
2. Switch the Properties Grid to the Events category. Set up an event handler for the `RowDataBound` event.
3. At the top of Code Behind of the document add the following line of code if you are using Visual Basic .NET:

```
Imports System.Data
```

4. Inside the event handler that VWD created for you, add the following code:

VB.NET

```
Protected Sub GridView1_RowDataBound(ByVal sender As Object, _
          ByVal e As System.Web.UI.WebControls.GridViewRowEventArgs) _
          Handles GridView1.RowDataBound
  Select Case e.Row.RowType
    Case DataControlRowType.DataRow
      Dim myRowView As DataRowView = CType(e.Row.DataItem, DataRowView)
      If Not Convert.ToBoolean(myRowView("Authorized")) Then
        e.Row.CssClass = "HighContrast"
      End If
  End Select
End Sub
```

C#

```
protected void GridView1_RowDataBound(object sender, GridViewRowEventArgs e)
{
  switch (e.Row.RowType)
  {
    case DataControlRowType.DataRow:
      DataRowView myDataRowView = (DataRowView)e.Row.DataItem;
      if (!Convert.ToBoolean(myDataRowView["Authorized"]))
      {
        e.Row.CssClass = "HighContrast";
      }
      break;
  }
}
```

5. Open Management.css from the Management theme folder and add the following CSS rule set:

```
.HighContrast, .HighContrast a
{
  background-color: Black;
  color: White;
}
```

6. Save changes to all open files and then request Reviews.aspx in the browser. From the drop-down list at the top, choose an item to display the reviews for that genre. When you have found a genre that has one or more reviews that have not been authorized yet (choose Indie Rock if you are using the database from this book's code download), you should see the item displayed with different background and text colors, as shown in Figure 14-7. If you don't see an unauthorized item, click the Title of a review first, clear the Authorized checkbox and then click the Update link.

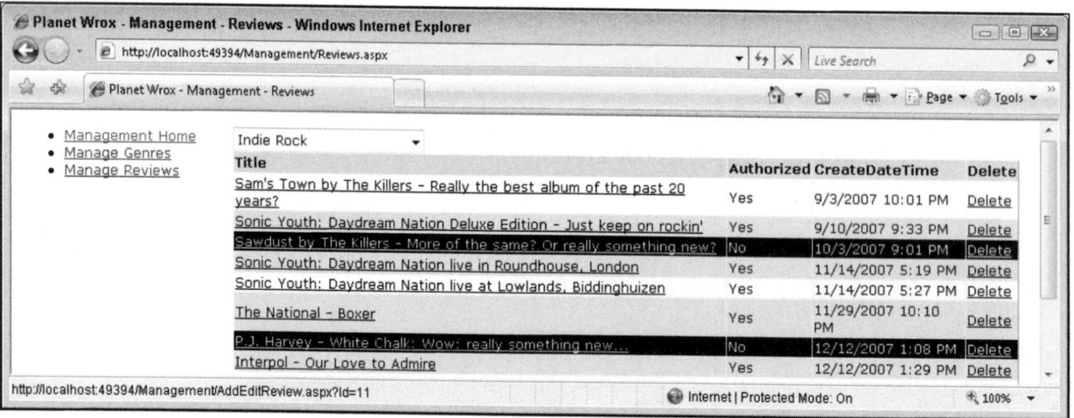

Figure 14-7

In Figure 14-7 you can see that two reviews are not authorized. To emphasize that, each row is displayed with a black background and white text.

How It Works

Although short, this exercise demonstrates a powerful way to hook into the different events of a control and change the presentation of the underlying control. To see how it works, take a look at the code:

VB.NET

```
Protected Sub GridView1_RowDataBound(ByVal sender As Object, _
         ByVal e As System.Web.UI.WebControls.GridViewRowEventArgs) _
         Handles GridView1.RowRowDataBound
  Select Case e.Row.RowType
    Case DataControlRowType.DataRow
      ...
  End Select
End Sub
```

C#

```
protected void GridView1_RowRowDataBound (object sender, GridViewRowEventArgs e)
{
  switch (e.Row.RowType)
  {
    case DataControlRowType.DataRow:
      ...
  }
}
```

The RowDataBound event gets passed an instance of GridViewRowEventArgs, a class that provides information about the row and data that are being bound at this stage. One of the properties of this class is the Row that represents the actual GridView row that is being added to the GridView. This row in turn contains a RowType enumeration property that you can test to see what kind of row is being added. This enumeration contains six different members that map directly to the different types of rows the GridView can contain: DataRow for normal and alternating rows, EmptyDataRow for empty data rows, Header and Footer for the header and footer rows that are placed at the top and bottom of the GridView, and so on. Since you want to change the appearance of an actual data row, the code in the Case block only fires for normal and alternating rows.

Inside the Case block, the following code is executed:

VB.NET

```
Dim myRowView As DataRowView = CType(e.Row.DataItem, DataRowView)
If Not Convert.ToBoolean(myRowView("Authorized")) Then
  e.Row.CssClass = "HighContrast"
End If
```

C#

```
DataRowView myDataRowView = (DataRowView)e.Row.DataItem;
if (!Convert.ToBoolean(myDataRowView["Authorized"]))
{
  e.Row.CssClass = "HighContrast";
}
```

The DataItem property contains a reference to the data item object that is being bound. When you are using a LinqDataSource control, the DataItem is actually a strongly typed instance of one of your LINQ to SQL objects, like a Review or a Genre. You see how this works later. But when you are using a SqlDataSource control, each row is presented as a DataRowView, a .NET object that encapsulates a row returned from the database.

Finally, the DataItem is cast to a DataRowView object and then it's indexed — using myRowView("Authorized") in VB.NET and myRowView["Authorized"] in C# — to get at the Boolean value for the Authorized column. If Authorized is False, the Row instance gets a new CssClass applied, which changes the background and text color of the entire row through CSS.

Because the Reviews page uses a `SqlDataSource` control you need to deploy some tricks to get at the actual data of the review. First you need to cast `DataItem` to a `DataRowView` and then you need to index that `DataRowView` and try to find the right `Authorized` column. Wouldn't it be much easier if you could directly access strongly typed objects like `Review` and `Genre` instances? You'll see how to do exactly this in the next exercise.

Try It Out Handling Events with Strongly Typed Objects

In this exercise you create another page for listing the various genres in your database, similar to the current Genres.aspx page in the Management folder. The page lists all the available genres together with a Delete button so you can delete them if you want. However, the Delete button will be disabled when the genre still has reviews associated with it.

1. Add a new Web Form called GenresLinq.aspx to the Management folder of the site. Make sure it's based on the Management master page. Set the page's `Title` to Events with the LinqDataSource.
2. Switch to Design View and then drag and drop a `GridView` control from the Toolbox to the page.
3. Connect the `GridView` to a `LinqDataSource` that in turn is bound to the `Genres` table. Ensure that Genres is selected in the Table drop-down list and then, in the Select list, make sure that the asterisk (*) is selected. Next, click the Advanced button and enable deletion of genres by checking the first checkbox on the Advanced Options dialog box and click OK. Your dialog box now looks like Figure 14-8.

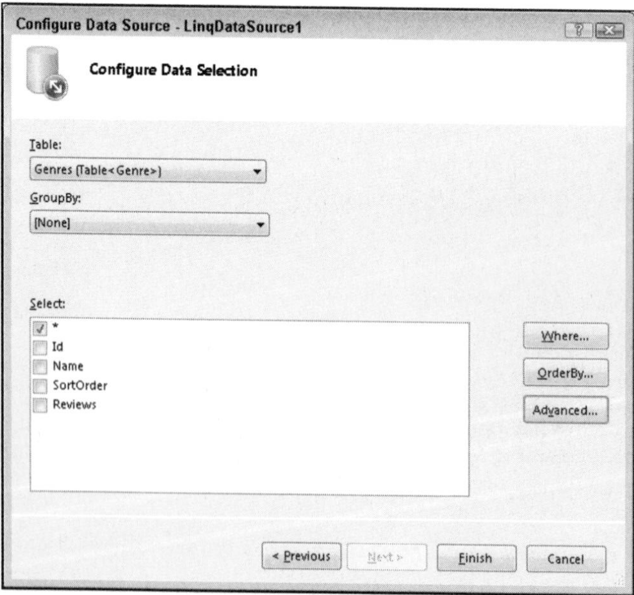

Figure 14-8

4. Click Finish to close the dialog box.

When you're done, you should have this code for the `LinqDataSource` control:

```
<asp:LinqDataSource ID="LinqDataSource1" runat="server"
```

```
    ContextTypeName="PlanetWroxDataContext" TableName="Genres" EnableDelete="True">
</asp:LinqDataSource>
```

5. Enable deleting on the `GridView` as well by selecting the Enable Deleting option on the control's Smart Tasks panel.

6. Still in the `GridView` control's Smart Tasks panel, click the Edit Columns link. Then click the Delete item in the Selected fields list, and finally click the blue link at the right side of the dialog box to convert the delete column into a `TemplateField`. Click OK to dismiss the dialog box. Your `GridView` should now consist of the following code:

```
<asp:GridView ID="GridView1" runat="server" AutoGenerateColumns="False" DataKeyNames="Id"
            DataSourceID="LinqDataSource1">
  <Columns>
    <asp:TemplateField ShowHeader="False">
      <ItemTemplate>
        <asp:LinkButton ID="LinkButton1" runat="server" CausesValidation="False"
                CommandName="Delete" Text="Delete"></asp:LinkButton>
      </ItemTemplate>
    </asp:TemplateField>
    <asp:BoundField DataField="Id" HeaderText="Id" InsertVisible="False"
                ReadOnly="True" SortExpression="Id"></asp:BoundField>
    <asp:BoundField DataField="Name" HeaderText="Name"
                SortExpression="Name"></asp:BoundField>
    <asp:BoundField DataField="SortOrder" HeaderText="SortOrder"
                SortExpression="SortOrder"></asp:BoundField>
  </Columns>
</asp:GridView>
```

7. Add an event handler to the `GridView` for its `RowDataBound` event using the Event category of the Properties Grid for the `GridView`.

8. Inside the event handler, write the following code:

VB.NET

```
Protected Sub GridView1_RowDataBound(ByVal sender As Object, _
          ByVal e As System.Web.UI.WebControls.GridViewRowEventArgs) _
          Handles GridView1.RowDataBound
  Select Case e.Row.RowType
    Case DataControlRowType.DataRow
        Dim myGenre As Genre = CType(e.Row.DataItem, Genre)
        Dim deleteButton As LinkButton = _
                             CType(e.Row.FindControl("LinkButton1"), LinkButton)
        deleteButton.Enabled = myGenre.Reviews.Count = 0
  End Select
End Sub
```

C#

```
protected void GridView1_RowDataBound (object sender, GridViewRowEventArgs e)
{
  switch (e.Row.RowType)
  {
```

```
        case DataControlRowType.DataRow:
          Genre myGenre = (Genre)e.Row.DataItem;
          LinkButton deleteButton = (LinkButton) e.Row.FindControl("LinkButton1");
          deleteButton.Enabled = myGenre.Reviews.Count == 0;
          break;
      }
    }
```

9. Save all changes and request the page in the browser by pressing Ctrl+F5. You should see a list with all the genres in the system similar to Figure 14-9. For most of the genres the Delete link should be disabled because they have associated reviews. However, because genres like Punk, Reggae, Industrial, and so on have no reviews attached to them, their Delete link is available. If all the Delete links are disabled, go to the Manage Reviews page and delete the reviews from at least one genre. Then when you reopen the GenresLinq.aspx page, you should see a list similar to Figure 14-9. Depending on the browser you are using, the Delete link may not appear as disabled. However, you still won't be able to click it.

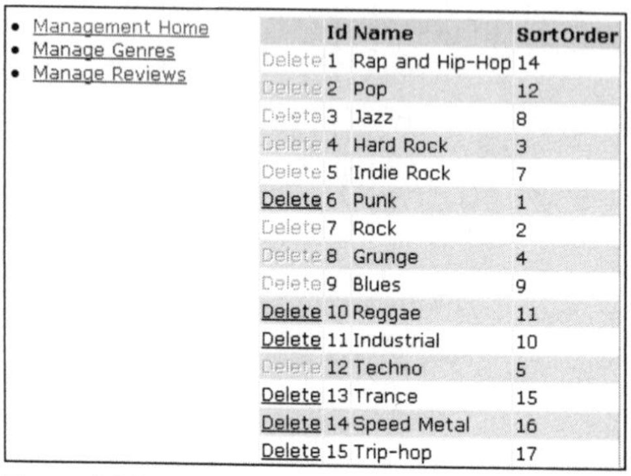

- Management Home
- Manage Genres
- Manage Reviews

	Id	Name	SortOrder
Delete	1	Rap and Hip-Hop	14
Delete	2	Pop	12
Delete	3	Jazz	8
Delete	4	Hard Rock	3
Delete	5	Indie Rock	7
Delete	6	Punk	1
Delete	7	Rock	2
Delete	8	Grunge	4
Delete	9	Blues	9
Delete	10	Reggae	11
Delete	11	Industrial	10
Delete	12	Techno	5
Delete	13	Trance	15
Delete	14	Speed Metal	16
Delete	15	Trip-hop	17

Figure 14-9

How It Works

Much of this exercise is similar to the previous one you did. You set up a `RowDataBound` event handler that fires for each row being added to the `GridView`. What's different is the way you access the data, and the way you use `FindControl` to search for the delete `LinkButton` in the `GridView`. Take a look at how the data is accessed first:

VB.NET

```
If e.Row.DataItem IsNot Nothing Then
  Dim myGenre As Genre = CType(e.Row.DataItem, Genre)
  ...
End If
```

C#

```
if (e.Row.DataItem != null)
{
  Genre myGenre = (Genre)e.Row.DataItem;
  ...
}
```

Because the `LinqDataSource` works with strongly typed objects, the `DataItem` property of `e.Row` contains a real `Genre` object, so you can cast this property to a true `Genre` instance and then access its properties. In this example, the code accesses the `Reviews` collection, which in turn has a `Count` property that indicates how many reviews the current `Genre` contains. If the count is zero, the genre can safely be deleted. In all other cases, the Delete button should be disabled. To understand the code that finds the button, you need to look at the markup for it first:

```
<asp:TemplateField ShowHeader="False">
  <ItemTemplate>
    <asp:LinkButton ID="LinkButton1" runat="server" CausesValidation="False"
                CommandName="Delete" Text="Delete"></asp:LinkButton>
  </ItemTemplate>
</asp:TemplateField>
```

By converting the delete column into a `TemplateField`, it's easier to see what the column contains. In this case, the column contains a `LinkButton` with its `CommandName` set to `Delete`, which makes it an automatic Delete button. Note that the `LinkButton` has its `ID` set to `LinkButton1`. This name is used inside the event handler to find the relevant button:

VB.NET

```
Dim deleteButton As LinkButton = _
                   CType(e.Row.FindControl("LinkButton1"), LinkButton)
deleteButton.Enabled = myGenre.Reviews.Count = 0
```

C#

```
LinkButton deleteButton = (LinkButton) e.Row.FindControl("LinkButton1");
deleteButton.Enabled = myGenre.Reviews.Count == 0;
```

Since each data row in the `GridView` contains a Delete button called `LinkButton1`, you cannot access this control directly using its name. Instead, you need to search for it in the current row using `e.Row.FindControl`. The `FindControl` method then returns a reference to the `LinkButton`, which you can then cast into a proper `LinkButton` instance.

Finally, the code determines if the button should be enabled or not by looking at the `Reviews` collection and its `Count` property. When there are no reviews, then the expression `myGenre.Reviews.Count = 0` will be `True`, and the button is enabled. Otherwise, the `Enabled` property is set to `False`, removing the option to delete the genre from the user interface.

With this code, you can easily prevent errors that may occur when you try to delete a genre that has associated reviews. However, you may not always be able to prevent an error from occurring during a CRUD operation against a data source control. For example, you may try to delete a genre that initially didn't have any reviews attached. However, right before you try to delete the genre, somebody else inserts a new review for it. When you then try to delete the genre you'll get an error because the genre is now linked to a review. In such cases, the data source controls enable you to diagnose the error that occurred and then take the necessary measures, like providing feedback to the user informing them that their CRUD operation didn't succeed.

Handling Errors that Occur in the Data Source Controls

In Chapter 17 you'll see a lot more about recognizing and handling errors that occur in your ASP.NET pages. That chapter demonstrates how to catch errors that may occur in your code, and then handle them by logging them or by informing the user. But since the data source controls expose error information as well, it's interesting to look at data access errors in this chapter.

Both the `LinqDataSource` and the `SqlDataSource` control give you information about errors (*exceptions* in .NET parlance) that may occur during one of the four CRUD operations. The four events that occur after the CRUD operation (`Selected`, `Inserted`, `Updated`, and `Deleted`) of the LinqDataSource all accept an instance of a class called `LinqDataSourceStatusEventArgs` whereas the same four events for the `SqlDataSource` receive an instance of `SqlDataSourceStatusEventArgs`. Figure 14-10 shows both these classes and their properties.

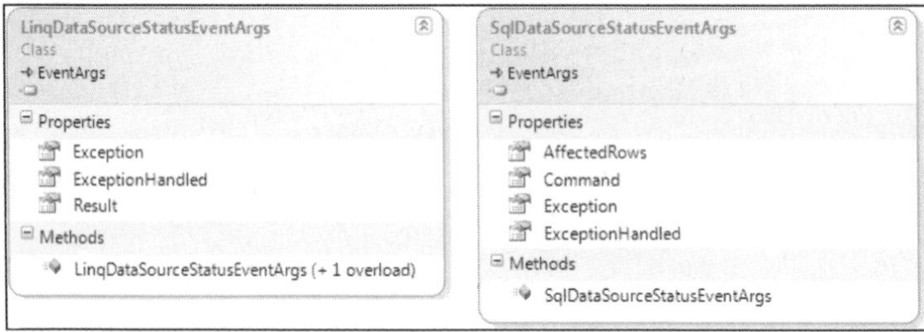

Figure 14-10

These two classes share two important properties: `Exception` and `ExceptionHandled`. The first contains the actual exception that occurred or `Nothing` (in VB.NET) or `null` (in C#) when everything goes according to plan and no error occurs. You can diagnose this error and take appropriate action. For example, you can inform the user that something went terribly wrong, or you can send an e-mail to the site's web master informing her about the error so appropriate follow up action can be taken.

If you decide to handle the error in the event handler of the data source control, you should set the `ExceptionHandled` property of the object to `True`. This signals to the ASP.NET run time that you are aware of the exception and have dealt with it adequately. If you omit setting this property, the run time forwards the exception, which is eventually displayed to the user.

In the following exercise you see how to make use of the `SqlDataSourceStatusEventArgs` class in the page Genres.aspx. Rest assured, you can apply the exact same principles from this section to events that are raised by the `LinqDataSource` control as well.

Try It Out Handling Errors When Deleting Rows

In this Try It Out you see how to deal with exceptions that occur in a `GridView` when deleting rows. You modify the original Genres page and display an error message when a user tries to delete a genre that still has reviews attached to it. This exercise mainly serves to demonstrate how to handle exceptions that may be thrown by the data source controls. From an end user's perspective, disabling the delete link when it's not appropriate as you did in an earlier exercise should take care of the problem in most circumstances, but there are still chances of someone else inserting a new review before you get the chance to delete your genre.

1. Open Genres.aspx from the Management folder.
2. Switch to Design View and from the Toolbox drag a `Label` control onto the `GridView`. This places the `Label` that will hold an error message above the `GridView`. Rename the `Label` to `lblErrorMessage` and delete its `Text` property. (Right-click the `Text` property in the Properties Grid and choose Reset. This removes the entire `Text` property and its value from the control's markup.) Set its `CssClass` to `ErrorMessage`. Finally, set its `EnableViewState` property to `False` to ensure the label doesn't maintain its text after postbacks. You should end up with this code:

```
<asp:Label ID="lblErrorMessage" runat="server" CssClass="ErrorMessage"
                EnableViewState="False"></asp:Label>
<asp:GridView ID="GridView1" runat="server" AllowPaging="True"
```

3. Open the Management.css file from the Management theme folder and add the following style rule:

```
.ErrorMessage
{
  color: Red;
  font-weight: bold;
}
```

4. Switch back to Genres.aspx, make sure the page is in Design View, and then click the `SqlDataSource` control once to select it. Then open its Properties Grid, switch to the Events category, and set up an event handler for the `Deleted` event by double-clicking the event name in the grid, visible in Figure 14-11.

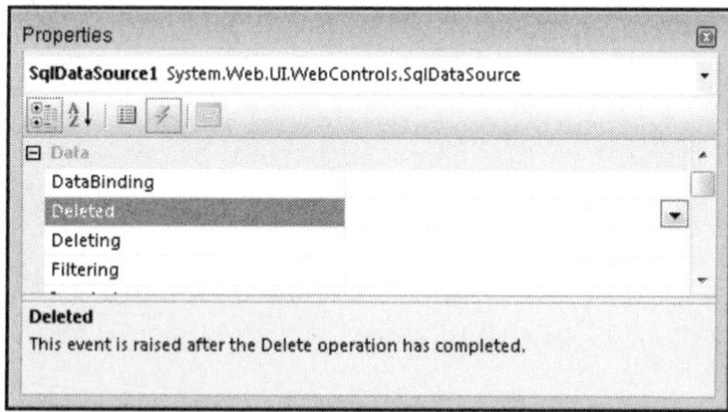

Figure 14-11

5. At the top of the Code Behind, add the following namespace:

VB.NET

```
Imports System.Data.SqlClient
```

C#

```
using System.Data.SqlClient;
```

6. Inside the event handler that VWD added for you, write the following code:

VB.NET

```
Protected Sub SqlDataSource1_Deleted(ByVal sender As Object, _
          ByVal e As System.Web.UI.WebControls.SqlDataSourceStatusEventArgs) _
          Handles SqlDataSource1.Deleted
  If e.Exception IsNot Nothing AndAlso _
              TypeOf (e.Exception) Is SqlException Then
    Dim myException As SqlException = CType(e.Exception, SqlException)
    If myException.Number = 547 Then
      lblErrorMessage.Text = "Sorry, you can't delete this genre because " & _
                  "it has associated reviews that you need to delete first."
      e.ExceptionHandled = True
    End If
  End If
End Sub
```

C#

```
protected void SqlDataSource1_Deleted(object sender, SqlDataSourceStatusEventArgs e)
{
  if (e.Exception != null && e.Exception is SqlException)
  {
    SqlException myException = (SqlException)e.Exception;
    if (myException.Number == 547)
    {
      lblErrorMessage.Text = @"Sorry, you can't delete this genre because
                  it has associated reviews that you need to delete first.";
      e.ExceptionHandled = true;
    }
  }
}
```

7. Save all your changes and then press Ctrl+F5 to open Genres.aspx in your browser. Try deleting a genre that you know has associated reviews, like Grunge. Instead of deleting the genre, the ASPX page now presents you with the error that is displayed above the `GridView` in Figure 14-12.

8. Click the Manage Reviews menu item in the Management menu and then select the Grunge genre from the drop-down list. Delete the reviews in the genre, or edit them and reassign them to a different genre.

9. Go back to Genres.aspx and try deleting the Grunge genre again. This time the genre is successfully deleted from the database.

10. To see the error you would get without this error handling, comment out the line in the Code Behind that sets `ExceptionHandled` to `True` using a single tick (`'`) in VB.NET and two forward slashes (`//`) in C#. Additionally, remove the `UpdatePanel` and its `ContentTemplate` element from Markup View of the Genres.aspx page. With an `UpdatePanel` in your page, the browser may swallow your exception. Without the `UpdatePanel`, it's much easier to see what's going on. Save your changes, open the page again in your browser, and try to delete a genre with reviews. You'll get a detailed ASP.NET error instead.

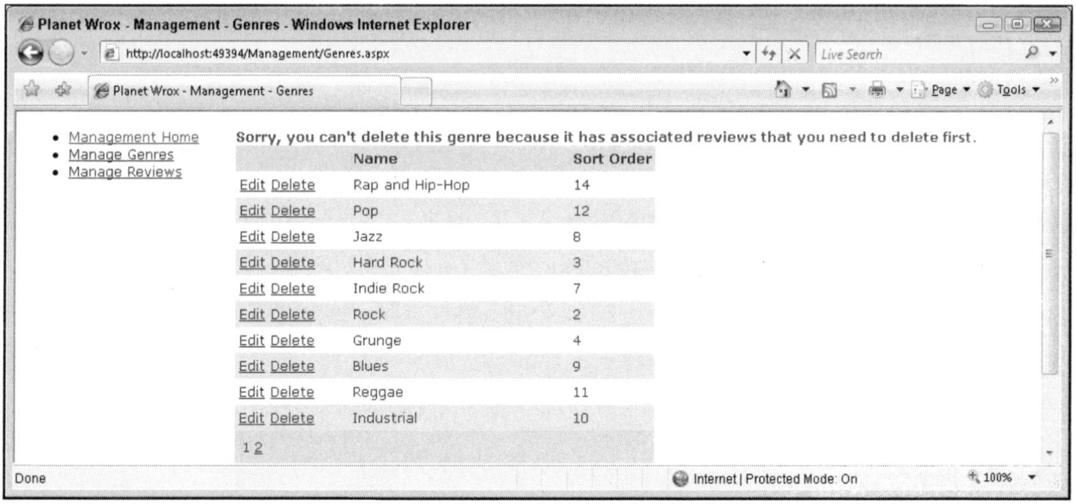

Figure 14-12

How It Works

When you click the Delete link in the `GridView` visible in Figure 14-12, the `GridView` triggers the `delete` command on the associated `SqlDataSource` control. As you have seen in previous chapters, this control tries to send a `DELETE` statement to the database. The database then tries to delete the requested genre from the database, but finds out that it can't because there are related reviews. This results in a *foreign key constraint error*; the genre cannot be deleted because its ID is used as a foreign key in another table.

This foreign key constraint error is then returned from the database and eventually ends up in the `Exception` property of the `e` argument of the `SqlDataSource1_Deleted` handler. The code then checks if there was an error (`e.Exception` is not `Nothing` / `null`) and checks the type of the exception to find out whether it's a `SqlException`:

VB.NET

```
If e.Exception IsNot Nothing AndAlso _
              TypeOf (e.Exception) Is SqlException Then
  ...
End If
```

C#

```
if (e.Exception != null && e.Exception is SqlException)
{
  ...
}
```

When you are working with a SQL Server database, as is the case in the Planet Wrox example, the errors thrown by the database are of type `SqlException` from the `System.Data.SqlClient` namespace that you imported in this exercise. This allows you to clearly separate database errors from other errors.

When SQL Server throws an error, it also passes an error number, which is stored in the `Number` property of the exception. To access that number, you need to cast the exception to a true `SqlException`, done with this code:

VB.NET

```
Dim myException As SqlException = CType(e.Exception, SqlException)
```

C#

```
SqlException myException = (SqlException)e.Exception;
```

Finally, the code checks the `Number` property. When it is `547`, it means that SQL Server threw a foreign key constraint error to indicate you cannot delete a genre because it still has associated reviews. When this is the case, the `Label` control's `Text` property is set, and finally the code sets `e.ExceptionHandled` to `True`. This tells the ASP.NET run time that the error has been dealt with, so the user won't get a nasty error page, but a nice and friendly error message at the top of the `GridView` instead. Note that for all other types of exceptions, the user still gets the default ASP.NET error message screen, also called the Yellow Screen of Death. Chapter 17 teaches you some techniques to log the error in a central location and present the user with a friendly, human readable error page instead.

The number `547` seems to be arbitrarily chosen, but it's the number that SQL Server returns for a foreign key constraint exception. In Chapter 17, which deals with debugging, you learn a few tricks that enable you to look into the exceptions that are thrown so you can diagnose the `Number` property for different kinds of exceptions.

In all the database examples you have seen so far, the code accesses the database for each and every request. Every time some data needs to be displayed, it's retrieved fresh from the database. Clearly, this can be a waste of time and resources like CPU cycles, especially if the data hasn't changed since the last time you accessed it.

In the final section of this chapter you are introduced to a technique called caching that can greatly improve the responsiveness and performance of your application.

Caching

Caching is one of the best and often easiest ways to improve the performance of an application. With caching, a *copy* of your data is stored in a location that can be accessed very quickly. The idea with caching is that fetching data from the cache should be faster than fetching it from the original data source. Therefore, most caching solutions store data in memory, which is usually the fastest way to get the data. The .NET cache is no exception, and allows you to store frequently accessed data in a special location in the computer's memory.

Usually, the caching principle takes the route displayed in Figure 14-13.

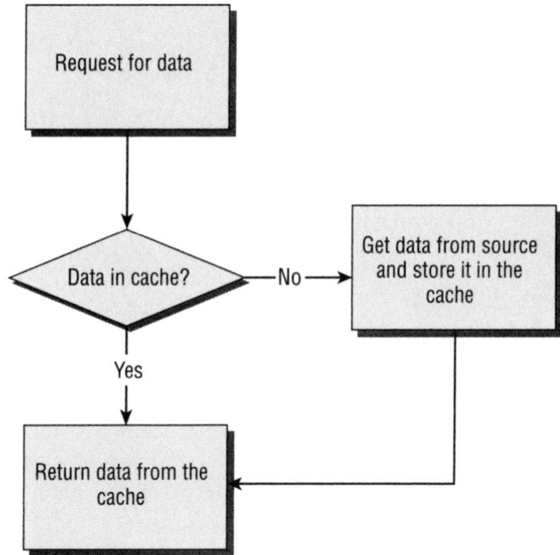

Figure 14-13

The application queries for some data — for example, a list of genres from the database. Instead of accessing the database directly, the cache is examined to see if it contains the requested data. If it does, the data is returned from the cache directly. If the data is not stored in the cache yet, it is retrieved from the data source, like a SQL Server database, a copy of the data is stored in the cache for later retrieval, and finally the data is returned to the calling code.

While caching is generally a great solution to improve your application, there are a few drawbacks that you need to be aware of. The following section explains a few common pitfalls you can run into when using caching. The section that follows then shows the different caching mechanisms you have available in your ASP.NET web applications.

Common Pitfalls with Caching Data

When working with cached data you run the risk of getting old — or stale — data. For example, when you cache the results of a query for all the genres in the database and use that data instead of getting it fresh from the database, you may not notice a new genre that another user has inserted in the table in the meantime.

Another issue with the cache is that you can't rely on an item being present in the cache. To minimize memory consumption for an application, the caching mechanism in ASP.NET automatically removes old and infrequently used items from the cache from time to time. Therefore, you shouldn't rely on items being in the cache, even if you insert them there on the application's startup.

In the next sections you see how to avoid these two problems.

Avoiding Stale Data

To avoid stale data that is no longer in sync with the original data in the database, you need a way to *invalidate the cache*. With cache invalidation, an item is removed from the cache so it can be recreated on the next request. To invalidate cache data, you have a number of options at your disposal. First of all, you can choose to set a short cache duration. For example, you could cache the Genres list in the database for, say, 10 minutes. If another user inserts a new genre during those 10 minutes, it won't show up in the web pages. However, after 10 minutes, the list is removed from the cache and recreated with fresh data the next time it is requested. You see how to use time-based caching later.

Another option to invalidate the cache is by using a cache dependency. With a cache dependency, you create a relationship between the cached item and the original data source. When the underlying data source changes, the cached item is invalidated so it can be recreated the next time it is requested. For example, you can cache the contents of a large text or XML file. Instead of reading the file every time you need it, you can insert it into the cache. You then hook it up to an instance of `CacheDependency` that will watch the source file for you. As soon as the file is changed, the item is removed from the cache and will be recreated on the next request. You see how to use the `CacheDependency` towards the end of this chapter.

You can also use a cache dependency when using a database like Microsoft SQL Server. This means that as soon as the data that is part of the cached query is changed, the cached item is invalidated. Database caching and invalidation is an advanced and broad subject. Scott Hanselman wrote about it in the chapter that deals with caching in *Professional ASP.NET 3.5*, published by Wrox (ISBN: 978-0-470-18757-9).

Don't Rely on the Data Being There

As you just learned, it's possible that items can be removed from the cache at different stages in the application's life cycle. They can be removed by the cache itself because the ASP.NET run time determines that the item is not used often enough and is thus taking up precious space unnecessarily. The entire cache is also cleared when the web application or web server restarts. But items can also be removed because of their dependencies. Therefore, you should never rely on the item being in the cache, even if you set it there yourself earlier in the application's life cycle.

Later in this chapter you see how to use the Cache API (Application Programming Interface; the way you can interact with the Cache functionality) to use the cache programmatically, but here's a quick example that retrieves an instance of a `Review` from the cache. The code doesn't assume the item is there, but checks the cache first:

VB.NET

```
Dim reviewId As Integer = Convert.ToInt32(Request.QueryString.Get("ReviewId"))
Dim myReview As Review

If Cache("MyReview" + reviewId.ToString()) Is Nothing Then
  Using db As New PlanetWroxDataContext()
    myReview = (From r In db.Reviews _
                Where r.Id = reviewId _
                Select r).Single()
  End Using

  Cache("MyReview" + reviewId.ToString()) = myReview
End If

myReview = CType(Cache("MyReview" + reviewId.ToString()), Review)
```

C#

```
int reviewId = Convert.ToInt32(Request.QueryString.Get("ReviewId"));
Review myReview;

if (Cache["MyReview" + reviewId.ToString()] == null)
{
  using (PlanetWroxDataContext db = new PlanetWroxDataContext())
  {
    myReview = (from r in db.Reviews
                where r.Id == reviewId
                select r).Single();
  }
  Cache["MyReview" + reviewId.ToString()] = myReview;
}

myReview = (Review) Cache["MyReview" + reviewId.ToString()];
```

In this code snippet the cache is searched for an item by its key, which is a combination of the static word `MyReview` and the ID of the `Review` being searched for. When the cache is empty (the search returns `Nothing` or `null`) the item is created using a LINQ query and then stored in the cache.

This is a good example of code that doesn't rely on the item being in the cache. Instead, it carefully checks the cache and creates the item first when it doesn't exist yet. You learn more about programmatically accessing the cache later in this chapter.

Using the cache API is not the only way to use the cache. The next section shows you the different ways of caching data in ASP.NET.

Different Ways to Cache Data in ASP.NET Web Applications

You can deploy a few different caching strategies in your ASP.NET applications, including output caching, caching with the built-in data source controls, and programmatic caching. All three options are discussed in the remainder of this chapter.

Output Caching

With output caching, the end result of a rendered page is cached. This means that the very first time a page is requested, its end result is added to the cache. Subsequent requests to the same page result in the same HTML being sent. Although this is fine for relatively static pages like the About page in the Planet Wrox site, this is typically not an ideal solution for dynamic pages. For example, imagine a dynamic page that shows the details for a Review based on the query string that is being passed to the page. The first time you request the page you may browse to something like:

```
http://localhost:12345/Reviews/ViewDetails.aspx?Id=23
```

ASP.NET generates a page showing review 23 and then caches the entire output of the page. So what happens when you then request this page?

```
http://localhost:12345/Reviews/ViewDetails.aspx?Id=58
```

Instead of seeing the review with an ID of 58, you end up with the same review with an ID of 23. To overcome this problem ASP.NET enables you to cache specific versions of a page. For example, you can instruct

Planet Wrox to cache a copy of the page for each unique query string field that it retrieves. For a page showing the details of a specific review, this is perfect. For each unique review, ASP.NET keeps a cached copy. This means that the database will only be hit the very first time a specific review is requested; subsequent requests will be served from the cache. In the next exercise you see how to create a details page that employs this caching strategy to avoid the same LINQ query that gets a review from being executed over and over again.

Try It Out — Output Caching

1. Start by adding a new page called ViewDetails.aspx in the Reviews folder of your web application. Make sure it's based on your custom template. There's no need to set a title, as it will be set programmatically.
2. In Markup View, add three `Label` controls to the `cpMainContent` content placeholder and name the controls as follows:
    - `lblTitle`
    - `lblSummary`
    - `lblBody`

    Delete the `Text` attribute and its value of all three labels.
3. Wrap `lblTitle` label in a `<h1>` element, and wrap the other two `Label` controls in a `<div>` element with their `class` attributes set to `Summary` and `Body`, respectively. You should end up with this code:

```
<h1><asp:Label ID="lblTitle" runat="server"></asp:Label></h1>
<div class="Summary"><asp:Label ID="lblSummary" runat="server"></asp:Label></div>
<div class="Body"><asp:Label ID="lblBody" runat="server"></asp:Label></div>
```

4. Switch to Design View and double-click the read-only area of the page to set up a handler for `Page_Load`,
5. Then add the following code to the `Page_Load` event handler that has been created for you:

VB.NET

```
Protected Sub Page_Load(ByVal sender As Object, ByVal e As System.EventArgs) _
            Handles Me.Load
  Dim reviewId As Integer = Convert.ToInt32(Request.QueryString.Get("ReviewId"))
  Dim myReview As Review

  Using db As New PlanetWroxDataContext()
    myReview = (From r In db.Reviews _
                Where r.Id = reviewId _
                Select r).Single()
    lblTitle.Text = myReview.Title
    lblSummary.Text = myReview.Summary
    lblBody.Text = myReview.Body

    ' Set the page title programmatically
    Me.Title = myReview.Title
  End Using
End Sub
```

C#

```
protected void Page_Load(object sender, EventArgs e)
{
  int reviewId = Convert.ToInt32(Request.QueryString.Get("ReviewId"));
  Review myReview;

  using (PlanetWroxDataContext db = new PlanetWroxDataContext())
  {
    myReview = (from r in db.Reviews
                where r.Id == reviewId
                select r).Single();

    lblTitle.Text = myReview.Title;
    lblSummary.Text = myReview.Summary;
    lblBody.Text = myReview.Body;

    // Set the page title programmatically
    this.Title = myReview.Title;
  }
}
```

6. Open the page All.aspx from the Reviews folder and delete the `GridView` that you created in the previous chapter. Replace it with a simple `Repeater` control that contains a single `Hyperlink`:

```
<asp:Content ID="Content2" ContentPlaceHolderID="cpMainContent" Runat="Server">
  <asp:Repeater ID="Repeater1" runat="server">
    <ItemTemplate>
      <asp:HyperLink ID="HyperLink1" runat="server"
          NavigateUrl='<%# "ViewDetails.aspx?ReviewId=" + Eval("Id").ToString() %>'
          Text='<%# Eval("Title") %>'></asp:HyperLink>
      <br />
    </ItemTemplate>
  </asp:Repeater>
</asp:Content>
```

7. Switch to the Code Behind of the page and replace the last two calls that used the `GridView` so they end up using the `Repeater` control instead:

VB.NET

```
Repeater1.DataSource = allReviews
Repeater1.DataBind()
```

C#

```
Repeater1.DataSource = allReviews;
Repeater1.DataBind();
```

8. Go back to the page ViewDetails.aspx and at the top of the page, right below the `@ Page` directive, add the following code:

```
<%@ Page Language="VB" MasterPageFile="~/MasterPages/MasterPage.master"
  AutoEventWireup="false" CodeFile="ViewDetails.aspx.vb" Inherits="Reviews_ViewDetails" %>
<%@ OutputCache Duration="300" VaryByParam="None" %>
```

9. Save all changes and then request All.aspx from the Reviews folder in your browser. Click the title of a review and you're taken to ViewDetails.aspx with the ID of the requested review in the query string.

10. Click the Back button and click a different review. Note that the text for the review is not updated and still shows the previous review. From the theme drop-down list, choose a new theme. Note that the page keeps displaying the old theme.

11. Switch back to VWD and modify the `OutputCache` directive:

```
<%@ OutputCache Duration="300" VaryByParam="ReviewId" %>
```

12. Open All.aspx again in the browser and click a review's title. From now on, clicking a review will correctly show the requested review. Under the hood, however, the entire page is still cached, minimizing the need to access the database to retrieve the review. If you still see the old page, press Ctrl+F5 or Ctrl+R in your browser to request a fresh copy of the page from the server.

    If you switch to a different theme, you'll notice that the page is still presented using the old theme.

How It Works

Most of the code in this exercise should be familiar by now. In the page ViewDetails.aspx you added a few labels that will hold relevant properties of the `Review`, like its `Title`, `Summary`, and `Body`. You wrapped these labels in client-side `<div>` elements with a `class` attribute so you can influence their styling from your CSS files if you want (although this wasn't shown in the example).

The code in the Code Behind for the file retrieves a single instance of `Review` based on the query string:

VB.NET

```
Using db As New PlanetWroxDataContext()
  myReview = (From r In db.Reviews _
              Where r.Id = reviewId _
              Select r).Single()
  ...
End Using
```

C#

```
using (PlanetWroxDataContext db = new PlanetWroxDataContext())
{
  myReview = (from r in db.Reviews
              where r.Id == reviewId
              select r).Single();
  ...
}
```

Note that the query uses the `Single()` operator to limit the query to a single `Review` instance.

The `Review` that is returned from the database is then used to fill the `Label` controls in the page, and the page's `Title`:

VB.NET

```
lblTitle.Text = myReview.Title
lblSummary.Text = myReview.Summary
lblBody.Text = myReview.Body

this.Title = myReview.Title
```

C#

```
lblTitle.Text = myReview.Title;
lblSummary.Text = myReview.Summary;
lblBody.Text = myReview.Body;

this.Title = myReview.Title;
```

Under normal circumstances, this code would fire for each request made to the page. Even if you requested the same review over and over again, the database would be accessed for each individual request. To minimize the overhead associated with a database call, the page uses an output caching strategy that caches the results for 5 minutes (300 seconds). Additionally, it takes care that a copy of the page is created for each individual `Review` object by using the `VaryByParam` setting:

```
<%@ OutputCache Duration="300" VaryByParam="ReviewId" %>
```

The `VaryByParam` attribute takes a semicolon-separated list of query string fields that you want to create separate cached copies for, giving you a great deal of flexibility in terms of the data that is being cached. This ensures that the ASP.NET run time only caches copies for unique pages, improving the speed for reviews that are requested often.

One of the problems with output caching is that it's often an all-or-nothing scenario. As you witnessed in the previous exercise, the entire page is cached for the first user that requests it. That page is then displayed to every user, regardless of the theme the user has selected. Although you could programmatically influence this behavior, there is an easier solution available: instruct the data source controls to cache data for you.

Caching with Data Source Controls

The biggest benefit of caching with the data source controls is that they only cache dynamic, database-driven data, and not the entire page. That allows you to keep other parts of the page dynamic, like a banner module or a personalized greeting welcoming the user. Caching is supported by design on all data source controls, except for the `LinqDataSource` control.

Caching with the data source controls is very easy: all you need to do is set the `EnableCaching` property and then specify a `CacheDuration`. The following code snippet shows a `SqlDataSource` control that caches its data for 10 minutes:

```
<asp:SqlDataSource ID="SqlDataSource1" runat="server" CacheDuration="600"
     EnableCaching="True"></asp:SqlDataSource>
```

What's cool about caching with the data source controls is that they are smart enough to see if you are making updates to the underlying data. So, when you have set up a `SqlDataSource` control to cache data for the `SelectCommand` for 20 minutes, but then make a change to the data by using the `InsertCommand`, `UpdateCommand`, or `DeleteCommand`, the cache is invalidated automatically. This only works when you execute the insert, update, or delete command against the exact same `SqlDataSource`. If you have one page that displays and caches a list with reviews (like All.aspx for example) and then have another page that is used to insert a new review (like AddEditReview.aspx in the Management folder) this won't work. After you have inserted a new review in the management section of the site, it won't show up in All.aspx until the cache has expired.

Besides the `CacheDuration` and `EnableCaching` properties, the data source controls provide more caching options. *Professional ASP.NET 3.5*, published by Wrox, gives you a detailed look at the advanced caching capabilities found in ASP.NET 3.5.

Code-free caching with the data source controls is useful in many situations. However, the data source controls cannot be used in every situation. What if you want to cache the results of data you get from a completely different source? What if you want to cache the contents of a text or an XML file that you frequently need to access? For those cases, ASP.NET gives you programmatic access to the cache.

Programmatic Caching

With programmatic caching, you can store items in the cache through VB.NET or C# code. Obviously, you can also access them again later. To store items, you use the `Add` or the `Insert` method or you index the `Cache` collection directly. The `Add` method is quite powerful (and complex) and allows you to specify a host of options that determine how long the item is cached, what priority it should have compared to other cached items, and based on what factors the item must be removed from the cache.

The `Insert` method on the other hand is much easier. It has a few short overloads that allow you to specify the cached item and associate it with a specific key. Another overload also allows you to define a dependency, as you'll see how to use in the next exercise.

You remove items from the cache using the `Remove` method that accepts the key of the cached item. You define this key when inserting the item using either `Add` or `Insert`.

To access the items in the cache, you have a few options available. First of all you can directly access the `Cache` collection:

VB.NET

```
myReview = CType(Cache("MyKey"), Review)
```

C#

```
myReview = (Review) Cache["MyKey"];
```

Here, the `Cache` collection is indexed using the key `MyKey`.

Additionally, you can use the `Get` method that expects the key:

VB.NET

```
myReview = CType(Cache.Get("MyKey"), Review)
```

C#

```
myReview = (Review) Cache.Get("MyKey");
```

Because Get is a method, the C# example now also uses parentheses around the cache key, making both examples look even more like each other. Under the hood, they result in the exact same item being returned.

Finally, you can access items in the cache using the Item property that also accepts the key of the cached item.

All three ways to access items in the cache always return a generic object. That means that if you know the type you are getting back from the cache, you should always cast it to the appropriate type before you can use its properties. The previous two examples show you how the item from the cache is cast to a strongly typed Review object first.

To give you an idea of how to use the cache programmatically, the next exercise shows you how to insert the contents of a file in the cache, so you don't need to read in the file every time you need it.

Try It Out Using the Cache API

In Chapter 9 you created the Contact form that uses the contents of a file as the body template for an e-mail. To avoid reading in the file every time an e-mail is sent, it's a good idea to cache the contents the first time you read them. Subsequent calls to the mail sending methods simply use the file body from the cache instead of reading in the file. To avoid the cached copy from getting out of date, you insert the item in the cache with a dependency on the original file. That means that if you change the file ContactForm.txt on disk, it will be removed from the cache automatically, and a fresh copy of it will be read the next time it's needed.

1. Open the user control ContactForm.ascx from the Controls folder.
2. Open the Code Behind of the control and at the top of the file, add the following Imports or using statement:

VB.NET

```
Imports System.Web.Caching
```

C#

```
using System.Web.Caching;
```

3. Locate the btnSend_Click event handler that is fired when the user tries to submit the form and change the code at the top of the handler that reads in the file so it ends up like this:

VB.NET

```
If Page.IsValid Then
 Dim fileName As String = Server.MapPath("~/App_Data/ContactForm.txt")
 Dim mailBody As String = String.Empty
 If Cache("ContactFormMailBody") Is Nothing Then
   mailBody = System.IO.File.ReadAllText(fileName)
   Cache.Insert("ContactFormMailBody", mailBody, New CacheDependency(fileName))
 Else
   mailBody = Cache("ContactFormMailBody").ToString() & vbCrLf & "(File from the cache)"
 End If
 mailBody = mailBody.Replace("##Name##", txtName.Text)
```

C#

```
if (Page.IsValid)
{
  string fileName = Server.MapPath("~/App_Data/ContactForm.txt");
  string mailBody = string.Empty;
  if (Cache["ContactFormMailBody"] == null)
  {
    mailBody = System.IO.File.ReadAllText(fileName);
    Cache.Insert("ContactFormMailBody", mailBody, new CacheDependency(fileName));
  }
  else
  {
    mailBody = Cache["ContactFormMailBody"].ToString() + "\r\n(File from the cache)";
  }
  mailBody = mailBody.Replace("##Name##", txtName.Text);
```

4. Save all your changes and open the page Default.aspx from the root of the site in your browser. From the About menu, choose Contact Us. Fill in the form and click the Send button. After a while you should get an e-mail in the mailbox of the account that is used in the Code Behind of the user control to send the e-mail message to.
5. Choose Contact Us from the About menu again, fill in the form, and click Send once more. After a while you should get another message (see Figure 14-14). However, this time the body of the mail message is tagged with the text (File from the cache) to indicate the file was retrieved from the cache and not from disk.
6. Go back to Visual Studio and make a change to the file ContactForm.txt. You can alter the text, or simply add a space; anything that makes the file "dirty." Save the changes to the file and then fill in the form again. This time around, you get the message without the notice about the cache, demonstrating that the file was read from disk again.

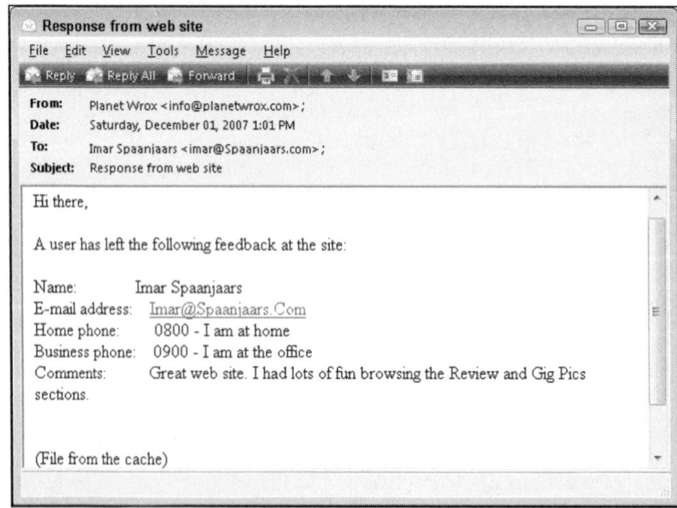

Figure 14-14

How It Works

When you click the Send button to submit the form to the server, the code in btnSend_Click fires. Instead of reading the mail body file from disk directly using ReadAllText as was the case previously, this code checks if the file is in the cache first:

VB.NET

```
Dim fileName As String = Server.MapPath("~/App_Data/ContactForm.txt")
If Cache("ContactFormMailBody") Is Nothing Then
  mailBody = System.IO.File.ReadAllText(fileName)
  Cache.Insert("ContactFormMailBody", mailBody, New CacheDependency(fileName))
Else
  mailBody = Cache("ContactFormMailBody").ToString() & vbCrLf & "(File from the cache)"
End If
```

C#

```
string fileName = Server.MapPath("~/App_Data/ContactForm.txt");
if (Cache["ContactFormMailBody"] == null)
{
  mailBody = System.IO.File.ReadAllText(fileName);
  Cache.Insert("ContactFormMailBody", mailBody, new CacheDependency(fileName));
}
else
{
  mailBody = Cache["ContactFormMailBody"].ToString() + "\r\n(File from the cache)";
}
```

When the item is not in the cache (Cache("ContactFormMailBody") in VB.NET returns Nothing or Cache["ContactFormMailBody"] in C# returns null) the file is read using ReadAllText and assigned to mailBody. The mail body (a string) is then stored in the cache using the Insert method. The first parameter of this method expects the unique cache key to identify the item (ContactFormMailBody in this example). As the second argument, it expects the actual data to be cached. Finally, it receives an instance of a CacheDependency class. One of the constructors of this class expects the physical path to a file that it should watch. In this example, it receives the variable fileName, which contains a path similar to C:\BegASPNET\Site\App_Data\ContactForm.txt. When that file changes, the item is removed from the cache automatically. Next time the contact form is sent, the file is read fresh from disk and stored in the cache for future use.

Practical Data Tips

Here are some practical data tips.

- Whenever you use the numerous style properties of the data-bound controls, consider using the CssClass property instead of setting the individual style properties directly on the style.

- The section about the control's life cycle has an exercise that shows you how to display the various events and the order they occur in. You could extend the example and write code for even more events. Additionally, you could add more controls to the page and handle their events as well to help you establish a solid understanding of those events. Because a good understanding of those events and their order is often critical in writing web applications, the time you put into this little research project is well spent.
- Whenever you are writing pages that access a database or other slow or scarce resources like files or web services, consider if they can benefit from caching. Although it's not that hard to add caching at a later stage, it's best to put it in as early as possible. That way, you know your caching code gets thoroughly tested and your application gains from the performance benefits that caching brings right from the start.

Summary

This chapter covered some of the more advanced topics on presenting data with the data controls that previous chapters deliberately skipped to allow you to focus on the core data access concepts. Now that you have a good understanding of data access in general, SQL, LINQ, the data-bound controls, and the various data controls like the `SqlDataSource` and `LinqDataSource` controls, it's much easier to see how you can modify the looks and behavior of your controls.

The chapter started off with a good look at the numerous style elements that most data-bound controls have. You learned how to configure styles such as `RowStyle` and `AlternatingRowStyle` to create a zebra effect on data-bound controls like the `GridView`. You also saw how you can use styles such as `EditItemStyle`, `HeaderStyle`, and `FooterStyle` to change the different areas in your data controls.

Although styling information is often applied to all rows in a data control at once, there are situations where you need to change the appearance of individual items in the control conditionally. You saw an example that used the `RowDataBound` event to change the background and text color of reviews that are currently unauthorized for publication. You also saw how to enable or disable the delete link for the genres `GridView` to stop users from deleting genres that still have reviews connected to them.

To help you understand the various events that you have at your disposal and the order in which those events fire, you followed the Try It Out exercise "Seeing the Page and Controls Life Cycles at Work" that showed you how to write the name of the event to a `Label`. Although the example is far from complete (there are many more events that you could handle) it shows you the basic concept for determining the order of events. Whenever you are unsure about some events, when they fire, or if they fire at all, you can use the concepts from the exercise to find out the exact events and their order.

The chapter closed with a discussion of the various caching capabilities that ASP.NET supports. You saw an example of output caching that caches the output of an entire page. To enable a dynamic page to be cached (for example, a page that changes the data it displays based on a query string or other variable) you can use `VaryByParam` to instruct the ASP.NET run time to cache a copy of every page with a unique query string.

Besides output caching, you can also cache data at the data source control level. All you need to do is set a few properties and the ASP.NET run time takes care of the rest.

If you need precise control over the cache, you can access it programmatically. The `Cache` object exposes various methods that let you insert, access, and remove data that is stored in the cache. Using a `CacheDependency` class you can create a relation between a resource, like a physical file on disk, and the cached item. When the resource changes, for example, because you add some text to a text file, the item in the cache is invalidated automatically which means the resource should be read from its original location the next time it's needed.

With caching, you have come to the end of this chapter that showed you some advanced topics on handling data in an ASP.NET web application. The following chapter shows you how to protect some of this data — for example, the Management folder — to unauthorized users by implementing ASP.NET security.

Exercises

1. Imagine you have a simple Web Form with a single `Button` on it. If you click the `Button` in the browser, it causes a postback and at the server its `Click` event is triggered. What happens first? The `Page` control's `Load` event or the `Button` control's `Click` event?
2. The `GridView` allows you to alternate colors (and other style information) for the rows it displays. How would you set up the `GridView` so it alternates between rows with a black background and white text and rows with a white background and black text?
3. What's the proper way to avoid an exception that you handled in a data-bound control's event in the Code Behind from being displayed in the page?

Security in Your ASP.NET 3.5 Web Site

Until now you have created pages in your web site that are accessible to all visitors to your site. You don't have a way to block certain resources like ASPX files or even whole folders for specific users. That means, for example, that currently anyone can access your Management folder and start messing with the genres and reviews in the system.

Clearly, this is not something you'd want in a production web site. So, you need to think of a good security strategy to stop unwanted users from accessing specific content. You also need to look at a mechanism that allows users to sign up for a new account and at the same time allows you to designate certain users as managers of your web site and grant them special access rights.

ASP.NET 3.5 ships with all the tools you need to create a solid and safe security mechanism. In this chapter you learn how to make use of these tools in your ASP.NET web site.

In particular, this chapter examines:

- Important terminology you'll encounter when dealing with security
- The ASP.NET application services that enable security
- How you can let users sign up for an account for your site using built-in server controls
- How users can independently reset their passwords or request new ones
- How you can manage the users and roles in your database at development time
- How you can present different content to different users based on their access rights in the system

Before you start looking at how security is implemented in the ASP.NET Framework, you need to understand a few important terms that you'll come across in every discussion on security.

Introducing Security

Although security can be quite a complex subject, it often revolves around three important questions:

- Who are you?
- How can you prove that?
- What are you allowed to do in the system?

Identity: Who Are You?

An identity is what makes you, *you*. The answer to what an identity is depends on the context it is used in. As a citizen of a country, your identity revolves around your person, your official name and birth date, and maybe even a social security number. However, for a web site like `p2p.wrox.com`, Wrox's community web site, your identity may be as little as your name and e-mail address.

No matter what you include in an identity, it is a way to refer to you. But how does anyone else know you? And how can they be sure it's really you when you log on to a web site for example? This is where authentication enters the game.

Authentication: How Can You Prove Who You Are?

Authentication is about providing evidence about who you are. When you need to register for a library card, you may need to show your passport to prove that the name you registered the card under really belongs to you. With a web site like `p2p.wrox.com` you need to provide an e-mail address and a password. Together these two pieces form the evidence that prove your identity. There are many other mechanisms used for authentication, including high-tech fingerprint or iris scans, smart cards and tokens (where the evidence is stored on something tangible), and so on. However, in light of the discussion on security of ASP.NET web sites, this chapter sticks to an e-mail address and password for authentication.

Authorization: What Are You Allowed to Do?

Depending on who you are, a system grants you more or fewer privileges to access certain areas. Think about the highly secured headquarters of a national security agency in an action movie, for example. Even if the main character is allowed to enter the building, he is often not allowed to enter specific areas because he lacks the proper authorization (the fact they eventually gain access in those movies using a 2-minute hack in the system is beside the point here).

To determine what a user is allowed to do, a system needs to know two things: the *permissions* for the current user and the *authorization rules* for the resource a user is trying to access.

The permissions for the user are based on its user name (the identity it represents) and the *roles* (or security groups) the user is optionally assigned to. Similarly, resources can be opened up or blocked for specific users or roles. When there is a match between the current user and the access rules for the resource a user is trying to access, the user is granted access. If the user is blocked specifically, then access is denied. So, for example, imagine a file that is only accessible to the user Tom and the group Developers. The user Tom can access that file, regardless of whether he is in the Developers role or not. At the same time, the user Jacqueline *has* to be in the Developers role in order to access the file.

You see how to work with these concepts in the remainder of this chapter.

The implementation of these security concepts in ASP.NET is done with the so-called *application services* that are discussed next.

An Introduction to the ASP.NET Application Services

Early versions of ASP.NET had some sort of support for security. However, they lacked the high-level controls and concepts that ship with ASP.NET 3.5. In ASP.NET 1.*x* applications you needed to write a lot of code to implement a solid security strategy. The downside of writing this code is that it was often pretty much the same in all your web sites. You were more or less forced to reinvent the wheel every time you wanted to go out for a drive.

These problems were solved with the advent of ASP.NET 2.0 that shipped with the application services, a software layer that sits between your web application and a data store and that enables you to use these services with little to no code.

ASP.NET ships with a number of services, of which the most important ones are:

- **Membership:** Enables you to manage and work with user accounts in your system.
- **Roles:** Enables you to manage the roles that your users can be assigned to.
- **Profiles:** Allows you to store user-specific data in a back-end database.

Figure 15-1 gives an overview of these services and shows how they are related to your application and the underlying data stores that the services may use.

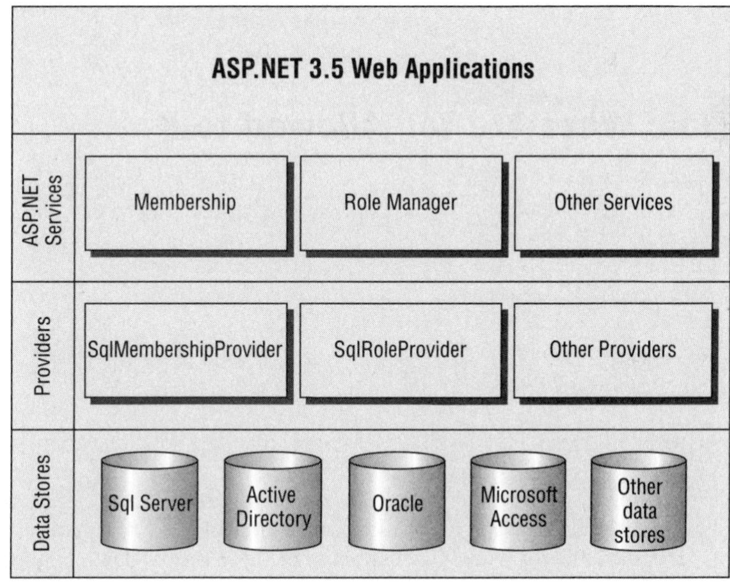

Figure 15-1

At the top of the diagram you see the ASP.NET 3.5 applications that represent the web applications that you build. These applications can contain controls like the login controls (discussed next) that in turn can talk to the ASP.NET application services like membership and profiles. To create a flexible solution, these services don't talk to an underlying data source directly, but instead talk to a configured *provider*. A provider is an interchangeable piece of software that is designed for a specific task. For example, in the case of the membership services, the membership provider is designed to work with users in the underlying data store. You can configure different providers for the same application service depending on your needs. For example, ASP.NET ships with a SQL Server provider that allows your Membership services to talk to a SQL Server database. This is an ideal provider for Internet-connected web sites like `PlanetWrox.com`. It also ships with an Active Directory provider that lets you create and manage users in Active Directory on Windows instead. This provider is best suited in closed networks, like an intranet.

Each provider needs a data store, represented by the bottom part of the diagram in Figure 15-1. Each provider is written to work with a specific data store. For example, the `SqlMembershipProvider` and the `SqlRoleProvider` are designed to work with a Microsoft SQL Server database.

In the remainder of this chapter, you see how to use the SQL Server membership provider and the SQL Server role provider. In the next chapter you'll work with the SQL Server profile provider. All three providers can be configured to use a single SQL Server database making it easy to centralize all your user data.

Ideally, you don't deal with these providers directly. Under normal circumstances, the different providers are configured for your web application at a central location. You then use these providers by talking to the application services. Although you could access these services directly from code, you usually use the ASP.NET built-in login controls to do the hard work for you. These controls are discussed next.

Introducing the Login Controls

The login controls that ship with ASP.NET 3.5 take away much of the complexity usually associated with writing a security layer in a web application. The available login controls effectively encapsulate all the code and logic you need to validate and manage users. These controls work by communicating with the configured provider through the application services, instead of talking to a database directly. To see how this works, the following exercise shows you how to create a simple Login and Sign Up page that allows a new user to create an account and then log in. The section that follows then looks at the seven login controls.

Try It Out — Creating Login and Sign Up Pages

In this exercise you finish the Login page that you created in Chapter 6. You also create a new page that allows a user to sign up for an account on the Planet Wrox web site.

1. Open up the page Login.aspx that you created in Chapter 6 from the root of the site and switch it to Design View.
2. Drag a `LoginStatus` control from the Login category of the Toolbox and drop it in the page.
3. Next, drag a `Login` control and drop it on the `LoginStatus`, so it ends up right above it. Both controls are visible in Figure 15-2 (the `LoginStatus` appears as a small Login link below the `Login` control).

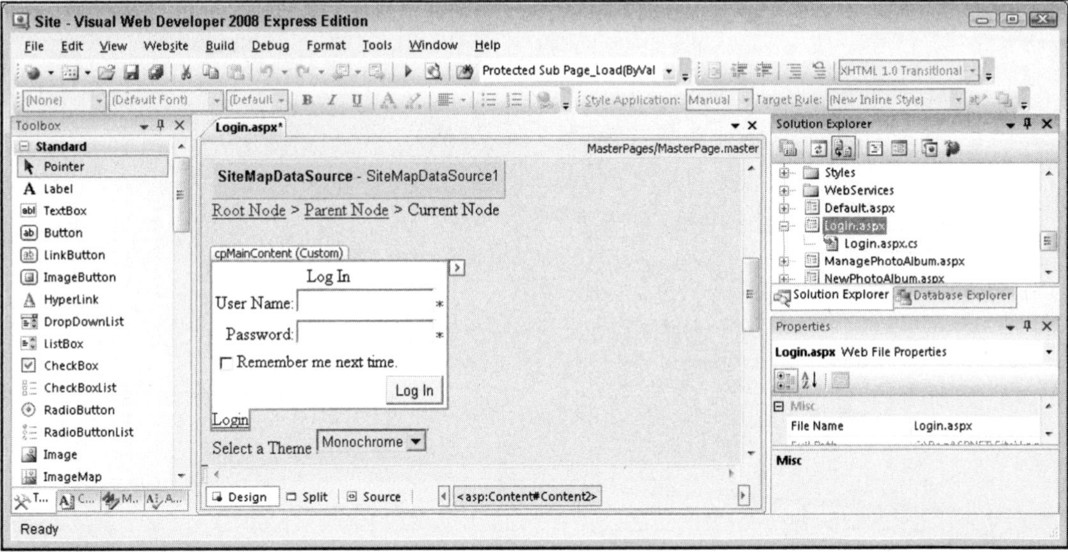

Figure 15-2

4. Open the Properties Grid for the `Login` control and set the two properties shown in the following table.

Property	Value
`CreateUserText`	Sign Up for a New Account at Planet Wrox Now!
`CreateUserUrl`	SignUp.aspx

5. In the root of the web site create a new page called SignUp.aspx based on your custom template and give it a `Title` of Sign Up for a New Account at Planet Wrox.

6. Switch the page to Design View and drag a `CreateUserWizard` from the Toolbox into the main content area for the page. Save and close the page.

7. Open the web.config file from the root of the site and locate the `<authentication>` element. Change the `mode` attribute from `Windows` to `Forms`:

```
<authentication mode="Forms"/>
```

8. Go back to Login.aspx and press Ctrl+F5 to open that page in your browser. You are greeted with a login box shown in Figure 15-3.

   Note that the Login status below the `Login` control is currently set to Login to indicate you are not logged in yet. If the text says Logout instead, verify that you set authentication to `Forms` in the web.config file.

9. Try to log in by entering a random user name and password. Obviously, this fails because you haven't created an account yet.

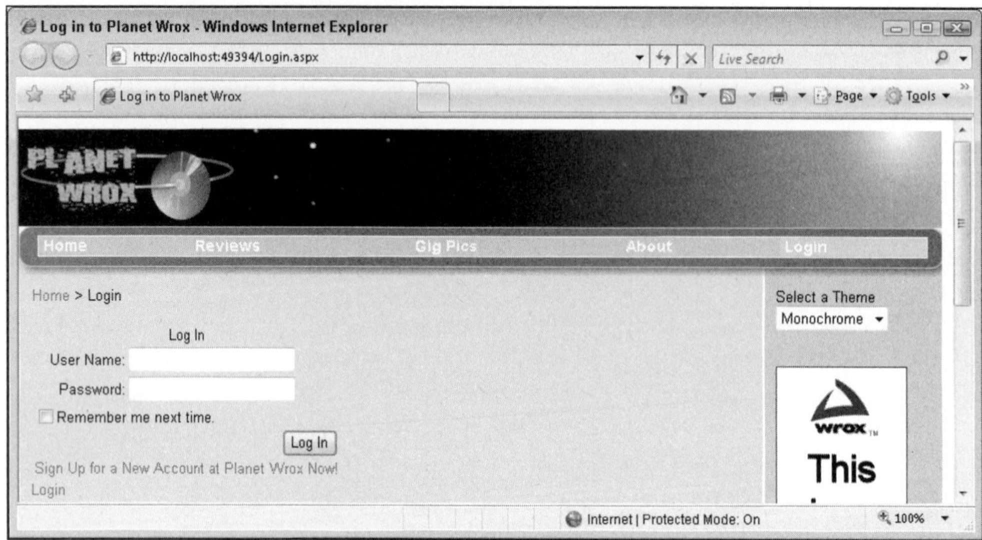

Figure 15-3

10. Follow the Sign Up link below the `Login` control to go to SignUp.aspx and then create an account by entering your personal details (see Figure 15-4). By default, the password needs to have a minimum length of seven characters and must contain at least one non-alphanumeric character. Please note that numbers are not considered non-alphanumeric characters so you need to make sure your password contains at least a character like # or $ or *. So for example, `Password` is not a valid password, while `Pass##Word` will be accepted. Note that the password is *case sensitive*. Write down the user name and password you just entered, as you'll need this account information again later.

    For the security question and answer, you can make up your own question with an answer. You need to supply the answer to the security question in case you lose your password.

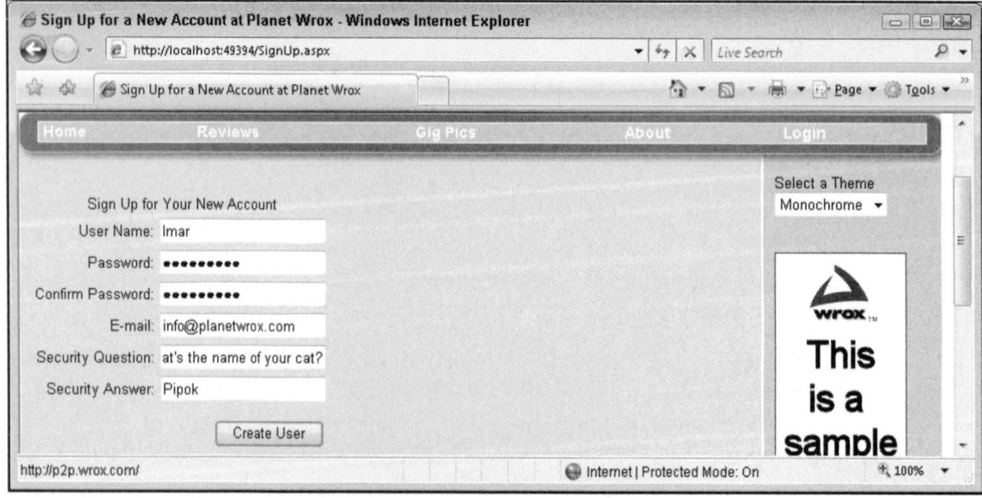

Figure 15-4

11. Click the Create User button to have the account created for you. When the page reloads, you get a confirmation that the account was created for you. Ignore the Continue button for now (you haven't written any behavior for it yet), but click the Login item from the main `Menu` or `TreeView` (depending on the theme you currently have selected) in the web site instead. You are taken to Login.aspx again where the `LoginStatus` control now indicates that you are logged in. When you create a new account, using the `CreateUserWizard`, you're logged in automatically, although you can change that behavior by setting the `LoginCreatedUser` property of the control to `False`. In Figure 15-5 you see the Logout link right below the `Login` control.

12. Click the Logout link and you'll be logged out, causing the `LoginStatus` to display the text Login again. In the `Login` control, enter the user name and password you entered in step 10 and click the Log In button. You're logged in and redirected to the home page. On the menu click Login to return to the Login page again. Note that the `LoginStatus` has changed and now shows Logout again, illustrating the fact that you successfully logged in.

    At this stage, being logged in doesn't add much value; all you see is the `LoginStatus` change from Login to Logout. However, later in this chapter you see how to offer different content to logged-in users.

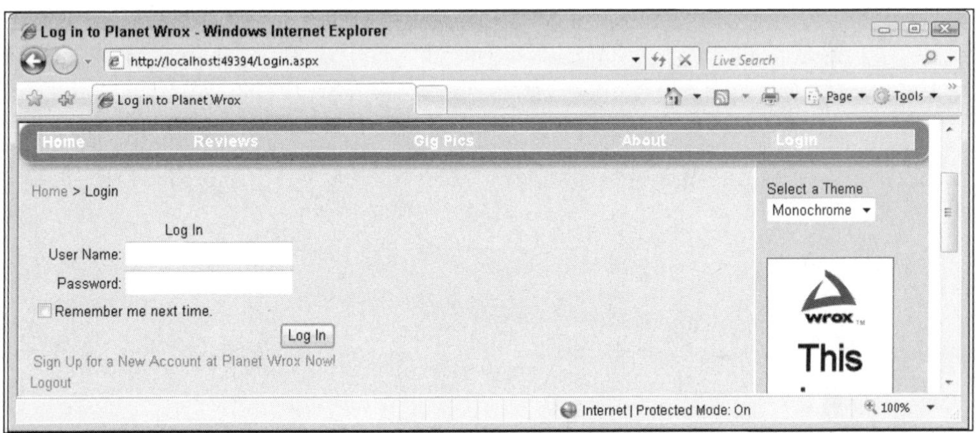

Figure 15-5

How It Works

Besides adding and configuring a few ASP.NET Server Controls, you didn't do any coding in this exercise. Still, you were able to implement a fully functional login procedure that allows a user to sign up for an account and then log in to the site. During sign up you supplied a user name and a password that you later use to log in to the Planet Wrox web site. So how does all this work? As you learned earlier, the ASP.NET controls talk to the configured application services providers; a software layer that sits between the login controls and the SQL Server database that keeps track of the users.

The very first time you try to log in (or use other login controls that require database access), the provider checks if your application is using a database with the necessary database objects like tables. By default, it checks the database by looking at a connection string called `LocalSqlServer`. You won't find this connection string in your web.config file though as it is defined in a file called machine.config located in the .NET Framework folder. You learn more about this file later. The connection string in that file looks like this:

```
<connectionStrings>
  <add name="LocalSqlServer" connectionString="data source=.\SQLEXPRESS;
```

```
            Integrated Security=SSPI;AttachDBFilename=|DataDirectory|aspnetdb.mdf;
            User Instance=true"
        providerName="System.Data.SqlClient" />
  </connectionStrings>
```

This is a connection string that targets SQL Server 2005 Express Edition, the free and lightweight version of Microsoft SQL Server. In Chapter 18 and Appendix B you'll see more examples of a connection string that targets the full versions of SQL Server.

You'll recall from Chapter 12 that a connection string that uses `|DataDirectory|` points to a database located in the App_Data folder of your web site. The providers take care of the database they need to operate correctly. If the aspnetdb.mdf database doesn't exist at the specified location the first time you use one of the login controls or the other application services, it is created for you automatically. To find out what the database looks like, go back to Visual Web Developer, click the App_Data folder, and then click the Refresh button on the toolbar to refresh the Solution Explorer's contents. You should see the new database as shown in Figure 15-6.

Double-click the new database in the Solution Explorer to open it in the Database Explorer window. Expand items like Tables and Views to get a list of database objects that have been added for you, visible in Figure 15-7 that shows some of the tables used for the application services.

After this database has been created successfully, the login controls can use it. For example, when you create a new account using the `CreateUserWizard` control, records are inserted in the `aspnet_Membership` and `aspnet_Users` tables. Similarly, when you try to log in, your user name and passwords are checked against these tables.

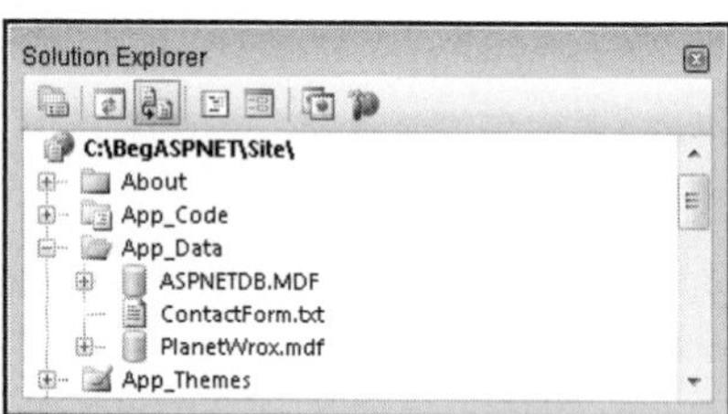

Figure 15-6

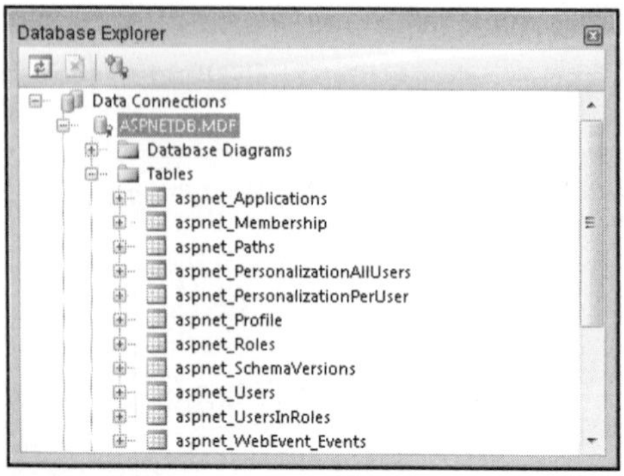

Figure 15-7

To force the ASP.NET run time to use forms-based authentication (for example, using controls like the `Login` control on a page and handing out cookies) you need to set the `mode` attribute of the authentication element to `Forms` in the web.config file:

```
<authentication mode="Forms" />
```

Other options for the `mode` attribute include `Windows` (where security is handled by Windows itself), `Passport` (using Microsoft's Passport services), and `None` which disables security altogether. In the remainder of this book, you'll use the `Forms` option exclusively.

The Remember Me Next Time option of the `Login` control is more forgetful than you may think. When you check this option you are logged in automatically the next time you visit the site. The first time you log in, the server sets a cookie that is saved for future sessions. However, this cookie expires after 30 minutes, which means a user returning to the site after that period needs to re-authenticate. To extend the period that users remain logged in you need to set the `timeout` attribute of the `<forms>` element that itself is a direct child of the `<authentication>` element in web.config. The `timeout` takes an integer value representing the timeout period in minutes. The following code sets the time-out to 24 hours (1440 minutes):

```
<authentication mode="Forms">
  <forms timeout="1440" />
</authentication>
```

Lower `timeout` values are generally considered safer as they don't provide unlimited or long-lasting access.

The database that ASP.NET creates for you in the App_Data folder makes it very easy to work with the various application services in a development scenario. However, when you need to roll out your application to a production server in your own network or with your Internet service provider (ISP) you may need more control over the database and the way it is accessed. Chapter 18, which deals with deployment, and Appendix B, which deals with SQL Server configuration, show this in more detail.

Now that you have seen how the login controls work in conjunction with the auto-generated SQL Server Express database, it's time to look at the controls in the Login category of the Toolbox in more detail.

The Login Controls

ASP.NET 3.5 ships with seven login controls, each serving a distinct purpose. Figure 15-8 shows the Toolbox with the login controls.

In the sections that follow, each of these controls is explained in more detail.

Figure 15-8

Login

As you saw in the previous exercise, the `Login` control allows a user to log in to the site. Under the hood it talks to the configured membership provider through the application services to see if the user name and password represent a valid user in the system. If the user is validated, a cookie is issued that is sent to the user's browser. On subsequent requests the browser resubmits the cookie to the server so the system knows it's still dealing with a valid user. The different settings for the membership provider (whether it uses cookies as described above, the default expiration policy for the cookie, and a few other settings) are all configured in the `<authentication>` element of the web.config file.

To create a fully functional login page, you only need the following control declaration:

```
<asp:Login ID="Login1" runat="server" />
```

However, in most situations you want to enhance the appearance and behavior of the control by setting one or more of the properties shown in the following table.

Property	Description
`DestinationPageUrl`	This property defines the URL the user is sent to after a successful login attempt.
`CreateUserText`	This property controls the text that is displayed to invite users to sign up for a new account.
`CreateUserUrl`	This property controls the URL where users are taken to sign up for a new account.
`DisplayRememberMe`	This property specifies whether the control displays the Remember Me option. When set to `False` or when the checkbox is not set when logging in, users need to reauthenticate every time they close and reopen the browser.
`RememberMeSet`	This property specifies whether the Remember Me option is initially checked.
`PasswordRecoveryText`	This property controls the text that is displayed to tell users they can reset or recover their password.
`PasswordRecoveryUrl`	This property specifies the URL where users are taken to get their (new) password.
`VisibleWhenLoggedIn`	This property controls whether the control is visible when the current user is logged in. True by default.

In addition to these properties, the control has a range of `Text` properties, such as `LoginButtonText`, `RememberMeText`, `TitleText`, and `UserNameLabelText` that are used to control the text that appears in the control and on its various child controls like the `Button` and `Label` controls that make up the user interface.

Just as with the data-bound controls, the login controls have numerous style properties that allow you to tweak their appearance. You're encouraged to check out the Styles category of the Properties Grid for the controls to see how you can set the various styling options. Remember, just as with the data-bound controls, you can move much of the styling information to skin and CSS files.

The `Login` control also exposes a few events that you typically don't need to handle, but that can come in handy from time to time. For example, the `LoggedIn` event fires right after the user has logged in and is a good place to send the user to another page dynamically if the `DestinationPageUrl` is not flexible enough.

LoginView

The `LoginView` is a handy control that lets you display different data to different users. It allows you to differentiate between anonymous and logged-in users, and you can even differentiate between users in different roles. The `LoginView` is template driven and as such lets you define different templates that are shown to different users. The following table describes the two main templates and the special `RoleGroups` element.

Template	Description
`AnonymousTemplate`	The content in this template is shown to unauthenticated users only.
`LoggedInTemplate`	The content in this template is shown to logged-in users only. This template is mutually exclusive with the AnonymousTemplate. Only one of the two is visible at any time.
`RoleGroups`	This template can contain one or more `RoleGroups` elements that in turn contain a `ContentTemplate` element that defines the content for the specified role. The role or roles that are allowed to see the content are defined in the `Roles` attribute that takes a comma-separated list of roles. The `RoleGroups` element is mutually exclusive with the `LoggedInTemplate`. That means that if a user is a member of one of the roles for the `RoleGroup`, the content in the `LoggedInTemplate` is not visible. Additionally, only content for the first `RoleGroup` that matches the user's roles is shown.

The `LoginView` control itself doesn't output any markup other than the content you define in the various child elements of the control, which means you can easily embed it between a pair of HTML tags like `<h1>`and `<li>`.

The following code snippet shows a `LoginView` control that defines content for three different users: anonymous visitors to the site, logged-in users, and users that have logged in *and* are members of the Managers role:

```
<asp:LoginView ID="LoginView1" runat="server">
  <AnonymousTemplate>
    Hi there visitor. Would you be interested in signing up for an account?
  </AnonymousTemplate>
  <LoggedInTemplate>
```

```
    Hi there visitor and welcome back to PlanetWrox.com.
  </LoggedInTemplate>
  <RoleGroups>
    <asp:RoleGroup Roles="Managers">
      <ContentTemplate>
        Hi there manager. You can proceed to the Management section.
      </ContentTemplate>
    </asp:RoleGroup>
  </RoleGroups>
</asp:LoginView>
```

You see more about creating and configuring roles later in this chapter.

LoginStatus

As demonstrated in the previous Try It Out exercise, the `LoginStatus` control provides information about the current status of the user. It provides a Login link when the user is not authenticated and a Logout link when the user is already logged in. You control the actual text being displayed by setting the `LoginText` and `LogoutText` properties. Alternatively, you can set the `LoginImageUrl` and `LogoutImageUrl` properties to display an image instead of text. Finally, you can set the `LogoutAction` property to determine whether the current page refreshes if the user logs out, or whether the user is taken to another page after logging out. You determine this destination page by setting the `LogoutPageUrl`.

Besides these properties, the control is capable of raising two events: `LoggingOut` and `LoggedOut` that fire right before and after the user is logged out.

LoginName

`LoginName` is an extremely simple control. All it does is display the name of the logged-in user. To embed the user's name in some text, such as `You are logged in as Imar` you can use the `FormatString` property. If you include `{0}` in this format string, it will be replaced with the user's name.

You see how this works in the next exercise that has you modify the Login and master pages for the site so they display relevant information about the user.

Try It Out Working with the Login Controls

In this exercise you hide the `Login` control on the Login.aspx page when the user is already logged in and display a message instead. Additionally, you add a text to the footer of the page that displays the name of the user together with an option to log out again.

1. Open Login.aspx and switch it to Design View. From the Toolbox, drag a new `LoginView` on top of the `Login` control so it's placed right above it in the page.
2. Open the Smart Tasks panel of the `LoginView` control and make sure that `AnonymousTemplate` is selected in the Templates drop-down list, visible in Figure 15-9.

   Any content you put in the control will be placed in the `AnonymousTemplate` area, as that is now the active template for the control in Design View.
3. Click the `Login` control once and then press Ctrl+X to cut it to the clipboard. Click inside the small white rectangle that represents the `LoginView` to position your cursor in the control and then press Ctrl+V to paste your `Login` control into your `LoginView`.

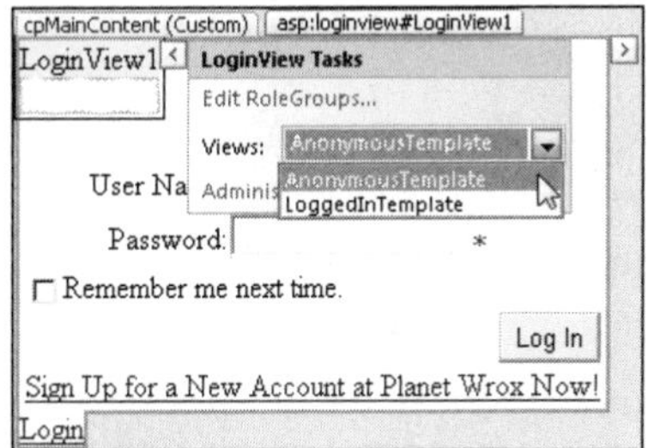

Figure 15-9

4. Open the Smart Tasks panel of the `LoginView` again and switch to the `LoggedInTemplate`. Click inside the small white rectangle of the control again and type the text `You are already logged in`.

5. Switch to Markup View and look at the code. The `Login` control should be placed inside the `AnonymousTemplate`, while the text you typed should be displayed within the `LoggedInTemplate` tags:

```
<asp:LoginView ID="LoginView1" runat="server">
  <LoggedInTemplate>
    You are already logged in
  </LoggedInTemplate>
  <AnonymousTemplate>
    <asp:Login ID="Login1" runat="server" CreateUserUrl="SignUp.aspx"
             CreateUserText="Sign Up for a New Account at Planet Wrox Now!">
    </asp:Login>
  </AnonymousTemplate>
</asp:LoginView>
```

6. Save and close the page, as you're done with it for now.

7. Open the main master page MasterPage.master in Markup View and locate the `Footer <div>` element at the bottom of the page. Remove the text `Footer Goes Here` and replace it with a new `LoginName` control by dragging it from the Toolbox into the `<div>` element. Set its `FormatString` property to `Logged in as {0}`.

8. From the Toolbox, drag a new `LoginView` control and drop it below the `LoginName` control, but still in the `Footer <div>`. Switch to Design View and on the Smart Tasks panel of the `LoginView` choose LoggedInTemplate from the Views drop-down list, and then in the white rectangle for the active `LoggedInTemplate`, drag and drop a new `LoginStatus` control.

9. Switch to Markup View again and wrap the code for the `LoginStatus` in a pair of parentheses. You should end up with the following code:

```
<div id="Footer">
  <asp:LoginName ID="LoginName1" runat="server" FormatString="Logged in as {0}"  />
  <asp:LoginView ID="LoginView1" runat="server">
    <LoggedInTemplate>
      (<asp:LoginStatus ID="LoginStatus1" runat="server" />)
    </LoggedInTemplate>
  </asp:LoginView>
  ...
</div>
```

10. Save all your changes and then request Login.aspx in your browser. Log in with the account and password you created in a previous exercise (you may need to log out first by clicking the Logout link). If you don't recall the user name and password, simply click the Sign Up link to create a new account first. Note that as soon as you are logged in, the footer displays the text visible in Figure 15-10.

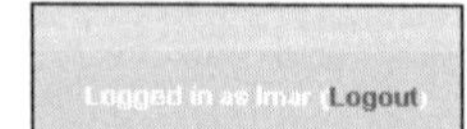

Figure 15-10

11. Click the Login item in the `Menu` or `TreeView` to go to the Login page. Instead of the `Login` control you should now see a message indicating you are already logged in.
12. Click the Logout link in the footer at the bottom of the page. The page refreshes and displays the `Login` control again. Additionally, the text from the footer has now disappeared.

How It Works

You started out by adding a `LoginView` to the Login page to wrap the `Login` control and a text message. If you only wanted to hide the `Login` control when the user is already logged in, you could simply set `VisibleWhenLoggedIn` to `False`:

```
<asp:Login ID="Login1" runat="server" VisibleWhenLoggedIn="false" />
```

However, in order to display a message when you are logged in and hide the `Login` control at the same time, you're much better off using the `LoginView`. Simply place the relevant content in the available templates and the control takes care of the rest.

The code in the footer of the master page contains a `LoginName` control that displays the name of the user that is logged in. It doesn't display anything for anonymous users. To control the text being displayed, you use the `FormatString` property:

```
<asp:LoginName ID="LoginName1" runat="server" FormatString="Logged in as {0}"  />
```

At run time, the `{0}` is replaced with the user's name.

By default the `LoginStatus` you added displays a link to allow users to log in and log out. Since the `Menu` or the `TreeView` already contains a link to the Login page, the footer uses a `LoginView` again to only display the Logout text when the user is currently logged in. If you want to add a Login link as well, you can extend the `LoginView` with an anonymous template and an additional `LoginStatus` or remove the entire `LoginView` so the `LoginStatus` is visible to all users.

Besides the controls you have seen that allow a user to log in and that use the current user's log-in status to show or hide relevant content, the Login category of the Toolbox contains three more controls that allow users to sign up for a new account on the site and to change an existing password or recover a lost password. These controls are discussed next.

CreateUserWizard

You briefly saw the CreateUserWizard at work in an earlier exercise. But the control has a lot more to offer than the standard behavior you saw in that exercise.

To start with, the control has a long list of Text properties, like CancelButtonText, CompleteSuccessText, UserNameLabelText, and CreateUserButtonText that affect the text used in the control. All properties have good (English) defaults, but you can change them if they don't suit your needs.

The control has a bunch of properties that end in ImageUrl like CreateUserButtonImageUrl. These properties allow you to define images for various user actions instead of the default buttons that the control generates. If you set any of these properties to a valid ImageUrl, you also need to set the corresponding ButtonType. For example, to change the Create User button to an image, you need to set the CreateUserButtonImageUrl to a valid image and set CreateUserButtonType to Image.

The default value for the ButtonType is Button, which renders as the standard, grey buttons by default. You can also set these properties to Link to have them rendered as standard LinkButton controls.

Additionally, the control exposes a number of useful properties that you may set to change its behavior and appearance, shown in the following table.

Property	Description
ContinueDestinationPageUrl	This property defines the page where users are taken when they click Continue.
DisableCreatedUser	Whether or not the user is marked as disabled when the account is created. When set to True, users cannot log in to the site until their account has been enabled. You see how to manually activate and deactivate user accounts later.
LoginCreatedUser	Whether or not the user is logged in automatically after the account has been created.
RequireEmail	Determines whether or not the control asks the user for an e-mail address.
MailDefinition	This property contains a number of subproperties that allow you to define the (optional) e-mail that gets sent to users after they sign up.

You may notice that the control doesn't have any properties to hide the security question and answer, or to change the strong password policy that requires users to type a password of at least seven characters, containing at least one non-alphanumerical character like # or *. Instead of changing these settings on the control, you need to configure them on the underlying provider. In the section "Configuring Your Web Application" later in this chapter you see how this works.

In the following exercise you see how to configure the MailDefinition element so the CreateUserWizard sends an e-mail message to the new user to confirm his account and send his user name and password for future reference.

Try It Out Sending Confirmation E-Mail with CreateUserWizard

For this exercise to work, you need to have configured the `<system.net>` element of the web.config file with a valid mail server name (as discussed in Chapter 9).

1. Add a new Text File to the App_Data folder and call it SignUpConfirmation.txt.
2. Add the following text to the file and then save and close it:

```
Hi <% UserName %>,

Thank you for signing up for a new account at www.PlanetWrox.Com.

To log in to the site, use the following details:

User name:        <% UserName %>
Your password:    <% Password %>

We look forward to your contributions.

The Planet Wrox Team
```

   Take care when typing the `UserName` and `Password` placeholders. They are wrapped in a pair of server-side tags (`<%` and `%>`), which are used to give special meaning to these placeholders.

3. Open SignUp.aspx and make sure it's in Design View. Then, on the Properties Grid of the `CreateUserWizard` control, locate the `MailDefinition` property and expand it. Click the `BodyFileName` property, click the ellipsis to browse for a file, and then select `SignUpConfirmation.txt`, which you created in the App_Data folder.
4. Set the `Subject` property to `Your New Account at PlanetWrox.com`. When you're done, the Properties Grid should look like Figure 15-11.
5. Save the changes and request SignUp.aspx in your browser. Enter the required details for a new account and click Create User to sign up for an account. If you get an error about specifying a `from` attribute on the `<smtp>` element, refer to Chapter 9. Make sure you enter a valid e-mail address or the mail server may still reject it.

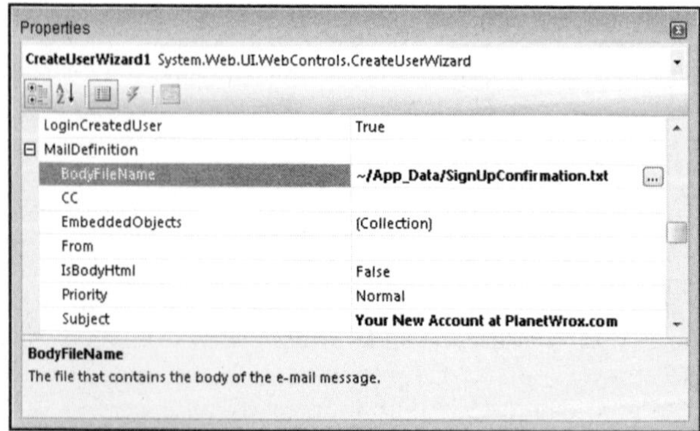

Figure 15-11

If your mail server requires you to use SSL, you have a problem. There is no way to set the `EnableSsl` property directly, as shown in Chapter 9. Instead, you should write your own code in the `SendingMail` event of the control to send your message using the same code to send e-mail as in the ContactForm.ascx control. You can access `e.Message` of the `SendingMail` event to get access to the message that needs to be sent.

6. After a while you should receive an e-mail that contains the welcome text you typed in step 2 (see Figure 15-12).

   Figure 15-12 shows the message with the user name and password placeholders replaced with the details that were entered in step 5.

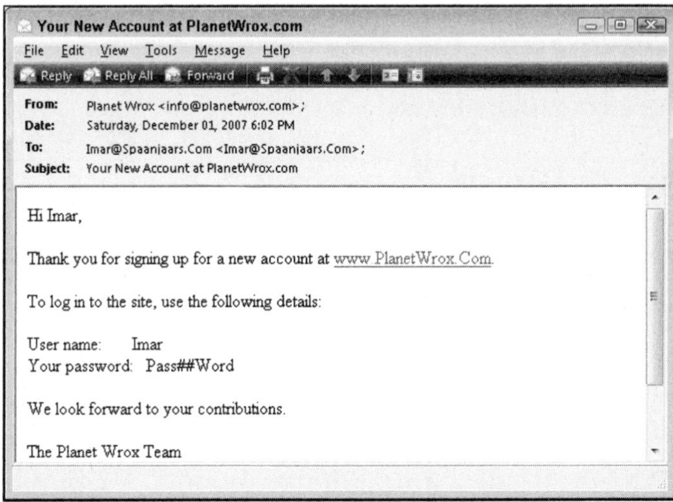

Figure 15-12

How It Works

The `CreateUserWizard` comes with built-in functionality to send a confirmation message to the user. It doesn't send the message until you specify the `<MailDefinition>` element. You use the `BodyFileName` property to point to a text file or an HTML file that is used as the e-mail's body.

Within this body you can use the special placeholders `<% UserName %>` and `<% Password %>`, which will be replaced automatically with the actual user name and password that the user entered in the signup form.

The `PasswordRecovery` control, discussed next, has similar functionality.

PasswordRecovery

The `PasswordRecovery` control allows users to retrieve their existing password (when the system supports it) or get a brand new auto-generated password. In both cases, the password is sent to the e-mail address that the user entered when signing up for an account.

Most of the properties of the `PasswordRecovery` should be familiar by now. It has a number of `Text` properties like `GeneralFailureText` (shown when the password could not be recovered) and

SuccessText that allow you to set the text that is displayed by the control. It also has properties that end with ButtonType, ButtonText, and ButtonImageUrl that allow you to change the look and behavior of the various action buttons of the control. You set the SuccessPageUrl to a page in your site if you want to send the user to another page when password recovery succeeds.

As with the CreateUserWizard, the PasswordRecovery also has a MailDefinition element that allows you to point to a file that you want to send as the mail body. You can use the same placeholders for the user name and password to customize the message. If you leave out the MailDefinition, the control uses a default mail body, as you'll see in the next exercise.

ChangePassword

The ChangePassword control allows existing and logged-in users to change their passwords. It has a host of properties that allow you to change things like text, error messages, and buttons, similar to the CreateUserWizard and PasswordRecovery controls. It also has a MailDefinition element that allows you to send a confirmation of the new password to the user's e-mail address.

Try It Out Implementing the Password Functionality

In this exercise you add PasswordRecovery and ChangePassword controls to the web site to allow users to change and recover their passwords. Since changing a password only makes sense for logged-in users, you add the ChangePassword control to its own page. In a later exercise in this chapter you protect this page so only authenticated users can access it.

1. Open up Login.aspx in Markup View and locate the closing </asp:Login> tag inside the <AnonymousTemplate>. Right after it, type two <br /> elements to create some room below the Login control:

```
<asp:Login ID="Login1" runat="server"  ... >
</asp:Login>
<br /><br />
```

2. Drag a PasswordRecovery control from the Toolbox into the code editor, right after the two <br /> elements you added in step 1.
3. Between the opening and closing tags of the PasswordRecovery control add a <MailDefinition> element and then set the Subject of the e-mail to Your New Password for PlanetWrox.Com. Your code should now look like this:

```
</asp:Login>
<br /> <br />
<asp:PasswordRecovery ID="PasswordRecovery1" runat="server">
  <MailDefinition subject="Your New Password for PlanetWrox.Com"></MailDefinition>
</asp:PasswordRecovery>
```

4. Save your changes and then close the file.
5. In the root of your site create a new Web Form based on your custom template and call it MyProfile.aspx. Set the Title of the page to My Profile.
6. Switch to Markup View and in the cpMainContent content placeholder create an <h1> element with its inner text set to My Profile. Right below the heading type some text which explains

that the My Profile page is used for things like changing passwords. Wrap the text in a pair of <p> tags to denote a paragraph.

7. Drag a `ChangePassword` control from the Toolbox and drop it after the closing </p> tag. You should end up with something like this:

```
<asp:Content ID="Content2" ContentPlaceHolderID="cpMainContent" Runat="Server">
  <h1>My Profile</h1>
  <p>The My Profile page allows you to make changes to your personal profile.
      For now, all you can do is change your password below.</p>
  <asp:ChangePassword ID="ChangePassword1" runat="server"></asp:ChangePassword>
```

8. Open Web.sitemap and add a new element under the About section. Let the `url` point to ~/MyProfile.aspx and set the `title` and `description` to `My Profile`. You should end up with this XML:

```
<siteMapNode url="~/About/Default.aspx" title="About" description="About this site">
  <siteMapNode url="~/About/Contact.aspx" title="Contact Us" description="Contact Us" />
  <siteMapNode url="~/About/AboutUs.aspx" title="About Us" description="About Us" />
  <siteMapNode url="~/MyProfile.aspx" title="My Profile" description="My Profile" />
</siteMapNode>
```

9. Save all changes and close all open files. Right-click Login.aspx in the Solution Explorer and choose View in Browser. Below the `Login` control you should now see the `PasswordRecovery` control, visible in Figure 15-13.

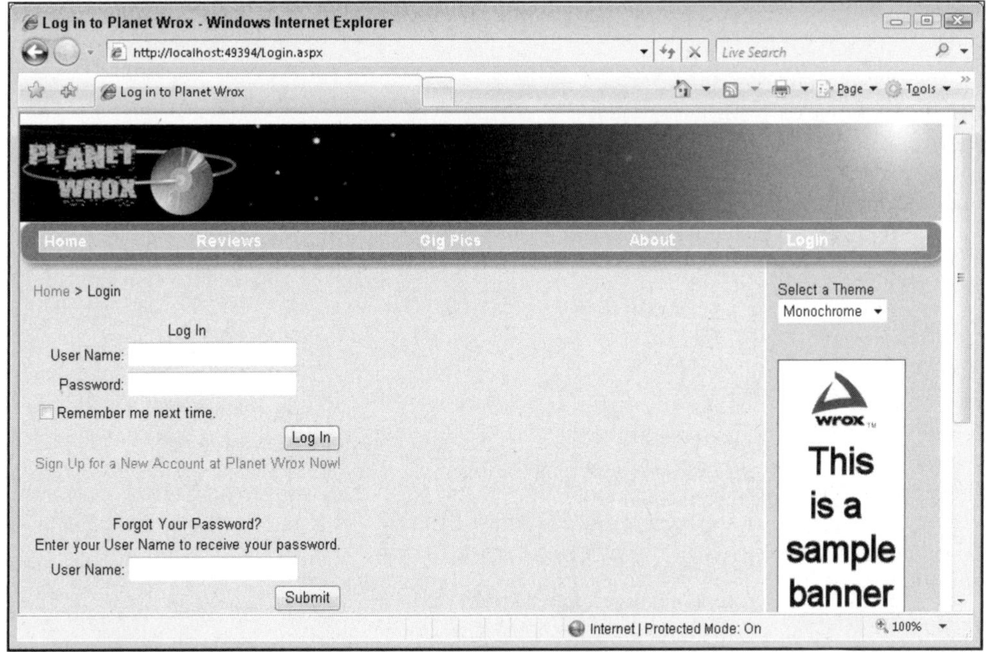

Figure 15-13

If you were already logged in, you need to click the Logout link first.

10. Enter your user name and click the Submit button. You're asked to enter the answer to the security question that you provided when you signed up for the account. Enter the answer and click Submit once more. After a while you should receive an e-mail message with your new, auto-generated password.

11. Use this new password to log in to the site. When you're in, choose the My Profile item from the `Menu` or the `TreeView`. The `ChangePassword` control visible in Figure 15-14 appears.

12. Enter the auto-generated password that was sent to you by e-mail, type a new password that is easier to remember, and then retype the same password. Finally, click Change Password. From now on, you can log in to the site using your new password.

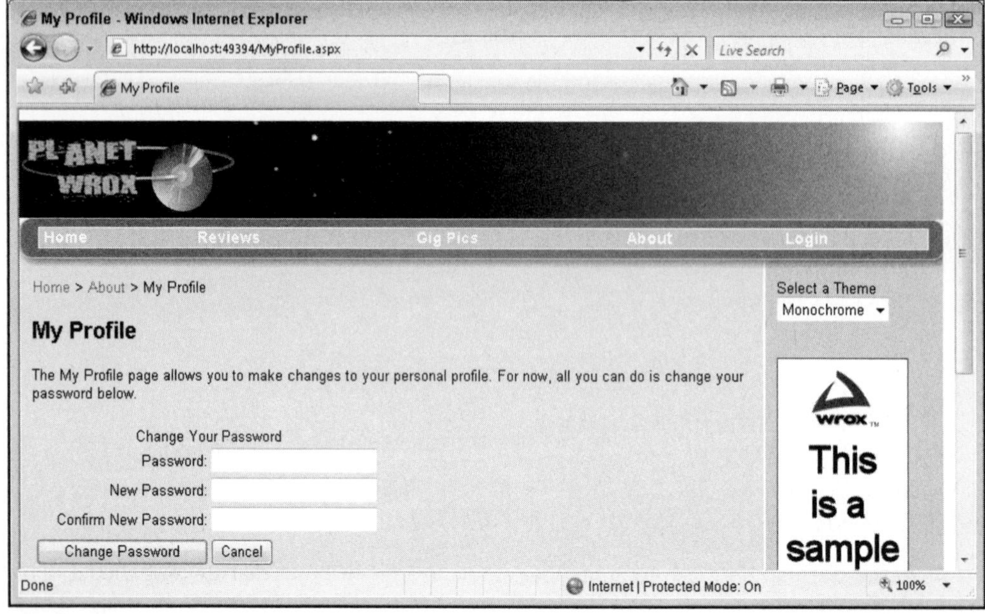

Figure 15-14

How It Works

By default, your passwords are stored in a *hashed* format in the database which means they cannot be retrieved. Hashing is an irreversible process that creates a unique fingerprint of your data. Because it's irreversible, there is no way to recreate the password from the hash, which makes it safer to store in a database. When you log in, the password you enter is also hashed and then the two hashes are compared to see if you are allowed to enter. Because the original password cannot be retrieved, the `PasswordRecovery` control generates a new password for you. It then sends this password to the e-mail address that is associated with the user name you entered. As the mail body it uses a standard template that contains the user name and the new password. To customize the mail body, you can point the `BodyFileName` of the `MailDefinition` to a text file that contains placeholders for the user name and password, just as you saw how to do with the `CreateUserWizard`.

You may have noticed that the login controls use a couple of defaults that you haven't been able to change so far. For example, the `CreateUserWizard` and `PasswordRecovery` controls always ask the user for a security question and answer as an additional layer of security. You also need to enter strong passwords with a minimum length of seven characters. You can change these settings for the entire application through the web.config file.

Configuring Your Web Application

Earlier in this chapter I discussed how the default connection string called `LocalSqlServer` is defined in the machine.config file so that it's effective by default in all web applications that you build. The same is true for many of the other settings that are relevant to the ASP.NET application services, like membership, roles, and profile. The machine.config contains the following settings for the membership services:

```
<membership>
  <providers>
    <add name="AspNetSqlMembershipProvider"
         type="System.Web.Security.SqlMembershipProvider, Version=2.0.0.0,
                        Culture=neutral, PublicKeyToken=b03f5f7f11d50a3a"
         connectionStringName="LocalSqlServer"
         enablePasswordRetrieval="false"
         enablePasswordReset="true"
         requiresQuestionAndAnswer="true"
         applicationName="/"
         requiresUniqueEmail="false"
         passwordFormat="Hashed"
         maxInvalidPasswordAttempts="5"
         minRequiredPasswordLength="7"
         minRequiredNonalphanumericCharacters="1"
         passwordAttemptWindow="10"
         passwordStrengthRegularExpression="" />
  </providers>
</membership>
```

This provider configuration features a number of interesting attributes that are described in the following table.

Attribute	Description
`connectionStringName`	This attribute points to the connection string for the application. Defaults to the LocalSqlServer connection you saw earlier.
`enablePasswordRetrieval`	This attribute determines whether users are able to retrieve their current password. This option cannot be set when `passwordFormat` is `Hashed`.
`enablePasswordReset`	This attribute determines whether a user is able to request a new password.

Continued

Attribute	Description
requiresQuestionAndAnswer	This attribute determines whether controls like CreateUserWizard and PasswordRecovery have the user enter a security question and answer.
applicationName	This attribute provides the unique name of the application.
requiresUniqueEmail	This attribute determines whether the system allows duplicate e-mail addresses for user accounts. When set to True, each user must provide a unique user name and a unique e-mail address.
passwordFormat	This attribute determines the way passwords are stored in the database. It supports the following formats: — Clear: Passwords are stored as plain text. — Encrypted: Passwords are encrypted in a reversible format that allows the system to retrieve the clear text representation of the password again. — Hashed: Passwords are encrypted with an irreversible, one-way algorithm. When the passwordFormat is Hashed, users cannot retrieve their original passwords anymore. They can only request a new, auto-generated password.
maxInvalidPasswordAttempts	This attribute specifies the number of times a user can enter an invalid password or invalid security answer before their account is locked.
minRequiredPasswordLength	This attribute determines the minimum length of the password.
minRequiredNonalphanumericCharacters	This attribute determines the minimum number of non-alphanumeric characters that must be included in the password.
passwordAttemptWindow	This attribute determines the time frame in minutes during which invalid password attempts are counted.
passwordStrengthRegularExpression	This attribute allows you to specify a custom regular expression to enforce a strong password.

To change these settings for the Planet Wrox application you could modify the machine.config directly. However, I strongly encourage you not to do this. Since this file applies to your entire machine, you may end up with a lot of unwanted side effects, or even render ASP.NET in a broken state.

Instead, you should reconfigure the `<membership>` element in the web.config file, and change the necessary attributes for the current application only. In the following exercise you see what it takes to reconfigure the membership provider for the Planet Wrox application.

Try It Out Configuring Membership

In this short exercise you see how to override the default behavior for the membership in the Planet Wrox site. When you have a copy of the configuration, you modify its settings to remove the security question and answer option and to change the rules for the password.

1. Locate the file machine.config, which by default you'll find in C:\Windows\Microsoft.NET\Framework\v2.0.50727\CONFIG. If you installed Windows in a different folder or drive, be sure to change the path accordingly. Don't worry if your system administrator doesn't allow you to access this file on your machine. If you can't access it, you can type the code from step 6 directly in the web.config file. Also note that the file is stored in the folder of the 2.0 version of the .NET Framework. The run time used in the ASP.NET 3.5 Framework is still version 2.0 and thus the files in the 2.0 configuration folder are used.
2. Open machine.config with Notepad and locate the `<membership>` element under `<system.web>` about three-quarters down in the file.
3. Copy the entire `<membership>` element to the clipboard.
4. Go back to VWD, open web.config, and paste the membership element right before the `<authentication>` element. Except for some different formatting (you could have the settings all on one line), you should end up with the configuration settings you saw at the beginning of this section.
5. Change `minRequiredPasswordLength` to `6` and set `requiresQuestionAndAnswer` to `false`.
6. Right before the `<add>` element, add a `<clear />` statement. When you're done, your configuration settings should look like this:

```
<membership>
  <providers>
    <clear />
    <add name="AspNetSqlMembershipProvider"
            type="System.Web.Security.SqlMembershipProvider, System.Web, Version=2.0.0.0,
                  Culture=neutral, PublicKeyToken=b03f5f7f11d50a3a"
        connectionStringName="LocalSqlServer"
        enablePasswordRetrieval="false"
        enablePasswordReset="true"
        requiresQuestionAndAnswer="false"
        applicationName="/"
        requiresUniqueEmail="false"
        passwordFormat="Hashed"
        maxInvalidPasswordAttempts="5"
```

```
        minRequiredPasswordLength="6"
        minRequiredNonalphanumericCharacters="1"
        passwordAttemptWindow="10"
        passwordStrengthRegularExpression="" />
  </providers>
</membership>
<authentication mode="Forms"/>
```

7. Save all your changes and request SignUp.aspx in the browser. Note that the security question and answer no longer appear in the Sign Up form as they did in Figure 15-4 at the beginning of this chapter.
8. Fill in the form but for the password fields, type something short like `pass`.
9. Click the Create User button. Note that the control now forces you to enter a password with a minimum length of six characters as you defined in web.config by showing the correct error message below the control, shown in Figure 15-15.
10. Enter a password of at least six characters with at least one non-alphanumeric character like `#` or `%` and click the Create User button again. This time your password is accepted and the account is created.

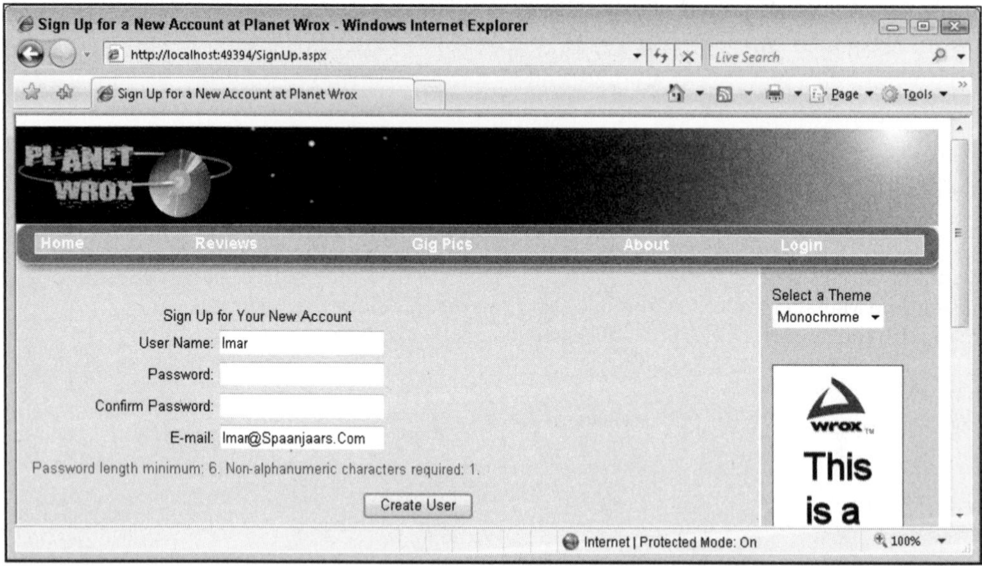

Figure 15-15

How It Works

The configuration settings for ASP.NET work in a hierarchical manner. This means that settings defined at a high level (for example, in machine.config) are applicable to all web applications on your computer. Without any modifications, the Planet Wrox web site inherits the settings defined in machine.config, including those for the membership provider. To change the behavior in a single web site, you need to create a copy of the original settings and then modify the necessary attributes.

However, in order to do that, you first need to *remove* the original settings. You do this with the `<clear />` element:

```
<providers>
  <clear />
  <add name="AspNetSqlMembershipProvider" ...
```

In this case, `<clear />` means as much as "remove any provider setting that has been added somewhere in the configuration hierarchy." So, right after the `<clear />` element, the `<providers>` element is considered empty, allowing you to add the same provider again, but this time with different settings.

Although this seems like a lot of work to change just a few settings, you'll find the ability to override the settings in your own web site to be of much more use when you need your application to talk to a different database system. Appendix B shows you how to do this.

So far you have seen how to let users sign up for an account so they can log in. But how can you differentiate between the different users in the system? How can you block access to specific folders like Management for unauthorized uses? You do this with the role manager, another application service that ships with ASP.NET.

The Role Manager

Although it's nice that your users can now sign up and log in to your site, it would be a lot more useful if you could differentiate between your users. That would enable you to grant access rights to one or just a few users to access the Management folder so only they can change your reviews and genres. With the Role Manager that ships with ASP.NET this is pretty easy to do. The Role Manager enables you to assign users to different roles. You can then use these roles to open or block specific functionality in your site. For example, you can block access to the Management folders to all users except for those in the Managers role. Additionally, you can display different content based on the roles users are in with the `LoginView` as you saw earlier.

Configuring the Role Manager

As with membership, the settings for the Role Manager are placed in config files. However, the Role Manager is not turned on by default, so you need to do that explicitly in the web.config file in the `<roleManager>` element that should be placed inside the `<system.web>` element in web.config:

```
<roleManager enabled="true" />
```

In a later exercise you see how to enable the roles with a management tool that is accessible from within VWD so you can enable roles without modifying the web.config file directly.

After you have enabled roles, you can assign users to different roles in a number of ways:

- Using the Web Site Administration Tool, generally referred to as the WSAT
- Programmatically using the RoleManager API (application programming interface)

The Web Site Administration Tool (WSAT) is used for a lot more, and is discussed in full detail in the next section. Managing roles using the Role Manager API is beyond the scope of this book. If you want to learn more about it, get a copy of Wrox's *Professional ASP.NET 3.5* (ISBN: 978-0-470-18757-9).

Managing Users with the WSAT

The WSAT tool ships with VWD and is available from the Website menu. The tool is used for the following tasks:

- Managing users
- Managing roles
- Managing access rules — for example, to determine what user can access which files and folders
- Configuring application, mail, and debug settings
- Taking the site off-line so users can't request any pages and get a friendly error message instead

The WSAT is only available from your local machine and is available as a menu shortcut in Visual Web Developer. As such, it's great for setting up the initial users and roles during development, but it isn't suitable for managing users in a production environment. To manage users in your production environment you can roll your own tool using the Membership and Role APIs or look into widely available open source solutions. Both solutions are outside the scope of the chapter, but for some ideas on creating your own management tool, pick up a copy of my book *ASP.NET 2.0 Instant Results* published by Wrox (ISBN: 978-0-471-74951-6). Although the book targets ASP.NET 2.0, you'll find that many of the concepts still apply to ASP.NET 3.5. Alternatively, take a look at *Professional ASP.NET 3.5*, which deals with the different APIs in great detail. If you are using Windows Vista or Windows Server 2008, you can also manage your users and roles through IIS, the web server. You see more of this in Chapter 18.

Some of the changes you make with the WSAT are persisted in the web.config file for the application. Other settings, like users and roles, are stored in the database for the configured provider.

In the next exercise you see how to start and use the WSAT. You see how to create a new role and a new user account, and how to assign that user to the role.

Try It Out Using the WSAT to Manage User Accounts and Roles

To protect your Management folder from users that are not authorized to access it, you need to create a role that is allowed to access this folder. After you have set up this role, you can grant all users in that role access to the folder while keeping all other users out. In this exercise you learn how to create the Managers role and assign a user to it. In a later exercise you see how to limit access to the Management folder to Managers only.

1. From within VWD, choose Website ➪ ASP.NET Configuration. Your browser opens and displays the Web Site Administration Tool, shown in Figure 15-16.
2. In the top-right corner you see a Help link that takes you to a help file describing how you can use the tool. Right below the logo of the application you see four tabs: Home, Security, Application, and Provider. The Home tab takes you back to the start page you see in Figure 15-16. The Application tab is used to configure different application settings while the Provider tab allows you to reconfigure the chosen provider for the application. In this exercise, all that's important is the Security tab, so go ahead and click it. You should see the screen displayed in Figure 15-17.

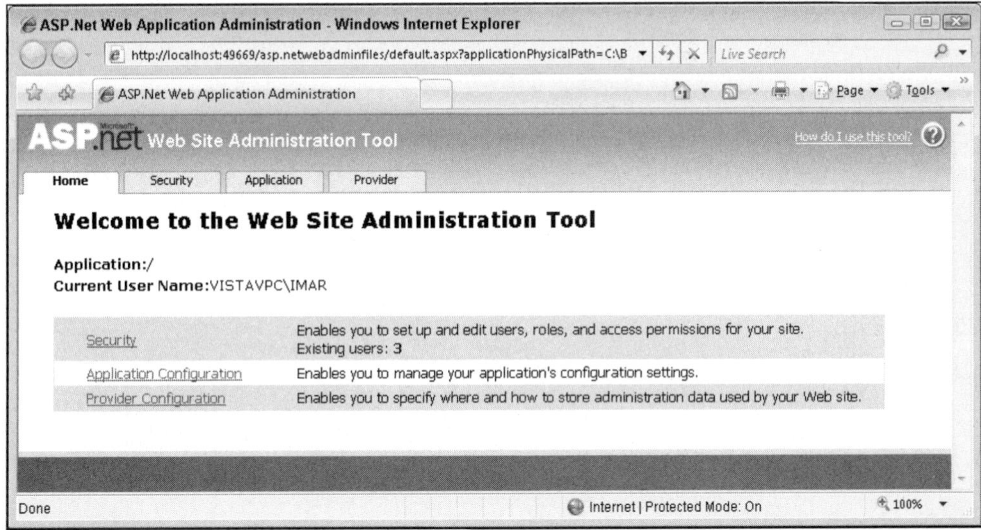

Figure 15-16

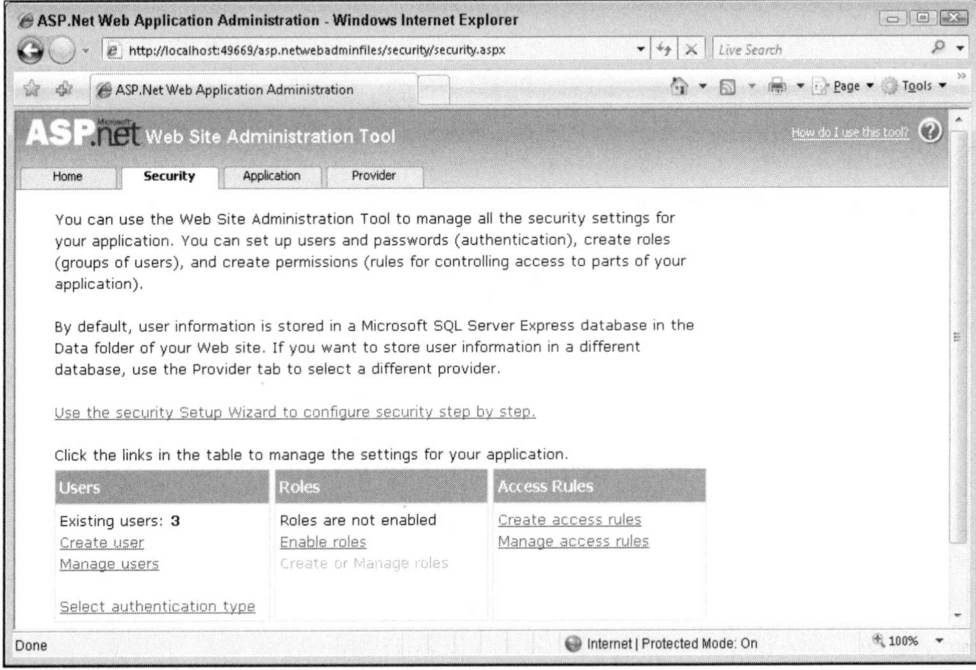

Figure 15-17

3. The bottom part of the screen is divided in three parts: Users, Roles, and Access Rules. You see how to use the Users and Roles in this exercise. The Access Rules is used to block or open up specific parts of your web site to users or roles. You won't see how to use it in this chapter, but instead you'll learn how to change some of these settings in web.config directly in a later exercise.

4. Make sure that under Users you see the Create user and Manage users links. If you don't see them, but you see a note about Windows authentication instead, click the Select authentication type link, then select From the internet, and finally click Done. Your screen should now look like Figure 15-17.

5. In the Roles section, click the Enable roles link. The screen reloads and now offers a link with the text Create or Manage Roles. Click that link to open the Create New Role window visible in Figure 15-18.

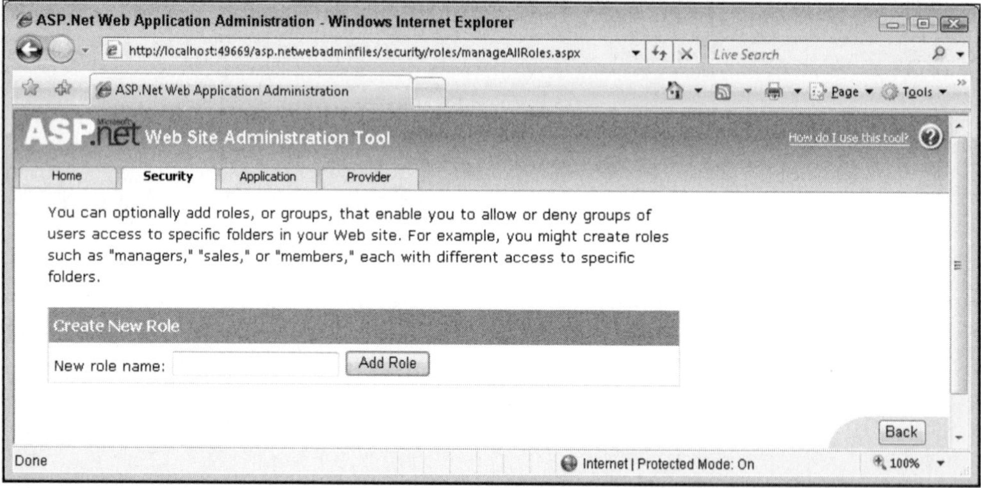

Figure 15-18

6. Enter Managers as the new role name and click the Add Role button. You should see the new role appear. Click the Back button at the bottom of the page to return to the main Security page.

7. Click the Create User link. You're taken to a page that allows you to enter the details for a new user and assign that user to the Managers role at the same time. Fill in the details as in Figure 15-19.

   As a password, enter something that meets the password rules you configured earlier. A password like `Manager##123` will do. You can choose your own e-mail address instead of the PlanetWrox.com account. Also, don't forget to check the Managers role name in the list of roles on the right.

8. Click Create User to add the user to the system and then click Continue on the confirmation page. At the bottom of the page click the Back button until you reach the main Security page.

9. On the Security page click the Manage users link. You are taken to a page that shows a list of all available users in the system, shown in Figure 15-20.

   From here you can edit, enable, disable, or delete existing users. For example, if you previously set `DisableCreatedUser` to `True` in the `CreateUserWizard`, you can enable the user here by checking the checkbox in front of the user name, visible in Figure 15-20. You can change the roles that are assigned to the user by clicking the Edit roles link. Also, using the filter controls and the alphabet above the user list, you can quickly search for a specific user in case you're dealing with a lot of user accounts.

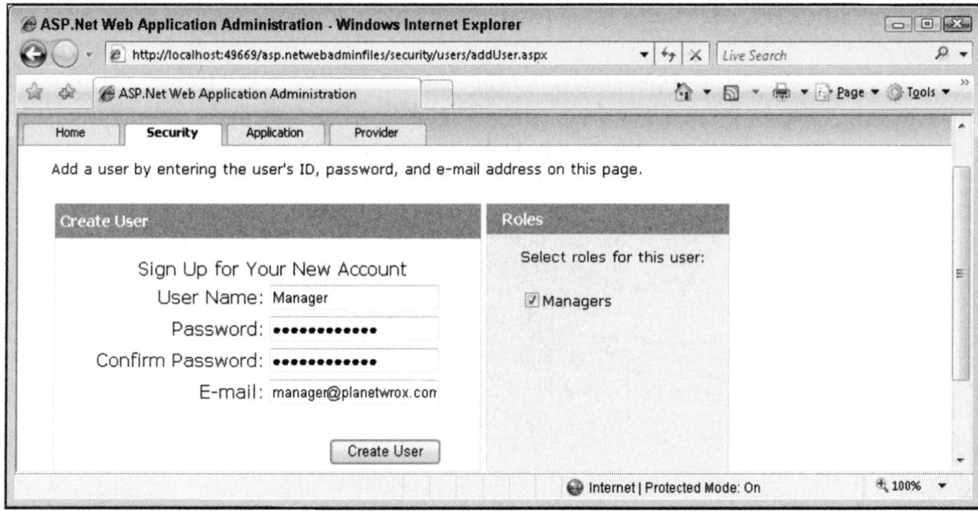

Figure 15-19

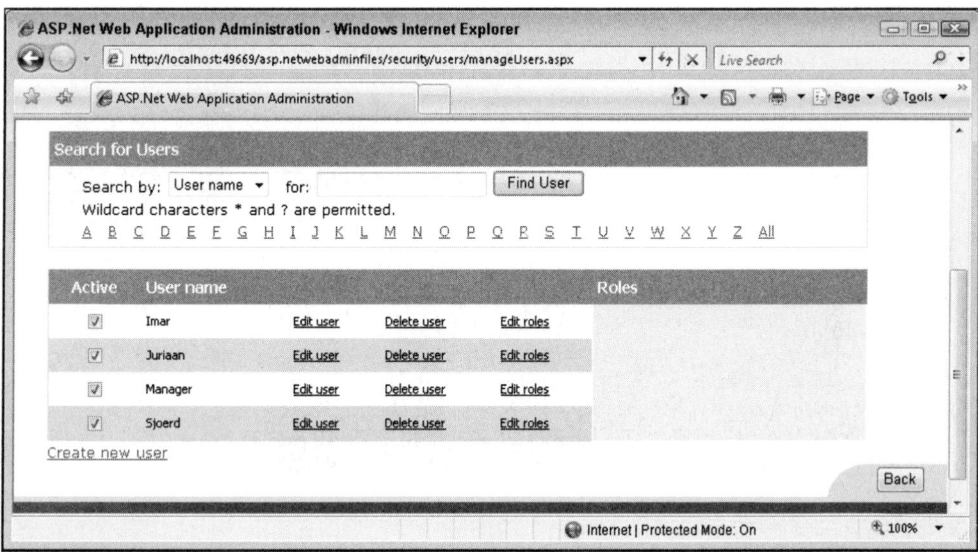

Figure 15-20

10. To see where your user and role ended up, close the browser and go back to VWD. On the Solution Explorer, double-click the `ASPNETDB.MDF` database in the `App_Data` folder to open it in the Database Explorer window. Then expand the Tables node, right-click the `aspnet_Roles` table, and choose Show Table Data. The role you created in step 6 should be listed. Open up some of the other tables like `aspnet_Membership` and `aspnet_UsersInRoles` and inspect the data they contain. In the first table you should see the user account you created in steps 7 and 8 while the latter table contains a relation between the new role and user account.

How It Works

Just like the login controls, the WSAT eventually talks to the provider you configured in the web.config file. In the case of the Planet Wrox application it means it talks to the `AspNetSqlMembershipProvider` which in turn talks to a SQL Server Express database identified by the `LocalSqlServer` connection string. The users and roles you create are stored in the various `aspnet*` tables in the database. Users that you create using the WSAT end up in the exact same location as those created with the `CreateUserWizard` control. In fact, the WSAT uses a `CreateUserWizard` to let you create a new user account. This means that any user you enter in the WSAT is able to log in using your standard Login.aspx page. In a later exercise, you use the Manager account you created in this exercise to log in to the site and access the Management folder.

In order to use the role you created in this exercise you have a few options at your disposal. First, you can use the role name to block access to specific folders in your web application through settings in the web.config file. Secondly, you can use the role in controls like the `LoginView` to present different content to different users. Finally, you can use the Role API to check whether the current user is in a specific role. This gives you fine control over the content or functionality you can offer to certain privileged users. You see how to block access to the Management folder and modify the `LoginView` next, while using the Role API is discussed in a later exercise.

Configuring the Web Application to Work with Roles

On the Security page of the WSAT you saw a section called Access Rules. This part of the tool allows you to block or open up resources in your site. It allows you to define rules such as, "This folder is blocked for anyone except for users in the Managers role," or, "Anyone can access this file, except for the Members role and the Joe account." The tool is quite intuitive to use, so it isn't difficult to set up the different rules. However, it has one downside: it stores the security settings in different web.config files, one for each subfolder you configure.

This makes it somewhat difficult to get an overview of all the different security settings. Fortunately, ASP.NET also allows you to configure the same settings in the main web.config using `<location>` elements. A `<location>` element has a path property that points to a file or folder you want to configure differently. You can use the `<location>` element for other settings from web.config as well (for example, you could set the `theme` attribute of the `<pages>` element for the Management folder in the main web.config). For the following exercise, you'll only set the child elements of `<location>` to those related to security.

Try It Out — Blocking Access to the Management Folder

Obviously, you don't want just anyone to mess with the reviews and genres that you have posted on your web site. Therefore, it's important to block access to the Management folder to anyone except Managers. In this exercise you see how to modify web.config to block the folder so only the user account you assigned to the Managers role earlier can access this folder and the files it contains.

1. Open the web.config file at the root of the site. Scroll all the way down to the closing `</configuration>` tag and right before it type a `<location>` element. Add a `path`

attribute to the element and set its value to `Management`. Note that IntelliSense kicks in to help you complete the element and find the attribute. Your code should now look like this:

```
    </mailSettings>
  </system.net>
  <location path="Management"></location>
</configuration>
```

2. Complete the configuration by entering the following XML settings:

```
  </system.net>
  <location path="Management">
    <system.web>
      <authorization>
        <allow roles="Managers"/>
        <deny users="*"/>
      </authorization>
    </system.web>
  </location>
</configuration>
```

3. Save and close the web.config file.
4. Open the main master page for the site (MasterPage.master) in Design View and scroll down to the end of the file. Select the `LoginView` control and open its Smart Tasks panel. At the top of the panel, click the Edit RoleGroups link, shown in Figure 15-21.

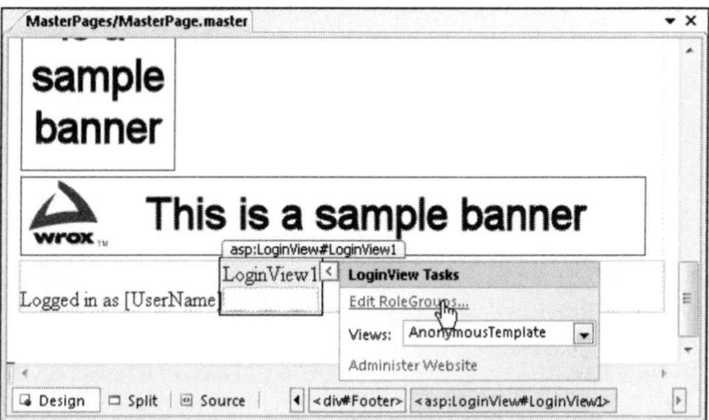

Figure 15-21

5. In the dialog box that opens, click the Add button to insert a new `RoleGroup` and then set the `Roles` property of this group to Managers, as shown in Figure 15-22.
6. Click OK to insert the `RoleGroup` and return to Design View.
7. Still on the Smart Tasks panel of the `LoginView`, choose RoleGroup[0] - Managers from the Views drop-down list. This switches the current template of the control to the `RoleGroup` for Managers, so you can add content that is only visible to Managers.

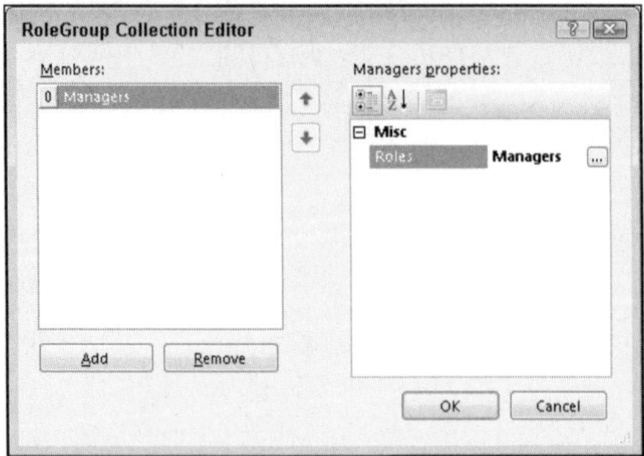

Figure 15-22

8. Drag a HyperLink control from the Toolbox and drop it into the LoginView. Using the Properties Grid, set the Text property of this HyperLink to Manage Site and set the NavigateUrl to ~/Management/Default.aspx. (You can use the URL picker for the HyperLink by clicking the small button with the ellipsis on it.) Switch to Markup View and after the HyperLink control type the word **or** followed by a LoginStatus control that you can drag from the Toolkit, or copy from the existing code in the LoggedInTemplate.

   When you are ready your LoginView should contain the following code:

```
<asp:LoginView ID="LoginView1" runat="server">
  <RoleGroups>
    <asp:RoleGroup Roles="Managers">
      <ContentTemplate>
        <asp:HyperLink ID="HyperLink1" runat="server"
                NavigateUrl="~/Management/Default.aspx">Manage Site</asp:HyperLink> or
          <asp:LoginStatus ID="LoginStatus1" runat="server" />
      </ContentTemplate>
    </asp:RoleGroup>
  </RoleGroups>
  <LoggedInTemplate>
    (<asp:LoginStatus ID="LoginStatus1" runat="server" />)
  </LoggedInTemplate>
</asp:LoginView>
```

9. Save all your changes and then request the home page (Default.aspx) for the site in your browser. Verify that you are currently not logged in (check the Footer of the page and if necessary click the Logout link).

10. Click the Login link on the Menu or TreeView and then log in with the Manager account you created earlier in this chapter. Make sure you don't check the Remember Me option. The page refreshes and now shows the Manage Site link in the Footer of each page (see Figure 15-23).

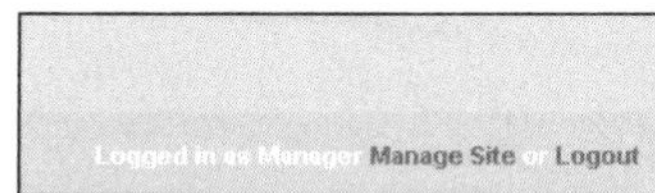

Figure 15-23

11. Click the Manage Site link to open the Management section of the web site. Copy the current URL of the page from the browser's address bar to the clipboard. Click the Back button of your browser to go back to the home page and then click the Logout button in the footer. Close your browser and open a new instance again. (You can do this from the start menu or your desktop if you have a shortcut there, or right-click a page in VWD and choose View in Browser.)

12. Paste the address you just copied in the address bar of the browser window and press Enter. Instead of going to an address like:

```
http://localhost:49666/Management/Default.aspx
```

you are taken to the Login page:

```
http://localhost:49666/login.aspx?ReturnUrl=%2fManagement%2fDefault.aspx
```

Note that the page you initially requested (Management/Default.aspx) is now appended to the query string. The forward slashes (/) in the address have been encoded to their URL-safe counterpart: `%2f` automatically. Log in with your Manager account and you should see the Management section appear again.

How It Works

There are a couple of interesting things you need to look at in this exercise. First, look at the settings you added to the web.config file to limit access to the Management folder:

```
<location path="Management">
  <system.web>
    <authorization>
      <allow roles="Managers"/>
      <deny users="*"/>
    </authorization>
  </system.web>
</location>
```

When the ASP.NET run time processes the request for a page, it checks the various configuration files to see whether the current user is allowed to access that resource. For requests to files in the Management folder, it encounters the rule set in the `<location>` element. It starts scanning the various rules (`allow` and `deny` elements with `roles` or `users` attributes to specify the users or roles that are affected by the rule) and as soon as it finds a rule, it stops the scanning process. If no rule is satisfied, access is *granted*! Therefore, it's important to end the rule with a deny rule to block all other users that haven't been granted access previously.

When an unauthenticated user logs in, the first rule won't match because the anonymous user is not a member of the Managers role. The user is then denied access because of the deny rule that blocks all users (indicated by the asterisk [*]).

After you logged in as a Manager and requested the same resource, the rule set was scanned again. The run time then found the `allow` element that grants access to the Managers role and immediately lets you in. The final rule that blocks access to all other users is never even checked anymore.

In addition to specific roles or user names and the asterisk (`*`) to refer to all users you can also use the question mark (`?`) to refer to unauthenticated, or anonymous users. So, for example, to let any logged-in user access the Reviews folder regardless of the role they are in, and block access to all other users, you can add the following `<location>` element to your configuration file:

```
<location path="Reviews">
  <system.web>
    <authorization>
      <deny users="?"/>
    </authorization>
  </system.web>
</location>
```

This denies access to all users that are not logged in. Because of the default rule that grants access to the resource if the current user is not matched by an earlier rule, all logged-in users can successfully access files in the Reviews folder.

You can specify multiple roles or user names in the roles and user elements by separating them with a comma.

It's important to understand how the `RoleGroups` element of the `LoginView` works. Although you can specify multiple `RoleGroup` elements that may all apply to a certain user, only *the first that matches* is displayed. Consider a user called Marcel assigned to the group WebMasters and to the group Managers and a web page with the following `LoginView`:

```
<asp:LoginView ID="LoginView1" runat="server">
  <RoleGroups>
    <asp:RoleGroup Roles="Managers">
      <ContentTemplate>
        <!-- Content for Managers here -->
      </ContentTemplate>
    </asp:RoleGroup>
    <asp:RoleGroup Roles="WebMasters">
      <ContentTemplate>
        <!-- Content for WebMasters here -->
      </ContentTemplate>
    </asp:RoleGroup>
  </RoleGroups>
```

With this code, the user Marcel only sees the content of the first `RoleGroup`, even though he is also assigned to the WebMasters group.

Programmatically Checking Roles

Although it's easy to use the `LoginView` control to change the content a user is allowed to see at run time, this isn't always enough. There are times where you need programmatic control over the data you are presenting based on someone's role membership. You can access information about roles for the current user in a number of ways. First of all, you can access the `IsInRole` method of the `User` property from the current page or user control like this:

VB.NET

```
If User.IsInRole("Managers") Then
  ' This code runs for Managers only
End If
```

C#

```
if (User.IsInRole("Managers"))
{
  // This code runs for Managers only
}
```

Alternatively, you can access the `Roles` class that contains a number of static methods that you can access directly. The following code is functionally equivalent to the previous example:

VB.NET

```
If Roles.IsUserInRole("Managers") Then
  ' This code runs for Managers only
End If
```

C#

```
if (Roles.IsUserInRole("Managers"))
{
  // This code runs for Managers only
}
```

The biggest difference between the two is that for the latter option to work, you need to have the Role Manager enabled. Since that's the case in the Planet Wrox web site, you can choose any of these two methods. For custom solutions, where you are not using a role provider but your own custom solution, you can only use the first code construct.

Besides the `IsUserInRole` method, the `Roles` class contains a lot of other methods that allow you to work with roles programmatically. For example, you can create and delete roles, assign users to and remove users from roles, and you can get a list of users that are assigned to a certain role. For more information about the Roles API, check out the MSDN documentation or pick up a copy of *Professional ASP.NET 2.0 Security, Membership, and Role Management* by Stefan Schackow (Wrox, ISBN: 978-0-7645-9698-8).

In the following exercise you learn how to modify the photo albums page so users logged in as Managers are able to delete pictures from a photo album. Other users won't be able to delete a picture as the Delete button will be hidden for them.

Try It Out Checking Roles with IsUserInRole at Run Time

Although you could potentially recreate this example by using a `LoginView` with different templates and `RoleGroups`, the following exercise uses a programmatic check for the user's role to hide or show the Delete button. This makes it easier to modify the code later so that owners of a specific photo album can delete their own pictures as well.

1. Open Default.aspx from the PhotoAlbums folder in Design View and locate the `LinqDataSource2` control that is used to manage the pictures in a photo album. Open its Smart Tasks panel and then enable deleting by selecting the Enable Delete item.
2. Switch to Markup View and then locate the `<ItemTemplate>` element of the `ListView` that is used to display the pictures.
3. Between the `Label` control and the closing `</li>` tag add a `Button` with its `CommandName` and `Text` properties set to `Delete`. Set the Button's `ID` to `DeleteButton`. The button should end up like this:

```
    <asp:Label ID="DescriptionLabel" runat="server" Text='<%# Eval("Description") %>' />
    <asp:Button ID="DeleteButton" CommandName="Delete" runat="server" Text="Delete" />
  </li>
```

4. Switch to Design View again, select the `ListView`, and open its Properties Grid. Switch to the Event category and then double-click the `ItemCreated` event to set up an event handler for that event.
5. Add the following code to the event handler that Visual Web Developer added for you in the Code Behind of the file:

VB.NET

```
Protected Sub ListView1_ItemCreated(ByVal sender As Object, _
             ByVal e As System.Web.UI.WebControls.ListViewItemEventArgs) _
             Handles ListView1.ItemCreated
  Select Case e.Item.ItemType
    Case ListViewItemType.DataItem
      Dim deleteButton As Button = CType(e.Item.FindControl("DeleteButton"), Button)
      deleteButton.Visible = Roles.IsUserInRole("Managers")
  End Select
End Sub
```

C#

```
protected void ListView1_ItemCreated(object sender, ListViewItemEventArgs e)
{
  switch (e.Item.ItemType)
  {
    case ListViewItemType.DataItem:
      Button deleteButton = (Button)e.Item.FindControl("DeleteButton");
      deleteButton.Visible = Roles.IsUserInRole("Managers");
      break;
  }
}
```

6. Save your changes and then request the page in your browser by pressing Ctrl+F5. If you're still logged in, click the Logout link first in the footer at the bottom of the page.
7. Choose one of the photo albums from the drop-down list. The page reloads and shows the pictures in the photo album. Since you're not logged in, the Delete link is not visible. Click the Login link in the main `Menu` or `TreeView` and log in with the Manager account you created earlier in this chapter.
8. Go back to the main Photo Albums page (choose Gig Pics in the menu) and choose a photo album from the list. Figure 15-24 shows how each picture is now associated with a delete button that deletes the picture when clicked.
9. Click the Logout link in the footer again and go to the Login page. Log in with the account you created first in this chapter that is not a member of the Managers role. Go back to the Gig Pics page and choose a photo album from the list. Even if you are logged in with a valid account, you still cannot delete pictures, as you are not assigned to the Managers role.

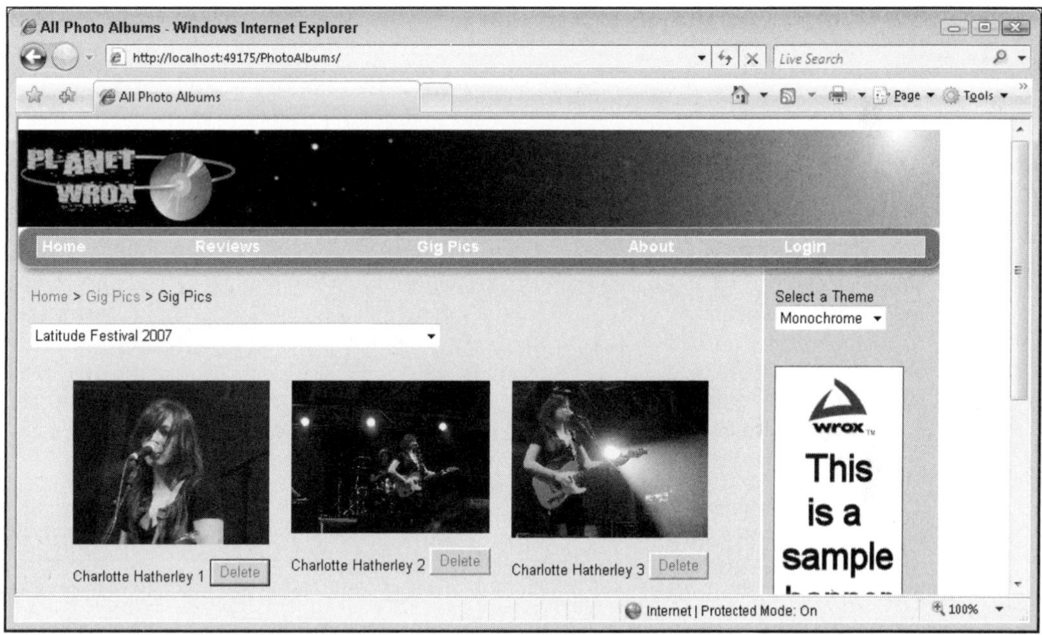

Figure 15-24

How It Works

Most of the code in this exercise shouldn't be new to you. You have seen how you can delete items with the `LinqDataSource` and `ListView` controls. You also learned how to handle the `ItemCreated` event and search for controls in an item using `FindControl`.

What's new in this example is the way you check whether the current user is a member of the Managers group:

VB.NET

```
Dim deleteButton As Button = CType(e.Item.FindControl("DeleteButton"), Button)
deleteButton.Visible = Roles.IsUserInRole("Managers")
```

C#

```
Button deleteButton = (Button)e.Item.FindControl("DeleteButton");
deleteButton.Visible = Roles.IsUserInRole("Managers");
```

The `IsUserInRole` method returns a Boolean that indicates whether the current user is a manager. When the method returns `True`, it means that the `Visible` property of the `Button` is set to `True`. When the method returns `False`, the button is hidden and the user is not able to delete pictures from the photo album.

Practical Security Tips

The following list provides some practical security tips.

- Although the concept of security is introduced quite late in the chapter, you shouldn't see it as an afterthought. To ensure you create a solid and secure application you should keep security in mind from the very early stages of your web site development. Deciding whether you want to have areas that are only accessible to certain users, and whether you are going to force users into getting an account for your site before they get access is best done as early as possible. The later in the process you introduce these concepts, the more difficulties you'll face when integrating this functionality.
- Try to group resources like ASPX pages under folders that represent roles in your system. Take, for example, the Management folder in the Planet Wrox web site. All pages related to the management of your site are packed together in a single folder, making it very easy to block the entire folder with a single `<location>` element in the web.config file. When the files you want to protect are scattered throughout your web site, you'll need more time to configure the application, and you'll end up with an unclear view of the active security settings.
- When you create roles to differentiate between users on your web site, try to limit the number of different roles your system has. You'll find that your system becomes much easier to manage with only a handful of logically grouped roles than with a large number of roles with only one or two users in them.

Summary

Security in your ASP.NET site can be implemented with several techniques, including Windows authentication (where the web server takes care of authentication) or third-party authentication (where an external service like Microsoft Passport takes care of validating the user). Last, you can use Forms authentication, which is the de facto standard for many of today's ASP.NET web sites.

In general, authentication encompasses three important concepts: identity, authentication, and authorization. Identity describes who you are and represents you on a web site. During the process of authentication, you hand over proof that verifies your identity. With ASP.NET web sites, this proof is sent in the form of a user name and password that are then validated against a user data store. Authorization deals with the things you are allowed to do within the system. For example, as an anonymous user you are not allowed to access the files in the Management folder of the site. As soon as you log in with an account that does have the correct permissions, you can browse to these files successfully.

The Membership provider allows you to create and manage users in a central database. Users can create their own accounts using controls like the `CreateUserWizard` or you can manage the user accounts using the built-in Web Site Administration Tool. With the login controls users can independently manage their own account: they can retrieve a lost password or change their existing password. The other login controls, like `LoginName`, `LoginView`, and `LoginStatus` allow you to display different content to anonymous and logged-in users, and even let you differentiate between users in different roles.

Roles are managed with the WSAT as well, so you can assign user accounts to different roles as you saw in this chapter. You can then open specific resources in your web site to members in a certain role. For example, with a simple `<location>` element in the web.config file you blocked access to the Management folder for all users that are not a members of the Managers role.

The various login controls allow you to customize the content that users get to see. In Chapter 16 you discover how to take this one level further, by creating dynamic pages that adapt based on the user that is accessing them.

Exercises

1. What's the difference between authentication and authorization?
2. Right now the Management folder is blocked for all users except those in the Managers role. What change do you need to make to the web.config file if you want to open up the folder for the user John and all people in the Editors role?
3. Imagine you have a web site that features a Login page with a single `Login` control. What change to the `Login` control do you need to make to send users to MyProfile.aspx in the root after they log in?
4. What's the difference between the `LoginView` and `LoginStatus` controls? When would you use each one?

Personalizing Web Sites

There is only one thing that beats good content on the web — good *personalized* content. In the era of information overload and the huge amount of competitive sites, it's important to know your visitors and understand the possibilities you have to present personalized content. With a good personalization strategy you can create a web site that lives up to your user's expectation by presenting them with exactly the data they are looking for. Personalization is useful for many different scenarios: on a sports site you use it to highlight activities from the user's favorite team. On a site that deals with programming, you can personalize content by showing the user examples in their preferred programming language(s) only. On a news web site, you can let a user choose one or more news categories (World, Local, Sports, Business, Financial, and so on) and target the content you show them based on these preferences. You can take this one step further by sending them e-mail updates when a new article is posted in one of those categories.

However, personalization goes further than just storing personal preferences and adapting the content to these preferences. With personalization you can also keep track of other user details, like names, date of birth, visits to the site, items users bought in an online shop, and so on. You can then use these details to further personalize web pages, creating a closer relationship with your visitor.

In the Planet Wrox web site, personalization is implemented simply yet effectively. The Reviews page only shows the reviews for those genres that the user is interested in. To see all the available reviews, users can still visit the All.aspx page but by visiting the personalized page, they only see reviews in genres they really like.

Additionally, users can enter personal details about themselves, like first and last name, and a short biography. These details will be shown in the Photo Albums section of the site so you know who uploaded a particular photo album.

To allow you to add personalization features to a web site, ASP.NET 3.5 ships with an application service called Profile. With the Profile service you can store data for a particular user with very few lines of code.

The chapter looks at the following personalization topics:

- The Profile feature that ships with ASP.NET
- How to create and consume a user's profile in a web site

- How you can recognize your users and how to serve them customized content
- How you can access the profile of other users in the site

By the end of this chapter, you'll have enough knowledge about the personalization features brought by the Profile to create dynamic and personalized web sites.

Understanding Profile

The ASP.NET Profile is another application service that ships with ASP.NET. It enables you to store and retrieve information about users to your site that goes beyond basic information like an e-mail address and password that users can enter during sign-up, as you learned in the previous chapter. With Profile, you can store information like a first and last name, a date of birth, and much more, as you'll see later in this chapter. By keeping track of the user that the data belongs to, ASP.NET is able to map that data to a user the next time she visits your site, whether that be minutes or weeks later. The cool thing about Profile is that it allows you to store data for registered users as well as anonymous users. So, even if your visitors haven't signed up for an account, you can recognize them and store information about them.

You access the properties of the Profile through a clean API with virtually no code. All you need to do is define the information you want to keep track of in the central web.config file and then the Profile feature takes care of the rest. All interaction with the database to retrieve or store the profile information in the database is handled automatically for you.

Enabling Profile in your web application is a simple, three-step process:

1. Define the information you want to store for a user in the web.config file.
2. Based on this information, the ASP.NET runtime generates and compiles a class for you on the fly that gives you access to the properties you defined in step 1. It then dynamically adds a property called Profile to the pages in your web site, so you can easily access the Profile from every page in your site.
3. In your application you program directly to this generated class to get and store the Profile information for the current user.

The Profile by default is connected to a logged-in user although you can also save profile data for unauthenticated users as you'll see later in this chapter.

Because data about the logged-in user is stored in a cookie, your users need to have browsers that support cookies for the ASP.NET Profile feature to work correctly.

In the following section you see how to define the profile properties in web.config, and how to use the new Profile in your web pages.

Configuring the Profile

You define a profile for your web site in the web.config file by creating a `<profile>` element as a direct child of the `<system.web>` element. Between the `<profile>` tags you need to create a `<properties>` element that is used to define the properties you want to expose from your Profile object. There are two types of properties: simple properties and complex properties, referred to as profile groups.

Creating Simple Profile Properties

You define simple properties as direct children of the `<properties>` element using an `<add />` element. The following example demonstrates how to create a property that can be used to hold a user's first name and one to hold a date of birth. The `FirstName` property can be accessed and set for anonymous users as well, whereas the date of birth property is only accessible to logged-in users:

```
<system.web>
  ...
  <profile>
    <properties>
      <add name="FirstName" allowAnonymous="True" />
      <add name="DateOfBirth" type="System.DateTime" />
    </properties>
  </profile>
```

Because properties are by default of type `System.String`, there's no need to define an explicit `type` on the property for simple properties like a first name. However, for other types like a `DateTime`, a `Boolean`, or an `Integer`, you need to define the type explicitly using the `type` attribute and its *fully qualified name* including its namespace. The following table lists the most common attributes of the `<add />` element that influence the properties of a profile.

Attribute	Description
`name`	This attribute defines the name of the property, like `FirstName`, `DateOfBirth`, and so forth.
`type`	This attribute sets the full .NET type name of the property, like `System.String`, `System.Boolean`, `System.DateTime`, and so on.
`allowAnonymous`	This attribute specifies whether the property can be set for anonymous users. The default is `False`. To set this attribute to True, you also need to enable `anonymousAuthentication`, discussed later in this chapter.
`defaultValue`	This attribute defines the default value for the property if it hasn't been set explicitly. When you leave out this attribute, the profile property has as its default value the default value for the underlying type (for example `null` for a `String`, 0 for an `Int32`, and so on).
`readOnly`	This attribute specifies whether the profile property can be changed at run-time. The default is `False` which means you can read from and write to the property.

Besides simple properties, you can also create profile groups that allow you to group other simple properties together.

Creating Profile Groups

Profile groups serve two distinct purposes: first, they allow you to logically group related properties. For example, you can create a group called `Address` that in turn has properties like `Street`, `PostalCode`, and `City`.

Groups also allow you to have properties with the same name, but located in a different group. For example, you can have two groups called `VisitAddress` and `PostalAddress` that both feature properties like `Street` and `PostalCode`, making it easier for a developer using your Profile object to find the relevant information.

To create a profile group you add a `<group>` element to the `<properties>` element of your profile and then specify a name. The `<group>` element then contains one or more simple properties. The following example shows a profile group for a `PostalAddress`:

```
<properties>
  <add name="FirstName" />
  <group name="PostalAddress">
    <add name="Street"/>
    <add name="PostalCode"/>
    <add name="City"/>
    <add name="Country"/>
  </group>
</properties>
```

You can have multiple groups within the `<properties>` tags, but you can only have one level of groups. This means that you can't nest a `<group>` element in another `<group>` or `<add />` element.

Using Non-standard Data Types

In addition to the data types listed earlier like `String`, `DateTime`, and `Integer`, you can also use your own types you have defined (in the App_Code folder, for example).

As with the built-in .NET types, you need to refer to your type using its fully qualified name that includes the namespace and the class name. Imagine you have a type called `Preference` that contains various properties related to the user's preference. To include this type in the Profile you need to wrap it in a namespace first:

VB.NET

```
Namespace PlanetWrox
  Public Class Preference
    Private _favoriteColor As String
    Public Property FavoriteColor() As String     ' You need full properties in VB.NET
      Get
        Return _favoriteColor
      End Get
      Set(ByVal value As String)
        _favoriteColor = value
      End Set
    End Property
    ' Other properties here
  End Class
End Namespace
```

C#

```
namespace PlanetWrox
{
```

```
  public class Preference
  {
    public string FavoriteColor {get; set;}       // You can use automatic properties in C#
    // Other properties here
  }
}
```

You can then refer to the type in a Profile property:

```
<add name="Prefs" type="PlanetWrox.Preference" />
```

A situation where you need a different syntax to refer to a type in the Profile setup is when you are using generics. Chapter 5 discusses how to use generics to store role names using a generics list of strings:

VB.NET

```
Dim roles As New List(Of String)
...
roles.Add("Members")
```

C#

```
List<string> roles = new List<string>();
...
roles.Add("Members");
```

To give your profile a property that is of a generic `List` type, you need to use some special syntax. The following setting in web.config creates a profile property called `FavoriteGenres` that stores the user's favorite genres as a `List (Of Integer)` in VB.NET and as a `List<int>` in C#:

```
<add name="FavoriteGenres" type="System.Collections.Generic.List`1[System.Int32]" />
```

The first part of the `type` attribute looks quite normal. The `List` class lives in the `System.Collections.Generic` namespace so it makes sense that you need to specify that here as well. However, right after the class name (`List`) you see `` `1``. This is not a typo, but the .NET way to refer to generic types in plain text. To define a property that is based on a generic type you need to use the back tick (`), usually found to the left of the 1 key on your keyboard. The `` `1`` is then followed by a pair of square brackets that contains the actual type you want to use for the list. The type specified in this Profile property is identical to its VB.NET and C# counterparts that are defined as follows:

VB.NET

```
Dim FavoriteGenres As New List(Of Integer)
```

C#

```
List<int> FavoriteGenres = new List<int>();
```

You'll see how to make use of this and other Profile properties in the following exercises. First, you'll learn how to define the Profile in web.config in the next Try It Out exercise. Later exercises show you how to work with these properties, and how to use the various methods of the `List` class.

Try It Out — Creating a Profile

In this exercise you see how to create a profile that is capable of storing a user's first and last name, a date of birth, a short biography, and a list of IDs of the user's favorite genres. This list is later used to show only the reviews that match the user's interest.

1. Open the web.config file from the root of the site and locate the opening `<system.web>` tag.
2. Add a new `<profile>` element below this tag.
3. Complete the `<profile>` element so it ends up looking like this:

```
<system.web>
  <profile>
    <properties>
      <add name="FirstName" />
      <add name="LastName" />
      <add name="DateOfBirth" type="System.DateTime"/>
      <add name="Bio" />
      <add name="FavoriteGenres"
                   type="System.Collections.Generic.List`1[System.Int32]" />
    </properties>
  </profile>
<roleManager enabled="true"/>
```

4. Save the web.config file by pressing Ctrl+S. As soon as you save the file, a background process starts to generate a class file that is used for the Profile. After the class file has been created and compiled successfully, you can access the Profile programmatically through the Profile property of the `Page` class.
5. To test the Profile, open the My Profile page you created in the previous chapter. Double-click the page in Design View to set up an event handler for the `Load` event and add the following code:

VB.NET

```
Protected Sub Page_Load(ByVal sender As Object, ByVal e As System.EventArgs) _
              Handles Me.Load
  Profile.FirstName = "Your First Name"
  Profile.LastName = "Your Last Name"
End Sub
```

C#

```
protected void Page_Load(object sender, EventArgs e)
{
  Profile.FirstName = "Your First Name";
  Profile.LastName = "Your Last Name";
}
```

6. As soon as you type the dot (.) after `Profile`, an IntelliSense list shows up, showing you the available Profile properties (see Figure 16-1).

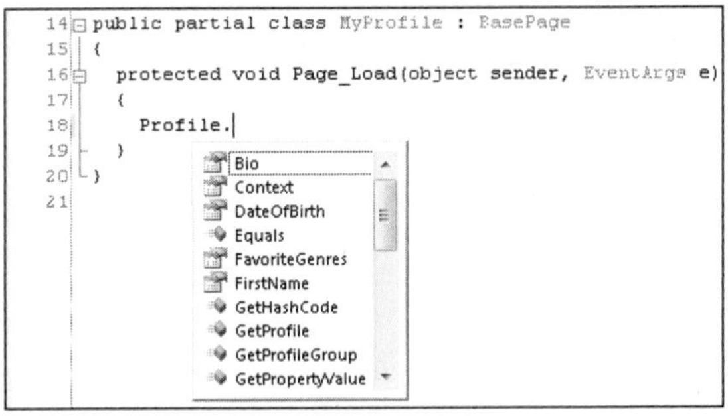

```
public partial class MyProfile : BasePage
{
  protected void Page_Load(object sender, EventArgs e)
  {
    Profile.
  }
}
```


Figure 16-1

7. When you are finished typing the code, save and close the file as you're done with it for now.

   If nothing shows up when pressing the dot, choose Build ➪ Build Solution from the main menu or press Ctrl+Shift+B. This forces VWD to start a recompilation of the application, including the special class for the Profile. You'll see more about compilation in Chapter 18. After a delay of a few seconds, the properties should now appear in the IntelliSense list for the Profile property of the Page class. If they still don't show up, check the Error List (choose View ➪ Error List from the main menu to open up the Error List) to verify that you didn't make any mistakes in the web.config file.

8. Switch back to the web.config file and scroll all the way to the end. Create a copy of the `<location>` element that blocks access to the Management folder for unauthorized users and paste it right below the existing element. Then modify the copy so it blocks access to the file MyProfile.aspx in the root of the site to all unauthenticated users. You should end up with these settings:

```
  </location>
  <location path="MyProfile.aspx">
    <system.web>
      <authorization>
        <deny users="?"/>
      </authorization>
    </system.web>
  </location>
</configuration>
```

9. In the Solution Explorer, right-click the file MyProfile.aspx and choose View in Browser. You can only view this file when you're logged in; if you weren't logged in previously, you are taken to Login.aspx first. Login with the user name and password you created in the previous chapter and click Login. You're taken back to MyProfile.aspx. Although you don't see anything new in the page, the code in `Page_Load` has run and has created a profile for you in the database.

10. To see this profile, close your browser and go back to Visual Web Developer. Open the Database Explorer window and expand the Tables element of the `ASPNETDB.MDF` database. Locate the table `aspnet_Profile`, right-click it, and choose Show Table Data. You should see something similar to Figure 16-2.

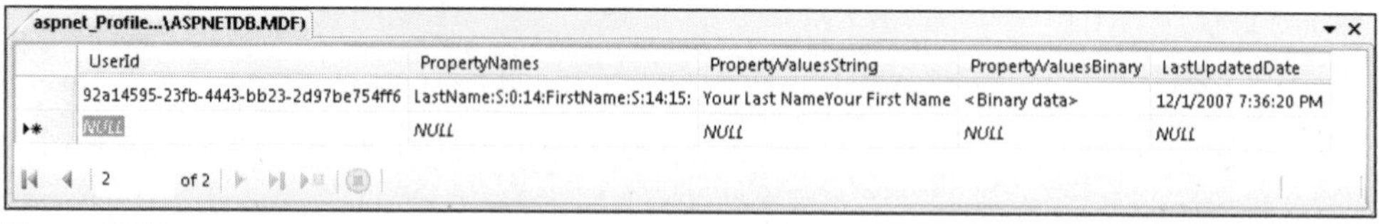

aspnet_Profile...\ASPNETDB.MDF)

	UserId	PropertyNames	PropertyValuesString	PropertyValuesBinary	LastUpdatedDate
	92a14595-23fb-4443-bb23-2d97be754ff6	LastName:S:0:14:FirstName:S:14:15:	Your Last NameYour First Name	<Binary data>	12/1/2007 7:36:20 PM
▸*	NULL	NULL	NULL	NULL	NULL

2 of 2

Figure 16-2

This figure shows the Profile data for a single user. The first and last name you entered in step 5 are stored in the column `PropertyValuesString`. Because of the special format this data is stored in, you shouldn't modify this data manually. Instead, you should use the Profile object to change the underlying data.

How It Works

When you define properties for the Profile in web.config, the ASP.NET run time creates a class for you in the background. This class, called `ProfileCommon`, gives you access to the strongly typed properties like `FirstName`, `LastName`, and `FavoriteGenres`. The `ProfileCommon` class is then made accessible to the `Page` through its `Profile` property. `ProfileCommon` inherits from `ProfileBase`, the base class defined in the .NET Framework that contains the behavior to access the Profile in the database by talking to the configured provider. The provider in turn takes care of all the hard work of persisting the data in the configured database. Just as the Membership and Role providers you saw in previous chapters, the Profile provider by default uses the database defined in the `LocalSqlServer` connection string. Appendix B teaches you how to change this behavior and have the provider use a different database.

To define properties you use `<add />` elements with a `name` attribute and an optional `type` if the property is of another type than `System.String`:

```
<add name="FavoriteGenres" type="System.Collections.Generic.List`1[System.Int32]" />
```

This property sets up a list that can store `Integer` values to hold the user's favorite music genres. You'll see how to use this property in a later exercise.

After you have set up the Profile in web.config and the background class has been compiled, you can access the Profile in code. For example, you can now set properties like `FirstName` through code:

VB.NET

```
Profile.FirstName = "Your First Name"
```

C#

```
Profile.FirstName = "Your First Name";
```

Although not used in the previous exercise, you access properties in a group in pretty much the same way. All you need to do is prefix the property name with the group name. Given the example of a `PostalAddress`, you would store the street for that address like this:

VB.NET

```
Profile.PostalAddress.Street = "Some Street"
```

C#

```
Profile.PostalAddress.Street = "Some Street";
```

Changes made to the Profile are saved automatically for you during `EndRequest`, an event that fires very late during the ASP.NET page life cycle. This way, you can change the Profile during many of the stages of the life cycle without having to worry about explicitly saving the Profile manually.

In Figure 16-2 you can see how a single record is used to store the entire profile. The first column contains the unique ID of the user the profile belongs to. The second column contains a list of property names that are saved for the current user, together with a starting index of the value and a length. For example, for the last name you see:

```
LastName:S:0:14
```

This states that the value for the `LastName` property, which is stored in the `PropertyValuesString` column, starts at position zero and has a length of fourteen characters. The letter between the `LastName` and the start index defines the column the data can be found in: `S` means the `PropertyValuesString` column, whereas `B` indicates the `PropertyValuesBinary` column, which is used to store complex objects in a binary format. This dense format enables the Profile provider to store many different properties in a single column, which eliminates the need to mess with the database schema any time the profile changes.

You'll learn more about reading from and writing to the Profile in the following section.

Using the Profile

As you saw in the previous section, writing to the Profile is easy. To change a property like `FirstName`, all you need is a single line of code. The Profile keeps track of the changes you have made to it, and, if necessary, automatically saves the changes during `EndRequest`. Reading from the Profile is just as easy; all you need to do is access one of its properties. The following snippet shows how to fill a `TextBox` with the first name from the profile:

VB.NET

```
txtFirstName.Text = Profile.FirstName
```

C#

```
txtFirstName.Text = Profile.FirstName;
```

Retrieving properties in a group is almost identical. To access the `Street` property discussed in a previous example, you need this code:

VB.NET

```
txtPostalAddressStreet.Text = Profile.PostalAddress.Street
```

C#

```
txtPostalAddressStreet.Text = Profile.PostalAddress.Street;
```

Accessing the `FavoriteGenres` property is slightly different. Since this property is a collection, you shouldn't access it directly. Instead you use its methods and properties to get data in and out. The following example clears the entire list first, and then adds the IDs of two genres to it:

VB.NET

```
Profile.FavoriteGenres.Clear()
Profile.FavoriteGenres.Add(7)
Profile.FavoriteGenres.Add(11)
```

C#

```
Profile.FavoriteGenres.Clear();
Profile.FavoriteGenres.Add(7);
Profile.FavoriteGenres.Add(11);
```

The following exercise shows you how to store basic data in the Profile. You'll see a real-world implementation of using the `FavoriteGenres` list in a later exercise.

Try It Out Storing Basic User Data in the Profile

In this exercise you modify the Profile page so a user can enter her first and last name, birthday, and a short biography.

1. Open MyProfile.aspx again and switch to Code Behind. Remove the two lines of code in `Page_Load` that set the user's first and last name.
2. Switch to Design View and, right above the `ChangePassword` control, add an HTML table of five rows and three columns by choosing Table ➪ Insert Table.
3. In the second column of each of the first four rows, drag `TextBox` controls and rename them, from the first to the last row, `txtFirstName`, `txtLastName`, `txtDateOfBirth`, and `txtBio`. Figure 16-3 shows you where the `TextBox` controls should be placed exactly.
4. In the first column of each of the first four rows, drop `Label` controls and set their properties as follows so each label is associated with a `TextBox` in the same row.

ID	Text	AssociatedControlID
lblFirstName	First Name	txtFirstName
lblLastName	Last Name	txtLastName
lblDateOfBirth	Date of Birth	txtDateOfBirth
lblBio	Biography	txtBio

5. In the second cell of the fifth row, drag a button, set its `ID` to `btnSave` and its `Text` to Save Profile. Design View should look like Figure 16-3.

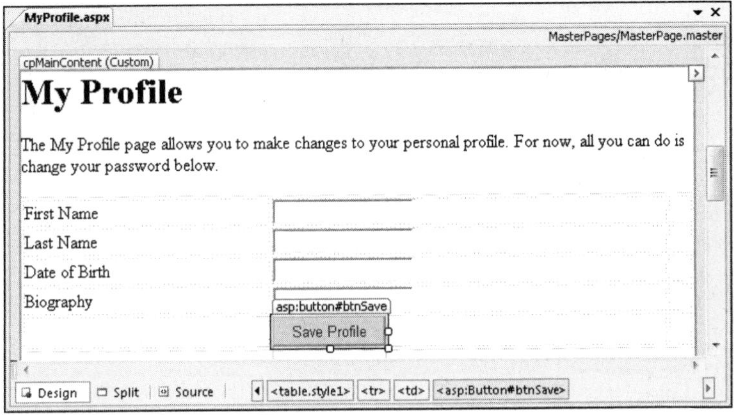

Figure 16-3

6. In the last column of each of the first three rows, drag `RequiredFieldValidator` controls. Set their properties as follows, so each validator lines up with a `TextBox` in the same row:

ControlToValidate	Display	Error Message
`txtFirstName`	`Dynamic`	`First name is required.`
`txtLastName`	`Dynamic`	`Last name is required.`
`txtDateOfBirth`	`Dynamic`	`Date of birth is required.`

7. Next to the validator for the `DateOfBirth` box, drag a `CompareValidator` and set its properties as follows:

Property	Value
`Display`	`Dynamic`
`ErrorMessage`	`Please enter a valid date.`
`ControlToValidate`	`txtDateOfBirth`
`Operator`	`DataTypeCheck`
`Type`	`Date`

8. Set the `TextMode` of the `txtBio` control to `MultiLine` and set its `Width` and `Height` properties to `300px` and `75px`, respectively.

9. Modify the text above the table to indicate that users can now do more than just change their password alone. Design View should look like Figure 16-4.

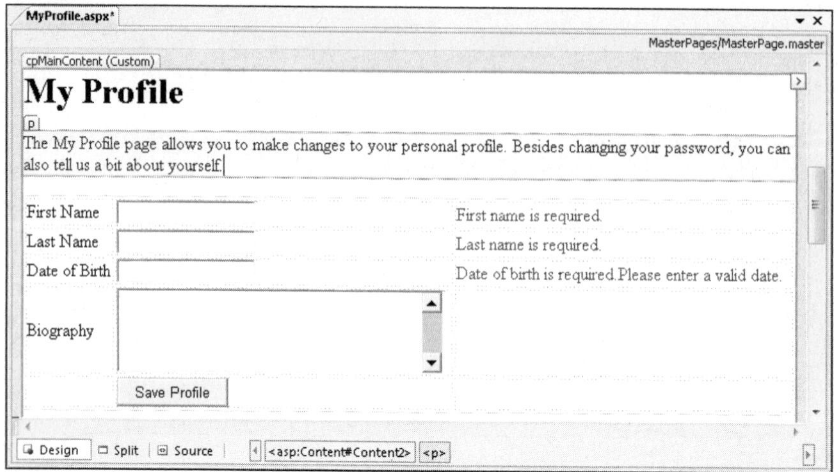

Figure 16-4

10. Double-click the `Button` and in the `Click` event handler that VWD added for you, write the following code:

VB.NET

```
Protected Sub btnSave_Click(ByVal sender As Object, ByVal e As System.EventArgs) _
                     Handles btnSave.Click
  If Page.IsValid Then
    Profile.FirstName = txtFirstName.Text
    Profile.LastName = txtLastName.Text
    Profile.DateOfBirth = DateTime.Parse(txtDateOfBirth.Text)
    Profile.Bio = txtBio.Text
  End If
End Sub
```

C#

```
protected void btnSave_Click(object sender, EventArgs e)
{
  if (Page.IsValid)
  {
    Profile.FirstName = txtFirstName.Text;
    Profile.LastName = txtLastName.Text;
    Profile.DateOfBirth = DateTime.Parse(txtDateOfBirth.Text);
    Profile.Bio = txtBio.Text;
  }
}
```

11. In the `Page_Load` event handler of the same page, add the following code that fills in the text box controls with the data from the profile when the page loads:

VB.NET

```
Protected Sub Page_Load(ByVal sender As Object, ByVal e As System.EventArgs) _
                  Handles Me.Load
  If Not Page.IsPostBack Then
```

```
    txtFirstName.Text = Profile.FirstName
    txtLastName.Text = Profile.LastName
    txtDateOfBirth.Text = Profile.DateOfBirth.ToShortDateString()
    txtBio.Text = Profile.Bio
  End If
End Sub
```

C#

```
protected void Page_Load(object sender, EventArgs e)
{
  if (!Page.IsPostBack)
  {
    txtFirstName.Text = Profile.FirstName;
    txtLastName.Text = Profile.LastName;
    txtDateOfBirth.Text = Profile.DateOfBirth.ToShortDateString();
    txtBio.Text = Profile.Bio;
  }
}
```

12. Save all changes and request the page in the browser. If you're required to log in first, enter your details and click the Login button. You should then see the My Profile page reappear with the data you entered for the first and last names in the previous Try It Out exercise already filled in. Change that data into your details and click the Save Profile button.

13. Close your browser, and then request MyProfile.aspx again. Note that your changes have been persisted between the two browser sessions.

How It Works

Much of what you have seen in this exercise should be familiar by now. The page contains a number of `TextBox` controls that are validated using `RequiredFieldValidator` and `CompareValidator` controls. Additionally, the `Label` controls are hooked up to their respective `TextBox` controls using the `AssociatedControlID` property. This makes it easy to put focus on the controls in the browser because clicking a `Label` now puts the cursor in the associated `TextBox`.

When you click the Save Profile button, the values are retrieved from the four `TextBox` controls and stored in the profile. When the page loads the first time, the reverse of this process takes place: the controls are pre-filled with the values from the Profile. In order to avoid overwriting the data that the user has entered, the code only gets the data from the profile when the page initially loads, and not during a postback:

VB.NET

```
If Not Page.IsPostBack Then
  txtFirstName.Text = Profile.FirstName
  ....
End If
```

C#

```
if (!Page.IsPostBack)
{
  txtFirstName.Text = Profile.FirstName;
  ...
}
```

Although the example itself is pretty trivial, it lays out a nice foundation for a more advanced scenario using the generics `List` of integers to store the user's preference for certain music genres. You can then use this list of favorite genres to limit the list with Reviews to those the user is really interested in. You'll see how to store the user's preference in Profile in the following exercise; a later exercise shows you how to use the saved data again.

Try It Out Storing Genre Preferences in the Profile

In this exercise you learn how to fill the `FavoriteGenres` property of the user profile. In order to let the user choose their favorite genres, you'll display a `CheckBoxList` that is hooked up to a `LinqDataSource` that retrieves the available genres. When the user saves the data, the items that the user checked are then stored in the Profile.

1. In MyProfile.aspx, add a table row above the one with the Save Profile `Button`. To do this, right-click the row with the button and choose Insert ➪ Row Above from the context menu that appears.
2. In the first cell of the new row, drag a `Label` and set its `Text` to Favorite Genres.
3. In the second cell drag a `CheckBoxList` control from the Standard category of the Toolbox.
4. Hook up the control to a new `LinqDataSource` using its Smart Tasks panel. In the Configure Data Source Wizard for the new data source control, choose the PlanetWroxDataContext and then choose the Genres table from the Table drop-down list. In the Select list, check only the items for the `Id` and `Name` columns. Click the OrderBy button, choose Name from the Sort by drop-down list and click OK. Your Configure Data Source dialog box now looks like Figure 16-5.

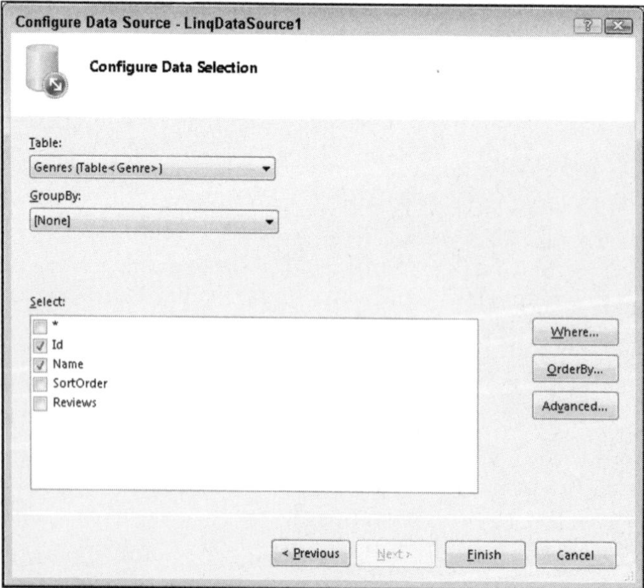

Figure 16-5

5. Click Finish to close the dialog box. Back in the Data Source Configuration Wizard for the `CheckBoxList` control, choose `Name` as the data field to display and keep `Id` as the data field for the value. Both are shown in Figure 16-6.

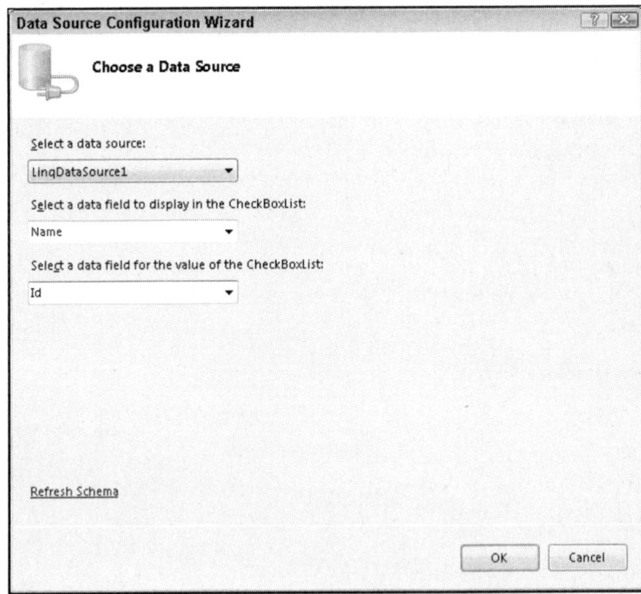

Figure 16-6

The code for the `LinqDataSource` control and the `CheckBoxList` should look as follows:

```
<asp:CheckBoxList ID="CheckBoxList1" runat="server" DataSourceID="LinqDataSource1"
            DataTextField="Name" DataValueField="Id">
</asp:CheckBoxList>
<asp:LinqDataSource ID="LinqDataSource1" runat="server"
                  ContextTypeName="PlanetWroxDataContext" OrderBy="Name"
                  Select="new (Id, Name)" TableName="Genres">
</asp:LinqDataSource>
```

6. In Design View, click the `CheckBoxList` control once, open its Properties Grid, and switch to the Events category. Double-click the `DataBound` event and then add the following code in the Code Behind to pre-select the items in the list based on the user's Profile settings:

VB.NET

```
Protected Sub CheckBoxList1_DataBound(ByVal sender As Object, _
                   ByVal e As System.EventArgs) Handles CheckBoxList1.DataBound
  For Each myItem As ListItem In CheckBoxList1.Items
    Dim currentValue As Integer = Convert.ToInt32(myItem.Value)
    If Profile.FavoriteGenres.Contains(currentValue) Then
      myItem.Selected = True
    End If
  Next
End Sub
```

C#

```
protected void CheckBoxList1_DataBound(object sender, EventArgs e)
{
  foreach (ListItem myItem in CheckBoxList1.Items)
  {
    int currentValue = Convert.ToInt32(myItem.Value);
    if (Profile.FavoriteGenres.Contains(currentValue))
    {
      myItem.Selected = true;
    }
  }
}
```

7. Extend the `btnSave_Click` handler with the following code so it also saves the user's preferred genres:

VB.NET

```
Profile.Bio = txtBio.Text
' Clear the existing list
Profile.FavoriteGenres.Clear()

' Now add the selected items
For Each myItem As ListItem In CheckBoxList1.Items
  If myItem.Selected Then
    Profile.FavoriteGenres.Add(Convert.ToInt32(myItem.Value))
  End If
Next
```

C#

```
Profile.Bio = txtBio.Text;
// Clear the existing list
Profile.FavoriteGenres.Clear();

// Now add the selected items
foreach (ListItem myItem in CheckBoxList1.Items)
{
  if (myItem.Selected)
  {
    Profile.FavoriteGenres.Add(Convert.ToInt32(myItem.Value));
  }
}
```

8. Save all your changes, request the Profile page in your browser, and log in when required. You should see the list of genres displayed in the browser, each one preceded by a check box. Select a couple of your favorite genres and then click the Save Profile button. Browse to another page and then choose My Profile again from the main `Menu` or `TreeView`. The genres you selected should still be selected in the page, as shown in Figure 16-7.

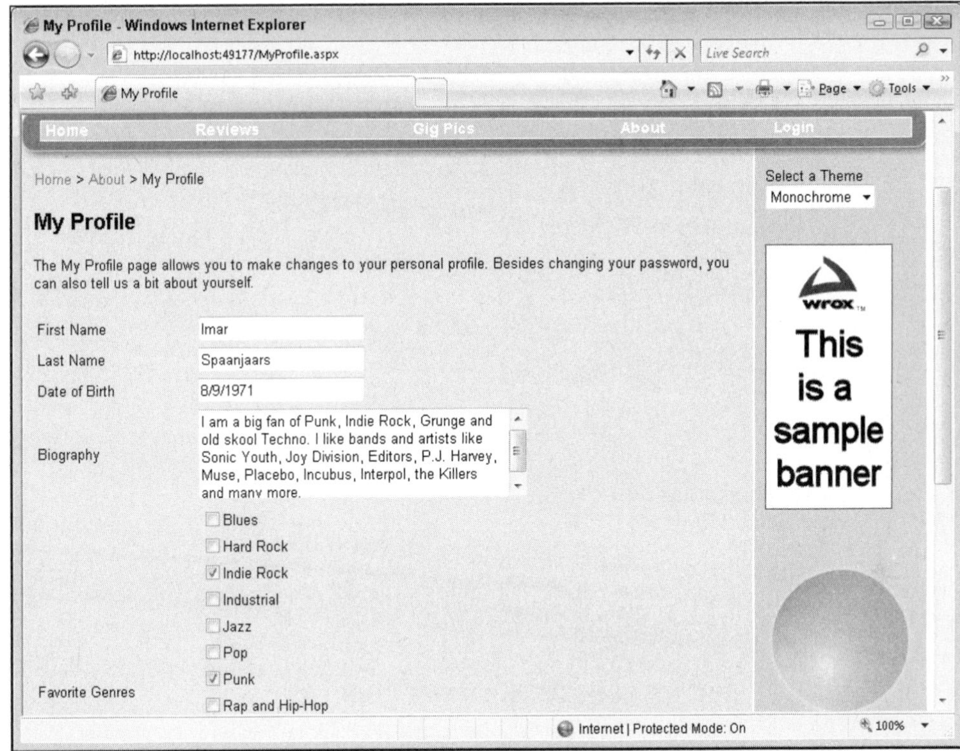

Figure 16-7

How It Works

Earlier you defined the `FavoriteGenres` property in the Profile as a generic list that can hold integer values. Because this property is a `List`, you do not assign values to it directly; instead, you use its methods like `Add` and `Clear` to add and remove items. Because each genre ID should only be stored in the list once, the list is cleared before the selected items are added again when the user presses the Save Profile button:

VB.NET

```
Profile.FavoriteGenres.Clear()
```

C#

```
Profile.FavoriteGenres.Clear();
```

Then when the list is empty, the IDs of the selected genres are added:

VB.NET

```
For Each myItem As ListItem In CheckBoxList1.Items
  If myItem.Selected Then
    Profile.FavoriteGenres.Add(Convert.ToInt32(myItem.Value))
  End If
Next
```

C#

```
foreach (ListItem myItem in CheckBoxList1.Items)
{
  if (myItem.Selected)
  {
    Profile.FavoriteGenres.Add(Convert.ToInt32(myItem.Value));
  }
}
```

This code loops through all the items in the `CheckBoxList`. The `Selected` property determines whether the user has selected the item in the Profile page. If it has been selected, the value of the genre is retrieved, converted to an `Integer` (an `int` in C#), and then added to the `FavoriteGenres` list using the `Add` method.

That's really all you need to store complex data like a list of favorite genres in the users' Profile. All you need to do is add a bunch of numbers to a list. The .NET run time then takes care of persisting the Profile in the database and making it available again in subsequent pages.

Of course, the list with favorite genres isn't really useful until you actually make use of it in the site. In the next exercise you see how to use the list to limit the list of `Reviews` that users initially see when they visit the default Reviews page.

Try It Out Using the Profile in the Reviews Page

Currently your site has two pages in the Reviews folder that are capable of displaying reviews: AllByGenre.aspx and All.aspx. In this exercise, you modify the page Default.aspx so it displays yet another list of reviews. However, this time the list with reviews is limited to those belonging to the genres that the user has selected in the My Profile page. When anonymous users see the page, they get a message that they haven't set their favorite genres yet.

1. Open Default.aspx from the Reviews folder in Markup View.
2. Add the following code that creates a nested `Repeater`:

```
<asp:Content ID="Content2" ContentPlaceHolderID="cpMainContent" Runat="Server">
  <asp:Repeater ID="Repeater1" runat="server">
    <HeaderTemplate>
      <p>Below you find a list with Reviews for your favorite music genres.</p>
    </HeaderTemplate>
    <ItemTemplate>
      <h3><asp:Literal ID="Literal1" runat="server"
                Text='<%# Eval("Name") %>'></asp:Literal></h3>
      <asp:Repeater ID="Repeater2" runat="server" DataSource='<%# Eval("Reviews")%>'>
        <ItemTemplate>
          <asp:HyperLink ID="HyperLink1" runat="server" Text='<%# Eval("Title") %>'
               NavigateUrl='<%# "ViewDetails.aspx?ReviewId=" + Eval("Id").ToString() %>'>
          </asp:HyperLink><br />
```

```
      </ItemTemplate>
    </asp:Repeater>
  </ItemTemplate>
</asp:Repeater>
<asp:PlaceHolder ID="plcNoRecords" runat="Server" Visible="False">
  <p>Sorry, no Reviews were found. You either didn't set your favorite genres
       or you may need to log in first. </p>
</asp:PlaceHolder>
<p>You can change your genre preferences <a href="~/MyProfile.aspx"
              runat="server">here</a>.</p>
</asp:Content>
```

You can create the `Repeater` controls manually by writing the necessary code, or you can drag and drop them from the Data category of the Toolbox. The inner `Repeater` contains a `HyperLink` control that points to the ViewDetails.aspx page that you created in Chapter 14.

3. Double-click the page in Design View to set up a `Load` handler and add the following code:

VB.NET

```
Protected Sub Page_Load(ByVal sender As Object, ByVal e As System.EventArgs) _
                Handles Me.Load
  Using myDatabaseContext As PlanetWroxDataContext = New PlanetWroxDataContext()

    Dim favGenres = From genre In myDatabaseContext.Genres _
                    Order By genre.Name _
                    Where Profile.FavoriteGenres.Contains(genre.Id) _
                    Select New With {genre.Name, genre.Reviews}

    Repeater1.DataSource = favGenres
    Repeater1.DataBind()

    Repeater1.Visible = Repeater1.Items.Count > 0
    plcNoRecords.Visible = Repeater1.Items.Count = 0
  End Using
End Sub
```

C#

```
protected void Page_Load(object sender, EventArgs e)
{
  using (PlanetWroxDataContext myDatabaseContext = new PlanetWroxDataContext())
  {
    var favGenres = from genre in myDatabaseContext.Genres
                    orderby genre.Name
                    where Profile.FavoriteGenres.Contains(genre.Id)
                    select new { genre.Name, genre.Reviews };
    Repeater1.DataSource = favGenres;
    Repeater1.DataBind();

    Repeater1.Visible = Repeater1.Items.Count > 0;
    plcNoRecords.Visible = Repeater1.Items.Count == 0;
  }
}
```

4. Save all your changes and then request the page in the browser. If you selected one or more genres in the Profile page previously, and there are reviews available for those genres, you should see a list similar to Figure 16-8.

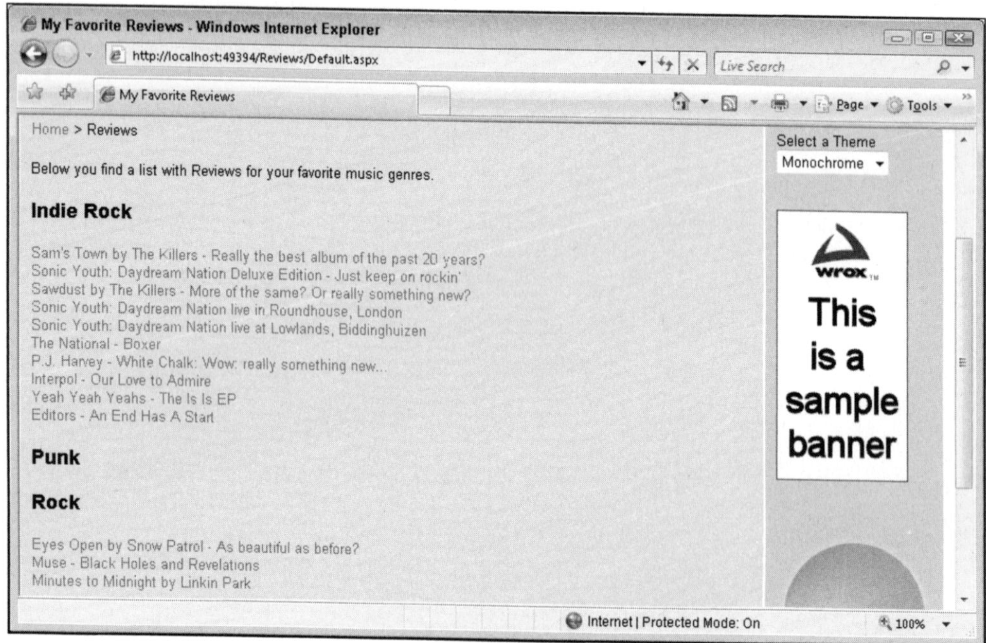

Figure 16-8

If you haven't set any preferred genres, or none of them contain any reviews or you're not logged in, you get the message shown in Figure 16-9.

By clicking the link in the message you are taken to the My Profile page so you can set or change your preferred genres. Unauthorized users will be asked to log in or sign up for an account before they can access the Profile page.

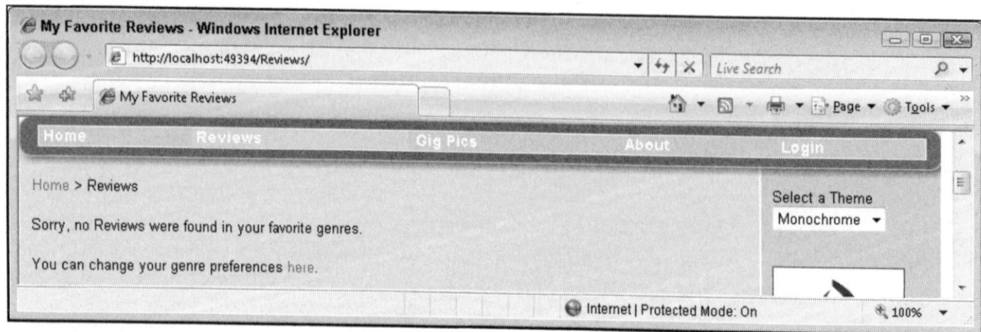

Figure 16-9

How It Works

The code in the Code Behind executes a LINQ query that retrieves all the reviews that belong to the user's favorite genres. For anonymous users, the list of favorite genres will be empty so they always get to see the message about setting their preferences in the Profile page.

The nested `Repeater` you added to the Default.aspx page in the Reviews folder looks similar to the code for the AllByGenre.aspx page that has a `Repeater` that contains a `BulletedList` control. Just as in that page, the nested `Repeater` gets its data from the outer `Repeater` with the `DataSource` attribute:

```
<asp:Repeater ID="Repeater2" runat="server" DataSource='<%# Eval("Reviews")%>'>
  ...
</asp:Repeater>
```

The nested `Repeater` then uses the list of `Reviews` to build up the hyperlinks that take you to the details page:

```
<asp:HyperLink ID="HyperLink1" runat="server" Text='<%# Eval("Title") %>'
          NavigateUrl='<%# "ViewDetails.aspx?ReviewId=" + Eval("Id").ToString() %>'>
</asp:HyperLink><br />
```

The `HyperLink` control gets its `Text` from the `Review` instance that it's bound to and uses its `Id` to build up the `NavigateUrl`. The `ToString` method is used on `Eval("Id")` to convert the value to a string before it's concatenated to the string that contains the URL. This is done to avoid type conversions in Visual Basic where `Eval("Id")` normally results in a number that you can't concatenate to a string directly.

To see how these controls get their data, you need to look at the Code Behind that uses a LINQ query:

VB.NET

```
Dim favGenres = From genre In myDatabaseContext.Genres _
                Order By genre.Name _
                Where Profile.FavoriteGenres.Contains(genre.Id) _
                Select New With {genre.Name, genre.Reviews}
```

C#

```
var favGenres = from genre in myDatabaseContext.Genres
                orderby genre.Name
                where Profile.FavoriteGenres.Contains(genre.Id)
                select new { genre.Name, genre.Reviews };
```

Except for the highlighted line of code and the variable name, this LINQ query is identical to the one used in AllByGenre.aspx. What makes this example special is the `where` clause that limits the number of reviews to those that the user is really interested in. Note how the `Contains` method of the generic `List` class is used here. Although at first it may seem that all genres and reviews are retrieved from the database into the ASPX page and then compared with the values in the `Profile` property, the reverse is actually the case. The LINQ engine is smart enough to collect all the IDs from the `FavoriteGenres` property first and then include them in the SQL statement that is sent to the database to fetch the requested genres and reviews. This means that filtering of the requested genres takes place at the database level, and not in the ASPX page. This in turn means that fewer records are transferred from the database to the ASPX page (only those that are really needed), which results in a better performance.

The Profile property FavoriteGenres returns an empty list, rather than throwing an exception for anonymous users. So, even users with no Profile can safely view this page. Instead of seeing any reviews, they get a message stating they haven't set their genre preferences yet, or that they need to log in first.

In the end of the Page_Load handler, some code determines whether to show or hide the Repeater and the No Results Label:

VB.NET

```
Repeater1.Visible = Repeater1.Items.Count > 0
plcNoRecords.Visible = Repeater1.Items.Count = 0
```

C#

```
Repeater1.Visible = Repeater1.Items.Count > 0;
plcNoRecords.Visible = Repeater1.Items.Count == 0;
```

If after data binding the outer Repeater the Items collection is still empty, it means no genres were found for the current user. If that's the case, the entire Repeater is hidden and the PlaceHolder is shown. However, if the Count property of the Items collection is larger than zero, the Repeater is made visible and the PlaceHolder is hidden.

In Chapter 13 you created a page called NewPhotoAlbum.aspx that lets users insert a new Gig Pics album. There are a few shortcomings with the current implementation of this page. First of all, anyone can insert a new album. There's no way to block anonymous users from creating a new album and uploading pictures.

Secondly, there is no easy way to add or remove pictures from an existing photo album. This also applies to the Managers of your site. So, even if someone uploads inappropriate pictures, there is no easy way for you to delete them. Now that you know more about security, this is pretty easy to implement, as you'll see in the following exercise.

Try It Out — Letting Users Manage Their Own Photo Albums

In this exercise you see how to block the NewPhotoAlbum.aspx and ManagePhotoAlbum.aspx pages from unauthenticated users. Additionally, you see how to record the name of the user that created the photo album and use that name later on to allow users to alter their own photo albums.

1. Open the Database Explorer, expand the PlanetWrox database and then locate the PhotoAlbum table. Right-click it and choose Open Table Definition. Add a new column called UserName, set its data type to nvarchar(256), and leave the Allow Nulls option selected. (There are already photo albums in this table without a valid UserName, so you can't make the column required at this stage unless you delete these photo albums and their related pictures from the database first.) Save the changes and close the table.
2. Open the LINQ to SQL Classes file PlanetWrox.dbml from the App_Code folder, right-click the PhotoAlbum class in the diagram and choose Delete. Next, from the Database Explorer, drag the PhotoAlbum table on the diagram again. By deleting and adding the table, the UserName column in the database now shows up as a property of the PhotoAlbum class (see Figure 16-10).
3. Save your changes and close the DBML file.

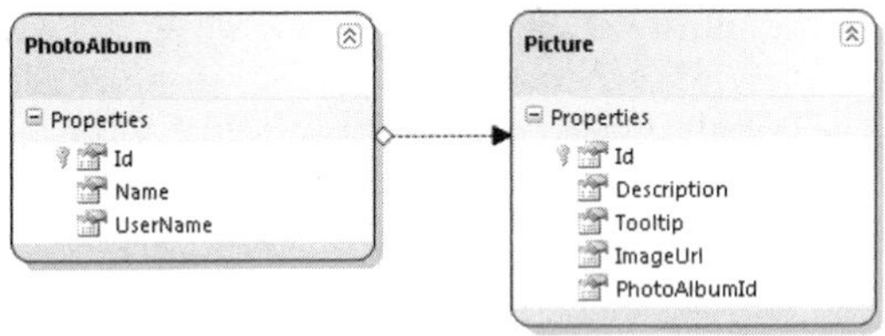

Figure 16-10

4. Open the web.config file and add the following two `<location>` elements to block access to the two referenced files for anonymous users:

```
    </location>
    <location path="ManagePhotoAlbum.aspx">
      <system.web>
        <authorization>
          <deny users="?"/>
        </authorization>
      </system.web>
    </location>
    <location path="NewPhotoAlbum.aspx">
      <system.web>
        <authorization>
          <deny users="?"/>
        </authorization>
      </system.web>
    </location>
  </configuration>
```

5. Save your changes and then close the web.config file.

6. Open NewPhotoAlbum.aspx in Design View, locate the `LinqDataSource` control, and set up an event handler for its `Inserting` event. Add the following code to the handler that VWD created for you:

VB.NET

```
Protected Sub LinqDataSource1_Inserting(ByVal sender As Object, _
             ByVal e As System.Web.UI.WebControls.LinqDataSourceInsertEventArgs) _
             Handles LinqDataSource1.Inserting
  Dim myPhotoAlbum As PhotoAlbum = CType(e.NewObject, PhotoAlbum)
  myPhotoAlbum.UserName = User.Identity.Name
End Sub
```

C#

```
protected void LinqDataSource1_Inserting(object sender, LinqDataSourceInsertEventArgs e)
{
  PhotoAlbum myPhotoAlbum = (PhotoAlbum)e.NewObject;
  myPhotoAlbum.UserName = User.Identity.Name;
}
```

7. Open Default.aspx from the PhotoAlbums folder in Markup View. Scroll all the way down to the bottom of the file and, right before the closing `</ContentTemplate>` tag of the AJAX `UpdatePanel`, drag a `HyperLink` control. Between its opening and closing tags put the text Edit Photo Album. Put two `<br />` elements in front of the `HyperLink` to create some room:

```
 <br /><br /><asp:HyperLink ID="HyperLink1" runat="server">Edit Photo Album</asp:HyperLink>
</ContentTemplate>
```

8. Switch to Design View, select the `ListView` control, and then set up a handler for its `DataBound` event that fires when the control is done with data binding. Complete the event handler with the following code:

VB.NET

```
Protected Sub ListView1_DataBound(ByVal sender As Object, ByVal e As System.EventArgs) _
                    Handles ListView1.DataBound
  Dim photoAlbumId As Integer = Convert.ToInt32(DropDownList1.SelectedValue)
  Using myDatabaseContext As PlanetWroxDataContext = New PlanetWroxDataContext()

    Dim photoAlbumOwner As String = (From p In myDatabaseContext.PhotoAlbums _
                                Where p.Id = photoAlbumId _
                                Select p.UserName).Single()

    If User.Identity.IsAuthenticated And (User.Identity.Name = photoAlbumOwner Or _
                User.IsInRole("Managers")) Then
      HyperLink1.Visible = True
      HyperLink1.NavigateUrl = "~/ManagePhotoAlbum.aspx?PhotoAlbumId=" & _
                  photoAlbumId.ToString()
    Else
      HyperLink1.Visible = False
    End If
  End Using
End Sub
```

C#

```
protected void ListView1_DataBound(object sender, EventArgs e)
{
  int photoAlbumId = Convert.ToInt32(DropDownList1.SelectedValue);
  using (PlanetWroxDataContext myDatabaseContext = new PlanetWroxDataContext())
  {
    string photoAlbumOwner = (from p in myDatabaseContext.PhotoAlbums
                          where p.Id == photoAlbumId
                          select p.UserName).Single();

    if (User.Identity.IsAuthenticated &&
              (User.Identity.Name == photoAlbumOwner || User.IsInRole("Managers")))
    {
      HyperLink1.Visible = true;
      HyperLink1.NavigateUrl = "~/ManagePhotoAlbum.aspx?PhotoAlbumId=" +
                          photoAlbumId.ToString();
```

```
    }
    else
    {
      HyperLink1.Visible = false;
    }
  }
}
```

9. Open the Code Behind of ManagePhotoAlbum.aspx. Add the following code to a `Page_Load` handler. If the handler isn't there yet, double-click the page in Design View to have VWD set one up for you.

VB.NET

```
Protected Sub Page_Load(ByVal sender As Object, ByVal e As System.EventArgs) _
          Handles Me.Load
  Dim photoAlbumId As Integer = Convert.ToInt32(Request.QueryString.Get("PhotoAlbumId"))

  Using myDatabaseContext As PlanetWroxDataContext = New PlanetWroxDataContext()
    Dim photoAlbumOwner As String = (From p In myDatabaseContext.PhotoAlbums _
                                    Where p.Id = photoAlbumId _
                                    Select p.UserName).Single()

    If User.Identity.Name <> photoAlbumOwner And Not User.IsInRole("Managers") Then
      Response.Redirect("~/")
    End If
  End Using
End Sub
```

C#

```
protected void Page_Load(object sender, EventArgs e)
{
  int photoAlbumId = Convert.ToInt32(Request.QueryString.Get("PhotoAlbumId"));

  using (PlanetWroxDataContext myDatabaseContext = new PlanetWroxDataContext())
  {
    string photoAlbumOwner = (from p in myDatabaseContext.PhotoAlbums
                              where p.Id == photoAlbumId
                              select p.UserName).Single();
    if (User.Identity.Name != photoAlbumOwner && !User.IsInRole("Managers"))
    {
      Response.Redirect("~/");
    }
  }
}
```

10. Save the changes to all open files (press Ctrl+Shift+S) and then request NewPhotoAlbum.aspx in your browser. If necessary, log in with an account you created earlier.

11. Enter a new name for the photo album and click Insert. At this stage, the photo album is saved, together with your user name. Proceed by adding a few images to your photo album.

12. Click Gig Pics from the main `Menu` or `TreeView` and then choose the new photo album you just created from the drop-down list. After the page has reloaded, your new photo album should be displayed, together with an Edit Photo Album link at the bottom of the screen. Clicking the link takes you to the ManagePhotoAlbum.aspx page that lets you add or remove pictures in your photo album.

13. Click the Logout link in the footer of the page. Then go to the Gig Pics page again and choose your new photo album from the drop-down list. Note that the Edit Photo Album link is now no longer visible.

How It Works

You started this exercise by adding a column for the user's name to the `PhotoAlbum` table. With this column, you can keep track of the user that created the photo album, giving you the opportunity to display data related to the user together with a photo album. Although you could manually add the `UserName` to the LINQ to SQL Classes file, it's often much easier to simply recreate the entire class as you did in this exercise. Whether this pays off, depends on the actual file you're working with. If you already made customizations (for example, renamed tables, relations, and so on) you're better off setting up the new property manually using the LINQ to SQL Classes designer surface.

In the New Photo Album page, you access the name of the current user with this code:

VB.NET

```
myPhotoAlbum.UserName = User.Identity.Name
```

C#

```
myPhotoAlbum.UserName = User.Identity.Name;
```

The `Page` class has a `User` property that represents the user associated with the current request. This user in turn has an `Identity` that in turn contains the user's `Name`. The `Name` is then assigned to the `UserName` property of the `PhotoAlbum` instance, which is retrieved from `e.NewObject`.

At this stage, the name is successfully stored in the database, together with the rest of the photo album. What's left is doing something useful with this name. The first place where you use this name is in the default page of the PhotoAlbums folder. There you used the following LINQ query to retrieve the `UserName` for a photo album:

VB.NET

```
    Dim photoAlbumOwner As String = (From p In myDatabaseContext.PhotoAlbums _
                                     Where p.Id = photoAlbumId _
                                     Select p.UserName).Single()
```

C#

```
    string photoAlbumOwner = (from p in myDatabaseContext.PhotoAlbums
                              where p.Id == photoAlbumId
                              select p.UserName).Single();
```

This code uses the `Single` method to retrieve the `UserName` for a single photo album; the one specified in `photoAlbumId`. The remainder of the code then determines the visibility of the Edit link if the current user is logged in and an owner of the photo album or a member of the Managers group. This way, both owners and all Managers can change existing photo albums.

The code in ManagePhotoAlbum.aspx performs a similar check to stop unauthorized users from accessing the page directly.

Other Ways of Dealing with Profile

In the final section of this chapter you see two other useful ways of dealing with the Profile feature in ASP.NET. First, you see how to use the Profile for anonymous users followed by a discussion on accessing the profile of a user other than the current user.

Anonymous Identification

The Profile feature is extremely easy to configure, yet very powerful. All you need to do to give logged-in users access to their profiles is create a few elements in web.config and the ASP.NET run time takes care of the rest. But what about anonymous users? What if you wanted to store data for your visitors who haven't signed up for an account or aren't logged in yet? For those users you need to enable *anonymous identification*. With anonymous identification, ASP.NET creates an anonymous user in the `aspnet_Users` table for every new visitor to your site. This user then gets a cookie that is linked to the anonymous user account in the database. On every visit, the browser sends the cookie with the request, enabling ASP.NET to associate a user, and thus a Profile, with the user for the current request.

To enable an anonymous profile, you need to do two things: turn on anonymous identification, and modify some or all profile properties to expose them to anonymous users.

Enabling anonymous identification is easy with the following element in web.config, directly under `<system.web>`:

```
<anonymousIdentification enabled="true" cookieName="PlanetWroxAnonymous" />
```

The `enabled` attribute turns on the feature, while the `cookieName` attribute is used to give the application a unique cookie name.

After you have turned anonymous identification on, the next step involves modifying properties under the `<profile>` element and setting their `allowAnonymous` attribute to `True`:

```
<add name="FavoriteGenres" type="System.Collections.Generic.List`1[System.Int32]"
            allowAnonymous="true" />
```

This Profile property can now be accessed through code for anonymous users as well. If you try to set a Profile property without the `allowAnonymous` attribute set to `True` for a user that is not logged on, you'll get an error. Reading from a property without this attribute set works fine as you saw in the Try It Out exercise "Using the Profile in the Reviews Page."

Once you have enabled Profile properties for anonymous users, reading from and writing to them is identical to how you deal with normal Profile properties. In the "Exercises" section at the end of this chapter, you find code to modify the current theme selector so it uses Profile for anonymous and logged in users.

Cleaning Up Old Anonymous Profiles

You may wonder what is happening with an anonymous user's profile when the associated user signs up for an account and becomes a registered user. The answer is: nothing. The old profile is discarded and the user gets a new profile that is associated with the registered account. This means that your `aspnet_Users` table can become quite large with old and unused anonymous user accounts. Fortunately, this is easy to fix. Whenever a user changes from an anonymous to an authenticated user (that is, when they log in), ASP.NET fires the `Profile_OnMigrateAnonymous` event that you can handle. You handle this event in a special file called Global.asax that is used for code that handles application or session-wide events. Inside an event handler for this event you can access two profiles for the same user: the old, anonymous profile that is about to get detached from the user and the new profile that is associated with the user who is currently logging in. You can then delete the old user account and its related profile data as you can deal with the new profile from now on. Although not used in the Planet Wrox web site, this event handler is also a perfect place to copy anonymous profile data from the old profile to the new one, as demonstrated by the following code:

VB.NET

```
Public Sub Profile_OnMigrateAnonymous(sender As Object, args As ProfileMigrateEventArgs)
  Dim anonymousProfile As ProfileCommon = Profile.GetProfile(args.AnonymousID)

  ' Copy over anonymous properties only
  Profile.AnonymousProperty = anonymousProfile.AnonymousProperty

  ProfileManager.DeleteProfile(args.AnonymousID)
  AnonymousIdentificationModule.ClearAnonymousIdentifier()
  Membership.DeleteUser(args.AnonymousID, True)
End Sub
```

C#

```
public void Profile_OnMigrateAnonymous(object sender, ProfileMigrateEventArgs args)
{
  ProfileCommon anonymousProfile = Profile.GetProfile(args.AnonymousID);

  // Copy over anonymous properties only
  Profile.AnonymousProperty = anonymousProfile.AnonymousProperty;

  ProfileManager.DeleteProfile(args.AnonymousID);
  AnonymousIdentificationModule.ClearAnonymousIdentifier();
  Membership.DeleteUser(args.AnonymousID, true);
}
```

Note that this code uses `Profile.GetProfile(args.AnonymousID)` to get an instance of the previous, anonymous profile of the user. This gets a reference to the profile of the user before she logged in.

The code then continues to copy over the existing, *anonymous* profile properties from the old to the new profile. In this example, only one property, called `AnonymousProperty` is copied. However, you can modify the code to copy more properties. Note that there is no point in copying over properties that are not accessible by anonymous users. Those types of properties cannot have been set previously, so there's nothing to copy.

The final three lines of code then delete the old profile, clear the anonymous user ID from the cookie and, finally, delete the old, anonymous user account from the database. When this code has finished, the old profile is migrated successfully to the new profile, and all the old profile stuff has been successfully deleted from the database and the user's cookies.

The `ProfileManager` class, that lives in the `System.Web.Profile` namespace that you need to import for the previous example to work, provides you with more useful methods to work with Profile. For example, you can use `DeleteInactiveProfiles` to delete profiles for users that have been inactive for a certain amount of time.

Looking at Other Users' Profiles

The examples you have seen so far use the Profile to access data for the *current* user. However, what if you need to display data for a different user? For example, what if you wanted to display a user's biography below a Gig Pics album? You won't be able to use the `Profile` property of the `Page` class in this case directly as it provides information about the current user, not about the user that created the photo album.

To solve this problem, the `ProfileCommon` class, the base class of the `Profile` property of the `Page` class, comes with a `GetProfile` method. The `GetProfile` method retrieves an existing Profile from the database if the name passed to it exists, or it creates a brand new profile if it doesn't exist yet. For example, to get the Manager's profile you can use this code:

VB.NET

```
Dim theProfile As ProfileCommon = Profile.GetProfile("Manager")
```

C#

```
ProfileCommon theProfile = Profile.GetProfile("Manager");
```

With the profile instance created, you can access its properties as you are used to. The following code assigns the `Bio` property of the Manager to the `Text` property of a `Label` control:

VB.NET

```
lblBio.Text = theProfile.Bio
```

C#

```
lblBio.Text = theProfile.Bio;
```

Being able to read someone else's profile is extremely useful. You can use it to show some of the properties of the Profile to other users, as you'll see in the last exercise of this chapter. However, you can also use similar code to update other users' profiles. For example, you could create a page in the Management section that allowed you to manage the profiles of the users that registered at your site. When you do modify other users' profiles, be sure to call the `Save` method when you're done. As you learned earlier, changes to the Profile are persisted in the database automatically. However, this only applies to the Profile of the current user. To change and persist the previously retrieved Manager's Profile, you can use this code:

VB.NET

```
theProfile.Bio = "New Bio for the Manager account here"
theProfile.Save()
```

C#

```
theProfile.Bio = "New Bio for the Manager account here";
theProfile.Save();
```

You'll see how to make use of this in the final exercise in this chapter.

In the following exercise you will put some of this in practice when you show the name of the user who created a specific photo album, together with its biography.

Try It Out Looking at Other Users' Profiles

The Default.aspx page in the PhotoAlbums folder currently displays the pictures in a specific photo album. You can't see which user created the photo album, so that would be a nice addition to the page. And to further improve the page, you can also display the user's biography together with the page.

1. Open the page Default.aspx from the PhotoAlbums folder again in Markup View. Scroll all the way down to the end of the file and locate the two breaks and the `HyperLink` you added in the previous exercise. Just before the breaks and the `HyperLink` control, drag a `PlaceHolder` control from the Toolbox. Inside this `PlaceHolder` drag two `Label` controls and then manually modify the code so it ends up like this:

```
    <asp:PlaceHolder ID="plcPhotoAlbumDetails" runat="server">
      <h2>Photo Album Details</h2>
      Created by: <asp:Label ID="lblUserName" runat="server" Text=""></asp:Label><br />
      About this user: <asp:Label ID="lblBio" runat="server" Text=""></asp:Label>
    </asp:PlaceHolder>
  <br /><br />
  <asp:HyperLink ID="HyperLink1" runat="server">Edit Photo Album</asp:HyperLink>
</ContentTemplate>
```

2. Switch to the Code Behind of the page and locate the `DataBound` event handler for the `ListView` control. Right after the `Else` (`else` in C#) block that hides the `HyperLink` control, add these lines of code that retrieve the profile for the user that created the photo album and then update the relevant labels:

VB.NET

```
    HyperLink1.Visible = False
  End If

  ' Display user's details
  If Not String.IsNullOrEmpty(photoAlbumOwner) Then
    Dim ownerProfile As ProfileCommon = Profile.GetProfile(photoAlbumOwner)
    lblUserName.Text = photoAlbumOwner
    lblBio.Text = ownerProfile.Bio
    plcPhotoAlbumDetails.Visible = True
  Else
    plcPhotoAlbumDetails.Visible = False
  End If
```

C#

```
    HyperLink1.Visible = false;
  }

  // Display user's details
  if (!string.IsNullOrEmpty(photoAlbumOwner))
  {
    ProfileCommon ownerProfile = Profile.GetProfile(photoAlbumOwner);
    lblUserName.Text = photoAlbumOwner;
    lblBio.Text = ownerProfile.Bio;
    plcPhotoAlbumDetails.Visible = true;
  }
  else
  {
    plcPhotoAlbumDetails.Visible = false;
  }
```

3. Save all your changes and then open Default.aspx from the PhotoAlbums folder in your browser.

4. From the drop-down list, choose a photo album you created and you should see the photo album details appear. If you don't see them, make sure you selected a recent photo album from the list. Because you added the `UserName` column to the database at a later stage, some of the photo albums don't have a user associated with them. If the Photo Album Details section remains hidden, create a new photo album and add one or more pictures to it. This ensures you have at least one photo album set with the `UserName` property. If you now select the photo album from the list, you should see the Photo Album Details, as displayed in Figure 16-11.

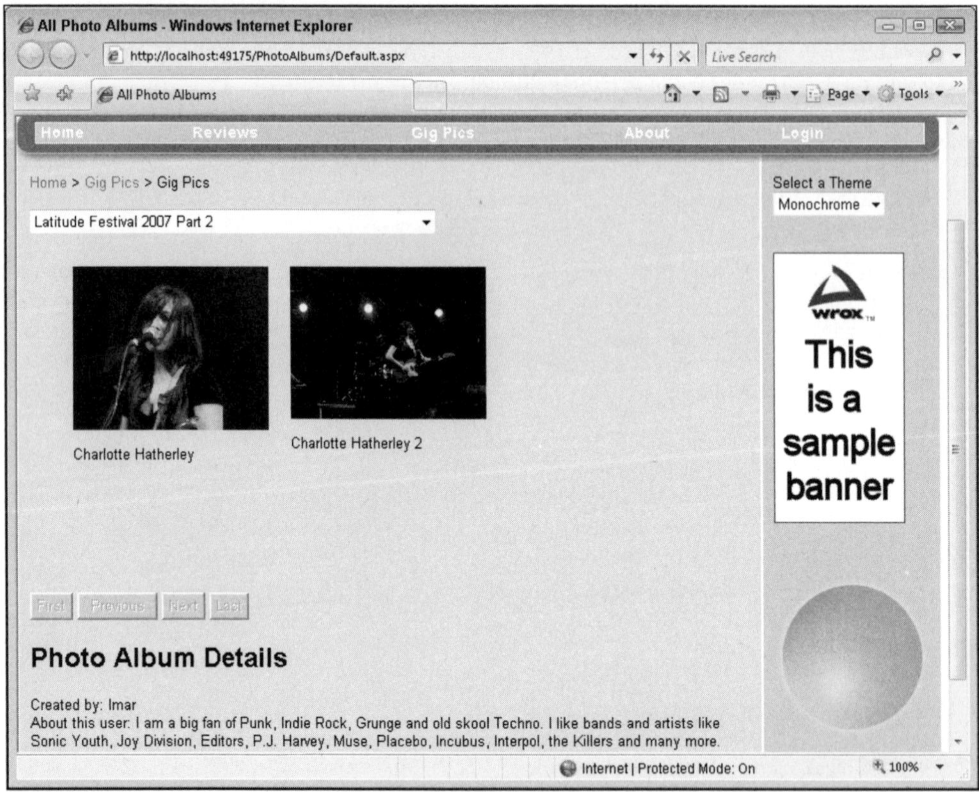

Figure 16-11

How It Works

Much of the code in this exercise has been discussed before. After adding a few `Label` controls in the Photo Album page, you retrieved the profile for the owner of the album with this code:

VB.NET

```
Dim ownerProfile As ProfileCommon = Profile.GetProfile(photoAlbumOwner)
```

C#

```
ProfileCommon ownerProfile = Profile.GetProfile(photoAlbumOwner);
```

This code gets a reference to an existing profile using `GetProfile`. The class that is returned is of type `ProfileCommon`; the underlying data type of the `Profile` property. When you have the reference, working with it is almost identical to working with normal profiles. The only difference is that you must call `Save` to persist any changes made to the Profile in the database as you saw earlier.

Practical Personalization Tips

The following list provides some personalization tips.

- Don't try to access the Profile in the Login page, as it isn't available yet. The Profile is instantiated early in the page's life cycle, so when a `Login` control authenticates you in a Login page, it's too late to associate the user's Profile with the current request. Use the `GetProfile` method of `ProfileCommon` instead or redirect to another page.
- Carefully consider what to store in Profile and what is better stored in your own database tables. Although the single-record structure that ASP.NET uses to store your profile offers you a quick and convenient solution, it's not the most efficient solution, especially not with large amounts of data. Don't try to store complete reviews or even photo albums in Profile, but use your own database tables instead.
- The current implementation of Profile makes it difficult to query data from the `aspnet_Profile` database in your own queries. For example, it's difficult to answer queries like: "Give me all users that prefer the Rock genre" because all the data is stored in a single column. To work around these issues, you can use a different Profile provider that you can download from the Sandbox section of the official ASP.NET web site: `www.asp.net/downloads/sandbox/`.

Summary

In this chapter you learned how to use the Profile feature that ships with ASP.NET 3.5 to store user related data. You can use Profile to keep track of data for authenticated but also for anonymous users.

Setting up a profile is a pretty straightforward operation. You need to create a `<profile>` element in the web.config file with a `<properties>` child element and then add one or more properties using `<add />` elements. To group related properties you use the `<group>` element.

When you set up the profile, you access its properties through the `Profile` property of the `Page` class. This always accesses the profile for the current user. Any changes you make to this profile are persisted for you automatically at the end of the ASP.NET life cycle.

By design, Profile properties are only accessible to logged-in users. However, you can easily change this by turning on anonymous identification.

To access the Profile of a user other than the one associated with the current request, you can use the `GetProfile` method. Any changes made to this profile are not persisted automatically, so you must call `Save` to send the changes to the database.

Now that your pages contain more and more code, chances are that bugs and problems will creep into your application. In the following chapter you learn how to use exception handling to avoid those problems from ending up in the user interface. You also learn how to debug your code, so you can fix problems before they occur.

Exercises

1. The favorite theme feature you created earlier would be a great candidate for a `Profile` property. What property would you need to add to the profile in web.config to make this possible?

2. To set the favorite theme in the `BasePage`, you need to access the Profile in a special way. Instead of accessing the profile on the `Page` class, you access it through the `HttpContext` like this:

VB.NET

```
Dim myProfile As ProfileCommon = CType(HttpContext.Current.Profile, ProfileCommon)
```

C#

```
ProfileCommon myProfile = (ProfileCommon) HttpContext.Current.Profile;
```

Given this code, how can you rewrite `Page_PreInit` so it gets the preferred theme from the Profile instead of from the cookie?

3. What else do you need to change to finalize storing the theme in Profile instead of a custom cookie?

17

Exception Handling, Debugging, and Tracing

You can't make an omelet without breaking eggs and you cannot write code without creating bugs. No matter how hard you try and how good you are, your code will contain problems that affect the behavior of your web site.

Of course you should strive to minimize the impact of these bugs, aiming for a "zero bug count." To aid you in this, the ASP.NET run time and Visual Web Developer provide you with a number of tools.

First of all, the languages supported by .NET implement *exception handling*, a methodology to identify and handle errors that occur at run time. By handling these errors, you can present your users a friendly error message. At the same time you can log these errors, giving you a chance to fix them before they reoccur. In this chapter you see how exception handling works, and how to log your errors by e-mail.

Before your code goes into production you need to write and debug it first. To help you debug your code, VWD comes with a rich toolset that includes ways to step through your code line by line, look at your variables and objects at run time, and even change them as you go. The toolset also provides you with valuable information about the *execution path* your code follows: the path that your application takes through your code, following methods, event handlers, `If` and `Else` statements, and so on.

In particular, this chapter looks at the following topics:

- How to write code that is able to detect and handle errors that occur at run time, at the same time shielding your users from the error details and give them an understandable explanation instead
- How to detect errors that occur on your production machine so you can take counter measures
- What debugging is and what debugging tools Visual Web Developer offers
- What tools you can use to gain information about your system while it's running in a development or production environment

Exception Handling

Whenever you write code, there is a chance things won't turn out as expected, resulting in non-compatible code, a crash, or otherwise unexpected behavior of your application. Things can go wrong for a large number of reasons: you introduced a typo in your code, the database server you're connecting to at run time suddenly goes down, you got your logic mixed up and accidentally deleted all records from a database table instead of just one, you try to delete a record from a database table that still has associated records, you try to write a file to a folder without proper permissions, your users enter incorrect data, and so forth.

In order to understand these problems and think of ways to anticipate, avoid, and handle them, you first need to understand the different types of errors that may occur in your web application. Once you understand the main differences, the remainder of this section is spent discussing ways to prevent and solve them.

Different Types of Errors

You can broadly categorize errors into the following groups:

- **Syntax errors:** Errors that are caused by typos or missing keywords, for example.
- **Logic errors:** Errors in applications that seem to run fine but that produce unexpected or unwanted results.
- **Run-time errors:** Errors that cause the application to crash or behave unexpectedly at run time.

Each of these categories is discussed in the following sections, together with information on avoiding and fixing them.

Syntax Errors

Syntax errors, or *compile errors*, are the easiest to find and fix because they happen during development. The IDE tells you when an error occurs and often prevents you from running the application. Syntax errors are caused by simple typos, missing or duplicate keywords and characters, and so on. The following examples all show errors that are caught at development time by the *compiler*. A compiler is a program that turns the human readable code you write in VB.NET or C# into machine readable code that can be executed.

VB.NET

```
mailBody = mailBody.Repalce("##Name##", txtName.Text)       ' Replace is misspelled

Response.Write()                                             ' Required parameter for the
                                                             ' Write method is missing

If i > 10                                                    ' Missing keyword Then
  ' Do something here
End If
```

C#

```
mailBody = mailBody.Repalce("##Name##", txtName.Text);     // Replace is misspelled

Response.Write();                                          // Required parameter for the
                                                           // Write method is missing

if (i > 10)                                                // Missing opening brace or
                                                           // extraneous closing brace
  // Do something here
}
```

Compile errors are always displayed in the Error List (accessible through the View ➪ Error List menu) that is shown in Figure 17-1.

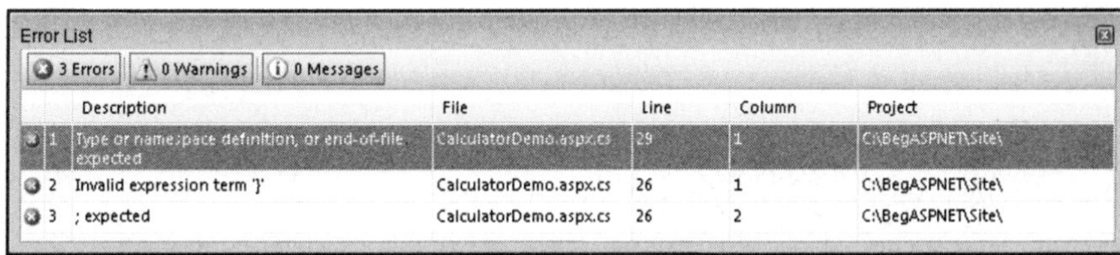

Error List

3 Errors | 0 Warnings | 0 Messages

	Description	File	Line	Column	Project
1	Type or namespace definition, or end-of-file expected	CalculatorDemo.aspx.cs	29	1	C:\BegASPNET\Site\
2	Invalid expression term '}'	CalculatorDemo.aspx.cs	26	1	C:\BegASPNET\Site\
3	; expected	CalculatorDemo.aspx.cs	26	2	C:\BegASPNET\Site\

Figure 17-1

You can force the compiler to give you an up-to-date list of all the compilation errors in your site. To do this, from the main menu choose Build ➪ Rebuild Web Site.

To go to the location where the error occurred so you can fix it, double-click the error in the Error List.

Logic Errors

Logic errors are often harder to find because they compile fine but only happen during the execution of your code. Consider the following buggy example:

VB.NET

```
Dim fromAddress As String = "you@yourprovider.com"
Dim toAddress As String = txtEmailAddress.Text
myMessage.From = new MailAddress(toAddress)
myMessage.To.Add(new MailAddress(fromAddress))
```

C#

```
string fromAddress = "you@yourprovider.com";
string toAddress = txtEmailAddress.Text;
myMessage.From = new MailAddress(toAddress);
myMessage.To.Add(new MailAddress(fromAddress));
```

Although it's easy to see what the problem is in this example (the `To` and `From` addresses are mixed up), it may be harder to find in a file with 250 lines of code. Additionally, since the compiler happily accepts your mistake, you won't notice the error until you see a message in your Inbox that you thought you sent to your visitors.

The best way to track down and solve logic errors is using the built-in debugging capabilities of VWD. You get an in-depth look at these tools later in the chapter.

Run-time Errors

Run-time errors occur at run time, which makes them incredibly difficult to track. Imagine you have a site that contains a bug that's hidden somewhere in a page. You haven't found it yet, but one of your visitors did and she gets a nasty error message (more on those later) instead. What can you do? Probably not much, as there's a fair chance your visitor won't even inform you about the mistake.

So, it's important to have a good error handling strategy that enables you to avoid errors when possible, and that handles them gracefully and optionally logs relevant information for you when they occur.

The following section deals with detecting and handling errors, or *exceptions* in .NET parlance; later in this chapter, you learn how to log errors and shield your users from ugly pages with detailed exception messages.

Catching and Handling Exceptions

Normally, when serious exceptions occur, the user is presented with an error message. For example, if you try to send a message to a mail server that isn't up and running, or doesn't allow you to connect to it, you'll get an exception that provides details about the exception. By default, this exception bubbles up all the way to the user interface where it's presented as a so-called Yellow Screen of Death, a reference to Windows' "blue screen of death" that you get when Windows crashes. You'll see a real example of this error in the next exercise.

Obviously, it's a lot better if you can anticipate the exception and write some code that prevents the exception from appearing in the user interface. You could, for example, display a nicely formatted message to users instead, informing them the message could not be sent at this moment.

Fortunately, support for these kinds of scenarios is integrated deeply in the .NET programming languages like C# and Visual Basic .NET. In these languages, you can make use of `Try Catch Finally` blocks (`try catch finally` in C#) where code that could potentially throw an exception is wrapped in a `Try` block.

When an exception occurs, the remainder of the code in the `Try` block is skipped and some code in a `Catch` block can be run to deal with the error. You can have multiple `Catch` blocks that all deal with specific exceptions, but only one will fire as you'll see in a later exercise.

A `Try` or a `Catch` block can be followed by a `Finally` block. Code in a `Finally` block is *always* fired, regardless of whether an exception occurred or not.

Both `Catch` and `Finally` blocks are optional, although you always need at least one of them.

The code in the following example tries to send an e-mail and then sets the `Text` property of a `Label` to the value of the variable `userMessage`. The `userMessage` variable is assigned a value in either the `Try` block (when the code executed successfully) or in the `Catch` block (when an error occurred). Either way, this `userMessage` is always assigned to the `Label` in the `Finally` block:

VB.NET

```
Dim userMessage As String
Try
  mySmtpClient.Send(myMessage)
  userMessage = "Message sent"
Catch ex As Exception
  userMessage = "An unknown error occurred."
Finally
  lblMessage.Text = userMessage
End Try
```

C#

```
string userMessage;
try
{
  mySmtpClient.Send(myMessage);
  userMessage = "Message sent";
}
catch (Exception ex)
{
  userMessage = "An unknown error occurred.";
}
finally
{
  lblMessage.Text = userMessage;
}
```

In this code example, the `Catch` block is set up to handle an exception of type `System.Exception`, the base class of all exceptions in the .NET Framework. This exception is sent to the `Catch` block in the `ex` variable. Since this example doesn't use the `ex` variable at all, you could leave it out altogether:

VB.NET

```
Catch
  userMessage = "An unknown error occurred."
End Try
```

C#

```
catch
{
  userMessage = "An unknown error occurred.";
}
```

The ability to specify an Exception type is useful when you think your code can encounter more than one exception. In that case, you can have multiple Catch blocks for different exception types. The following code is able to handle a specific SmtpException exception that may occur during the mail sending operation, while it's also capable of catching all other exceptions using its generic Catch block:

VB.NET

```
Try
  mySmtpClient.Send(myMessage)
Catch smtpException As SmtpException
  lblMessage.Text = "Sorry, an error occurred while sending your message."
Catch ex As Exception
  ' Something else went wrong.
End Try
```

C#

```
try
{
  mySmtpClient.Send(myMessage);
}
catch (SmtpException smtpException)
{
  lblMessage.Text = "Sorry, an error occurred while sending your message.";
}
catch (Exception ex)
{
  // Something else went wrong.
}
```

The order of the exception handling blocks is important. .NET scans the list of Catch blocks and only fires the code in the first block that matches a specific type of exception. In the above example, when an SmtpException occurs (which is a subclass of Exception) it will be caught by the Catch block that handles exceptions of type SmtpException. Although an SmtpException *is* also an Exception, the code in the last Catch block won't be fired anymore as only the first matching Catch block is handled. Therefore, if you'd reverse the order of the catch blocks in this example, the more generic Exception block would be executed, and the SmtpException block would never fire.

In the following exercise you see how to use Try and Catch in your code.

Try It Out Handling Exceptions

You'll try out the Try Catch code in a separate page in the Demos folder so you can closely watch its behavior. When you understand how it works, you'll modify the ContactForm.ascx user control and incorporate the exception handling code. The reason the code is not applied to the user control directly is because it uses an Ajax UpdatePanel that shields users from the dirty details of an exception by default.

1. Create a new file in the Demos folder and call it ExceptionHandling.aspx. Base the page on your custom template and set its Title to Exception Handling Demo.
2. Add a Label control to the main content area and call it lblMessage.

3. Switch to the Code Behind and add either an `Imports` or a `using` statement to the code:

VB.NET

```
Imports System.Net.Mail
```

C#

```
using System.Net.Mail;
```

4. Switch to Design View and set up an event handler for the `Load` event of the page by double-clicking the read-only area if the page. Add the following code to the event handler. Notice how this code is almost identical to the code you added in the ContactForm.ascx user control, so you can save yourself some typing by copying parts of the code from that file. The string with `"InvalidMailServer"` in the `SmtpClient` object's constructor is intentional to create an exception. Because you won't have a mail server called `InvalidMailServer` you get an exception when you try to send a message to this server:

VB.NET

```
Protected Sub Page_Load(ByVal sender As Object, ByVal e As System.EventArgs) _
                Handles Me.Load
  Dim myMessage As MailMessage = New MailMessage()
  myMessage.Subject = "Exception Handling Test"
  myMessage.Body = "Test message body"

  myMessage.From = New MailAddress("you@yourprovider.com")
  myMessage.To.Add(New MailAddress("you@yourprovider.com"))

  Dim mySmtpClient As SmtpClient = New SmtpClient("InvalidMailServer")
  mySmtpClient.Send(myMessage)
  lblMessage.Text = "Message sent"
End Sub
```

C#

```
protected void Page_Load(object sender, EventArgs e)
{
  MailMessage myMessage = new MailMessage();
  myMessage.Subject = "Exception Handling Test";
  myMessage.Body = "Test message body";

  myMessage.From = new MailAddress("you@yourprovider.com");
  myMessage.To.Add(new MailAddress("you@yourprovider.com"));

  SmtpClient mySmtpClient = new SmtpClient("InvalidMailServer");
  mySmtpClient.Send(myMessage);
  lblMessage.Text = "Message sent";
}
```

Don't forget to change the `From` and `To` e-mail addresses.

5. Press Ctrl+F5 to open up the site in your browser. You should see the "yellow screen of death" with the error message, displayed in Figure 17-2.

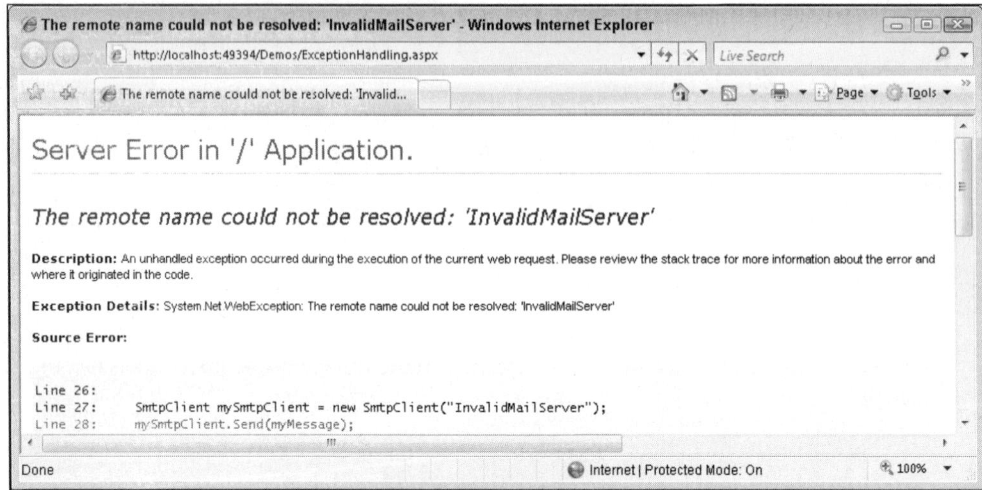

Figure 17-2

Note that the Exception Details section tells you that a `System.Net.WebException` occurred.

6. Go back to VWD and wrap the code that sends the message and sets the `Label` control's `Text` in a `Try Catch` block:

VB.NET

```
Dim mySmtpClient As SmtpClient = New SmtpClient("InvalidMailServer")
Try
  mySmtpClient.Send(myMessage)
  lblMessage.Text = "Message sent"
Catch ex As Exception
  lblMessage.Text = "An error occurred while sending your e-mail. Please try again."
End Try
```

C#

```
SmtpClient mySmtpClient = new SmtpClient("InvalidMailServer");
try
{
  mySmtpClient.Send(myMessage);
  lblMessage.Text = "Message sent";
}
catch
{
  lblMessage.Text = "An error occurred while sending your e-mail. Please try again.";
}
```

7. Save your changes and request the page in your browser again. You should now see a user-friendly error message, visible in Figure 17-3.

   The exception that is thrown is now caught in the `Catch` block. Instead of getting an error page with all the technical details of the exception, the user now gets a friendly message explaining something went wrong.

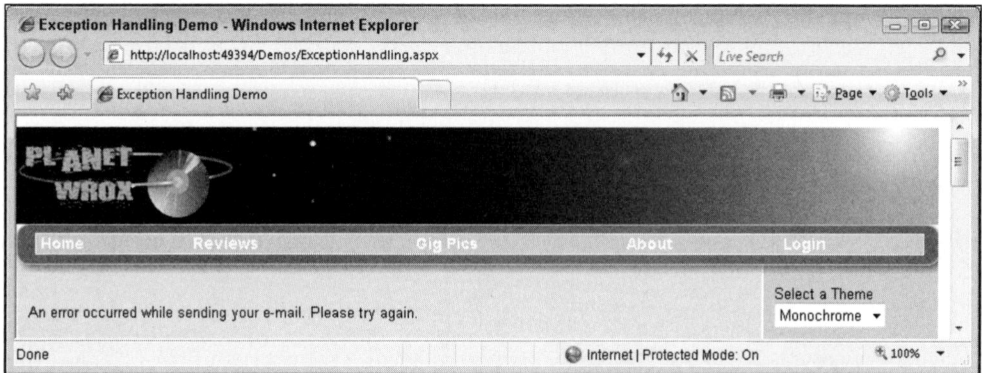

Figure 17-3

8. Go back to your code and remove the parameter from the `SmtpClient` constructor:

VB.NET

```
Dim mySmtpClient As SmtpClient = New SmtpClient()
```

C#

```
SmtpClient mySmtpClient = new SmtpClient();
```

By removing the server name from the constructor, mail will be sent through the default SMTP server that you defined in the web.config file in Chapter 9.

9. Save your changes and request the page again. You'll now get a message indicating that the message was sent successfully.

10. Open ContactForm.ascx from the Controls folder, switch to its Code Behind, and wrap the `Send` method in the following `Try Catch` block:

VB.NET

```
Dim mySmtpClient As SmtpClient = New SmtpClient()
Try
  mySmtpClient.Send(myMessage)
Catch ex As Exception
  lblMessage.Text = "An error occurred while sending your e-mail. Please try again."
End Try
```

C#

```
SmtpClient mySmtpClient = new SmtpClient();
try
{
  mySmtpClient.Send(myMessage);
}
catch (Exception ex)
{
  lblMessage.Text = "An error occurred while sending your e-mail. Please try again.";
}
```

From now on, whenever an error occurs during the sending of the e-mail, your users will get a normal error message instead of the full error detail page that .NET displays by default.

How It Works

When an exception occurs at run time, .NET checks if the code is wrapped in a `Try Catch` block. If that's the case, it scans the list of `Catch` blocks for an `Exception` type that matches the exception being thrown. Only the first `Catch` block that matches the `Exception` is being called; all remaining `Catch` blocks are ignored. Code in the `Try` block following the line that caused the exception is not executed anymore.

In this exercise, the code was set up to handle the general `Exception` type. Since this type is the base type of all exceptions, it will be fired for all exceptions, regardless their type. But as you learned before the exercise, you can have multiple `Catch` blocks, each one dealing with a specific type of exception.

With these `Try Catch Finally` blocks you can write code that helps you deal with errors that you think might happen in your code. It's always a good practice to wrap code that might throw an error in a `Try Catch` block so you can deal with it gracefully. Some examples of code that may throw an exception include:

- **Sending e-mail:** The mail server may be down, or you may not have the permissions to access it.
- **Accessing a database**: The server may be down, you may not have permissions, you may get errors due to foreign key constraint violations as you saw in Chapter 14, and so on.
- **Trying to write an uploaded file to disk**: The disk may be full, you may not have the necessary permissions to write to disk, or you are providing an invalid file name.

Although `Try Catch` blocks are great to avoid exceptions from bubbling up to the user interface, you should use them with care, as they come at a cost. A `Try Catch` block is generally slower than code without it, so you shouldn't use a `Try Catch` block for errors you can avoid otherwise. Consider the following example that divides two numbers:

VB.NET

```
Dim value1 As Integer = Convert.ToInt32(txtValue1.Text)
Dim value2 As Integer = Convert.ToInt32(txtValue2.Text)
Try
  result = value1 / value2
  lblResult.Text = result.ToString()
Catch ex As DivideByZeroException
  lblResult.Text = "Sorry, division by zero is not allowed."
End Try
```

C#

```
int value1 = Convert.ToInt32(txtValue1.Text);
int value2 = Convert.ToInt32(txtValue2.Text);
try
{
  result = value1 / value2;
  lblResult.Text = result.ToString();
```

```
}
catch (DivideByZeroException ex)
{
  lblResult.Text = "Sorry, division by zero is not allowed.";
}
```

In this example, the code is set up to expect a `DivideByZeroException` exception. This exception is thrown when `value2` contains the value `0`. It's much better to write code that checks for this value before the division is carried out, instead of letting an exception occur:

VB.NET

```
If (value2 <> 0) Then
  result = value1 / value2
  lblResult.Text = result.ToString()
Else
  lblResult.Text = "Sorry, division by zero is not allowed."
End If
```

C#

```
if (value2 != 0)
{
  result = value1 / value2;
  lblResult.Text = result.ToString();
}
else
{
  lblResult.Text = "Sorry, division by zero is not allowed.";
}
```

Of course it would even be better if you had placed a `CompareValidator` on the page, making sure that `txtValue2` could never contain the value zero. Chapter 9 explained how to use this control.

Although `Try Catch` blocks are useful to catch exceptions that you anticipate, what about errors you don't? How can you deal with unexpected errors? Because they are unexpected, you won't know when they occur, so it's difficult to write code to handle them.

To solve this problem, the next section shows you how you can globally log unhandled exceptions and send information about them by e-mail. This way, you know they occurred, giving you, the page developer, a chance to fix them before they happen again.

Global Error Handling and Custom Error Pages

To shield your users from the technical details of the exception, you should provide them with a user-friendly error page instead, preferably in the same style as your application. Fortunately, ASP.NET enables you to define *custom error pages*, ASPX pages that are shown to the user when an exception occurs. You can map different types of errors (server errors, page not found errors, security problems, and so forth) to different pages.

You define the error page or pages you want to show in the `customErrors` element of the web.config file. A typical element looks like this:

```
<customErrors mode="On" defaultRedirect="~/Errors/Error500.aspx">
  <error statusCode="404" redirect="~/Errors/Error404.aspx" />
  <error statusCode="500" redirect="~/Errors/Error500.aspx" />
</customErrors>
```

The `mode` attribute determines whether a visitor to your site gets to see a detailed error page or not. The attribute supports the following three values:

- `On`: Every visitor to your site always sees the custom error pages when an error occurs.
- `Off`: The custom error page is never shown and full error details are displayed on the page.
- `RemoteOnly`: With this setting, the full error details are shown to local users, while all other users get to see the custom error page. This is the preferred setting because it allows you to see error messages on your site during development, while your users are always presented with the custom error page.

Within the opening and closing tags of the `customErrors` element you define separate `< error />` elements, one for each HTTP status code you want to support. The previous configuration defines two custom pages: one that is shown when the requested page could not be found (the 404 status code) and one that is shown when server errors occur (the 500 code).

For all other HTTP status codes you haven't defined explicitly, you use the `defaultRedirect` attribute to designate the custom error page.

Although custom error pages shield your users from the exception details, they don't help in informing *you* that an exception occurred. All these pages do is hide the real error and show a page with a custom error message instead. To be notified about these exceptions, you need to write some code that looks at the exception and then sends you an e-mail with the details. Alternatively, you could write code that inserts the error details in a database, or writes them to a text file.

ASP.NET offers you a handy, central location to write code that is triggered when an exception occurs. You write this code in a special event handler called `Application_Error` inside the Global.asax file, a special file (note the .asax extension) that lets you write code that is triggered in response to events that are applicable site-wide, like the start of the application, or the start of a request for a resource. Inside this event handler you can collect relevant data about the exception, stick it in an e-mail message, and send it to your own Inbox. This gives you detailed information about exceptions that occur on your site, aiding in fixing the problem as soon as possible. You'll see how to write this code in the next exercise.

Try It Out Handling Exceptions Site Wide

In this exercise you learn how to write code in the Global.asax file to send the exception message by e-mail. Additionally, you see how to create global error pages that are shown to your user in case of an error.

1. Right-click the web site in the Solution Explorer and choose Add New Item. In the list with templates, select Global Application Class. Leave its name set to Global.asax and click Add.

2. At the top of the code of the file, right after the `Application` directive, add the following `Import` statement. Note that when adding an `Import` statement like this, both VB.NET and C# use the keyword `Import`, rather than `Imports` and `using` that you normally use in Code Behind:

VB.NET

```
<%@ Application Language="VB" %>
<%@ Import Namespace="System.Net.Mail" %>
```

C#

```
<%@ Application Language="C#" %>
<%@ Import Namespace="System.Net.Mail" %>
```

3. Inside the `Application_Error` handler that should already be present in the Global.asax file, add the following highlighted code that is triggered whenever an unhandled exception occurs in your site. If the handler isn't there, make sure you type all the code from the following snippet, including the parts that are not highlighted:

VB.NET

```
Sub Application_Error(ByVal sender As Object, ByVal e As EventArgs)
  If HttpContext.Current.Server.GetLastError() IsNot Nothing Then
    Dim myException As Exception = _
                HttpContext.Current.Server.GetLastError().GetBaseException()
    Dim mailSubject As String = "Error in page " & Request.Url.ToString()
    Dim message As String = String.Empty
    message &= "<strong>Message</strong><br />" & myException.Message & "<br />"
    message &= "<strong>StackTrace</strong><br />" & myException.StackTrace & "<br />"
    message &= "<strong>Query String</strong><br />" & _
                   Request.QueryString.ToString()& "<br />"
    Dim mySmtpClient As SmtpClient = New SmtpClient()
    Dim myMessage As MailMessage = New MailMessage("you@yourprovider.com", _
                 "you@yourprovider.com", mailSubject, message)
    myMessage.IsBodyHtml = True
    mySmtpClient.Send(myMessage)
  End If
End Sub
```

C#

```
void Application_Error(object sender, EventArgs e)
{
  if (HttpContext.Current.Server.GetLastError() != null)
  {
    Exception myException = HttpContext.Current.Server.GetLastError().GetBaseException();
    string mailSubject = "Error in page " + Request.Url.ToString();
    string message = string.Empty;
    message += "<strong>Message</strong><br />" + myException.Message + "<br />";
    message += "<strong>StackTrace</strong><br />" + myException.StackTrace + "<br />";
```

```
    message += "<strong>Query String</strong><br />" + Request.QueryString.ToString() +
               "<br />";
    SmtpClient mySmtpClient = new SmtpClient();
    MailMessage myMessage = new MailMessage("you@yourprovider.com",
               "you@yourprovider.com", mailSubject, message);
    myMessage.IsBodyHtml = true;
    mySmtpClient.Send(myMessage);
  }
}
```

Don't forget to change the two e-mail addresses that are passed to the `MailMessage`'s constructor. The first address represents the sender's address, while the second one holds the recipient's address.

4. Save all your changes and close the Global.asax file.

5. Next, open up the web.config file and locate the `customErrors` element that should be present in the file. Notice how in your file the element is commented out as it appears in green text. Cut the element, and paste it again outside the comment tags (`<!--` and `-->`) so the element becomes active. Then modify the element as follows:

```
<customErrors mode="On" defaultRedirect="~/Errors/Error500.aspx">
  <error statusCode="404" redirect="~/Errors/Error404.aspx" />
  <error statusCode="500" redirect="~/Errors/Error500.aspx" />
</customErrors>
```

Don't forget to change the `mode` attribute from `RemoteOnly` to `On`. Save and close the configuration file.

6. Create a new folder in your website and call it Errors.

7. Inside this new folder, create two new Web Forms and call them Error500.aspx and Error404.aspx, respectively. Make sure both of them are based on your custom template so they are using the main master page and inherit from `BasePage`.

8. Set the `Title` of Error404.aspx to File Not Found. Inside the content placeholder for the main content add the following markup:

```
<asp:Content ID="Content2" ContentPlaceHolderID="cpMainContent" Runat="Server">
  <h1>File Not Found</h1>
  <p>The page you requested could not be found. Please check out the
    <a href="~/" runat="server">Homepage</a> or choose a different page from the menu.</p>
  <p>The Planet Wrox Team</p>
</asp:Content>
```

9. Repeat this process for the Error500 page, but set its `Title` to An Error Occurred and enter the following content:

```
<asp:Content ID="Content2" ContentPlaceHolderID="cpMainContent" Runat="Server">
  <h1>Un unknown error occurred</h1>
  <p>An error occurred on the page you requested. The error has been logged and
```

```
                  we'll fix it ASAP.</p>
    <p>The Planet Wrox Team</p>
</asp:Content>
```

10. Save the changes to all open files by pressing Ctrl+Shift+S and then close them. Right-click Default.aspx in the Solution Explorer and choose View In Browser. Once the page has finished loading, request a nonexistent page like DefaultTest.aspx by changing the address bar of the browser to something like `http://localhost:49169/DefaultTest.aspx`. Obviously, the DefaultTest.aspx page does not exist, so you get an error. But instead of a detailed error page, you should now get the error page you defined and created in this Try It Out, shown in Figure 17-4.

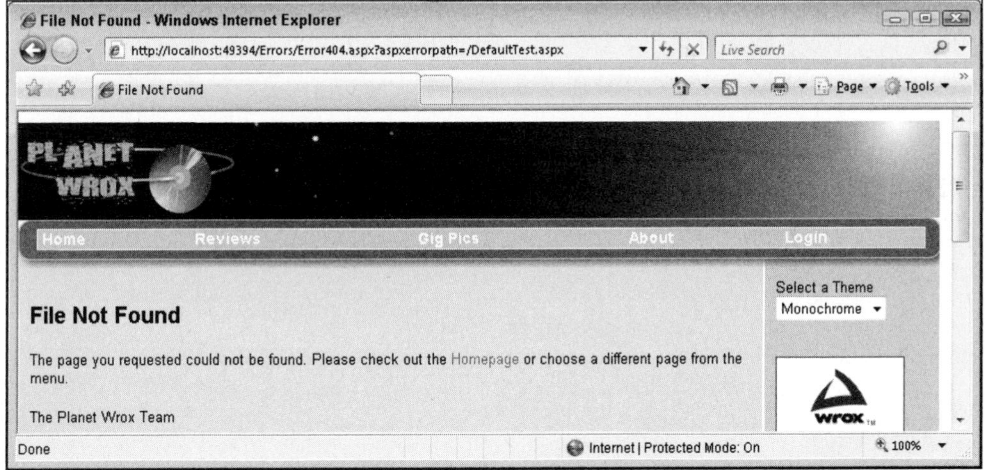

Figure 17-4

Additionally, you should also get a message by e-mail that provides more details about the error. Figure 17-5 shows the message you get when you request a page that does not exist.

Note that the Message indicates the page that does not exist.

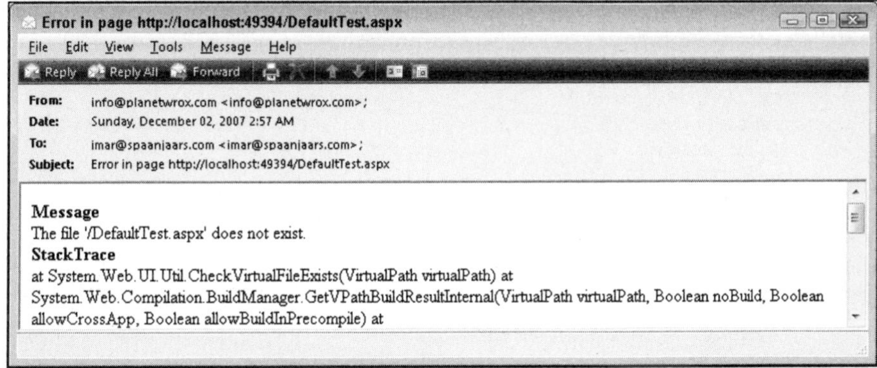

Figure 17-5

How It Works

There are two important parts worth examining in this exercise. The first part is the way the ASP.NET run time hides the Yellow Screen of Death with the error details from the user with the use of custom error pages. This serves two purposes. First, it helps you protect potentially private data like passwords or information about database connections that may end up in the error message. Second, it shields your users from cryptic error messages they probably don't understand anyway and gives you the chance to display a good-looking error page instead that integrates with the site's look and feel.

The only thing you need to do to make this work is enable custom errors in the web.config file and provide one or more pages you want to display for the errors that may occur in your site. The configuration element lets you set up different pages for different exceptions:

```
<customErrors mode="On" defaultRedirect="~/Errors/Error500.aspx">
  <error statusCode="404" redirect="~/Errors/Error404.aspx" />
  <error statusCode="500" redirect="~/Errors/Error500.aspx" />
</customErrors>
```

When .NET encounters a 404 exception (for example, you requested a page that could not be found), you are taken to the Error404.aspx page. The name and content of this page are completely up to you, giving you the option to provide your own explanation to the user about what went wrong. Note that this only works for file types that are registered with ASP.NET, like .aspx files. It won't work out of the box for .html files or images.

A server exception, like the exceptions you have seen so far, is associated with a status code of 500. Whenever your code crashes for some reason, users are taken to Error500.aspx that explains something went wrong.

The other part of this exercise is the code in Global.asax that fires when an exception occurs. In that case, the event handler `Application_Error` is triggered. Within this handler, you can retrieve the exception that occurred with this code:

VB.NET

```
If HttpContext.Current.Server.GetLastError() IsNot Nothing Then
  Dim myException As Exception = _
          HttpContext.Current.Server.GetLastError().GetBaseException()
```

C#

```
if (HttpContext.Current.Server.GetLastError() != null)
{
  Exception myException = HttpContext.Current.Server.GetLastError().GetBaseException();
```

To get at the root exception that caused the problem in the first place, you need to call `GetBaseException()` on the `Exception` that is returned by `Server.GetLastError()`. This `Exception` instance, stored in the `myException` variable, then gives you access to useful information like `Message` and `StackTrace`. In the previous exercise, the `StackTrace` displayed in the error e-mail contains information that really isn't of any interest to you. However, with other exceptions, like the one thrown by an incorrect configuration of the mail server or a division by zero exception, the `StackTrace` gives you information about the file that generated the error, the method that caused it, and even the line number in the code, making it easy to find the error and fix it.

The remainder of the code creates an e-mail message with the error details. It also adds information about the query string with this code:

VB.NET

```
message &= "<strong>Query String</strong><br />" & Request.QueryString.ToString() &
                "<br />"
```

C#

```
message += "<strong>Query String</strong><br />" + Request.QueryString.ToString() +
                "<br />";
```

Knowledge of the query string helps in debugging a problem if values from the query string are used. You could extend the code in `Application_Error` and add other useful information like cookies and form collections. For more information about accessing these kind of collections, pick up a copy of *Professional ASP.NET 3.5* published by Wrox. Alternatively, look into ELMAH — the Error Logging Modules and Handlers project at `http://code.google.com/p/elmah/`, an open source project run by Atif Aziz that is aimed at handling and logging exceptions.

Although the ability to handle and log exceptions at run time is useful, it's of course better to prevent them from happening in the first place. To write solid code, with as few bugs as possible, you need good tools to help you understand the execution of your code so you can debug it. VWD comes with excellent debugging tools that aid you in this process. You see what these tools are and how to use them in the next section.

The Basics of Debugging

Debugging is the process of finding and fixing bugs in your code. Although that may sound easy, it often isn't. Some bugs are very obvious and easy to spot and thus easy to fix. Others are much harder to find and require knowledge about the execution environment of your program. The debugging tools that ship with Visual Web Developer help you understand this execution environment by giving you direct access to the inner workings of your program or web page.

Debugging with VWD is like snapping your fingers to stop the time. When you do that, everything halts, except for you, so you can walk around in your code, investigate variables, look into objects, try out methods, and even execute new code. To tell VWD where to halt, you need to set one or more *breakpoints* in your code. When the code under the breakpoint is about to be executed, VWD stops the execution of the application (usually a web page, a user control or code in the App_Code folder) and then puts focus back on VWD so you can diagnose the code and its environment.

You set a breakpoint by pressing F9 on the line of code where you want execution to halt. Instead of the F9 shortcut key, you can also click the margin of the code, where the big dot appears in Figure 17-6, or you can choose Debug ➪ Toggle Breakpoint from the main menu. Pressing F9, clicking the same spot in the margin, or choosing the menu item again toggles the presence of the breakpoint. To clear all breakpoints in your entire web site, press Ctrl+Shift+F9.

To give you an idea of how debugging works, and what it can do to help you, the following exercise shows you the basic operations of debugging. Later parts of this chapter give you a detailed look at the numerous debugging tools and windows that ship with Visual Web Developer.

Try It Out Debugging Your Application

In this exercise you'll debug the Calculator you created in a previous chapter. If you don't have the file, refer to Chapter 5 that explained how to create this file, or download the code for this chapter from `www.wrox.com`. The debugging exercises in this chapter assume you are using Internet Explorer as your browser. If you are using a different default browser, such as Firefox or Opera, the debugging experience will be largely the same although you may find that VWD does not always get the focus automatically while breaking into your code.

1. Open the page CalculatorDemo.aspx from the Demos folder and switch to Code Behind.
2. Click the first line of code in the `btnCalculate_Click` handler that checks the length of the two `TextBox` controls. Then press F9 to set a breakpoint. The line gets highlighted, as shown in Figure 17-6, and a colored dot appears in the margin of the Document Window.

```
Demos/CalculatorDemo.aspx.cs
Demos_CalculatorDemo            btnCalculate_Click(object sender, EventArgs e)
protected void Page_Load(object sender, EventArgs e)
{

}
protected void btnCalculate_Click(object sender, EventArgs e)
{
  if (txtValue1.Text.Length > 0 && txtValue2.Text.Length > 0)
  {
    double result = 0;
    double value1 = Convert.ToDouble(txtValue1.Text);
    double value2 = Convert.ToDouble(txtValue2.Text);
```

Figure 17-6

3. Press F5 to open the web site in your browser and start the debugging process. Alternatively, choose Debug ➪ Start Debugging from the main menu. If you get the dialog box in Figure 17-7, click OK to have VWD modify the web.config file for you.

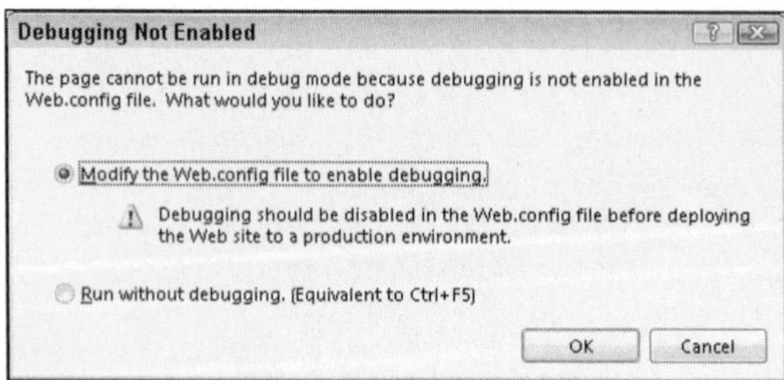
Debugging Not Enabled
The page cannot be run in debug mode because debugging is not enabled in the Web.config file. What would you like to do?
Modify the Web.config file to enable debugging.
Debugging should be disabled in the Web.config file before deploying the Web site to a production environment.
Run without debugging. (Equivalent to Ctrl+F5)
OK
Cancel

Figure 17-7

Depending on your browser's setup, you may be confronted with the dialog box shown in Figure 17-8.

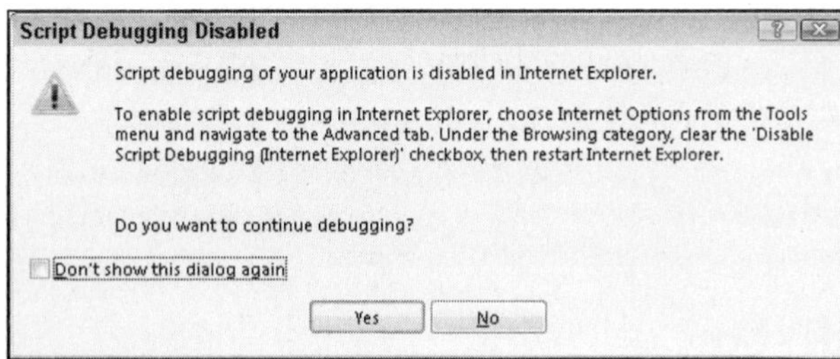

Figure 17-8

You may get this dialog box if you haven't set up Internet Explorer to allow debugging client-side script, something you need in later exercises in this chapter. If you get this dialog box, follow the instructions it displays and then click the Yes button when you return to VWD. If you configured Internet Explorer according to the instructions, you won't see this dialog box again. Don't worry if you don't get this dialog box at all; you only get it when you need to change something to your set-up.

4. The page should load normally, showing you the two `TextBox` controls, the `DropDownList`, and the `Button`. Enter `5` in the first text box, `7` in the second, and then click the Calculate button. Instead of getting the answer in your browser, you are now taken back to Visual Web Developer. If you're not taken back to VWD directly, you may need to switch to it manually. You'll see the taskbar icon of VWD flash to get your attention.

5. In VWD, the line with the breakpoint is now highlighted in yellow. Additionally, you see a yellow icon in the document margin to indicate this line of code *is about to be executed*. However, before it does, you get a chance to look at your controls, variables and other elements that make up the execution environment. The behavior you see here differs for C# and VB.NET. For example, to see the values you entered in the `TextBox` controls in a C# web site, hover your mouse over the `Text` properties in the highlighted lines. You'll see a small tooltip appear that displays the value you entered. When you do the same in VB.NET, all you see is the length of the value you entered in the text box.

   The behavior in VB.NET is slightly different. To see the value you entered in the `TextBox` control, use your mouse to highlight the code `txtValue1.Text` and then hover your mouse over that selection. You'll now see the value appear in a tooltip, just as in Figure 17-9.

Demos/CalculatorDemo.aspx.cs

Demos_CalculatorDemo | btnCalculate_Click(object sender, EventArgs e)

```
protected void Page_Load(object sender, EventArgs e)
{

}
protected void btnCalculate_Click(object sender, EventArgs e)
{
  if (txtValue1.Text.Length > 0 && txtValue2.Text.Length > 0)
  {                          txtValue1.Text | "5"
    double result = 0;
    double value1 = Convert.ToDouble(txtValue1.Text);
    double value2 = Convert.ToDouble(txtValue2.Text);
```

Figure 17-9

6. Hover your mouse over some of the variables in the code like `result` and `value1`. Note that you *won't* get a tooltip, because the code hasn't reached the point where these variables are declared. As far as the debugger is concerned, they don't exist.

7. To advance in the code, press F10. This steps over the selected line, executing it. Keep pressing F10 until the line that declares the `value2` variable is highlighted. When you now hover your mouse over `value1`, the tooltip appears, indicating that `value1` now contains the value `5.0`.

8. Hover your mouse over the `SelectedValue` property in the `Select Case` (in VB.NET) or `switch` statement (in C#). Note that the tooltip shows you the value you selected in the drop-down list (the plus symbol). Even if this line of code hasn't been executed, the `SelectedValue` has been assigned a value earlier so you can look at it here.

9. Press F10 a few more times and note that the code steps into the `Select Case` or `switch` block. Keep pressing F10 until you reach the line that assigns a value to `lblResult`. Hover your mouse over the `result` variable (you need to highlight the `result` variable first with your mouse if you are using VB.NET) and note that it displays the number `12`, the outcome of the calculation, shown in Figure 17-10.

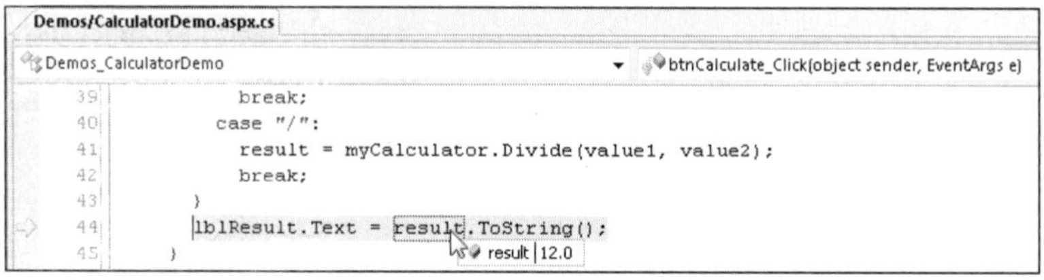

```
Demos/CalculatorDemo.aspx.cs
Demos_CalculatorDemo                    btnCalculate_Click(object sender, EventArgs e)
          break;
        case "/":
          result = myCalculator.Divide(value1, value2);
          break;
      }
      lblResult.Text = result.ToString();
    }                     result | 12.0
```

Figure 17-10

10. Finally, press the F5 key. By pressing this key, the code continues until it finds the next breakpoint. Since you haven't defined another breakpoint in your code, the remainder of the code in the `Click` event handler is executed and the result is displayed in the page.

How It Works

Whenever you press Ctrl+F5 to view a page in a browser as you have done up until this chapter, nothing special happens. VWD simply opens the browser, which then requests the page from the built-in web server. However, when you press F5 instead, VWD gets in debugging mode and respects the breakpoints you have set in your code. Whenever a breakpoint is hit, execution of the code is stopped so you can look at the code and its execution environment that gives you access to variables, controls, methods, and much more. Note that the code on the line with the breakpoint has not been executed at this point. You need to step through it, using F10, F11, or F5, for example, to execute it.

Before you can debug your code, you need to configure the application to support it. You do this by setting the `debug` attribute of the compilation element in web.config to `true`:

```
<compilation debug="true">
```

If you're using Visual Basic, you may see two additional attributes on this element: `strict` *and* `explicit`*. By default,* `strict` *is set to* `false` *which means Visual Basic will do silent casts and conversions for you. The* `explicit` *attribute is set to* `true`*, which means you need to declare all your variables before you can use them. For most scenarios, these defaults are fine.*

Whenever you start debugging and the `debug` attribute of the `<compilation />` is set to `false`, you get the dialog box shown in Figure 17-7 offering to turn it on for you. To avoid the overhead this setting brings, you should always set it to `false` on a production server.

In this exercise you also learned how to use the *data tips*, the small tooltip windows that appear when you hover your mouse over selected variables. For simple types, such as an `Integer` or a `String`, all you see is the variable's value. For complex types, such as results returned from a LINQ query, you get a much richer data tip, providing you with a lot more detail.

Useful as the debugging data tips may seem, they are only a small part of the rich debugging features. In the next section you get an overview of all the debugging tools that ship with Visual Web Developer.

Tools Support for Debugging

With a number of short cut keys and menu items, VWD lets you move around the code that you are debugging, giving you the option to execute code line by line or larger blocks of code at once. Additionally, the IDE provides you with a lot of windows that allow you to diagnose and change the execution environment, including the values of variables at run time. You'll see how to move around code first, which is followed by a discussion on the numerous debugging windows.

Moving around in Debugged Code

When your code has halted on a breakpoint, you can use a number of keyboard shortcuts to determine what to do next. The following table lists the most common short cuts.

Key	Description
F5	Press this key to start debugging, as demonstrated in the previous exercise. When pressed during debugging, the code will continue until the next breakpoint is hit, or until all code is finished executing.
F11	Press this key to execute the current line and step into a method that's being called if possible. You see how this works later.
F10	Press this key to execute the current line without stepping into the code that is being called, unless that code itself contains a breakpoint.
Shift+F11	Press this key combination to complete the code in the current method and return to the code that initially called it.
Shift+F5	Press this key combination to stop debugging. This closes the browser and returns you to VWD.
Ctrl+Shift+F5	Press this key combination to restart the debugging process.

In addition to these keyboard shortcuts, you can also use the Debugging toolbar shown in Figure 17-11, which offers similar functionality.

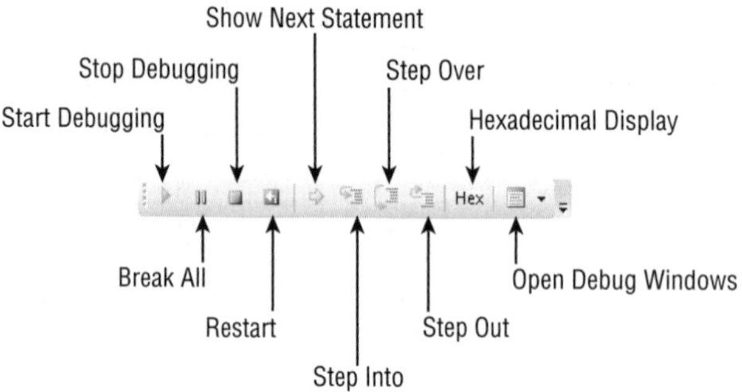

Figure 17-11

This toolbar should appear automatically when you start debugging, but if it doesn't, right-click an existing toolbar and choose Debug.

While you are debugging your code in VWD, you have a number of debugging windows at your disposal that are discussed in the following section.

Debugging Windows

The numerous debugging windows enable you to watch the variables in your application and even change them during run time. Additionally, they provide you with information about where you are in the application and what code was previously executed. All this information helps you understand the execution flow of your application.

You access all the debugging windows through the Debug ➪ Windows menu option. Not all of them are available in the Express Edition of Visual Web Developer. Also, to access most of the windows, your application must be in debug mode first. The next sections show you the different windows you have available. In the exercise that follows, you get a chance to work with them so you understand how to use them and why they are useful.

Watching Variables

Knowing the values of your variables is critical to understanding your application. To help you with this, VWD offers three debugging windows that provide you with useful information. All these windows support changing the value of your variables at run time, allow you to use data tips to dig deeper into the objects, and allow you to copy and paste data so you can reuse it somewhere else.

The Watch Window

This is probably the most important window for you to keep an eye on. It allows you to watch all your variables and dig into them. Figure 17-12 shows the Watch window that is currently watching the `value1` variable used in the calculator page while the `value2` variable is being added to the list.

There are a few different ways to add your variables to the Watch window. First of all, you can click the Watch window once and then start typing a variable name. You can then press Ctrl+Space to bring up the IntelliSense list, making it easy to complete the variable's name. Alternatively, you can right-click a variable in the Document Window and choose Add Watch. And finally, you can highlight a variable in the Document Window and then drag it into the Watch window.

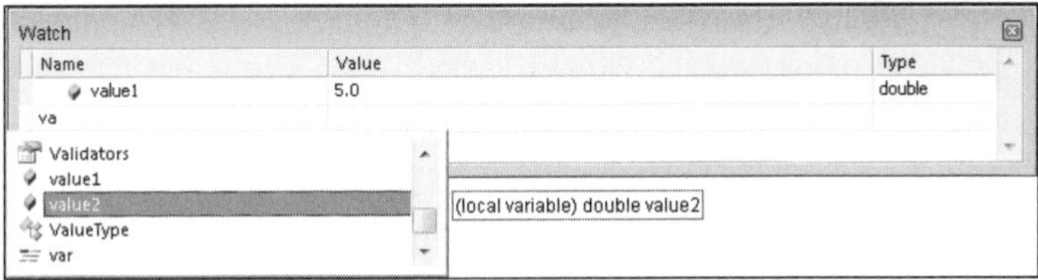

Figure 17-12

When your variables are in the Watch window, you can change their values to influence the execution of your code. For example, you could change the value of the `value1` variable to a different number, changing the outcome of the calculation. To change a value, double-click it in the Watch window on the Value column. Alternatively, right-click the watched variable and choose Edit Value.

Besides showing variables' values, you can also use the Watch window to execute code. For example, you could call `ToString()` on the `value1` variable to see what its string representation looks like. To do this, double-click the variable name in the Watch window so it becomes editable and then add `ToString()` as shown in Figure 17-13.

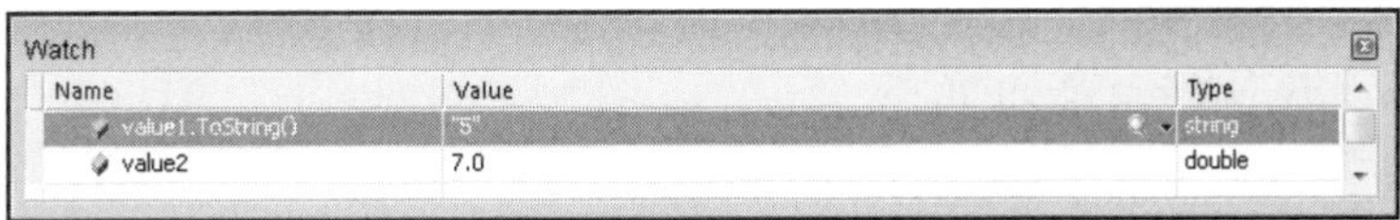

Figure 17-13

You are not limited to calling `ToString` in the Watch window. Any expression that has a result can be executed here. However, the Immediate window, discussed later, is much more appropriate for executing code on the fly.

Besides the Watch window, the Autos and Locals windows are available. They work more or less the same as the Watch window.

The Autos Window

The Autos window is only available in the commercial versions of Visual Studio and not in the Express Edition. Since it's so similar to the Watch window, this isn't really a problem. The Autos window shows the variables used by the current and previous code statements and is updated automatically as you step through the code.

The Locals Window

The Locals window is also similar to the Watch and Autos window, but the Locals window shows all variables that are currently in scope (can be "reached") by the code that is currently executing. This is a useful window, as it shows you all relevant variables without requiring you to add them manually.

Other Windows

Besides windows to watch variables, Visual Web Developer has a few other useful windows available.

The Breakpoints Window

The Breakpoints window gives you an overview of all breakpoints you have set in code throughout your entire web site. Unfortunately, this window is not available in the Express Edition, so you manually have to find breakpoints by looking at the actual code.

Call Stack Window

The Call Stack window provides you with information about the order in which your code has been executed or called. Each call from one piece of code into another is placed on a *stack of calls* that you can navigate. It looks a bit cryptic at first, but once you understand how it works, it enables you to jump through your code quite easily. Figure 17-14 shows the Call Stack window inside the `Add` method of the `Calculator` class.

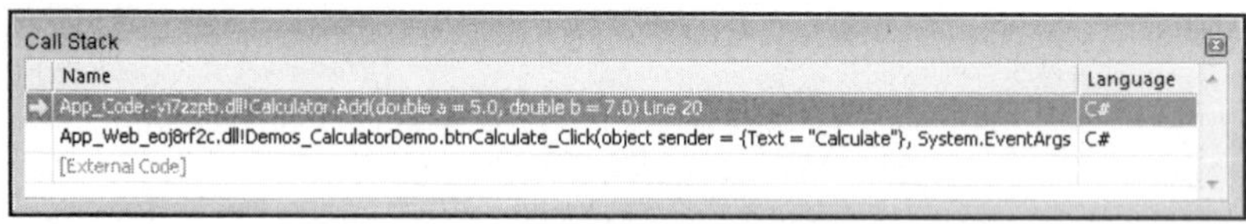

Figure 17-14

In the highlighted line you can see that `Calculator.Add` is the currently active code. Right below it you see `btnCalculate_Click`, the event handler in the Calculator page that called the `Add` method. Double-clicking a line in the Call Stack window takes you to the appropriate code location.

Immediate Window

The last interesting debugging window is the Immediate window. This window lets you execute code as if you had written it in a page. You can use this window to test expressions, see what functions return, and so on. For example, when you are in debug mode, you can enter the following command in the Immediate window:

VB.NET

```
? New Calculator().Add(3, 4)
```

C#

```
? new Calculator().Add(3, 4);
```

The question mark is used to output to the Immediate window. The code then instantiates a new `Calculator` instance and directly passes the values `3` and `4` to its `Add` method. The code will be executed, the `Add` method returns `7` which is then printed in the Immediate window.

This window is great for quickly testing out code. Instead of writing code you want to test in a page, you can type it directly in the Immediate window and see its output.

In the following Try It Out exercise, you'll see these debugging windows at work.

Try It Out — Extensive Debugging

In this exercise you look at all the debugging windows that have been discussed earlier. Since a lot of windows and options are available, you won't see a detailed discussion of every step in the process. Instead, you're encouraged to experiment. Try adding more variables to the Watch window, type your own code in the Immediate window, and so on. Experimenting is the best way to discover the large number of debugging capabilities in VWD.

1. Open the CalculatorDemo.aspx page again and then press Ctrl+Shift+F9 to clear all previously set breakpoints. Click Yes to confirm the deletion.

2. Click the line that declares the variable `value1` and press F9 to set a breakpoint. Your Document Window should look similar to Figure 17-15, which shows the Document Window for the C# project.

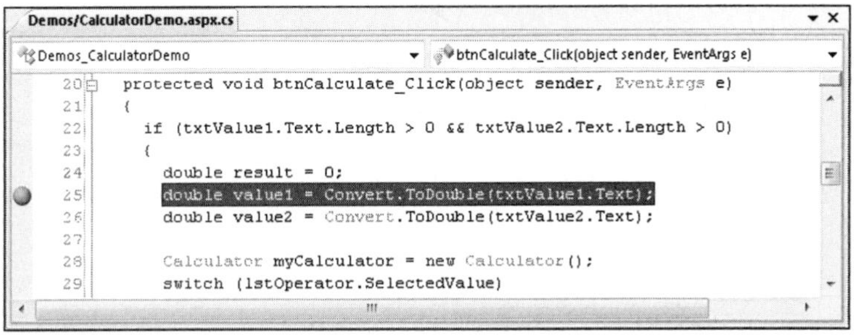

```
Demos/CalculatorDemo.aspx.cs
Demos_CalculatorDemo          btnCalculate_Click(object sender, EventArgs e)
20  protected void btnCalculate_Click(object sender, EventArgs e)
21  {
22    if (txtValue1.Text.Length > 0 && txtValue2.Text.Length > 0)
23    {
24      double result = 0;
25      double value1 = Convert.ToDouble(txtValue1.Text);
26      double value2 = Convert.ToDouble(txtValue2.Text);
27
28      Calculator myCalculator = new Calculator();
29      switch (lstOperator.SelectedValue)
```

Figure 17-15

3. Press F5 or choose Debug ➪ Start Debugging from the main menu to start debugging the application. Enter the number `5` in the first text box, ensure that the plus sign is selected in the drop-down list, and enter `7` in the second text box. Then click the Calculate button and VWD breaks at the breakpoint you set in the previous step.

4. If you weren't taken there automatically, switch back to VWD. Hover your mouse over the `lstOperator` variable that is used below the current breakpoint and notice how VWD displays a data tip with a plus (+) symbol in front of it. This means you can expand the item to get detailed information about the variable. Figure 17-16 displays the expanded data tip.

   If you are using VB.NET, you need to double-click the `lstOperator` variable in the Document Window first to select it, and then hover your mouse over it.

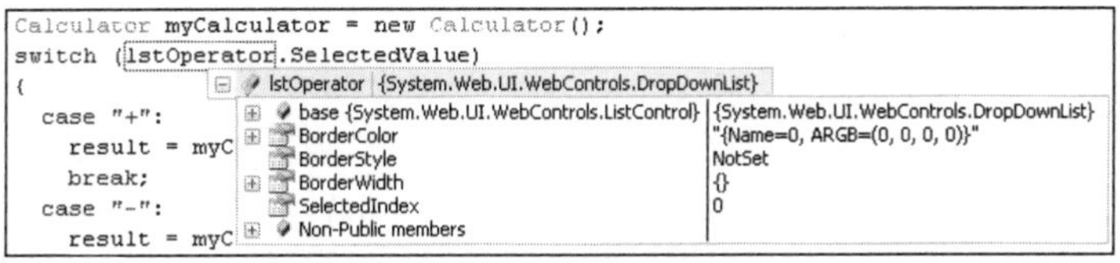

```
Calculator myCalculator = new Calculator();
switch (lstOperator.SelectedValue)
{
  case "+":
    result = myC
    break;
  case "-":
    result = myC

lstOperator {System.Web.UI.WebControls.DropDownList}
  base {System.Web.UI.WebControls.ListControl}  {System.Web.UI.WebControls.DropDownList}
  BorderColor     "{Name=0, ARGB=(0, 0, 0, 0)}"
  BorderStyle     NotSet
  BorderWidth     {}
  SelectedIndex   0
  Non-Public members
```

Figure 17-16

Note that you can expand other items (like the `DropDownList` control's base class) to get at other relevant data. Go ahead and expand the base item. Once you do that, you'll see relevant properties of the `ListControl`, including its `SelectedValue` that is set to "+" if you didn't change it in step 1.

5. Right click `txtValue1` in the code at the top that checks the length of the `TextBox` controls and choose Add Watch. The variable is added to the Watch window where you can expand it similar to how you expanded the data tip. Expand the item and you'll see, for example, that the `Text` property is set to `"5"`.

6. Double click the value `"5"`, change it to `"12"` (including the quotes), and press Enter.

7. Open the Locals window. (Choose Debug ➪ Windows ➪ Locals if the window isn't visible yet.) Press F10 to execute the line under the breakpoint. This gets the value from `txtValue1`, converts it to a double, and assigns it to `value1`. Look at the `value1` variable in the Locals window. Note that it now contains `12.0`, the value you assigned to the `Text` property of the text box in the previous step, now converted to a double.

Locals

Name	Value	Type
this	{ASP.demos_calculatordemo_aspx}	Demos_CalculatorDemo {ASP.demos_calculatordemo_aspx}
sender	{Text = "Calculate"}	object {System.Web.UI.WebControls.Button}
e	{System.EventArgs}	System.EventArgs
result	0.0	double
value1	12.0	double
value2	0.0	double
myCalculator	null	Calculator

Figure 17-17

Note that the value of the `value1` variable has changed color as well. This means that the item has recently been changed. Also note that because all of this is happening at the server during a postback, the browser is unmodified, and the text box still shows the value 5. Only when the page has finished rendering to the browser will you see the new value show up.

In Figure 17-17 you also see the other variables that are currently in scope, like `result`, `myCalculator`, and `this` (`Me` in Visual Basic) that contains a reference to the page that is currently being executed.

8. Press F10 once more so `value2` is updated as well. Note that the color of the value in the Locals window is changed to red to indicate the value has changed. This makes it easy to see what variables are modified by a statement.

9. Press F10 until you reach the line that calls the `Add` method on the `Calculator` class. Instead of pressing F10 to execute that line, press F11. This steps into the `Add` method so you can see how it performs the calculation. Inside the `Add` method, you can hover over the method's arguments to see their values, as demonstrated in Figure 17-18.

```
public double Add(double a, double b)
{                                       b | 7.0
  return a + b;
}
```

Figure 17-18

10. Choose Debug ➪ Windows ➪ Call Stack to bring up the Call Stack window and note that the `Add` method was called by the `btnCalculate's Click` handler, shown in Figure 17-19.

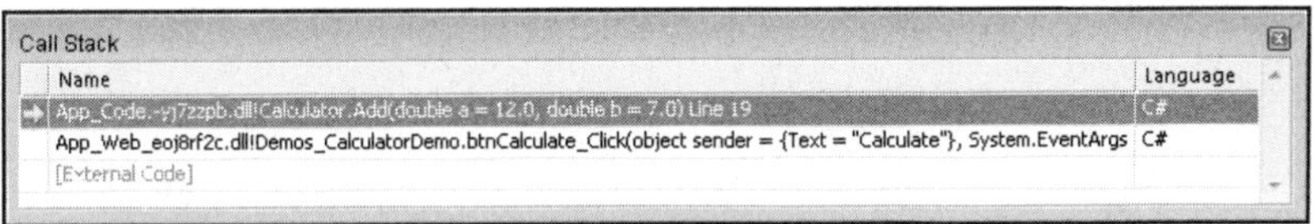

Figure 17-19

11. Double-click the second line in the Call Stack window and you'll be taken back to the Calculator page. Note that this doesn't execute any code; all it does is show you the relevant code. Double-click the first line and you'll be taken to the `Add` method code again.
12. Press Shift+F11 to step out of the `Add` method and return to the calling code in the calculator page. If you take another look at the Call Stack window you'll see the line for the Add method is now removed from the call stack.
13. Open the Immediate window (choose Debug ➪ Windows ➪ Immediate) to test out some code. In the window, type the following and press Enter:

VB.NET

```
? New Calculator().Multiply(4, 12)
```

C#

```
? new Calculator().Multiply(4, 12);
```

The Immediate window displays the outcome of the calculation, as shown in Figure 17-20.

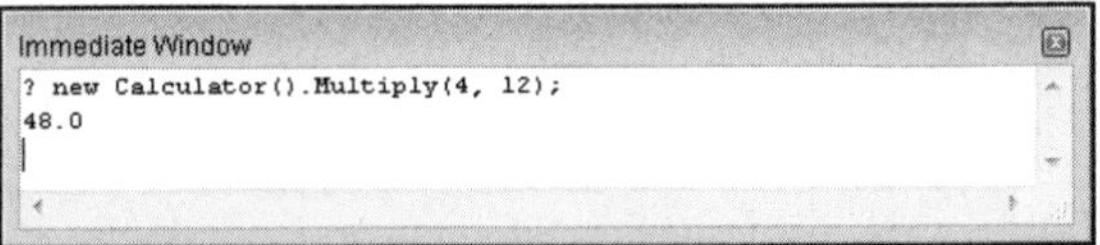

Figure 17-20

14. Finally, press F5. This executes the remainder of the code in the page. The focus will be put on the browser again that now displays the outcome of the calculation in the `Label` control. If everything turned out as planned, you should see the number `19`: the sum of `12` (the new value you entered for `txtValue1.Text` in step 6) and `7` (that you entered in step 3).

How It Works

As demonstrated in a previous Try It Out exercise, when you put a breakpoint in your code, execution is halted as soon as the line with the breakpoint is about to be executed. From there, you can jump around in your code, investigate variables, and execute statements. In this exercise you saw how to step in and over code using the F10 and F11 shortcut keys. You usually use F10 to execute a line if you're not interested in the underlying code that is being called. You use F11 if you want to see the code that is being executed as you saw how to do with the `Add` method.

The data tips and Watch and Locals windows are invaluable tools in examining and changing variables and values. For example, even though you entered `5` in the first text box in the browser, you were able to change that value to `12` during debugging. Any changes you make while debugging are propagated to the rest of the code that still needs to be executed.

The Immediate window lets you try out small snippets of code. This can be useful to try out some ideas, without the need to write it in the code window and debug it. In this exercise, you wrote some code that created a new `Calculator` instance, called the `Multiply` method and outputted the value using the question mark.

VB.NET

```
? New Calculator().Multiply(4, 12)
```

C#

```
? new Calculator().Multiply(4, 12);
```

Although most of the debugging capabilities in ASP.NET 3.5 and Visual Web Developer 2008 already existed in previous versions, this new release comes with a major new feature in debugging: debugging client-side script.

Debugging Client-Side Script

So far, you have used the debugging tools to debug ASPX pages and Code Behind. However, that's not all there is to it. Visual Studio 2008 now has great support for debugging client-side JavaScript as well. Debugging client-side JavaScript requires that you use Internet Explorer and won't work correctly with other browsers like Firefox or Opera. The cool thing about debugging client-side JavaScript in VWD is that you already know how to do it. You can use the same familiar tools that you have seen in this chapter to debug both server-side and client-side code.

The JavaScript that is eventually used by the page in the web browser can come from a lot of different sources. You can have JavaScript in external script files, embedded in the page, in a master page, and even server controls can emit their own JavaScript. This makes it difficult sometimes to break in the right code, as you don't always know where it comes from. Fortunately, VWD has a great solution for this; it lets you set breakpoints in the final HTML being displayed in the browser. To show you in what file you're adding breakpoints or what code you are debugging, VWD updates the Solution Explorer and displays a list of all files containing client-side script that you can step through as soon as you are in debug mode. Breakpoints you set in these files during debugging are preserved when possible, making debugging a smooth experience.

The easiest way to learn the new client-side JavaScript debugging possibilities is by trying them out, so the next exercise dives right in and shows you how to debug the web service test page that you created in Chapter 10.

Try It Out Debugging JavaScript in Internet Explorer

You need to use Microsoft Internet Explorer to carry out the following exercise because most of the features shown in this Try It Out exercise only work with that browser. If Internet Explorer is currently not your default browser, right-click a page in the Solution Explorer and choose Browse With. Select Internet Explorer in the Browsers list and choose Set as Default. You can click Cancel to close the dialog box and VWD still remembers your default browser setting. When you're done with this exercise, you can switch back to your favorite browser using the exact same steps.

1. Open the file NameService.cs or NameService.vb from the App_Code folder. Locate the `HelloWorld` web method and set a breakpoint on the first line of code in the method that returns the personalized greeting. Close the file.
2. Open WebServices.aspx from the Demos folder and switch to Markup View. Locate the `HelloWorld` JavaScript method, click the line that declares the `yourName` variable and press F9 to set a breakpoint, visible in Figure 17-21.

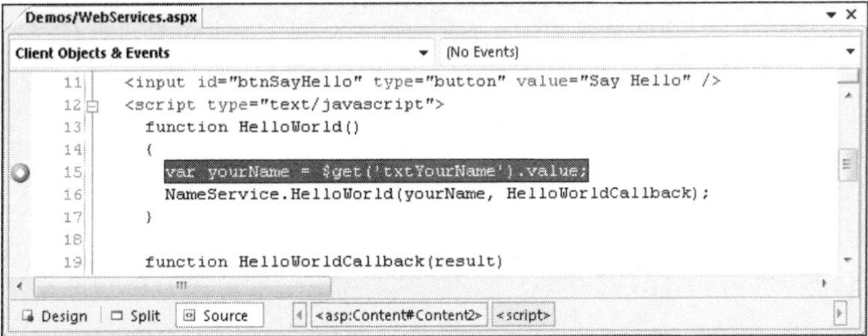

Figure 17-21

3. Press F5 to start debugging. The page will load in the browser and you get a `TextBox` control and a `Button`. Enter your name in the `TextBox`, and click the `Button`. As soon as you click it, focus is put back on Visual Studio, and the code halts in the JavaScript code block. Press F10 to execute the highlighted line and assign the name you entered to the `yourName` variable. Then hover your mouse over that variable and you'll see a data tip appear.
4. Open the other debugging windows and notice how they all behave identically to what you saw before. You can add JavaScript variables to the Watch window to look at their values, enter JavaScript in the Immediate window for evaluation, and so on. Also note that the Solution Explorer has changed, showing the active client-side files containing script right above the web project (see Figure 17-22).
5. Double-click WebServices.aspx under the Windows Internet Explorer node that has appeared in the Solution Explorer. At first, the file may look like before. But if you look closely, you can see that this is no longer the original source file with ASP.NET controls mixed up with other markup, but the final HTML rendered in the browser. To warn you that you are looking at the final file, and not the original source, VWD has added the text `[dynamic]` and a lock icon to the tab for the file above the Document Window, shown in Figure 17-23.

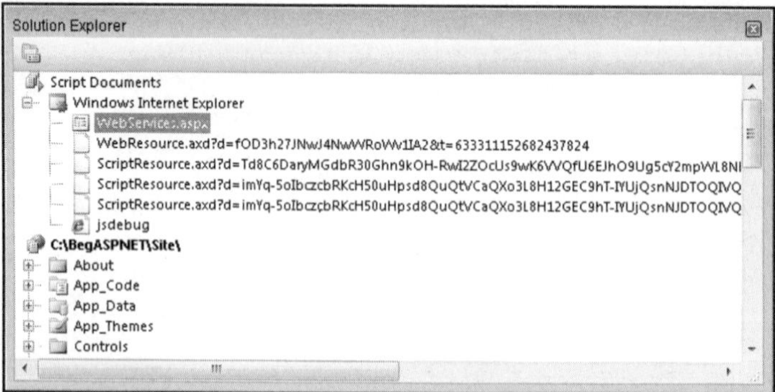

Figure 17-22

```
WebServices.aspx [dynamic]
Client Objects & Events          (No Events)

      <span id="ctl00_SiteMapPath1"><a href="#ctl00_SiteMapPath1_SkipLink"><img alt="Skip N


  <input id="txtYourName" type="text" />
  <input id="btnSayHello" type="button" value="Say Hello" />
  <script type="text/javascript">
    function HelloWorld()
    {
      var yourName = $get('txtYourName').value;
      NameService.HelloWorld(yourName, HelloWorldCallback);
    }

    function HelloWorldCallback(result)
    {
      alert(result);
```

Figure 17-23

What's really nice about this is that even though you are looking at a run time file, Visual Web Developer is still able to relate this run-time file with the original source. This means you can set breakpoints in the run-time file, and they'll be remembered in the original source so they are available for the next debugging session.

6. To see how this works, set a breakpoint on the line with the `alert` statement in the `HelloWorldCallback` handler, visible in Figure 17-23. Once the code returns from the web service that is being called in this exercise, you'll return to this handler again, so you can investigate the value returned by the service.

7. Press F5 to continue executing code. The name you entered in the text box is retrieved and then sent into the `HelloWorld` method of the service. Since you added a breakpoint there in step 1, the code should stop again, allowing you to look at the variable `yourName` passed to the web method. Although this exercise itself is pretty simple, a lot of magic just happened under the hood. You stepped from some client-side code running in the browser into code running in a web service at the server, all from the same IDE.

8. Press F5 again and you'll be taken back from the server-side web service into the client-side code where you can see the result of the web service in the `HelloWorldCallback` handler.

9. Press F5 once more. The code will complete and shows a JavaScript alert window with a greeting containing your name, just as it did in Chapter 10.

10. Close your browser, go back to VWD again, and open the file WebServices.aspx by double-clicking it in the Solution Explorer. This opens the original source file, and not the dynamic version you saw in step 5 of this exercise. Locate the `HelloWorldCallback` handler in the WebServices.aspx file. Note that the breakpoint you set in step 6 has been persisted.

How It Works

There are a few interesting points to take away from this exercise. First of all, you should understand the notion of *dynamic files*, or *run-time files*. These files are the final result from your ASPX pages and give you insight in the final HTML, CSS, and JavaScript that ends up in the browser. This is a great help, as it gives you a total view of all relevant content. Remember, the final markup displayed in the browser comes from a variety of resources, including master pages, content pages, external CSS and JavaScript files and from the various server controls that live in your page. The ability to look at the combined result from a single location makes it easy to see how everything fits together.

Another important point to remember from this exercise is how the IDE offers you fully integrated debugging features, from the client-side code in the user interface, all the way up into the server. To make it easy to set breakpoints, VWD doesn't restrict you to adding them in pages at design time only; instead it also allows you to set them in the dynamic run-time files. When you stop debugging, VWD tracks the new breakpoints for you, finds out to what source file they belong and adds them there again for you, so they are available for the next debugging session.

Although you may not realize it as everything is taking place on the same computer and in the same IDE, you are crossing many boundaries when debugging like this. First, VWD enables you to debug client-side script in the browser, so you can hook into that even before any data is sent to the server. When you press F5 in step 7, the code continues and sends the value to the server where it was used in the `NameService`'s `HelloWorld` method. Once that server-side web method is done, execution returns to the client again, enabling you to break on the alert statement that shows the message from the web service.

Useful as debugging may be during the development of your site, it lacks the capability to investigate the behavior of your site while it's running in production. Fortunately, ASP.NET has a solution for that as well: tracing.

Tracing Your ASP.NET Web Pages

Without tracing, finding out the values of variables, objects, the execution path your code follows, and so on at run time is problematic at best. You would probably add a `Label` control to the page, and then write information to it like this:

VB.NET

```
Dim value2 As Double = Convert.ToDouble(txtValue2.Text)
lblDebug.Text &= "The value of value2 = " & value2.ToString() & "<br />"
```

C#

```
double value2 = Convert.ToDouble(txtValue2.Text);
lblDebug.Text += "The value of value2 = " + value2.ToString() + "<br />";
```

Although this certainly works, it's quite cumbersome. First, you need to write a lot of code to make this work. Secondly, you end up with an ugly `Label` control in your page that you shouldn't forget to remove when you're done doing your debugging or tracing. And finally, when you're ready, you should remove all the code that sets the `lblDebug` label. You could take the easy way out by setting the `Label` control's `Visible` property to `False`, but you would still take the performance hit of assigning the text to the `Label` control.

Tracing in ASP.NET solves all of these problems. It lets your pages, controls, and code write information to a central location, called the Trace, which can then be shown in the browser. Tracing is built into the ASP.NET Framework, which means you can use it without any manual coding. Additionally, you can add your own information to the trace. In the following section you see how to use the built-in Tracing capabilities, giving you a wealth of information about your page. In a later exercise you see how to add your own information to the trace.

Using the Standard Tracing Capabilities

Without much work, you can get a lot of information about the way your pages execute. All you need to do is enable tracing for your pages. You can do this at the page level, or at the application level. With tracing enabled at the page level, you can choose one or more specific pages you want to trace. Application-level tracing is useful if you want to look at multiple pages at the same time. This may help you, for example, to find slow pages in your website.

Tracing with Individual Pages

To enable tracing in a page, you need to set its `Trace` attribute in the `Page` directive to `True`:

```
<%@ Page ........ Trace="True" %>
```

When you run a trace-enabled page, you get a long list of details at the bottom of the page. Figure 17-24 shows the ASP.NET Trace for the calculator demo page you have been working with in this chapter.

The trace provides a lot of details about your current page. At the top you find a summary of the request details, including the current date and time, the method used to retrieve this page (GET or POST), and the status code (status 200 in Figure 17-24, to indicate success).

Below that you see the Trace Information section. The ASP.NET `Page` class writes to the trace when you enable it. This is similar to the demo page you wrote in Chapter 14 that wrote to a `Label` control from the numerous events triggered during the page's lifecycle.

By default, the data is sorted by time, putting the events in the order in which they occurred. You can also sort them on the category (more on categories in the section that deals with adding your own information to the trace) by changing the `TraceMode` from `SortByTime` to `SortByCategory`:

```
<%@ Page ........ Trace="true" TraceMode="SortByCategory" %>
```

A little further down the page you see the *control tree*, which presents a hierarchical view of the controls in your page and their size.

Below the control tree you see the details for a number of important collections, including the Query String, Cookies, Form, Headers, and Server Variables. Additionally, you see information you may have stored in Session or Application state. Being able to see these collections can be a great aid in figuring out a problem. For example, if you have a page that is supposed to read from a cookie, but that crashes as soon as the page loads, you can look at the Cookies collection and see if the page receives the data you expect. These collections are invaluable tools in understanding the execution of your page and can really aid in finding and fixing bugs in your code.

Page-level tracing means you need to enable tracing on every page you want to trace. It also means that you need to disable it on every page after you're done. Because this can be cumbersome in a large site, ASP.NET also allows you to trace the entire application.

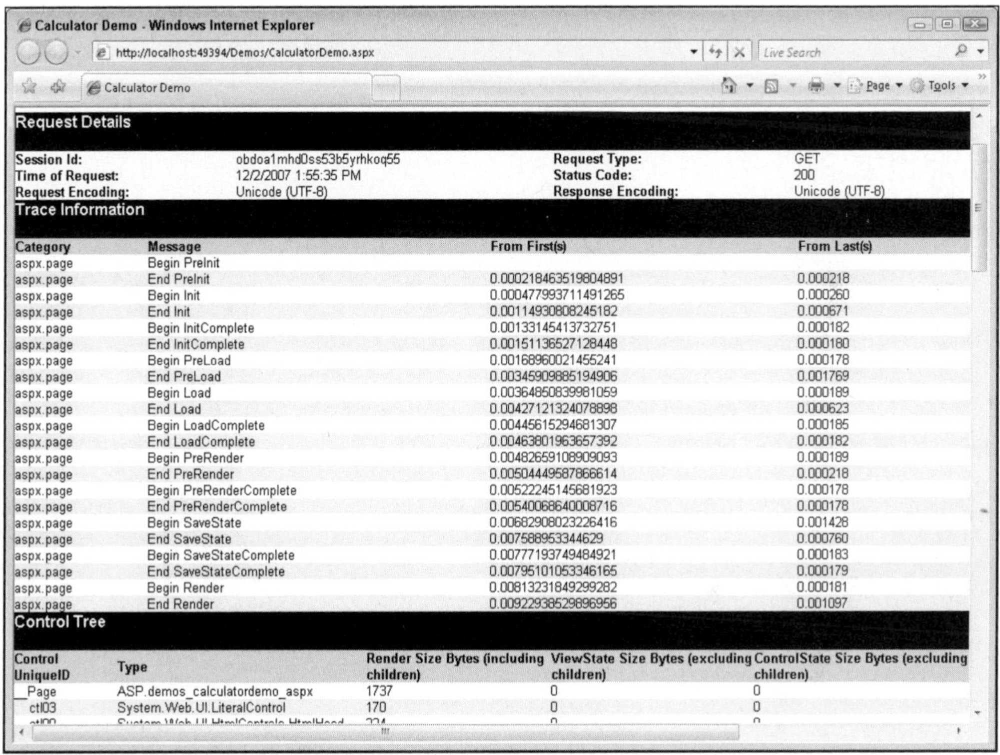

Figure 17-24

Tracing the Entire Web Site

You can enable tracing for the entire web site by changing trace settings in the web.config file. You do this by creating a `<trace />` element under `<system.web>`. The following table lists the most important attributes that the `<trace />` element takes.

Attribute	Description
`enabled`	This attribute determines whether or not tracing is enabled for the application. By default, tracing is disabled, so you need to set this attribute to `True` explicitly.

Continued

Attribute	Description
traceMode	This attribute determines the order in which items are sorted in the trace output. It works identically to the TraceMode attribute of the Page directive.
requestLimit	This attribute determines the number of trace requests that ASP.NET keeps available.
pageOutput	This attribute specifies whether the trace information is displayed on the page. When set to False (the default) you can only access the tracing information using Trace.axd that is discussed later.
localOnly	This attribute specifies whether the special Trace.axd handler is accessible from the local host only. From a security point of view, you're best off to leave this set to True, which means the trace is not available to outside users.
mostRecent	This attribute determines whether old trace records are discarded when the number of trace request hits the requestLimit. When set to False, tracing is disabled automatically when the requestLimit is hit.

When you have enabled tracing, there are two ways to read the trace information. When you have set pageOutput to True, the trace information is appended to each page, similar to what you saw with page-level tracing.

However, to make tracing less obtrusive, you can disable pageOutput and then request tracing information using a special file called Trace.axd. This is a virtual file, which means you won't find it in your web site when you go looking for it. However, the ASP.NET run time knows it should provide you with tracing information when you request this special page.

You see how this works in the following exercise.

Try It Out Enabling Tracing for the Entire Site

In this exercise you see how to enable site-wide tracing. First, you make a few changes to the web.config file. You'll then browse your site, filling the trace log with your page requests. Finally, you request the special Trace.axd page to see the available Trace log information.

1. Open web.config and locate the opening <system.web> tag. Right after it, add the following configuration information to enable tracing:

```
<trace
  mostRecent="true"
  enabled="true"
  requestLimit="100"
  pageOutput="false"
  localOnly="true"
/>
```

   This enables the trace, but doesn't add its output to the page. Instead you need to request the special Trace.axd page to see the trace information. Additionally, you make your system a little more secure by only allowing requests for the trace information from the local machine.

2. Save and close web.config. Then right-click Default.aspx in the Solution Explorer and choose View in Browser.
3. Click around the site, opening pages, changing the theme, filling in the contact form, and so on.
4. After you have requested at least five pages, change the address bar of your browser as follows so it requests the special Trace.axd page:

```
http://localhost:49394/Trace.axd
```

Your port number may be different, but it's important that you request the page Trace.axd on localhost. Note that this address assumes you configured the site with / as the Virtual Path as you learned how to do in Chapter 7. If you haven't done that, select the web site in the Solution Explorer, open its Properties Grid and set Virtual Path to /. Then request the Trace.axd file again. You should get a page similar to Figure 17-25.

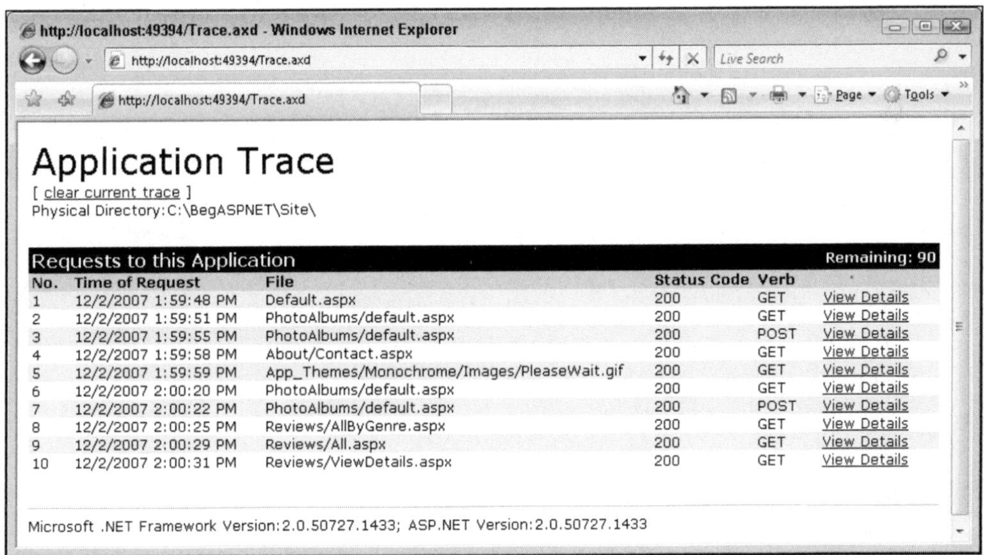

Figure 17-25

5. The list of traces is sorted based on time, from oldest to newest. Click the View Details link you see in Figure 17-25 for an ASPX page, like Contact.aspx. You get a page similar to the one shown in Figure 17-24.

How It Works

The ability to see trace information for pages that have been requested is extremely valuable. The information can help you understand the flow of information from and to a web page. For example, the trace information for the Contact.aspx page also shows the information that users have entered in the text box controls on the page. To see what this information looks like, click the View Details link for an item you want to zoom in on.

Although the information that ASP.NET traces for you automatically is extremely useful, you're not limited to just this information. You can also add your own information to the Trace log.

Adding Your Own Information to the Trace

Besides the standard information that the ASP.NET runtime adds for you, you can also add your own information to the trace. This is useful if, for example, you want to see the value of a variable, or want to find out if a specific event fires or not, and when it fires exactly.

You can add information to the trace by using the `Trace` class. This class exposes two useful methods: `Write` and `Warn`. Both do pretty much the same thing: they add information to the trace that you can optionally put in a category you can make up yourself. The only difference between `Write` and `Warn` is that messages written by `Warn` appear in red. You could use the `Warn` method for unexpected situations as the message will draw more attention.

In the following exercise you see how simple it is to add your own information to the trace using the `Warn` and `Write` methods.

Try It Out — Adding Trace Data to Your Pages

In this exercise you add some custom information to the ASP.NET trace. You'll use the `Write` method to write out trace information in a normal page execution, and use the `Warn` method for unexpected scenarios.

1. Open CalculatorDemo.aspx, switch to its Code Behind, and locate the `Click` handler for the Calculate button.
2. Right before the `Select Case` (VB.NET) or `switch` statement(C#), add the following `Trace.Write` call:

VB.NET

```
Trace.Write(String.Format("Performing the calculation with the {0} operator", _
            lstOperator.SelectedValue))
Select Case lstOperator.SelectedValue
```

C#

```
Trace.Write(string.Format("Performing the calculation with the {0} operator",
            lstOperator.SelectedValue));
switch (lstOperator.SelectedValue)
```

3. Near the bottom of the event handler, modify the `Else` statement for the check that ensures that both `TextBox` controls contain a value:

VB.NET

```
Else
  lblResult.Text = String.Empty
  Trace.Warn("Custom Category", _
             "TextBox controls are empty; time to add Validation controls?")
End If
```

C#

```
else
{
  lblResult.Text = string.Empty;
  Trace.Warn("Custom Category",
           "TextBox controls are empty; time to add Validation controls?");
}
```

4. Enable tracing for this page explicitly. You can do this by setting the `Trace` attribute of the `Page` directive in Markup View:

```
<%@ Page ... Trace="true" %>
```

5. Save all your changes and request the calculator page in the browser by pressing Ctrl+F5. Enter two numbers and click the Calculate button. Note that your custom information is added to the trace, between the `Begin Raise PostBackEvent` and `End Raise PostBackEvent` trace entries. Note also that the Category is missing.

6. Clear the text from both `TextBox` controls in the browser and click the Calculate button again. The trace information should now be easier to spot because of its different color and own category name, as shown in Figure 17-26.

7. Go back to Visual Web Developer once more and disable tracing. You need to change this at the page level (remove the `Trace` attribute from the `Page` directive of the Calculator page) and at the site level in web.config. Save all your changes and request the Calculator page again. Note that the page still functions correctly, but no longer outputs the trace information.

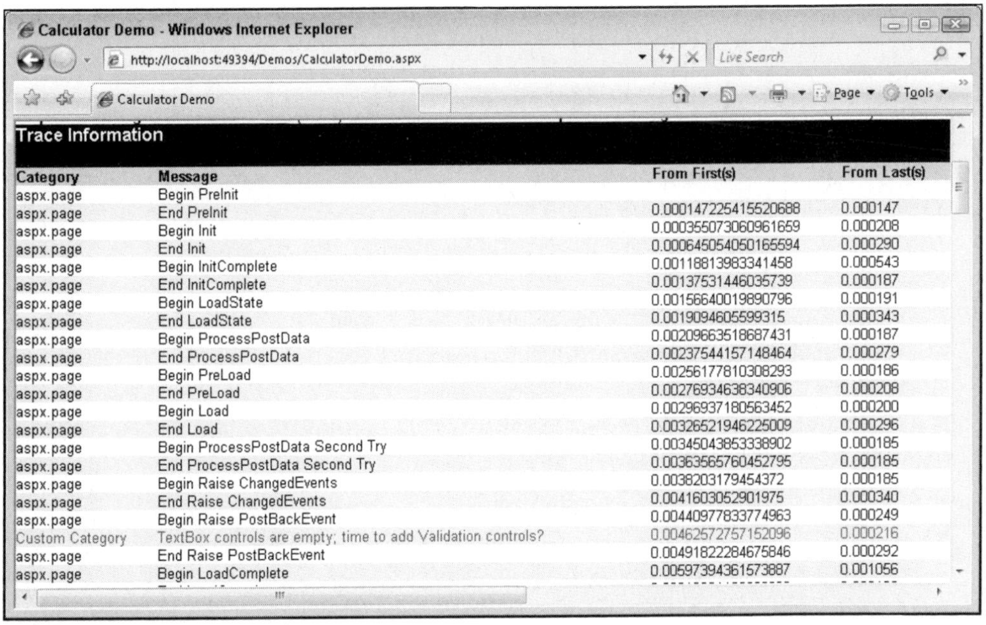

Calculator Demo - Windows Internet Explorer
http://localhost:49394/Demos/CalculatorDemo.aspx

Trace Information

Category	Message	From First(s)	From Last(s)
aspx.page	Begin PreInit		
aspx.page	End PreInit	0.000147225415520688	0.000147
aspx.page	Begin Init	0.000355073060961659	0.000208
aspx.page	End Init	0.000645054050165594	0.000290
aspx.page	Begin InitComplete	0.00118813983341458	0.000543
aspx.page	End InitComplete	0.00137531446035739	0.000187
aspx.page	Begin LoadState	0.00156640019890796	0.000191
aspx.page	End LoadState	0.0019094605599315	0.000343
aspx.page	Begin ProcessPostData	0.00209663518687431	0.000187
aspx.page	End ProcessPostData	0.00237544157148464	0.000279
aspx.page	Begin PreLoad	0.00256177810308293	0.000186
aspx.page	End PreLoad	0.00276934638340906	0.000208
aspx.page	Begin Load	0.00296937180563452	0.000200
aspx.page	End Load	0.00326521946225009	0.000296
aspx.page	Begin ProcessPostData Second Try	0.00345043853338902	0.000185
aspx.page	End ProcessPostData Second Try	0.00363565760452795	0.000185
aspx.page	Begin Raise ChangedEvents	0.0038203179454372	0.000185
aspx.page	End Raise ChangedEvents	0.00416030529019975	0.000340
aspx.page	Begin Raise PostBackEvent	0.00440977833774963	0.000249
Custom Category	TextBox controls are empty; time to add Validation controls?	0.00462572757152096	0.000216
aspx.page	End Raise PostBackEvent	0.00491822284675846	0.000292
aspx.page	Begin LoadComplete	0.00597394361573887	0.001056

Figure 17-26

How It Works

The `Write` and `Warn` methods of the `Trace` class allow you to write additional information to the trace. The ASP.NET run time keeps track of the information and displays it together with the rest of the Trace info, either directly at the bottom of the page in the browser with page-level tracing, or through the special Trace.axd page you saw earlier.

The `Write` and `Warn` methods each have three overloads. The first one (shown only with `Write` in the previous example) accepts a single string that is displayed in the Message column. The second overload also accepts a category name as demonstrated with the `Warn` method. The final overload, not shown in the previous Try It Out exercise, also accepts an `Exception` object whose message will be added to the trace output. This is useful to trace the information of an exception in a `Catch` block.

Tracing and Performance

Although it may seem that leaving `Warn` and `Write` statements in your code on your production system may hurt performance, this isn't the case. Since you can disable tracing in the web.config file by setting the `enabled` property of the `trace` element to `false`, you effectively eliminate the performance overhead of tracing.

A Security Warning

Tracing can be very useful, but leaving trace information in your production environment can lead to information disclosure. Therefore, you should always either disable tracing by setting its `enabled` attribute in web.config to `False`, or at least by setting the `localOnly` to `True`. In Chapter 18 you learn a trick that enables you to make this change for all sites on your production server, making it easy to block access to the trace functionality.

Practical Debugging Tips

The following list provides some practical tips to help you debug your application.

- Never leave `debug="true"` in the web.config file for the site in a production environment. Always set it to `false` to improve performance and ensure solid operation of your site. In Chapter 18 you see an even better solution to ensure this setting is never set to true on a production server.
- Try to avoid *swallowing* exceptions in a `Catch` block. You may be tempted to wrap your code in a `Try/Catch` block and then leave the entire `Catch` block empty. Although this certainly avoids exceptions showing up in the user interface, it makes debugging extremely difficult. Because you are no longer aware a problem occurs, you also cannot write code to prevent the error from happening in the first place. The general rule here is: Catch errors that you can handle successfully, for example by displaying a message to the user. If you can't handle the exception in your code, let it bubble up and log it in the `Application_Error` event handler so you know that the exception occurred.

- If you need to re-throw an exception in a `Catch` block, don't use `Throw ex` (`throw ex` in C#), but use `Throw` (`throw` in C#) only. When you use `Throw ex`, you make it difficult to track the path the code has followed before the exception occurred. Here's the code:

VB.NET

```
Try
  ...
Catch ex As Exception
  Throw ex              ' Bad example; you lose track of the source of the exception
  Throw                 ' Good example; forwards the exception and maintains the call stack
End Try
```

C#

```
try
{
  ...
}
catch (Exception ex)
{
  throw ex;             // Bad example; you lose track of the source of the exception
  throw;                // Good example; forwards the exception and maintains the call stack
}
```

- Try to avoid exception handling when possible. As you saw in this chapter, it's much better (and faster) to simply avoid an exception in the first place. For example, the `DivideByZeroException` exception can easily be avoided by checking for a value of zero before carrying out the division.

Summary

No matter how carefully you program, your site is likely to contain some bugs or throw exceptions at run time. To minimize these exceptions and build a site that runs as smooth as possible, there are a number of things you can do.

First of all, you can use exception handling techniques, where you write code that is able to catch exceptions that you foresee and handle them appropriately. Sometimes, updating a simple label to inform the user something went wrong is enough. In other cases, for example when the database server is down, there isn't much you can do. For those cases, the code that sends error messages by e-mail may come in handy, as it allows you to detect and analyze problems even if you're not logged in to the server.

To help you write code with as few bugs as possible, Visual Web Developer offers you a great set of debugging tools. The ability to break into your code and analyze and change the execution environment is a great time-saver. On top of that, you have the smooth debugging experience that allows you to debug from client-side code all the way into the server. Together, they make VWD a great tool in your bug-slashing adventures.

But even if you have debugged your application thoroughly, there's still a chance your site may have issues in production, whether they are related to performance, logic errors, or other unexpected reasons. In those cases, you can use the ASP.NET tracing facilities that let you track information about running pages. Analyzing this trace information can bring you a long way in fixing the underlying issues.

Now that your web site is complete and hopefully bug-free, the next step is to put it online. You'll see how to deploy your ASP.NET web site in the next chapter.

Exercises

1. What's the difference between debugging and tracing?
2. Imagine you have some code that could potentially throw an exception. For example, you try to send an e-mail message to a mail server, or write a file to disk while you're not sure if you have the right permissions to do so. What kind of exception handling strategy would you use to avoid the exception from being displayed in the browser? What code would you need?
3. You're taking over a web site that has been built by another developer who had never heard of exception handling. Your client is complaining about the quality of the site and the large number of "yellow screens of death" that users see. Besides analyzing the code for the entire application, what would be a quick solution to get information about the errors and the locations where they occur? And how can you shield the site's users from the dirty details of the exception messages?

Deploying Your Web Site

Congratulations! The fact that you're reading this chapter probably means you now have a full-featured, database-driven ASP.NET web site that is ready to release into the wild. It's an exciting time for you and your project. Pretty soon your application will be used and judged by your target audience.

To make your web site accessible to users on the Internet, you need to publish it to a production server that is connected to the Internet. What kind of server this is and where it is located depends on your own requirements and budget. You can host the site on a home server in your attic with a private Internet connection or you can host it with an external (and often commercial) party with a direct connection to the Internet backbone.

Either way, some work needs to be done to get your site from its development location at C:\BegASPNET\Site to a location where it's accessible over the Internet.

This chapter deals with a few topics related to successfully deploying your web application. You'll learn about the process from preparing your application in the development environment to actually running and testing it at your production server.

In particular, this chapter looks at the following topics:

- How to ease the deployment process through simple changes to your code and configuration
- How to prepare your site for deployment by creating a copy using Visual Web Developer's built-in copy tools
- How to install and configure a web server and your web site on your target machine
- How to avoid common errors you may get when deploying a site
- How to copy data stored in your SQL Server 2005 databases to the target server

The chapter then ends with a list of things you need to take care of when deploying an application. You can use this checklist to help you make sure you configure your production site in the most secure and optimal way.

Preparing Your Web Site for Deployment

When you're working on the first edition of your web site in a development environment, managing the site and its source code is pretty straightforward. You only have a single version of the site's source, making it easy to maintain. However, as soon as you put your site in production, you now have two versions of the site: one running in the production environment and the one you use for development. This makes it difficult to keep things synchronized. For example, you probably use a different database and connection string in your production environment. You're also likely to use different e-mail addresses for the e-mail that is sent by the site. Finally, you may want to disable sending the error e-mails from the Global.asax files in a development environment. If you make all of these changes in the code directly when you put your site live, there's a fair chance that you'll overwrite some settings during the next update, which can lead to unwanted results.

This section shows you how to make managing different versions of the same web site a little easier. You see how to move some of the hardcoded settings, like e-mail addresses, to the web.config file. The code in your application then reads these values at run time. The only difference between your development and production environments is a single configuration file, making it easy to have different settings in both environments.

Avoiding Hardcoded Settings

So far the pages and user controls you have built used some hardcoded settings for things like e-mail addresses. For example, ContactForm.ascx, the User Control that sends out an e-mail, uses the following code to set the recipient and sender information:

VB.NET

```
myMessage.From = New MailAddress("you@yourprovider.com", "Sender Name Here")
myMessage.To.Add(New MailAddress("you@yourprovider.com", "Receiver Name Here"))
```

C#

```
myMessage.From = New MailAddress("you@yourprovider.com", "Sender Name Here");
myMessage.To.Add(New MailAddress("you@yourprovider.com", "Receiver Name Here"));
```

Hardcoding settings in this manner makes it difficult to give them different values in different environments. Every time you want to roll out your site to production, you need to make sure you're not accidentally overwriting settings you changed for the production environment.

Fortunately, ASP.NET comes with a great solution to avoid these kinds of problems: the web.config file, *expression syntax*, and the `ConfigurationManager` class you use to read from the web.config.

The web.config File

You've used the web.config file a number of times in this book to store information about connection strings, profile and membership information, and so on. What you haven't seen is the `<appSettings>` element that allows you to store data in a key/value pair using `<add />` elements. The `<appSettings>` element allows you to store simple information, like an e-mail address, and retrieve that value by its key. For example, to store an e-mail address, you can add the following to the web.config file:

```
<appSettings>
  <add key="FromAddress" value="webmaster@planetwrox.com" />
</appSettings>
```

The `<appSettings />` element is placed outside the `<system.web>` element in the web.config file, yet still within the parent `<configuration />` element.

Obviously, you need a way to access the data in `<appSettings />` at run time. You can do this in a couple of ways, including expression syntax and using the `ConfigurationManager` class, both of which are discussed next.

Expression Syntax

Expression syntax allows you to bind control properties to resources, like those found in the `<appSettings>` element in web.config, connection strings, and localization resource files. To display data from the `<appSettings>` element, you use the following syntax where *`AppSettingKeyName`* refers to a key you define in web.config:

```
<%$ AppSettings:AppSettingKeyName %>
```

For example, to display a copyright notice on your pages in a `Literal` control, you can add the following setting to web.config:

```
<add key="Copyright" value="Copyright by Wrox" />
```

You can then display this text in a `Literal` control like this:

```
<asp:Literal ID="litCopyright" runat="server" Text="<%$ AppSettings: Copyright %>" />
```

To make it even easier to set properties like `Text` as in the example above, VWD comes with the Expression Editor. To access this dialog box, select a control in Design or Markup View, open its Properties Grid and then click the ellipsis for the (Expressions) item, shown in Figure 18-1. You may find that the (Expressions) item does not always show up when in Markup View. If that's the case, switch to Split View or Design View first.

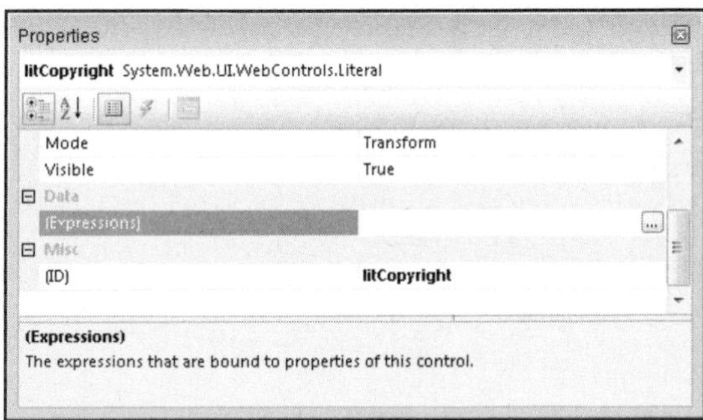

Figure 18-1

The Expressions dialog box opens, enabling you to bind control properties to expressions. To bind the `Text` property of the `Literal` control to an application setting, first click Text on the left side of the dialog box, choose AppSettings from the Expression Type drop-down list on the right, and finally choose the right AppSetting from the drop-down list in the Expression Properties section. Figure 18-2 shows the complete Expressions dialog box for a `Literal` control used to display the copyright text.

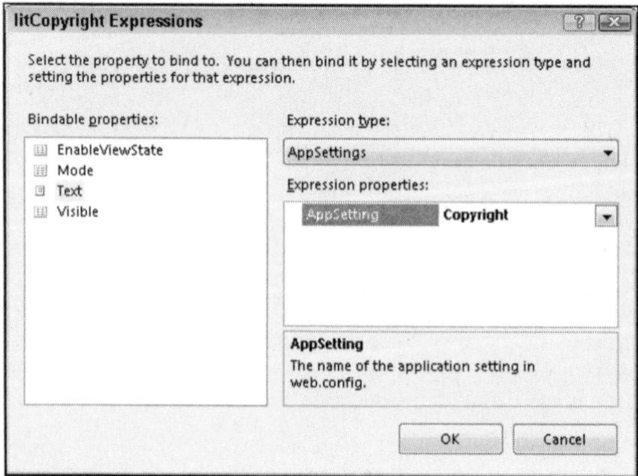

Figure 18-2

When you click OK, VWD modifies the `Text` property of the `Literal` so it contains a reference to the correct application setting.

Getting values from the web.config using expression syntax is useful, but may not cover all your needs. Therefore, it's good to know you can retrieve the values programmatically as well. To do this, you can use the `ConfigurationManager` class.

The ConfigurationManager Class

The `ConfigurationManager` class from the `System.Configuration` namespace provides access to data that is stored in configuration files. It has special support for the `appSettings` and `connectionStrings` elements of the web.config file, enabling you to retrieve data from those sections with a single line of code. The following snippet shows you how to retrieve the `FromAddress` section from the `appSettings` element:

VB.NET

```
Dim fromAddress As String = ConfigurationManager.AppSettings.Get("FromAddress")
```

C#

```
string fromAddress = ConfigurationManager.AppSettings.Get("FromAddress");
```

The `Get` method always returns data as a string, so you'll need to convert it to a proper type if you're expecting anything other than a string. For example, if you have stored a Boolean value in web.config like this:

```
<add key="SendMailOnError" value="true" />
```

you need to use the following code to retrieve and convert the value:

VB.NET

```
Dim sendMail As Boolean = _
  Convert.ToBoolean(ConfigurationManager.AppSettings.Get("SendMailOnError"))
```

C#

```
bool sendMail = Convert.ToBoolean(ConfigurationManager.AppSettings.Get("SendMailOnError"));
```

Although you can access the `ConfigurationManager` class in your code directly (provided you have imported the `System.Configuration` namespace), I prefer to create static, read-only properties in a custom configuration class that accesses the web.config to get the values. You'll see how to do this in the following exercise.

Try It Out Moving Application Settings to the Configuration File

In this exercise you create a class with a few properties that get their values from the web.config file. You'll then use the properties of this class in your code to replace the hardcoded values that were used earlier.

1. Inside the App_Code folder, create a new class file and call it AppConfiguration.vb or AppConfiguration.cs. In C#, remove the constructor code, highlighted in the following code block:

```
public AppConfiguration()
{
  //
  // TODO: Add constructor logic here
  //
}
```

   Because the class is going to have static properties exclusively, you don't need the constructor.

2. Inside this class, right after the class declaration, create a new `Shared` (`static` in C#), read-only property that returns the `FromAddress` from the web.config file. Recall from Chapter 5 that a `Shared` / `static` member (like a method or a property) operates on the class itself, and not on an instance of that class.

VB.NET

```
Public Class AppConfiguration
  Public Shared ReadOnly Property FromAddress() As String
    Get
      Dim result As String = ConfigurationManager.AppSettings.Get("FromAddress")
      If Not String.IsNullOrEmpty(result) Then
        Return result
      End If
      Throw New Exception("Appsetting FromAddress not found in web.config file")
    End Get
  End Property
End Class
```

C#

```
public class AppConfiguration
{
  public static string FromAddress
  {
    get
```

```
    {
      string result = ConfigurationManager.AppSettings.Get("FromAddress");
      if (!string.IsNullOrEmpty(result))
      {
        return result;
      }
      throw new Exception("Appsetting FromAddress not found in web.config file");
    }
  }
  ...
}
```

3. Repeat the previous step, but this time create the following three properties by creating a copy of `FromAddress`:

```
FromName
ToAddress
ToName
```

   Don't forget to rename all three occurrences of `FromAddress` into the new property name.

4. Still inside the `AppConfiguration` class, create a Boolean property called `SendMailOnError`:

VB.NET

```
Public Shared ReadOnly Property SendMailOnError() As Boolean
  Get
    Dim result As String = ConfigurationManager.AppSettings.Get("SendMailOnError")
    If Not String.IsNullOrEmpty(result) Then
      Return Convert.ToBoolean(result)
    End If
    Throw New Exception("Appsetting SendMailOnError not found in web.config file")
  End Get
End Property
```

C#

```
public static bool SendMailOnError
{
  get
  {
    string result = ConfigurationManager.AppSettings.Get("SendMailOnError");
    if (!string.IsNullOrEmpty(result))
    {
      return Convert.ToBoolean(result);
    }
    throw new Exception("Appsetting SendMailOnError not found in web.config file");
  }
}
```

5. When you're ready with the five properties, save and close the AppConfiguration file.

6. Open the Code Behind of ContactForm.ascx in the Controls folder and locate the code that sets the From and To addresses and replace the hardcoded values with their `AppConfiguration` counterparts:

VB.NET

```
myMessage.From = New MailAddress(AppConfiguration.FromAddress, AppConfiguration.FromName)
myMessage.To.Add(New MailAddress(AppConfiguration.ToAddress, AppConfiguration.ToName))
```

C#

```
myMessage.From = new MailAddress(AppConfiguration.FromAddress, AppConfiguration.FromName);
myMessage.To.Add(new MailAddress(AppConfiguration.ToAddress, AppConfiguration.ToName));
```

7. Save your changes and close the file.

8. Open the Global.asax file and wrap the entire code in `Application_Error` in an `If` check that ensures that `SendMailOnError` is set to `True`:

VB.NET

```
Sub Application_Error(ByVal sender As Object, ByVal e As EventArgs)
  If AppConfiguration.SendMailOnError Then
    If HttpContext.Current.Server.GetLastError() IsNot Nothing Then
      ...
    End If
  End If
End Sub
```

C#

```
void Application_Error(object sender, EventArgs e)
{
  if (AppConfiguration.SendMailOnError)
  {
    if (HttpContext.Current.Server.GetLastError() != null)
      ...
    }
  }
}
```

9. Open web.config and replace the existing `<appSettings />` element with the following, and change the e-mail address for `FromAddress` and `ToAddress` to your own:

```
<appSettings>
  <add key="FromAddress" value="webmaster@planetwrox.com" />
  <add key="FromName" value="Planet Wrox" />
  <add key="ToAddress" value="webmaster@planetwrox.com" />
  <add key="ToName" value="Planet Wrox" />
  <add key="SendMailOnError" value="true" />
</appSettings>
```

10. Save all your changes and close any open files. Press Ctrl+F5 to open the home page in your browser. Go to the Contact page and fill in the contact form. You should receive an e-mail at the address you specified in step 9.

11. Request a nonexistent page in your browser. For example, change the address in the browser's address bar to DefaultTest.aspx. You should receive an e-mail with the exception details, just as in Chapter 17.

12. Go back to Visual Web Developer, open web.config, and change the setting for `SendMailOnError` from `true` to `false`:

```
<add key="SendMailOnError" value="false" />
```

13. Save all your changes, and again request a page that doesn't exist. Because you changed the `SendMailOnError` setting, you shouldn't get an e-mail with the exception details.

How It Works

The properties of the `AppConfiguration` class look into the web.config file for the requested application settings. When the setting is not defined or does not contain a value, each property throws an exception. This is useful to detect missing application settings at an early stage. Instead of silently returning an empty value, you now get an exception that reminds you to add the required application setting.

At run time, the code accesses these properties like this:

VB.NET

```
myMessage.From = New MailAddress(AppConfiguration.FromAddress, AppConfiguration.FromName)
```

C#

```
myMessage.From = new MailAddress(AppConfiguration.FromAddress, AppConfiguration.FromName);
```

Because the properties have been defined as `Shared` (`static` in C#), you can access them directly on the `AppConfiguration` class, without the need to create a new instance of `AppConfiguration` first.

Although you could access the `<appSettings>` element in web.config directly in the code (for example, you could use `ConfigurationManager.AppSettings.Get("FromAddress")` to get the e-mail address in ContactForm.ascx directly), I prefer to wrap the `<appSettings>` elements in shared properties in their own class. This solution gives you IntelliSense on the `AppConfiguration` class, making it easy to see what configuration properties are available. It also enables you to write centralized code that throws exceptions when the required application settings cannot be found. If you access web.config directly in your own code, you would need to check for valid values every time you access a setting.

The same principle is used for the `SendMailOnError` setting. When an exception occurs at run time, the code in `Application_Error` now consults the `SendMailOnError` property. This property in turn checks the `<appSettings>` element of web.config to determine if an error message should be e-mailed or not. Because the `SendMailOnError` property is a Boolean, the code uses `Convert.ToBoolean` to convert the string returned from the web.config file into a Boolean.

By storing values in web.config instead of hardcoding them, your site becomes easier to maintain and deploy. When you go live, all you need to do is create a copy of web.config for your production environment and change a few settings.

With the hardcoded application settings moved to the central web.config file, the next step in the deployment process is creating a copy of your web site.

Copying Your Web Site

During development of your site you use the built-in web server that ships with Visual Web Developer. While this server is great for local development, you can't use it in a production environment, as it only listens to requests coming from localhost. To put your site in production, you need to deploy it to a machine that runs IIS — Internet Information Services, Microsoft's professional web server. In this section you see how to prepare your site so it can be run under IIS. Later in this chapter you see how to install and configure IIS.

To deploy your site to a production server, the deployment targets shown in the following table are available, right from within VWD.

Deployment Option	Description
File system	This option allows you to create a copy of the site on the local file system of your development machine or networked machine. This option is useful if you want to move the files manually to your production server later.
Local IIS	This option allows you to create a copy of your site that will run under your local IIS installation.
FTP	This option allows you to send the files that make up your web application to a remote server directly using FTP.
Remote Server	This option allows you to send the files that make up your web application to a remote IIS server. For this option to work, the remote server needs to have the Front Page Server Extensions installed. Check out the documentation that comes with IIS or consult the administrator of your remote server for more help with this option.

If you are using a commercial version of Visual Studio, you can access these four deployment options from the two main ways of deployment that VWD offers: Copy Web Site and Publish Web Site. If you're using the free Express Edition, you can only use Copy Web Site.

Creating a Simple Copy of Your Web Site

The Copy Web Site command simply creates a copy of your site using any of the four transportation options. This is a great way to quickly copy your site to another location, including your production server or even to a portable media device like a USB stick that you can take with you. You can access the Copy Web Site option from the Solution Explorer's toolbar shown in Figure 18-3 or from the main Website menu.

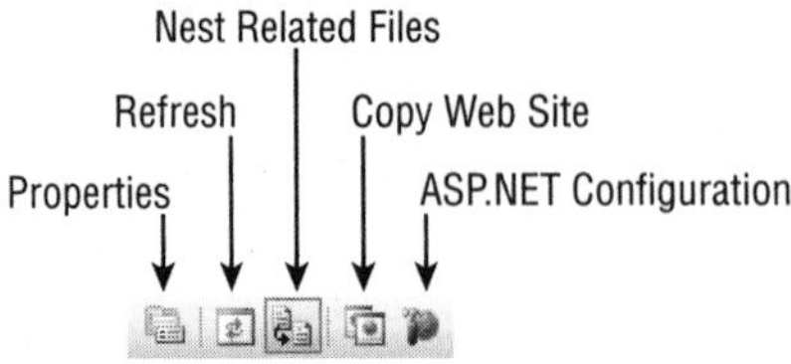

Figure 18-3

Before you create a copy of your web site, it's a good idea to check the state of your web site. You should do a full recompile where VWD compiles all the code and pages in your web site. This helps you detect any problems in your web site before you deploy it to a production environment.

Deploying a site is also a good moment to do some housekeeping. To avoid slowing down the deployment process and to keep your site as lean and clean as possible, you should delete the files from your web site that you don't need in production.

In the next exercise you see how to use the Copy Web Site command to create a copy of the entire Planet Wrox project. In a later exercise you use this copy again when you configure IIS for your production web site.

Try It Out Using the Copy Web Site Option

In this exercise you use the Copy Web Site option together with the Local File System option to determine the destination location of the copy. The other three transportation options (FTP, Local IIS, and Remote IIS) work similarly. The biggest difference with these options is that they ask you for details about the destination, like a user name and password, or the IIS web site you want to use. With the copy you create in this exercise, you can manually create an IIS web site, something you'll see how to do later in this chapter.

1. Close all open files in Visual Web Developer and then choose Build ➪ Rebuild Web Site from the main menu. Doing so forces VWD to recompile the entire application even if it already had compiled some parts of it. VWD lists any problems your site may have in the Error List. To verify your site is error free, open the Error List (choose View ➪ Error List from the main menu) and make sure you don't have any compile errors. Fix any errors you may have in your site.

2. When the Error List is empty, choose Website ➪ Copy Web Site or click the Copy Web Site icon on the Solution Explorer's toolbar shown in Figure 18-3.

3. At the top of the dialog box, click the Connect button to bring up a dialog box that lets you choose the destination location for your site.

   At the left site of the dialog box, make sure that File System is selected. Then on the right side, locate the folder C:\BegASPNET, click it once to select it, and then click the Create New Folder button; the button with the yellow folder icon at the top-right corner of the dialog box. Type Release and press Enter to apply the new name. Figure 18-4 shows the final dialog box.

   Finally, click Open to choose C:\BegASPNET\Release as the destination location for your copy operation.

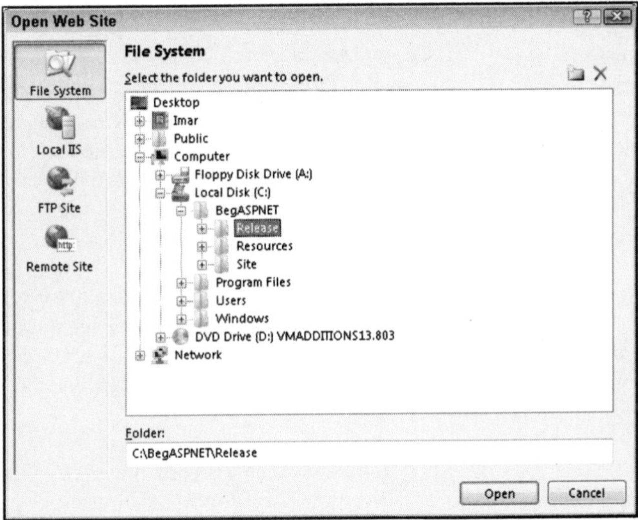

Figure 18-4

4. In the Copy Web Site dialog box, put the focus on the list at the left by clicking a file or folder and then press Ctrl+A to select all files in the Source Web Site list.

5. Click the Synchronize Selected Files button (the one with the two arrows facing opposite directions) between the two lists, visible in Figure 18-5. This starts the synchronization process. Because the folder displayed on the right side is empty, all files from the left list are copied to the right. When copying is complete, your dialog box should look like Figure 18-5.

6. Next, open a Windows Explorer window and browse to C:\BegASPNET\Release. Verify that all relevant files that make up your site are there.

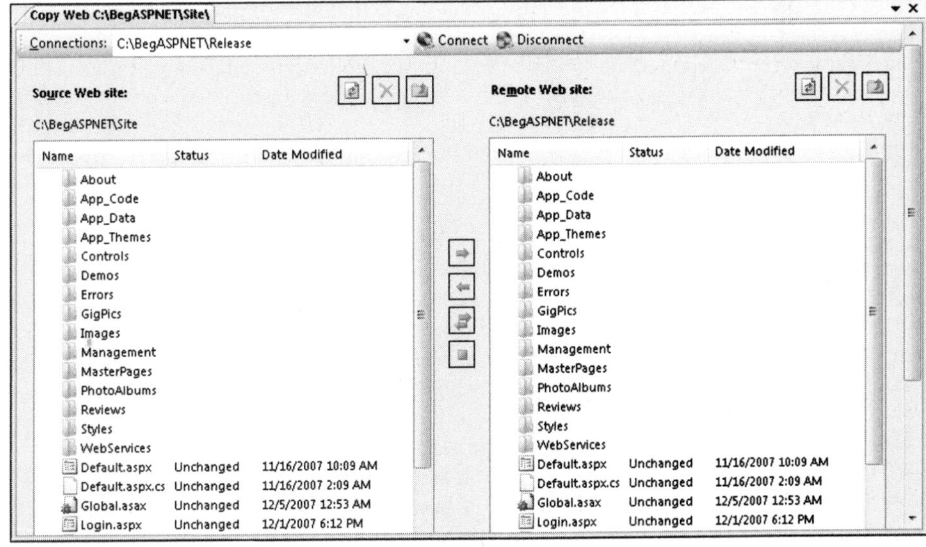

Figure 18-5

How It Works

The Copy Web Site option simply creates a copy of all files that make up your site. It can create a copy of the site at different locations, including the local file system, an FTP server, and an IIS server. In this exercise, you created a copy at a local hard drive. The first two buttons with blue arrows between the two file lists in Figure 18-5 allow you to copy files from the source to the remote location or vice versa. The third button, with the two arrows, allows you to synchronize, rather than just copy over the files. This means that if you run Copy Web Site again, VWD is able to determine which files have changed since the last time you ran it and only copy over those files.

In this exercise you opted to copy the files to the local system. This is a great way to create a copy that is detached from the development environment that can be run on your local machine. You can of course copy the same set of files to another machine using an FTP program, a USB stick, and so on. Also, if you host your site externally, your hosting provider may offer a web-based interface to upload these files to their server.

The good thing about this copy option is that it *synchronizes* your files. When you create a copy on your local system this may not seem like a big deal, but when you're creating the copy over a slow FTP connection, you'll be glad this tool only uploads new and changed files, and leaves unmodified files untouched.

The detached local copy enables you to make modifications to a few files first (like web.config) and then upload everything to your host.

Publishing Your Web Site

The Publish Web Site command, only available in the commercial versions of Visual Studio and not in the Express Editions, is similar to the Copy Web Site option in that it creates a copy of the web site you can use for deployment. However, it's different in that it allows you to *precompile* the application, which means all the code in the Code Behind of your ASPX pages, controls, code files in App_Code, and so on are compiled into *.NET assemblies*; files with a .DLL extension in the bin folder of your site. The main benefits of precompiling are source protection (others with access to the server can't look into your source) and an increased performance the very first time a page is requested. Pages that are not precompiled are compiled on the fly when they are requested the first time, which takes a little bit of time. Remember that regular visitors to your site will never be able to see the source of your application. All they'll be able to see is the final HTML that gets sent to the browser.

The Publish Web Site command is available from the Build menu and brings up the dialog box shown in Figure 18-6.

Clicking the ellipsis at the end of the target location brings up the same dialog box shown in Figure 18-4, allowing you to choose a target location. When the option Allow This Precompiled Site to Be Updateable is selected, VWD compiles all your VB.NET and C# code into .NET assemblies and places them in a bin folder that it creates at the root of your site. It leaves the markup in ASPX and ASCX files alone. However, with this option turned off, *all the markup code is compiled into .DLL files as well.* The actual files still need to be deployed to the server, but their content has been replaced with a placeholder text: "This is a marker file generated by the precompilation tool, and should not be deleted!" When the page is requested by a browser, the ASP.NET run time finds the appropriate content in the assemblies in the bin folder and serves its content as if it were a normal page. This latter option is especially great if you want to prevent other people from altering your site. Since all the source and markup is compiled into .DLL files, there is no way to change it on the server anymore, other than uploading a new set of published files.

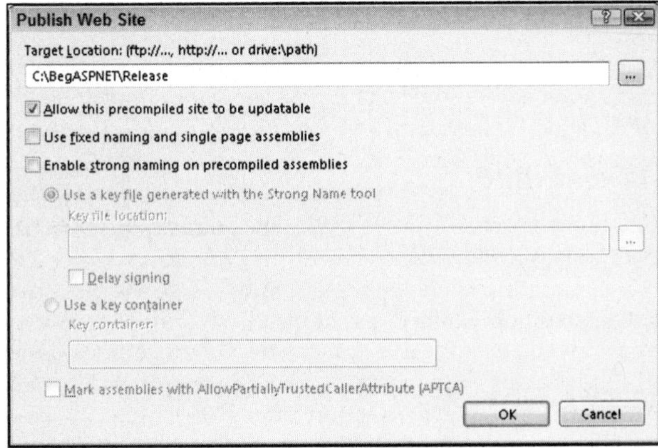

Figure 18-6

Copying or publishing your web site to a new folder on your local system is only one step of the deployment process. The next part is configuring the web server so it knows where to look for your files.

Running Your Site under IIS

Up until now, you've been using the built-in web server that ships with Visual Web Developer to debug and test your application. However, since requests to this server are limited to those coming from the localhost to minimize security implications, you'll need to use IIS, which comes with most major Windows versions. In order to have your web site run under IIS, you need to perform the following steps:

1. Install and configure IIS.
2. Install and configure the .NET Framework 3.5.
3. Configure security settings.

Depending on the current state of your system, some of these actions are optional. In the following sections you see how to carry out these steps.

Installing and Configuring the Web Server

Although IIS ships with most Windows versions, it's not installed by default, so you need to install it first. You also need to make sure that your version of Windows supports IIS. For IIS to be supported on Windows XP, you need to have Windows XP Professional, and not the Home edition. And although the Starter and Home Basic versions of Windows Vista ship with some parts of IIS, you can't run ASP.NET pages on them, so you need at least the Home Premium edition. On the server-based versions of Windows, IIS is fully supported.

To install and configure IIS on your Windows machine, you need to be logged on as an Administrator. If the account you use to log on to your machine does not have administrative privileges, you need to ask your administrator to install and configure IIS for you.

In addition to installing IIS, you'll also see how to create and configure the web site in IIS. Because of the way security works under Windows, your site probably won't work immediately after you configure IIS unless you change some of the security settings under Windows. You see how to do this in two later sections: "Understanding Security in IIS" and "Configuring the File System."

Making Sure IIS Is Installed

In this section, you'll see how to make sure that IIS is installed on the most important Windows versions: Windows XP, Windows Vista, Windows Server 2003, and Windows Server 2008. The procedure to check this and to install IIS is different for each version of Windows, so the sections below guide you through the different options. You should pick the one that matches your operating system.

Windows XP and Windows Server 2003

You install IIS through the Add or Remove Programs section, which you can access through the control panel or by choosing Start ➪ Run and then entering **`appwiz.cpl`**. When you're in the Add or Remove Programs dialog box, you need to click the Add/Remove Windows Components button at the left side of the dialog box to bring up the Windows Component Wizard, shown in Figure 18-7.

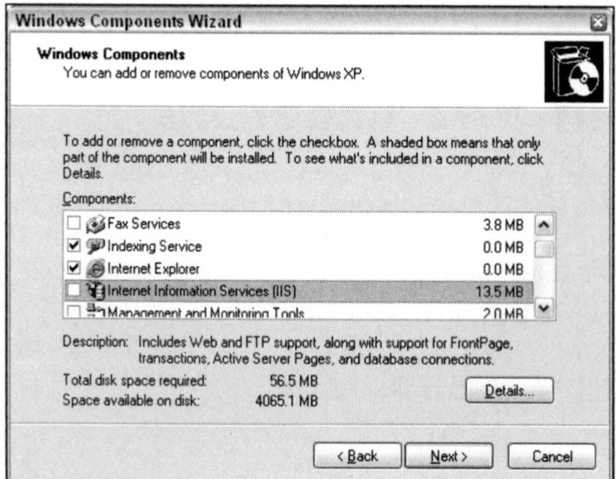

Figure 18-7

On Windows XP you should see the Internet Information Services (IIS) item directly in the list with components. For Windows Server 2003, click Application Server first and then click the Details button.

On Windows Server 2003, check the ASP.NET item. For both Windows XP and Windows Server 2003, verify that Internet Information Services (IIS) is selected and then click the Details button. Check at least the following items:

- Common Files
- Internet Information Services Snap-In (called Internet Information Services Manager on Windows Server 2003)
- World Wide Web Service

You don't need the SMTP server for the examples in this book (since you can use your ISP's external mail server) so you can uncheck the SMTP Service option. Not installing the SMTP server is a good security practice that helps minimize the security risks typically associated with installing IIS.

After you've selected the World Wide Web Service option, click its own Details button and ensure that at least World Wide Web Service is selected as well. The other items are optional.

Complete the Windows Component Wizard by following the on-screen steps. You may be asked for your Windows installation media. Once you have finished the Windows Component Wizard, reboot your machine and log in again. IIS is now ready to be run. You can proceed with configuring ASP.NET in the section "Installing and Configuring ASP.NET."

Windows Vista

You install IIS through the Programs and Features section, which you can access through the control panel or by clicking Start, typing `appwiz.cpl` in the Search box, and pressing Enter. When you're in the Programs and Features dialog box, click the link Turn Windows Features On Or Off to bring up the Windows Features dialog box, shown in Figure 18-8.

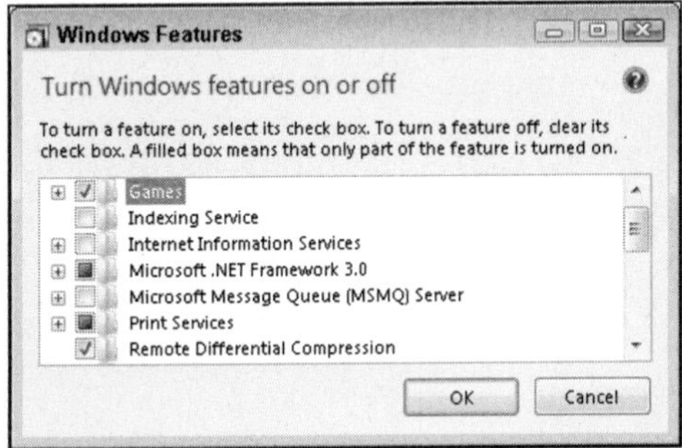

Figure 18-8

Click the Internet Information Services item to select it. This also selects some of its required subfeatures. Then expand World Wide Web Services ➪ Application Development Features and select ASP.NET. This causes some of the other Development features to be selected as well.

Finally, click OK and Windows installs the requested features for you. You can proceed with configuring ASP.NET in the section "Installing and Configuring ASP.NET."

Windows Server 2008

You install IIS through the Programs and Features section, accessible through the control panel or by clicking Start, typing `appwiz.cpl` in the Search box, and pressing Enter. When you're in the Programs and Features dialog box, click the link Turn Windows Features On Or Off to bring up the Server Manager, shown in Figure 18-9.

Right-click the Roles item in the tree on the left and choose Add Roles. Follow the on-screen instructions and install the role Web Server (IIS). When you get to the screen where you can choose the various Role Services, make sure you at least select ASP.NET under the Application Development node, as shown in Figure 18-10.

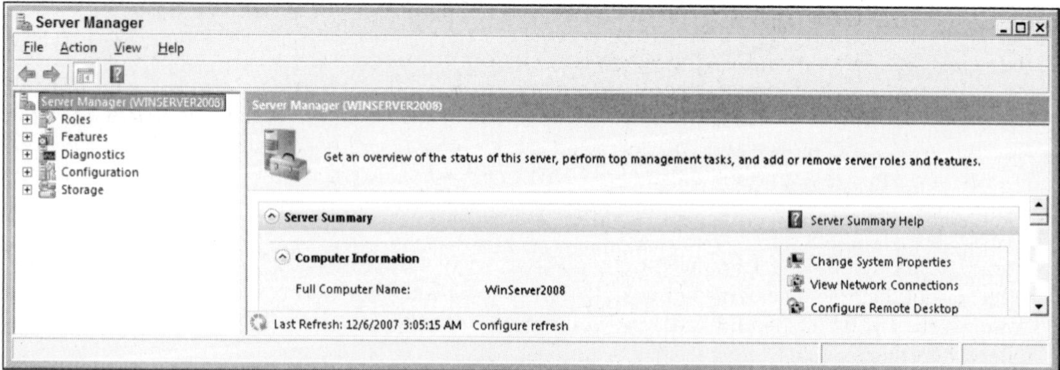

Figure 18-9

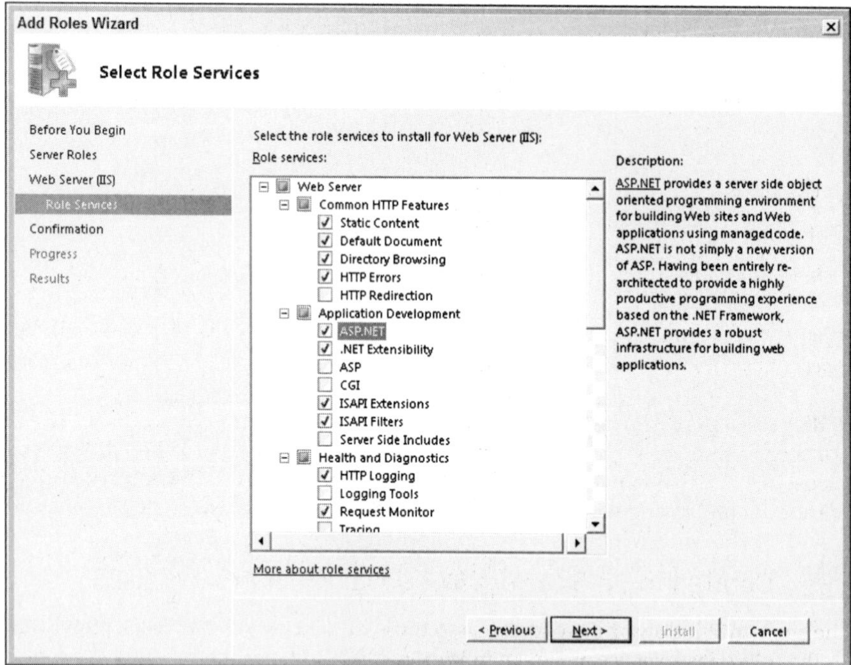

Figure 18-10

This in turn selects a number of other features that are required by IIS and ASP.NET.

Continue the Roles Wizard by clicking Next until Windows starts installing the required files for the selected roles. When everything is ready, you may need to reboot your computer. When you log back in, IIS is ready for use.

When IIS is installed successfully, you need to make sure you have the Microsoft .NET Framework version 3.5 installed.

Installing and Configuring ASP.NET

If you installed Visual Web Developer 2008 (any edition) on your target machine, you already have the .NET Framework 3.5 installed. Otherwise, you need to download it from the Microsoft site at `http://msdn.microsoft.com/net`. Follow the Download link or use the search option and search for "download framework 3.5." Make sure you download the 3.5 version, and not an earlier version of the .NET Framework. After you have downloaded the .NET Framework, run the installer and follow the on-screen instructions.

If you already had the .NET Framework 3.5 on your machine and installed IIS *afterward*, you need to tell IIS about the existence of the Framework. Normally, this is done during installation of the .NET Framework. If you installed IIS later, you would need to do this manually. To register ASP.NET in IIS follow these steps:

1. Open a command prompt. To do this in Windows XP or Windows Server 2003, choose Start ➪ Run, type `cmd`, and then press Enter. On Windows Vista and Windows Server 2008, click Start, type cmd in the search box, and then press Ctrl+Shift+Enter to start the command prompt with elevated permissions. When you confirm the action, the command prompt will open normally.
2. Navigate to the .NET Framework version 2.0 folder by entering the following command:

```
cd \Windows\Microsoft.NET\Framework\v2.0.50727
```

   Press Enter.

3. Enter `aspnet_regiis -i` and press Enter again.

   After a while you should get a message that ASP.NET was installed successfully.

Note that the 2.0 in the Framework version number is not a mistake; web sites created with the .NET Framework 3.5 still run under the 2.0 version of the ASP.NET run time that you are configuring here.

Now that IIS and the .NET Framework have been installed and configured correctly, the next step is to create your web site under IIS. You'll see how to do this in an upcoming Try It Out exercise. Again, you should choose the one that matches your operating system. After the following Try It Out exercise, you learn more about configuring security permissions for your system.

Try It Out Configuring a Site with Windows XP or Server 2003

Most of the steps in Windows XP are identical to those in Windows Server 2003. However, the screens you see in the following exercise are taken in Windows XP and might be slightly different on Windows Server 2003. Because Windows XP only allows you to run one web site at a time, you'll modify the default web site in this exercise. Make a note of any changes you make, so you can revert to the old site you had configured if you want to.

1. Open the Internet Information Services Manager. You find this item in the Administrative Tools section of the control panel. Alternatively, you can click Start ➪ Run, type **inetmgr**, and press Enter. The Internet Information Services Manager appears.
2. In the navigation tree, expand your server, and then expand the Web Sites node until you see the Default Web Site, shown in Figure 18-11.

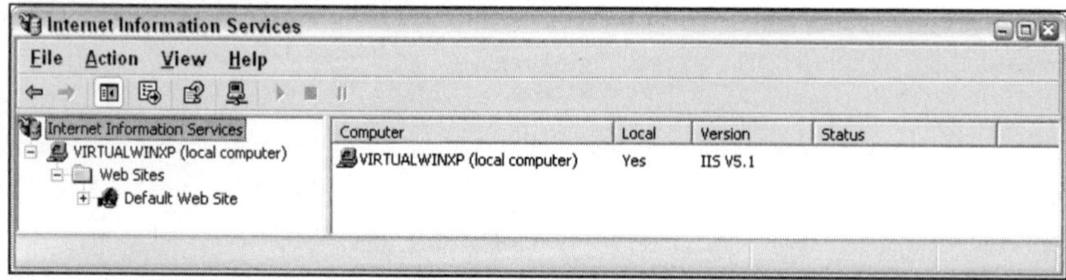

Figure 18-11

3. Right-click the Default Web Site and choose Properties. Switch to the Home Directory tab and in the Local Path area, click the Browse button and browse to the Release folder you created earlier at C:\BegASPNET\Release. When you're done, your dialog box should look like Figure 18-12.

4. Next, make sure that the right version of ASP.NET is selected. To do this, switch to the ASP.NET tab and ensure that the selected version in the drop-down list is 2.0.50727. If you don't see this option at all, refer to the section "Installing and Configuring ASP.NET" earlier in this chapter.

5. The next thing to check is to make sure that IIS is configured to use a sensible default document; the document that is served when you request just a folder name or the root of the site. The Planet Wrox site uses Default.aspx which is the most common default document name. To check this, switch to the Documents tab. If Default.aspx is not listed, click the Add button, enter Default.aspx, and then click OK to add the item to the list. Finally, use the up arrow button to move the item to the top of the list, as shown in Figure 18-13.

6. Click OK to apply your changes. If you get a dialog box about overriding the values for any child nodes, simply click OK to avoid this setting being applied to child nodes.

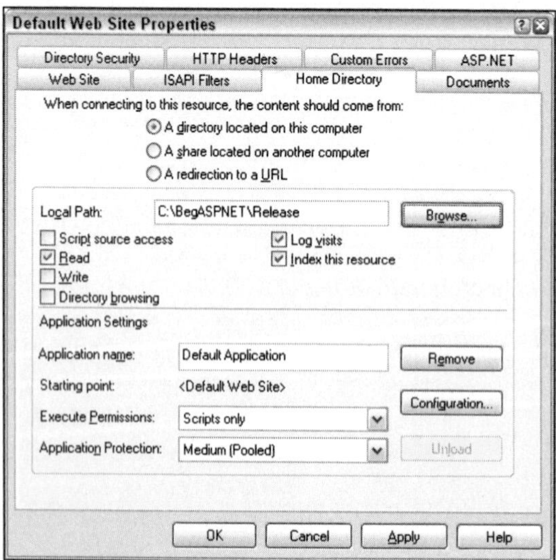

Figure 18-12

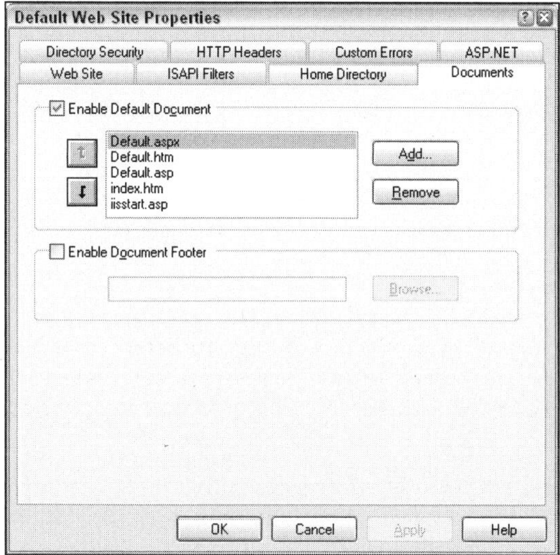

Figure 18-13

7. If you are using Windows Server 2003, there is one final action you need to perform: make sure ASP.NET is allowed to run. To do this, click the Web Service Extensions node of the Internet Information Services under your server name. You should see a list with Web Service Extensions that are currently available on your machine. Make sure that ASP.NET v2.0.50727 is set to Allowed.

At this point, IIS is configured correctly. However, your site probably won't work yet because you still need to configure the file system. You'll see how to do this after the next Try It Out exercise (which explains how to configure IIS in Windows Vista or Server 2008) and the explanation at the end of it.

Try It Out Configuring a Site with Windows Vista or Server 2008

In this exercise you see how to configure the standard "Default Web Site" that ships with IIS. While it's possible to create more than one site under IIS on Windows Vista and Windows Server 2008, this option is not discussed here. Contact your system administrator or read the help that comes with IIS to learn more about creating multiple web sites under IIS. Most of the steps in Windows Vista are identical to those in Windows Server 2008. However, the screens you see in the following exercise are taken in Windows Vista and may be slightly different on Windows Server 2008.

1. Open the Internet Information Services Manager. You find this item in the Administrative Tools section of the control panel if it's in Classic View. Alternatively, click Start, then type **inetmgr** in the Search box, and press Enter.
2. Expand the tree on the left until you see the Default Web Site, as shown in Figure 18-14.
3. Right-click the Default Web Site item in the tree on the left and choose Advanced Settings. You can open the same dialog box by clicking Advanced Settings in the Actions pane on the right of Figure 18-14.

Figure 18-14

4. In the Advanced Settings dialog box, click the Physical Path property, then click the ellipsis to open up a folder browser, select the folder C:\BegASPNET\Release, and click OK. Click OK again to close the Advanced Settings dialog box.

5. What's really cool about IIS on Windows Vista and Server 2008 is that its Management console gives you access to a lot of ASP.NET Configuration options. In Figure 18-14 you see the items you can access from here, including .NET Profile, .NET Roles, .NET Users, Application Settings, and Connection Strings. To see how this works, double-click the .NET Users item. You should see the user accounts you have created earlier. Double-clicking a user allows you to manage the roles for that user. Similarly, double-clicking the Application Settings item allows you to change the e-mail addresses you moved to web.config earlier in this chapter.

6. Next you need to make sure that IIS is configured to use a sensible default document; the document that is served when you request a folder name or the root of the site. The Planet Wrox site uses Default.aspx which is the most common default document name for ASP.NET web sites. To check this, double-click the Default Document option in the IIS list, visible in Figure 18-14. Then make sure that Default.aspx is present and at the beginning of the list. If the item is not there or it's not at the beginning of the list, manually type it in the text box at the beginning of the list and then click the Apply link in the Actions pane on the right (see Figure 18-15).

7. You can now close the Internet Information Services Manager, as the site is configured correctly as far as IIS is concerned. However, it still won't run correctly as you need to configure security permissions on the file system, as you'll see later.

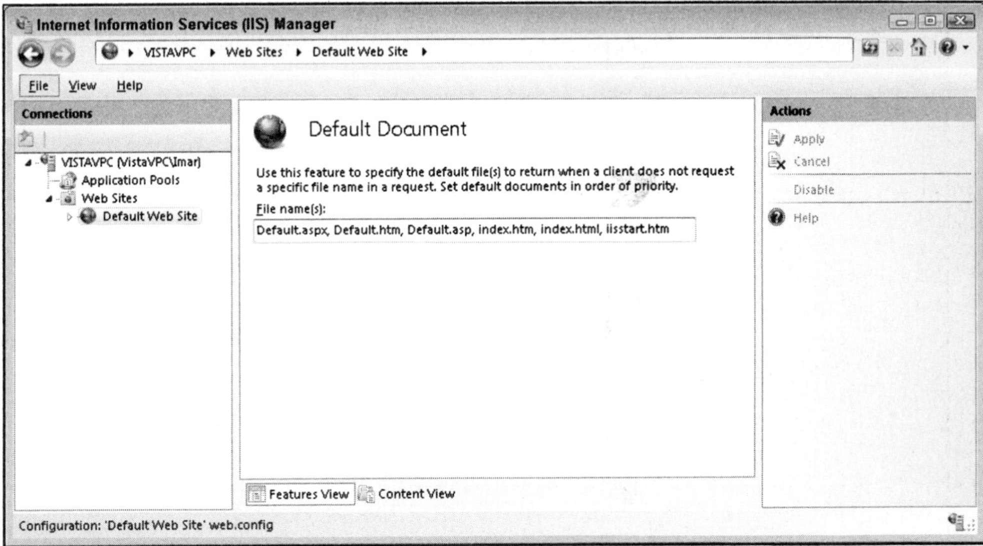

Figure 18-15

How It Works

Whether you chose the Windows XP / 2003 or the Vista / 2008 version of this Try It Out exercise, the steps you performed are pretty much the same. You started by configuring a web site in IIS. Each new IIS installation has a Default Web Site, the site that listens to `http://localhost` by default. In Windows XP you're stuck with this site but other operating systems allow you to create multiple sites.

Next, you pointed the root of the site to the Release folder that contains your web site. With that mapping set up, IIS is able to see what files to serve when you request a URL like `http://localhost`. It means that a URL like `http://localhost/Login.aspx` is mapped to the physical file at C:\BegASPNET\Release\Login.aspx.

At the end of the exercise you configured a default document, the file that is served when you request a URL without an explicit file name, like `http://localhost` or `http://localhost/Reviews`. By configuring Default.aspx as the default document, IIS will try to find and serve a file with that name instead.

The final thing you need to do to make sure your site runs on your local IIS installation is configure the security settings. This is discussed in the following two sections.

Understanding Security in IIS

Because of the seamless integration of the built-in web server in Visual Web Developer 2008, you may not realize what happens under the hood, and what security settings are in effect. In order to use resources in your site, like ASPX files, Code Behind files, the database in the App_Data folder, and the images in your site, your web server needs permissions from Windows to access those resources. This means that you need to configure Windows and grant access to those resources to the account that the web server uses. But what exactly is that account? The specific account that needs permission depends on a number of factors, including the version of Windows, whether you run your site under IIS or with the built-in web server, and on a number of settings within IIS.

In most cases, however, there are only two scenarios to consider: using the built-in web server or using IIS as your web server.

In the former case, the account that the built-in web server uses is the account you use to log on to your Windows machine. This account is usually something like `DomainName\UserName` or `MachineName\UserName`. Logged in with this account on Windows, you start up VWD 2008, which in turn starts up the built-in web server. This means that the entire web server runs with your credentials. Since it's likely you're an Administrator on your local Windows machine and have permissions to access all files that make up your site, things probably just worked fine so far without any changes to the security settings.

In the latter case, where IIS is used, things are quite different. By default, an ASP.NET application under IIS runs with a special account created when you installed IIS. This account is called ASPNET on Windows XP, while Windows Vista and Windows Server 2003 and 2008 use an account called Network Service. In addition to the account used for ASP.NET applications, you also need to configure an account used by the web server for resources that are not related to ASP.NET directly, like images, CSS files, and so on. The following table lists the accounts used by the built-in web server, ASP.NET, and IIS for non ASP.NET-related files.

Your OS	Using Built-In Server	ASP.NET Account	Web Server Account
Windows XP	DomainName\UserName or MachineName\UserName	ASPNET	IUSR_*MachineName*
Windows Vista	DomainName\UserName or MachineName\UserName	Network Service	IUSR
Windows Server 2003	DomainName\UserName or MachineName\UserName	Network Service	IUSR_*MachineName*
Windows Server 2008	DomainName\UserName or MachineName\UserName	Network Service	IUSR

Note that Windows XP and Windows Server 2003 use a *_MachineName* suffix for the account name, where *_MachineName* refers to the name of your machine. Windows Vista and Server 2008 simply use IUSR.

For example, if you want to configure IIS on Windows Vista, you need to use Network Service as the ASP.NET account and IUSR (without the *_MachineName* suffix as XP and 2003 have) as the Web Server account.

After you discovered the accounts that you need to configure, the final step is to configure the file system.

NTFS Settings for Planet Wrox

Regardless of the account you are using, you'll need to make changes to the Windows file system, so the web server is allowed to access your resources. This is only necessary when your hard drive is formatted using NTFS and not with FAT or FAT32, the older Microsoft file systems. You'll see how to determine the type of your drive in an exercise later in this section.

To successfully configure your NTFS file system for the Planet Wrox web site, you need to grant the following permissions to the web server accounts that you determined in the previous section.

Folder Name	Permissions	Explanation
Release (Located at C:\BegASPNET\)	List folder contents; Read	The web server and the ASP.NET accounts need to be able to read all the files and folders that make up the web site. Child folders, like Reviews, need to be set up to inherit these settings.
App_Data GigPics (Located at C:\BegASPNET\)	Modify; List folder contents; Read; Write	The ASP.NET account needs to be able to read from and write to the Microsoft SQL Server 2005 databases in the App_Data folder. It also needs to be able to save the uploaded images in the GigPics folder.

In the following exercise you learn how to configure the security settings for these folders.

Try It Out Configuring the File System

In this exercise you see how to configure the file system for the Planet Wrox web site. The exercise shows you screenshots from Windows Vista, but the other flavors of Windows have similar screens. Search Windows help for "security settings NTFS" or contact your administrator if you're having problems carrying out the following steps.

1. Start by opening a Windows Explorer and then locate your C drive. Right-click it and choose Properties. Verify that under File system you have NTFS. If you see the older FAT or FAT32 file systems you can skip this entire Try It Out, as FAT doesn't allow you to change security settings.
2. In the same Windows Explorer window, browse to the Release folder at C:\BegASPNET\Release, visible in Figure 18-16.

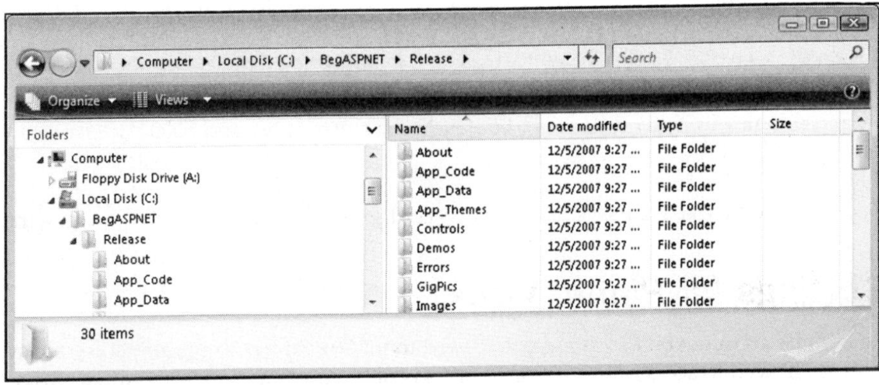

Figure 18-16

3. Right-click the Release folder, choose Properties, and then switch to the Security tab. If you don't see the Security tab on Windows XP, close the dialog box and then choose Tools ➪ Folder Options from the main menu. Click the View tab and then scroll all the way down in the Advanced settings list. Make sure that Use simple file sharing (Recommended) is *not* checked. Then open the Properties dialog box of the Release folder again. You should now have the Security tab, shown in Figure 18-17.

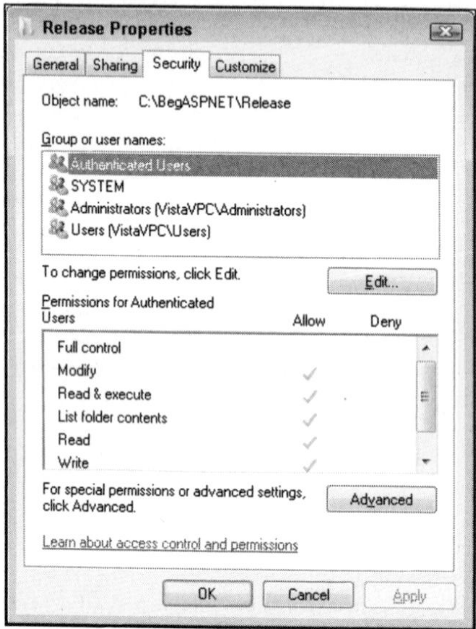

Figure 18-17

4. By default, the Release folder inherits its settings from its parent folder (C:\BegASPNET), which in turn gets its settings from the root of your C drive. To break this inheritance chain, click the Advanced button to open the Advanced Security Settings dialog box. For Windows Vista and Windows Server 2008, click the Edit button on the Advanced Security Settings dialog to turn this screen into Edit mode.

   You should get a screen similar to Figure 18-18.

5. Clear the Include Inheritable Permissions From This Object's Parent option (the setting is labeled "Inherit from parent the permission entries that apply to child objects" in Windows XP and "Allow inheritable permissions from the parent to propagate to this object and all child objects" in Windows Server 2003). Click OK. You'll get a dialog box that asks you if you want to Copy or Remove the existing settings. Choose Copy and then close all dialog boxes until you're back in the Release Properties dialog box visible in Figure 18-17.

6. The next step is adding accounts. In Windows Vista and Server 2008, click the Edit button visible in Figure 18-17, and then click the Add button. In Windows XP and Server 2003 you can click the Add button directly. Type the name of the ASPNET or Network Service account, depending on the version of Windows you are using. Instead of typing in the name manually you can also search for the account. To do this, click Advanced and then click the Find Now button. Once the correct account is in the text box, click the OK button.

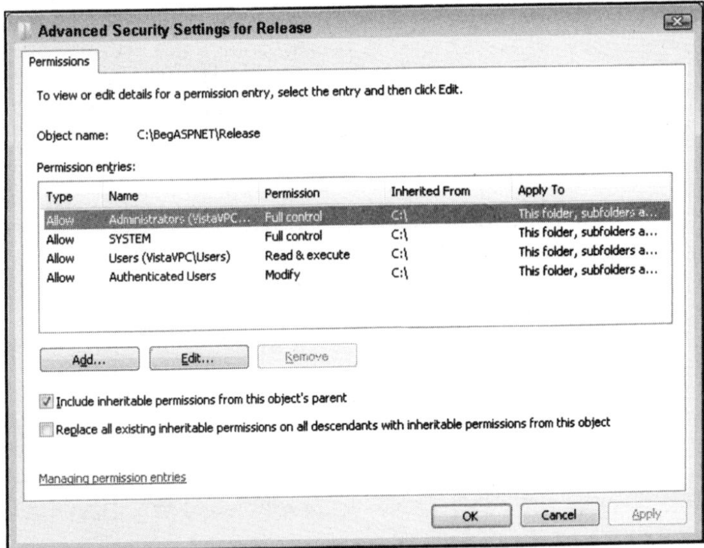

Figure 18-18

If you don't see the ASPNET account on Windows XP, make sure you installed and registered the .NET Framework correctly. When in doubt, run the `aspnet_regiis -i` *tool as shown earlier.*

With the account selected in the Group or user names list, ensure that only List Folder Contents and Read are selected.

Repeat this step, adding the IUSR or IUSR_MachineName account depending on your Windows version. Your dialog box should end up similar to Figure 18-19.

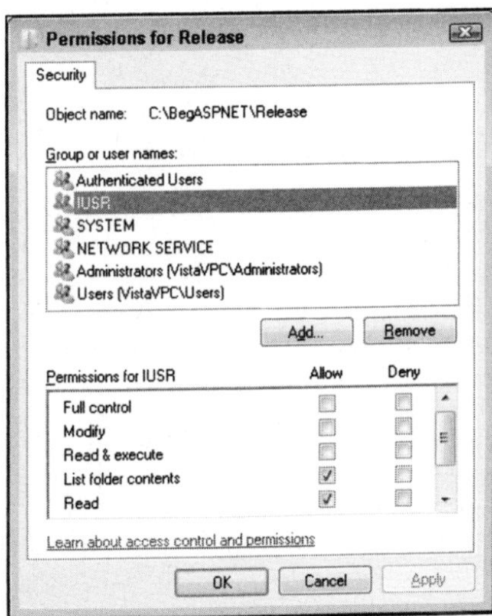

Figure 18-19

7. Close all open dialog boxes except for the Release Properties dialog box shown in Figure 18-17.

8. Click the Advanced button to open the Advanced Security Settings dialog box again. When you're using Windows Vista or Windows Server 2008, click the Edit button in the Advanced Security Settings dialog box to put it in Edit mode. Select the second checkbox you see in Figure 18-18. This forces Windows to apply the same security settings to all subfiles and -folders, replacing all existing settings. Click OK and then confirm the changes that will be made. Finally, click all remaining open dialog boxes.

9. Back in Windows Explorer, right-click App_Data from the Release folder, open its Security settings, and then change the permissions for the ASPNET or Network Service account by adding Modify and Write permissions (Read & Execute get selected automatically as well). For Windows Vista and Windows Server 2003 you need to click the Edit button first to bring the Properties dialog box in editable mode. Repeat this step for the GigPics folder.

10. At this stage, your web site should now work. To verify this, open a browser and go to `http://localhost`. You should see the Planet Wrox web site appear. To verify that everything is in order, browse through the site by requesting pages from the main menu, filling in the contact form, creating a new Album, uploading pictures and so on. If you get an error, refer to the section "Troubleshooting Web Server Errors."

    If you still can't make it work, try configuring the file system for the Everyone group. Although, from a security point of view, this is not the recommended group to use in a production environment, it may help you in finding out whether it's a security issue or not. If it works for the Everyone account, it's indeed security-related, so you need to make sure you configured the correct accounts.

How It Works

On a standard Windows system all files and folders are protected using the Windows NTFS file system. To ensure proper operation of your web site you need to grant the account used by the web server the necessary permissions to the files and folders of your web site. For most files and folders, Read permission is enough. However, for two folders you need to change the permissions. Both App_Data and GigPics are written to at run time so you need to grant Modify and Write permissions to these folders.

Troubleshooting Web Server Errors

When you are trying to configure your web server, you may run into a number of problems. This section lists the most common problems and provides a fix for them. You should realize there are a large number of possible reasons for the errors you may get, so it's impossible to cover them all here.

- **It is an error to use a section registered as allowDefinition='MachineToApplication' beyond application level:** You get this error when your web site is not at the root of the web server, or you haven't configured the folder as a separate application. Given the current configuration for the Planet Wrox site, you get this error when, for example, you map your site in IIS to C:\BegASPNET and then browse to `http://localhost/Release`. To fix this error, make sure that the root of your IIS web site points to the folder that contains your main web.config file; C:\BegASPNET\Release in this case. You get the same error when you open an incorrect folder in VWD. For example, when you open C:\BegASPNET and then browse to the /Site folder. Instead, open C:\BegASPNET\Site as the web site in VWD.

- **HTTP Error 401.3–Unauthorized:** You get this error when the account used by the web server does not have permission to read the files on disk. To fix these problems, refer to the section "Configuring the File System" earlier in this chapter and configure the correct permissions.
- **Failed to update database "C:\BEGASPNET\RELEASE\APP_DATA\ASPNETDB.MDF" because the database is read-only:** You get this error when either the database files have been marked as read-only, or if the account used by the web server is not allowed to write to the database files. In the former case, open the file's Properties in Windows Explorer and verify that the Read Only checkbox is cleared. In the latter case, ensure that the account used by ASP.NET has at least Modify permissions on the App_Data folder.
- **HTTP Error 403.14–Forbidden:** Although this error seems to suggest a problem with NTFS permissions at first, it's often caused by an incorrect or missing default document. If you get this error, ensure that the site or folder you are accessing contains a document called Default.aspx and that you configured that document name as a default document in IIS.
- **HTTP Error 404.0–Not Found:** You get this error when you try to request a file or folder that doesn't exist, like `http://localhost/DoesNotExist` or `http://localhost/DoesNotExist.gif`.
- **An error has occurred while establishing a connection to the server. When connecting to SQL Server 2005, this failure may be caused by the fact that under the default settings SQL Server does not allow remote connections. (provider: Named Pipes Provider, error: 40–Could not open a connection to SQL Server):** You can get this error for a number of reasons. Although the error message mentions SQL Server 2005 explicitly, you can also get the same error for SQL Server 2000. Usually, this error is caused by problems reaching the configured database server. You can get it when you misspelled the server's name in a connection string, the server is down, or the server can only be reached from the local machine and cannot be contacted over the network. To make sure that SQL Server is running correctly, open the Services section of the Administrative Tools (that you find in the Control Panel). Then look under SQL Server and verify that SQL Server is started. Appendix B explains SQL Server security in great detail and provides solutions to these problems.

If you run into a problem you can't solve, turn to the Wrox community site at `http://p2p.wrox.com`. You'll find many helping hands (including mine) that understand your problem and can help you find a solution for it.

When you are deploying to a machine that also has SQL Server 2005 Express Edition installed, you are done with the deployment process now. However, if you're dealing with a different SQL Server, the only thing that's left to do is to make sure your new Release site has the required data. You'll see how to do this next.

Moving Data to a Remote Server

Releasing a site to IIS on your local machine is pretty straightforward. You simply copy the data to a new location, configure IIS, change a few security settings and that's it. Because the site continues to use SQL Server 2005 Express Edition, it will run fine.

If you need to move your site to an external server or host, things are not so easy. Although copying the files that make up your site is usually extremely simple using an FTP program, copying data from your

SQL Server 2005 database to your host is quite often a bit trickier. This is because most web hosts don't support SQL Server 2005 Express Edition, so you can't just simply copy the .mdf files to the App_Data folder at your remote host. Instead, these hosts often offer the full versions of SQL Server, which you can access either with a web-based management tool or with tools like SQL Server Management Studio (for SQL Server 2005) and Enterprise Manager (for SQL Server 2000).

To make it easy to transfer data from your local SQL Server 2005 database into a SQL Server database of your web host, Microsoft has created the Database Publishing Wizard.

Using the Database Publishing Wizard

The Database Publishing Wizard allows you to create a .SQL script that contains all the information required to recreate your database and its data at a remote server. Recreating this data is a two-step process:

1. Create a .SQL script from your local SQL Server database.
2. Send this script to your hosts and execute it there.

The first step is described in detail in the next exercise. I won't show you how to run the script at your host because this is different from host to host. Instead, I will give you some general pointers so you know what to look for with your host.

Try It Out Exporting the Planet Wrox Database

You can access the Database Publishing Wizard from the Database Explorer window (the Server Explorer in paid versions of Visual Studio). Once you have completed the wizard, you'll have a .SQL file that contains all the necessary SQL code to recreate the database at a different server.

1. With the Planet Wrox project loaded in VWD, choose View ➪ Database Explorer (or View ➪ Server Explorer).
2. Right-click the PlanetWrox.mdf database and choose Publish to Provider to invoke the Database Publishing Wizard. If you get a welcome screen, click Next and ensure that your database is selected and that Script All Objects in the database is selected, and then click Next. The dialog box shown in Figure 18-20 appears.
3. In this screen, you can choose between two options. The first allows you to create a text file with the necessary SQL statements, while the second option allows you to talk to your shared hosting provider over the Internet directly. If your host supports this, they can give you the necessary information to set up a Provider here. For now, choose Script to File and click the Next button.
4. In the step that follows, accept all defaults shown in Figure 18-21 and click Next once more.
5. Click Finish and the wizard will generate the SQL script for you. Open the file in Notepad and look at the SQL statements it contains. Although most of it probably looks like gibberish to you, it can be used as is to recreate the database on a compatible SQL Server 2005 database.

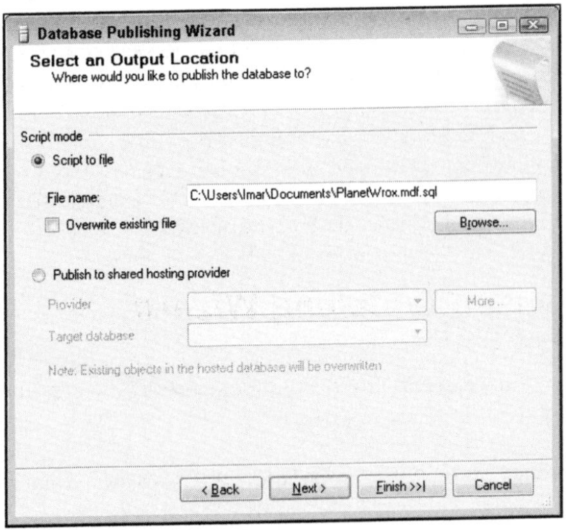

Figure 18-20

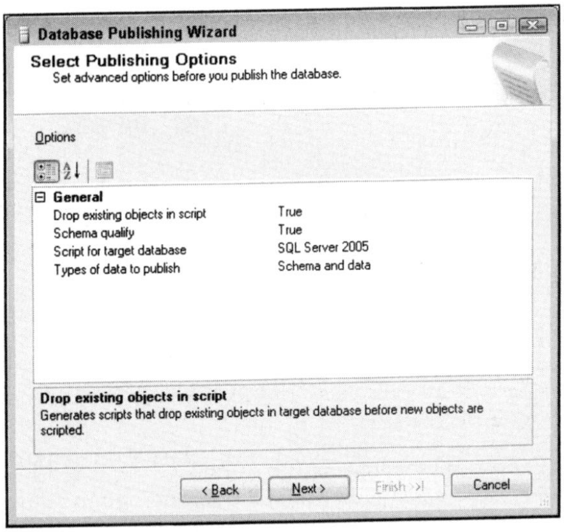

Figure 18-21

How It Works

The contents of a database can be separated in two categories: the structure of the database and the actual data. When the Database Publishing Wizard runs, it investigates the structure of your database first and creates SQL `CREATE` statements for all the items it finds in your database, like the tables you created in earlier chapters. It then creates INSERT statements that recreate all records like Reviews, Genres, and even users in the target database. By clearing the Script All Objects checkbox at the beginning of the wizard, you can selectively choose parts of your database allowing you to script only a few tables, for example.

At the end, the wizard assembles all the SQL statements and saves them to a single .SQL file. This file is now ready to be run at your host to recreate the database.

Recreating the Database

Although every host has its own rules and procedures when it comes to providing access to their SQL Server, they can be grouped in three categories.

First, there are some hosts that don't give you remote access to their database and require you to submit a SQL file so they can execute it for you. In this case, you don't have to do anything other than send the file and wait for the host to create your database.

The second category contains the hosts that allow you to execute SQL statements through a web interface. You typically log in to your online control panel and then execute the SQL statements created by the Database Publishing Wizard, either by uploading the file or by pasting its contents in a text area in a web page. Regardless of the method, you then end up with a database that you can access from your application. How this works exactly is different with each host, so consult the hosting service's help or support system for more information. There are some known issues with web-based database management tools from some providers, resulting in errors when you try to run the generated SQL file. Although the file itself is technically valid, the tool may still run into issues with it. If that's the case, contact your ISP for help on resolving the issue.

The final category contains hosts that allow you to connect to their SQL Server over the Internet. This allows you to use tools like SQL Server Management Studio to connect to the database at your host right from your desktop and execute the SQL scripts remotely.

The SQL Server Management Studio also has a free Express Edition that you can download from the Microsoft site (http://msdn.microsoft.com/vstudio/express/sql). This tool works pretty much the same as its commercial counterpart that ships with the paid versions of SQL Server 2005 and is an invaluable tool for anyone working with SQL Server databases.

After your database is recreated at your target server, you need to reconfigure your ASP.NET application to use the new database by changing the connection strings in your web site. For this to work, you need to modify two connection strings: the PlanetWroxConnectionString1 you created in an earlier chapter, and the LocalSqlServer connection string that the ASP.NET Application Services use by default. The easiest way to accomplish this is to clear the old connection string and then add a new one. How your connection string must look depends on the database you are using and its configuration. For many examples of proper connection strings, check out www.connectionstrings.com. The following snippet provides a simple example that reconfigures your application to use a database server called DatabaseServer. This example requires that you to log in with a user name and password:

```
<connectionStrings>
  <clear />
```

```
    <add name="PlanetWroxConnectionString1" connectionString="Data
           Source=DatabaseServer;Initial Catalog=PlanetWrox;User Id=YourUserName;
           Password=YourPassword;" providerName="System.Data.SqlClient"/>
    <add name="LocalSqlServer" connectionString="Data
           Source=DatabaseServer;Initial Catalog=ASPNETDB;User Id=YourUserName;
           Password=YourPassword;" providerName="System.Data.SqlClient"/>
  </connectionStrings>
```

This points both the connection string for the PlanetWrox database with the Reviews and Albums tables and the ASPNETDB database that contains Membership, Roles, and Profile information to a different SQL Server. Consult Appendix B for more information about configuring your ASP.NET application and SQL Server to operate with each other. Appendix B also explains how you can incorporate the data of the ASPNETDB database into your own, which is useful if your host charges you extra for each separate database.

At this stage, you're pretty much done configuring your newly created web site. Congratulations! However, before you relax and start enjoying your new web site, read the following checklist that helps you secure your site and improve its performance.

The Deployment Checklist

Instead of ending this chapter with general practical tips about deployment, this section gives you a practical list of things to check when you're ready to put your web site in production.

- ❑ Make sure you don't have debugging enabled in the web.config file. This causes unnecessary overhead and decreases performance of your web site as code executes slower and important files cannot be cached by the browser. To ensure debugging is disabled, open the web.config file you are using for your production environment, and verify that `debug` is set to `false`:

```
<compilation debug="false">
```

- ❑ Make sure you have turned on custom errors by setting the `mode` attribute of the `customErrors` element in web.config to either `On` or `RemoteOnly`. In the first case, everyone sees your custom error pages while in the second case, only users local to the web server can see the error details. Never leave the `mode` set to `Off`, as doing so can lead to information disclosure. The following snippet shows a safe configuration of the `customErrors` element:

```
<customErrors mode="On" defaultRedirect="~/Errors/Error500.aspx">
  Optional <error /> elements go here
</customErrors>
```

- ❑ Disable tracing, or at least limit the trace information to users coming from the local machine. The following `<trace>` element from web.config blocks tracing for users coming from machines other than the web server itself. Additionally, it stops the trace information from appearing in the page:

```
<trace mostRecent="true" enabled="true" requestLimit="1000"
          pageOutput="false" localOnly="true"/>
```

- Consider setting the `retail` attribute of the deployment element in machine.config to `true`:

```
<configuration>
  <system.web>
    <deployment retail="true"/>
  </system.web>
</configuration>
```

  - This section is used to indicate this is the shop-ready version of your web site and changes all three previous items to a secure setting: debugging and tracing are disabled, while error messages are only accessible to local users.
  - To make this change, you need to be logged in as an Administrator on your system. Also, be sure to make a backup copy of the file first. Because it serves as the root configuration file for all your ASP.NET web sites, you don't want to mess up this file.
- Scan your site for important files that may contain sensitive information (like Word or text documents) and either exclude them from the release version or consider moving them to the App_Data folder. Files in that folder cannot be accessed directly. However, your own code can still access the files as you saw in Chapter 9.
- Make sure you turn on error logging. With the error logging code you created in the previous chapter, you are notified whenever an error occurs, allowing you to proactively keep an eye on your server, fixing errors before they get a chance to happen again.
- If you are using themes in your site, make sure you remove either the `theme` or the `styleSheetTheme` attribute from the `<pages>` element in web.config. The Planet Wrox web site uses themes, but you added the `styleSheetTheme` attribute to enable design-time support in Visual Web Developer. On your production server all you need is this:

```
<pages theme="Monochrome">
  ...
</pages>
```

  This way, the page won't include the same style sheet twice.

What's Next

Now that you have finished your first ASP.NET web site, I am sure you are looking forward to creating your next site. The Planet Wrox site can serve as a basis for new sites you will build. You probably won't use any of its pages in your site directly, but hopefully this book and the Planet Wrox web site inspired you enough to build a new web site on your own.

Because this book is aimed at beginners, I haven't been able to provide you with a lot of in-depth information on some important topics. Some subjects that have their own chapter in this book easily warrant an entire book on their own. For example, topics like CSS, Ajax, and LINQ are so extensive that Wrox has published many books about them. Now that you've mastered the basics of these technologies, you can dig deeper into them using the following books in the Wrox Professional series:

- *Professional CSS: Cascading Style Sheets for Web Design* (ISBN: 978-0-7645-8833-4)
- *Professional AJAX* (ISBN: 978-0-471-77778-6)
- *Professional LINQ* (ISBN: 978-0-470-04181-9)
- *Professional ASP.NET 3.5* (ISBN: 978-0470-18757-9)
- *Professional ASP.NET 2.0 Design: CSS, Themes, and Master Pages* (978-0-470-12448-2)

Of course the web is also a good place for more information. The following URLs may be helpful in your search for more information about ASP.NET and its related technologies:

- `p2p.wrox.com`: The public discussion forum from Wrox where you can go for all your programming-related questions. This book has its own category on that site, allowing you to ask targeted questions. I am a frequent visitor of these forums and I'll do my best to answer each question you may have about this book.
- `imar.spaanjaars.com`: My own web site where I keep you up to date about various web programming–related topics.
- `www.asp.net`: The Microsoft community site for ASP.NET technology. Go here for news on ASP.NET, additional downloads, and tutorials.
- `msdn.microsoft.com/asp.net`: The official home for ASP.NET at the Microsoft developers web site that gives you a wealth of information on ASP.NET.

Summary

Obviously, deployment is an important action at the end of the development cycle of your new web site. However, it's unlikely that you only deploy your site once. As soon as you release the first version of your site, you'll think of other new and cool features you want to add, making the development of your site a never-ending story. To accommodate for this, you need to make your site easy to deploy.

One way to do this is by moving hardcoded configuration settings to web.config, giving you a single location to change parameters for the site in your development and production environments.

When you're ready to roll out your site, it's a good idea to create a copy of your site and clean that up before you send the files to your target server. Copying and then publishing a site is a breeze with the Copy Web Site and Publish Web Site commands.

Since you will deploy your site against IIS, you need to understand some important settings of this web server. In this chapter you saw how to configure the default web site and make some configuration changes. Because of the way security works in Windows and IIS, you also need to configure your hard drive so that the accounts used by the web server can read the files in your site, and write to specific folders like App_Data and GigPics.

The chapter closed with a short discussion of the Database Publishing Wizard, a tool that allows you to create a scripted copy of your database that you can use to restore your database on a remote server. Appendix B digs deeper into configuring and connecting to remote database servers.

Exercises

There are no exercises in this chapter, as the Planet Wrox site is now completely finished. However, your biggest challenge starts now: building web sites with the knowledge you gained from this book. If you ever build a site with the information from this book and want to share it with me, please contact me through my web site. Have fun!

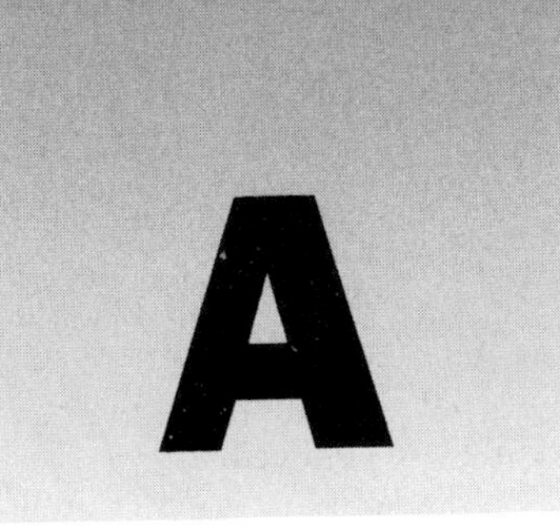

Exercise Answers

Chapter 1

Exercise 1 solution

The markup of a page in VWD contains the raw and unprocessed source for the page, including the HTML, ASP.NET Server Controls, and programming code. The web server then processes the page, executing the code in the page and then sends out the final HTML to the browser.

Exercise 2 solution

XHTML and HTML are related since XHTML is a version of HTML rewritten with XML rules. Where HTML is much more relaxed, XHTML forces the programmer to write code that conforms to XML rules, such as correct capitalization, closed tags, and attributes that are enclosed in quotes.

Exercise 3 solution

The easiest way to store HTML fragments that you use often is to select them in the code window and then drag them to a free space on the Toolbox. When the item is added, you can rename it to give it a more meaningful name. Now you can simply double-click an item or drag it from the Toolbox into your page whenever you need it.

Exercise 4 solution

There are a number of ways to reset part of the customization changes you may have made, including:

- Resetting the Window layout by choosing Window ➪ Reset Window Layout.
- Resetting the Toolbox by right-clicking it and choosing Reset Toolbox.
- Resetting all settings of VWD with the Import and Export Settings menu under the Tools main menu.

Exercise 5 solution

To change the property of a control on a page, you can click the control in Design or Markup View and then use the Properties Grid (which you can bring up by pressing F4) to change the value of the property.

Alternatively, you can change the property directly in the Document Window.

Chapter 2

Exercise 1 solution

A number of files fall in the web files category, including .aspx files (Web Forms that end up as pages in the web browser), .html files (that contain static HTML for your site), .css files that contain Cascading Style Sheets information and .config files that contain configuration information for the web site. Refer to the table with the different file types in Chapter 2 for a complete list of files.

Exercise 2 solution

When you want to make a piece of text both bold and italicized you need to select the text and then click the Bold button in the Formatting toolbar. Next you need to click the Italic button. The final HTML code in the page should look like this:

```
<b><i>Welcome to Planet Wrox</i></b>
```

Exercise 3 solution

The first way is using the Solution Explorer. Right-click your project, choose Add Existing Item and then browse for the item(s) you want to add.

Secondly, you can drag and drop files from Windows Explorer or from your desktop directly into a VWD project.

As a third alternative, you could put the files directly in the project's folder using Windows Explorer. For example, files you add to the folder C:\BegASPNET\Site become part of your web site automatically. If you don't see the new files appear in VWD directly, click the Refresh icon on the Solution Explorer toolbar.

Exercise 4 solution

In VWD, you have three different views on your code: Design View, Markup View (also referred to as Source View or Code View), and Split View. The first gives you an impression of how your web page is going to look in the browser, while the second view shows you the raw markup. Split View enables you to see both views at the same time.

VWD also has different views for other files. For example, programming code for an ASPX page is generally referred to as the Code Behind view or simply the Code Behind.

Chapter 3

Exercise 1 solution

The biggest benefit of an external style sheet is the fact that it can be applied to the entire site. Simply by changing a single rule in that file, you can influence all pages in your site that make use of that rule. With embedded or inline styles, you need to manually change all the files in your site. External style sheets also make it much easier to reuse a certain style with many different elements in your site. Simply create a class or an ID selector and reuse that wherever you see fit.

Exercise 2 solution

The rule can look like this:

```
h1
{
  font-family: Arial;
  color: Blue;
  font-size: 18px;
  border-top: 1px solid blue;
  border-left: 1px solid blue;
}
```

Note another shorthand version of the border property. This one looks similar to the border property you saw earlier in this chapter that allowed you to set the size, style, and color of the border at once. In this rule, `border-top` and `border-left` are used to change the left and top borders only; the other two directions, the bottom and right border, are not affected by this rule.

Exercise 3 solution

The second declaration is more reusable in your site as it denotes a Class selector as opposed to an ID selector. The latter can only be used once in a single page by an element that has a matching `id` attribute: `MainContent` in this example. The Class selector `BoxWithBorders`, on the other hand, can be used by multiple elements in a single page, as you are allowed to apply an identical `class` attribute to multiple elements in a page.

Exercise 4 solution

VWD lets you attach a style sheet in the following ways:

- Type in the required `<link>` element in the `<head>` of the page in Markup View directly.
- Drag a CSS file from the Solution Explorer into the `<head>` section of a page in Markup View.
- Drag a CSS file from the Solution Explorer and drop it onto the page in Design View.
- Use the main menu Format ⇨ Attach Style Sheet and then browse to your CSS file.
- Use the Manage Styles or Apply Styles windows and click the Attach Style Sheet link.

Chapter 4

Exercise 1 solution

The mechanism that enables controls to maintain their state is called ViewState.

Exercise 2 solution

The ASP.NET run time stores the values for the controls on a hidden field called `__VIEWSTATE`. This hidden field is sent with each postback to the server, where it's unpacked and then used to repopulate the controls in the page with their previous values.

Exercise 3 solution

The `DropDownList` only allows a user to make a single selection whereas the `ListBox` allows for multiple selections. In addition, the `DropDownList` only shows one item in the list when it's not expanded, while the `ListBox` is capable of displaying multiple items simultaneously.

Exercise 4 solution

In order to have a `CheckBox` control submit back to the server when you select or clear it in the browser, you need to set the `AutoPostBack` property to `True`:

```
<asp:CheckBox ID="CheckBox1" runat="server" AutoPostBack="True" />
```

Exercise 5 solution

Many of the ASP.NET Server Controls let you change colors using properties like `BackColor` and `ForeColor`. Additionally, you can use `BorderColor`, `BorderStyle`, and `BorderWidth` to change the border around a control in the browser. Finally, to affect the size of the control, you need to set its `Height` and `Width` properties.

Exercise 6 solution

Instead of setting individual style properties as listed in the previous exercise, you're much better off setting the `CssClass` property that points to a style sheet. This way, your pages become easier to maintain, as style-related information is stored in a single place: in the style sheet. At the same time, your page loads faster as not all the style information is sent for each control on each request. Instead, the browser reads in the style sheet once and keeps a locally cached copy.

Chapter 5

Exercise 1 solution

Both the `Byte` and the `SByte` data types are designed to hold small, numeric values. Both of them take up exactly the same amount of computer memory, so you're probably best off using the `Byte` data type. Because it doesn't allow you to store negative numbers, it's clear from the start that it can only contain a number between `0` and `255`. However, it's much better not to store someone's age, but the date of birth instead. That way, you can always extract the age from the date of birth by comparing it with today's date, as demonstrated by the following example:

VB.NET

```
Dim albertsBirthday As DateTime = New DateTime(1879, 3, 14)
Dim age As Integer = DateTime.Now.Year - albertsBirthday.Year        ' displays 129 in 2008
```

C#

```
DateTime albertsBirthday = new DateTime(1879, 3, 14);
int age = DateTime.Now.Year - albertsBirthday.Year;                  // displays 129 in 2008
```

Exercise 2 solution

This code looks a little tricky because it uses an expression and an assignment in one condensed line of code. Because of the order in which things are executed, the expression is evaluated first, followed by the assignment. In the original code, this means that `ShoppingCart.Items.Count > 0` is evaluated first. This is an expression that checks if the `Count` property of the `Items` collection in the shopping cart is greater than zero. As you learned in this chapter, this results in a Boolean expression with either the value `True` or `False`. This Boolean value is then assigned to the `Visible` property of the `Button` control, making it visible or hidden. When you expand the code a little, it's easier to see what's going on:

VB.NET

```
Dim canShowButton As Boolean = False
If ShoppingCart.Items.Count > 0 Then
  canShowButton = True
End If
DeleteButton.Visible = canShowButton
```

C#

```
bool canShowButton = false;
if (ShoppingCart.Items.Count > 0)
{
  canShowButton = true;
}
DeleteButton.Visible = canShowButton;
```

Exercise 3 solution

To create a specialized version of `Person`, you need to create a second class that inherits the `Person` class and extend its behavior by adding the `PhoneNumber` property.

VB.NET

```
Public Class PersonWithPhoneNumber
  Inherits Person
  Private _phoneNumber As String
  Public Property PhoneNumber() As String
```

```
      Get
        Return _phoneNumber
      End Get
      Set(ByVal value As String)
        _phoneNumber = value
      End Set
    End Property
  End Class
```

C#

```
public class PersonWithPhoneNumber : Person
{
  public string PhoneNumber { get; set; }
}
```

Chapter 6

Exercise 1 solution

The `ContentPlaceHolder` element should be placed in the master page. It defines a region that content pages can fill in. The `Content` control should be placed in a content page that is based on the master page. It is used to supply the content for the `ContentPlaceHolder` element that it is connected to.

Exercise 2 solution

To link a `Content` control to its `ContentPlaceHolder` in the master page, you need to set the `ContentPlaceHolderID`:

```
<asp:Content ID="Content1" ContentPlaceHolderID="IdOfContentPlaceHolder" Runat="Server">
</asp:Content>
```

Exercise 3 solution

There are a few ways to do this. First, you can create a named skin with a different CSS class in the same skin file. You then hook up this named skin to the control you want to change:

```
<asp:Button runat="server" SkinID="RedButton" CssClass="RedButton" />
```

The `Button` control in the ASPX page should then set the `SkinID` to `RedButton`:

```
<asp:Button ID="Button1" runat="server" Text="Button" SkinID="RedButton" />
```

Alternatively, you can disable theming on the `Button` control and give it a different CSS class directly in the ASPX page:

```
<asp:Button ID="Button1" runat="server" EnableTheming="False" CssClass="RedButton"
     Text="Button" />
```

In both solutions, you need a CSS class that sets the background color:

```
.RedButton
{
  background-color: Red;
}
```

Exercise 4 solution

A `StyleSheetTheme` is applied early in the page's life cycle. This gives controls in the ASPX page the opportunity to override settings they initially got from the `StyleSheetTheme`. This means that the `StyleSheetTheme` just suggests the look and feel of controls, giving the individual controls the ability to override that look. A `Theme` on the other hand overrides any settings applied by the controls. This allows you as a page developer to enforce the look and feel of controls in your site with the settings from the theme. If you still need to change individual controls, you can disable theming by setting `EnableTheming` to `False`.

Exercise 5 solution

There are three ways to set the `Theme` property in an ASP.NET 3.5 web site. The first option is to set the property directly in the `@ Page` directive so it applies to that page only:

```
<%@ Page Language="C#"  ...... Theme="Monochrome" %>
```

To apply a theme to all pages in your site, you set the `theme` attribute of the `<pages>` element in the web.config file:

```
<pages theme="Monochrome">
```

The final option you have is to set the theme programmatically. You have to do this in the `PreInit` event of the `Page` class, which you can handle in individual pages in your site or at a central location using the `BasePage` as you did in this chapter.

Exercise 6 solution

A base page allows you to centralize behavior for all the pages in your site. Instead of recoding the same functionality over and over again in every page, you move this code to the base page so all ASPX pages can use it. When you implement the theme switcher, all you have to do is write some code in the central `BasePage` class. All pages in your site that inherit from this `BasePage` class then correctly set the selected theme, without the need for any additional code.

Chapter 7

Exercise 1 solution

To change the items of the `Menu` control, two main groups of style properties are available. The properties in the first group all start with `Static` and refer to the main menu items that are shown when the page first loads. The `StaticMenuStyle` applies to the entire menu, while `StaticMenuItemStyle`, `StaticHoverStyle`, and `StaticSelectedStyle` are used to change the appearance of the actual menu items in various states (normal, when moused over, and when they are the active menu item).

For the subitems, the same style properties are available, but they all start with Dynamic instead of Static.

Exercise 2 solution

To redirect a user to another page programmatically, you can use Response.Redirect and Server.Transfer. The first option sends a redirect instruction to the browser and is thus considered a client-side redirect. Server.Transfer, on the other hand, takes place at the server, allowing you to serve a different page without affecting the user's address bar.

Exercise 3 solution

To display a TreeView that doesn't have the ability to expand or collapse nodes, you need to set the ShowExpandCollapse property of the TreeView to False.

Chapter 8

Exercise 1 solution

A standard property uses a normal backing variable to store its value, whereas a ViewState property uses the ViewState collection for this. A normal property is reset on each postback, whereas a ViewState property is able to maintain its value. This advantage of the ViewState property comes at a cost, however. Storing the value in ViewState adds to the size of the page, both during the request and the response. A normal property doesn't have this disadvantage. You should carefully consider what you store in ViewState to minimize the page size.

Exercise 2 solution

To make the property maintain its state across postbacks, you need to turn it into a ViewState property. The required code is almost identical to that of the NavigateUrl, but it uses the Direction data type instead of a string. For the VB.NET example, just modify the highlighted Get and Set parts of the property. For the C# example, you need to remove the automatic property and replace it with the following code.

VB.NET

```
Public Property DisplayDirection() As Direction
  Get
    Dim _displayDirection As Object = ViewState("DisplayDirection")
    If _displayDirection IsNot Nothing Then
      Return CType(_displayDirection, Direction)
    Else
      Return Direction.Vertical ' Not found in ViewState; return a default value
    End If
  End Get
  Set(ByVal Value As Direction)
    ViewState("DisplayDirection") = Value
  End Set
End Property
```

C#

```
public Direction DisplayDirection
{
  get
  {
    object _displayDirection = ViewState["DisplayDirection"];
    if (_displayDirection != null)
    {
      return (Direction)_displayDirection;
    }
    else
    {
      return Direction.Vertical;  // Not found in ViewState; return a default value
    }
  }
  set
  {
    ViewState["DisplayDirection"] = value;
  }
}
```

With this `ViewState` property, you no longer need the private field `_displayDirection` that was initially declared outside the property in the `Banner` user control.

Exercise 3 solution

Using a custom data type like the `Direction` enumeration has two benefits over using numeric or string data types. Because of the way IntelliSense helps you select the right item, you don't have to memorize magic numbers or strings like 0 or 1. Additionally, the compiler helps you check the spelling, so if you type `Direction.Vrtical` instead of `Direction.Vertical` you get an error at development time.

Chapter 9

Exercise 1 solution

First, you need to write a property in the Code Behind of the user control, similar to the `DisplayDirection` property you created in the previous chapter for the Banner control. This property could look like this:

VB.NET

```
Private _pageDescription As String
Public Property PageDescription() As String
  Get
    Return _pageDescription
  End Get
  Set(ByVal Value As String)
    _pageDescription = Value
  End Set
End Property
```

C#

```
public string PageDescription { get; set; }
```

You then need to modify the control declaration. For example, in Contact.aspx, you can modify the control like this:

```
<uc1:ContactForm ID="ContactForm1" runat="server" PageDescription="Contact Page"/></p>
```

Note that the `PageDescription` property contains a short description of the containing page. Obviously, you can put whatever text you see fit to describe the page in the property.

Finally, you need to add the `PageDescription` to the subject or body of the e-mail message. The following code snippet shows you how to extend the subject with the value of this new property:

VB.NET

```
myMessage.Subject = "Response from web site. Page " & PageDescription
myMessage.From = New MailAddress("you@yourprovider.com", "Sender Name Here")
```

C#

```
myMessage.Subject = "Response from web site. Page " + PageDescription;
myMessage.From = new MailAddress("you@yourprovider.com", "Sender Name Here");
```

From now on, this custom page description is added to the subject of the mail message.

Exercise 2 solution

If you don't inspect the `IsValid` property, your system is vulnerable to invalid data. Users can disable JavaScript in their browser and submit invalid data directly into your page. By checking the `IsValid` property you can tell whether or not it's safe to continue with the submitted data.

Exercise 3 solution

The `From` property of the `MailMessage` class is of type `MailAddress`, meaning that you can directly assign a single instance of this class to it. Since you can potentially have more than one recipient, the `To` property is a *collection* of `MailAddress` objects, and so you need to use the `Add` method to add instances of `MailAddress` to the `To` property.

Exercise 4 solution

To call a client-side validation function, you need to set the `ClientValidationFunction` property of the `CustomValidator` like this:

```
<asp:CustomValidator ID="CustomValidator1" runat="server"
      ClientValidationFunction="ValidatePhoneNumbers" >*</asp:CustomValidator>
```

The client function that you need to add to the markup of the page must have the following signature:

```
function FunctionName(source, args)
{}
```

The `source` argument contains a reference to the actual `CustomValidator` control in the client-side HTML code. The `args` argument provides context information about the data and allows you to indicate whether the data is valid or not. The names of the arguments don't have to be `source` and `args`; however, when using these names, the client-side function looks as close to its server-side counterpart as possible. Another common naming scheme, used for almost all other event handlers in ASP.NET, is to use `sender` and `e` respectively.

Exercise 5 solution

To tell the validation mechanism whether the data you checked is valid or not, you set the `IsValid` property of the `args` argument in your custom validation method. This applies to both client- and server-side code. The following snippet shows how this is done in the client-side validation method for the ContactForm.ascx control:

```
if (txtPhoneHome.value != '' || txtPhoneBusiness.value != '')
{
  args.IsValid = true;
}
else
{
  args.IsValid = false;
}
```

Chapter 10

Exercise 1 solution

The `ScriptManager` control is a required component in almost all Ajax-related operations. It takes care of registering client-side JavaScript files, handles interaction with Web Services defined in your web site and it's responsible for the partial page updates. You usually place the `ScriptManager` directly in a content page if you think you need Ajax capabilities on only a handful of pages. However, you can also place the `ScriptManager` in a master page so it becomes available throughout the entire site.

When you have the `ScriptManager` in the master page you can use the `ScriptManagerProxy` to register individual Web Services on content pages. Since you can only have one `ScriptManager` in a page, you can't add another one in a content page that uses your master page with the `ScriptManager`. The `ScriptManagerProxy` serves as a bridge between the content page and the `ScriptManager`, giving you great flexibility as to where you register your services.

Exercise 2 solution

You can let your users know a partial page update is in progress by adding an `UpdateProgress` control to the page. You connect this control to an `UpdatePanel` using its `AssociatedUpdatePanelID`. Inside the `<ProgressTemplate>` you define whatever markup you see fit to inform your user an update is in progress. A typical `<ProgressTemplate>` contains an animated icon, some text, or both.

Exercise 3 solution

To create a script-callable Web Service, you first need to add a Web Service file to your site using the Add New Item dialog box. The Web Service you create inherits from `System.Web.Services.WebService`, the class that defines the default behavior for all Web Services.

When you create the Web Service, you need to add the `ScriptService` attribute to it:

VB.NET

```
<System.Web.Script.Services.ScriptService()> _
<WebService(Namespace:="http://tempuri.org/")> _
<WebServiceBinding(ConformsTo:=WsiProfiles.BasicProfile1_1)> _
<Global.Microsoft.VisualBasic.CompilerServices.DesignerGenerated()> _
Public Class NameService
  Inherits System.Web.Services.WebService
```

C#

```
[System.Web.Script.Services.ScriptService]
public class NameService : System.Web.Services.WebService
```

Finally, you need to decorate each method within this class that you want exposed as a web method with the `WebMethod` attribute:

VB.NET

```
<WebMethod()> _
Public Function HelloWorld(ByVal yourName As String) As String
```

C#

```
[WebMethod]
public string HelloWorld(string yourName)
```

Chapter 11

Exercise 1 solution

The `DELETE` statement fails because there is a relationship between the `Id` of the `Genre` table and the `GenreId` of the `Review` table. As long as this relationship is in effect, you cannot delete genres that still have reviews attached to them. To be able to delete the requested genre, you need to delete the associated reviews first, or assign them to a different genre using an `UPDATE` statement.

Exercise 2 solution

The relationship between the `Genre` and `Review` tables is a one-way relationship. The relationship enforces that the `GenreId` assigned to a review must exist as an `Id` in the `Genre` table. At the same time, it blocks you from deleting genres that have reviews attached to them. However, the relationship doesn't stop you from deleting records from the `Review` table.

Exercise 3 solution

To delete reviews with an `Id` of 100 or less, you need the following SQL statement:

```
DELETE FROM Review WHERE Id <= 100
```

Exercise 4 solution

Before you can delete the genre, you need to reassign the existing reviews to a new genre first. You can do this with the following `UPDATE` statement:

```
UPDATE Review SET GenreId = 11 WHERE GenreId = 4
```

This assigns the `GenreId` of `11` to all reviews that previously had their `GenreId` set to `4`. This in turn means that the genre with an ID of `4` no longer has any reviews attached to it, so you can remove the genre with the following SQL statement:

```
DELETE FROM Genre WHERE Id = 4
```

Chapter 12

Exercise 1 solution

The best control for this scenario is `GridView`. It's easy to set up and has built-in support for paging, updating, and deleting of data. Together with a `DetailsView` control you can offer your users all four CRUD operations.

Exercise 2 solution

For a simple, unordered list, you're probably best off using a `Repeater` control. The biggest benefit of the `Repeater` control is that it emits no HTML code on its own, allowing you to control the final markup. A downside of the control is that it doesn't support editing or deletion of data, which isn't a problem if all you need to do is present the data in a list. Chapter 13 shows you how to use the `Repeater` control.

Exercise 3 solution

A `BoundField` is directly tied to a column in your data source and offers only limited ways to customize its appearance. The `TemplateField`, on the other hand, gives you full control over the way the field is rendered. As such, it's an ideal field for more complex scenarios — for example, when you want to add validation controls to the page, or if you want to let the user work with a different control, like a `DropDownList` instead of the default `TextBox`.

Exercise 4 solution

You should always store your connection strings in the web.config file. This file has an element called `<connectionStrings>` that is designed specifically for storing connection strings. By storing them in web.config, you make it very easy to find your connection strings and modify them. If you store them at the page level, you have to search through your entire project for the relevant connection strings.

You can access the connection strings using expression binding syntax. For example, to set the connection string in a `SqlDataSource`, you can use code like this:

```
ConnectionString="<%$ ConnectionStrings:PlanetWroxConnectionString1 %>"
```

Chapter 13

Exercise 1 solution

To get the 10 most recent reviews from the system, your query needs two important LINQ constructs: first it needs an `Order By` (`orderby` in C#) clause to order the list in descending order. It then needs to use the `Take` method to take the first 10 reviews from that result set:

VB.NET

```
Dim recentReviews = (From myReview In myDataContext.Reviews _
                    Order By myReview.CreateDateTime Descending _
                    Select New With {myReview.Title, myReview.Genre.Name}).Take(10)

GridView1.DataSource = recentReviews
GridView1.DataBind()
```

C#

```
var recentReviews = (from myReview in myDataContext.Reviews
                    orderby myReview.CreateDateTime descending
                    select new
                    {
                      myReview.Title,
                      myReview.Genre.Name
                    }).Take(10);

GridView1.DataSource = recentReviews;
GridView1.DataBind();
```

This code also uses the `New` keyword (`new` in C#) to create a new, anonymous type that only contains the review's title and the genre's name.

Exercise 2 solution

The biggest benefit of the `ListView` control is that it combines the strengths of those other data controls. Just like the `GridView` control, the `ListView` control makes it easy to display data in a grid format that users can edit from within the grid. Additionally, the `ListView` control allows you to insert new records, behavior that is found in controls like `DetailsView` and `FormView` but not in `GridView`.

Finally, the `ListView` control gives you full control over the markup that gets sent to the browser, an important feature that only the `Repeater` control gives you out of the box.

Exercise 3 solution

First you would need to change the Default.aspx page so it links each thumbnail to a detail page and passes the ID of the Picture to this new page. In the `<ItemTemplate>` of the `ListView` control in Default.aspx add this `HyperLink` control around the `Image` control that was already there:

```
<asp:HyperLink ID="HyperLink1" runat="server"
        NavigateUrl='<%# "PictureDetails.aspx?Id=" + Eval("Id") %>'>
```

```
<asp:Image ID="Image1" runat="server" ImageUrl='<%# Eval("ImageUrl") %>'
        ToolTip='<%# Eval("ToolTip") %>' />
</asp:HyperLink>
```

Note that the `NavigateUrl` is built up from the static text `PictureDetail.aspx?Id=` and the ID of the picture in the database.

Then create a new page called PictureDetails.aspx page and add an `Image` control in the markup:

```
<asp:Content ID="Content2" ContentPlaceHolderID="cpMainContent" Runat="Server">
  <asp:Image ID="Image1" runat="server" />
</asp:Content>
```

Finally, you need to execute the following LINQ query in the `Load` event of the page in the Code Behind to set the `ImageUrl`:

VB.NET

```
Protected Sub Image1_Load(ByVal sender As Object, ByVal e As System.EventArgs) _
        Handles Image1.Load
  Dim pictureId As Integer = Convert.ToInt32(Request.QueryString.Get("Id"))

  Using myDataContext As New PlanetWroxDataContext()
    Dim imageUrl As String = (From picture In myDataContext.Pictures _
                              Where picture.Id = pictureId _
                              Select picture).Single().ImageUrl

    Image1.ImageUrl = imageUrl
  End Using
End Sub
```

C#

```
protected void Page_Load(object sender, EventArgs e)
{
  int pictureId = Convert.ToInt32(Request.QueryString.Get("Id"));
  using (PlanetWroxDataContext myDataContext = new PlanetWroxDataContext())
  {
    string imageUrl = (from picture in myDataContext.Pictures
                      where picture.Id == pictureId
                      select picture).Single().ImageUrl;
    Image1.ImageUrl = imageUrl;
  }
}
```

This code gets the ID of the picture from the query string first and then feeds it to the LINQ query. The `Single` method is used to retrieve a single picture from the `Picture` table whose `ImageUrl` is then used to display the image in the browser.

Chapter 14

Exercise 1 solution

The `Load` event of the `Page` always fires before user-triggered events like a `Button` control's `Click`.

Exercise 2 solution

To alternate the odd and even rows you need to set up a `RowStyle` and an `AlternatingRowStyle`. You then need to set their respective `BackColor` and `ForeColor` properties:

```
<asp:GridView ID="GridView1" runat="server" ... >
  <AlternatingRowStyle BackColor="White" ForeColor="Black" />
  <RowStyle BackColor="Black" ForeColor="White" />
  <Columns>
    ... Column definition here
  </Columns>
</asp:GridView>
```

Remember that embedding style information like this can lead to page bloat and results in pages that are difficult to maintain. Moving the style definition to a separate CSS file and using the `CssClass` of the styles would be a much better solution. Your CSS file should contain these selectors:

```
.AlternatingRowStyle
{
  background-color: white;
  color: black;
}

.RowStyle
{
  background-color: black;
  color: white;
}
```

With these CSS selectors you need to modify the `GridView` styles as follows:

```
  <AlternatingRowStyle CssClass="AlternatingRowStyle" />
  <RowStyle CssClass="RowStyle" />
```

Exercise 3 solution

The various data-bound controls can raise exceptions that you can handle in their event handlers. Once you have dealt with the exception appropriately, you need to set the `ExceptionHandled` property of the `e` argument to `True`. The following code snippet shows how a `Label` control is updated with an error message. The `ExceptionHandled` is then set to stop the `Exception` from getting passed on into the user interface where it would otherwise result in a "yellow screen of death."

VB.NET

```
Protected Sub SqlDataSource1_Deleted(ByVal sender As Object, _
          ByVal e As System.Web.UI.WebControls.SqlDataSourceStatusEventArgs) _
          Handles SqlDataSource1.Deleted
```

```
    If e.Exception IsNot Nothing Then
      lblErrorMessage.Text = "We're sorry, but something went terribly wrong while " & _
                 "deleting your genre."
      e.ExceptionHandled = True
    End If
  End Sub
```

C#

```
protected void SqlDataSource1_Deleted(object sender, SqlDataSourceStatusEventArgs e)
{
  if (e.Exception != null)
  {
    lblErrorMessage.Text = @"We're sorry, but something went terribly wrong while
             deleting your genre.";
    e.ExceptionHandled = true;
  }
}
```

Chapter 15

Exercise 1 solution

Authentication is all about proving your identity to a system like a web site. After you have been authenticated, the authorizations you have then determine what it is you can and cannot do in the system.

Exercise 2 solution

To expand the access to the Management folder for John and all users in the Editors role, you need to expand the current `roles` attribute to include Editors, and add an additional `allow` element with its `users` attribute set to `John`:

```
<system.web>
  <authorization>
    <allow roles="Managers, Editors"/>
    <allow users="John"/>
    <deny users="*"/>
  </authorization>
</system.web>
```

The `roles` attribute allows you to specify multiple roles separated by a comma. In order to grant the John account you need to add an additional `allow` element and then fill in John's name in the `users` attribute.

From a maintainability perspective, it would be a lot better to add John to the Managers or Editors role if possible. However, you may end up giving John more rights than you want (he could then access anything that a Manager or an Editor could access). Generally, it's best to manage users through roles as much as possible, but it's good to know that you can grant individual accounts the necessary rights as well (or explicitly take those rights away using a `deny` element).

Exercise 3 solution

If you want to redirect all users to the same page, all you need to set is the `DestinationPageUrl`:

```
<asp:Login ID="Login1" runat="server" DestinationPageUrl="~/MyProfile.aspx">
```

When a user is logged in successfully, she's taken to MyProfile.aspx automatically.

Exercise 4 solution

The `LoginStatus` simply displays a simple text that indicates whether the user is logged in or not. By default the text that is displayed is Login when the user is currently not logged in, and Logout when the user is already logged in. Clicking the link either sends the user to the default Login page, or logs the user out.

The `LoginView` is somewhat similar in that it displays different content depending on whether the user is currently logged in. However, because the control is completely template driven, you can fully control the content that is displayed. To enable you to differentiate between different user roles, you can use the `RoleGroups` element to set up templates that are only shown to users in specific roles.

Chapter 16

Exercise 1 solution

You would implement the favorite theme as a `String` property and call it `FavoriteTheme`. To ensure that you always have a valid theme, you could also set a default value. Finally, you should make the property accessible to anonymous users. Your final `Profile` property could end up like this:

```
<add name="FavoriteTheme" defaultValue="Monochrome" allowAnonymous="true" />
```

Exercise 2 solution

Given the syntax you saw in the question, you could now access the new property and use it to change the current theme in the BasePage:

VB.NET

```
Private Sub Page_PreInit(ByVal sender As Object, ByVal e As System.EventArgs) _
          Handles Me.PreInit
  Dim myProfile As ProfileCommon = CType(HttpContext.Current.Profile, ProfileCommon)
  If Not String.IsNullOrEmpty(myProfile.FavoriteTheme) Then
    Page.Theme = myProfile.FavoriteTheme
  End If
End Sub
```

C#

```
private void BasePage_PreInit(object sender, EventArgs e)
{
```

```
    ProfileCommon myProfile = (ProfileCommon) HttpContext.Current.Profile;
    if (!string.IsNullOrEmpty(myProfile.FavoriteTheme))
    {
      Page.Theme = myProfile.FavoriteTheme;
    }
  }
```

Exercise 3 solution

To finalize the theme selector using Profile, you also need to change the code in the master page. Instead of storing the user-selected theme in a cookie, you should now store it in Profile instead. Change the code in Page_Load as follows:

VB.NET

```
If Not Page.IsPostBack Then
  Dim selectedTheme As String = Page.Theme

  If Not String.IsNullOrEmpty(Profile.FavoriteTheme) Then
    selectedTheme = Profile.FavoriteTheme
  End If
  If lstPreferredTheme.Items.FindByValue(selectedTheme) IsNot Nothing Then
    lstPreferredTheme.Items.FindByValue(selectedTheme).Selected = True
  End If
End If
Select Case Page.Theme.ToLower()
```

C#

```
if (!Page.IsPostBack)
{
  string selectedTheme = Page.Theme;
  if (!string.IsNullOrEmpty(Profile.FavoriteTheme))
  {
    selectedTheme = Profile.FavoriteTheme;
  }
  if (lstPreferredTheme.Items.FindByValue(selectedTheme) != null)
  {
    lstPreferredTheme.Items.FindByValue(selectedTheme).Selected = true;
  }
}
switch (Page.Theme.ToLower())
```

You can then simplify the code in `lstPreferredTheme_SelectedIndexChanged` in the master page to:

VB.NET

```
Protected Sub lstPreferredTheme_SelectedIndexChanged(ByVal sender As Object, _
            ByVal e As System.EventArgs) Handles lstPreferredTheme.SelectedIndexChanged
  Profile.FavoriteTheme = lstPreferredTheme.SelectedValue
  Response.Redirect(Request.Url.ToString())
End Sub
```

C#

```
protected void lstPreferredTheme_SelectedIndexChanged(object sender, EventArgs e)
{
  Profile.FavoriteTheme = lstPreferredTheme.SelectedValue;
  Response.Redirect(Request.Url.ToString());
}
```

To enable Profile for anonymous users, you need to enable anonymous identification with the following element in web.config, directly under `<system.web>`:

```
    <anonymousIdentification enabled="true" cookieName="PlanetWroxAnonymous" />
```

Chapter 17

Exercise 1 solution

Debugging is the process of watching your code execute in the development environment, investigating variables and looking into objects in order to understand the execution path of your code, looking for bugs with the aim to fix them. Debugging usually takes place at development time in your Visual Web Developer IDE.

Tracing, on the other hand, provides you with information on the run-time execution of your code. As discussed in this chapter, you can use tracing to get information about events that fire and the order they fire in. Additionally, you can add your own information to the trace. Since disabling tracing through configuration greatly minimizes the performance overhead associated with it, you can leave your trace calls in the code, making it easy to disable and enable tracing whenever you need it.

Exercise 2 solution

The best way to stop a possible exception from ending up in the user interface is to wrap your code in a `Try/Catch` block. That way you can display an error message to the user in case something goes wrong. Your code could end up looking like this:

VB.NET

```
Try
  ' Execute code here to send an e-mail or write to a file.
Catch ex As Exception
  lblErrorMessage.Text = "Something went wrong while executing the requested operation"
End Try
```

C#

```
try
{
  // Execute code here to send an e-mail or write to a file.
}
catch (Exception ex)
```

```
{
  lblErrorMessage.Text = "Something went wrong while executing the requested operation";
}
```

Exercise 3 solution

To understand which exceptions occur in the site and find out where they occur (that is, what pages or code files are causing the exceptions) you can log all exceptions using some code in the `Application_Error` event handler. The exception details you can intercept in this method should help you understand the cause of the exception, which in turn should help finding a fix for them.

To prevent your users from seeing the "yellow screen of death" error messages, you need to use custom error pages. You should create a simple Web Form that tells the user something went wrong. To tell the ASP.NET run time to show the contents of that file instead of the error message, you need the following element in your web.config:

```
<customErrors mode="On" defaultRedirect="~/Errors/AllOtherErrors.aspx">
  <error statusCode="500" redirect="~/Errors/Error500.aspx" />
</customErrors>
```

This element sets up a special page for error code 500 that occurs when your code crashes unexpectedly. When other exceptions occur, like a "Page not found" error, users are sent to the more generic AllOtherErrors.aspx page.

Configuring SQL Server 2005

This book assumes that you are using Microsoft SQL Server 2005 Express Edition as the database for the Planet Wrox project. SQL Server 2005 Express Edition is great for development because it's free, relatively lightweight, and easy to use. However, in a production environment it doesn't always cut it because it isn't designed to handle lots of users simultaneously. In cases where the Express Edition is not enough, you need to look at its bigger brothers: the commercial versions of SQL Server 2005, like the Standard or Enterprise Editions. In this appendix you will learn about security in SQL Server 2005, how to enable your SQL Server 2005 database and your ASP.NET 3.5 application to work together, and how to obtain and use SQL Server Management Studio Express, a free tool from Microsoft that lets you manage your database.

Although this appendix doesn't discuss SQL Server 2000, you'll find that most of the concepts apply to this older version of SQL Server as well. In fact, you can even use SQL Server Management Studio Express to manage your SQL Server 2000 database.

In addition to configuring your SQL Server and ASP.NET 3.5 application to work together, this appendix also shows you how to configure a SQL Server database to support the ASP.NET 3.5 application services. This is necessary if you want your application to use your own, custom database instead of the aspnetdb.mdf database that is generated for you automatically.

Configuring SQL Server 2005

Before you can configure your database, you need to be aware of the different security concepts that are inevitably associated with databases and web applications. In Chapter 18 you learned how the different computer accounts used by the web server play a big role when configuring security settings for the file system, and that's not different when connecting to SQL Server. In the following section, you get a quick primer on the different ways to connect to SQL Server. In the section that follows you see how to attach your .mdf database files to SQL Server followed by a discussion of configuring your application and database so they can talk to each other.

Terminology and Concepts

When you connect to a SQL Server database, SQL Server needs to know who you are, so it can enforce the correct access policies on the objects like tables in the database. SQL Server 2005 supports two different authentication mechanisms: SQL Server Authentication and Windows Authentication (often called Integrated Security). Both come with a few advantages of their own and require you to write different connection strings to connect to SQL Server. In the following section you see the two most common connection strings, but you're advised to visit `www.connectionstrings.com` for an extensive list of possible connection strings.

SQL Server Authentication

With SQL Server Authentication, SQL Server takes care of user management. You manage the users for your SQL Server database with SQL Server Management Studio, either the Express Edition (which you'll see how to obtain and use a little later in this appendix) or the full versions that ship with the commercial versions of SQL Server 2005.

To connect your web application to a SQL Server 2005 that uses SQL Server authentication, you need to pass a user name and password in the connection string of your application. A typical connection string looks like this:

```
Data Source=ServerName;Initial Catalog=DatabaseName;User Id=UserName;Password=Password;
```

In this case the Data Source addresses an *unnamed instance* of SQL Server: the server is addressed by its name alone. Recall from Chapter 12 that it's also possible to install SQL Server as a *named instance*. With a named instance, the name of the server is followed by the name of a particular SQL Server instance. For example:

```
Data Source=ServerName\InstanceName;Initial Catalog=DatabaseName;
    User Id=UserName;Password=Password;
```

The counterpart of SQL Server Authentication is Windows Authentication, which is discussed next.

Windows Authentication

With Windows Authentication, the Windows OS takes care of user management. All interaction with the database is done in the context of the calling user so the database knows who's accessing the system. You still need to map a Windows account to a SQL Server account so SQL Server can determine whether the account has sufficient permissions. I'll show you how to do this later.

A typical connection string using Windows Authentication looks like this:

```
Data Source=ServerName;Initial Catalog=DatabaseName;Trusted_Connection=True
```

Instead of specifying a user name and password you add `Trusted_Connection=True` to the connection string to indicate you want to connect to the server with the user context of the calling user.

Since both methods eventually do the same (they allow you to connect to SQL Server), you may wonder which one of the two you should use.

Choosing between Windows and Server Authentication

In general, it's recommended to use Windows authentication. The fact that you don't need to use a password in the connection string means your application will be a bit safer. You don't need to send the password over the wire, and it's also not stored in a configuration file for your application.

However, SQL Server Authentication is a bit easier to set up. Since you specify the user name and password explicitly, you don't need to know the final user account that your application runs under.

Later in this appendix you see how to use one of these two authentication mechanisms to connect to your database. However, you need to look at something else first: the tools used to manage SQL Server.

Using SQL Server Management Studio

You use SQL Server Management Studio to manage your databases. It enables you to attach and detach databases to your SQL Server; create new database objects like tables in existing databases; select, create, edit and delete data; and much more. If you are using a commercial version of SQL Server 2005, you already have access to SQL Server Management Studio, as it comes bundled with the database engine. If you are using the free Express Edition of SQL Server, you need to download SQL Server Management Studio Express first. This Express edition of the database management tool is similar to its commercial counterpart and it allows you to carry out most if not all of your database management tasks.

Obtaining and Installing SQL Server Management Studio Express

You can download SQL Server Management Studio Express from the following page at the Microsoft site: `http://msdn2.microsoft.com/en-us/express/bb410792.aspx`. Alternatively, you can go to the main downloads page at `www.microsoft.com/downloads` and search for "SQL Server Management Studio Express."

After you have downloaded the Management Studio setup file, double-click it to start the installation process and then follow the on-screen instructions. After installation is finished, you can start up SQL Server Management Studio from the Start Menu. You'll be presented with a screen similar to Figure B-1 that allows you to select a SQL Server instance you want to log in to.

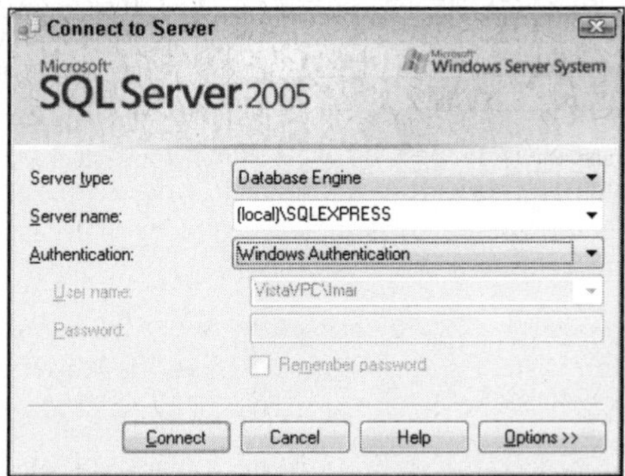

Figure B-1

Depending on the database server you are connecting to, you can log in with Windows Authentication using your current Windows account or you can choose SQL Server Authentication from the Authentication drop-down list and enter a user name and password. After you log in, you get a screen similar to Figure B-2 that allows you to manage your SQL Server instance.

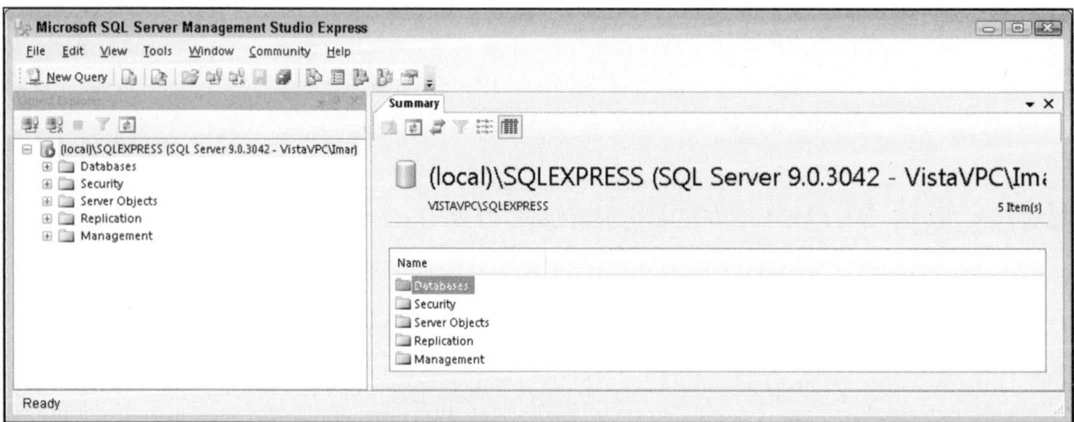

Figure B-2

If you are having trouble connecting to a remote SQL Server (for example, an instance of SQL Server that is not on the same physical server as the one you're running Management Studio on), you may need to enable SQL Server for remote connections first. This is discussed next.

Enabling Remote Connections in SQL Server

When working with SQL Server 2005, you may receive the following error: An error has occurred while establishing a connection to the server. When connecting to SQL Server 2005, this failure may be caused by the fact that under the default settings SQL Server does not allow remote connections.

Although you may also get this error when the database server is down or not responding, you also get this error when SQL Server is not configured for remote connections. In a default installation, SQL Server only allows local applications to connect and blocks remote connections automatically. To resolve this, and grant remote systems access to the database as well, follow these steps:

1. Open the SQL Server Configuration Manager from the Microsoft SQL Server 2005 Start menu item. Depending on the version of SQL Server you're using, this item may be located under the Configuration Tools sub menu.
2. In the window that appears, locate your instance of SQL Server under the SQL Server 2005 Network Configuration item and click it to display the list with available protocols. Figure B-3 shows the list for a SQL Server instance called SQLEXPRESS.
3. In the list with protocols on the right, right-click Named Pipes and choose Enable if its status is currently set to Disabled.
4. Repeat the previous step, but this time configure TCP/IP.

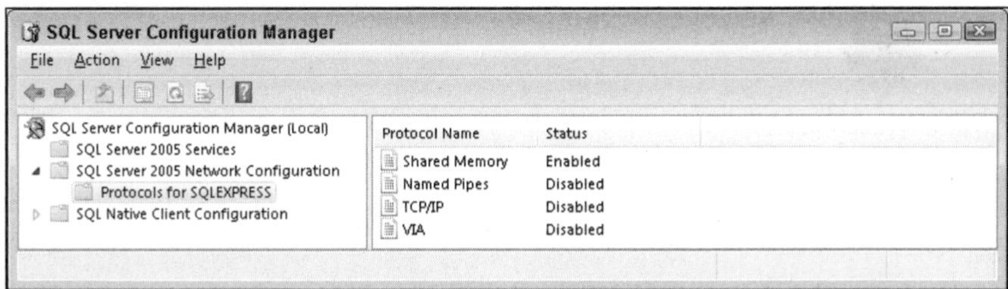

Figure B-3

5. Restart SQL Server. You can do this by right-clicking the server in the Object Explorer of SQL Server Management Studio (shown in Figure B-2) and choosing Restart. If you get an error about security permissions, you may need to reboot your computer instead.

SQL Server now allows incoming connections from remote machines. However, before you can actually use your databases, you need to attach them to SQL Server first. This is described in the following section.

If you have trouble connecting to SQL Server, make sure that SQL Server is running. To verify this, open the Control Panel and then open the Administrative Tools section (you need to put the Control Panel in Classic View to see this item in Windows Vista). Next, open the Services item and then verify that the SQL Server instance you are connecting to is running. If you installed SQL Server Express on your local machine, the service is called SQL Server (Express).

Attaching Databases to SQL Server

SQL Server Express allows you to work with database files in two ways: you can either attach them at runtime using a special attribute in the connection string, or you can attach them using tools like Management Studio before you start using the database. With the full versions of SQL Server, you always need to attach your databases as described in this section.

You've been using the first option in all database-related chapters so far. The Planet Wrox connection string you used looks like this:

```
<add name="PlanetWroxConnectionString1" connectionString="Data Source=.\SQLEXPRESS;
     AttachDbFilename=|DataDirectory|\PlanetWrox.mdf;Trusted_Connection=True;
     User Instance=True" providerName="System.Data.SqlClient" />
```

This connection string points to a database called PlanetWrox.mdf located in the web site's App_Data folder (determined by `|DataDirectory|`). The connection string instructs SQL Server to attach this database file to SQL Server on the fly when it's used. When the database is no longer needed, it is detached again.

This is a great solution for local development because it allows you to easily use SQL Server databases, create and use new ones, and move them around from project to project. However, with a production database this option isn't good enough and you need to attach the database to SQL Server first. The following steps explain how to attach the PlanetWrox.mdf database to an instance of SQL Server in case you have the need. You can follow the exact same steps to attach a database to an instance of SQL Server Express Edition, which may be handy if you want to use SQL Server Management Studio to perform maintenance tasks in SQL Server that you cannot do in Visual Studio (managing users and roles, for example).

1. Create a folder that will hold your new database, like C:\Data\SqlServer.
2. Move the files PlanetWrox.mdf and aspnetdb.mdf and their associated .ldf files from the web site's App_Data folder at C:\BegASPNET to this new folder.
3. Enable Modify permissions on the folder where the database resides (C:\Data\SqlServer) for the account used by SQL Server (which is the Network Service account by default, even on Windows XP) and for your own account. Chapter 18 explained how to set these permissions.
4. Open SQL Server Management Studio (any version will do) and log into your SQL Server instance you want to attach the database to. If you are using Windows Vista, you have to run this process as an administrator. To do this, right-click the Management Studio menu item in the Windows Start Menu and choose Run as Administrator. Regardless of how you started SQL Server Management Studio, you should see a screen similar to Figure B-2.
5. Right-click the Database node shown in Figure B-2 and choose Attach.
6. In the dialog box that follows, click the Add button and then select the .mdf file you moved to C:\Data\SqlServer in step 2.
7. Click the value in the Attach As column and type PlanetWrox as the new name that will be given to the database. Once you're done, your dialog box should look like Figure B-4.
8. Click OK to attach the database to SQL Server. If you get an error, make sure your own account (or the Users group you are part of) and the ASPNET or Network Service account both have Modify permissions on the C:\Data\SqlServer folder and the .mdf files this folder contains.

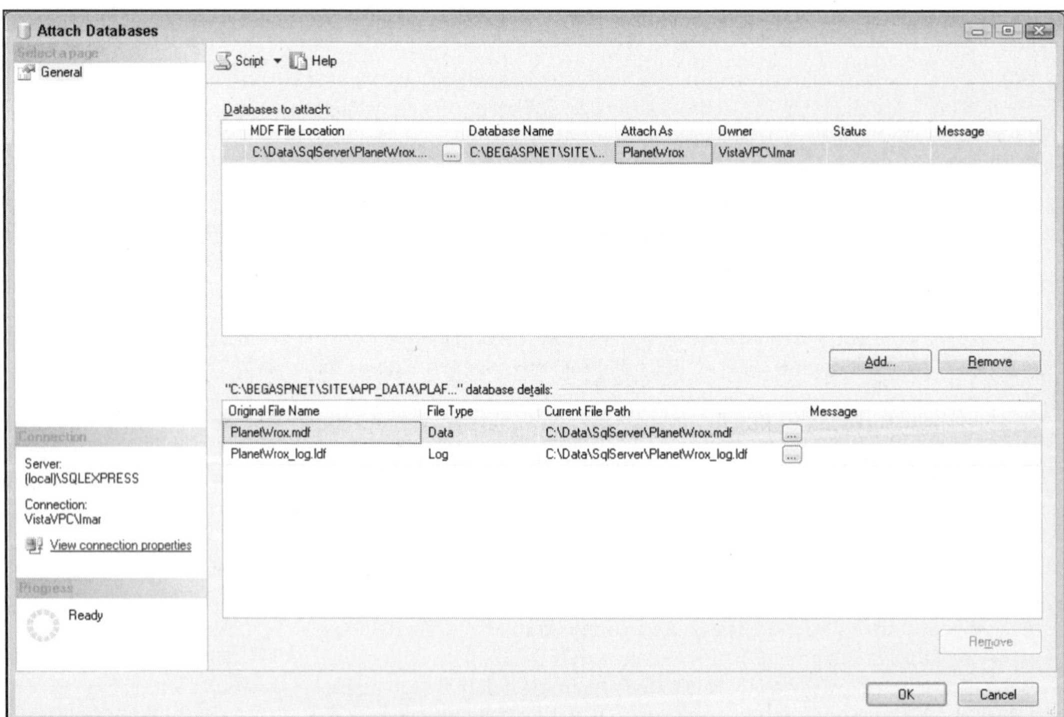

Figure B-4

9. Your database is now accessible under the Databases node of Management Studio's Object Explorer. If you expand the Databases element and then look into your database you should see familiar items like Tables that you also saw in the Database Explorer in Visual Web Developer earlier in the book. Figure B-5 shows the attached database and its tables.

10. Repeat steps 5 through 8, but this time attach the aspnetdb.mdf database. In step 7 type aspnetdb as the new name for the database.

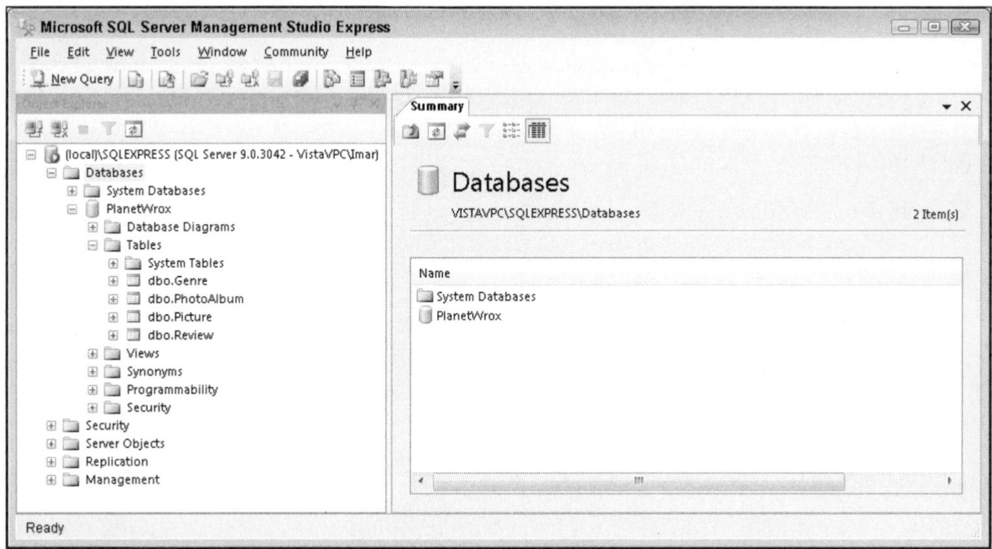

Figure B-5

At this stage, only administrative accounts (Windows administrators or the built-in SQL Server administrative account called SA) have access to the database. In order to have the Planet Wrox web site work with these two databases, you need to configure both SQL Server security and your web site. You see how to do this next.

Connecting Your Application to SQL Server 2005

In the following section, I'll show you how to connect to SQL Server from two different but common scenarios: using SQL Server Authentication and using Windows Authentication when IIS and SQL Server are on the same server. For both scenarios you'll see how to configure SQL Server, the Planet Wrox web site, and if necessary, your Windows accounts.

You're likely to use the first scenario when dealing with an external hosting company that hosts your site. When web hosts offer SQL Server, they often use SQL Server Authentication and as such require you to pass a user name and password to the database server.

The second scenario is useful if you host the site and have both SQL Server 2005 and IIS on the same machine.

More advanced scenarios, like using Windows Authentication with IIS and SQL Server on two different machines, are beyond the scope of this appendix. For more information about configuring and securing SQL Server, get yourself a copy of *Beginning SQL Server 2005 Administration* (Wrox, ISBN: 978-0-470-04704-0) or *Professional SQL Server 2005 Administration* (Wrox, ISBN: 978-0-470-05520-5).

Scenario 1 — Using SQL Server Authentication

From a configuration point of view, this is probably the easiest scenario to configure: all you need to do is make sure that your SQL Server installation supports SQL Server authentication, create a user in SQL Server, and then use that account in the connection string of the Planet Wrox web site. To do this, follow these steps:

1. In SQL Server Management Studio, right-click the server name in the Object Explorer shown in Figure B-2, choose Properties, and switch to the Security category. The dialog box shown in Figure B-6 appears.

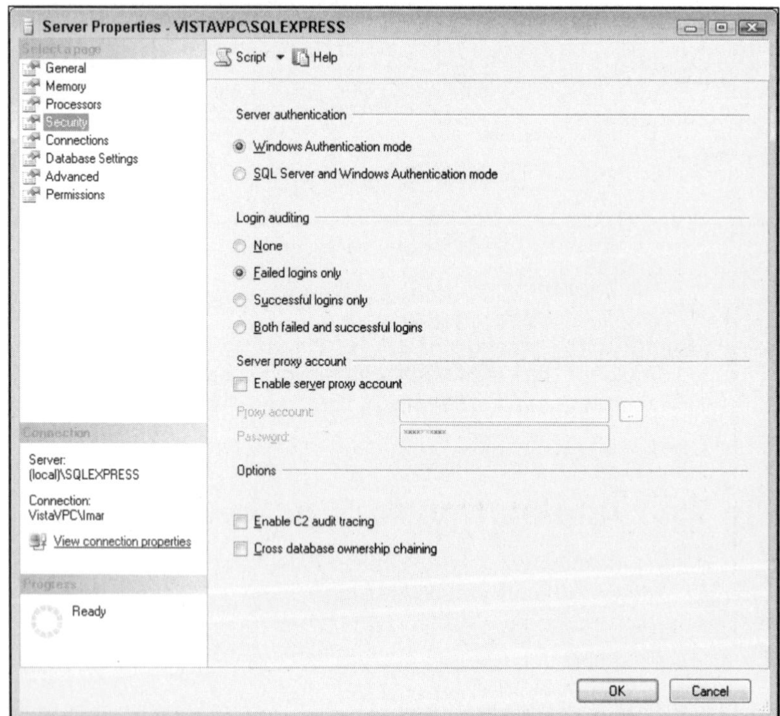

Figure B-6

2. If not already selected, choose the SQL Server and Windows Authentication Mode item at the top of the screen. Before you click OK, click the Help link at the top of the screen and read a bit more about SQL and Windows Authentication, and determine if you really need SQL Server Authentication. Windows Authentication is more secure than SQL Server authentication, so you're advised to use that option whenever possible.

3. Restart SQL Server. You can do this by right-clicking the server in the Object Explorer and choosing Restart. If you get an error about security permissions, you may need to reboot your computer instead.

4. Back in SQL Server's Management Studio's Object Explorer, expand the server's Security node visible in Figure B-2. Make sure you choose the one directly under your server name, and not the one belonging to a specific database. Right-click on Logins and choose New Login.

5. Type a Login name, then select the SQL Server Authentication option, and type a password. In this and the following examples, I'll use PlanetWroxUser as the user name, and Pa$$w0rD (with a zero instead of the letter o) as the password.

6. Clear the Enforce Password Expiration. This also deselects User Must Change Password At Next Login. Your dialog box should end up looking like the one in Figure B-7.

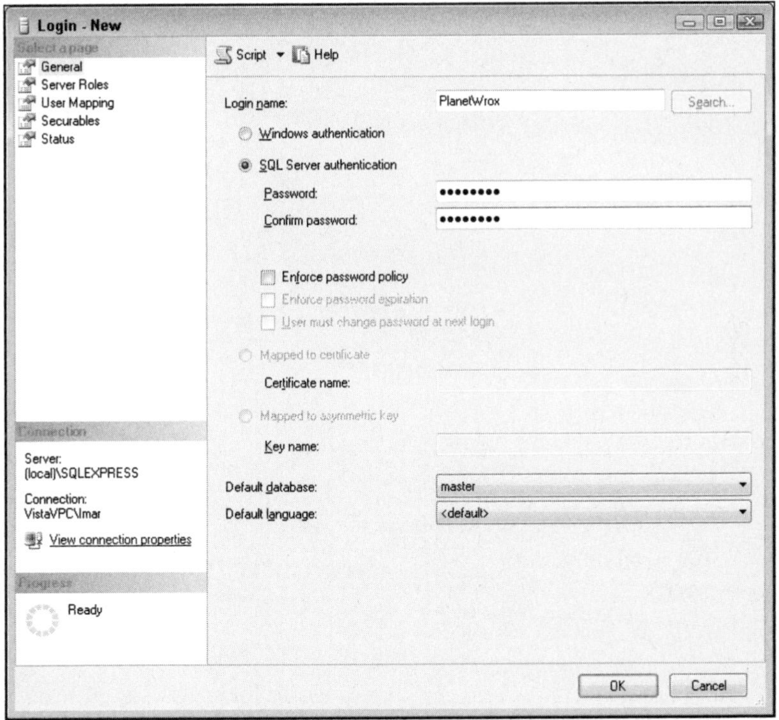

Figure B-7

If you want to learn more about the individual settings on this screen, click the Help button at the top of the screen.

7. Click OK to create the new account.

With the account created, the next phase is to give this new account the proper permissions to your database:

1. On the Object Explorer, expand Databases, then the PlanetWrox database, followed by the Security node. Finally, expand the Users node, right-click it, and choose New User.
2. In the User name text box, type **PlanetWroxUser**.
3. In the Login name text box, type **PlanetWroxUser** again. Alternatively, click the ellipsis button, then click Browse, and select the user from the list that has appeared.
4. At the bottom of the screen, you see a box labeled Database Role Membership. In this box, you can choose a number of roles that you can grant to your new user. The rule here is: give users as little permissions as possible. A good choice is db_datareader and db_datawriter that allows the account to both read from and write to tables in the database, so check these two options, visible in Figure B-8.

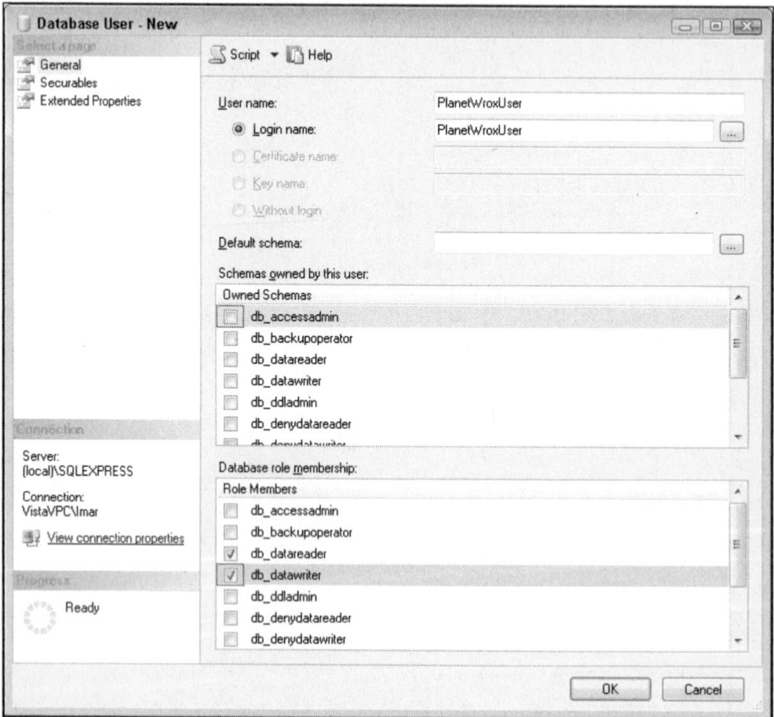

Figure B-8

Check out SQL Server's Books Online for more information about the various roles.

5. If you want to set fine-grained security options for your database objects, click the Securables option you see in the left-hand part of Figure B-8. This dialog box allows you to determine permissions for the user account on objects in your database like tables, views, and stored procedures. For the Planet Wrox web site, you don't need to make any changes in this dialog box.
6. Finally, click OK to assign the PlanetWroxUser account to the db_datareader and db_datawriter roles.
7. Repeat the previous five steps, but now configure the aspnetdb database that you attached earlier. When you get to step 5, select all the roles that start with aspnet_. These are the roles that are used by the ASP.NET application services and grant the new user account just enough permissions to support the various application services like Membership and Roles. There's no need to select any of the other roles.
8. You can close SQL Server Management Studio for the moment as you're done with it.

Now that SQL Server and your user accounts are configured correctly, the final phase is to configure the web site to use this new user account.

1. Open the web.config file of the PlanetWrox application from the C:\BegASPNET\Release folder.
2. Modify the `<connectionStrings>` element as follows:

```
<connectionStrings>
  <clear />
  <add name="PlanetWroxConnectionString1" connectionString="Data Source=ServerName;
            Initial Catalog=PlanetWrox;User ID=PlanetWroxUser;password=Pa$$w0rD"
       providerName="System.Data.SqlClient"
  />
  <add name="LocalSqlServer" connectionString="Data Source=ServerName;
            Initial Catalog=aspnetdb;User ID=PlanetWroxUser;password=Pa$$w0rD"
       providerName="System.Data.SqlClient"
  />
</connectionStrings>
```

   Don't forget to replace the value in the `Data Source` with a valid server name. Depending on your server and configuration, this could be as simple as `(local)` to point to a SQL Server on the local machine, `DatabaseServer` to point to a server called DatabaseServer on the network, or something like `DatabaseServer\Sql2005` that points to a named instance called Sql2005 on a machine DatabaseServer.

3. Save the changes and then open the site by starting your browser and going to `http://localhost` (or the address you configured in Chapter 18). Everything should still work but the site now no longer uses the databases in the App_Data folder, but uses the SQL Server you defined in your connection strings instead.

If you get an error when browsing to the site, you may need to turn off custom errors in web.config (set it to `RemoteOnly` instead of to `Off`) to see the actual error message. Possible reasons for an error are an incorrect user name or password, an incorrect server name in the connection string, and an incorrectly configured database role membership for the PlanetWroxUser account.

Scenario 2 — Using Windows Authentication with IIS and the Database on the Same Machine

This is a common scenario, especially when you're running your site on a local machine you control yourself. Both the web server (either IIS or the built-in development web server) and SQL Server run on the same physical machine. This scenario makes it easy to use Windows Authentication because both the web server and SQL Server can use the same Windows account. To configure your server for this scenario, follow these steps:

1. Determine the account used by your web server. Refer to Chapter 18 for precise details on how to do this, but generally your own account is used when running your site under the built-in web server. You need the ASP.NET account when using IIS on Windows XP or the Network Service account when using IIS on Vista or a server edition of Microsoft Windows. I am using the account Network Service in the remainder of this section.
2. Next, you need to map this Windows account to a SQL Server account. To do this, open SQL Server Management Studio and log in to your SQL Server instance. Expand the Security node for the server (and not of an individual database), as shown in Figure B-2. Then right-click Logins and choose New Login.
3. Click the Search button to bring up the Select User or Group dialog box, shown in Figure B-9.
4. Click the Advanced button and then the Find Now button to bring up a list with user names.
5. Select the user account you need to configure from the list and then click OK twice to return to the New Login dialog box, which should now have the correct login name selected, as shown in Figure B-10.
6. Click OK to create the new user account.

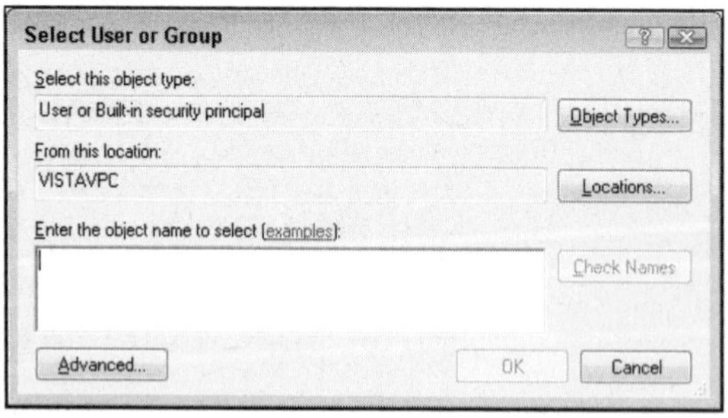

Figure B-9

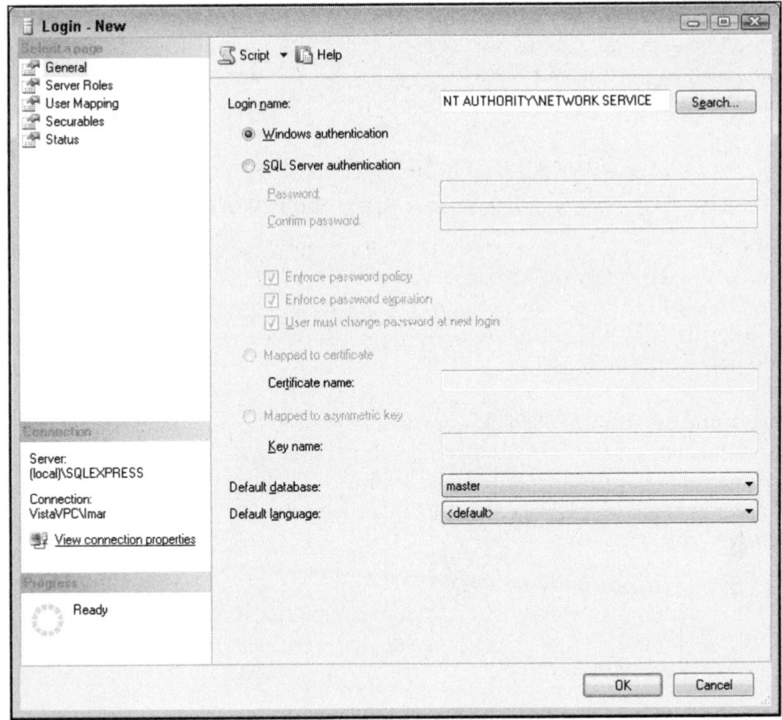

Figure B-10

With the account created, the next step is to give this new account the proper permissions to your database.

1. Open the Security node of the PlanetWrox database and then expand the Users node, right-click it, and choose New User.
2. In the User name text box, type Network Service (or the account name you configured earlier).
3. For the Login name text box, click the ellipsis button and then click Browse so you can select a user name. Choose the NT Authority\Network Service account (or the account name you configured earlier).
4. At the bottom of the screen, you see a box labeled Database role membership. In this box, you can choose a number of roles that you can grant to your new user. The rule here is: give users as little permissions as possible. A good choice is db_datareader and db_datawriter that allows the account to both read from and write to tables in the database, so check these two options, shown in Figure B-11.

Check out SQL Server's Books Online for more information about the various roles.

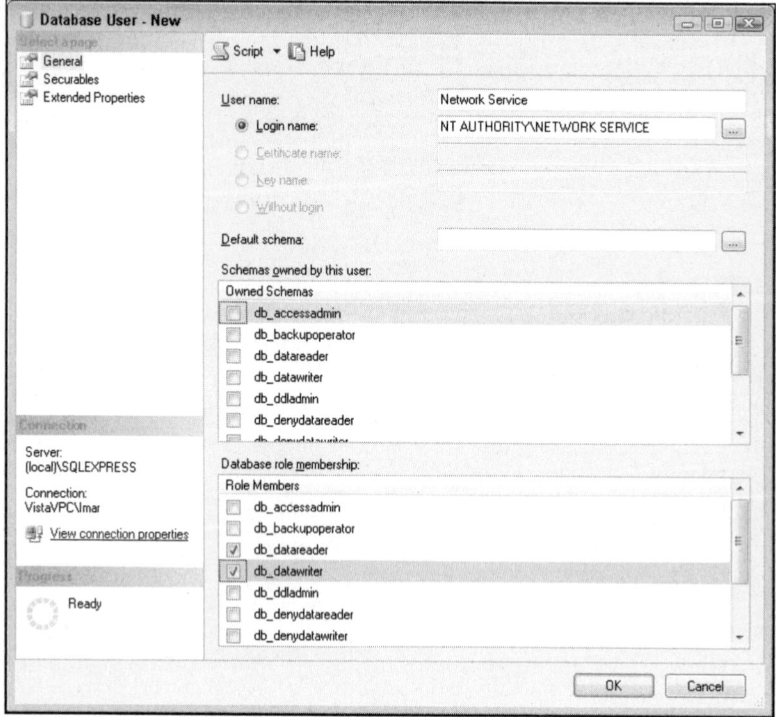

Figure B-11

5. If you want to set fine-grained security options for your database objects, click the Securables option visible in Figure B-11. This dialog box allows you to determine permissions for the user account on objects in your database like tables, views, and stored procedures. For the Planet Wrox web site, you don't need to make any changes in this dialog box.
6. Finally, click OK to assign the Network Service account to the db_datareader and db_datawriter roles.
7. Repeat steps 1–6, but now configure the aspnetdb database that you attached earlier. When you get to step 5, select all the roles that start with aspnet_. These are the roles that are used by the ASP.NET application services and grant the new user account just enough permissions to support the various application services like Membership and Roles.

Now that SQL Server and your user accounts are configured correctly, the final step is to configure the web site to use this new user account.

1. Open the web.config file of the PlanetWrox application from the C:\BegASPNET\Release folder.
2. Modify the `<connectionStrings>` element so it ends up like this:

```
<connectionStrings>
  <clear />
```

```
    <add name="PlanetWroxConnectionString1" connectionString="Data Source=ServerName;
              Initial Catalog=PlanetWrox;Trusted_Connection=True"
         providerName="System.Data.SqlClient"
    />
    <add name="LocalSqlServer" connectionString="Data Source=ServerName;
              Initial Catalog=aspnetdb;Trusted_Connection=True"
         providerName="System.Data.SqlClient"
    />
  </connectionStrings>
```

Don't forget to replace the value in the Data Source with a valid server name. Depending on your server and configuration, this could be as simple as `(local)` to point to a SQL Server on the local machine, `DatabaseServer` to point to a server on the network called DatabaseServer or something like `DatabaseServer\Sql2005` that points to a named instance called Sql2005 on a machine called DatabaseServer.

3. Save the changes and then open the site by starting your browser and going to `http://localhost` (or the address you configured in Chapter 18). Everything should still work as expected, but the site now no longer uses the databases in the App_Data folder, but it uses the SQL Server defined in your connection strings instead through Windows Authentication, as identified by the `Trusted_Connection=True` attribute in the connection string.

   If you get an error when browsing to the site, you may need to turn off custom errors in the web.config file (or set it to `RemoteOnly`) to see the actual error message. Possible reasons for the error are an incorrect server name in the connection string and an incorrectly configured database role membership for the Network Service account.

Once you find out the correct account and have configured SQL Server correctly, using Windows Authentication isn't that hard. In fact, your connection string now becomes a little easier and more secure, as you don't need to store a user name and password in it anymore.

Configuring Application Services

Earlier in this book you learned that the ASP.NET application services make use of a SQL Server 2005 database that is reached by using a connection string called `LocalSqlServer`. The application services then ensure that a new database called aspnetdb.mdf is created in your web site's App_Data folder the very first time you use one of the application services like Membership or Profile.

What if you don't want to use the default aspnetdb.mdf database but rather one of your own? Or what if you rather not rely on a local SQL Server Express database to be created for you, and instead want to get your membership, role, and profile data from your own, dedicated server?

In such cases, you need to reconfigure your application (through the web.config file) and tell it where your database is located. There are two ways to accomplish this: overriding the `LocalSqlServer` connection string, and overriding the settings for the various application services. However, before you look at these two options, you need to know how you can prepare a custom database for the ASP.NET application servicess.

Configuring Your Database for the Application Services

When the aspnetdb database is created for you in the App_Data folder, it already contains a number of objects like tables and stored procedures (snippets of SQL code that can be executed at the server). If you want to use your own database instead of the default one, you need to prepare your database for the application services first. The Microsoft .NET Framework ships with a handy tool designed specifically for this task. You find this tool, called aspnet_regsql, in the following location:

```
%windir%\Microsoft.NET\Framework\v2.0.50727
```

You should type `%windir%` exactly as shown here in the address bar of a Windows Explorer and it will automatically expand to your Windows folder. To execute the tool, simply double-click aspnet_regsql.exe in the folder. This starts the ASP.NET SQL Server Setup Wizard. Click Next twice to reach the screen that allows you to select a SQL Server and a database (see Figure B-12).

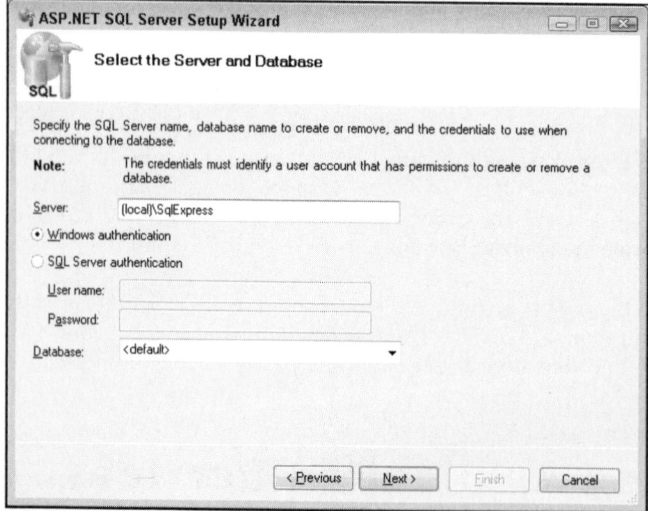

Figure B-12

Enter the name of your database server (like `(local)\SqlExpress` for your local SQL Server Express Edition) and then select a database from the drop-down list in the bottom half of the screen. If you don't see your database listed, you may need to attach it first. Attaching databases is described earlier in this appendix.

Once you have selected your database, click Next twice and the tool creates the necessary objects in your database. You can click Finish to close the Wizard as you're done with it.

The GUI version of the tool that you just saw adds support for all application services in one fell swoop. If you want to control what gets created exactly, open up a command window, navigate to `%windir%\Microsoft.NET\Framework\v2.0.50727`, type **aspnet_regsql /?**, and then press Enter to get a (long) list of options. Scroll up in the option list to see all the available possibilities. At the very least you need to define the following options to add support for an application service:

- **-S:** Allows you to set the SQL Server name.
- **-E:** Indicates you want to use Windows Authentication to connect to SQL Server.
- **-A:** This option must be followed by one or more letters to indicate support for the different application services, like m for Membership, r for the Role manager, and p for Profiles.
- **-d:** Defines the name of the database that must be configured. If you leave out this name, the tool uses the default aspnetdb database.

To execute a command that creates support for Membership, the Role manager, and Profiles against a local SQL Server instance called SqlExpress in the database PlanetWrox, you need to execute the following command:

```
aspnet_regsql -S (local)\SqlExpress -E -A mrp -d PlanetWrox
```

After a while you get a message indicating that the requested services were configured successfully.

Whether you used the wizard or the command line interface, from now on the database you configured can be used for ASP.NET application services.

Overriding the LocalSqlServer Connection String

This is the easiest and quickest path to using a different database. All you need to do is overwrite the `LocalSqlServer` connection string and have it point to your new database. You already saw what this connection string looked like earlier in this chapter, but here it is again so you can see how it works:

```
<connectionStrings>
  <clear />
  ...
  <add name="LocalSqlServer" connectionString="Data Source=.\SQLEXPRESS;
              Initial Catalog=aspnetdb;Trusted_Connection=True"
      providerName="System.Data.SqlClient"
  />
</connectionStrings>
```

Note that the `<connectionStrings>` element contains a `<clear />` element. This element is used to clear out all previously defined connection strings, including the `LocalSqlServer` connection string defined in machine.config. The configuration file then defines a new connection string with the same name, but with a different connection string. In this example the connection string points to an attached database called aspnetdb on a local SqlExpress named instance. When the application services need to connect to SQL Server, they find the connection string `LocalSqlServer`, which then enables them to connect to the SQL Server that you have defined.

Overriding the `LocalSqlServer` connection string is a quick solution to have your ASP.NET web application use a different server. However, this solution brings two disadvantages. First, it feels a bit awkward to have a connection string called `LocalSqlServer` pointing to a remote server. Secondly, this option doesn't allow you to completely override the settings for the configured provider. You can avoid both problems by reconfiguring the application services in web.config as you'll see how to do next.

Overriding the Settings of the Application Services

Overriding the settings of the different providers in the web.config file gives you the most flexibility. Not only does it allow you to point the various application services to a new database connection, it also allows you to change the other settings that each provider supports. To override the settings for the Planet Wrox application, you need to give each configured provider (Membership, Role Manager, and Profile) its own `<provider>` setting. The file machine.config, located at `%windir%\Microsoft.NET\Framework\v2.0.50727\CONFIG` gives you an example of how the different providers need to look.

If you want to override all three providers for the Planet Wrox application so they use the standard `PlanetWroxConnectionString1` instead of the default `LocalSqlServer`, you need to add the following configuration information to the web.config file. When you add these settings, make sure you overwrite all current settings that are already present in the file. In order for this to work you need to configure the PlanetWrox database for the application services using aspnet_regsql as explained earlier.

```
<profile>
  <providers>
    <clear />
    <add
      type="System.Web.Profile.SqlProfileProvider, System.Web, Version=2.0.0.0,
                              Culture=neutral, PublicKeyToken=b03f5f7f11d50a3a"
      name="AspNetSqlProfileProvider"
      connectionStringName="PlanetWroxConnectionString1"
      applicationName="/"
    />
  </providers>
  <properties>
    <add name="FirstName" />
    <add name="LastName" />
    <add name="DateOfBirth" type="System.DateTime"/>
    <add name="Bio" />
    <add name="FavoriteGenres" type="System.Collections.Generic.List`1[System.Int32]"
            allowAnonymous="true"
    />
  </properties>
</profile>

<roleManager enabled="true">
  <providers>
    <clear />
    <add
      type="System.Web.Security.SqlRoleProvider, System.Web, Version=2.0.0.0,
                          Culture=neutral, PublicKeyToken=b03f5f7f11d50a3a"
      name="AspNetSqlRoleProvider"
      connectionStringName="PlanetWroxConnectionString1"
      applicationName="/"
    />
```

```
  </providers>
</roleManager>

<membership>
  <providers>
    <clear />
    <add
      type="System.Web.Security.SqlMembershipProvider, System.Web, Version=2.0.0.0,
                       Culture=neutral, PublicKeyToken=b03f5f7f11d50a3a"
      name="AspNetSqlMembershipProvider"
      connectionStringName="PlanetWroxConnectionString1"
      enablePasswordRetrieval="false"
      enablePasswordReset="true"
      requiresQuestionAndAnswer="false"
      applicationName="/"
      requiresUniqueEmail="false"
      passwordFormat="Hashed"
      maxInvalidPasswordAttempts="5"
      minRequiredPasswordLength="6"
      minRequiredNonalphanumericCharacters="1"
      passwordAttemptWindow="10"
      passwordStrengthRegularExpression=""
    />
  </providers>
</membership>
```

Each application service has a `<providers>` section that allows you to define one or more providers for the service. The `<clear />` element is used once again to remove any previously defined providers from the configuration hierarchy. Each provider is then added using an `<add />` element. Note that each configuration section uses `connectionStringName="PlanetWroxConnectionString1"` to point to the custom connection string defined in the same web.config file. Also note that you can change any of the other settings that the provider supports.

All the provider configuration settings have an attribute called `applicationName` which is set to `/`. This is the name that each application uses to look in the database for the requested users, roles, and so on. You can make up another name if you like, but it's important that all configured providers use the same `applicationName` or they'll end up looking for the wrong information. Without a matching `applicationName`, the services won't be able to relate records from one service to another. This in turn leads to a mismatch among users, roles, and their profile in the database.

With these reconfigured application services, you no longer need the `LocalSqlServer` connection string you may have added to web.config earlier in this appendix.

After you have saved the modified web.config, your site should continue to run as normal. However, the application services now make use of the PlanetWrox database, instead of a separate aspnetdb database.

Index

A

B

C

D

G

H

I

J

K

L

M

Q

R

S

T

U

V

W

X

Z

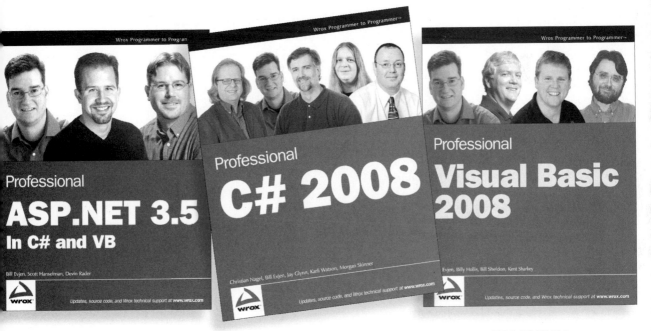